THE PROCESS

2020 EDITION

Integrating Valuations and Biases into a Winning Fantasy Baseball Formula

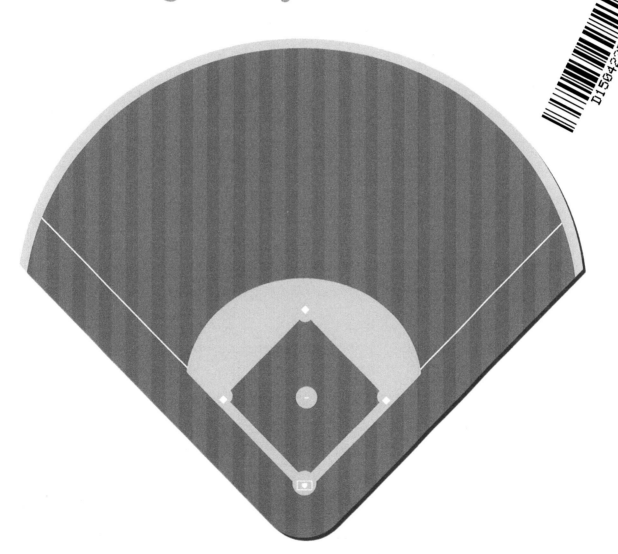

JEFF ZIMMERMAN AND TANNER BELL

Acknowledgements

From Jeff

Here are the people I'd like to thank:

Every leaguemate I've ever had. You've made me the competitor I'm today.

David Appelman, Paul Sporer, and Meg Rowley for putting up with me at FanGraphs and for the use of some content.

Beyond the Boxscore, Royals Review, RotoWire, Baseball America, ESPN, FanGraphs, MLBTradeRumors, BaseballHQ, Hardball Times, CBS, and Fantrax for allowing me to write there over my career.

Rob Silver for reading through the book and offering suggestions before publishing.

Greg Ambrosius and everyone at NFBC for helping compile the FAAB bids.

Jared Cross for supplying the Steamer projections.

Dylan Higgins for doing the editing. God bless his soul.

Clay Link for writing the intro.

My two kids, Ruby and Cole. You are the love of my life and keep me going every day.

And most of all, Tanner. After the first edition, especially getting it to the paper format, I wasn't sure we'd have a 2020 edition. It was especially helpful to come up with ideas since we were co-managers on a couple of teams. It seemed weird when a day went by and we didn't correspond in some way.

Thanks again, Jeff

From Tanner

Thank you to Dylan Higgins for editing this edition of the book. Thank you to anyone who had a hand in contributing data and ideas to this project, especially Jared Cross and the Steamer Projections team. Thank you to the fine folks that put on the various NFBC competitions and make the data so freely available to study. Without that fine arena, much of the research in this book would not be possible.

Thank you to many of the fine fantasy analysts that have at some point offered words of praise, research ideas, and constructive criticism. Special thanks to Clay Link, Rob Silver, Mike Gianella, Rudy Gamble, Al Melchior, Fred Zinkie, Vlad Sedler, and Eno Sarris.

I'm very grateful for all those in the fantasy baseball community that continue to surprise me with their generosity and willingness to help. Thanks to Mike, Rudy, and Rob for all your work, much of which has helped me form ideas you see here. Thank you to the folks at Fantrax, OnRoto, and FanGraphs for providing great data to use. Thank you to those that have given a total unknown the opportunity to work with them – Reggie, Clave, Dixon, Bryan Curley, Mike Podhorzer, and Eno Sarris.

To all my AL-only home league competitors, I'm going to win that league one of these years. Kris, thanks for gently prodding me to play for higher and higher stakes.

Mom and Dad, thanks for supporting my lifelong love of baseball. I love you.

My family – Jess, Jane, Ali, Cam. I love you all.

And thank you, Jeff. Another year, another book that I hope pushes the boundaries of fantasy baseball research. Here's to many more.

Contents

Foreword

By Clay Link

Rob Silver wrote the foreword for the first edition of *The Process*. Going from Rob Silver to myself is like going from Carlos Correa to Jack Mayfield or from Mike Trout to Michael Hermosillo. A big net loss, to be sure, but I'm honored nonetheless that Jeff and Tanner would ask me.

I've had the privilege of knowing Jeff Zimmerman for several years, since shortly after I first broke into the fantasy industry as a student intern at RotoWire. I have gotten to know him even better in recent years while competing against him in the League of Alternative Baseball Reality (LABR) and am proud to call him a friend. Jeff is not only one of the smartest and nicest people in the fantasy baseball world, but he's also one of the most driven and transparent. Nobody has this game completely figured out, but Jeff will be damned if he's not going to try to solve this thing. Jeff's also going to show his work, because he doesn't just want to figure this out for himself. He wants to elevate everyone's understanding of the game and of themselves as rotisserie players. He wants to elevate the conversation.

What lies in these pages is the most thorough tackling of the larger questions of rotisserie baseball that you'll find anywhere in this world (physical or digital). Jeff and Tanner examine concepts such as cognitive biases and measurement of intrinsic value, they dig into the tricky, inexact science of FAAB, and they also introduce new ideas and theories. They weigh the pros and cons of numerous valuation systems. They dispel myths and narratives with historical evidence. Do players over 30 really come with more downside? How much does past production really matter? Are first- and second-round pitchers really more risky than hitters in that range? Over at RotoWire, we produce a fantasy baseball annual, but the vast majority of that magazine is the A-Z player section, which provides season outlooks for 1,200-plus individual players. You will find individual player analysis and 2020 fantasy baseball cheat sheets there as well, but what Jeff and Tanner do in *The Process* is look at broader concepts and strategies and get to the heart of what goes into our fantasy baseball decision-making — the good and the bad, the smart and the ill conceived.

Jeff and Tanner provide the tools you need to succeed in rotisserie baseball and provide the blueprint along with those tools so that you can understand the concepts for what they actually are and not just in the abstract. What they do such a good job of is making this information digestible. One of the very first things said in this book is "don't be intimidated," and while that may seem impossible for some after a quick glance at the table of contents, they do a tremendous job of explaining these concepts and making them relatively easy to grasp. This is not a slog to get through. In fact, if you have a passion for rotisserie baseball, I think you will find this to be quite the page-turner. If you're new to the game and don't really know where to start with your own research, this is a great place to begin. Jeff and Tanner have provided the knowledge base from which to build.

Baseball is a constantly evolving game, and *The Process* has been updated to reflect the current landscape. The additions to this year's version are excellent, and Jeff and Tanner have taken a critical look at their own work and removed some things that they determined were of little practical value in hindsight. What bleeds through when reading *The Process* is what we should all strive for as fantasy players; passion, accountability, objectivity, level-headedness, and always looking for that extra edge and striving for a deeper understanding of ourselves and this silly game we love. Jeff's life's work is in fantasy baseball, and to see someone as motivated, passionate, and good as he is at this, who's still very much grounded and eager to turn over the next stone, is motivating. This is a deep dive into the countless, shifting variables and theories of rotisserie baseball, stripped of the subjectivity and narratives; a labor of love if I've ever seen one.

New in This Year's Book

What follows are the notable additions to this 2020 edition of *The Process*. We've inserted small ideas, corrected typos, and clarified some existing ideas, but won't necessarily call those out here.

Foreword (pg. 1-2) - We are fortunate enough to have Clay Link write the foreword to this year's edition. Clay is the MLB editor for RotoWire and has been one of the most successful fantasy baseball owners in the fantasy sports industry over the past two seasons. In 2018, he won The Great Fantasy Baseball Invitational, finished eighth out of over 1,700 teams in the 2018 NFBC Online Championship competition, and placed second in the Tout Wars Head-2-Head league. He repeated that second place Tout Wars Head-2-Head finish in 2019.

Find an Advantage (pg. 12-13) - A brief section on finding an advantage and knowing one's strengths.

The F-ing Ball (pg. 17-18) - Brief discussion of the elephant in the room, the juiced baseball, and understanding how a juiced ball in 2019 and non-juiced ball in 2018 affect Steamer projections, along with references to the standings gain points and pERA measures in the appendices.

Projecting Holds (pg. 34-35) - Updated analysis of the top Saves + Holds earners from the 2019 season.

Rookie Variance (pg. 49-50) - New study looking at the variance in rookie hitter projections versus non-rookie projections and how to apply this when attempting to value and draft rookie hitters.

Valuation Methods (pg. 76) - Due to the fact that neither of the authors regularly utilize the percentage valuation method and our lack of confidence in being able to adequately explain the nuances of the calculations, we have elected to remove the detailed explanation of how to calculate PVM valuations.

Standings Gain Points Example Final Equations (pg. 85) - Added brief explanation and example of how to use the SGP factors and example equations in Appendix H. This example formula can be used to shortcut the process and value players without going through the entire SGP process.

Z-score Example Final Equations (pg. 92-93) - Added brief example of what a final z-score calculation looks like. Once an owner has performed a z-score calculation, this example formula can be used to shortcut the process on future valuation runs.

Comparison of SGP and Z-score Auction Values (pg. 94-96) - New study comparing valuation results from the SGP and z-score methods. The study highlights the differences for both hitters and pitchers and where the two valuation systems differ most on the extremes.

Are Closers or Starters Cheaper in the Auction or in Free Agency (pg. 105-107) - New study attempting to shed light on the age-old argument of if it's cheaper to acquire saves in the draft or via free agency.

What is Multi-position Eligibility Worth? (pg. 109-111) - Added several more paragraphs to the argument as to why multi-position eligible players are more valuable.

Consider Previous Production (pg. 124-132) - New study seeking to understand if and the extent to which previous fantasy production levels indicate the likelihood of better returns on investment in the future.

Catcher Strategy (pg. 139-140) - Added several new paragraphs on the strategy of waiting to draft catchers until the later stages of the draft.

Historic Results for Closers (pg. 142-143) - Important new information about the Saves environment, changing closer usage patterns, and closer turnover rates.

Finding a Helper (pg. 143-145) - Added a section about tips and benefits of working with a partner manager during the season.

Draft-only Strategy (pg. 151-152) - Added two new tips: "The Mike Fiers Rule" and "Default Stat Rule of Thumb."

Studies of Weekly Valuations for the 2017 and 2018 Seasons (pg. 162-182) - Updated study to now include the results of the 2018 season. Expanded study to include both 12-team and 15-team leagues.

ADP and Weekly Valuations (pg. 182-184) - New addition to the weekly valuation study to also incorporate expected weekly earnings from various ADP ranges.

What Does an Average Weekly Statistic Line Look Like (pg. 184-187) - New addition to the weekly valuation studies that demonstrate what weekly stat lines look like and what they are worth.

FAAB Spending Trends (pg. 187-190) - Updated for 2019 NFBC Main Event FAAB transactions.

How Valuable are Two-Start Pitchers (pg. 190-191) - Updated study which includes both 2017 and 2018 results. Expanded study to include both 12-team and 15-team leagues.

The Split Changes During the Season (pg. 192) - Removed this concept from the book.

In-Season Tools (pg. 205-207) - New section on the MLB news monitoring, lineup and batting order, projected starting pitcher, and weekly projection tools used by the authors to identify free agent targets and set lineups each week.

Mid-to-Late May (pg. 208-210) - Updated listing of hitters demoted during the 2019 season. Added significant discussion of the MLB Super Two deadline and its applicability to fantasy baseball.

FAAB Procedure (pg. 216-217) - Added discussion of the importance of each owner establishing a consistent and repeatable FAAB process to run through each weekend.

Specific Bidding Strategies (pg. 221-227) - Added a concept on "FAAB Binning Strategy" and different categories of players to target. Discussed overlap of the binning strategy with the costing strategy from the 2019 edition of *The Process*. Added 2019 charts of NFBC Main Event FAAB trends.

The Balancing Act of Player Valuation (pg. 228) - New section discussing how owners can find a balance between maximizing short-term value and long-term value on their rosters.

What to Consider for Weekly Lineups (pg. 239-241) - Added tables that can be used to quickly identify the earnings a player is expected to lose by missing one game in a 7, 4, or 3-game lineup period.

Lineup Setting Strategies (pg. 241) - New tip about monitoring MLB lineups.

Utility Advantage (pg. 242) - New tip about setting a lineup to give the owner the most flexibility to react to late news or injuries.

Studying Success Factors and Winning Owners (pg. 249-278) - Comprehensive new study of the final standings, all owner acquisitions, and all owner drops of the 2018 NFBC Main Event. This study seeks to confirm that successful owners are demonstrating behaviors consistent with the recommendations of this book.

Oh, and we also found a Melvin Upton reference that we changed back to B.J. Upton.

About the Book

The Process is a mix of theory, strategy, technical skills, soft skills, and tools for fantasy baseball. It focuses on the common variations of rotisserie baseball (auctions and drafts, deep and shallow, mixed and only leagues), but we briefly delve into points and head-to-head leagues as well. We'll assume the book-buyers have an interest in the more technical aspects of fantasy baseball. We're not going to hold back on the level of detail, but when good work has already been done on a topic, we won't rehash it. We'll just point to where that work lives and layer on our own interpretations.

The Process follows a chronological approach to winning a league. It begins with a detailed discussion of how to formulate projections and then moves into discussions about playing time. Consideration of risk and its effects on projections and valuations is an ongoing theme.

Then, *The Process* uses the projections as a calculation input for dollar valuations and player rankings. Theoretical discussions of value, replacement level, and strategy are included. Next up are the three main valuation techniques: standings gain points, z-scores, and the percentage valuation method.

Next, we investigate player prices and how and when value appears outside of the draft and how this should affect an owner's draft strategy and in-season management. After establishing an understanding of value, it's time to monitor the preseason and know what to look for and how to properly adjust draft rankings or auction price points.

We also move on to draft and auction strategy, including how to construct a cheat sheet, preparations, and specific strategies.

In-season management is an underappreciated skill. We outline how an owner can make their way through the season and how one's mindset should shift at certain mile markers. We'll dive into free agent auction budgeting, determining who to add and drop, and how to squeeze the most value from the waiver wire.

Finally, we've included reference material. The back of the book contains standings information and SGP calculations for a variety of league types as well as early projections for the 2019 season.

Don't Be Intimidated

This book is the brainchild of two authors who have moderate-to-severe obsessions with rotisserie baseball. A lot of potential work and effort goes into perfecting *The Process*. Each aspect outlined will not be for everyone, as it's just what we believe is optimal. But an owner can enjoy many of the benefits by closely following what is outlined. Pick what works and add in new wrinkles over time. We certainly didn't start out here. *The Process* has been and will continue to be a living and adapting work.

It's Not Finished … Sort of (A Work in Process?)

The idea behind this book was to create an ever-evolving guide as the games of baseball and fantasy baseball evolve. The hope is to never be done. When we locked down the initial 2019 edition, many additional topics were noted to be included, refined, or analyzed further in this 2020 edition.

Some, but not all, of the 2019 player examples, stories, and statistics were updated. If the example still works, it stayed. Other areas were updated to give another year of context. We hope the advice and strategies given are so sound that, over the years, the vast majority of advice will remain and the examples will simply be churned over with fresher and more relevant names.

Additionally, please let us know of any additions or subtractions that would be helpful or satisfy curiosity. We are here to provide a usable source beyond the static newsstand magazine. We aren't going to provide sleeper lists or player previews -- which might grow stale or irrelevant -- like other sources. Our goal is to provide the guidance and stats to stay ahead of these sources. This is a "teach a man to fish" type of situation. We gladly welcome all feedback.

Overall Themes

The game of fantasy baseball is made up of countless decisions. A major goal of this book is to reduce the subjectivity that many owners bring into their decision-making process. A significant portion of fantasy advice available to readers represents "feelings" or "beliefs." However, little of that advice translates those thoughts into objective information like projections, valuations, and rankings. This book seeks to do that, but it must be recognized that probability, uncertainty, and cognitive biases are obstacles to that goal.

Probability

Probability underlies all of the technical and strategic decisions owners make playing fantasy baseball. They might consider the probability of a hitter exceeding his projection, of a closer losing his job, of a minor leaguer being called up before the All-Star break, of a pitcher getting injured, or of a high draft pick being traded to another league. Yet it is often forgotten.

Nothing in baseball is set in stone. Even Bartolo Colon eventually retired. Owners will often boil their decisions down to, "Who's better, Player A or Player B?" Instead, the better question is, "What are the odds that Player A outearns Player B the rest of the season?"

Those two questions seem to be asking the same thing, but the "what are the odds" question is a different way of thinking about the same problem. As discussed in detail in the projections section, a player's projected stat line is not a set number, despite being listed next to his name like a fact.

The major benefit to asking, "What are the odds that Player A outearns Player B?" is that the mind immediately wanders into different scenarios and types of risk. There are considerations like the chances a player over or underperforms, falls into a platoon, loses his job, is surpassed by another player, drops or rises in the lineup, and many more. An owner can begin to recognize the complexity of Player A and Player B's situations, making them less prone to biases and poor decisions. An owner might come to the conclusion that Player B is the better player, but that given the surrounding factors and risks, Player A actually has a better chance of out-earning him.

Studying launch angles and calculating values can provide insight, but at the end of the day, owners are really betting on the likelihood of certain outcomes, not unlike the chances that a coin lands on heads or that the dice roll doesn't come up snake eyes.

Baseball statistics are involved, but owners are also making decisions in the context of their opponents' actions. If a competing owner overstates the probability of Player A succeeding, they will draft Player A first or pay more for him at an auction. If, on the other hand, the owner understates the probability of Player B succeeding relative to other owners, they will miss out on Player B.

An owner's job is to figure these probabilities and find where the market is misvaluing or misinterpreting these players' probable outcomes.

The point of The Process is that it's an involved system requiring calculations and judgment at many steps along the way. An owner should not invest solely in evaluating players from a baseball perspective like many fantasy articles and guides are inclined to do. Instead, an owner should strive to become a well-rounded player who is skilled in all aspects of the decision-making process.

Understanding how a major league player's approach change leads to a new batted ball profile that in turn leads to more extra-base hits and run production is one skill (technical baseball knowledge). The best owners then take that new information and interpret what it means in the player's major league context. How does this newfound skill level affect the player's projected playing time? How is his job safety affected? What does the change in this player's playing time mean for other players? These questions and estimates are another skill (understanding the MLB landscape and estimating probabilities).

Uncertainty

Once an owner creates a projection, it is just that: a projection with a possible outcome range. This range of outcomes is tough for some fantasy owners to accept.

Oddly, the maps used to predict the path of a hurricane are a good analogy for baseball projections. The map depicts a range of locations which the hurricane might strike. It might even have probabilities listed or shaded across the map, suggesting certain outcomes are more likely than others. The path depicted is probably wide, suggesting that the exact outcome is unknown, but that experts have varying degrees of confidence in a range of outcomes.

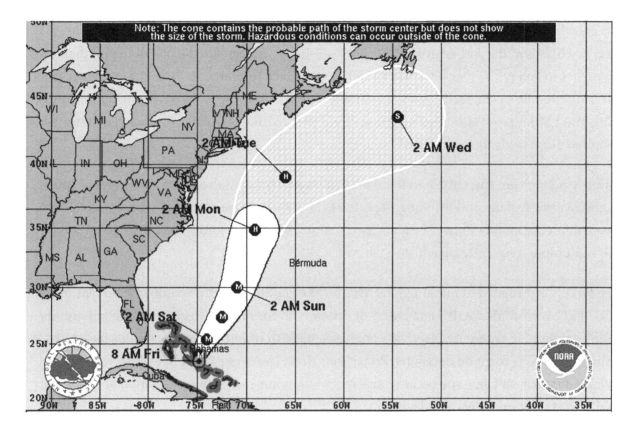

Such hurricane graphics are not all that dissimilar from a set of baseball projections. Weather simulations are the output of a system that runs countless scenarios and simulations based on statistical inputs. That's how a powerful baseball projection engine develops its final projections. Player performance is impossible to predict precisely, but we can develop a range of possible outcomes and determine the likelihood of certain scenarios coming to be.

Cognitive Biases

The decisions fantasy owners make are susceptible to cognitive biases, or mental traps to which the human brain is prone. Think of them as blind spots to making an optimal decision.

Confirmation bias is a well-known cognitive bias. This is the tendency for a person to seek out information that supports the decision they want to make. A simple example could be an owner considering a pickup of two different players. It may only take a positively worded tweet or a passing sentence in a long article about one of the players to tip the scales.

Meanwhile, a lengthy and well-researched article focusing solely on the downside of the same player will be quickly dismissed.

Recency bias is perhaps the most powerful cognitive bias in the realm of fantasy baseball. Recency bias is at the core of every "buy-low-sell-high" debate. It's the invisible pull that leads an owner to believe a hitter on a one-week hot streak is a fundamentally different player from his projection. It's what leads owners to ignore a period of three years over which Jose Altuve outearned Mike Trout and to assume one down year (2018, which included a knee injury which required surgery) is the new player.

Fantasy owners are susceptible to these mental traps. Throw in the fact that many will spend hours reading articles and listening to podcasts, and these biases can cement themselves into overconfidence, another bias. Humans tend to think they know more than they do and that they are right more frequently than history shows.

The Process is designed to minimize the likelihood of falling victim to confirmation bias, recency bias, and overconfidence. It's fact-based. It doesn't call for making decisions based on tidbits of information. It's more involved. It's not susceptible to recency bias because it's based on using projections to guide decisions. Projections don't overweight recent events. Finally, overconfidence isn't an issue because an owner following *The Process* is aware that probability and uncertainty underlie each decision.

Find an Advantage

Any team can be average. The owner just needs to draft using a recent average draft position listing, which should give them an average team. Owners can also follow the industry's suggestions, just like anyone else. Acting like everyone else will lead to mediocre results.

This book will give hints on gaining advantages, but each owner must find their own edge in the limited time they have to spend on their team. The same strategy won't work for everyone. Some are in direct conflict. Someone can't both churn their roster each week and be patient holding onto players waiting for slumps to end. Certain strategies don't fit well with certain owners.

The key is to find one advantage and implement it. Choose to focus on something that works for you. Then find another one and use it. Small advantages will add up over a season.

Don't waste time where an advantage can't be gained. An owner who is horrible at negotiations should not be sending out dozens of trade offers. Instead, their time may be best spent watching pitching debuts for pitch mix changes.

One way to find an advantage is to zig when everyone else is zagging. If everyone in the league over-values prospects, feel free to roster older players. If others are over-bidding for this week's two-start pitchers, start looking two weeks ahead. Don't compete with 11 other owners doing the same thing. Work smarter, not harder.

By following the crowd, anyone can be average. Owners have to find niches where they can incrementally improve their team.

Projections

To place fantasy values on players, owners need to create a unique projection for every player who may be relevant, given their league settings and depth, in the upcoming season. While several inputs combine to create a projection, the main goal is to create an accurate future estimate of a player's statistical performance for the league's categories. Some of the best minds in the game create projections by hand after examining each player (e.g. Larry Schechter and Jeff Erickson). Others have created personal stat-based projections (e.g. Mike Podhorzer and Todd Zola). Still, others use some combination of those approaches (e.g. Rob Silver). The key is to come up with a quality projection, limited by each owner's personal time, and then insert that projection into a valuation formula.

The projected stats provide a solid backbone to finding which players are valuable in different league formats. High-walk players gain a huge advantage in on-base over batting average leagues. Adding holds as a sixth pitching category allows an entirely new type of player to earn value and expands the pitching pool by 33%. Not every valuation applies to every league setting. There's no single magic formula.

With projections, there are two inputs: talent and playing time. Each needs to be treated as an independent input. With the talent projection part, it's the percentage chance an event will happen in each plate appearance or inning pitched. For example, the frequency at which a player will strike out or hit a home run. Once the talent projection is determined, an owner multiplies that rate by the second component, the expected playing time during the upcoming season.

If an owner projects a player will score 0.162 runs per plate appearance with 620 plate appearances, the player would have a 100-run projection (0.162 * 620 = 100).

Adjusting the talent and playing time inputs should split the off-season. Early in the off-season, owners should focus on the talent projections. Once spring training gets underway and rosters begin to take shape, owners can fine-tune the playing time projections.

While it takes more work to break projections into these two inputs, owners avoid the biases and subjectivity that can creep into dealing with final stat lines (e.g. 35 home runs and 110 RBI). When preseason buzz starts to send a player rocketing up the ADP boards, owners have to ask themselves, "Have the player's skills changed? Or is he coming into more playing time?" If the answer is "no" to both questions, it's likely the move up draft boards is just due to the hype and not a change in true value.

Talent Component

Once popular projection systems (e.g. Steamer) start becoming available, owners should determine if the underlying talent projections need tweaking. While 95% of them will likely not change at all, this is the point in the process where an owner should add in their own scouting adjustments (more on this later).

An example could be that a pitcher may have struggled for a couple of months with an injury. The injury worsened, and he was forced to the injured list, then he came back throwing bullets for the last two months. While there may be some injury-related concern about his playing time going forward, an owner may also want to adjust the pitcher's talent projection to approximate the production over the last two months.

Some public projections may already make such an adjustment, but most don't. Most will include and weight the two-month period when the player struggled with the injury the same as the two-month dominant period.

It cannot be stressed enough that if an owner thinks a player will perform better or worse than expected, they need to come back and adjust the talent projections. These talent projections create the backbone for all player values. Don't just adjust the player's ending stat line or just add dollars to the player's valuation.

For example, say during spring training a player states that he will steal more bases during the coming year and an owner believes him. The owner decides to boost his yearly total by 50% (e.g. 30 steals as opposed to the projected 20). Instead of guessing if this jump equates to a two-round value jump or is worth spending $5 more during an auction, the owner just needs to adjust the talent projection to determine the exact value increase.

An owner can create a simple shortcut for some last-minute talent adjustments. The owner could perform some tests to determine when he adjusts for X stolen bases, the player's value changes by Z.

Keep in mind that the more unique the league's settings, the more difficult it becomes to find complete talent projections. For example, it's nearly impossible to find pitcher Quality Start and Hold projections. Because this hurdle exists, owners who make a one-time effort to find usable talent projections will be a step ahead of their competitors.

Several talent projection systems exist and each one will flaunt its greatness. Here's a list of available projections we know of, although there are probably twice as many.

- ATC (Ariel Cohen)

- Baseball HQ

- Marcels

- Mastersball (Todd Zola)

- PECOTA (Baseball Prospectus)

- Projecting X (Mike Podhorzer)

- Steamer

- The BAT (Derek Carty)

- Zips (Dan Szymborski)

Projection creation is a straightforward process with small differences existing between the various projections. The variations are based on the underlying data used and input weighting. Some projections are based on the traditional major and minor league stats while others include batted ball data and pitch velocity. Some are purely data-driven while others include quite a bit of human input.

What each one provides is a starting point or a baseline projection for each player. Most systems treat players uniformly. They are not aware of and will not make adjustments for specific situations, like the earlier injured-pitcher example. There are pros and cons to this approach. A significant benefit is that treating players consistently avoids biases that can creep into looking at players one-by-one. The downside is that situational and contextual information, as with the injured pitcher scenario, is real. A fantasy owner's personal judgment can provide valuable input in these situations.

The F-ing Ball

The baseball is juiced. And then it's not. And then it might be again. But maybe it's not. These are the plot lines over the baseball the past several years and up through this year's postseason. We had no desire to create a huge IF-THEN-ELSE qualifier on the advice in this book and on how owners should adjust to the constantly changing ball.

With so many unknowns, here is how the information in this book was constructed and how it's potentially affected by the ball.

- The Steamer league scoring environment is based 70% off 2019 numbers and 30% off the 2018 environment. These are the historical values.

- The standings gain points information in Appendix H include both the 2018 and 2019 values for owners to refer to and to pick and choose their own poison.

- The pERA and pitch value information in Appendix E is based on the juiced 2017 and 2019 ball. The same information in Appendix F is based on the non-juiced 2016 and 2018 ball. The big difference is that the information in Appendix E will favor ground-ball pitchers more than the information in Appendix F.

Combining or Aggregating Projections

There is a theory that is typically named "wisdom of the crowds." It's the idea that a bunch of independent thinkers can attack a problem with diverse approaches, and that when all of these different approaches are combined, the aggregate is an optimal way of solving the problem. This is a big reason why ADP has value. It's not just a measure of market perception, it's also an indication of what "the crowd" thinks.

Similarly, combining multiple projection sets into one can be a valuable tool, especially if an owner is not able to take the time to formulate their own. FanGraphs' Depth Charts projection system is an example of this. It combines Steamer and Zips into one system, with playing time estimates formulated by the FanGraphs staff.

Creating or Adjusting Projections

Assume an owner downloaded Steamer's 2018 preseason projections for Mike Trout, J.D. Martinez, and Ronald Acuna. The projections would have looked like this:

Player	Team	G	PA	AB	H	AVG	R	HR	RBI	SB
Mike Trout	LAA	144	634	510	157	.308	111	38	106	20
J.D. Martinez	BOS	126	538	479	137	.285	80	32	97	3
Ronald Acuna	ATL	105	433	397	111	.280	49	14	54	21

To establish a baseline projection for each player, simply divide each counting stat by the number of plate appearances. This will give the owner ratios like "AB per PA," "H per PA," and "R per PA." Dividing the number of projected plate appearances by the games played projection converts plate appearances to "PA per G." Here's what this would look like for the three:

Player	G	PA/G	AB/PA	H/PA	AVG	R/PA	HR/PA	RBI/PA	SB/PA
Mike Trout	144	4.40	0.804	0.248	.308	0.175	0.060	0.167	0.032
J.D. Martinez	126	4.27	0.890	0.255	.285	0.149	0.060	0.180	0.006
Ronald Acuna	105	4.12	0.917	0.256	.280	0.113	0.032	0.125	0.048

Here's the beauty of breaking projections down into the talent and playing time components. Before the 2018 season, there was great debate about when Ronald Acuna would be called up. Some argued he might break camp with the team. Others thought he'd be up two weeks into the season (to gain an extra year of player control). Still, others said the Braves had no incentive to bring him up until the Super Two deadline in late-May or early-June (to avoid an extra year of arbitration).

If an owner had a talent projection for Acuna, they just needed to multiply that projection by each scenario's estimated plate appearances to determine the final projected stat line:

Player	G	PA	AB	H	AVG	R	HR	RBI	SB
Ronald Acuna	155	639	586	164	.280	72	20	80	31
Ronald Acuna	141	581	533	149	.280	66	19	73	28
Ronald Acuna	95	391	359	100	.280	44	13	49	19

This process of breaking a projection down into the talent and playing-time components is like what happens with Steamer projections. That projection set is used as a base for Razzball and the aforementioned FanGraphs Depth Chart projections. Rudy Gamble of Razzball adjusts the base Steamer talent projections and then layers on his own playing time estimates and projections for statistics Steamer doesn't project (e.g. Saves, Holds, Quality Starts, etc.).

As previously stated, many player projections provide enough accuracy; they don't need adjustments. Others do. The following situations can provide a guide for when to adjust them.

Adjusting Pitcher Projections

Almost all disagreements between projections and expectations involve pitchers, and most of those disagreements center on ERA. Most projection systems base their estimates on their walk and strikeout rates with a heavy amount of batted ball regression.

Batted ball data is messy. So many factors influence a struck ball, making it nearly impossible to know how much of a particular event is the pitcher's responsibility, or how much is due to the ballpark, defense, hitter, weather, or even something like crazy Aunt Mary yelling insults from the stands. Be wary of any tout who points to a single factor as the cause of a pitcher's batted ball luck. It's never just one factor.

The second conflict point focuses on small samples. Pitchers can instantaneously change their talent level. They can gain or lose velocity, add or drop a pitch, change their pitch mix, or even adjust their mechanics. Small tweaks, if they stick, can lead to immediate talent changes.

The goal coming out of the projection process is to have the best one-line projection based on the owner's evaluation process. If the owner thinks a pitcher will outperform his projection, he should change the projections so that the valuation process can provide a correct value compared to other pitchers.

The following are some instances in which an owner needs to adjust a pitcher's projections.

Pitchers Stuck Between Starting and Relieving

Projections systems really have a tough time creating a pitcher's projection when he splits time between starting and relieving. Generally speaking, pitchers have more success pitching out of the bullpen where they only have to face a hitter once and can max out their velocity. In these situations, it's as if two different pitchers exist and there should be two different projections for the player. Many projection systems conflate the roles by combining both projections into a single value.

Jared Cross, the mind behind Steamer projections, has stepped forward and provided separate projections for the separate roles. While these are based on historical differences, owners may want to dive a little more into each pitcher's results to see if their spread is more or less than the projection.

An example of this was when Wade Davis made the transition from replacement-level starter to lights-out closer. As a starter, he posted a career 4.57 ERA. Since moving to the bullpen, his ERA has averaged 2.03 (including a rough 2018). Normally the ERA difference is around one run lower throwing out of the bullpen. Davis, however, has just a two-run difference.

When Davis made the transition from starter to reliever in 2013, many of the projection systems were using his starting stats to estimate his relieving numbers. The problem was that even in that first season, the contrast was noticeable with a 5.97 starter ERA and a 0.90 reliever ERA (in a limited sample).

The transition from reliever to starter can have the opposite effect. As a starter, a pitcher can't go 100% for six innings. The starter may try, but slowly his velocity will drop. For example, here's Danny Duffy's velocity as he made the transition to starter in 2016.

Note: The closely spaced games are when the pitcher threw out of the bullpen while the evenly spaced games are starts.

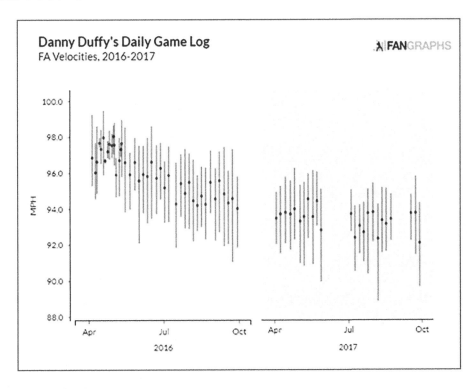

Most projection systems have no idea these pitchers are transitioning between roles. In Duffy's case, it would have been difficult to know after the 2016 season if his velocity would continue to decline had he stayed a reliever, but his shift to becoming a starter cemented a decreased velocity.

By incorporating the pitcher's starter/reliever splits, an owner can improve their projections.

For example, Danny Duffy posted a 3.88 ERA in 2017 as a full-time starter. Below are his 2016 stats during his transition from reliever to starter. xFIP is used as an ERA estimator because it uses strikeout and walk values and heavily regresses batted ball data.

Role	xFIP
Reliever	3.31
Starter	3.84

Duffy displayed an xFIP around 3.80 as a starter in 2016, right in line with his ERA of 3.88 the following season.

Similarly, Duffy's xFIP in the second half of 2016 was indicative of his ERA to come.

Split	xFIP
April	4.05
May	3.45
June	3.51
First half	3.49
Second half	4.04

Coming into the 2017 season, an ERA around 4.00 would have been a reasonable expectation for Duffy when starting.

Gaining or Losing Fastball Velocity

While changing roles can lead to a change in velocity, it's not the only cause. Pitchers naturally lose velocity as they age or come off an injury. Miraculously, some discover an extra tick. Owners need to be able to value such pitchers at their new velocity.

One method is to compare the results for the time frame when the pitcher threw at the new velocity and when they didn't. It's the same procedure when a pitcher changes roles. Owners should concentrate on strikeout and walk numbers and their ERA estimators first because they stabilize faster.

A better method exists but it takes a little more time. Go to the player's page at FanGraphs.com, navigate to the Game Logs, and select the past three seasons from the Dashboard tab.

Copy the same data from the Pitch Type tab and verify that the dates match. Group the results by different velocity ranges. The pitcher's ERA, WHIP, K/9, BB/9, etc. can be calculated for the different velocity groupings.

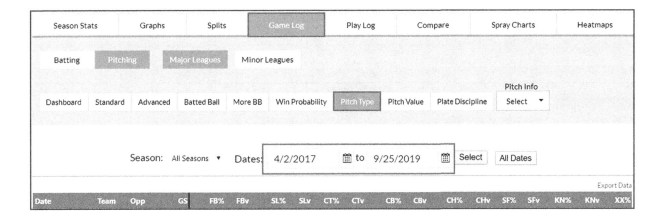

For a more visual representation, navigate to the player's Graphs tab, then choose the Pitch Velocity graphs. Finally, overlay specific statistics on the graph so an owner can gauge the effect of velocity on the pitcher's output. To do this, click the Advanced stat drop-down and choose the measure to add to the graph.

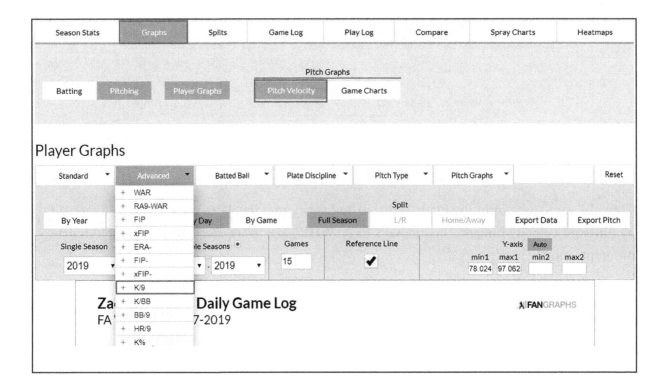

For example, overlaying K% or K/9 on the chart gives a more visual representation of velocity's effect on those measures.

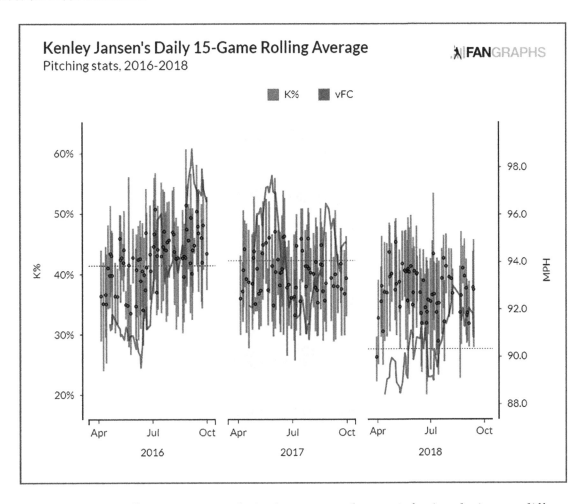

This process is especially important early in the season when a pitcher's velocity can differ significantly from the previous season.

New Pitch

Adding a new effective pitch has the potential to transform a pitcher into a top talent. However, it's difficult to determine if the new pitch can transform an average pitcher into one of the league's best.

In 2017, Luis Severino developed a changeup and Robbie Ray added a curve. Both were either late-round selections in fantasy drafts that year or not drafted at all in some leagues. With the additional pitches, they went from waiver fodder to finishing as top-10 starters.

New pitches can also present a problem. Every pitcher seems to be trying out a new (or the same) one every preseason. Hello Chris Archer and his changeup.

One method to determine the pitch's possible effect is to sit down and watch the pitcher. Does the pitch seem to visually make the pitcher better? By how much? Certainly, most owners do not have a scouting background, but they can still determine how the pitcher is using the pitch. Is it being used to attack batters with two strikes? Is the pitcher using the pitch when he's behind in the count? If the pitch seems to be effective as more than a lightly used token threat, an unscientific solution is to bump up the strikeout rate 0.5 K/9 to 1.0 K/9 and the ERA down by 0.25 to 0.50. These conservative changes allow the pitcher to move up in the final valuations, especially if other owners are utilizing unadjusted projections.

Some owners may not be comfortable in their own scouting abilities but will trust what they see or hear elsewhere. This can be problematic because most announcers and writers have no scouting ability either, but many owners will base their decisions on these non-scouts. To gain more comfort in their ability, an owner doesn't need to take any action while doing their scouting but can instead just keep track of their personal reports and see how they stack up to actual results.

An owner probably can't check in on each of these pitchers in the preseason, so they may need to pick and choose the pitchers who can benefit the most. Most of the time, it will affect two-pitch pitchers who are trying to add an average or better third pitch to help them navigate a lineup for a second or third time.

Once the season has started, owners have detailed Statcast pitch information to indicate how a pitch is performing[1]. Owners need to determine if a new pitch is near or above the average historic swinging strike rate benchmarks. Swinging strike rate (i.e. the percentage of pitches at which opposing batters swing and miss) has a high correlation to strikeout rate, and the hope for the pitcher and fantasy owners is for the new pitch to generate strikeouts.

---

[1] https://fantasy.fangraphs.com/pitch-type-peripherals-benchmark-update-with-matt-cain/

Pitch	GB%		SwgStr%	
Type	Good	Above Avg	Good	Above Avg
SI	47.9%	50.5%	4.8%	5.6%
CU	45.4%	50.0%	9.5%	10.5%
FS	44.4%	49.4%	15.5%	16.3%
FT	44.9%	47.7%	4.5%	5.2%
CH	44.4%	46.7%	11.9%	13.7%
SL	41.2%	44.0%	13.0%	14.4%
FC	40.0%	42.4%	8.7%	9.1%
FF	34.2%	37.4%	5.6%	6.4%

Additionally, the pitch's batted-ball results can help or hurt a pitcher's performance. Yet the only batted-ball results found to be predictive are ground-ball (or fly-ball) rates.

Ground-Ball Rate

With so much information to digest, only ground-ball rates -- not line-drive or fly-ball rates -- are needed to analyze batted-ball data. First, the stringers collecting the batted-ball data will more often correctly label ground balls as opposed to line drives or fly balls. Second, a low ground-ball rate is a perfect proxy for a high fly-ball rate. Generally speaking, if a pitcher increases his ground balls, then there will be a corresponding decrease in fly balls or vise versa.

One of the great inefficiencies in fantasy baseball markets is extreme fly-ball pitchers. Many sources ignore them and focus on pitchers with 50% or higher overall ground-ball rates. This approach is wrong for several reasons.

The natural instinct is to assume home runs result only from fly balls, so all fly balls are bad. The fact of the matter is, if a fly ball doesn't go for a home run, it's likely an out. Additionally, the rate of easy-to-catch infield pop-ups tends to jump with higher fly-ball rates. These cans-of-corn won't come close to being home runs and are automatic outs. A pitcher can thrive at the fly-ball extreme just like heavy ground-ball pitchers.

If a pitcher isn't a ground ball or fly ball pitcher, they're not generating easy outs, or worse, they're a line-drive pitcher.

As for the benchmarks, a pitcher has to produce a GB% of lower than 30% or greater than 55% in order to be considered a true fly ball or true ground ball pitcher, respectively. While the 50% GB% benchmark is easy to remember, no significant batted-ball improvement happens from 50% to 55%.

Another item to consider is that the improvement in results a pitcher would see in going from being an average fly-ball pitcher to an extreme fly-ball pitcher aren't linear, they're logarithmic. The same holds true for improvements in ground-ball rate.

The final inputs which may contribute to a pitcher generating weak contact are the individual pitches above or below the batted-ball thresholds. It's easy to simply look at the overall ground-ball rate, but an equal mix of above and below ground-ball pitches makes the pitcher's overall resulting ground-ball rate look average.

J.A. Happ is a perfect example. In 2017, he had a middle-of-the-pack 47% ground-ball rate. His most frequently thrown pitches were his four-seamer, coming in at a 21% ground-ball rate (a great fly-ball pitch), and a sinker at 61% (a great ground-ball pitch). Both pitches produced above-average results, but when combined, his overall ground-ball rate was unexciting. Most fantasy owners would expect some regression from his 3.53 ERA to one near 4.00, which was close to his ERA estimators, but his varied pitch mix provides a reason to believe that he can outperform ERA estimators.

Pitchers who throw four-seam fastballs and mix in a curve or sinking changeup fall into this pitcher group (the four-seamer tends to generate fly balls while the pitches with drop generate ground balls). For example, in 2018, Trevor Bauer had a fastball with a 28% ground-ball rate and a curve with a 60% rate, but his overall ground-ball rate was 45%. Another example is Zack Greinke. His four-seamer had a 32% ground-ball rate and his changeup was at 71%, for an overall 45%. In both instances, the pitcher posted an ERA well below their ERA estimators.

Jeff Zimmerman created his own ERA estimator, pERA, to take these individual pitch differences into account. It's another tool for owners to utilize to find pitcher targets. The values have been provided in Appendices E and F, where Appendix E is based upon the more hitter friendly baseball used in 2017 and 2019, while Appendix F is based upon the baseball used in 2016 and 2018.

Change Pitch Mix/Lose a Bad Pitch

Fantasy touts can focus too much on pitchers improving a pitch. Instead of improving a pitch, pitchers can take a step forward by throwing fewer crap pitches or junking a pitch altogether. Some pitchers have thrown a pitch for years, getting out amateur or low-minors hitters. Once in the majors, the pitch's effectiveness declines and it shouldn't be thrown. But maybe the pitcher is attached to this pitch and keeps throwing it anyway. If a pitcher has a loaded arsenal, he can just drop the junker.

Maintaining Improvements

As fast as a pitcher can break out, they can also turn into a pumpkin. This is especially true for non-prospects. They had just one aspect of their game that made them relevant (e.g. a velocity bump), so one small negative change can have them headed to independent ball.

For example, Pitcher X gains two ticks on his fastball which helps all his pitches play up. He's loved everywhere but he ends up landing on the IL because his arm can't take the workload. He loses the velocity and is back to being a Quad-A arm.

Owners must not get stuck on a pitcher's value but instead continue to adjust it as the pitcher changes.

Tom Glavine Clones

Glavine was historically great at not allowing home runs when runners got on base. With no runners on base, he allowed 1.1 HR/9. Once runners got on base, he posted a 0.6 HR/9 over his career. He'd just prefer to walk the batter then give them a pitch to drive. Not giving in to the hitter with runners on allowed him to post a 3.87 ERA, which was significantly lower than his 4.40 FIP and 4.57 xFIP. Glavine is the most extreme pitcher when looking at this trait, but it did allow him to post an ERA about 0.5 runs lower than his ERA estimators.

Nolan Ryan Clones

While Nolan Ryan will go down as one of the greatest pitchers of all time, he wasn't nearly as productive from the stretch. The main reason was his strikeout rate dropping from 27.3% to 22.6%.

Some pitchers have a deceptive or velocity-gaining windup and are bland from the stretch. Not being their best with runners on base is a horrible combination and can lead to an ERA higher than a pitcher's ERA estimators.

Bad Fastball

A pitcher can consistently get hit around and maintain a higher than expected BABIP if their fastball does nothing. A pitcher needs their fastball to either:

1. Miss bats via movement or speed.

2. Generate an above-average number of ground balls or popups.

3. Be perfectly placed at the zone's edges or at the hitter's weak points.

An ideal fastball would do all three. If the pitch does none of them, the hitter can just sit on the fastball and crush it.

An example of this was Logan Webb in 2019. He could get a decent number of swings and misses with his change and curve, but his sinker got destroyed.

Only the Fastball for Strikes

Besides having a bad fastball, a pitcher can struggle when the only pitch they can throw for called strikes is their fastball. If they get strike one, they can then throw their breaking balls out of the strike zone and hope the hitter will chase them. But if they don't get strike one, the hitter can just sit back and wait on the fastball and crush it.

These pitchers accumulate strikeouts but look unlucky when comparing their high ERA to their ERA estimators. Michael Pineda exemplifies this pitcher type.

The key idea to remember here is that an owner should expect a pitcher's ERA to regress to their ERA estimators, but in this instance, it may not be due for the typical regression. It's something to research further when a pitcher is getting hit around.

Starter with Two Pitches

Michael Pineda had another problem; he largely relied on only two pitches. With a limited arsenal, hitters immediately see both his pitches. They can start timing both and know if they need to lay off others.

Mitchel Lichtman found in a study[2] that pitchers with only two pitches perform worse than those with a three- or four-pitch repertoire.

---

[2]   https://mglbaseball.com/2013/11/11/ttop-and-a-starting-pitchers-repetoire/

While a few pitchers can post a decent season with just a couple of pitches (e.g. Rich Hill), no top-tier pitcher has thrived with just two pitches over longer periods of time. As such, their upside is limited.

For reference, Jeff listed the starters who rely on two pitches 85% or more of the time at FanGraphs.[3]

Random Pitch Mix

Johnny Cueto has been a bit of an enigma as he has posted great batted-ball data for years with no obvious explanation. After examining his results in detail, he doesn't get hit around differently when ahead or behind in the count. The reason is that he'll throw any pitch in any count. Hitters just don't know what's coming and can't square the pitch up.

These random number generators, while effective, are quite rare. Most pitchers, even the league's best, lean heavily on their plus breaking pitches to put hitters away. When trying to explain a lower-than-expected ERA, this explanation should be the last area an owner should examine. Again, Jeff has already listed such pitchers in a FanGraphs article.[4]

Rockies Starters

An owner needs to have a plan on how they'll use Rockies pitchers. Is the league deep enough where they will be started every time at home and away (e.g. NL-only league)? Or will the owner just use them for their road starts?

Owners need to come to grips with this decision when projecting playing time. If the pitcher will be used only half the time, their projection should include only half the innings. It's basically a home/away platoon, so a replacement level of production needs to be incorporated. But there is a twist: when adjusting projections for Rockies pitchers to account for part-time usage, owners should use the pitcher's road projections.

Another issue to consider is the extra roster spot. This spot has some value. It's at least worth $1 in auction value as an extra replacement level player can be rostered and utilized. For owners with deep benches, the penalty is less.

---

[3]   https://fantasy.fangraphs.com/fantasy/two-pitch-starters/
[4]   https://fantasy.fangraphs.com/fantasy/two-pitch-starters/

This penalty doesn't just apply to Rockies pitchers. If an owner isn't going to use a pitcher at home or against several specific opponents, then some playing time drop and production increase can be applied.

For example, if an owner isn't going to use a Baltimore pitcher at home and on the road at Boston or New York, a lower playing-time projection should be used in conjunction with a better performance projection.

Closers (Saves + Holds)

Simply put, dealing with closers is a necessary mess in Roto leagues that count saves. There are so many variables that influence the save total, so a lot of owners take one of two approaches to eliminate the hassle. They either use a couple of early-round picks on closers, or they go to the other extreme and ignore the category.

Saves

When projecting saves, owners need to analyze each team's situation and pick which one of the following saves projection totals to use. On average, a team has around 40 saves a season. The following table can be used as a guide for projecting saves, based on the skill level of the pitcher and the quality of the MLB team. Projecting a great closer on a playoff team for 36 saves allows for that stud to lose some saves when overworked or on a short IL stint.

Closer Level	Playoff	Middling	Bad
Great	36	32	28
Decent	32	30	24
Ok W/ No Replacement	24	26	28
Setup Man Better Than Closer	12	12	12
Committee	10	10	10

The following are the definitions used for Closer Level in the above table:

Great: Projected for an ERA of 2.75 or less.

Decent: Projected for an ERA between 2.75 and 3.25.

OK w/ No Replacement (Fernando Rodney class): ERA > 3.25. In a normal bullpen, these closers would get replaced when they struggle. With no obvious replacement, they continue to hold the job.

Setup Man Better Than Closer: Projected ERA > 3.25 but there is a replacement with a projected lower ERA. These situations become tenuous immediately unless the manager has come out and named one of the arms a fireman (e.g. Taylor Rogers and Josh Hader). For owners scrounging for saves, they may want to focus on these setup men.

Committee: A mess. Two or more arms are contending to be the closer. These situations are pure gambles, especially when the heir apparent struggles.

As for the team grouping, these can be done a couple of ways. As one option, an owner can group the teams by his gut. There is nothing wrong with this approach. For those owners who want to go complete nerd, they can use preseason projected win totals. Using CAIRO and FanGraphs preseason win projections, the divisions are simple:

Bad (sellers): Projected for 78 or fewer wins. Only 10% of these teams reached the 90-win total needed for the playoffs.

Middling: Projected for between 79 and 83 wins. A breakout or bust could put these teams on either side of the spectrum.

Good: Projected for 84 or more wins. As teams push to play over .500, they are going to be buyers.

Projecting Holds

Holds are a total pain and nearly impossible to project. The key to estimating holds is to focus on talent. In the vast majority of holds leagues, saves are also counted. Many times, the two categories are even combined into one stat. If we just look at the 2019 season, here are the top 30 pitchers ranked by saves + holds.

Rank	Name	HLD	SV	SV+HLD	ERA	WHIP
1	Josh Hader	6	37	43	2.62	0.81
2	Kirby Yates	0	41	41	1.19	0.89
3	Taylor Rogers	10	30	40	2.61	1.00
4	Roberto Osuna	0	38	38	2.63	0.88
5	Sergio Romo	17	20	37	3.43	1.11
6	Raisel Iglesias	3	34	37	4.16	1.22
7	Aroldis Chapman	0	37	37	2.21	1.11
8	Craig Stammen	31	4	35	3.29	1.16
9	Will Smith	0	34	34	2.76	1.03
10	Brad Hand	0	34	34	3.30	1.24
	Average 1-10	**6.7**	**30.9**	**37.6**	**2.82**	**1.04**
11	Andrew Miller	28	6	34	4.45	1.32
12	Ryan Pressly	31	3	34	2.32	0.90
13	Kenley Jansen	0	33	33	3.71	1.06
14	Liam Hendriks	8	25	33	1.80	0.96
15	Shane Greene	10	23	33	2.30	1.01
16	Zack Britton	29	3	32	1.91	1.14
17	Brandon Workman	15	16	31	1.88	1.03
18	Ian Kennedy	1	30	31	3.41	1.28
19	Sean Doolittle	2	29	31	4.05	1.30
20	Jake Diekman	31	0	31	4.65	1.42
	Average 11-20	15.5	16.8	32.3	3.05	1.14
21	Hector Neris	2	28	30	2.93	1.02
22	Adam Ottavino	28	2	30	1.90	1.31
23	Will Harris	26	4	30	1.50	0.93
24	Matt Barnes	26	4	30	3.78	1.38
25	Alex Colome	0	30	30	2.80	1.07
26	Yusmeiro Petit	29	0	29	2.71	0.81
27	Felipe Vazquez	0	28	28	1.65	0.93
28	Ty Buttrey	26	2	28	3.98	1.27
29	Michael Lorenzen	21	7	28	2.92	1.15
30	Aaron Bummer	27	1	28	2.13	0.99
	Average 21-30	**18.5**	**10.6**	**29.1**	**2.63**	**1.09**

The group of the top 10 pitchers is composed primarily of closers, with the average being roughly seven holds and 31 saves. The allocation of saves-to-holds roughly evens out (17 saves to 16 holds) for those ranked 11th-20th and then flips towards holds (19 holds to 11 saves) for those ranked 21st-30th. The ERA and WHIP marks for those ranked 21st-30th were nearly the same as the top 10. Several of the more talented arms that historically were earning saves, like Vazquez and Hendriks, have made the transition from setup man to closer.

The point to take from this exercise is that good relievers will get saves and/or holds, but knowing the exact mix is nearly impossible. Looking back at the last four seasons, here are the average number of saves + holds for relievers based on their Steamer-projected ERA.

Projected Steamer ERA	2016 Holds + Saves	2017 Holds + Saves	2018 Holds + Saves	2019 Holds + Saves
< 3.00	26.7	24.8	31.0	23.0
3.00 to 3.25	15.8	18.4	24.0	18.0
3.25 to 3.50	12.5	13.9	21.1	13.7
3.50 to 3.75	8.2	13.0	13.3	13.5
3.75 to 4.00	5.3	9.2	8.9	7.8

Owners in leagues that use saves + holds need to focus on the pitchers with a projected ERA under 3.25. Historically, these pitchers have produced the most holds (and saves). Use the above numbers for projecting saves + holds for non-closers, knowing at some point the reliever may move into the closer's role and start getting saves.

Playing Time

Playing time is the second major projection input. As the player-talent projections become more refined, accurate playing time adjustments are where owners can gain an edge. Owners should find a source(s) that constantly updates playing-time projections, or personally adjust them.

Many different variables contribute to estimating how often a player is on the field. Free agents have been waiting longer and longer to sign. Injuries happen. Lineup positions are unsettled.

Three playing-time variables exist: chunk, sporadic, and team-based. Chunk means that a set amount of time exists when the player will not be available. Examples of this are a known major stint on the injured list (IL), time in the minors, or a suspension. With sporadic, the player is expected to be available all season but will not play every day. The erratic playing time could be a righty-lefty platoon or a history of nagging injuries (e.g. Ryan Braun). With team context adjustments, a player's teammates help determine his value by pushing him up and down the lineup or going through the lineup based on the team's ability to score runs.

Chunk

Chunk consists of known missed playing time. It requires more calculations but can provide the owners who do those calculations a better idea of the production they'll get during the season. The key component is knowing the amount of missed time. Player X is expected to miss the season's first four weeks from an injury. Owners don't have to take a complete zero for this time frame. Instead, they can use a replacement player until the injured player returns. Replacement players are the players readily available on a team's bench or waiver wire.

Calculating the replacement player stats is simple. If the league's historic data exists, find five-to-ten regulars owned but on various team's benches. Average the stats from this group and it will be close to the stats available while the better player is unavailable.

Going back to the 2017 15-team Tout Wars Mixed Auction, here are five bench hitters and their averaged 2017 stats.

Name	HR	R	RBI	SB	AVG
Brandon Drury	13	41	63	1	0.267
Danny Valencia	15	54	66	2	0.256
Kolten Wong	4	55	42	8	0.285
Joe Mauer	6	51	43	0	0.273
Joc Pederson	21	56	50	1	0.245
Replacement Player	12	51	53	2	0.265

The replacement player is far from good. If the bench players were good, they'd be starting. At least an owner gets these stats until this other player returns to the lineup.

This objective approach to determining what the bench or waiver wire will truly look like is the preferred method because it will capture any biases the league has for or against certain player types. For example, if the league over-values strikeout pitchers and power hitters, the replacement-level adjustment should reflect the fact that only low-WHIP pitchers or high-batting-average hitters are available.

Most leagues aren't ongoing from year-to-year. Fortunately, there is another solution to determine the replacement level. The owner will need to proceed with this book's steps and create an initial complete draft list. The owner can then take the first 10 or so players who didn't make the list and average their stats. This average will represent the replacement level player. The owner can go back and adjust the projections for the players who will miss a known chunk of time.

Sporadic

These players have historically missed time (mainly from injuries) but it is usually a day or two at unknown points. Ryan Braun fits into this category, as he seems to always be sitting for this or that ailment. Another player to consider is a defensive liability who gets pulled late in games. Jose Martinez, J.D. Davis, and Kyle Schwarber were all consistently removed him in favor of defensive replacements in close games.

For players expected to miss sporadic time, replacement-level production may or may not be added depending on the league rules.

In daily lineup leagues, a replacement can be substituted when a player isn't starting. With this adjustment, the owner needs to know their own level of diligence in checking and updating their lineups, especially at the time when daily lineups become available. If an owner just checks and sets their daily lineups once in the morning based on who does or doesn't have a game that day, the owner may want to stay away from players who sporadically miss time.

In weekly leagues, the owner must simply set their lineup and hope the player plays as much as possible. Again, seeing a player sit and not being able to change the lineup is not for everyone. Owners need to acquire players based on their own risk tolerance.

Some players, mainly oft-injured pitchers, fall into both these Chunk and Sporadic groups. Rich Hill is an example of this pitcher type. No reasonable owner expects "Blister Boy" to start 30-plus games. He's likely to spend time on the IL at some point. The problem is that owners don't know for sure when the injury will occur. Worse, owners don't know if a particular injury will be the short, sporadic type or a significantly larger chunk type. In daily lineup leagues, Hill can be replaced. In a weekly league, there is a good chance the owner will just get a big fat zero for the missed start and will then have to replace Hill for a larger chunk of time, too.

For these pitchers, their final projection should contain the pitcher's own projection, the replacement-level projection, and a small amount of missed starts. The exact percentage of missed time to factor into the projection can't be known but docking 5% to 10% is a reasonable buffer.

For example, going back to Rich Hill, an owner might estimate he'll make 60% of his possible starts, leaving owners with a replacement pitcher 30% of the time, and missed starts about 10% of the time.

Team-based

Platoon

Projecting playing time while factoring in the team context is tough. A common issue owners have to deal with are platooning hitters. The platoon starts when one hitter struggles against same-sided pitching but destroys opposite-handed pitching. This hitter shares time with a hitter who doesn't struggle against the same-pitcher handedness. This second hitter may or may not struggle against same-handed pitching.

For example, hitter A may have a .400 OPS against left-handed pitching but a .900 OPS against right-handed pitching. He's perfect for the platoon. Player B could be the opposite of Player A and has posted a .900 OPS against lefties and .400 OPS against righties. Or he could have a .700 OPS against both handedness pitchers. Either way, the two players will be sharing at-bats.

Through some previous research, a hitter needs a minimum .600 projected OPS to continue hitting against both pitcher handedness before he's at risk of a platoon. A fantasy owner can use this difference to find a potential platoon situation. For reference, a full list of hitters and their projected OPS against each pitcher handedness is included in Appendix D.

Another situation to look for are outfields with too many bodies (e.g. Tampa Bay Rays). To keep everyone happy, the team may set up a platoon situation.

Once a platoon has been established, both players lose a ton of value in weekly lineup leagues. On average, the strong-side hitter (i.e. the one facing right-handed pitching) will start two-thirds of the games, and the one on the short side of the platoon will start the rest of the time. The hitter on the short side is unplayable and the strong-side hitter will likely only be usable in 15-team or deeper leagues.

Another factor to consider with platoon hitters is that their playing-time risk is not just related to losing entire games played. They're also likely to lose at-bats late in games as they get swapped out due to a new pitcher's handedness.

Owners in weekly leagues can try to get a few more plate appearances out of the hitter by examining the upcoming weekly lineups to see which pitcher they'll be facing.

In weekly lineups, no replacement-level production can be added. In daily lineups with decently sized benches, these platoon hitters are golden since the owner can control the matchups and maximize every plate appearance.

In recent history, teams that have no problems implementing a hitting platoon are the Athletics, Rays, Cubs, and Dodgers, but any team may use one if their available personnel allows it.

With all of this said, owners must keep in mind the changing landscape of the major leagues. Teams have begun experimenting with "opener" pitchers instead of the traditional starter role. Likewise, the percentage of innings consumed by starting pitchers continues to fall, regardless of the use of "openers." This means there is a diminishing return to using platoon hitters. As the likelihood of starters or openers coming out of games early increases, attempting to time the use of platoon bats will become a less viable solution.

Platooning Starting Pitchers

While pitchers can't get platooned by their MLB team, they can by their fantasy owners. Will an owner start a pitcher every time at Colorado? The same may be asked of pitchers in the AL East.

Will they be started against New York and Boston and at the launching pads in Toronto and Baltimore? A team will play each division opponent about 20 times during a season. By the time a season's over, an AL East starting pitcher could be benched nearly half the time.

Using the AL East as an example, the Tampa Bay Rays play 20 games each against New York and Boston and 10 games at Toronto and at Baltimore. That's a total of 60 games where the Rays play against dangerous opponents or in dangerous hitters' parks. A Rays pitcher may need to be benched for 37% (60/162) of his projected starts and have a replacement-level player's stats added in.

With Colorado starters, it may be a simple 50% replacement-level adjustment. Many owners make a guesswork Colorado adjustment or find the math too hard and just ignore pitchers from Colorado. If fantasy owners take the time to make detailed calculations and estimates to build in the replacement-level adjustment, a truer valuation can be obtained.

If short on time, simply ignoring Rockies pitchers isn't unreasonable, especially considering Colorado's history of not developing quality starters, but that trend seems to have turned around in 2018.

Rookie Promotions

Another team-based situation an owner must deal with is rookie promotions. Prospect projections work like players who will miss a set amount of time (chunk) from an injury. They should be evaluated using a projection that includes the prospect's own MLB projection and the replacement-level projection while they're toiling in the minors.

The key to setting a call-up date comes down to several variables.

1. Quality of player
2. Levels removed from majors
3. Team needs and finances
4. Position

Owners need to come to their own comfort level for when they assume a player will be called up. In some instances, the owner's risk tolerance level may be too low, and they miss out on the top prospects.

Unforeseen Adjustments

The discussion of playing time risk to this point has dealt with known playing-time adjustments. Owners can plan around them. The problem is that other events occur which are unknown to start the season, especially injuries. These unknown events could all be added in to lower the projected playing time, but there is no need as the risk is about the same for each player. When risks are different for certain players, adjustments should be made. The next section discusses these other types of risks and how to respond.

Valuation Risks

Many decisions must be made involving player risk, and not just the injury and playing-time risk already discussed. Risk (or uncertainty) can be a positive or negative factor for a given player. The problem is that risk often gets inserted at draft or auction time as owners decide on the fly how much to adjust a player's value. This is a dangerous approach.

The risks might already be included in that single stat line. But if an owner believes the player needs more or less risk added to their final projection, which is not already accounted for, it should be added before entering the value calculation process.

Two overall risks areas exist:

1. Risks within the player's profile
2. Risk the player adds to the owner's fantasy team

The key here is to identify individual players or a group of players who have a risk that isn't already incorporated into their basic projections and then adjust the projections.

Too much emphasis may be focused on getting the correct projection. Why the need to bake all of these factors into the projected stat line? The reason for the emphasis now is that, during a draft, owners will have merely a minute to decide which player to add with various other factors to absorb. Owners don't have time to correctly account for risk while on the clock. But with risk baked into the projection and then valuation, the stressed owner can focus on other factors.

Another issue arises later in a draft when player values flatten out. The draft ranking is based on a single stat line. A small adjustment could change a player's value 20 to 30 spots. Without formally adjusting the projection and seeing the effect on the player's value, adjusting the player's rank on the fly becomes too subjective. It's best to determine a player's risk-adjusted value before the draft.

Adding risk's impact is even more important in an auction where the decision isn't between several players but comes down to a yes-or-no decision on just one player at a time. The owner creates a dollar value they are comfortable paying. They don't immediately get the option of paying the same amount for a different player.

Below are some risks which exist and how to adjust the player's projection accordingly. In most instances, a final simple adjustment is provided to the playing time, so owners can quickly go through their players and make the changes.

Individual Risks

Sucking Risk - Hitters

Players who can't hit major-league pitching don't normally play. To find the level of production needed to keep a major-league job, non-rookie (played at least 25 games in the majors and Triple-A from 2015 to 2017) OPS stats were compared. Here are the stats ordered by the defensive spectrum (most-difficult positions to play are towards the top):

Position	Median	Average
C	.628	.632
SS	.622	.618
2B	.647	.622
3B	.633	.628
OF	.644	.639
1B	.635	.654
All	.641	.636

It's not surprising to see the OPS increase as the positions get easier to play, but it is a little surprising how little the values vary. As for setting a baseline for major-league production replacement level, a .635 OPS is used. Any major leaguer with an OPS below .635 looks to be below average and could be replaceable.

With the baseline set, here is how often hitters of various OPS projections exceed that .635 level:

Projected OPS +/- .025	.600	.635	.650
.550	44%	36%	31%
.600	47%	38%	33%
.650	59%	47%	42%
.700	76%	65%	61%
.750	87%	82%	78%
.800	95%	91%	91%
.850	98%	96%	95%
.900	99%	97%	97%
.950	100%	100%	100%

Let's apply this table to the real-life example of Byron Buxton. Coming into the 2017 season, the Steamer projection estimated Buxton's OPS at .758, meaning there was a near-82% chance Buxton would keep on OPS over .635. However, Buxton did not come close to the .635 cutoff and posted a .383 OPS in 94 plate appearances before getting demoted. While the chance wasn't huge for a collapse, it was non-zero, and Buxton was the unlucky one with the horrible start to the season.

The bottom line is that owners should start considering the potential for lost playing time if a player's projected OPS is below .800. An owner could strictly adhere to this projected OPS baseline to identify players at risk of losing playing time due to collapse, but a better approach is to consider each individual circumstance.

Going into 2018, the level of sucking risk was different for the Yankees than it was for the Padres. It's relative to the team *and* the alternatives that are available. The Yankees had lineup flexibility and options like Brett Gardner, Ronald Torreyes, Miguel Andujar, Gleyber Torres, and Brandon Drury waiting in the wings, not to mention their potential to trade for other help if needed.

As soon as one of the bench players' projected OPS exceeded a struggling starter (Neil Walker), the switch could be made -- even if Walker was producing above the typical cutoff sucking risk level of .635.

Examining the 2018 preseason projections, Walker was projected for an OPS of .750 and Gleyber Torres was at .720. An owner might have estimated that there was a 33% chance that Walker sucked, dropping his OPS well below .750, or that Torres would exceed his projection so much that a switch would be made.

For the Padres, assume Manuel Margot is projected for .715 OPS and Franchy Cordero is projected for .680. That's close to the same, only a .035 difference. Again, an owner might estimate a 33% chance of Cordero surpassing him. But then Travis Jankowski is added into the mix, and his projection is .620. Maybe that suggests a 5% chance Jankowski surpasses Margot. With the combination of Cordero and Jankowski, there would be a combined 38% risk of Margot losing playing time.

Sucking Risk - Pitchers

The consideration of pitchers sucking risk differs in a couple of ways from hitters. The biggest difference is that with pitchers, their role can change from a starter, second starter (thank you Rays), long reliever, setup man, closer, and opener (thanks again, Rays). In addition to any number of possible role changes at the MLB level, the pitcher can be demoted to the minors. Pitcher roles and levels are in flux a lot more than those of hitters.

Generally, bad starters either get demoted to the minors or become long relievers. Below are the median ERAs for MLB starters who spent at least 20 innings starting in both the minors and majors in a season from 2015 to 2017. Also, the ERA from those who both started (min 40 IP) and relieved (min 20 IP) in the majors.

Stat	Moved to and From Minors	Moved to and From the Bullpen
ERA	5.26	5.14
WHIP	1.50	1.42

When a starter performs with an ERA over 5.00 and a WHIP over 1.40, they are at risk of getting moved to the bullpen or the minors.

Most owners aren't going to be intentionally starting a pitcher with an ERA over 5.00, but it's impossible to know which starter will break down and underperform to this level. What an owner can do is calculate the odds this might occur.

The following table shows the calculated likelihood that a pitcher with a given projected ERA will be able to keep his ERA below the 5.00 danger zone.

Projected ERA	ERA < 5.00
< 3.25	100%
3.25 to 3.50	87%
3.50 to 3.75	91%
3.75 to 4.00	85%
4.00 to 4.25	89%
4.25 to 4.50	83%
4.50 to 4.75	80%
4.75 to 5.00	48%

Except for the game's elite arms, most rosterable starters have around a 10-20% blowup chance. Generally, pitchers stay around their projected ERA.

As previously stated, reliever roles are fickle. Here are the odds a team's initial closer could keep their job and why (source[5]):

ERA Range	Whole Season	Poor Performance	Injury	Other
< 2.50	70%	10%	10%	10%
2.50 to 3.00	48%	9%	39%	4%
3.00 to 3.50	35%	31%	18%	16%
>3.50	31%	28%	19%	22%

Besides the few elite options, less than half of all closers keep their job all season. Valuing closer risk and the saves they can generate is perilous with no perfect solution. The central issue is that approximately 30 pitchers at any time are generating saves and usually all are owned. While any hitter has the chance to drive in runs, and any pitcher can get strikeouts, not just any pitcher can get saves.

---

[5]   https://fantasy.fangraphs.com/how-teams-initial-closers-performed/

Should owners spend an early-round pick on a closer who has a 30% chance of losing his job? Should owners wait for even worse options that are even more likely to lose their job? Should they allocate valuable roster bench spots to speculate on closers-in-waiting? Should owners wait until a new closer gets named and are forced to spend 30% or more of their FAAB on the closer? Or does the owner ignore the mess altogether and dump saves? It's a balancing act for sure, and it's a topic to be addressed later in the book.

Salary

There are exceptions that make a player immune to sucking risk, such as having a large contract. Bad contracts happen. The deal is that the MLB teams don't usually eat these sunk costs. Instead, they just keep playing the subpar player. Ryan Howard. Albert Pujols. Chris Davis. Victor Martinez.

While these players drag down their real-life teams, they receive guaranteed playing time that they take away from young players with their league-minimum contracts. This playing time floor can help fantasy teams.

Here are the top 10 largest contracts in which teams sat or released a healthy hitter:

Name	Salary Eaten ($m)
Chris Davis	$92
Rusney Castillo	$73
Hector Olivera	$67
Jose Reyes	$48
Yasmany Tomas	$47
Carl Crawford	$43
Alex Rodriguez	$42
Jason Bay	$38
Pablo Sandoval	$36
B.J. Upton	$33

One interesting note is that three of the top five contracts eaten were for Cuban defectors. Chris Davis set a high mark near $92 million, but the high mark may be less than $50 million for former MLB regulars.

The point is that it's rare for players with contracts comparable to these to be benched. Many of these examples are several years old, with only Davis being recently added. Healthy hitters with large contracts have a safe plate appearance floor. For reference, Appendix G contains known large contract information an owner can use to identify players with a potentially safer playing time floor.

Performance Variance Risk

To this point, incorporating much of the risks covered requires an adjustment to playing time. The player's talent level projection was left constant. But the fact of the matter is, there is a great deal of uncertainty within that talent level projection.

It's difficult (impossible) to know or accurately predict which hitters will exceed or fall short of their talent level projections. If an owner can do that, they should start their own projection system. What can be done is to study and analyze the types of players that are more susceptible to variation.

"Small sample size" is a commonly repeated mantra around baseball. This is because the smaller the sample, the wilder the variation can be. Players that strike out a lot or walk a lot have far fewer balls in play than free-swingers who make good contact. Fewer balls in play will lead to more variable outcomes. The following table shows the standard deviation for OPS at a given projected strikeout rate. Hitters are grouped into those who are projected to strike out less than 16%, between 16-26%, and more than 26% of their plate appearances.

OPS	< 16% K%	16% K% to 26%	> 26% K%
>.800	.095	.100	.123
.700 to .800	.097	.112	.106
.600 to .700	.096	.122	.121
< .600	.055	.147	.113

Moving from left-to-right across the chart, it's apparent those that strikeout less than 16% of the time have noticeably less variance in their OPS (between 10 to 30 points) than the hitters with higher strikeout rates.

Different hitter talent level (OPS) ranges are shown to help illustrate that the variation risk is just as high for good and bad hitters.

While walks can result in positive fantasy events like runs and stolen bases, they also result in fewer opportunities to put the ball in play and have the potential to add volatility. However, the analysis in the following table shows that players with higher walk rates do not necessarily demonstrate this.

OPS	< 6% BB%	6% BB% to 10% BB%	>10% BB%
>.800	.106	.100	.110
.700 to .800	.114	.110	.091
.600 to .700	.112	.121	.128
< .600	.141	.131	N/A

What happens if the values are combined? Putting strikeouts and walks together into a measure of overall plate discipline, the K%-BB% table below shows results like the K% previous table. The worse the plate discipline, moving left-to-right across the table, the more volatility is shown in OPS.

OPS	< 10% K%-BB%	10% to 15% K%-BB%	>15% K%-BB%
>.800	.104	.101	.113
.700 to .800	.102	.108	.114
.600 to .700	.098	.128	.114
< .600	.057	.150	.134

The effects in the tables above are not enormous, but the takeaway for owners should be that when all else is equal, a player with better plate discipline tends to be a more consistent and reliable producer.

Rookie Variance

In every draft, an owner or two gambles on rookie hitters. They dream of the upside of Juan Soto for little to no cost. Most times, these rookies get targeted later in drafts for their upside. More recently, rookies like Vladimir Guerrero Jr. and Eloy Jimenez have been drafted with very high picks. Several questions come from this phenomenon. Are rookies more volatile than established hitters? By how much? Does the rookie's upside offset the possible downside? Do rookie projections differ from MLB regulars? These questions deserve an answer.

All hitters with a Steamer projection (2010 to 2018) were collected and then their projected OPS was compared to their actual OPS results (min 50 PA). The average difference, standard deviation, and the 25th and 75th percentile differences were calculated for players of various ages and rookie statuses. An adjustment was made to the Steamer projections in order to control for the effect of the juiced ball, which would have distorted the results in certain years.

Hitter	Avg OPS Diff	Std Dev	75th PercentileOPS Diff	25th Percentile OPS Diff	Count
Rookies	.023	.127	.097	-.054	659
Non-Rookies	-.005	.112	.058	-.062	3,567
<= 25 (non-rookies)	-.008	.108	.057	-.062	563
26 to 30	.002	.113	.067	-.057	1,719
31 to 35	-.010	.110	.051	-.069	1,050
> 35	-.018	.112	.048	-.076	219

Rookies have the most variance but, on average, they outperform their projections. Some obvious bias exists in the data sample in that minor leaguers who haven't taken a developmental step forward aren't going to be promoted. Those who make a developmental improvement will outperform their projections. The deviation is still quite a bit more than the other player groups, so rookies have a nice upside compared to the downside.

Besides the rookies, the downside for players over 30 is significant. Note the 25th percentile OPS difference is lower below zero than the 75th percentile is greater than zero. While some fantasy analysts may be seem to be ageists, there is a reason. Hitters in their 30s shouldn't be ignored. Instead, owners need to understand there is more downside risk.

Stolen Base Variance

Plate discipline can also have an impact on stolen base numbers. Stolen bases are heavily dependent upon how frequently a player can reach first base, something that is greatly affected by both walk rate and strikeout rate. The more a player strikes out, fewer balls are put into play, making the player more susceptible to BABIP variance.

The tables that follow are hypothetical calculations to illustrate plate discipline's stolen base effect. Forgive some of the calculations. For the sake of simplicity, assumptions are made about certain events like sacrifice flies and hit-by-pitches. Factors that affect the hitter's first-base frequency are walks, BABIP, and not striking out (e.g. can get on via fielder's choice).

This first table demonstrates what 5% incremental changes in the walk rate will do to a full-time hitter (600 plate appearances). Notice that a 5% change in walk rate translates to 22 additional times on base.

PA	BB%	AB	H	AVG	TOB
600	18%	477	126	0.265	234
600	13%	507	134	0.265	212
600	8%	537	142	0.265	190
600	3%	567	150	0.265	168

The next table holds the walk rate constant and displays various combinations of strikeout rate and BABIP. An 8% shift in strikeout rate cannot be expected but would result in a sizeable 27 more times on base. Also, notice that a 40-point jump in BABIP results in 16 more times on base.

PA	K%	BB%	BIP	BABIP	AB	H	TOB
600	22%	8.5%	399	0.340	534	156	207
600	22%	8.5%	399	0.300	534	140	191
600	22%	8.5%	399	0.260	534	124	175
600	30%	8.5%	349	0.340	534	139	190
600	30%	8.5%	349	0.300	534	125	176
600	30%	8.5%	349	0.260	534	111	162
600	14%	8.5%	445	0.340	534	171	222
600	14%	8.5%	445	0.300	534	154	205
600	14%	8.5%	445	0.260	534	136	187

So how much do these extra times on base matter? The following table displays the frequency of stolen base attempts by some of the more prolific 2019 base stealers. For example, Adalberto Mondesi attempted a steal every 2.5 stolen base opportunities (number of plate appearances the player reached first or second base with no runner on the base ahead of him).

PLAYER	SB	SBO	SBA	%	SBO/SBA
Mallex Smith	46	200	54	27%	3.7
Adalberto Mondesi	43	126	50	40%	2.5
Jonathan Villar	40	261	49	19%	5.3
Ronald Acuna Jr.	37	256	46	18%	5.6
Trea Turner	35	264	40	15%	6.6
Elvis Andrus	31	217	39	18%	5.6
Jarrod Dyson	30	175	34	19%	5.1
Christian Yelich	30	266	32	12%	8.3

Based on the above table, it's reasonable to see plate discipline and BABIP increasing or decreasing a player's stolen base opportunities by 40 or so opportunities. Depending on the base stealer involved, an owner could easily expect a corresponding change of 5-10 stolen base attempts.

Players' Minor League Options

Players with minor league options are at risk of being demoted and losing playing time. Wading through this risk is difficult though because player options are tough to explain, understand, and track. The extremely simplified version is that a player can be moved to and from the minor leagues for a few seasons before becoming a free agent. Here is the definition according to MLB.com[6]:

> *Players on a 40-man roster are given three Minor League "options." An option allows that player to be sent to the Minor Leagues ("optioned") without first being subjected to waivers. When a player is optioned to the Minors for a span of more than 20 days, he loses an option.*

---

[6]   http://m.mlb.com/glossary/transactions/minor-league-options

Upon being optioned to the Minor Leagues, a player must remain there for a minimum of 10 days before he is eligible to be recalled to the Major League roster. The exception to that 10-day minimum is if the player is recalled as the corresponding move made when his club places an injured player on the Major League injured list. In this exception, there is no minimum number of days in which the optioned player must remain in the Minors."

This definition is quite confusing and it's one of the simpler versions available. The key point is that some younger players can be taxied between the minors and majors based on the team's needs.

RosterResource.com eliminates much of the confusion surrounding options by doing the legwork and showing the options remaining for each player (example). During the 2019 season, this same information became available on Fangraphs, under the RosterResource area of the site (example).[7]

Options especially come into play with spring training position battles. Teams may say either of two similarly talented players could get the starting job. Nine times out of 10, the player with options heads to the minors.

This happened at the beginning of 2018 when Teoscar Hernandez started the season in the minors after the Blue Jays acquired Curtis Granderson and Randal Grichuk in off-season moves. Neither of the veterans could be sent to the minors without having to clear waivers. Because of his remaining options, Hernandez drew the short straw and was sent down, despite likely being more talented than either Granderson or Grichuk.

Many sources will mention and bring up playing time battles in spring training. Owners should give the hitters with available options a hit to their playing time.

This can be hard to do. It might seem incorrect. After all, there will be many fantasy analysts shouting that the player with minor league options is an amazing sleeper. Buzz will build. The player will be flying up the ADP ranks, etc. As counterintuitive as it seems, dock the player playing time. MLB teams don't pay attention to hype, especially from the fantasy baseball community. What MLB teams do care about is trying to see what might be left in the tank for aging veterans while they have the option to keep young talent protected in the minor leagues.

---

[7]   https://www.rosterresource.com/mlb-kansas-city-royals

Defense

Fantasy analysis doesn't often delve into defense, but there is a common narrative in baseball that good defense will keep a player's bat in the lineup. A quick study shows to what degree that narrative is true.

The following table presents the results of a study using 2010 to 2017 preseason Steamer hitter projections. Hitters were examined who had a projected OPS between .650 and .750 and saw their actual OPS drop below .650. They're subpar or underperforming hitters. The table compares the projected versus actual plate appearances grouped by previous season defensive value (defensive UZR and the positional adjustment are combined).

Defensive Value + Positional Adjustment	Projected PA	Actual PA	PA Retained
< -5	363	287	79%
-5 to 0	227	143	63%
0 to 5	225	163	72%
5 to 10	368	349	95%
>10	429	448	104%

A significant plate appearance drop occurs when a player has a defensive and positional value under five.

UZR plus the positional adjustment is available at the FanGraphs defensive leaderboards. An owner can use these measures to adjust a player's playing time on the account of defensive ability.

It is important to use the same data across the board for all players. Do not pick and choose which players to investigate. Owners should be careful not to fall into the trap of only looking up the fielding data for players believed to be good fielders or those players "they like." There will be players an owner "doesn't like" that have good fielding measures. Failure to apply this test uniformly will lead to biased results.

Notice from the previous table that the plate appearance projections are somewhat low. Owners won't serve themselves well to draft players projected for only 300-400 plate appearances. Here are the results when the same analysis is performed on hitters projected for at least 500 plate appearances:

Defensive Value + Positional Adjustment	Projected PA	Actual PA	PA Retained
< -5	607	347	57%
-5 to 5	563	321	57%
> 5	580	482	83%

Owners should expect average and below-average hitters to see a drop in their playing time as they underperform. The hitters who can play good defense will maintain a good chunk of their playing time, regardless of performance.

It is worth pointing out that a struggling player maintaining their playing time is both a blessing and a curse. They'll have a longer leash to dig out of extended slumps, but those struggling ratio stats, like batting average, can have a very detrimental effect on a fantasy team's place in the standings.

Injury Risk

Pet peeve time. Fantasy analysts love to speak very emphatically about who is and who isn't an injury risk. Many of these analysts speak of injury with little to no understanding of the underlying data regarding who is or isn't at risk. Some experts have explored the subject, but the most detailed of the work has been done by some poor soul named Jeff Zimmerman. Maybe some readers have heard of him. The following is the basic outline of his work.

Pitcher Injury Risk

Every study done on pitcher injuries shows that the single greatest predictor of future injuries is past injuries. If a pitcher has pain in his throwing shoulder, he's likely to have future pain.

Pitchers are divided into two groups:

1. Presumably perfectly healthy pitchers
2. Everyone else

The presumed perfectly healthy pitchers have two qualities:

1. **Under 30 years old.** As pitchers age, the chance for injury just keeps going up. Few aces have been able to throw full seasons after the age of 30.

2. **No throwing-related injury in the past three seasons.** About 95%+ of all pitcher IL stints relate to throwing in some way. An example of a non-throwing injury is when Noah Syndergaard went on the IL for hand, foot, and mouth disease in 2018. Injuries to the leg and core can affect a pitcher's throwing motion and lead to more time on the injured list.

Now, there will be exceptions within the two groups. There always are. The key for an owner is finding the balance between talent and health.

Hitter Injury Risk

One of the most difficult ideas for most owners to wrap their head around is that there are no injury-prone hitters. Besides a few noted exceptions, the data behind past injuries leading to future injuries just doesn't exist for hitters the same way it does for pitchers.

Unless a hitter has a known injury coming into the season (a chunk playing time adjustment), most regulars should get a full plate appearance projection. If a chunk adjustment is necessary, make the move and change the playing time projection. Don't do what most owners will do and simply make a mental adjustment on the fly. Don't half-ass it on draft day.

Giancarlo Stanton is the recent poster child for being an injury-prone hitter. For years, he suffered unfortunate injuries: a knee injury that required surgery, breaking a bone in his hand, and being hit in the face by a pitch. Owners were flocking to the hills. Then he went two seasons without an IL stint. Then he was hurt for most of the 2019 season. Nelson Cruz used to have this same injury label until he didn't, playing all of 2014-2017 without an IL stint.

Here's a little math to show how some hitters get the injury label. First, 40% of all hitters will spend time on the IL for some reason each season. With a random distribution of injuries, here are the number of hitters who will spend time on the IL in consecutive seasons. Assume eight hitters on 30 teams or 240 total regulars.

Year 1	96
Year 2	38
Year 3	15
Year 4	6

Six poor saps will, through random luck, experience four consecutive seasons with an IL trip. They will for sure get the injury-risk label. These "injury-prone" players are great to target because they often go for a discount. Now, they still may get hurt (there's a 40% chance), but so could any other hitter.

As previously stated, there are exceptions. The following are more than just the standard "bad luck" and should be considered as a true risk factor for hitters.

- **Chronic Injuries.** Some hitters have issues that just won't heal, and the player will be a regular on the IL. Examples are David Wright and Miguel Cabrera with their backs and Albert Pujols with his knees.

  Picking out the chronic guys are easy once the same injury reappears for multiple seasons. It's the transition season which is tough.

  Coming into 2017, owners had to decide if Miguel Cabrera's back trouble was going to be ongoing or if it would finally heal. It showed up again and his value tanked. When in doubt, owners might as well go the conservative route and limit the plate appearances for repeated injuries in the same area of the body.

- **Older Hitters.** Research has shown older hitters are more likely to go on the IL and spend more time on it once there. The difference could be a few plate appearances and can be quickly adjusted in the playing time values.

- **Aggressive Play Injuries.** These hitters go all out all the time and seem to be banged up a few times a season from their aggressive play. Think Kevin Kiermaier, Bryce Harper, and A.J. Pollock. As for now, there is no way of using public data to determine if their past injuries can predict future injuries, but it can't be ruled out either. Each owner is going to need to make their own call if they will take these past injuries into account.

Playing Through Injuries

For fantasy owners, this player group provides a ton of value. Here's how they do it.

A player gets hurt but can play through the injury, which means no time on the injured list. Meanwhile, the injury drops the hitter's production by 10%. The hitter cannot provide 100% production, but his 90% performance level is better than most other hitter's 100%, so the team keeps playing him.

When projection systems create their projections for the following season, they don't know the hitter played sub-optimally for a while. The final projection will not be as high as it should otherwise be.

An example this past season was Mike Trout in 2018. He injured his wrist in early August, played through it for a while, went on the IL, then came back struggling but finally got himself going. In every month except August, he posted an OPS between 1.039 and 1.236. In August, it was just .873.

Fantasy Team-Based Risk

Some risks don't relate to the player's value as an individual but can greatly affect an owner's chances of being able to construct a winning team.

Too Many Resources in a Single Player

Mike Trout is easily the best player in real baseball and possibly in fantasy depending on the league rules. There is no one even close. In a single-season auction league, he could easily cost a team 20% of its budget. It's great to secure a player like Trout, but the problem is that if he gets hurt, as he did in 2017 to 2019, a team loses 20% of their production for a couple months. Does this risk need to be factored into a player's value?

Before answering the question, keep in mind that this specific team-based risk only applies to auction drafts where an owner must concentrate many resources to acquire the top players. In snake drafts, everyone is taking on the same risk with highly valued players and it doesn't cost premium resources to draft Mike Trout. Owners aren't given the option to choose between the first overall pick or three selections in the second round.

Before considering how to account for this concentration of risk, here are some IL statistics to be mindful of. These are hitters projected for more than 500 plate appearances from 2010 to 2017:

- 41% of hitters went on the IL
- The average number of IL trips per player was 0.56
- They lost 19.9 days on average
- 25.5% of all hitters spent more than 30 days on the IL
- 11.6% spent more than 60 days on the IL
- 5.7% spent more than 90 days on the IL

It's pretty staggering to think that on average a player will lose 20 days to the IL and that there's a greater than 25% chance the owner will be losing a star player at least 30 days and a greater than 10% chance they'll be on the shelf for more than 60 days.

These injury rates are not reflected in many playing time projections. Take a look at any projection system and an owner will likely see all the top players projected for 150+ games.

Think about Mike Trout again. Owners need to exercise caution when deciding to invest in a player like that. In an auction format, purchasing a player like Mike Trout will leave a team with relative weakness in other spots, whether it's weaker starting players or a subpar bench. Losing Mike Trout and replacing him with that lack of depth could sink a season.

This is not to suggest it's foolish to pursue the best players, but making educated decisions about risk management is what fantasy baseball is all about. If an owner has a higher tolerance for risk, there's nothing wrong with concentrating so many resources (20% of an owner's budget) in a player like Trout.

Those that have a smaller appetite for risk might consider a spread-the-risk auction strategy. As will be discussed in a later case study, owners should leave themselves the option to invest in players who unexpectedly become valuable. In all but the deepest formats and AL- or NL-only leagues, valuable players appear.

The obvious risk-spreading strategy is to spend evenly on all players. Of a $260 total budget, $175 might be spent on hitting. Spreading that across 14 players suggests about $12-$13 per player. This is a perfect spreading-the-risk strategy.

This approach closes the door to capitalize on value during the draft and the season. Any good owner has a list of $1-$2 end-of-draft targets they expect will earn $5-$10. Don't close the door on that possibility. Instead of spending $12-13 on each player, push the concentration of talent and risk somewhat by investing in players worth around $20 so owners can still capitalize on those dollar days scenarios.

Further, there will normally be some price mismatch with early or late inflation during the auction. Owners need to quickly spot these differences. Savvy owners learn to balance the differences between concentrating risk and still getting value. Those that do often win.

Research (and probably common sense) tells us there's a greater chance a $12 player ends up above replacement level at the end of the year than a $1 player. With that in mind, having a team comprised entirely of $12-$13 players actually prevents an owner from being able to churn the bottom part of their roster in search of value. It would be very difficult (and perhaps stupid) to drop a $12 player for a risky speculation on the waiver wire. But if the decision is instead between a $1 player and the risky speculation play, the decision is a lot more practical.

Single Player, Single Category Risk (Rotisserie leagues only)

This topic could be called Billy Hamilton Roulette. Hamilton historically provided value in only one category, but that total alone was enough in some years for the owner to finish near the top spot for the category. Hamilton was good for 55+ steals for four straight seasons from 2014-2017. His fantasy value has since mostly dried up, but his story may have relevance in upcoming seasons for players, like Mallex Smith, that specialize in gobs of stolen bases and offer little else.

In Hamilton's case, he had several factors driving down his value, like sucking risk (.634 OPS ins 2017, .626 in 2018, and now .564 in 2019) and declining stolen-base success rate (from highs approaching 90% to 82% in 2017, 77% in 2018, 79% in 2019). While both of these factors were in play, the biggest risk was from injury. With all an owner's stolen bases wrapped up with a single player, an injury will sink the owner's season if it prolongs for months. An owner won't find 30+ steals on the waiver wire. With the scarcity of steals, they'd be lucky to find five.

This single category risk obviously exists with closers and their precious saves as well. Another category which historically faced the same increase risk is home runs. With the new live ball, home runs are more plentiful. At various times in the past, home runs were harder to come by.

Even though there is more risk with these players, it doesn't mean owners should completely stay away. There will always be a price where the stolen-base stud will be a good value. Such a player might end up being a must-add for an owner who has already selected too many players who don't steal bases.

The bottom line here is that anytime an owner concentrates too much production of one category in a single player, they continue to add risk to their team.

Closing Thoughts on Risk

All the discussions above are little incremental adjustments an owner can make. Implementing one of the suggestions is not going to put an owner on the path to fantasy greatness.

Instead, it's the many little things that add up. Avoid the player that'll miss 75 PAs due to sporadic health issues. Draft the player that doesn't lose his job to sucking risk over one that misses half the season. Secure an extra 6-10 stolen bases. Avoid the pitcher whose ERA blows up.

And remember, at risk of beating a dead horse, the key to adjusting for these risks is to update a player's projection and have that feed into the player's valuation. Then make informed decisions using the updated value. Never just "bump a guy up a few spots."

Valuations and Rankings

The Concept of Value

When we talk about player valuations, it's important to understand that there are two types of value. The first can be thought of as a player's theoretical or intrinsic value. This is the type of value we are trying to determine by using a valuation system like standings gain points (SGP) or z-scores. Based on a player's projected statistics in relation to all other players' projected statistics, he is worth X dollars.

The second type of value is the market value, or what other individuals are willing to pay for the player. A player can have an intrinsic value of $30, but if others don't agree with the projection or are unwilling to spend $30 at an auction, that intrinsic value doesn't mean much. Average Draft Position (ADP) and average auction values (AAV) are examples of specific market values. Perceptions about players, narratives, and the "sexiness" of owning a player all fuel market value.

A valuation system might kick out a theoretical projected value of $14 for a well-publicized minor leaguer who everyone wants to own. The player's extra demand could push his auction value to $20.

Having an understanding of the intrinsic and market values allows an owner to make optimal decisions. If an owner believes a player is worth a 4th-round pick but can determine from ADP that he's likely to still be available in the 6th round, they can plan and make better use of their resources.

Market Values Move Fast

Intrinsic values move slowly, if at all. They shouldn't change on a day-to-day basis unless meaningful news about an injury, a demotion, a trade, or some other effect on playing time occurs. Intrinsic value is not affected by a 4-for-4 performance or a three-home-run game. It should primarily be driven by what is expected of the player going forward.

Conversely, market values are continually changing based on recent news, notable performances, and general "buzz" about a player. They can change quickly, dramatically, and irrationally.

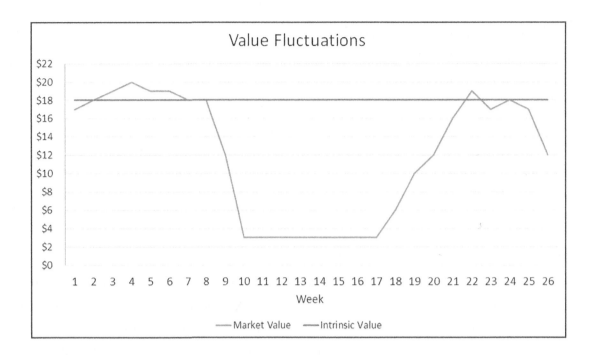

The big reason for the difference in variability is that market values are susceptible to many cognitive biases that creep into owners' decision-making processes. Ideas like recency bias, bandwagon effect, confirmation bias, and the gambler's fallacy can affect market value.

Intrinsic value can see through that noise. It's an objective calculation process that can arrive at a more realistic depiction of what a player is truly worth. Make decisions based on intrinsic value. Unless there is a benefit to be had (e.g. market value is low, and the player can be cheaply acquired), avoid letting market value affect behavior.

Measurement of Intrinsic Value

The true measure of a player's value compares his production to other players. More specifically, the player's value is his production level over the replacement level players. Here are some other inputs needed to determine a player's value:

- The player's projection
- The projections of other players
- The league scoring system
- The number of owners and roster size

The Player's Projection

Obviously, the player's projected stat line is a significant component of his value, but a player's value goes much deeper than these few stats.

The Projections of Other Players

A simple way to think through why other players' projections affect a player's value is to assume the world is full of outfielders who hit 20 home runs. In this world, the player that can hit 30 home runs doesn't provide a team with 30 dingers. Instead, think of this player as though he provides 10 more home runs than the replacement-level player. It is those 10 home runs above and beyond the freely available 20 which provide value.

The ability to determine (or approximate) the replacement-level player is why every player projection matters.

The League Scoring System

A league's settings determine a player's intrinsic value. For example, players will be valued differently in a league that uses AVG as opposed to an OBP league.

The Number of Owners and Roster Sizes

Both league and roster sizes are needed to determine where the replacement level falls. The freely available players on a waiver wire will be different in a 10-team league with no bench players than a 15-team league with five bench spots.

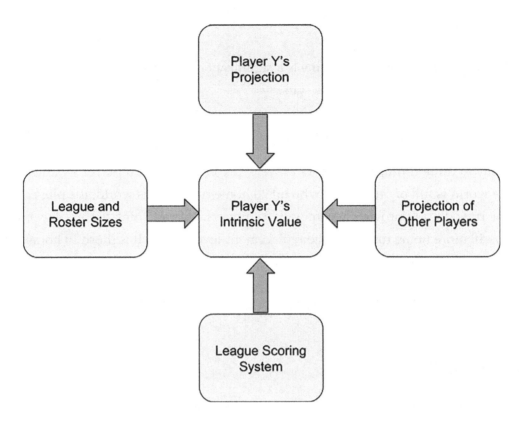

Once each of these inputs is known, it's time to use a valuation system to determine each player's intrinsic value and formulate rankings to be used in an auction or draft.

Valuation System Overview

Three popular methods of calculating player valuations will be discussed: standings gain points (SGP), percentage valuation method (PVM), and the z-score method. While they differ in the approach to determine a value, some base theories underlie their value creation.

First, all three systems convert a player's baseball statistics into some other consistent measure. This is needed because it's very difficult to compare the value of 30 home runs to 100 RBI and even more difficult to compare those counting stats to ratio stats like an ERA of 3.50 or a WHIP of 1.20. The valuation systems convert the stats to standings gain points, percentages, or z-scores.

Next, all valuation systems need to account for and identify replacement-level players. The value of a 90 R, 30 HR, 100 RBI first baseman doesn't lie in those raw numbers. If a 65 R, 18 HR, 70 RBI first baseman can be freely added from the waiver wire, then that may be replacement level for the league.

In this case, the first player's valuable stats are 25 R (90 - 65), 12 HR (30 - 18), and 30 RBI (100 - 70). Let's call these differences "stats over replacement level." Every player better than the replacement-level player at their position is considered "draftable" or "ownable."

Each of the valuation systems requires determining the replacement level. For each player "above replacement level," their associated "stats over replacement level" are thrown into a larger pool. At this point, the valuation systems start to differ in their approach, but at a very high level, they take these "stats over replacement level" and assign a value to them.

Where Do Player Values Come From?

If an owner has never participated in an auction or calculated their own dollar values, they might be curious as to where the dollar value assignments come from. For some reason, baseball auction drafts have historically used a $260 team budget. In a 12-team league, this means there is $3,120 that can be spent on players.

Of that $3,120, a certain portion will be spent on hitters and the rest on pitchers. The allocation of the league budget between hitting and pitching spending is known as the hitter-pitcher split, or just "the split." The split's intricacies will be examined later, but a typical split allocates 67% to hitters and the remaining 33% to pitchers. Thus, of the budget, $2,090 should be assigned to hitter valuations ($3,120 * 0.67) and $1,030 to pitchers.

Again, the main valuation systems convert a player's baseball statistics into some other consistent measure. To better weave some concepts together, it's best to think of it as "convert a player's baseball statistics above replacement level into some other consistent measure." Remember, the 30-home-run hitter might only be producing 12 home runs of value.

For example, the SGP valuation system might determine the draftable pool of hitters has a combined 300 "standings gain points" above replacement level and that Mike Trout accounts for seven of them. This means Trout should have 2.33% (7 / 300 = 0.0233) of the league hitting value assigned to him, or $48.77 (0.0233 * $2,090). The PVM and z-score valuation methods follow similar approaches.

Do Snake Draft Owners Need to Use a Valuation System?

The procedure will start getting more mathy as the focus transitions to auction values. And whether it's because an owner hates math or doesn't play in an auction league, they might be asking themselves, "Why do I need dollar values? I only play in snake draft leagues." It's a fair question.

The main benefit of calculating player dollar values is that it makes hitters directly comparable to pitchers. It was mentioned previously that somewhere around 67% of spending in an auction is on hitters. The dollar value conversion is the easiest way to account for this hitter-pitcher split. If owners don't apply this split through a dollar value, they will need some other way to decrease the importance or priority they place on pitcher statistics.

Another nice advantage of using dollar values is that they mean something to us. Comparing a $40 player to a $35 player is easier to do than comparing a 7.76 standings gain points player to a 6.80 player. As humans, we're used to making decisions based on monetary values. In a fast-paced auction, each split-second faster an owner can cut from making decision is important.

Finally, there's a whole world of fantasy research and advice that refers to dollar valuations. These articles are among the most helpful, insightful, and instructional pieces of content owners come across. Owners don't want to shut themselves off from these great resources just because they don't think in terms of player dollar values. Owners can go the extra mile, using whatever valuation system they prefer, and calculate player dollar values.

Replacement Level

Before an owner gets into a specific valuation method, it's important to understand the concept of replacement level. The replacement level concept is the same regardless of the valuation method used. While the replacement level was briefly discussed in the Projections section, the following will not be as brief.

Here's a classic example that can be used to illustrate the importance of replacement level. Assume a two-team draft in which each team drafts two players. An owner must draft one outfielder and one infielder and the only category of importance is home runs. This is the available player pool:

Outfielders		Infielders	
Player Name	Projected HR	**Player Name**	Projected HR
Outfielder A	45	**Infielder A**	20
Outfielder B	40	**Infielder B**	5

If an owner is blessed with the first pick in this draft, who would they select? It's a little counterintuitive, but the best selection is Infielder A. Selecting him gives an owner a 15 HR advantage over the replacement/last player available at the position.

The owner won't land the player with the most home runs, but the second-round pick is still going to be Outfielder B with 40 HR. the owner's team total will exceed the opponent.

Selection	Player Name	Projected HR	Selection	Player Name	Projected HR
#1	Infielder A	20	#2	Outfielder A	45
#3	Outfielder B	40	#4	Infielder B	5
	Total HR	60		Total HR	50

The technical term for this concept is marginal production. In fantasy sports, it's referred to as statistics over replacement level. It is the value or statistical production one player earns over the position's replacement player. Infielder A has a higher marginal production than Outfielder A, even though Outfielder A has the most actual home runs.

A player's statistics over replacement level are the true measure of their value. It is not just their raw statistical totals.

Replacement Level and Positional Adjustments

Owners certainly have heard folks saying, "I'd rather have this shortstop than that outfielder because he plays at a scarce position." Valuing positional scarcity is another important reason to understand and properly determine replacement level. How owners determine the replacement level at a given position determines the necessary positional adjustment.

Going back to the simplistic outfielder/infielder example, infielders are the scarce commodity. The home runs from infielders are scarcer than outfield home runs. Notice that *no positional adjustment* really takes place. The statistics over replacement level calculation *is the positional adjustment.*

Outfielders				Infielders			
Player Name	Proj HR	Repl Lvl HR	HR Over Repl	Player Name	Proj HR	Repl Lvl HR	HR Over Repl
Outfielder A	45	40	5	Infielder A	20	5	15
Outfielder B	40	40	0	Infielder B	5	5	0

It cannot be stressed enough: The replacement level adjustment **IS THE POSITIONAL ADJUSTMENT.** Any valuation system (SGP, z-score, PVM) takes this adjustment into account. No further position adjustment is needed. Manual or on-the-fly adjustments that owners make because of a player's position is double counting.

The Myth of Positional Adjustments

Owners will hear fantasy analysts mention positional adjustments or scarce positions. We just looked at why this theory can be misleading. But an even bigger misunderstanding is that for most leagues, the only positional adjustment that takes place when owners adjust for replacement level is for catchers, and that's only if playing in a two-catcher league.

One position which may start needing a position adjustment in deeper leagues is outfield. In 15-team or deeper leagues, finding full-time outfielders off the waiver wire is becoming tougher as teams platoon more and more. This is a trend owners should monitor.

Leagues that use corner infield, middle infield, and utility slots end up minimizing the difference between positions. These flexible roster spots eat away at any difference in replacement level that truly exists between the positions.

How can this be? Assume a scenario where first basemen were much stronger statistically than third basemen. When owners allow for a corner infield position in a 12-team league, the corner infield spots will be filled by a first baseman after filling the first base spots. At some point, even the 13th-best third baseman will be better than the first basemen being placed into the CI spots. For example, there may be a point at which owners would rather have the 13th third baseman than the 20th first baseman. The only way a significant positional adjustment can occur would be if owners preferred all of the top-24 first basemen (all 12 first base starters plus 12 more to be slotted at corner infield) to the 13th-best third basemen. That difference just doesn't happen.

When 12 utility players are thrown into the mix, any difference that exists between corner infielders, middle infielders, and outfielders erodes. The only significant difference that remains is the difference between catchers and the other positions, and that difference only exists because the 20th (in 10-team, two-catcher leagues), 24th (in 12-team, two-catcher leagues), and 30th (in 15-team, two-catcher leagues) catchers suck. Terribly.

Pitcher Replacement Level

Setting the pitcher replacement can require … how to best put it, some … guesstimating. While in theory a positional adjustment should not be needed, one may be needed between starters and closers, depending on the league setup.

The first step involves determining if the league has designated roster spots for starters and relievers. If it does, the splitting is simplified. In most cases, a closer's contributions are worth less than a starter's, meaning it is advantageous to place any relief-pitcher-eligible starters into the reliever group. The other starting pitchers will be in the starter group. The replacement level is then determined for each of the two pitching position buckets.

When designated SP and RP slots do not exist within the league rules, owners must decide if the pitchers need to be divided for valuation purposes. In points-based leagues, the answer is likely no, because a point is a point, no matter how it's achieved. There is no need to understand if a given point came from a starter or a reliever.

In roto leagues that counts Saves, tracking replacement level for both starters and relievers is warranted, even in leagues that don't designate SP and RP positions. In theory, all the pitchers could just be grouped together into a single valuation list (there are no formal requirements on the number of starters or relievers to be rostered). But if an owner uses and follows just these rankings, two things could happen:

1. They will likely not have winning bids on any closers, as the prices will be too high.
2. Several closers marked as below replacement level will end up being drafted.

These situations could put owners in a dangerous situation that should be avoided, such as having to adjust values on the fly and make arbitrary decisions while in a stressful situation.

To be clear, the authors of this book differ in how to best resolve this problem. One point of view is that special treatment to account for a league's irrational behavior is to do nothing different in the process. This will allow the owner to know the extent they are overpaying for players. The owner can minimize the amount they veer away from their theoretical values.

The opposing point of view is that not attempting to plan for this situation can leave an owner unprepared and confused about prices during the draft. To avoid this scenario, and to make sure an owner can be on similar ground to his competition, he may choose to pool any save-generating relievers into one group. All the other pitchers, starters and non-closers, get placed in another group.

Defining the groups in this way allows the owner to specify replacement levels for Save-generating pitchers and for all other pitchers. Just like what happens with catchers, these distinct replacement levels allow for Save-generating pitchers to be placed on par with all the other pitchers, should their values come out on the low side.

There are other techniques and theories an owner should consider if attempting to manipulate the value of relief pitchers. See the section "Advanced Valuation and Rankings Thoughts" for further discussion of closer valuations.

Hitter-Pitcher Split

This is one of the most misunderstood topics in fantasy baseball. Nobody likes to talk about it. Nobody fully understands it. Most know it exists. Nobody knows why, or how it's arrived at, or if we can change it, or how to properly change it. So, let's talk about it.

In general, the hitter-pitcher split is a decision about how much of an owner's draft resources to allocate to hitters versus pitchers. As mentioned earlier, a common team draft budget in an auction is $260, and the typical hitter-pitcher split is generally something like 67% of the budget to hitting and 33% to pitching, meaning a team should spend around $174 ($260 * 0.67) on hitters and $86 ($260 * 0.33) on pitchers.

Although not as transparent, the hitter-pitcher split is also relevant to draft leagues. This requires some intermediate steps to see, but it is there. Through data modeling, draft selections can be converted into an auction or dollar value. The very first pick in the entire draft is worth more than the second, a second-round pick is more valuable than a third-rounder, and so on. After converting draft positions to dollar values, more resources will have been expended on hitting than pitching.

This shouldn't be surprising if you think about it. Owners generally load up the first round with hitters. They push pitchers to the end of the first round and delay grabbing a starter. This behavior is the split at work.

The split's big pitfall is that if misapplied, it can easily result in misleading valuations, which leads to bad decisions, which leads to blowing the draft, which leads to losing the league. It's better to observe the league-wide split than it is to significantly manipulate one's own spending split. It's generally not helpful to change to a drastic split. It's rarely a strategic advantage.

Thinking Through the Split

Because a lot of misinformation exists on the topic and there's no definitive proof on the matter, throw all preconceived notions aside and try to think through the problem.

To start, consider the scoring system of a typical rotisserie league. Most leagues include five hitting categories and five pitching categories. The points available in hitting are equal to the points available for pitching.

STOP. Knowing just that information, the baseline split should be 50-50, with half the points coming from hitting and the other half from pitching.

To deviate from 50-50, an owner needs specific reasons.

One of the most common stories around is that the split settled 67-33 because there are more roster spots for hitters than pitchers. The traditional roster sizes of 14 starting hitters and 9 pitchers suggests a 61-39 split (14 / (14 + 9) = 60.8%). "That's how we got to 67-33," people will say.

But does that make sense? Not particularly. Scoring is still 50-50 between hitting and pitching, regardless of the number of players. And how did 61-39 go to 67-33? What justified that additional shift?

Consider this hypothetical league and scenario with half of all points from hitting and the other half from pitching. Imagine fourteen hitters are drafted, but only one pitcher is drafted per team.

In addition, in this made-up league, the hitting points are spread among five categories (R, HR, RBI, SB, AVG) but the pitching points come in only one category (Ks), but the pitching points are just weighted to be five times as important (half of all points still come from pitching). Assume all other typical rules and conventions apply (e.g. points in pitching are evenly distributed down to 1 as there is a decline in the standings).

In this theoretical league, assume the top pitcher is projected for significantly more strikeouts than the second-best pitcher (think about prime Randy Johnson or Pedro Martinez or Clayton Kershaw).

How much should an owner spend on that top pitcher? Think about it and come up with an answer.

If an owner could all but guarantee first place in pitching points and have secured half of all possible points, he could be willing to spend up to half of his budget (50%) to get that one player.

Therefore, roster sizes should not inherently affect the split.

Of course, that was a cherry-picked scenario. There are many qualitative factors to consider.

- With half of all possible points concentrated into one player, should an owner adjust for that additional risk? It seems like spreading the risk across many players may make investing in hitting wiser in the long run?

- Injury risk is just one component of overall risk. How does it affect pitchers differently than hitters?

- How accurately can an owner predict the statistics? Said another way, how volatile are player performances in these categories? Sure, the pitcher is projected to win strikeouts going away, but is that a steady and predictable category? Can players have significant increases or decreases in all the scoring categories?

- The draft is not our only access to players for the season. What kinds of free-agent pitchers become available? What about hitters?

These are the factors that should justify a deviation from 50-50. It's complicated. It's not just roster sizes. It's not just injury risk. It's not just performance risk. It's not just the ability to replace players during the season. It's all of them together combined into one big judgment mess.

The following two statements are true:

1. We are less accurate at predicting the pitchers that will end the season in the ownable player pool (e.g. the top 108 pitchers in a 12-team league) than the ownable hitters.

2. More pitching value appears in the free-agent pool during the season than hitting value.

These two factors make much more sense for a split shifted to favor investing in hitters.

Later in the book, there is a closer look at how undrafted value from hitters and pitchers appears during the year. The important idea to understand now is that it's easier to capture pitching value during the season than it is to pick up hitter value. The fantasy community is decent at identifying and drafting the players who will end up in the pool of top-50 hitters at the season's end, but they're worse at drafting top-50 pitchers.

Deep Thoughts on the Hitter-Pitcher Split

The split is full of confusion because it is spoken about as if there is only one hitter-pitcher split, but there are three levels of the split to be mindful of.

First, there is the theoretical 67-33 split) which most owners use. This will be called the "estimated league split" (ELS). Most fantasy owners will employ similar draft prep or use a resource which assumes similar values.

The second option is the optimized version of the "estimated league split." Let's call this the "optimal league split" (OLS). We all default to something like 67-33. By searching for information published on the split, an owner will realize no authoritative resources exist which have researched the optimal split. If nobody is studying this concept and nobody's attempting to change it, what are the odds that 67-33 is really the perfect balance?

Finally, we have the individual team's split (ITS). This split is very different from "deciding that I will base all calculated dollar values using the assumption that 67% of resources will be spent on hitting." This concept states, "given the ELS, I plan to spend $200 (or 76.9%) of my $260 on hitters." An owner can still spend 60%, 70%, or 80% of their budget on hitting even under a league-wide split of 67-33.

The ELS is an important valuation process input. Owners can look at past drafts and attempt to calculate the split from actual spending to get a more accurate measure, but an owner should require a lot of evidence before deviating from something like 65-35, 67-33, or 70-30.

Under no circumstances should an owner change the ELS in their valuations because of their own draft plan. Changing the ELS without justification will result in having wildly different player values from all other owners in the league. This will lead to thinking all hitters are overvalued and all pitchers are undervalued, or vice versa.

Back to the optimal league split. It was mentioned that there's little-to-no research on the OLS, so here's another thought experiment. The previous section contained factors that are valid reasons for deviating from a 50-50 split. The one factor which carries the most validity is that fantasy owners are not as good at identifying the draftable pitchers compared to draftable hitters. More viable pitchers are available through the waiver wire than hitters.

Assume a hypothetical 12-team league that doesn't follow the standard 14-hitter and 9-pitcher rosters. This league starts 12 hitters and 10 pitchers. Instead of the typical 12-team league drafting 168 hitters (12 teams of 14 hitters) and 108 pitchers (12 teams of 9 pitchers), this league drafts 144 hitters and 120 pitchers.

Is this actionable? What adjustment might an owner make?

It's likely that this league wouldn't make a drastic adjustment to the actual split, so the ELS can remain around 67-33.

But what about the OLS? We just established that a big reason we pushed the default 50-50 split to 67-33 is that more pitchers are available during the season than hitters. But we largely got to that 67-33 split mostly using leagues that draft 9 pitchers. This hypothetical league drafts more pitchers.

How good are the owners in this league (or the fantasy community) at identifying the top 120 pitchers? Where are those extra 12 pitchers going to come from? Within those additional 12 pitchers, at least a couple of them will be drafted who will end up within the year's top-108 pitchers. One of those pitchers from the top 109 through the top 120 might end up as a top-50 or even a top-25 pitcher.

The more players that are drafted, the lower the likelihood that significant value enters the league during the season. Owners are not perfect at drafting, but the more players owners can select, the more chances they have to grab one of the top players. If owners get only 120 selections, they might only correctly identify 45 of the top 50 in end-of-season earnings. But if they got 150 chances, they might identify 48 of the top 50 players.

If a league drafts 150 pitchers instead of 108, the split should move toward 50-50. How much toward 50-50? The research does not exist to say definitively, but it's worth noting.

If an owner doesn't think the typical 67-33 ELS is correct in theory, they can calculate two sets of player values - one calculated at the ELS and another using what they believe is the Optimal League Split. This new OLS valuation set represents theoretical dollar values. In this scenario, the ELS can be thought of as an approximation of ADP or what opposing owners will do. The owner can then look for differences between the standard 67-33 split price and the theoretical value.

ADP is a measure or approximation of "market value." This is the price an owner has to pay to secure a player. A projection-based valuation might indicate that a star catcher in a 15-team two-catcher league is a top-10 player. If his ADP is only 35, an owner won't have to pay the top-10 price tag. Similarly, a set of 60-40 OLS values might indicate that an ace pitcher is the most valuable player in fantasy baseball, but an owner won't need to pay that full price if the ELS values tell a different story.

Challenging the Basic Tenet of the Hitter-Pitcher Split

The entire theory of the hitter-pitcher split is built upon the assumption it makes sense to group all hitters and all pitchers together into groups. Owners surmise the "all hitters" group is more reliable to project than the "all pitchers" group. But does it make sense?

What if hitters and pitchers can't be grouped evenly into "all hitter" and "all pitcher" buckets? What if a certain class of hitter is more reliable than a given class of pitcher? Should all pitchers be treated the same? Are pitchers with 200 career innings pitched more or less reliable than those with 1,000? Are those with 95-mph fastballs different than those with 89 mph fastballs? Are owners better at predicting the top 10 than the top 108?

If there were reasons to believe a specific pitcher or type of pitcher was subject to more reliable end-of-season valuations, that player group should be allocated more of the 67-33 split than they would otherwise receive, and their valuation would rise accordingly.

A great example of this is Clayton Kershaw entering the 2016 campaign. Kershaw was coming off his best season. He was 27 years old and had improved each season. An honest debate existed whether Trout or Kershaw should be the first overall pick.

Many arguing for Kershaw stated that at the end of the season, 50 percent of value comes from pitchers. If an owner used a 50-50 split to price Kershaw, his value would skyrocket past any hitter, even Trout.

Kershaw was infallible. He'd had only one IL stint in his eight-year career. Risk didn't apply to him. He was a safe pitcher. An owner could pluck him out of the 67-33 split because those rules didn't apply… until they did. He went on to accumulate five IL trips in the next three years.

Owners should exercise extreme caution before believing a given player is more reliable or less risky than others.

Valuation Methods

Two of the most popular methods for assigning dollar values to projections or actual results are the standings gain points (SGP) and z-score methods. Detailed descriptions of how to perform these calculations are included in the pages that follow.

A third popular approach for calculating values is the Percent Valuation Method (PVM). This is the method most famously used by Todd Zola. Todd's writeup can be found here. Because this is not an approach used by the authors of this book, we feel it best to defer to Todd's expertise on describing the system.

Standings Gain Points

First published by Alex Patton and famously used by Art McGee in his book, *How to Value Players for Rotisserie Baseball*, the standings gain points method of valuing players is likely the most popular of the valuation approaches. What follows is a brief overview of the process. If an owner is looking for a more in-depth discussion of the procedure, they should read Larry Schechter's book, *Winning Fantasy Baseball*. They can also read here[8] if they're looking for step-by-step instructions on using Microsoft Excel to perform SGP calculations.

The standings gain points method analyzes a league's past standings data in order to determine how much of each scoring category it takes to move up one spot in the category and therefore one spot in the overall standings. The analysis will result in a calculation called "SGP factors" or "SGP denominators."

Examine the example standings and SGP factors for 12-team leagues in the following table. Look closely at the runs category. Notice the SGP factor at the bottom of the table is 19.39 runs. This indicates that, on average, 19 runs should move a team up one point in the standings. If an owner goes through the runs column, they can see this is mostly true. For most spots, adding 18-20 runs would indeed leap a team over the next team in that category.

---

[8] https://www.smartfantasybaseball.com/e-book-using-standings-gain-points-to-rank-players-and-create-dollar-values/

Roto Points	Batting Average	Runs	Home Runs	RBI	Stolen Bases
12	.278	1,131	323	1,105	182
11	.274	1,100	307	1,071	165
10	.272	1.080	298	1,051	154
9	.270	1,061	290	1,032	146
8	.268	1,045	283	1,016	139
7	.267	1,031	277	999	133
6	.265	1.015	270	983	127
5	.264	1,000	263	966	121
4	.262	982	256	946	114
3	.260	961	247	925	107
2	.258	934	236	899	98
1	.254	888	219	852	83
SGP Factor	0.0019	19.39	8.31	20.34	7.85

There is an argument that the SGP valuation method is not as mathematically sound as the other valuation systems presented in this book, but part of its appeal is that it is based upon actual standings data that also captures league behavior, tendencies, and the effect of all the player acquisitions that occur during the season. The other valuation systems determine player values at a specific point in time and do not have a method of incorporating actual league behavior.

How to Calculate SGP Factors

The first step in the SGP calculation process is to obtain final standings information for several years of a league. Three years of history is sufficient if an owner can get their hands on it.

After gathering the data, sort through it to group all first-place finishers in each category together, all of the second-place finishes together, etc. Then calculate the average it took to finish in each place. Here's an example of what the batting average standings data might look like:

Place	2018	2017	2016	2015	2014	Average
1st	.277	.271	.279	.279	.277	.277
2nd	.273	.268	.275	.276	.274	.273
3rd	.271	.266	.273	.273	.272	.271
4th	.269	.264	.271	.271	.270	.269
5th	.268	.262	.269	.270	.269	.268
6th	.266	.261	.267	.268	.267	.266
7th	.264	.259	.266	.267	.266	.264
8th	.263	.257	.264	.265	.265	.263
9th	.261	.256	.263	.264	.263	.261
10th	.259	.254	.261	.262	.261	.259
11th	.257	.252	.259	.260	.259	.257
12th	.254	.248	.254	.256	.256	.254

This example data shows that it takes a .277 batting average to finish in first place in a 12-team league, whereas a .254 AVG will finish in dead last. This means 23 points of batting average (.277 - .254 = 0.023) separates 11 places in the standings (from 1st to 12th). Some quick division tells takes about 0.0021 batting average points to move up one spot in the standings (0.023 / 11 = 0.0021).

An owner would repeat this calculation for each scoring category their league uses.

$$\text{(First Place Total - Last Place Total) / (Number of Teams - 1)}$$

$$= (.277 - .254) / (12 - 1)$$

$$= 0.0021$$

This 0.021 calculation might be referred to as an SGP factor or SGP denominator (more on that soon). They'll be referred to as SGP factors for the rest of the book.

This is a very simple calculation. Too simple, in fact. It's flawed, and better ones can be created. This approach's major flaw is the failure to account for outliers. Standing's outliers pose a problem for the SGP method, as they distort the SGP calculations.

The standings produce a bunching near the middle allowing more mobility up and down the rankings. At the top and the bottom of the standings, the gaps between teams are larger. One or two teams usually run away with a category and a few lag behind.

Eliminate Outliers from Standings

While it's true that an owner would need to accumulate more stats than other outlier teams to finish first in a category, it would be misleading to include the outliers in a calculation of what it takes to move up one average spot in the standings.

There are a couple of ways to deal with this problem. One is to use the SLOPE Excel formula to calculate the SGP factors. This function will calculate the slope of the line of best fit through the standings data. This can minimize the effect of outliers but doesn't eliminate the problem.

Using the SLOPE function on the batting average data shown above would yield an SGP factor of 0.0019 (compared to 0.0021 with the simpler calculation). Seeing a lower SGP factor makes sense. A calculation that includes the outliers will make it seem like one's likelihood of moving up in the standing is lower than an owner would encounter in most scenarios.

A more aggressive treatment for outliers is to exclude them from the calculations altogether. An owner could apply a non-biased rule by eliminating the top and bottom two teams from the standings, or they could use judgment to carefully eliminate clear outliers from the calculations. The more judgment applied to the calculations, the more personal bias is added to the calculations. Owners shouldn't pick and choose. Appendix H includes SGP factors for a variety of league types (12-team, 15-team, draft and hold, with transactions, batting average, OBP, etc.). To be consistent, the authors elected in calculating the SGP factors for these leagues to eliminate the top and bottom two teams from 12-team leagues and the top and bottom three from 15-team leagues.

Valuing Players with SGP Factors

Once an owner has determined these SGP factors, they then convert each player's projected stat line into a projected standings gain points. The calculations that follow demonstrate how to calculate SGP for an individual player. An owner needs to use Microsoft Excel or a similar software application to perform these calculations efficiently for all players.

Projected Stat / SGP Factor = Projected SGP

For example, Mike Trout's 2018 projection converted to SGP would have looked like this:

	R	HR	RBI	SB
Projected 2018 Stats	114	39	105	22
Divided by SGP Factor	19.39	8.31	20.34	7.85
Equals Projected SGP	5.87	4.69	5.16	2.80

SGP For Rate Statistics

The SGP calculation for batting average (or any other rate statistic, like ERA or WHIP) is more involved. For a counting stat, each additional run scored by a player contributes an additional run scored to the team's total. The benefit is clear.

Rate stats are not so clear. What is the effect of adding a .280 hitter to a team? And further still, what is the effect if he gets 600 at-bats? How does a person evaluate him against a .290 hitter projected for only 500 at-bats?

To approximate the effect on a team's batting average, assume a fantasy-league-average for an entire team of players (for example, many leagues start 14 hitters). Remove one player from that league-average team (down to 13 hitters now) and add back the stats for the player being evaluated.

Reviewing the hypothetical standings on the last page, it looks as though the average team in the league had a batting average of around .266. Most league hosting sites don't track or display the number of at-bats that lead to that .266 average, but looking at the projections for the top 168 hitters for the upcoming season can create an approximation, assuming that value came out to 87,567 at-bats or 522 at-bats per player.

A 13-player team of players with 522 at-bats would calculate to 6,786 at-bats.

Knowing those players posted a league-average .266 BA, we know they'd have 1,805 hits (1,805 / 6,786 = .266).

Assuming Mike Trout has a projection for a .299 BA on 157 hits and 523 at bats, the adjusted team batting average would be ((1,805 + 157) / (6,786 + 523)) = .2684.

The revised .2684 average indicates Trout raised the team average 0.0024. The BA SGP factor of 0.0019 would give Trout a BA SGP of 1.26 (0.0024 / 0.0019).

Finishing the SGP Calcs, Determining Replacement Level

Here is Mike Trout's complete SGP calculation that we've walked through::

	AVG	R	HR	RBI	SB	Total
Projected SGP	1.26	5.87	4.69	5.16	2.80	19.78

This is his raw or unadjusted standings gain points. Owners need to repeat these calculations for every player.

Owners should then identify the top 168 hitters (assuming a 12-team league and 14 offensive players) based on their league's roster requirements. This process means identifying 12 players at each infield position, 12 more corner infielders, 12 more middle infielders, 60 outfielders, 24 catchers, and 12 more utility players to comprise the top 168 players. (Since his process is difficult to describe, here's a short video demonstrating how to do this in Excel.[9])

Once the top 168 are established, identify the last player at each position that is still within the top 168. These are the replacement-level players at each position.

Continuing with the Trout example, assume an Alex Gordon-like player is the replacement level outfielder. His SGP calculations might be:

	AVG	R	HR	RBI	SB	Total
Projected SGP	(0.26)	3.46	2.29	3.59	0.89	9.96

Recall the discussion of stats over replacement level. Owners can remove Gordon's SGP from Trout's total to determine the true value of Trout's production. Owners don't have to calculate the stats over replacement for each category. All they care about is the total SGP over replacement.

	SGP
Mike Trout (Raw)	19.78
Replacement Level (Kepler)	(9.96)
Mike Trout (SGP over Replacement)	9.82

---

[9]   https://www.youtube.com/watch?v=j0ztlMHwPiU&t=5s

It goes without saying, but this same adjustment applies to each outfielder, including Gordon. Gordon receives an SGP over a replacement of 0.

When an owner performs this task on other players, they need to subtract out the replacement-level SGP of the player at the same position (e.g. subtract the replacement-level SGP of a 1B from all the 1B, subtract the SS from all SS, etc).

Assigning Value

Once SGP over replacement is calculated for each player, owners need to determine the total positive standings-gain-points-over-replacement for the entire draftable player pool. Owners can do this by sorting the data and summing each player's SGP over replacement with a positive number. Only the draftable players (e.g. the top 168) should have a positive or zero SGP over replacement. Players outside the draft pool have a negative SGP over replacement.

An owner may finish this exercise and calculate a total of 406 "draftable" standings gain points. This 406 total will be used for further calculations.

Remember that this example assumes a 12-team league. Assigning the typical $260 team budget means that a total of $3,120 (12 * $260) can be spent in the auction. A section in this book on the hitter-pitcher split comes later, but 67% of the league's spending will be allocated toward hitters in this example.

This suggests a total of $2,090 will be spent on hitters (12 * $260 * 0.67) and that each SGP over replacement is then worth about $5.15 of value ($2,090 / 406 Total SGP over Repl).

It follows that Mike Trout is worth $50.57 (9.82 SGP over Repl * $5.15).

Assigning $1 of Value to Replacement Level

A very common variation on the calculation of values is to assign a $1 price tag to the replacement level player at each position. This approximates the auction draft rules that a bid must be at least $1 on each player.

This adjustment is simple. Instead of assigning all $2,090 of value to the draftable player pool, an owner must first subtract $1 for each drafted player. In a 168-hitter league, $168 needs to be set aside for the player baseline ($1 for each), and then have $1,922 remaining to allocate based upon SGP over replacement level. This adjustment results in each SGP being worth $4.73 instead of $5.15.

SGP for Pitchers

The process outlined above is largely the same for pitchers. A key difference is pitchers have two rate stats, ERA and WHIP, in which a lower number is more valuable than a higher number.

Here are some example standings data for 12-team leagues and their calculated SGP factors. Notice how the ERA and WHIP factors are negative numbers. The negative value accounts for a lower number pointing to better performance.

Roto Points	Wins	Strikeouts	Saves	ERA	WHIP
12	108	1,519	113	3.261	1.146
11	102	1,467	104	3.399	1.175
10	99	1,431	97	3.489	1.192
9	96	1,401	92	3.567	1.207
8	94	1,375	87	3.632	1.219
7	91	1,347	82	3.696	1.231
6	89	1,319	76	3.760	1.242
5	86	1,291	71	3.822	1.254
4	84	1,257	64	3.894	1.266
3	80	1,223	56	3.970	1.281
2	76	1,172	44	4.077	1.299
1	69	1,082	28	4.234	1.328
SGP Factor	3.10	34.70	6.87	(0.0785)	(0.0145)

Error Checking

There is a lot of math to step through to calculate a dollar value. One misstep along the way can lead to unusual values. Given the task's importance (fake baseball!), owners need to incorporate some error checking into the process.

The best thing an owner can do to detect an error is to calculate the total dollar values assigned to the draftable (or above replacement level) players. If they are in a standard 12-team league with 14 roster spots, this overall total would be the players with the top 168 dollar values.

The total value of those players MUST be equal to the amount of money allocated toward hitting. In the example we just walked through, the top 168 players should add up to $2,090.

If owners find this isn't true, the issue usually lies with how replacement level was set. They need to go back and verify how they determined the replacement-level player at each position, especially when corner infield, middle infield, and utility players are thrown in.

After an owner has checked the replacement level, they need to verify they are subtracting the replacement-level SGP from players at the same position. This can be tedious but important. If the dollar values do not equal $2,090 (or the appropriate amount as adjusted for league size, league budget, and hitter-pitcher split), owners cannot rely on the values for individual players.

League-Specific Standings vs. Larger Sample Size

One of the big appeals of the standings gain points approach is that it is a model of a specific league's past behavior. It considers the competitors' preferences and incorporates those into rankings and valuations tailored to the league.

Alarm bells should be going off for some owners right now. An experienced fantasy baseball player knows to put qualifiers about small sample size on player statistics. They might hear some of the greatest minds in fantasy baseball talking about SGP, which in its basic form uses the standings from just one league. Talk about a small sample size.

Just because home run power or stolen bases ended up concentrated on a few teams in the league in past seasons does not mean that it's indicative of "long-term owner biases." Drafts and auctions are dependent on so many variables, owners should hesitate to value players based solely on a handful of years of standings data solely from one league. Thankfully, there are some reliable sources of publicly available standings data from which to draw.

Publicly Available Standings Information

The National Fantasy Baseball Championship (NFBC) is an online rotisserie competition that offers a variety of formats. There are 12-team leagues and 15-team leagues. Many of these leagues allow for in-season moves via free-agent acquisition bidding (FAAB, more on this later), but some of the leagues are "draft and hold" wherein no in-season moves are allowed. Owners draft a team of 50 players and cannot add or drop during the year. Summarized standings information for these leagues is available in Appendix I. SGP factors for these specific NFBC league types are available in Appendix H.

If owners are interested in performing their own standings analysis, they can find the 12- and 15-team standings data here[10]. There they'll see references to the various league types, like "Main Event" and "Online Championships." The Main Event leagues are 15-team leagues and the Online Championships are 12-team leagues. Both use the standard 5x5 rotisserie categories.

Example Final Equations

The process outlined above can be expedited if, for example, a pair of helpful authors analyzed the standings of popular league types and calculated the SGP factors. The SGP factors can then be inserted into a sample final equation. This final equation can be added to a spreadsheet of projections easily.

Listings of SGP factors for various league types along with sample formulas to calculate individual player SGP totals can be found in Appendix H.

For example, here are the SGP factors in Appendix H for a 12-team mixed league, as calculated from the NFBC Online Championship:

	R	HR	RBI	SB	AVG	W	K	SV	ERA	WHIP
SGP Factor	20.8	8.4	19.0	5.8	0.0016	2.8	31.7	5.0	-0.0707	-0.0135

$$\text{SGP Average Formula} = ((1795 + H) / (6768 + AB) - 0.265) / 0.0016$$

$$\text{SGP ERA Formula} = (((526 + ER) * 9) / (1187 + IP) - 3.99) / -0.0707$$

$$\text{SGP WHIP Formula} = ((1459 + HA + BB) / (1187 + IP) - 1.230) / -0.0135$$

These SGP factors and ratio formulas can be translated into this equation and used to calculate the total SGP an individual player is projected for:

---

[10]   https://playnfbc.shgn.com/standings_overall

$$(R - \text{Repl R}) / 13.7 + (HR - \text{Repl HR}) / 5.6 + (RBI - \text{Repl RBI}) / 15.2 +$$
$$(SB - \text{Repl SB}) / 4.5 + ((1665 + H) / 6454 + AB) - 0.258) / 0.0013$$

The player being evaluated has his projections for R, HR, RBI, SB, H, and AB added into the formula. Then the positionally adjusted replacement level statistics are inserted for the "Repl" arguments. This will give the SGP above replacement for a player.

Weaknesses of SGP

While SGP is the most famous method of valuing players, it's also the method with the most significant weaknesses. As mentioned, a small sample size can be an issue. There is no ideal answer on the number of years of standings data to use in the calculations. If the league has been around for 20 years, does it make sense to calculate the SGP factors on 20 years of data? Doubtful.

This decision is made more difficult by the fact that the MLB statistical environment has changed in recent years. Home runs, stolen bases, and pitcher usage have dramatically changed. To calculate SGP across these different environments would be a flawed approach.

Obtaining standings data is also a significant hurdle, especially for non-standard leagues or new leagues. Owners can work around the newly formed league issue by drawing standings data from public standings information data like the NFBC, but if their league uses categories like OBP, OPS, Quality Starts, or Holds, there are no large data sets from which to draw.

The last problem is one of theory. When an owner compares a set of SGP rankings to z-scores or percentage value method rankings, they will look very similar, but some question the mathematical soundness of the SGP calculations. There are assumptions built into the use of SGP that must be true for the calculations to hold up. For example, if an owner neglects stolen bases the entire draft and then adds a player projected for 30 steals in the late rounds, they can't really expect to move up four spots in the standings (30 steals / 7.85 SB factor). They need to accumulate a baseline number of stolen bases before the SGP factor can be relied upon.

On some level, this last problem is true of any valuation method. No valuation method is perfect. Once a draft starts, values should not be the sole input into the decision-making process. Team construction cannot be ignored and slowly takes precedence as the draft or auction proceeds.

Don't get the wrong idea here. SGP is tried and true. It is used by many of the best and winningest fantasy baseball players around. These weaknesses can be overcome, especially in leagues with standard scoring systems.

Z-score

Z-score measures how many standard deviations data is from the data set's mean. When evaluating baseball projections, an owner calculates a z-score for each player in each of the league's scoring categories. These deviations measure how far above or below average a player is in each category.

To determine z-scores:

1. Obtain player projections.
2. Calculate the average projections for the draftable player pool.
3. Calculate each category's standard deviations of those projections for the same draftable player pool.
4. For each player, subtract the average projection (#2) from their projected stat line to arrive at stats over average.
5. Divide that "stats over average" measure by the standard deviation for each scoring category.
6. Convert z-scores to dollar values.

The Advantage of Z-scores Over SGP

Z-scores offer one major advantage over the SGP method: they do not require standings information. All that is needed to calculate rankings are projections. The system is more flexible and able to accommodate newly formed leagues or those with unusual scoring systems.

Z-scores for Ratio Stats

Think back to our investigation of SGP. The value calculations in SGP incorporate team context. The value of a player is determined based on how they will affect a fantasy team in the standings. Conversely, z-score calculations ignore team context. Player values are calculated entirely from comparing one player to the pool of other players.

For this reason, owners need a different method to calculate a player's ratio stats values (batting average, ERA, WHIP). Owners can't determine value based on a hitter's effect on the team's average. They need to come up with another solution.

The method used needs to weigh a .300 average over 600 at-bats more heavily than a .300 average over 200 at-bats. Once the batting average (or WHIP or ERA) is known for the draftable pool of players, the best way to weight a better average is to simply determine the number of hits each player would have above what the average player would have had in the same amount of playing time (think of this as "Hits over Average" or "HOA").

Assume the top 168 hitters had a combined batting average of .266. Using the example of a .300 hitter with 200 AB, the calculations would look like this:

Sample Player:	.300 * 200 AB = 60 H
Average Player:	.266 * 200 AB = 53.2 H
Hits over Average:	60 H - 53.2 H = 6.8

And for a .300 hitter with 600 AB, the calculations would look like this:

Sample Player:	.300 * 600 AB = 180 H
Average Player:	.266 * 600 AB = 159.6
Hits over Average:	180 H - 159.6 H = 20.4

A shortcut is to subtract the batting average of the average player from the sample player's average, then to multiply that result by the playing time (at-bats) of the sample player:

$$(.300 - .266) * 600 = 20.4$$

Note, the calculations for pitchers (or for any ratio stat, like ERA and WHIP, where a lower score is better) are flipped. The player's ratio is subtracted from the average player's ratio. For example, in evaluating a pitcher with a 3.75 projected ERA over 180 innings pitched in a league where the average player has a 4.00 ERA, the calculation would be:

$$(4.00 - 3.75) * 180 = 45$$

Calculate the Averages for the Draftable Player Pool

For example, the pool of all draftable players is the population we want to compare each individual player against. It does an owner no good to compare a player to a minor leaguer that might be called up and have 50 plate appearances. We only want to compare players against who we project will be in the top 168 hitters (in a standard 12-team league).

The averages for the top 168 hitters might look something like this:

	AVG	HOA	R	HR	RBI	SB
Top 168 Hitters	.266	0.29	76	23	78	10

Note, the Hits Over Average (HOA) almost appears to be a batting average, but it's not. That is the average of the HOA for the top 168 players. This number should theoretically be zero. The fact that it is not zero highlights a difficulty in using the z-score system - its iterative calculations. This issue is explored more in coming pages. An HOA near zero is safe to use. Anything far from zero should be investigated.

Calculate the Standard Deviation for the Draftable Player Pool

Use Microsoft Excel or another spreadsheet application to calculate the standard deviation of the draftable player pool (e.g. top 168) for the same statistical categories (STDEV is one Excel function to use).[11]

The standard deviations would look something like this:

	HOA	R	HR	RBI	SB
Top 168 Hitters	9.88	14.47	8.46	17.69	9.52

Subtract the Average Projection from Each Player's Projection

This procedure will need to be performed for each player. Here's an example of what Mike Trout's calculation would look like:

---

[11] https://support.office.com/en-us/article/stdev-function-51fecaaa-231e-4bbb-9230-33650a72c9b0

	HOA	R	HR	RBI	SB
Projected 2018 Stats	17.88	114	39	105	22
Subtract Top 168 Average	0.29	76	23	78	10
Equals Stats Over Average	17.59	38	16	27	12

Divide Stats Over Average by Standard Deviation

Perform this calculation for each player as done here with Trout:

	HOA	R	HR	RBI	SB
Stats Over Average	17.59	38	16	27	12
Divide by Standard Deviation	9.88	14.47	8.46	17.69	9.52
Equals Z-Score	1.78	2.63	1.89	1.53	1.26

This calculation gives Trout a total of 9.09 z-scores across the five categories.

Determining Replacement Level

After calculating the z-score for each player, an owner then has completed player rankings and the framework through which to calculate dollar valuations. The process to convert z-scores into dollar values is identical to the process used for standings gain points.

Sort the z-score calculations to identify the top 168 hitters (assuming a 12-team league) based on the league's roster requirements. Verify the top 168 hitters who meet the league's roster requirements (e.g. 12 players at each infield position, 12 more corner infielders, 12 more middle infielders, 60 outfielders, 24 catchers, and 12 more utility players). Again, this video demonstrating how to do this in Excel[12] will be helpful.

Once this draftable pool of players is determined, identify the last player at each position that is still within the top 168. This is the replacement level player at the position.

Going back to our example with Mike Trout, let's assume the z-score process identifies Mikie Mahtook as the replacement-level outfielder. His z-score calculations might look like this:

---

[12]   https://www.youtube.com/watch?v=j0ztlMHwPiU&t=5s

	ZHOA	ZR	ZHR	ZRBI	ZSB	Total Z
Projected Z-score	(0.64)	(0.41)	(0.83)	(0.57)	(0.00)	(2.45)

The twist with z-scores is that the replacement level players will likely show negative z-scores. Under the SGP method, counting categories will always contain positive numbers.

The negative numbers don't change. The next step is to determine Mike Trout's z-score over replacement level. Just like with SGP, this is done by subtracting the z-scores of the replacement-level player. However, because those numbers are negative, it has the effect of adding them to Mike Trout's z-score calculations. In essence, all outfielders' z-scores are bumped up by the negative numbers associated with the replacement-level player.

	Z-score
Mike Trout (Raw)	9.09
Replacement Level (Mahtook)*	-2.45
Mike Trout (Z over Replacement)	11.54

*Subtracting the negative z-score is the same as adding the number.

This same adjustment would be applied to each outfielder and a similar replacement-level positional adjustment would be performed on every player.

Owners must be careful to adjust the player's replacement-level z-score for the same position (adjust for the replacement-level z-score of a 1B from all the 1B, SS from all SS, etc.). This is similar to the replacement-level adjustment performed under the other valuation systems. The adjustment should be similar for all positions except catcher in leagues utilizing infield, corner infield, middle infield, or utility lineup spots.

Converting Z-scores to Dollar Values

The sum of all z-scores over the replacement level for the draftable player pool will be used to assign player values. If the replacement level adjustment is performed correctly, only players in the draftable player pool should display a positive z-score over replacement. Players outside the draft pool should display negative z-scores over replacement.

Calculate the total z-scores over the draftable player pool replacement level. Think of these as "useful z-scores" (only players that should be drafted are "useful").

Let's assume this exercise was completed and it was determined that there are 493 "draftable" or "useful" z-scores over replacement.

Just like with the SGP example, we'll assign the typical $260 budget per team, meaning there is a total of $3,120 to be spent on players. Assume that 67% of league spending will be allocated toward hitters.

This split means a total of $2,090 will be spent on hitters (12 * $260 * 0.67) and that each z-score over replacement is worth about $4.24 of value ($2,090 / 406 Total SGP over Repl).

Mike Trout would then be worth $48.93 (11.54 z-score over Repl * $4.24).

Assigning $1 of Value to Replacement Level

In order for replacement-level players to be valued at exactly $1, see this same section in the SGP valuation method area of the book. The same method can be used for the z-score process of valuing players.

Example Final Equations

To help visualize the final z-score equation for a specific player, here is a sample hitter formula:

$$(R - 69.6) / 13.8 + (HR - 19.9) / 7.2 + (RBI - 69.8) / 14.6 + (SB - 8.4) / 7.9 +$$
$$(((AVG - .261) * AB) - 0.3) / 9.1$$

The following bullets will help to illustrate what is happening in the formula:

- 19.9 = Average HR for the player pool.
- 7.2 = Standard deviation for the player pool in the HR category.
- .261 = Average batting average for the player pool.
- 0.3 = HOA adjustment previously mentioned to average out at-bats. Theoretically should be zero, as previously noted.
- 9.1 = Standard deviation in hits above average.

Here is a sample pitcher formula:

$$(K - 199.5) / 54.4 + (W - 7.0) / 3.92 + (SV - 7.1) / 11.6 + (((1.23 - WHIP) * IP) - 0.33) / 9.8 + (((3.63 - ERA) * IP) + 6.23) / 45.5$$

The Difficulty with Z-scores

The theory and steps behind the z-score methodology are sound. It's a mathematical approach used to evaluate much more complicated issues than fantasy baseball.

The issue an owner runs into when applying this process is that it uses iterative or cyclical calculations. This makes the spreadsheet calculations significantly harder to build out, especially if the goal is to automate the process.

The calculation's iterative aspect revolves around determining the averages for the top 168 players. This calculation is one of the first and most significant steps performed in the z-score method. But how can an owner know who the top 168 players are before they start?

And that's why it's complicated. The calculation process must be run through at least twice: once to determine a rough estimate of who the draftable players are and then one more time to refine that determination. Making matters more confusing is that if the iterations of calculations are continually run, they may result in a slightly different pool of players each time.

There are two ways an owner can take this. One way is to get frustrated. The second, more productive course of action is to recognize that all these calculations give us a false sense of precision. The fact that three or four players move in or out of the draftable pool is not anything to worry about.

Additional Reading on Z-Scores

- **Part I: Standard Scores**[13] (Mays Copeland, lastplayerpicked.wordpress.com)
- **Part II: Positional Adjustments**[14] (Mays Copeland, lastplayerpicked.wordpress.com)
- **Part III: Dollar Values**[15] (Mays Copeland, lastplayerpicked.wordpress.com)
- **Part IV: Iterations**[16] (Mays Copeland, lastplayerpicked.wordpress.com)

---

[13] https://lastplayerpicked.wordpress.com/how-the-price-guide-works/part-i-standard-scores/
[14] https://lastplayerpicked.wordpress.com/how-the-price-guide-works/part-ii-positional-adjustments/
[15] https://lastplayerpicked.wordpress.com/how-the-price-guide-works/part-iii-dollar-values/
[16] https://lastplayerpicked.wordpress.com/how-the-price-guide-works/part-iv-iterations/

- **Fantasy Value Above Replacement: Part One**[17] (Zach Sanders, fangraphs.com)

- **Fantasy Value Above Replacement: Part Two**[18] (Zach Sanders, fangraphs.com)

- **Fantasy Value Above Replacement: Part Three**[19] (Zach Sanders, fangraphs.com)

- **Fantasy Value Above Replacement: New and Improved!**[20] (Zach Sanders, fangraphs.com)

Comparison of SGP and Z-score Auction Values

While SGP and z-score have their own advantages and disadvantages in terms of calculating values, the question then becomes how the resulting values differ among players. There is no way the values will be the same under both methods, especially with one method taking historic results as a significant input and the other being entirely forward-looking based upon the projections. The following analysis seeks to determine if there is much of a difference between the resulting values.

The comparison was created using the 2019 Steamer projections with FanGraphs playing time estimates taken right before the season started. A 15-team league and a 63-37 hitter pitcher split were used. The SGP factors used were the 15-team, standard mixed league factors from last year's edition of *The Process.*

Hitters

The dollar valuations from the two methods were compared for all players with at least 200 projected plate appearances (331 players in total) and position scarcity was not accounted for. The r-squared between the two data sets was .996. Note, r-squared is a statistical term measuring the extent the variance of a given variable explains the variance in another variable. A variance of 1.000 would mean that all the movements in SGP are explained by movements in z-scores. Translating this, an r-squared of .996 is damn near perfect. The hitter study should end there but more evidence can't hurt.

The maximum difference in dollar values between the systems was only $3.10, with the range of value differences ($SGP - $z-score) being $4.60 (from $3.10 to -$1.50). This difference isn't much

---

[17]   https://fantasy.fangraphs.com/value-above-replacement-part-one/
[18]   https://fantasy.fangraphs.com/value-above-replacement-part-two/
[19]   https://fantasy.fangraphs.com/value-above-replacement-part-three/
[20]   https://fantasy.fangraphs.com/basebal-fantasy-value-above-replacement/

considering these were only exhibited on extreme player examples. For comparison, here are the average statistics of the 10 players who deviated the most between the two methods.

Group of 10 Largest Differences	R	HR	RBI	SB	AVG
Favors SGP	71.7	12.2	56.0	32.8	.262
Average	56.1	15.7	56.4	6.7	.256
Favors Z-score	79.1	25.7	87.2	2.8	.291

The SGP approach gives more value to the speedsters while the z-score favors power hitters and those hitters with a high batting average. To the extent a player is not an extreme speedster or a bat-controlling power hitter, the two systems will tend to agree on a valuation.

One conclusion to take away is that speedsters may see the highest variation in perceived value at drafts and auctions. If it is known that competing owners utilizing SGP to rank players could be pushing up steals more than others.

Pitchers

When it comes to pitchers, there is not as much overlap between the two systems. All pitchers projected for at least 30 innings (458 pitchers) were included in the study. The r-squared between the two systems was .710. This larger unexplained variance can also be seen with the extreme range in the difference from $8.60 to -$13.30.

Group of 10 Largest Differences	W	K	SV	WHIP	ERA
Favors SGP	9.5	146.0	0.0	1.41	4.77
Average	4.9	81.9	2.3	1.33	4.13
Favors Z-score	1.6	31.5	0.0	1.27	3.88

Fortunately, none of these pitchers are good, with SGP favoring horrible bulk starters and z-score favoring below-average non-closer relievers. It is not surprising to see starters favored by the backward-looking SGP system that incorporates final standings into its calculations.

To refine the study and limit the sample, the maximum valuation of the two systems was taken and then the top 200 pitchers were re-compared. These are the pitchers most likely to be rostered.

The range in the results barely moved, going from $8.30 to -$12.10, and the r-squared only improved to .730. Here are how the extreme values compare for this group of players:

Group of 10 Largest Differences	W	K	SV	WHIP	ERA
Favors SGP	10.0	157.9	0.0	1.37	4.56
Average	6.8	114.9	5.1	1.26	3.80
Favors Z-score	2.6	55.5	0.0	1.21	3.39

The z-score approach suggests it might be ideal to use good middle relievers, but league history points to bad starters having the edge. There are also often league innings pitched minimums to keep in mind. The true optimal strategy likely lies somewhere in the middle.

The last area for comparison is closers. All closers projected for 10 or more saves were compared. The range of differences was from $3.70 to $-7.10 with an r-squared of 0.79. Here are the extreme values disagreements for closers:

Group of 10 Largest Differences	W	K	SV	WHIP	ERA
Favors SGP	3.4	74.6	13.3	1.21	3.36
Average	3.3	73.7	24.3	1.24	3.58
Favors Z-score	3.3	69.6	32.4	1.27	3.95

There has been a little twist of fate, with SGP now favoring the more talented closers while z-score tries to get any save, regardless of ratios.

These extreme differences can make pitcher values fluctuate wildly in a draft or auction. SGP hopes to emulate owner tendencies (at least in the NFBC Main Event), and those tendencies are to use as many starters as possible while ruining their team's ratios.

Most computer-generated auction values use a valuation method like z-score to create their dollar amounts. Fantasy owners should know that these programs might over-value relievers and closers compared to the actual final standings approach utilized by SGP.

Common Valuation Mistakes

There are several key mistakes that can be made when performing one of these valuation methodologies. If an error is made, the results will be inaccurate dollar values that could lead to poor decisions.

Overvaluing Projections and Valuations

After an owner invests a significant amount of time going through the projection and valuation process, it's very easy to lose sight of the bigger picture. The end goal is to win the league, to have the most points in the standings, to accumulate the most stats relative to the opponents.

Projections and valuations are a powerful tool in achieving those goals, but overreliance on these tools can be a problem. The proverb about not being able to see the forest for the trees applies here.

Think about the process we've outlined. Mire over projections. Playing time projections and talent projections. Consider team influences and the environment. Convert projections to very specific SGP factors, z-scores, or percentages. We're talking numbers out to four or five decimal places in some calculations. Sum up all of those calculations and run them through an allocation exercise we're not sure of (hitter-pitcher split). Maybe it's 65-35, 67-33, or 70-30. Then calculate a dollar value out to two decimal places. Yes, Mike Trout is worth exactly $50.57.

Hopefully, alarm bells go off and the house-of-cards analogy comes to mind. A dollar value calculation is layers upon layers of assumptions, guesses, and uncertainty. It's a false sense of security. It's putting a very precise number on top of a very imprecise process.

This is not to devalue the importance of these practices. Going through these exercises allows an owner to make the best possible and most informed decisions.

To illustrate how projections can give a false sense of security and precision that isn't there, assume the stat line for Player A below. Then assume Player A has the bounces go his way over the course of the season (and becomes "Player A+"). He doesn't even have a dramatic skill change; he just gets a few nice breaks. Those extra breaks amount to five extra hits over the season, a couple of extra HR, an extra SB, and a handful of extra R and RBI.

	AVG	R	HR	RBI	SB	$ Value
Player A	.283	75	23	92	2	$8.04
Player A+	.293	80	25	99	3	$14.31

If an owner compared Player A's preseason projection and the actual stat line (player A+), they might think that the projection was pretty damn good—it's almost dead on. But if the owner only looked at the preseason value and compared it to the actual end of season value, they would probably think the projection was very inaccurate. A few extra breaks are worth more than $6 of value. Imagine how significant the effect a dramatic skill change or increase in playing time can produce.

Player values are fluid. Don't take them as gospel. Spending time focused on results is futile and owners can better use their time on the lookout for the significant qualitative factors (like changes in approach, risk, or projected playing time) that will impact the player's value. These qualitative factors' effect can be immense. They are a lot more meaningful than sweating over whether or not five hits and two home runs change a player's projection.

Modeling League Behavior, Not Determining Player Value

This is a common scenario. An owner gets curious and Googles "how to calculate fantasy baseball player values." They come across SGP, z-scores, or PVM and then spend hours on formulating values specific to their league. The excitement is high. The spreadsheet is nearly complete. They hit the enter key and race to look at the calculated player values and are very confused and disappointed by what they see.

Most owners go through this process and expect to see values that mirror the way "their league behaves." And if the values don't look right, they go on a quest to "make the values look like the way their league behaves." This is wrong. The goal is to compare ADP to their rankings, find an edge, and determine where ADP is wrong.

If league-mates vastly over-value sluggers and bid through the roof on them, an owner should not come up with quick patches to the valuation process that fixes home run prices. It's a point where the owner needs to recognize this for what it is, a chance to buy up other undervalued resources that other owners don't properly value.

The SGP, z-score, and PVM processes are designed to calculate the true worth of a player's projection. They *are not* tools to approximate what other owners will do.

Allocating More (or Less) Than the League Budget to Player Values

After completing the valuation process, the most important error check is to verify that the sum of all the above-replacement-level players agrees to the league spending budget. Again, in a 12-team league with a $260 budget that drafts 14 hitters and 9 pitchers, the total values for the top 168 hitters (12 * 14) and top 108 pitchers (12 * 9) should be $3,120.

Further, the money allocated to hitting and pitching should also be verified. Using the same $3,120 example, if a 67-33 hitter-pitcher split was used, the owner should double-check that the top-168 hitters have a combined value of $2,090 and the top-108 pitchers have a combined value of $1,030.

If it is determined that the combined values do not agree to $3,120, the problem is very likely something to do with how replacement level was determined. There are probably not 168 hitters and 108 pitchers above the line where replacement level was drawn.

This is a common problem for snake draft leagues. It's easy to think, "I've made it through most of the valuation processes. I'm not in an auction, so I don't need to go all the way through to calculating dollar values." The problem with this thinking is that until dollar values are calculated, the hitter-pitcher split has not been applied.

Remember that we typically apply 65-70 percent of the total spending budget to hitters. This is important to do, even in a draft. Weighting needs to be applied to hitters, so an owner doesn't end up over-drafting pitchers.

A pitcher with a combined 5.25 standings gain points over replacement is not directly comparable to a hitter with a combined 5.25 SGP. For this reason, it's a good exercise to convert SGPs into dollar values. Once that is done, a $20 hitter is directly comparable to a $20 pitcher.

Advanced Valuation and Rankings Thoughts

The topics that follow are more advanced manipulations an owner might consider including in their valuation process.

Variations on the Hitter-Pitcher Split

At the risk of beating a dead horse, there is still more to be said about the confounding hitter-pitcher split. Both the SGP and z-score valuation methods calculate the utility for hitters and pitchers, and those measures are then taken and squeezed into a box that assumes a league-wide split of something near 67-33. To illustrate, here are example above replacement-level SGP totals for hitters and pitchers for a 12-team league heading into the 2018 season:

Player Type	Standings Gain Points	Percent of Total
Hitters (top 168)	406	55%
Pitchers (top 108)	336	45%
Total	742	100%

Before they are adjusted, the draftable hitters project for 406 standings gain points while pitchers project for 336. Shouldn't these numbers be equal? Or at least around 50-50?

This is a flaw that critics of SGP like to point out. One reason the flaw exists is that SGP factors are determined using end-of-season results. Those year-end standings include the effects of the many adds, drops, and trades made throughout the season. They are not solely based on draft results and preseason projections.

SGP works around this confusing issue by using a 67-33 (or similar) split, regardless of the split demonstrated solely in the preseason calculations.

The z-score section of this book suggests a similar safeguard of forcing all hitter z-scores into a 67% split of the league budget and all pitchers into the 33% side.

Another apparent logical flaw in SGP was alluded to earlier but can be explored more here. The SGP system assumes a minimum level of stats are in place for each team. In order for an 8.3 home run SGP factor to be relevant, or for a team to move up in the standings after earning 8.3 home runs, the team needs to be "in the thick" of the standings. A team with 12 horrible power hitters doesn't move up in the standings when an additional 8.3 home runs are secured.

The problem is that SGP does not offer a measure of what the minimum level of stats are. An owner should generally be in the ballpark if a balanced team is drafted, but this is a definite gray area in an approach that is otherwise objective and calculated.

The pursuit of finding the perfect hitter-pitcher split and the perfect method of valuing players is a bit like finding WAR in baseball. There are many intelligent people using a variety of theories and methods to determine a player's overall value. All parties are on the same team and headed in a similar direction but use different paths to the final destination.

While the overall process may be confusing and overwhelming at times, the generated values are light years ahead of an ordinal rank. In the end, the values will end up being very similar. Owners need to find a method they agree with and logically understand.

Deciding to Punt or Ignoring a Category in Roto

Ignoring a Category

Ignoring is often confused with punting. Ignoring a category means when given a choice between two players of similar value, the player with the less desirable category will be passed over. With pitchers, it may be those with a low WHIP as owners chase strikeouts. Or, with batters, an owner might choose to ignore AVG or OBP as they chase higher HR totals. By going with this strategy, owners accept a bad finish in the category but are not actively pursuing a guaranteed zero.

Punting

Punting a category means the owner accepts a last-place finish in that category. If they accept this finish, they need to make sure they don't half-ass it and get some production within the category. They need to finish dead last and by a large margin. Any other result suggests the owner could have performed better in the non-punted categories if they had only invested even less in the punted category.

The first step is to calculate all player valuations without including the category being punted. By excluding the category from the value calculations, money that had previously been allocated to that punted category will be reallocated to the remaining categories. The rankings will not look like any other industry rankings, but that is the advantage being sought. The owner will be able to focus on the remaining categories and can hopefully dominate them.

In almost every 5x5 rotisserie league, punting two categories—such as Wins and Strikeouts by drafting all relievers—is a recipe for failure. The strategy can put the owner in the top half or top third of the league but leaves them highly susceptible to an owner or two that are balanced enough to win. It's practically impossible to recover a last-place finish in two categories.

Categories to Punt

Saves: This statistic is the easiest to punt during the auction and season. One cautionary note is that with MLB's environment shifting so that starters are not going as deep into games, many more relievers become valuable fantasy players. If targeting some middle relievers, go for those without any possible Saves value attached to them, as their price will be lower.

Stolen Bases: With steals becoming increasingly rare, focusing on hitters with just the four other offensive categories will save some draft and post-draft headaches.

AVG/OBP: This one can be a little difficult to envision but it is a completely workable tactic that opposing managers will not suspect. In drafts, it may require the owner to wait a round or two for hitting. The top hitters will usually have some batting average skills, meaning it may be a good idea to draft a pitcher in the first round or to sit out on the top hitters in an auction, waiting for better values. Target the top end pitching and get the Joey Gallos later.

Other Punting Considerations

If an owner decides to punt one category, they must take care to not ignore or put themselves at risk of finishing poorly in another puntable category. If punting Stolen Bases, the owner needs to make sure they have plenty of Saves.

Some leagues have more than the standard five categories. Some even go as far as 10x10. In these instances, punting (and probably ignoring) categories is a more desirable strategy. With the extra categories, many skills overlap—like home runs, slugging percentage, and even OPS. Owners should focus on these correlated categories. Categories that are independent of others -- like Saves, Holds, and Stolen Bases -- can be punted.

A little side note on punting Holds or Saves: Reliever roles can be interchangeable during the season (as seen on page 28), with guys moving back and forth between the closer and setup roles. Punting Saves may be a desirable method as preseason rankings focus on Saves. Information on Holds is much harder to find. Many of the top Holds guys become closers. Owners with these new-found closers need to make an immediate decision. Do they want to join the Saves game, or should they trade the closer off as each Save is wasted? If they want to just stay in the Holds game, they can trade the new closer for the old closer, if healthy, and both owners remain happy.

In head-to-head category leagues, depending on the rules, punting may be the best possible strategy. This is especially true where the setup of the league is that teams that win the most categories get a single win for the week. In these instances, punting Wins and Strikeouts is a viable strategy. Here, an owner can attempt to sweep the hitting categories while dominating

WHIP and ERA to earn a "W" that week. Be careful and know the league rules since most leagues have a minimum innings pitched threshold.

In head-to-head leagues where each category victory represents a win in the standings (e.g. a team can go 7-3 in one week), a combination of a more balanced strategy early in the year with a more punt-based strategy as the league playoffs approach can give an owner the best chance of winning. The balanced strategy early in the season will maximize the chances of earning a top seed in the playoffs. The punt strategy then maximizes the likelihood of winning the head-to-head matchups in the playoffs.

Owners must beware of other teams' punting strategies in these formats. Be sure to anticipate the opponent's strategy and identify if there are any easy ways to attack those punted categories (having a single stolen base specialist on the bench can help knock out an opponent who is also punting steals).

Auction Cheat Code

Note: If an owner is in a draft, they can ignore this auction-only section.

A huge underlying assumption of valuations is that owners agree and will all be picking from the same above-replacement-level player pool. And for 95% of the pool, this is true. The focus here is on that last 5%. A difference of a few plate appearances in a projection can move a hitter above or below replacement level, so it's simply not going to happen that all owners agree perfectly on the player pool.

A handful of players bid on in each auction are ones that other owners have no interest in rostering. Each below-replacement-level player rostered means an above-replacement-level player can no longer be rostered.

What should an owner do with this information? If by the end of the auction there are 15 below-replacement-level players selected, 15 players from the owner's valuation spreadsheet cannot be selected. If those 15 unrostered players from the valuation sheet had a projected value of $30, that money is being wasted being allocated to them. Those funds should instead be spread to the most valuable players or just evenly across the remaining rosterable player pool.

To account for the fringe differences, most owners can assume one team's worth of players does not need values assigned to them. Through historical tests, in 15-team leagues, about 30 players are bid on who aren't on a given owner's auction list. In 12-team AL or NL-only leagues, that number drops to about 15 players.

The reason for the discrepancy is that in deeper leagues, just about any player on an MLB roster who sees the lineup with any regularity is owned. The shallower the league, the more divergent player opinions can come into play. Though not tested, the authors suspect two full teams of unvalued players may be unowned in 10- or 12-team mixed league auctions.

This process of allocating money from unrostered players to those that are rostered is not exactly the same as "going one dollar more." This process makes sure the league's budget goes to only the desired players who will be rostered. Evenly distributing the exact amount helps for a consistent game. This step takes advantage of different valuations to help allocate the total dollar pool to the players who will be rostered.

Owners need to decide if they want to eliminate a team's (or two) worth of players from the overall pool *and* how much value they think will be bid on those players (likely only $1-$2). The total amount of money bid on these players can then be reallocated to the players above replacement level the owner anticipates will be rostered.

By doing this, the valuations of all players increase. This can be used to justify going an extra dollar or two early in the auction on star players.

Alternate Method for Valuing Closers

As mentioned earlier, setting separate replacement-level players for Save-generating pitchers and all other pitchers can help level the valuations when an owner believes their league pushes the values of closers up too high.

Another approach would be for the two pitcher pools to have their own replacement level and their own portion of the budget (instead of a hitter-pitcher split, it becomes a hitter-reliever-starter split).

An owner can look at recent years' auction results to estimate what the league's hitter-reliever-starter split is. Instead of a 67-33 split of $3,120 (12 teams * $260), an owner might find a 60-10-30 split where $1,872 is spent on hitters, $312 on closers, and $936 on starters.

Using the league's historical split will give the owner a better understanding of whether a reliever is a decent value within the league's context.

The splitting of resources is one of the few areas of disagreement between this book's authors. While theoretically there would be no hitter-reliever-starter auction split, there is one, just like with hitters and pitchers. If an owner doesn't take into account the split, they'll have to drastically overpay from their calculated prices in order to roster hitters or closers. All other owners will be on a different pay scale.

With that said, this extra splitting of values arguably ventures into the territory of "modeling league behavior, not determining player value." The ideal solution to this is likely to calculate one set of values with a traditional split and another set with the observed hitter-reliever-starter split. But that is a lot more work and a lot of information to absorb during a fast-paced auction. The benefit of using only the additional split is that it makes decision-making much easier during stressful times of the auction. There is only so much information an owner can absorb while on the clock.

One principle emphasized in this book is to not overpay. However, if this mantra is followed too strictly and other owners are willing to go $1 more, the tight owner must either overpay or completely miss out on bedrock players. Without further splitting the pitcher pool, all closers may look overpriced. If owners use league-historical splits to calculate player values, they can have a better understanding of under- and overpriced closers and can then avoid or minimize the need to overpay.

Are Closers or Starters Cheaper in the Auction or in Free Agency

Starters of varying quality will always be available on the waiver wire. Andrew Cashner will be out there throwing every five days, but a reliever in line for saves probably won't be. Perceived scarcity creates a premium for those potential saves-earners whenever a closer's job changes hands. The in-season free agency bidding for these players can become quite fierce, so the authors tested to see if it is more cost-efficient to pay for closers in the draft and pick up starters via FAAB, or vice versa.

Using the 2018 NFBC Main Event results, both closers and non-closers had their average ADP compared to the average FAAB spent for comparable pitchers. The ADP was converted to auction dollars and those dollar values were then adjusted for the weeks remaining in the seasons to account for less available FAAB and rosterable time being available.

Trying to get a handle on FAAB spent is… frustrating. It's almost impossible. Using the 38 competitive leagues of the Main Event was intended to help obtain a better composite of public opinion. Even with using so many leagues, the data was still noisy.

The research shows that any pitcher looking like they will get Saves, even only a small amount or ones that have a low chance of retaining the job, will go for a $50 minimum, regardless of when during the year the role change occurs. The bid amounts only go up from that baseline, especially earlier in the season (sometimes extremely so).

Another aspect of the in-season costing model is if the pitcher has any kind of talent, the FAAB cost jumps by about $2.50 for an equivalent $1 of auction money spent for similar talent.

For example, say the pitcher had the talent of a $10 or 12th-round player (144th overall pick). The expected FAAB spent would be about $75 ($50 + $2.5 *10). Again, FAAB behavior is wild and this model breaks down often, especially early in the season. Here are the top 10 "closers" by total dollars spent across all the 2018 Main Event leagues.

Name	Week	AVG	Saves
Hunter Strickland	2	$389	14
Jacob Barnes	3	$206	2
Tyler Clippard	8	$168	7
Hector Rondon	12	$130	15
Jose Alvarado	10	$119	8
Seranthony Dominguez	9	$125	16
Joakim Soria	12	$87	16
Nate Jones	9	$159	5
Matt Albers	3	$68	1
Keynan Middleton	2	$70	6

As a group, they averaged nine Saves over the course of the season.

Using the same modeling theory for starters, it works out that a $45 baseline needs to be implemented, but that baseline dollar value drops as the pitcher quality decreases. There is no $50 baseline. Instead of a $2.50 of FAAB per auction dollar ratio, the price increases quicker with a $3.50 increase for each extra dollar of expected production.

The following table illustrates the effect of the two FAAB cost models. Note that the valuation break-even point or cross over, where it costs the same amount of FAAB for a closer and a starter, is at around pick 250.

Draft Pick	Equivalent Auction Cost	Adjusted Auction to FAAB Cost	Expected Closer FAAB	Expected Starter FAAB
25	$25.1	$96	$113	$133
50	$19.0	$73	$98	$112
100	$13.0	$50	$83	$91
150	$9.5	$37	$74	$78
200	$7.0	$27	$68	$70
250	$5.1	$20	$63	$63
300	$3.5	$13	$59	$57
350	$2.1	$8	$55	$53
400	$1.0	$4	$52	$48

In all fairness, the difference on the higher end players isn't much. Neither starters or closers are cheaper in the draft compared to the waiver wire, so owners might just focus on talent and not roles when making this decision. The values at the lower end of the model, or for the worst players, differ more, suggesting paying for crappy closers via FAAB is more costly than paying for crappy closers at the auction.

Again, the costing models and FAAB behaviors can break down at the extremes. This prevents us from finding clear-cut conclusions on the topic, but the following rules of thumb still apply:

1. Don't spend more than $100 on any pitcher, starter or closer, as similar deals come along.

2. Develop or locate a reasonable projection for the pitcher and find comparables. Use this chart for restraint. "Should I really pay $100 in FAAB for the equivalent of a $2 pitcher?"

3. Stay out of early bidding frenzies. It's a long season and the FAAB saved (avoid wasting) by avoiding dangerous bidding situations can be utilized later.

Understand the Valuation Goal

Following a strict process and adhering to the principles of calculating value from one of these systems will help an owner to arrive at a set of values that measure both intrinsic and theoretical value. A valuation system's goal is *not* to estimate or predict the market value a league will place on players.

An owner might look at those intrinsic values and say, "But in my league, the top starting pitchers are drafted much earlier than that. These values aren't accurate. I need to adjust them."

Fight that urge. Owners need to understand both theoretical value *and* market value in order to make optimal decisions. Resist the urge to combine the two values into one measure.

Consider League Rules, Intricacies

Many of the examples in this book use a "standard league." It's fair to say that no such standard league exists. Many home leagues are far from standard. Even the well-known industry leagues like LABR, Tout Wars, and the recently created Great Fantasy Baseball Invitational (TGFBI) can differ in their setup.

League rules can have a significant impact on valuations and an individual owner's decision-making process. Take TGFBI, for instance. The league, created by Justin Mason, had only one catcher position in 2018 (it switched to two catchers in 2019).

The one-catcher rule meant an owner needed to adjust the replacement-level catcher in the valuation method used. Instead of replacement level being the 30th catcher (2 * 15 teams), it had to be set at the 15th catcher. This difference has a huge effect on the valuation of catchers.

It's important for owners to tailor their valuations to their individual league. Owners might assume all the contestants in TGFBI properly accounted for this rule. After all, they're fantasy baseball analysts. But quite a few managers did not make the proper catcher adjustment in 2018. If industry "experts" are not all making this adjustment, owners can bet many managers in the typical home league are not either.

Keep the Valuation Spreadsheets and Formulas

The valuation work done in the preseason can largely be re-used in-season by replacing the season-long projections with rest-of-season projections. An owner should keep the preseason version, delete the information, and create an in-season version. This new version can be used to help pinpoint valuable in-season free-agent targets.

Valuing Multi-Position Eligible Players

Players that are eligible at multiple positions present a unique valuation challenge. For example, it seems each year there is one player that will qualify at catcher even though they won't play catcher at all in the upcoming season. That same player might also qualify as a first baseman. Similarly, there are a plethora of guys each season who qualify at both 1B and OF or at 2B and SS.

It's already been explained that a player's value is determined by his statistics relative to the replacement-level player at the same position. How do we account for this other factor?

The first thing to do is to assign the player to the weakest position for which they qualify. Or, said another way, the shallowest or worst offensive position. This means that if a player qualifies at catcher and first base, his value should be determined as if he is a catcher only.

The landscape can change from year-to-year, but the historic positional hierarchy is:

1. First base
2. Outfield
3. Third base
4. Second base
5. Shortstop
6. Catcher

And realistically, the catcher should be well below the others, because there is a significant gap from shortstop to catcher.

Placing a player at the weakest available position for which he's eligible will result in the highest value being assigned to him. This hypothetical player's statistics are the same, whether he's labeled a catcher or an outfielder. But the replacement level at one position is different than the other, that the player's "stats over replacement" or "usable stats" are higher if he's compared to the catcher pool instead of the outfielders.

What is Multi-Position Eligibility Worth?

To be clear, this question is not asking, "How much more will this player be worth if slotted as a catcher instead of an outfielder?" This question is asking, "Does the fact that a player qualifies at more than one position have a value? If so, how can we quantify it?"

There is indeed value there. Below are scenarios in which adding a player with positional flexibility can benefit an owner, along with examples of how to extract value from each situation.

1. **Flexibility during the draft.** Imagine an owner drafts a 2B/OF eligible player in the first round. Then a valuable 2B-only player falls to them in the second round. They don't have to think twice about this like they might have if they had already taken another 2B-only player.

2. **Take additional risks during the draft.** The owner drafts an SS/2B eligible player early on. The draft progresses. Middle infielders are getting scarce, to the point where competitors are reaching to avoid being left with scraps. This leaves a valuable OF on the board. The owner is no better equipped to take the OF and risk that they'll be able to find a satisfactory MI later. Given that they can slide this SS/2B player to either position, they just need a decent option at either SS or 2B. The owner can capitalize on someone at either position falling, whereas other teams might be handcuffed.

3. **Better ability to work around injuries.** Say an owner's 3B gets injured. Fortunately, they have a player that's 2B/3B eligible. This means that when going to the waiver wire, the owner is not just looking for a 3B. They might quickly realize that the available 2B are far more intriguing than the 3B.

4. **Take advantage of major call-ups.** A strong set of corner infielders are drafted. A hotshot prospect 3B is called up. If one of the corner infielders happens to be OF eligible, the owner can still work this player into their lineup.

5. **Maximize games played.** In weekly lineup leagues, a player who will play seven games in a given week has a major advantage over one who plays only five. The more flexibility an owner has with positional eligibility, the easier it will be for them to shift players around in their lineup to utilize more seven-game guys each week.

6. **Free up a roster spot.** Imagine having an extra roster spot opponents don't have. What would that mean over the course of the season? It would be hard to imagine this not having several dollars' worth of value due to the extra speculating and holding of players an owner can execute. Having a player that is eligible at both SS and 2B allows an owner to not have to roster back-up players at both 2B and SS. If an injury occurs to a middle infielder, regardless of whether it's a 2B or an SS, the owner can handle the situation.

Take a moment to think critically about these observations. While slight, these are advantages. It seems like there is definitely value in position eligibility. But the value only comes into play *if* an owner is mindful of the additional eligibility *and* is able to exploit the additional flexibility.

There is an opposing viewpoint that additional eligibility is not worth anything because "a player's statistics are worth what they're worth" and to add additional value to a player is fundamentally wrong. The authors agree with the opposing view that there is no inherent value in the eligibility itself. Extra statistics do not get added to team totals simply for having the player. The value lies in what such a player allows a team to do. But it's still up to the owner to capitalize on the eligibility. That is the difficult part.

Stepping back, the question at hand is, "How much more would an owner expect to add in stats over the course of the season because of a player's additional flexibility (or lack thereof)?" Once the amount of stats expected to be gained is determined, the stats can be converted into standings gain points to determine their value. It does not take much to start seeing an increase in value. For example, an additional 3 runs, 1.2 HR, 3.1 RBI, and 1.2 SB was worth about 1 SGP (a quarter SGP in each of the four counting categories) in a 2018 15-team NFBC team league. It's not hard to imagine being able to accumulate those extra statistics by being able to take better advantage of 7-game weeks instead of being stuck with a 6-game week. In looking at end-of-season values, 1 SGP is worth somewhere between $0.70-$1.70. The added flexibility could be worth even more, but this seems like a conservative estimate to add 1 SGP to a multi-position eligible player.

On the other hand, DH-only players get a bad rap and see their value squashed by not having a position besides the UTIL slot. Removing 1 SGP from a DH-only player's auction value is perfectly reasonable.

A multi-position eligible player is worth more to a strategic manager than he is to a lackadaisical manager. A player like Bryce Harper has pretty much the same value to any team. He can only be played in the OF and is relatively locked into the lineup. It takes skill, planning, and active management to squeeze value from players with multi-eligibility.

How to Adjust Rankings Properly

The ideal way to adjust rankings or valuations is to do so via a change to the underlying projections. Do not directly edit the final values. Making manual adjustments directly to the rankings opens an owner up to making arbitrary decisions. These will lead to moving up players an owner likes and harming players they don't.

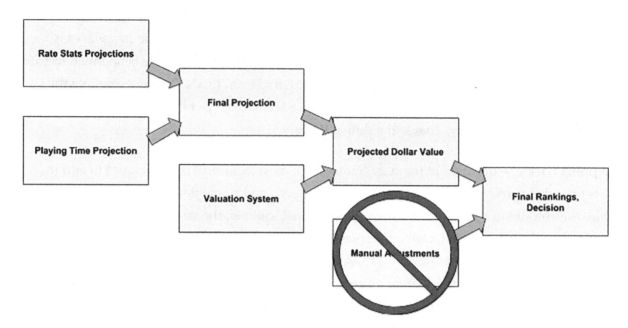

Besides the arbitrary nature of the adjustments, another problem with this manual tweaking of players is that it often results in double counting of factors. Do any of these thoughts sound familiar when adjusting a player's ranking?

- His batting average is probably going to be below .230. Move him down.

- Stolen bases are hard to come by. Bump him up a few spots.

- This guy pitches in Colorado. Move him down.

These are all examples of double counting factors that are already taken into account. A player's batting average is an input in the calculation of his projected dollar value. A bad batting average is already reflected in his calculated price. The stolen bases of all players were already incorporated into the calculation of the values. A player's home field is already accounted for in any worthwhile projection system.

The most objective ways to move a player up or down rankings are:

1. Go back to the original rate stat projections. Make a change to the underlying rate stat projections (skill projections) if there is a reason to believe the player will perform better or worse than estimated.

2. Make manual adjustments to playing time estimates.

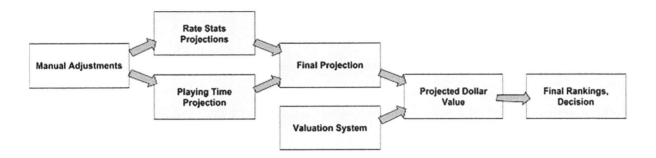

Consider Values and Costs

To this point, a lot has been discussed about the formulation of projections and values. These values provide only half of the equation when selecting players in a draft or auction. Each decision involves the weighing of benefits (value) and costs (when to select, how much to pay, opportunity cost).

Lots of fantasy advice focuses only on a player's value or cost, but it's knowledge of both inputs that make an educated decision to draft a player. In the preseason, owners have to expend draft capital (auction dollars or draft picks) to obtain value. During the season, the costs are either FAAB or waiver wire priority (not a significant cost).

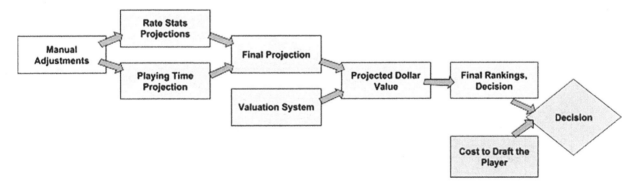

Owners should invest in a player (in the preseason or during the season) if the value to their team exceeds the cost required to obtain the player. The value minus the cost to obtain a player is the excess value.

$$\text{Value - Cost = Excess Value}$$

The best method of determining the investments to make is to compare the excess value from one decision to the excess value to be captured from another decision. Owners should make investments in players that maximize the excess value Player A offers in relation to Player B.

Preseason Values and Costs

Values and costs are clear when it comes to auction leagues. If the player shows a projected value of $30 and he can be won for $28 in the auction, it makes sense to make the purchase (unless the same $28 could instead be used to capture a $32 player).

Things are less clear in a draft scenario. It's arguably not important to consider cost in a snake draft. But an owner could convert a draft pick slot to a dollar value using the formula below (from Jeff's FanGraphs article),[21] where the "ln" in the formula is the natural logarithm of the draft pick.

$$((.1126 *\#\_of\_Teams) - 10.37)*\ln(draft\_pick) + 53$$

PICK	12-team Value	15-team Value	PICK	12-team Value	15-team Value
1	$53.0	$53.0	16	$28.0	$28.9
2	$46.8	$47.0	17	$27.5	$28.4
3	$43.1	$43.5	18	$26.9	$27.9
4	$40.5	$41.0	19	$26.4	$27.4
5	$38.5	$39.0	20	$26.0	$27.0
6	$36.8	$37.5	21	$25.5	$26.6
7	$35.5	$36.1	22	$25.1	$26.2
8	$34.3	$35.0	23	$24.7	$25.8
9	$33.2	$33.9	24	$24.3	$25.4
10	$32.2	$33.0	25	$24.0	$25.1
11	$31.4	$32.2	26	$23.6	$24.7
12	$30.6	$31.4	27	$23.3	$24.4
13	$29.9	$30.7	28	$23.0	$24.1
14	$29.2	$30.1	29	$22.6	$23.8
15	$28.6	$29.5	30	$22.3	$23.5

---

[21]   https://www.fangraphs.com/fantasy/adp-to-auction-values-process/

This information can be useful in leagues that allow trading of draft picks, as an owner can gauge the cost of a draft pick.

Also, the table and formula can be used to convert reliable ADP data into approximate auction values. There are not reliable resources an owner can turn to in order to see actual average auction values. Most host and fantasy information providers just provide estimated or suggested auction values, but reliable and aggregated ADP data does exist.

Opportunity Cost

Remember the TGFBI fantasy league. In 2018, the league rules allowed for an owner to have up to five players on the injured list at one time. Unlike the league setting dictating only one starting catcher, this IL rule did not directly affect player values. However, it was a significant factor to consider and highlights another type of cost: opportunity cost.

Opportunity cost is the missed opportunity an owner incurs by choosing one option over another. The cost of choosing Player A is not just the cost of drafting Player A, it is also the lost chance to have drafted Player B or Player C.

It is very difficult to quantify opportunity cost, but its effects can be obvious in certain circumstances. The TGFBI's IL rules offered one such instance.

Prior to the 2018 season, several very interesting and talented players were expected to open the season on the injured list—Michael Brantley, Michael Conforto, and Alex Reyes, to name a few. When a valuation is calculated for players expected to miss part of the season, the price will tend to come out on the low end. Earlier demonstrations in this book showed how only minor changes in playing time and performance can hamper a player's value.

The ability to place these players on the fantasy IL and subsequently have the freedom to speculate on early-season breakouts (more on these later) is a benefit that isn't quantified in a straight player valuation. The following table illustrates the decision here:

Option A	Option B
Player X ($10)	Player Y ($9)
	Ability to speculate on free agents

Assume Player Y is expected to miss the first two months of the season. When deciding based purely on preseason valuations, Player X's $10 projected value seems like the obvious choice. Risk-averse managers might also say things like, "Player Y isn't worth the risk in not knowing when he'll return."

However, if the owner has done his due diligence, has waded through the fluff, and truly believes an early June return is possible, that fact should be reflected in the playing time projection. If that returns a $9 valuation, the risk is already incorporated into that $9 valuation.

The selection of Player Y also comes with the intangible benefit of having a free roster spot to use for speculation.

One other item to consider is the rate at which the value gets realized during the season. Using the playing time estimates and the valuations from the previous table, the earnings would likely come as follows:

	April	May	June	July	August	September	Total
Player X	$1.67	$1.67	$1.67	$1.67	$1.67	$1.67	$10.00
Player Y	Injured	Injured	$2.25	$2.25	$2.25	$2.25	$9.00

When considering the earnings rate and the ability to have a free roster spot, Player Y looks more interesting.

Points Leagues

There's a dirty little secret about points leagues that most of the fantasy baseball community either doesn't realize or is hesitant to admit. There is no such thing as a "standard" points league. Unless an owner is playing in a default scoring league at a major site like ESPN, points leagues are like fingerprints. They're unique, and they need to be treated as such.

The uniqueness means there is no reason to read points league advice articles, to follow points league "experts," or to consume generic points league content.

The problem with seeking advice is the source has no understanding of unique league scoring formats. It's borderline negligent to give out points league advice. Sure, there are generalities common across leagues, but to answer a question like, "Points league: Player A or Player B?" is irresponsible. Avoid such advice at all costs.

To elaborate, it just takes one subtle points league scoring system tweak to significantly affect a player's value. If the cost of a hitter strikeout is changed from -1 to 0 or from -1 to -2, that is meaningful.

The variation in rotisserie leagues can be dramatic, but there's far more commonality and there are conventions in place making it reasonable to dispense advice. "Roto," "5x5," "OBP league," "4x4," or "standard roto with quality starts instead of wins" are simple ways to communicate the important details. Those conventions do not exist in points leagues.

The truth about points leagues is that an owner simply has to do all the work on their own.

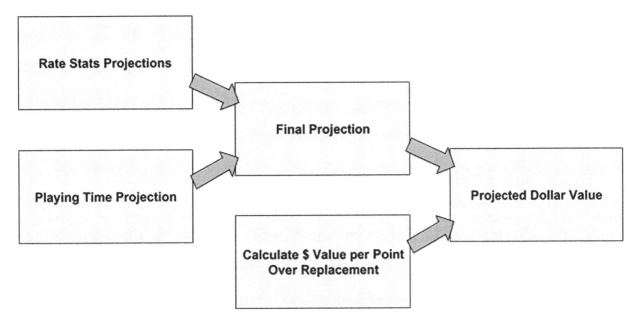

It's possible to take shortcuts. It's not necessary to formulate projections from scratch. Instead, an owner can download a strong set like Steamer. But it's imperative that an owner perform a custom calculation of projected dollar values that are based specifically on the league's scoring system.

The process is the same as for a rotisserie league, just with a different valuation system. The complexities of standings gain points, percentage valuation, and z-scores are gone. They are replaced by a simple calculation of the value of "points over replacement."

An author experienced a very odd phenomenon in two points leagues in which he participated. In each case, he ran a projection system through the league scoring settings and adjusted for replacement level. It then became very clear that pitching was extremely important.

As the new guy in each league, one of which was composed of fantasy baseball analysts, he assumed the veterans would have figured out the importance of pitching and clawed to get a top ace. But that never happened. Throughout the drafts, he stockpiled top arms while others spent their resources on hitters.

Great pitching options, worth more than hitters in his projected values, were available well into the draft. These deals went on for so long that he became uncomfortable and began to significantly question his value calculation method.

He had participated in enough rotisserie leagues to know how things work. But in a points format and in a league with a unique scoring system, it can become very difficult to trust one's work when other owners (with experience in the league) are pursuing such a different strategy. The end results in both of these leagues were championships. The valuations were correct.

The point to hammer home is that owners should be prepared for this misunderstanding in a points league. Situations can arise where it seems like everyone else is wrong. It's not unusual, especially if competitors have not done the work to develop customized rankings.

Is a Hitter-Pitcher Split Necessary in a Points League?

Think back to the rotisserie discussion on the hitter-pitcher split. Although most leagues end up with a split around 67-33, it was concluded that the starting point for a split should be 50-50 due to the rotisserie scoring structure providing that half of the possible points come from hitting and the other half from pitching.

But there is no such convention in a points league! There is no rule that says 50 percent of points come from pitching. If rankings are tailored to the league's scoring system, it might happen that well over 50% is designed to come from pitchers. Because points leagues tend to use unique scoring systems, attempting to apply the default 67-33 split may be misleading.

If prior seasons' standings data is available, an owner should do their homework to determine what percent of league scoring comes from hitting and what percent is from pitching. This will set the baseline from which to set the split. The owner may determine that scoring is nearly 50% from hitters and 50% from pitchers, or it might be determined that 40% of points are from hitters and 60% from pitchers.

Recall the factors that led us to deviate from 50-50 in rotisserie leagues. We might be more accurate at projecting hitters than pitchers, and it may be true, depending on league settings, that significantly more pitching value may arise during the season.

If the owner determines that the scoring split is near 50-50 and roster sizes and availability of free agent pitching seems like a typical rotisserie league, using a 67-33 split seems reasonable. However, if there is a significant slant toward pitching, the owner should deviate from the 40-60 hitter-to-pitcher scoring and may want to estimate that a 57-43 split is called for.

If an owner wishes to apply these theoretical splits, it is recommended that the Hitter-Pitcher split section of this book be reread, particularly the "Deep Thoughts on the Hitter-Pitcher Split" subsection.

Draft & Auction Strategy

Overview

A large percentage of the offseason work previously discussed is to prepare an owner to make clear timely decisions on draft or auction day. For many owners, the draft season is fantasy baseball's pinnacle. It's a period of several hours that will dramatically control the course of the season.

The following steps will help an owner to prepare the necessary reference information for the draft, as well as to help shape the plans and strategies the owner will use when drafting or bidding on players.

Draft Value Sheet

Step 1. Add ADP

Once an owner has his individual player values calculated, it's time to find where these values diverge from everyone else's views. An owner creates their own personal sleeper and bust list. This comparison list will be called the Draft Value Sheet and will be an owner's focus until the draft or auction ends.

Determining which players project to provide surplus value cannot be done without considering how the rest of the industry and/or the rest of the owners in a given league are valuing players. Personal and industry values must be compared in both drafts and auctions.

Ideally, an owner wants to compare their rankings to the ADP and/or rankings from the host league's website. Many other owners will be too lazy to do their own draft research and will just use the website's preset rankings or ADP. An owner who puts in a little more effort can run circles around this crowd.

This next step can take some time, but the personal ranks and website ADP need to be lined up. Sometimes ADP isn't yet available for an early draft, so use any available ADP.

Before matching a set of industry rankings to the owner's personal rankings, the industry values need to be translated to a dollar value. The easiest method is for an owner to match their calculated player values to the industry order. For example, if the industry takes Player

X as the fifth player off the board, he needs to get assigned the owner's fifth-highest calculated dollar value even if the owner has that fifth-highest value assigned to Player Y. Most of the time, the players won't be at the same values, but the differences will be small. The key is to find the biggest differences. These will be the biggest breakout and busts for the owner to target or avoid.

Industry rankings, especially on major websites, are not going to be far off each other. Their goal is to be average, not different or better. One major source states they need to adjust their values if they get too far off the rest of the industry. Because of this bias to not be different, the first public rankings will have a ton of influence as other sources anchor to these values.

Because of this herd effect, don't assume all the websites are right and the individual owner is wrong. If an owner still has reservations about their personal values, refer to the NFBC's ADP. These owners have hundreds, if not thousands, of dollars on the line, and they will have a better pulse on an actual player's value.

While the owner is obtaining information, some additional information can be helpful. For those in drafts, consider including the high and low pick at which players have been selected (NFBC data includes this data). For auctions, include the league's historic auction bids if they are available. These numbers will not be used until it is time for final draft prep, but an owner doesn't want to be chasing down data as draft day nears.

Step 2: Churn Draft Value Sheet to Determine Values

The key at this point is to find and verify valuation differences. Certain differences will be obvious, especially if the owner's league has different roster requirements such as one or two catchers. For other differences, some digging needs to be initiated to determine why valuations diverge. The reason may be in playing time, risk tolerance, or other factors. However, an owner could realize the player's projections are incorrect and need adjustment. The key is to adjust the projections instead of indiscriminately moving players in the rankings, as discussed in the "How to Adjust Rankings Properly" section.

Early in the offseason, many valuations are guesses since few free agents have signed and no trades have been executed. Around the time pitchers and catchers report to spring training, analysts know most MLB teams' compositions and can make accurate playing-time projections. Most owners will then rest on their laurels as the regular season nears. Keeping track of position and bullpen battles can give an owner a huge advantage.

Additionally, ADP values will change during the offseason as savvy owners start to push up the price of bargains. Updating the ADP list will point to new value differences to investigate.

Updating and recycling the list doesn't need to happen daily or even weekly. Instead, it's a personal discovery time to get comfortable with the players who owners will likely roster. Many times, these aren't the hottest names. An owner needs to again decide if they want a "cool" team or a winning team. Most times, it can't be both.

Draft/Auction Day Changes

Sheet Additions (Draft)

Two pre-draft steps can be completed to help immensely on draft day.

Step 1. If available, use high, average, and low average ADP to determine the likelihood a player will be available at a certain draft pick.

This step may not be possible if current high and low draft positions don't exist. These ADP values need to be inserted into Jeff's article published at FanGraphs (link).[22]

With these percentages in hand, each owner can then gamble on how far they will let the availability rate drop. This rate will be different for different owners and their risk tolerance. Some may not want the likelihood a player will be available to drop under 90% while others may take a chance all the way down to 50% or lower.

Step 2. Determine players to skip for value buys.

This step determines how most drafts are won or lost. Simply, it's playing the odds in getting an early-round pick in a later round.

For example, Player X has a 2nd-round valuation but normally he goes in the 4th round. Here's a chance for a value grab. Even if Player X is the top value on the owner's board in round 2, the owner passes on him and takes the chance he's available in round 3. The availability values in Step 1 help with these decisions.

---

[22]   https://fantasy.fangraphs.com/adp-availability-workbook/

If the draft percentage is not available, the owner will need to go with their gut. As a rule, owners need to split the difference between when a player is being drafted and where their valuation places the player. For example, if a player has a 6th-round value but is being drafted in the 10th round, draft him in the 8th round. If the rounds can't be split evenly, go down a round. So if the value was the 6th and the ADP suggest an 11th-round value, draft in the 9th round.

Don't try to get too fancy and let the player drop too far. Owners shouldn't feel bad about drafting their highest-rated player. It will feel much worse if such a player falls into the hands of an opposing manager.

Early in the draft, few if any of these values will exist. Owners will just be taking the highest-rated player. It's not until later when the highest values need to be skipped over. It feels great getting a 5th-round value in the 7th.

Consider Previous Production

The fantasy tout pair of Colton and the Wolfman (Glenn Colton and Rick Wolf) have used their "SMART system and Rules of Engagement[23]" to much success over the years. One of their mantras is that age matters and they urge owners to "pay for prime players (loosely defined as 26-32) with a proven track record." Besides the pair, other successful fantasy players religiously follow the "with a proven track record" rule.

To test the validity of these beliefs and the extent to which performance in prior years matters, all preseason Steamer projections from 2010 to 2018 were analyzed and compared to both previous seasons' actual performances and the actual performances for the season being projected. The 2018 15-team, average league standing gains points were used to determine values, assuming a 63%/37% hitter pitcher split.

Previous Hitter Production

Comparisons for hitters were performed for the actual results of the previous season, the average results from the previous two seasons, and the maximum level of production observed in the past three years.

---

[23]   https://www.fantasyalarm.com/smart

Here are the results of the analysis when players are grouped by the actual results of the previous season:

Projected Return	Previous Season Return	Average Projected Return	Average Actual Return	Difference	% of Projected Return
> $30	> $30	$35	$25	($10)	71%
	< $30	$33	$18	($15)	54%
$20 to $30	> $30	$24	$23	($1)	95%
	$20 to $30	$24	$15	($9)	62%
	< $20	$23	$14	($9)	59%
$10 to $20	>$20	$15	$12	($3)	80%
	$10 to $20	$14	$9	($5)	67%
	< $10	$13	$6	($7)	45%
$0 to $10	> $10	$6	$4	($2)	63%
	$0 to $10	$4	$0	($4)	(4%)
	< $0	$4	($1)	($5)	(24%)

Here are the results when players are grouped by the average results from the previous two seasons:

Projected Return	Previous 2-year Average Return	Average Projected Return	Average Actual Return	Difference	% of Projected Return
> $30	> $30	$35	$26	($9)	75%
	< $30	$34	$18	($16)	52%
$20 to $30	> $30	$26	$24	($2)	94%
	$20 to $30	$24	$15	($9)	65%
	< $20	$23	$15	($8)	66%
$10 to $20	>$20	$15	$11	($4)	71%
	$10 to $20	$14	$10	($4)	74%
	< $10	$13	$7	($6)	49%
$0 to $10	> $10	$7	$4	($3)	58%
	$0 to $10	$5	$1	($4)	28%
	< $0	$4	($2)	($6)	(38%)

And here are the results when players are grouped by their maximum level of production in the last three seasons:

Projected Return	Previous 3-year Max Return	Average Projected Return	Average Actual Return	Difference	% of Projected Return
> $30	> $30	$35	$23	($12)	66%
	< $30	*	*	*	*
$20 to $30	> $30	$24	$18	($6)	75%
	$20 to $30	$23	$14	($9)	60%
	< $20	$23	$15	($8)	65%
$10 to $20	>$20	$14	$10	($4)	72%
	$10 to $20	$13	$10	($3)	74%
	< $10	$14	$0	($14)	2%
$0 to $10	> $10	$5	$3	($2)	53%
	$0 to $10	$4	($1)	($5)	(32%)
	< $0	$4	($3)	($7)	(86%)

* Not enough samples in this player grouping to draw conclusions from.

In almost every grouping of preseason valuations for each of one, two, and three previous years, players with higher levels of previous production outperformed the players with lesser levels of performance. While the authors had never considered using previous production, they do now. These are eye-opening results.

This study seems to fly in the face of previous sections of the book where rookies are touted as potential bargains. Keep in mind, the earlier study in the book focused on OPS. It is possible that rookie hitters outperform their projected OPS measures but fall short in playing time and the accumulation of counting stats. Because they don't have previous MLB experience, this study suggests owners should not focus on the top projected rookies and instead focus on rostering rookies at the end of drafts or in the dollar days, where the downside can be minimized and owners may still be able to capture the upside variance previously discussed.

Here are the linear regression r-squares using the projected value and the various measures of previous production. The goal is to find which measure of previous value should be used.

Projected Return	Actual Return	Previous Season	Previous 2-year Average	Previous 3-year Max
>$30	0.01	0.08	0.08	0.03
$20-$30	0.01	0.03	0.02	0.03
$10-$20	0.03	0.04	0.04	0.05
$0-$10	0.02	0.04	0.04	0.05

As can be seen in the previous table, the results for the previous two-year averages and previous seasons are similar. The authors recommend using the average of the last two seasons because it also happens to be the measure used for pitchers.

Recall that a projection is comprised of both a playing time component and a skill component. It seems most likely to the authors that playing time changes more rapidly and dramatically than skills, and that these results are being driven by the playing time component of projections. This suggests that last season's playing time or the average of the past two seasons' playing time is more accurate.

In order to determine if these results are being affected by playing time, the Steamer projected plate appearances were compared to each player's actual and previous season's plate appearances.

Projected PA Range	Previous Season PA	Projected PA	Actual PA at EOS	Actual / Previous Season PA	Actual / Projected PA
> 700	690	715	593	86%	83%
650-700	653	669	609	93%	91%
600-650	594	626	570	96%	91%
550-600	509	575	504	99%	88%
500-550	449	527	465	104%	88%
450-500	435	475	431	99%	91%
400-450	368	426	374	102%	88%
350-400	344	374	330	96%	88%
300-350	322	324	293	91%	90%
250-300	275	274	280	102%	102%
200-250	246	224	234	95%	104%
150-200	196	175	204	104%	117%
100-150	162	124	170	105%	137%

The projected plate appearance values were optimistic, meaning projections will tend to overstate earnings. Interestingly, most players also lost playing time from the previous season, but the effect seems less than the overstatement by projections. From the authors' knowledge, Steamer is one of the more conservative projection systems, so other projections may be even more optimistic with playing time.

Because the projections seems to overstate playing time, it may seem like an average of the past two seasons may be most accurate, but comparing the r-squared for all projections over 100 PA, the projection-to-actual has a value of .48 while the average value is only .46 (previous season to next season is .34). Despite the room for improvement, the projected playing time is still more accurate than some other measures.

Going back to the projected value versus actual value produced, overall optimistic playing time is likely the cause of all groups of players missing their projections. Still, hitters who haven't previously reached their projected threshold perform worse than those with similar projections that have done it before.

Previous Pitcher Production

The same dataset of Steamer projections was used, and the same analysis was performed for pitchers, but with one change; only two years of data was used to determine the maximum value of previous performance. Pitchers change so much during a season, let alone looking three years into the past. Some numbers may seem off because of rounding.

Here are the results of the analysis when players are grouped by the actual results of the previous season:

Projected Return	Previous Season Return	Average Projected Return	Average Actual Return	Difference	% of Projected Return
> $30	> $30	$36	$37	$1	103%
	< $30	$31	$31	($0)	99%
$20 to $30	> $30	$25	$23	($2)	91%
	$20 to $30	$24	$26	$3	112%
	< $20	$24	$19	($6)	77%
$10 to $20	>$20	$15	$15	($11)	96%
	$10 to $20	$14	$11	($3)	78%
	< $10	$13	$8	($5)	62%
$0 to $10	> $10	$6	$6	$1	109%
	$0 to $10	$5	$3	($2)	63%
	< $0	$4	$1	($3)	21%

Here are the results when players are grouped by the average results from the previous two seasons:

Projected Return	Previous 2-year Average	Average Projected Return	Average Actual Return	Difference	% of Projected Return
> $30	> $30	$37	$39	$3	108%
	< $30	$31	$25	($7)	79%
$20 to $30	> $30	$24	$25	$0	102%
	$20 to $30	$24	$25	$0	102%
	< $20	$23	$17	($7)	72%
$10 to $20	>$20	$15	$12	($3)	82%
	$10 to $20	$14	$12	($2)	84%
	< $10	$14	$10	($4)	73%
$0 to $10	> $10	$6	$4	($2)	69%
	$0 to $10	$5	$2	($2)	52%
	< $0	$4	$3	($1)	83%

And here are the results when players are grouped by their maximum level of production in the last two seasons:

Projected Return	Previous 2-Year Max	Average Projected Return	Average Actual Return	Difference	% of Projected Return
> $30	> $30	$36	$37	$1	103%
	< $30	$32	$30	($1)	96%
$20 to $30	> $30	$25	$24	($1)	97%
	$20 to $30	$23	$26	$3	111%
	< $20	$23	$8	($15)	35%
$10 to $20	>$20	$15	$13	($2)	85%
	$10 to $20	$13	$10	($4)	73%
	< $10	$13	$9	($4)	71%
$0 to $10	> $10	$4	$2	($2)	54%
	$0 to $10	$5	$4	($1)	75%
	< $0	$3	$2	($1)	63%

Top-end pitchers (those projected for more than $20 in value), on average, meet their projections more than hitters of the same category. Paying for these elite arms seems like a safe bet (shhh!). With the high variation in Wins, the results can fluctuate, but on average they are relatively safe investments. Well, almost.

Pitchers who have not recently reached a $20 value are horrible investments. These pitchers have historically provided only half their projected return. Also, the $10-$20 range of projected pitchers have been horrible investments. Again, those with previous success do somewhat better than those that haven't but not by much.

Here are the pitcher linear regression r-squares using the projected value and the various measures of previous production.

Projected Return	Actual Return	Previous Season	Previous 2-year Average	Previous 2-year Max
> $30	0.11	0.23	0.31	0.22
$20 to $30	0.05	0.12	0.15	0.18
$10 to $20	0.03	0.10	0.09	0.11
$0 to $10	0.03	0.11	0.14	0.13

The key with this r-squared table is to pair it with the corresponding value study above where players from projected dollar ranges met or exceeded expectations. For example, not only is the 0.31 r-squared for the "Previous 2-year average" grouping the highest measure in the previous table, it also corresponds to one of the best returns; where the pitchers that exceeded $30 of production in the average of the prior two seasons exceeded the earnings they were projected for. As mentioned in the hitter study, this averaging of the past two seasons also shows strong r-squared values, meaning owners can treat hitters and pitchers the same when considering previous performance.

The following table shows the relationship between projected and actual innings pitched.

Projected IP Range	Previous Season IP	Projected IP	Actual IP at EOS	Actual / Previous Season IP	Actual / Projected IP
> 220	237	227	230	97%	101%
200-220	211	207	191	91%	92%
180-200	185	189	167	90%	88%
160-180	155	170	148	95%	87%
140-160	129	150	130	101%	87%
120-140	105	132	116	110%	88%
100-120	93	110	104	112%	95%
80-100	75	89	83	111%	93%
60-80	65	67	59	91%	88%
40-60	51	52	47	92%	90%
20-40	36	33	37	103%	112%

Like with hitters, the raw Steamer projections tend to project more playing time than actually transpires. Most pitchers only reach 90% of their innings projections, but it's notable that the workhorses appear to achieve innings pitched right in line with their projections. Still, when investing in top arms, look for a two-year track record to help limit the downside risk.

Values (Auction)

In auctions, the key is to buy $320 in players with a $260 budget. Owners need to average approximately $3 of surplus value per player to accomplish this. Without being able to identify these deals, owners will come out of the auction with an average team at best. Follow these additional steps to those already completed

Step 1. If desired, ensure the Auction Cheat Code boost (discussed in the "Advanced Valuation and Rankings Thoughts" section) is calculated and translated to the ADP values (as discussed in the "Draft Value Sheet" section). The new cheater price points add a few extra dollars to help acquire the top talent.

Step 2. If available, collect the league's historic ranked auction values divided up by hitters, starters, and closers. These values bring to the surface the league owners' biases. Do certain owners over- or undervalue closers? Do the top players come at a premium? How soon and how long do the dollar days (where players go for only $1) last? How do catchers get valued?

Here's how to determine the best values going into the auction.

Process No. 1 - Only ADP is Available, Past Auction Data is Not Available.

The process is the same as outlined in Step 1 of creating the Draft Value Sheet. It's important this is completed for auction preparation in order to give some estimate of what actual auction prices may be. Here is a step-by-step process for hitters:

1. Collect the ADP for leagues with the same positions required to be filled in the auction (e.g. two catchers, five outfielders, etc.). If the league settings are different for the average draft data, the owner could get very misleading data for certain positions. If the league settings are not the same, the owner can instead collect ADP by each position.

2. The owner places his ranked hitter dollar amounts next to the hitter's ADP. If the ADP league settings are the same, the owner starts with the highest valuation next to the player with the highest ADP, his fifth-highest valuation next to the player with the fifth-highest ADP, etc. If the ADP league settings are not the same, this is done with the positional ADP data, position by position. The owner takes his highest catcher valuation and assigns it to the catcher that is highest on the ADP report. The owner takes his 20th-highest OF valuation and assigns it to the 20th OF on the ADP report, etc. The ADP hitters now have proxy dollar values.

3. The ADP-translated dollar values can now be compared to the owner's calculated dollar values to find deals.

Process No. 2 - ADP and Past Auction Values

When using both ADP and historic values, the procedural difference is that the two data points need to be averaged to anticipate the best deals.

Auctions are far from a perfect market and the historic values may include information about league tendencies and where to buy. Good deals may be found early on when owners are shy and don't want to pay up for the top few players, or leagues may show a tendency to greatly overpay for the top players, leaving significant value on middle- and lower-tier players. Going over big round numbers, like $50, can be a barrier for some people. Owners need to find the auction's historic soft spot. By knowing its weakness, owners can prepare themselves mentally to jump immediately or to be ready to wait a while for values to surface.

Pre-Draft Prep

Speed Up Pre-Draft Projection Churning (~1 month to 1 day before the auction)

An owner's overall rankings need to be continuously compared to the current average draft position for the league's drafting platform. This step is huge and probably the least utilized. It points an owner to the over- and undervalued players. By the time of the draft, an owner should have an idea of the players they'll likely be rostering.

Additionally, it allows the owner to determine if any player values differ from the owner's internal rankings. It's best to notice the values now instead of during the draft. Work out the difference now so no mid-draft second-guessing is needed. Owners should feel good with every player ranking. If they don't, adjust the projection to a more comfortable one. Player values are changing constantly and owners who stay up on these changes will have an advantage.

For example, Miguel Cabrera was tough to value before the 2018 season. Projections still liked him, but owners knew his constant back injuries could sap his power and playing time. Or all of that could be fine, and he could be top-30 hitter again. A wide range of outcomes existed and owners needed to go in and personally adjust the projection to their perception of the risk level. Once the risk was added in, Cabrera would have had a value which reflected the owner's tolerance. The value might seem low, but this value is where the owner feels safe to buy in. These decisions should be made well ahead of the draft. There isn't enough time to mull over things like this during the auction.

How to Use ADP

The Flaws of ADP

ADP by its very nature is groupthink. It's the combined thinking of many people, often over a large period of time (from January through March). This wisdom of the crowd approach can be helpful. Research has shown that many independent opinions, when combined, can improve accuracy over an individual's decision making.

This is where the value in ADP comes from. The thoughts of thousands of fantasy owners are a better measure than just one … or are they?

While ADP is a good measure of player value, some of the very benefits just mentioned are the weaknesses that can allow an owner to exploit ADP.

First, the order in which players are drafted is not necessarily the order in which players are valued. If an owner suspects a higher valued player can still be selected two rounds later, they would be wise to wait.

So ADP does not reflect everyone's thoughts on value. It's more a measure of this weird game theory dynamic of how far down fantasy owners can squeeze value from price and everyone else's price.

The second reason ADP is a flawed measure is it breaks the conditions required for the wisdom of the crowd to be true. ADP is not independent opinions. It's an echo chamber of people making decisions based on knowing the ADP. It's the opposite of an independent opinion.

Finally, it just takes one owner in a draft to overvalue a player to keep his ADP high even though the other 14 owners don't value him as much. Maybe the owner still believes the guy can hit 50 home runs or steal 50 bases like the previous season. Perhaps they're buying into the hype surrounding a young unproven talent that doesn't have a major league track record.

How to Exploit ADP

Now that we've stripped ADP of some of its glamor, we can take it for what it really is: simply a measure of what other people are doing. Or better yet, a measure of what other people have done. No more, no less.

The flaws discussed help illustrate a main weakness of ADP that is rarely mentioned: it's slow to respond to actual changes in value. Very slow. There are two reasons for this:

- ADP is often based on months of data
- Game theory is involved

With months of draft data involved, the recent drafts are not going to move the needle much. Moving ADP is like turning the Titanic around. It's a slow process.

135

The Process

On top of that, there is no incentive to jump players to their true expected value when drafting them. Assume the projection and value of Player X shows him as a top-100 player. If Player X has been drafted around pick 200 and months of ADP data reflects that it would be foolish to take him at pick 100. Rounds and rounds of cushion still exist. An owner might wait until pick 150 or even 180, depending on risk tolerance.

Many otherwise intelligent folks will be too conservative when it comes to "jumping" a player up the draft boards. They might say things like, "People are reaching way too far for him," or "I would never take him that early."

Stop. Think. One of two things could be happening. The player could just be a victim of overhyping, which certainly happens, or the people saying that are too invested in the ADP and they're not realizing that players' true values change faster than ADP will change.

If a player's projection suggests ADP is wrong, don't be afraid to jump on the player. Be aggressive. It only takes one other manager in the league to also believe in the player for him to be taken early.

ADP is like a boat that is slow to turn with a captain that has no incentive to turn the steering wheel as far as needed. ADP will move slower than it should. The following is how to exploit it.

Tips for Using ADP

The most important tip to keep in mind is to narrow the date range of the ADP source. The NFBC ADP data is great for this. The quantity of NFBC drafts really picks up as the season nears, so owners can get a sizeable number of drafts included in the calculations and still keep the date ranges to only several days. The NFBC also allows filtering of draft data to only show results from a certain time frame (e.g. the last month). This addition limits some of the slow-moving changes.

If an owner cannot filter the date ranges, keep an eye on the "Min" and "Max" pick data for players. This may be the more accurate measure of when a player will go, especially if his value is shifting rapidly.

Finally, know the competition and adjust the ADP accordingly. In a home league with a bunch of casual players that uses ESPN as the hosting site, using ESPN's ADP data as a measure of what league-mates will do is better than using detailed NFBC data.

136

Focus on Production Over Position: Ignoring Position Rankings & Tiers

The main concept on which to follow through is to use player dollar values, whether participating in a snake draft or an auction. Under all circumstances, try to stay away from ordinal positional rankings. Many owners consider the drop from the No. 1 to No. 2 player at a position to be the same from the no. 7 to No. 8. That might be true, but it's more likely that there isn't as much difference between No. 7 and No. 8. These drop-offs are specifically quantified in dollar values.

Additionally, owners shouldn't feel the need to fill a position. The positional scarcity has already been baked into the valuations. Just go off the values.

Owners shouldn't feel like they need a position filled at a certain spot in the draft like a first baseman by the third round. If the only first basemen are fourth-round values, wait until the fourth round to draft them. If those first basemen are taken in the third round, that's a good thing. There should be plenty of surplus value sitting there in the fourth.

Position Runs

Unprepared owners can create a run on a position, further pushing down the available values. These runs are fine. There are plenty of position players to go around and the disciplined owners should sit out of the run and just fill the spots later. It's better to get the twelfth-ranked first baseman at the right round than overpay for sixth-best one.

To further illustrate this point, here are projected hitter values from a 2018 15-team standard league. It's the classic sideways S curve (top half) with the shortstop values depicted in orange.

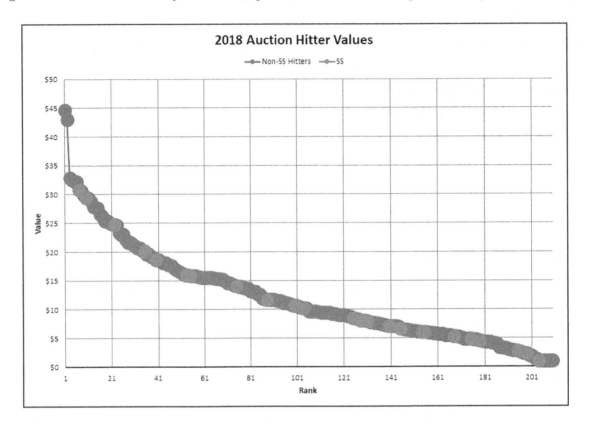

The graph shows how the talent drops quickly and somewhat curved from the first ranked player to around the 50th overall player. After that, the line takes a more linear descent. The key for a team is to pick up as many players in the non-linear section.

The gaps between the shortstop values aren't evenly distributed, with some $5 gaps early on. Additionally, there are a couple of instances where 20 players fall between two shortstops. These differences further show how ordinal positional ranks can be more of a hindrance than a help.

There is one exception where grouping players can be helpful. On the final auction value sheet, the players may be grouped by position to help locate them easier. However, decisions should be made from the dollar values associated with the players, not the positional rank. For the infield positions, it might be easiest to group by middle and corner infield.

Catcher Strategy

Catcher valuation and pricing can be one area where an owner can gain an edge on the competition. First, the number of catchers to be rostered must be considered. In just about all one-catcher formats, a starting Major League catcher can be rostered. The surplus ends in all two-catcher formats, causing their valuations to jump (because the replacement level is a part-time MLB player who is offensively challenged).

In leagues with a bid history, see where the catcher values have historically lied. Most likely, the values won't be found with the top few or the bottom. It's the middle tier that will provide surplus value.

When targeting middle-to-low end catchers, an owner should try to find a carrying trait where the player's value will come from and one that fits with their planned team construction. With catchers, it's likely to be power, batting average, or on-base percentage. It's rare for a mid-tier catcher to contribute significantly in more than one of these areas.

Depending on the number of teams in the league, there are several reasons why an owner might wait on drafting catchers until the later stages of the draft:

1. Catchers are the most likely players to get hurt. In a lineup where lineups are set for the week, it's better to have a low producing catcher out for the week than someone invested in with a significant draft pick.

2. With an increasing number of MLB teams deploying catcher time-shares or platoons of some sort, it's becoming easier to stream the position based on matchup. The authors were able to successfully deploy this strategy in a 15-team league during the 2019 season, meaning it can surely work in a 12-team or shallower league. Matchups can be cheaply exploited. There are usually a handful of catchers freely available that project better than replacement level for the upcoming week. There is also very little content available touting this group of players, meaning little competition on the waiver wire. It just takes a little bit of work each week to check for recent playing time trends.

3. Because of injuries and the low offensive level needed to become valuable, above-replacement catchers will emerge throughout the season. By grinding the bottom catchers, one of these players might break out and stick on a team as a valuable long-term contributor (think Christian Vazquez in 2019).

In leagues where bench space is not at an extreme premium, owners may want to have an additional catcher on the bench early in the season while they churn through several players trying to find the best two options.

Closer Strategy

Owners need to enter the draft or auction with a plan on how they'll handle closers. The problem with Saves is that only 30 or so pitchers are accumulating them at any point during the season.

The overall contribution from closers can be one (Saves) and sometimes up to three (ERA and WHIP) categories. As looked at earlier in the "Advanced Valuation and Rankings Thoughts" section, overpaying for closers on draft day may be tough to swallow, but it may be a better use of resources to pick them up in the draft than to spend a ton for them in FAAB. In some leagues, an owner may spend 25% or more of their FAAB budget on a popup closer, only to see the closer immediately lose the job or in some instances never truly get it (e.g. Tyler Clippard twice in 2018).

Owners may want to roster one trustworthy closer and then allocate several roster spots to closers in shaky situations.

For owners in waiver wire leagues, it may be completely impossible to get a newly promoted closer depending on the waiver priority order. Starting pitchers will always be available to fill roster voids, but closers won't be.

The key to effectively navigating the closer waters is to always think of the three main factors that go into any situation:

1. Projection & Value
2. Risk
3. Cost

Owners frequently lose their heads when it comes to investing in closers. Quite a bit has already been written on the irrationality of closer prices. They don't follow normal valuation models.

A viable compromise would to budget more resources to closers in the auction or draft. Know and anticipate that the prices will not be rational and plan for it.

Another compromise is to allocate more roster spots to closers. Instead of spending $30+ on two studs who may get hurt or be out of a job the next week, spend that $30 on five unsexy guys with jobs or close to a job, knowing that some may hit and others won't. The owner comes into the season with several options at closer and can search the waiver wire for cheap starters.

Another factor that should inform an owner's closer strategy is bench size. If a team is allowed six or more bench spots, they could roster several closers in waiting and hope for an injury, trade, or role change. If a team has only three spots, there is no way they can afford to roster a non-closer.

Underlying all of these strategies is a decision discussed in the valuation section of this book. Prices may seem more or less irrational depending on whether the owner elected one of these variations on valuing relievers:

- Set separate replacement levels for Save-generating and all other pitchers
- Using a variation of a 60-10-30 hitter-closer-starter split to allocate the league budget

An owner may find it best to use this additional split, but others won't. The same owner may split for one league and not another. It comes down to what process the owner feels best matches the league's context and history.

One way to make this assessment is to compare the non-separated or traditional pitcher ranks to the historic spending. The owner may find that no closer inflation exists and the two types of pitchers don't need separate budgets. The owner may also find evidence that the first closer off the board causes a major closer run where all owners panic and overpay. Finally, owners might observe that the league overvalues the elite arms and the lesser closers represent values.

Most owners have short memories as to how the closer market played out, and the previous season's results can have a major impact on the next season's rankings. If there was a lower than normal turnover rate, owners might spend up for the seemingly "safe" guys. In other seasons, no closer lasts and owners are gun-shy about paying for even the top guys. These may be other opportunities to exploit.

It's tough to find a universal answer on how to allocate closer resources. Good luck finding the personal balance.

Historic Results for Closers

The following tables will help demonstrate the changing Saves landscape and turnover in the closer role. Thanks to Smada (@smada_bb on Twitter) for help collecting the data below. The term incumbent refers to the pitcher who starts the season as a team's closer. The "Same Closer as Incumbent from Previous Year" refers to pitchers that begin a season as closer and recur as the closer to begin the following season. These numbers are higher than the "Incumbent Kept Job Until EOS" column because closers will frequently be injured or removed from the closer role during the season but still return to the role to begin the following season.

Year	Saves by Incumbent	MLB Saves	% Saves by Incumbent	Incumbent Kept Job Until EOS	EOS %	Same Closer as Incumbent from Previous Year	Same Incumbent %
2013	927	1,266	73.2%	15	50.0%		
2014	746	1,264	59.0%	11	36.7%	16	53.3%
2015	737	1,292	57.0%	11	36.7%	14	46.7%
2016	797	1,276	62.5%	11	36.7%	16	53.3%
2017	668	1,179	56.7%	10	33.3%	13	43.3%
2018	759	1,244	61.0%	5	16.7%	12	40.0%
2019	573	1,180	48.6%	7	23.3%	9	30.0%
Average	743.9	1,243	59.8%	10	33.3%	13.3	44.4%

Here is a breakdown of the number of players reaching certain saves thresholds the past several seasons:

Year	Players Getting Saves	Players Getting >= 4 Saves	Players Getting >= 9 Saves	Non-Incumbent >= 9 Saves
2013	130	42	37	10
2014	134	49	39	15
2015	145	47	37	15
2016	148	53	42	15
2017	162	52	40	15
2018	165	59	43	14
2019	199	64	38	16
Average	154.7	52.3	39.4	14.3

While the tables contain many pieces of useful information, here are a few main points.

- Few incumbents make it as the team's closer for the entire season and only accumulate 60% of all a season's saves, historically. Further, the percentage of saves earned by incumbents hit an all-time low or at least the low since this has been monitored in 2019.

- The number of closers who keep their role from the start to the end of the season has been cut in half from 15 in 2013 to just 7 this past season.

- The number of pitchers getting saves has skyrocketed from 130 in 2013 to 199 this past season. There was steady growth from 2013 to 2018, but the trend of bullpen-by-committee really took hold in 2019.

- Beware of and don't buy into the mindset that bullpen-by-committee means it's easier to pick up saves during the season. Accumulating saves for fantasy purposes from these committees will be challenging. The increased spread of saves is not increasing the number of closers getting nine or more saves. There is a small increase in players earning four or more saves, but the bulk of the increase is in those earning three or fewer saves.

Fantasy owners need to come to grips that the save landscape has changed dramatically in the past half decade and that it's probably not done changing.

Last Year's Notes

Go over last year's notes (if available) and see if anything sticks out to utilize, such as the room's early aggressiveness or owner tendencies.

Find a Helper

Draft Day

First off, adding a draft (or auction) day assistant should not necessarily make that assistant the team's co-owner. That decision should be made way before draft day. This person helps with the auction's hustle and bustle.

An owner can ask another fantasy enthusiast who is not in the league to help with the draft, offering to provide the same help for one of the helper's own drafts. Both owners feel no obligation to run the other owner's team while both gain the draft-day advantage.

The labor division is usually one owner making the verbal (or internet draft room-based) decisions while reading the room's faces and reactions. The team's helper needs to do the book work: writing down bids, looking for trends, monitoring rosters, marking off selected players, etc.

While the second role is not as exciting, their contribution becomes more and more important in the draft's second half. They can keep track of positional depth remaining or concentrate on the needs and resources of other teams. This additional hand becomes especially helpful when the auction bids are only $1 and there isn't always time for bookkeeping.

Complete Season

Adding a full co-owner, and not just a draft day assistant, can be a huge advantage during the season. If done properly, the team will have two minds to allocate the work of the season-long grind and a built-in backup to pick up the slack when real life takes one owner's focus. There will also be diverse opinions to locate potentially hidden gems, as well as a valuable sounding board or person to reign in an owner's bad ideas. Or the co-owner situation can be a nightmare that drives a wedge between two friends, especially if a substantial amount of money is involved.

The keys to combining heads are:

1. Start with one, maybe two leagues with a limited prize pool. If the owners can't get along in these simpler situations, make sure both can walk away with their friendship intact.

2. Evenly split the entry fee. Owners can't be pulling the "I have more money in it so I have more of a say" card. Also, decide how the prize money should be spent. Some owners may like to "let it ride" on bigger entry contests in the future, while others may want to use it for Magic cards or football leagues.

3. The most heated arguments the pair will get into are likely to occur during the draft or auction. It's tough enough for one person to pick a player in a minute, let alone two coming to a consensus. Both owners should pour over the pre-draft rankings and valuations together before the draft in order to know what's coming and identify potential disagreements when they have time to talk through them. This should result in a draft

or auction list in a rough order that both owners feel comfortable with. Avoid significant and repeated compromise on picks and instead, take turns letting one or the other have their pick. The worst-case scenario here is that half the team will be filled with players one owner likes and rest with the other owner's guys. This is preferred to a team of players that nobody likes and was the result of repeated compromise.

4. One member is going to be the more alpha personality, and both need to acknowledge it. Skilled fantasy players used to making their own executive decisions likely have a little alpha dog in them, so it might be tough for one to back down. The key is for the alpha to listen, go against their inner personality, and take the other player's advice.

5. Discuss a plan for how in-season FAAB and lineup setting will work and understand how much time each owner expects to spend on these processes. One owner is going to spend more time on the league and it's better to discuss this upfront than for animosity to build up. The owner who puts in more time just needs to understand the other owner isn't as detailed.

6. Let the other partner know of any move. Sometimes quick action is needed if a player gets hurt right before lineups lock, but it's important to still inform them. With this said, there is no need to go through all the weekly bids together. Instead, have one owner compile an initial add and drop list, then have the other owner tweak the options and layer in their desired players.

7. Have fun talking about fantasy baseball together.

Lock in the Player Values and Finalize Tracking Tools

Depending on the format of the owner's Draft Value Sheet (paper or electronic) and their skill level with a spreadsheet, there inevitably will be some time between when they must lock in their values and when the draft starts. Unfortunately, things can happen within this window that significantly affect valuations: a player gets hurt or a closer role gets decided. In these instances, some on the fly adjustments need to be made. Owners don't need to waste their limited mental energy re-running values for a player or two. Just cross off the player's name or make an educated guess about the effect of the event by looking at players expected to have similar stat lines. All the other owners will likely be making the same adjustment.

Tracking Tools

Besides creating player values, this is probably the most crucial step of draft preparation but one that is too often ignored. Some forms of this chart have been recommended by various touts, and for good reason: it works. It keeps a team balanced and focused. Here's the layout for a roto league. For a points-based league, ignore the counting stat columns.

Name	Hitters	Cost	HR	HR Projected	SB	SB Projected
	$40		23		10	
	$28		46		21	
	$24		69		31	
	$20		91		41	
	$17		114		52	
	$14		137		62	
	$11		160		73	
	$9		183		83	
	$7		206		93	
	$4		229		104	
	$3		251		114	
	$2		274		124	
	$1		297		135	
	$1		320		145	

Here's the layout for pitchers:

Name	Starters	Cost	K's	K's Projected
	$25		151	
	$12		302	
	$8		453	
	$4		604	
	$2		756	
	$1		907	
	$1		1,058	
Name	Closers	Cost	K's	K's Projected
	$17		1,209	
	$6		1,360	

While it may look complex, it has an elegant simplicity. Here are the values to be filled in before draft day. The player's cost is simply the price paid in an auction. In a draft, it is the dollar value given to the player. Each of the two or three player types (hitters, pitchers, closers) gets its own category with the average expected costs included.

Here is how each value is generated and maintained during the draft or auction.

- Projected Values: These are the amounts under the "Hitters," "Starters," and "Closers" columns in the previous table. These amounts are calculated by taking the top X valued hitters, starters, and closers and averaging their cost where X is the number of teams in the league. For example, assuming a 12-team league, the values of the top 12 hitters add up to $480. This averages out to $40 per player and becomes the first value. Continue this procedure for the rest of the players required to be drafted.

  Sum up all the values to ensure they agree to the team budget (e.g. $260). A dollar or two may need to be added or subtracted because of values being rounded to $1 increments. If an owner has decided to not create dollar values and just go with a ranking, give the rankings a dollar value. This division of resources allows for a balanced team with enough hitting and pitching to win.

- HR/SB/Strikeouts: These values are included to make sure a team is balanced. For these values, use last year's third-place finisher's values. It helps to provide a baseline to follow. If last year's values aren't available, the individual home run, stolen base, and strikeout values should still be tracked so owners can build a balanced team.

- In keeper formats, owners should fill in their keepers at their costs. This helps them know where they can spend and the stats still needed.

In auctions, the values can be adjusted to personal tastes. An owner may not want to buy just $1 players and could budget $2 for each slot. Maybe they want eight $30 players while filling up the rest of their roster with $1 players. Instead of an $8 starter, the owner wants to instead spend that money on another closer. These adjustments can be made, just be sure to adjust all values accordingly and to ensure the total budgeted spending matches the league's budget.

Owners may also adjust their preferences of the ideal pitcher-to-hitter mix at this point. An owner may have a strong ability to scour the waiver wire for up-and-coming hitting, so they'll transfer some dollars from the hitting budget to their pitching pool. Don't adjust the league-wide split (or ELS) at this point. That split determines the market price for all players. Only the owner's spending balance for his team is being changed (e.g. planning to spend $150 on hitting and $110 on pitching).

Most of this step has been done before putting in the final values. Again, if an owner has a limited amount of preparation time, they should use this table to help create a balanced team.

Backup Draft Values

Never assume the location will have the internet available or the computer will start up without requiring a two-hour long Windows update. Shit happens, and Murphy's Law works double time on draft day. Even in this digital age, it is best to have the information available on a second device like a tablet or phone. Owners don't want to be drafting out of a magazine.

Using Only a Paper Copy

Some owners prefer to use only paper rankings at a live event and ignore electronics except for obtaining news and viewing the overall draft board. Many owners may find the experience liberating, and with the information on paper, the owner can keep up with the few important trackable items (e.g. team pitcher-hitter balance and remaining budget).

Draft Day Strategy

Overview

An owner should adopt a value-only mindset. The value focus may seem to be overstated in this book, but it's to drive home a point. As insensitive as it sounds, owners must forget their "gut" and "feelings" and concentrate on the objective and tangible financial side. Many owners draft or bid according to how they think or feel a player will perform. The draft is not the time to weave in personal preferences or to abandon all the hard work done in draft preparation. Add those preferences into the projections. While draft or auction dynamics can adjust some decisions, owners shouldn't adjust much during the draft or auction. The key is to determine the inefficiencies in the room as quickly as possible and then exploit them.

Owners need to act non-emotionally, like stock traders. They know the values for all stocks, now they need to find the best deals. This is not for all owners. Some owners want their guys no matter the cost. These owners may need to come to grips with not getting "their" players if they want to win a competitive league.

This is another reason for doing the advanced draft preparation and studying of ADP. This will allow an owner to come to grips with the fact that they won't end up with a certain player. It's tough to have both a team of favorite players and great values.

Show Up Early

It's nice to show up 15 to 30 minutes before the draft or auction to get a decent seat, connect to the wireless network, grab a drink and snack, and shoot the shit. Being flustered drains an owner's energy.

Don't Get Wasted

For those who like to have a drink or twelve, try to limit oneself to one per hour during the draft or auction. Draft day may be one of the few times everyone gets together each year, but try to keep a straight head during the process.

Update Draft Value Sheet

The owner should update the Draft Value Sheet during the event. For drafts, this is simple: cross off the name of a drafted player. In an auction, the final bid value needs to be included. This value helps to spot trends such as inflation and differences in the pitcher-hitter split, and it can be used next year for draft preparation if values are not captured in an online draft room.

Focus on Talent, Not Positions for Two-thirds of the Draft

Positional adjustments have already been figured into the values, so concentrate on finding the best deals. This is achieved differently in drafts than in auctions, but an owner can find value in several ways. They don't need a top-five first baseman to win; they need better-than-projected production compared to the cost.

With position players, don't get caught up in a run at the position and overpay to get the next guy who is not a value. Learn patience and the deals will start revealing themselves as other teams fill their needs.

In rotisserie leagues, try to wait on filling the final two outfielder and possibly utility spots unless obvious values emerge. No team can perfectly balance the different hitting categories. Early exceptions exist for speed at first base or power from the middle infield, but the outfield is the one position that provides both stolen bases or home runs in the end game. Leaving these spots open allows the owner to pursue whatever category they lack by tapping into the diverse outfield pool.

Do the same with two to five pitchers. Recall the flat talent curve of middle-tier pitchers. Don't spend significant resources on these fungible assets during the auction or draft.

Prospects

These considerations should already be baked into the playing time projections but focus on talented players on contending teams that are in Double-A or Triple-A. For hitters, look for outfield prospects. Only one of the three outfielders must struggle or go on the IL for an outfield prospect to get promoted. Similarly, there will occasionally be well-publicized stories about infielders where the major league team has shifted them to different positions to increase the minor leaguer's chances of filling a hole. Favor these players over those cemented into one position.

The prospect market is unpredictable and largely based on how the previous year's market developed. If several high-profile prospects succeeded the season before, prices could be high. If the high-profile prospects busted, prices may be depressed. Owners should go in with a prospect cost plan and stick to it. Don't allocate valuable resources to players with an unknown promotion date when a similar player can be cheaply acquired.

Team Construction

The draft's primary decision driver should be to maximize value, but an owner must also remain mindful of their team's construction as the draft progresses. This requires monitoring stats drafted and those they still need, especially in the coveted categories like Stolen Bases and Saves. It may make sense to draft players that fulfill those category needs even ahead of higher-valued players if the pool is drying up. Owners should strike before hysteria sets in so as to not overpay.

Remain Balanced

Another way to avoid overpaying for certain player types is to seek balance throughout the draft. When values don't offer a clear player choice, acquire the hitter that contributes in all categories over the specialist. The specialists, like Billy Hamilton, put an inordinate amount of risk on the roster and can also close doors to deals later in the draft. With Hamilton in place, an owner may have to pass on a late-round bargain that derives his value from stolen bases to address other needs.

If an owner has a balanced team, they can sit back and let the draft come to them. They don't need to accept lesser values for team construction. Having a balanced team is analogous to having a poker hand with many outs. Value is king. Balance should be queen.

Draft-Only Strategy

Monitor the Queue

If drafting online, be wary of players showing up on the hosting site's upcoming draft queue. Unprepared owners are going to be picking from this list. If a value target appears on one of these lists, draft him quickly or someone else will snatch him up.

The Mike Fiers Rule

There is often a point in the draft when an owner has several acceptable draft targets lined up and all of them are selected right before the owner's pick, causing him to frantically find a player. This can easily result in the selection of an unwanted player like Mike Fiers, as one author not named Tanner did this past season.

In addition to a short-term queue, have a list of late-game darts queued up to grab when plans go astray. An owner will be less mad overpaying for their favorite sleeper than having drafted someone they don't even want.

Default Stat Rule of Thumb

As the draft gets into the double-digit rounds, the talent pool starts to level off and it becomes tougher to decide between similarly valued players. To help with this decision-making process, have a rule of thumb or two to fall back on. These can be simple tiebreakers like, "take the hitter with a higher batting average," or "take the pitcher with the highest strikeout rate."

The rules can be updated to fill in for team weaknesses as the draft progresses. For example, "pick the hitter on the better team to help with Runs and RBIs," or "pick the pitcher on the better team to get Wins." With limited time, a quick and easy rule should be decided on before the owner is on the clock so it can help make the one-minute decision.

Early in the draft, it might be best to focus on categories that are scarce during the season like steals or strikeouts. Another option would be to focus on rate stats and hope the team can catch up in counting stats as other teams lose focus later in the season.

Avoid switching the rule frequently during the draft. Pick a lane and stick with it. An owner that switches the rule of thumb each round ends up no better off than someone with no guiding lights.

Auction-Only Strategy

Auctions are completely different beasts. Owners that have previously done only drafts should be prepared for the unknown. The pace and non-sequential player evaluations make it unique. While different, it provides more value-finding opportunities.

With auctions, the final roster doesn't need to fit into a perfect mold, which is common in drafts. The team may have three first-rounders, or it can have 10 fifth-rounders. The roster's talent distribution doesn't matter. The key is to make sure the most talent is purchased at the cheapest price.

The key to finding value in the auction is to determine how the room will play. Here's the general flow:

1. **Timid owners may bid conservatively early to feel out the room.** This non-aggressive bidding can lead to some great values in the first few nominations. These deals disappear quickly. Don't be afraid to jump in and get some early values even if it means spending a decent portion of a budget on a couple of top-tier players.

    Some owners are reluctant to pay up early. Don't be. Just be reluctant to overpay. The money must be spent at some point. It's better to pay for a few solid anchors than overpay for replacement-level players.

    If an owner must nominate a player in the first few picks, it should be the owner's highest dollar value. It may be the only chance to get the desired player before inflation sets in. If the top players are already going for more than their values, just back off and wait on nominating this player until budgets shrink.

2. **The auction will generally force owners to follow two auction directions.** Every auction is unique. They will not follow only one format and there will be some degree of mixing these two general paths. Owners just need to concentrate on finding early values.

    a. The auction stays conservative with the top talent. Continue to roster unpriced stars with the knowledge that the middle-tier players will eventually go for more than expected. The owner will sit out the middle section of the action and wait for dollar days. The roster with the most value will consist of stars-and-scrubs.

    b. This auction format features the star player prices being 20% to 30% over the projected values. Owners need to have the willpower to stay out of these high bids and wait for future deals. With the average amount spent per player being ~$12 ($260 budget, 23 roster spots), owners can wait until the inflation amount starts dropping and not have to overpay.

No matter the inflation amount and desire to not overpay, owners must still spend their budget. Once all the first- and second-round talent is owned, owners need to come up with a plan to spend their remaining budget. The goal is to not go past the $20-dollar players without a plan for efficiently using their entire auction budget.

The owner can scratch out and pencil in new projected values in the "Hitters," "Starters," and "Closers" sections of the tracking tool that are consistent with their revised plan. For example, if the draft stays conservative and the owner grabs several $30-$40 players, corresponding amounts between the $24 and $7 players should be replaced with $1 slots. The values on the tracking tool should always stay in line with the $260 budget so an owner can determine when to correct course.

3. **A deal is a deal no matter if it's early or late.** Recall that a general rule is that the owner must acquire $320 worth of value for the $260 budget. Don't be afraid to pay up for several early high-priced players if the valuations support it and a chunk of that $60 surplus can be secured. Some owners don't like to put too much stock in a single player, but this risk is already baked into the valuations. Trust them.

4. **Make sure pitchers, hitters, and closers are being nominated and the bids are as expected.** While historic values exist for the pitcher/hitter split, there are always exceptions. A 33% spending difference on pitching instead of 35% won't throw an owner off, but 30% will be noticeable and affect bids.

   An owner can tell if the split has changed if they are showing every player of a certain category as a bargain and players from other categories as overpriced. If the split changes, owners will need to adjust on the fly as soon as they find out. The key is to find out early. To find out, an owner needs to see evidence from the three categories of players (hitters, pitchers, closers). To expedite the process, nominate from a player group that hasn't seen many nominations. Most of the time, it will be closers. Even though it may stop the auction's flow, jump to a new player group because other owners may be staying away as they hope for deals.

5. **Getting money off the table.** During the rest of the auction, especially when there is heavy inflation, get as much money spent by others so deals can materialize. An owner can nominate desired players that will likely be overvalued by others. Nominating these desired players allows a safety cushion if crickets (no other bids) happens and the owner is stuck with the player. This strategy can be performed early and late.

6. **Using nominations strategically.** As with everything in life, balance is better than a heavily weighted strategy. While getting money off the table has its benefits, nominations of players an owner sees as key to a strategy are also very important. At some point in the draft, it becomes more valuable for an owner to know if they'll end up with a specific player than it does to get more money off the table.

For example, an owner may have a player they feel will offer a very strong value. Perhaps the player is valued at $15 to them, but they suspect the player can be won for only $5. It could be very important to know if the owner has those extra $10 to use. Rather than waiting for the other $5 players to come around, the owner can strategically nominate this player early. They'll then know how much of that $10 surplus can be spent in other ways.

These decision points can happen many times during the draft. An owner should use nominations to determine the best course of action. At some point just getting $20 off the draft board is not very helpful, but learning about roster construction might be.

7. **Don't nominate under-$10 values in the auction's first half.** With most owners going with a stars-and-scrubs approach, wait for the low-cost players to get even cheaper.

   For example, an owner's projections and valuations have a pitcher valued at $12. The market has the pitcher valued around $8. While the owner could get $4 in surplus value by paying $8, the price may drop even more depending on the early inflation level.

8. **Consider going with "$2 days" instead of "$1 days."** In every auction, there are several players rostered who go for just $1. The problem is that an owner who goes into this section only able to make $1 bids will see their desired players being grabbed and must settle for players valued at $1. Having $2 to spend per player allows the owner to have a little more initial bid and can jump other $1 bids if a deal comes up. Allocating $10 instead of $5 for the last few picks could mean a lot more value rostered.

9. **Stay away from a bidding war.** Try to stay away from a needs-based major bidding war late in the auction. This back-and-forth bidding happens when two owners are going after the last best player at a position or with a certain skill set (like stolen bases). Avoid these situations by being proactive and sensing when a population is drying up. This can also be prevented by continuously nominating the owner's top players. Don't save a desired player for late and assume others don't know about the player. Others know and will be hoarding their money for him.

10. **If overwhelmed or in trouble, call for a break.** Everyone needs to go and this is an acceptable reason for a break. By taking a break, owners can clear their heads, catch up on bookkeeping, and see what they must do to round out their team.

11. **Note the auction's loser.** Most of the bids are just owners throwing out numbers with no emotional attachment. Then there are those bids between owners who just go back-and-forth with everyone else on the sidelines watching. The winner of the player should note the losing owner. They may be a nice willing trade partner down the road. This work should not be done with every player, just those where the loser obviously wanted the player in question.

Post Draft and Auction Strategy

After the draft has been completed, it's time to enjoy a refreshing beverage, preferably Yoo-Hoo, in anticipation of what's to come for the season. But before kicking back entirely, an owner should take some draft day notes of anything that sticks out. Capture these thoughts while they are fresh in the mind. These notes will be especially helpful if the league carries forward each year with many of the same managers.

Some of the draft information can be extracted from the raw data results but other thoughts can only be noticed and documented that day. One owner may be the prospect hound and voice his displeasure when others are rostered, but this won't be captured next offseason in looking at only the players selected. Other owners may have a favorite MLB team and take a high number of players from that roster. Some don't pay up for talent, others do. One owner may get drunk and bid erratically. These are things an owner should note for the following year.

In-Season Management

Much of this book's focus is draft-centric, which is not unlike how many owners invest their time managing their teams. Owners spend months preparing for the draft but will spend little-to-no time researching in-season decisions. This is a critical component of the game that should not be overlooked. A great draft sets the table for a good season, but in-season management is how owners jockey for position, close in on the leaders, and take home the title. The 26-week long season can be a grind. It's easy to lose focus on summer activities, vacations, and the start of the football season. But by staying true to *The Process* and by focusing on a few areas, owners can generate key in-season stats that will push them over the top.

The Thought Process Doesn't Change

The process of obtaining or formulating projections (both playing time and talent-based), calculating valuations, and exploiting differences in projected value from market costs should continue throughout the season.

Difficulties arise because owners need to make quicker decisions during the season and projections are subject to wild fluctuations, especially with playing time changes. It becomes a balance between not over-reacting and not acting fast enough. This is why some teams are good at drafting but can't seem to win.

Slow Down In-Season Decision-Making

Once the season starts, the decision-making process changes for many owners, although it shouldn't. In the preseason and during the draft, the mind tends to view decision-making as, "Which player should I select from this group?" whereas in-season the thought process becomes, "Should I add player A or player B?" -- even though they're still selecting Player A from a pool of free agents.

This thought process shift has a very fundamental effect on owners. There is research to support the idea that people are likely to treat a selection from a group of objects differently than an "A or B" decision.

Thinking Fast and Slow by Daniel Kahneman is a terrific book on decision-making and the way the human brain works. A key concept from the book is that people have both a fast and slow side to the brain. The fast side has been refined and trained over time to make decisions quickly using a shortcutted process. This is how we instinctively know two plus two is four and to turn the other way instead of heading down a dark alley. The brain instinctively makes these decisions without any effort or critical thinking needed.

The slow side of the brain allows people to dig more deeply into a problem, to study it, to analyze it. While the answer to 10 + 10 snaps into the mind, the brain won't even make a quick effort at a more complicated math problem like 13 x 67. It instinctively knows deep thinking is needed to solve that problem.

These concepts are anecdotal and dependent on the individual, but it seems owners love to agonize over preseason decisions but are quick to make snap judgments and knee-jerk decisions once the season starts.

Blame the fantasy industry. Enablers! While it might seem like lengthy articles focusing on all the reasons a player represents a sound investment would kick us over into the "slow brain," we end up focusing on snippets and anecdotes.

"Justin Turner changed his launch angle. There was a news article that Player B changed his launch angle. I'm going to pick him up."

"Pitcher Z has raised his swinging strike rate to 13%. I'm going to pick him up."

"Hitter H has a strikeout rate over 30%. I'd never roster him."

Or worse yet, "Player Q has hit .300 for the last week. I'm going to pick him up."

There is a place for shortcutting some decisions, but owners need to be mindful of the mental traps they can fall into and avoid problems when possible. Fantasy baseball decisions should not be made with the quick trigger system. They should be made with the slower, calculated, and methodical part of the brain.

Instead of "Player B changed his launch angle, I'm going to pick him up," the owner should think, "Player B changed his launch angle. How should I change the player's home run projection? If the player has truly improved his talent, does he also stand to gain more playing time? What would the revised projection be for this player? With that revised projection, what is his projected value? Do I have a player projected for less value that I can drop?"

Rest of Season Projections (RoS)

Projections feed into a valuation system. Valuations help to guide the owner's decisions. Just like the reliable full-season projections FanGraphs and other providers make available during the preseason, several rest-of-season (RoS) projections are available during the season. The best RoS projections are updated daily to account for the exact number of games remaining.

Running the RoS projections through the valuation model will yield similar dollar values to what one would see in the preseason. While this process can be time-consuming, it's hard to argue that following this process wouldn't result in better objective decisions, and that's the goal. Owners need a way to appeal to the slow and detailed brain and to avoid the pull to make quick and poor decisions, and referring to RoS projections is a great way to make that appeal.

The Strengths of RoS Projections

A player's true talent level does not change rapidly, therefore his projected stat line doesn't change quickly. It follows that his valuation based on RoS projections should not wildly fluctuate. Despite this, the *perception* and *behavior* regarding a player can change in the blink of an eye.

Consuming news, watching ESPN, listening to podcasts, or following fantasy analysts on Twitter will suck in even the most even-keeled owners and cause them to have feelings, positive or negative, about a player. These inputs make an owner more susceptible to cognitive biases than if objective inputs like RoS projections are used.

The human brain cannot effectively understand and weigh past performance properly against recent events. Most owners are either too quick to buy into or dismiss recent performance. A projection system can objectively weight and incorporate small samples appropriately.

If time allows, an owner should attempt to perform the same processes as in the preseason. Obtain a RoS projection. Dissect it into the talent-based component and the playing time component. The owner then should decide if they agree with that playing time projection. The talent and playing time components should be multiplied to determine the projected RoS numbers. Those statistics are run, along with the RoS projections, for all players through a valuation system to arrive at a dollar value.

If an owner does not have time to undertake this process for many players, they should at least consider diving in deeply on those players they're considering acquiring or dropping from their team.

The Weaknesses of RoS Projections

The process of running RoS projections through a valuation system and using the output to make decisions sounds all well and good, but there's a problem.

Think back to the discussion on projections. Recall that a projection is comprised of two significant inputs: the player's rate stat projections multiplied by the player's playing time estimate.

The amount of fluctuation in a player's rate state projections should be minimal once the season starts. Projections are often based on three years of projected stats. Those three years of data are not just thrown out the window if a player gets off to a hot start in the current season. This slow adjustment period is great for keeping owners from overreacting to small sample sizes, but it will completely miss on a player that has undergone a fundamental shift in approach and therefore has a new baseline talent level (players like J.D. Martinez, Justin Turner, and Max Muncy are recent MLB examples).

While RoS projections do include a playing time projection, which is a great convenience to the owner that doesn't have time to formulate their own estimates, this can be a weakness. Playing time estimates are highly subjective. They are a messy probability calculation that weighs a player's performance, other players on the same major league team, injuries, manager tendencies and quirks, the possibility of a trade, potential minor-league call-ups, and more. All these factors are constantly fluctuating. A well-informed owner that stays on top of MLB news can likely read the tea leaves more effectively than a RoS projection can. At the very least there will be many areas of disagreement where an owner can take advantage of differences in perceived value.

For these reasons, a heavy reliance on RoS projections means an owner will be slow to react. They will miss out on surprise players, but they'll presumably ignore many one-week wonders. Finding the balance of when to rely on RoS projections strengths and when to deviate from the projection because it isn't accounting for something is an important skill to develop.

Capturing Weekly (or Even Daily) Value

Owners have to admit that while using preseason valuations enables them to make more objective and better decisions in planning and executing a draft, there is an inherent weakness to consider. The very foundation of preseason valuations is an assumption that owners can invest in or avoid these players on a season-long basis only. Except for possibly the hitter-pitcher split, there is little consideration given in the preseason for what types of value will materialize during the season.

When it comes down to it, performance during each of the league's scoring periods are how players should be valued. If a league uses weekly scoring periods, an owner starts the player that is most likely to produce the most value in the coming week; they don't start the player projected for the most season-long value. And yet, little-to-no attention is given to weekly valuations.

Depending on league depth, it's very possible that an owner could generate more value by streaming hitters with good short-term playing time outlooks and favorable situations than a player projected for $3 of season-long value. Said another way, players projected for negative season-long values can outearn the $3 player if the cards are played correctly. Remember, it only takes a few home runs and other counting stats over the course of the year to increase earnings by several dollars.

Owners need to open their eyes to these different horizons. Keeping a player projected for $3 of season-long value on the roster all year can have an opportunity cost. The owner cannot capitalize on players with favorable matchups. The owner cannot speculate on free agents that might come into massive value. While the regimented owner may be thinking he's doing the right thing by keeping the $3 player rostered, teams strong at in-season management are gaining ground.

In different scenarios, we can anticipate that a given player will perform well enough to be rostered in a given week even though he's not worth owning in a season-long context. Perhaps a fringe player has a four-game series in Colorado, or perhaps a poor strikeout pitcher has two starts in a week against bad teams, or maybe a bench player is thrust into the starting lineup because a starter is injured. Each of these scenarios could push a player into consideration that wouldn't otherwise be desirable.

These and other scenarios are why countless "players to target" articles are written each week. Players move into and out of the ownable player pool all season long.

Many owners understand the fluctuations in player value. They usually make rational decisions to pick up players with good matchups, two-start weeks, or temporary playing time. But there are not many discussions about how to make these decisions. Owners are mostly left to use "feel" or to make "gut" decisions on these guys. A lot of effort is spent focusing on season-long valuations, but little is put into objectively making weekly decisions.

Recall from the valuation system discussions earlier in this book that calculating dollar values is not easy to do. It takes time, effort, skill, and caution. For those reasons, there aren't discussions of weekly and daily valuations for season-long leagues.

For daily valuations, owners can follow some DFS (daily fantasy sports) discussions of daily matchups. Remember that the DFS discussion is normally about the FanDuel or DraftKings scoring systems, not standard roto scoring. When an owner takes the advice for daily fantasy and applies it to a season-long game, the owner needs to ensure they understand the scoring differences.

The same season-long concepts hold true for the short timetables. To identify the most valuable players for a given week (or day), simply load up a weekly (or daily) projection for each player, determine replacement level, and run it through the valuation system of choice. This would be quite an undertaking to do on a weekly (or daily) basis, which is why so many people just eyeball it. "I think this guy going to Colorado is worth owning," or, "this two-start pitcher can help me." Those decisions might be correct, but let's take a closer look.

Studies of Weekly Valuations for the 2017 and 2018 Seasons

The studies of weekly valuations that follow were conducted with the actual weekly statistics for each player during the 2017 and 2018 MLB season. The work was initially performed on the 2017 season for inclusion in "The Process - 2019 Version," but we have since expanded the depth of the research. When more exhaustive research was performed on the 2018 season, it was not necessarily reperformed on the 2017 data. Please keep this in mind while reading this section, as the context of the data may flip between 2017 and 2018 valuations.

For the 2017 study, each player's stat line was run through the valuation process assuming a 12-team standard league (with 23 roster spots, 14 hitters, and 9 pitchers). This means 168 drafted hitters (12 * 14) and 108 drafted pitchers (12 * 9). Expanding this out to weekly lineups, there were 4,368 hitter weeks (12 * 14 * 26 weeks) and 2,808 pitcher weeks (12 * 9 * 26).

The 2018 study was performed for both 12-team and 15-team standard leagues. The 2018 MLB season had 27 weeks of data, resulting in 4,536 hitter weeks (12 * 14 * 27 weeks) in a 12-team league and 5,670 hitter weeks (15 * 14 * 27 weeks) in a 15-team league. There were 2,916 pitcher weeks (12 * 9 * 27) in a 12-team league and 3,645 pitcher weeks (15 * 9 * 27) in a 15-team league.

How Many Undrafted Players Earn Weekly Value?

If an owner looks hard enough, they can find interesting articles after the season regarding how well the fantasy community did at ranking players in the preseason. But this analysis ignores the weekly fluctuations in value that were just discussed. How well do we do at capturing weekly value? The following table shows how much of that weekly value is undrafted in a 12-team league.

| | Season-long Valuation | | | | Weekly Valuation | | | |
| | 2018 | | 2017 | | 2018 | | 2017 | |
	Count	Pct	Count	Pct	Count	Pct	Count	Pct
Undrafted Hitters that End in Top 168	52	31%	65	39%	2,224	49%	2,209	50%
Drafted Hitters that End in Top 168	116	69%	103	61%	2,312	51%	2,175	50%
Total Hitters	168		168		4,536		4,384*	

It's mentioned above that there are 4,368 hitter weeks. This study ended up with more than that due to some weeks where players tied at the replacement-level cutoff. It's difficult for players to end up with the same yearly stat line, but much more likely with a smaller weekly stat line.

Here are the same results for 15-team leagues:

	Season-long Valuation		Weekly Valuation	
	2018		**2018**	
	Count	**Pct**	**Count**	**Pct**
Undrafted Hitters that End in Top 210	54	26%	2,440	43%
Drafted Hitters that End in Top 210	156	74%	3,230	57%
Total Hitters	210		5,670	

When the evaluation period is the entire season, the fantasy community can predict the ownable (above replacement level) player pool with about 60-70% accuracy in 12-team leagues, which is not terrible. But shift that to weekly valuations and the accuracy drops to only 50% in 12-team leagues, meaning the players drafted in the preseason will only end up with half of the valuable weeks during the season!

This incredible realization means that in a 12-team league, half of the above-replacement-level weeks are available on the waiver wire.

The numbers are similar in 15-team leagues. The fantasy community can identify the best season-long valuations at about 75% accuracy in 15-team leagues, but only 57% of valuable hitter weeks will be drafted.

How did owners fare with pitchers in 12-team leagues?

	Season-long Valuation				Weekly Valuation			
	2018		**2017**		**2018**		**2017**	
	Count	**Pct**	**Count**	**Pct**	**Count**	**Pct**	**Count**	**Pct**
Undrafted Pitchers that End in Top 108	52	48%	46	43%	1,812	62%	1,816	65%
Drafted Pitchers that End in Top 108	56	52%	62	57%	1,107	38%	995	35%
Total Pitchers	108		108		2,919		2,811	

And in 15-team leagues?

	Season-long Valuation		Weekly Valuation	
	2018		2018	
	Count	Pct	Count	Pct
Undrafted Pitchers that End in Top 135	62	46%	2,199	60%
Drafted Pitchers that End in Top 135	73	54%	1,448	40%
Total Pitchers	135		3,645	

Owners are worse at predicting the ownable pitchers on a season-long basis, and they are much worse at capturing the value on a weekly basis. Nearly two-thirds of all valuable pitcher weeks go undrafted in the preseason in both 12- and 15-team leagues.

A large reason for this is the unpredictability of pitcher wins. Middle relievers and bad starters that pitch well and luck into a win can spike in a weekly valuation. An owner could argue this isn't predictable and cannot be captured, but it is important to keep in mind the amount of inefficiency owners demonstrate in capturing pitcher value. A closer look at this pitcher study follows shortly and will demonstrate the types of pitchers available in-season and their reusability. A detailed look at the value of two-start weeks is also included.

How Many Undrafted Hitters Earn Significant Weekly Values?

Setting the threshold for this study at only the top 168 hitters might not be that helpful. What if these undrafted hitters are only barely making it into the top 168? If they end up at 150 or worse, are owners really missing out on that much value? How do we do at predicting the top 100 players?

	Season-long Valuation				Weekly Valuation			
	2018		2017		2018		2017	
	Count	Pct	Count	Pct	Count	Pct	Count	Pct
Undrafted Hitters that End in Top 100	16	16%	28	28%	1,153	42%	1,139	44%
Drafted Hitters that End in Top 100	84	84%	72	72%	1,547	58%	1,464	56%
Total Hitters	100		100		2,700		2,603*	

This should be 2,600, or the top 100 players for 26 weeks, but keep ties in mind. With weekly stat lines, the 100th player tied with others in several instances.

Here is the same information for top-100 hitters in 15-team leagues.

	Season-long Valuation		Weekly Valuation	
	2018		2018	
	Count	Pct	Count	Pct
Undrafted Hitters that End in Top 100	12	12%	916	34%
Drafted Hitters that End in Top 100	88	88%	1,784	66%
Total Hitters	100		2,700	

The percent of undrafted players that sneak into the top-168 or top-210 in 12-team and 15-team leagues, respectively, drops significantly when the focus is narrowed to only the top-100 players. This was particularly true in 2018. The fantasy community's accuracy looks pretty good in that light. But still, there are significant quantities of top-100 weeks available during the season. Roughly 40-45% of the top-100 weeks are available via free agency in 12-team leagues, and over one-third of top-100 weeks are freely available in 15-team leagues.

And the results look even better when just the top bats are analyzed. Here are the top-50 results for 12-team leagues:

	Season-long Valuation				Weekly Valuation			
	2018		2017		2018		2017	
	Count	Pct	Count	Pct	Count	Pct	Count	Pct
Undrafted Hitters that End in Top 50	2	4%	9	18%	485	36%	489	38%
Drafted Hitters that End in Top 50	48	96%	41	82%	865	64%	811	62%
Total Hitters	50		50		1,350		1,300	

And the top-50 results for 15-team leagues:

	Season-long Valuation		Weekly Valuation	
	2018		2018	
	Count	Pct	Count	Pct
Undrafted Hitters that End in Top 50	2	4%	379	28%
Drafted Hitters that End in Top 50	48	96%	911	72%
Total Hitters	50		1,350	

Regardless of league size, few undrafted hitters crack the top 50 on a season-long basis, but the number of top-50 weekly performers who go undrafted is still significant. Nearly 40% and 30% of all top-50 hitter weeks are freely available during the season in 12-team and 15-team leagues, respectively.

The trend continues when narrowing the focus to the top 25. Our ability to predict the top-25 players is slightly better than our ability to predict the top 50. It is rare for an undrafted player to crack the top-25 season-long valuations, only four players did it in 2017 and none in 2018.

However, roughly one-third of the top-25 weeks came from the undrafted pool in 12-team leagues. More than 20% of the top-25 weeks were undrafted in 15-team leagues. Think about what an owner would pay for an additional top-25 hitter. Might owners invest more time on in-season management if they realized the amount of top-tier value that was available in-season?

For reference, the four undrafted hitters that made the season-long top 25 in 2017 were Aaron Judge (3rd-ranked hitter, 128 R, 52 HR, 114 RBI, 9 SB, .284), Ryan Zimmerman (18th, 90 R, 36 HR, 108 RBI, 1 SB, .303), Tommy Pham (22nd, 95 R, 23 HR, 73 RBI, 25 SB, .306), and Whit Merrifield (24th, 80 R,19 HR, 78 RBI, 34 SB, .288). All were taken well outside the top-300 players.

After seeing how inefficient owners are at capturing these valuable performances, one might be wondering, "Could or would I have even tried to own any of these players?" It's a fair question. After all, if a player only popped up for one top-25 week, he would still go unowned. He would explode for that week, everyone would reactively bid gobs of FAAB for him, and he'd never reach the same production level.

So what do these players look like, and did the performances recur in subsequent weeks?

2018			2017	
Player	# of Top 25 Weeks 12-tm	# of Top 25 Weeks 15-tm	Player	# of Top 25 Weeks 12-tm
Jesus Aguilar	6	6	Aaron Judge	9
Jed Lowrie	5	5	Ryan Zimmerman	7
Stephen Piscotty	4	Drafted	Scooter Gennett	6
Mallex Smith	4	Drafted	Cody Bellinger	6
Jurickson Profar	4	4	Justin Smoak	6
Miguel Andujar	4	6	Mark Reynolds	6
Matt Chapman	4	Drafted	Tommy Pham	6
Ketel Marte	3	Drafted	Jose Reyes	4
Adalberto Mondesi	3	4	Justin Bour	4
C.J. Cron	3	3	Avisail Garcia	4
Luke Voit	3	2	Aaron Altherr	4
Christian Villanueva	3	2	Marwin Gonzalez	4
Brandon Crawford	3	Drafted	Whit Merrifield	4
Mitch Moreland	3	2	Mike Zunino	4

There are many more players not shown above that popped for at least one top-25 week. Of those that had only one such week, many of them went on to post multiple top-50 and top-100 weeks, meaning they are not just one-hit wonders. These hitters had value for chunks of time that could be captured.

To further illustrate that undrafted hitters do appear for blocks of time in which they earn value, the following table shows the number of undrafted hitters that earned positive value in at least four weeks. Regardless of league size, there were 110 different players that earned value in at least 10 weeks of the season in both 2018 and 2017.

Positive Weeks	2018		2017
	# of Undrafted Players (12-tm)	# of Undrafted Players (15-tm)	# of Undrafted Players (12-tm)
24	0	1	0
23	1	2	0
22	1	3	1
21	1	5	1
20	2	11	7
19	6	17	12
18	11	24	15
17	16	35	24
16	25	48	29
15	31	61	43
14	46	75	52
13	64	86	67
12	78	90	82
11	94	102	95
10	118	113	112
9	134	134	126
8	151	146	141
7	168	165	158
6	191	185	176
5	216	205	198
4	237	226	231

How Many Undrafted Pitchers Earn Significant Weekly Values?

When performing a similar analysis on pitchers, if those who spike for positive weekly values end up ranked 90 or worse in a week, are owners really missing out on that much value? Here are the top-75 results for 12-team leagues:

	Season-long Valuation				Weekly Valuation			
	2018		2017		2018		2017	
	Count	Pct	Count	Pct	Count	Pct	Count	Pct
Undrafted Pitchers that End in Top 75	28	37%	30	40%	1,157	57%	1,178	60%
Drafted Pitchers that End in Top 75	47	63%	45	60%	868	43%	775	40%
Total Pitchers	75		75		2,025		1,953	

And here are the top-75 results for 15-team leagues:

	Season-long Valuation		Weekly Valuation	
	2018		2018	
	Count	Pct	Count	Pct
Undrafted Pitchers that End in Top 75	23	31%	1,056	52%
Drafted Pitchers that End in Top 75	52	69%	972	48%
Total Pitchers	75		2,025	

The improvement in accuracy from the top 108 to the top 75 is negligible. Still, roughly 40% of season-long value is undrafted, and a whopping 60% of weekly top-75 value can be had during the season in 12-team leagues. The accuracy rises when looking at 15-team leagues, but over 50% of the weekly top-75 values go undrafted.

What happens when the analysis is ratcheted up to the top 50 players on a season-long and weekly basis? Here are the top-50 results for 12-team leagues:

	Season-long Valuation				Weekly Valuation			
	2018		2017		2018		2017	
	Count	Pct	Count	Pct	Count	Pct	Count	Pct
Undrafted Pitchers that End in Top 50	14	28%	17	34%	707	52%	725	56%
Drafted Pitchers that End in Top 50	36	72%	33	66%	643	48%	577	44%
Total Pitchers	50		50		1,350		1,302	

Here are the top-50 results for 15-team leagues:

	Season-long Valuation		Weekly Valuation	
	2018		2018	
	Count	Pct	Count	Pct
Undrafted Pitchers that End in Top 50	13	26%	640	47%
Drafted Pitchers that End in Top 50	37	74%	710	53%
Total Pitchers	50		1,350	

Roughly one-third of season-long value was undrafted the past two seasons, but over half of the weekly values are still there for the taking in 12-team leagues. Similarly, nearly half of top-50 weekly values were available in free agency.

And lastly, the top-25 values. Recall that on average in 2017 and 2018, about one-third of weekly top-25 hitter performances went undrafted. Here are the top-25 pitcher results for 12-team leagues:

	Season-long Valuation				Weekly Valuation			
	2018		2017		2018		2017	
	Count	Pct	Count	Pct	Count	Pct	Count	Pct
Undrafted Pitchers that End in Top 25	2	8%	8	32%	324	48%	333	51%
Drafted Pitchers that End in Top 25	23	92%	17	68%	351	52%	317	49%
Total Pitchers	25		25		675		650	

Here are the top-25 results for 15-team leagues:

	Season-long Valuation		Weekly Valuation	
	2018		2018	
	Count	Pct	Count	Pct
Undrafted Pitchers that End in Top 25	3*	12%	280	41%
Drafted Pitchers that End in Top 25	22	88%	395	59%
Total Pitchers	25		675	

It is odd that more undrafted pitchers cracked the top 25 in a 15-team league than in a 12-team league. Upon closer review, this is due to some subtleties in replacement level differences. In 2018 12-team leagues, Jeremy Jeffress and Josh Hader were 16th and 24th, respectively. Mike Foltynewicz and Kyle Freeland just missed qualifying by finishing 26th and 27th, respectively. In 15-team leagues, Josh Hader was drafted but still finished 24th. Jeffress, Foltynewicz, and Freeland finished 15th, 22nd, and 23rd, respectively.

Roughly half of the top-25 week value is undrafted in 12-team leagues, and over 40% goes undrafted in 15-team leagues.

Any reasonable owner is surely looking at this data with skepticism. So, who were these undrafted pitchers that turned in top-25 weeks? And would anyone in their right mind have picked them up? Additionally, did these performances carry over into subsequent weeks of the player producing value?

2018			2017	
Player	# of Top 25 Weeks 12-tm	# of Top 25 Weeks 15-tm	Player	# of Top 25 Weeks 12-tm
German Marquez	8	Drafted	Luis Severino	11
Trevor Williams	7	7	Jason Vargas	7
Marco Gonzales	7	7	Alex Wood	6
Mike Minor	6	Drafted	Ervin Santana	6
Mike Foltynewicz	6	6	Chase Anderson	6
Jack Flaherty	6	6	Jimmy Nelson	6
Nate Eovaldi	6	6	Jose Berrios	6
Sean Newcomb	5	Drafted	Dan Straily	6
Reynaldo Lopez	5	5	CC Sabathia	5
Andrew Heaney	5	5	Trevor Bauer	4
Zack Wheeler	5	5	Zack Godley	4
Chris Stratton	5	4	Mike Clevinger	4
Mike Fiers (Boo!)	5	5	Jhoulys Chacin	4
Kyle Freeland	5	5	Alex Cobb	4
Anibal Sanchez	5	4	Patrick Corbin	4
Freddy Peralta	5	4	Eduardo Rodriguez	4
Wade Leblanc	5	5	R.A. Dickey	4
Eduardo Rodriguez	4	Drafted	Mike Fiers (Boo!)	4
Tyler Skaggs	4	4	Clayton Richard	4
Jakob Junis	4	5	Trevor Cahill	4
Ross Stripling	4	4		
Walker Buehler	4	4		
Kyle Gibson	4	4		

Although this study was performed on the 2017 and 2018 data, it's insightful to see the names in the context of what happened during 2019. Some of these names came and went, while others were clearly emerging and produced many more top-25 weeks when drafted the following season. The list appears to be a mix of talented pitchers and those who could be considered streamers. It's notable that not a single reliever had enough top-25 weeks to make this list. There are many more pitchers that popped for at least one top-25 week. Like hitters, they are not just one-hit wonders. These pitchers were valuable for many weeks.

To further illustrate that undrafted players do appear for blocks of time in which they earn value, the following table shows the number of undrafted pitchers who earned positive value in at least four weeks. There are many undrafted pitchers that earned value in at least 10 weeks of the season in both 2018 and 2017. Regardless of league size, well over 200 undrafted pitchers popped into positive earnings at least four separate times.

Positive Weeks	2018		2017
	# of Undrafted Pitchers (12-tm)	# of Undrafted Pitchers (15-tm)	# of Undrafted Pitchers (12-tm)
19	0	1	0
18	0	1	2
17	1	2	4
16	2	5	8
15	5	11	11
14	12	22	16
13	16	37	19
12	25	51	31
11	40	64	42
10	56	88	54
9	76	109	70
8	95	138	86
7	128	173	113
6	158	207	148
5	190	238	196
4	225	269	236

When Do Valuable Free Agents Appear?

It has now been demonstrated that a lot of value comes into a 12-team league after the draft via free agency or waivers. But when should owners be on the lookout for this talent? When does it appear during the season?

The following table shows the first positive-earning week for those undrafted hitters that landed on the list of ownable hitters at some point during the season. Here are the 2018 results for 12-team leagues:

4-Wk Period	Total	Pct	C	1B	2B	3B	SS	OF	DH
2018									
1	181	55%	38	18	20	22	18	61	4
2	42	13%	4	3	5	7	6	17	0
3	23	7%	11	3	2	0	2	5	0
4	31	9%	5	2	10	1	3	9	0
5	22	7%	4	1	1	2	2	12	0
6	17	5%	2	3	4	1	1	5	1
7	11	3%	1	1	0	0	2	7	0
Total	327	100%	65	31	42	33	34	116	5

Here are the 2017 results for 12-team leagues:

4-Wk Period	Total	Pct	C	1B	2B	3B	SS	OF	DH
2017									
1	190	55%	37	18	21	20	25	68	1
2	40	12%	5	1	4	5	5	19	1
3	31	9%	7	2	2	1	4	15	0
4	25	7%	1	3	5	4	4	8	0
5	25	7%	4	5	2	1	3	10	0
6	21	6%	5	1	1	3	0	10	1
7	12	4%	3	2	0	3	0	3	1
Total	344	100%	62	32	35	37	41	133	4

Here's the data for 15-team leagues:

2018									
4-Wk Period	**Total**	**Pct**	**C**	**1B**	**2B**	**3B**	**SS**	**OF**	**DH**
1	176	54%	38	13	26	24	18	55	2
2	43	13%	5	2	7	6	3	20	0
3	27	8%	10	5	1	0	5	6	0
4	27	8%	6	2	4	0	4	11	0
5	21	6%	3	2	1	4	1	10	0
6	18	6%	5	1	4	1	0	6	1
7	12	4%	1	0	2	0	2	7	0
Total	324	100%	68	25	45	35	33	115	3

And here is the data for the first week of earnings for undrafted pitchers in 12-team leagues:

	2018		**2017**	
4-Wk Period	**Pitchers**	**Pct**	**Pitchers**	**Pct**
1	170	46%	173	46%
2	77	21%	85	23%
3	44	12%	44	12%
4	30	8%	28	7%
5	16	4%	21	6%
6	21	6%	20	5%
7	11	3%	5	1%
Total	369	100%	376	100%

Here are the results for 15-team leagues:

4-Wk Period	2018	
	Pitchers	Pct
1	198	50%
2	72	18%
3	46	12%
4	31	8%
5	20	5%
6	20	5%
7	12	3%
Total	399	100%

There's a key takeaway from these tables, and it is that talent arrives early in the season then tapers off dramatically and slows to a steady trickle.

The problem is that most owners drafted a team they researched all off-season and they are ready to win with this team. Hopefully there were meaningful reasons behind why players were chosen. Now this data suggests owners need to be ruthless in making early-season cuts to roster the best in-season values. There is a balance to be found here. Owners need to take a hard look at what they liked about players in the preseason and make judgment calls about if those assumptions still hold true. Being too slow to adjust one's beliefs will cause the owner to miss out on these early values.

How is Value Recognized Over the Season?

Owners know a lot of value appears during the year, and they know it will first appear very early in the season. But is there still a steady stream of value throughout the entire season? Are there valuable free agents to pursue all year long?

The following table demonstrates the number of undrafted hitters that earn value in a given month. These calculations are performed on a weekly basis but are presented monthly to simplify the table. This means that if an undrafted hitter earned positive value for all four weeks of a given month, he'd be counted four times.

Here's the data for 12-team leagues in 2018:

2018								
4-Wk Period	Total	C	1B	2B	3B	SS	OF	DH
1	305	63	38	32	35	32	100	5
2	306	52	33	34	41	37	106	3
3	327	67	28	27	46	39	117	3
4	343	67	39	44	37	36	117	3
5	335	64	35	34	43	41	116	2
6	343	63	40	40	39	34	121	6
7	265	48	32	29	31	25	100	0
Total	2,224	424	245	240	272	244	777	22

Here's the undrafted hitters that earned value in the different months of the 2017 season:

2017								
4-Wk Period	Total	C	1B	2B	3B	SS	OF	DH
1	314	61	34	29	33	42	114	1
2	338	64	38	31	32	42	128	3
3	345	61	36	32	26	44	146	0
4	328	59	38	32	32	43	122	2
5	343	60	33	39	37	41	132	1
6	360	64	35	42	38	44	136	1
7	181	32	19	17	18	23	71	1
Total	2,209	401	233	222	216	279	849	9

Here's the data for 15-team leagues:

4-Wk Period	Total	C	1B	2B	3B	SS	OF	DH
2018								
1	334	67	34	48	41	36	104	4
2	349	58	27	54	50	38	118	4
3	355	71	21	39	52	48	122	2
4	363	80	32	52	47	44	108	0
5	368	72	35	50	52	47	111	1
6	380	73	43	55	40	43	122	4
7	291	53	37	32	35	34	100	0
Total	2,440	474	229	330	317	290	785	15

These undrafted hitters generally begin to earn value early in the season but the value streams steadily throughout the season at all positions. Let's look at the disbursement of value for pitchers in 12-team leagues:

4-Wk Period	2018	2017
1	246	249
2	256	275
3	268	297
4	270	270
5	282	283
6	272	272
7	149	141
Total	1,743	1,787

And here's the data for pitchers in 15-team leagues:

4-Wk Period	2018
1	298
2	315
3	328
4	327
5	341
6	327
7	263
Total	2,199

Those numbers are nothing short of incredible. In a given week, there are between 55 and 80 undrafted pitchers that theoretically earn positive value.

Roughly half to two-thirds of the pitchers who provide positive production went undrafted. It seems absurd on the surface but makes more sense if the owner considers the volatility a pitcher can experience when viewed on a one-week basis.

The Win statistic is valuable, but when a pitcher only gets one start in a week, it's unlikely they'll capture one, especially when compared to pitchers who get two starts. Further, a starter who is deficient in strikeouts or simply average in ratios is unlikely to produce much value.

For these reasons, streaming pitchers and pumping two-start arms into a lineup is a viable strategy. Many owners recognize this value, but it's nice to see some supporting evidence. If an owner can maximize the win potential and control ratios by streaming a starter, it's likely they're creating value. Streaming isn't easy, and it can result in blow-ups, but there are upwards of 80 undrafted pitchers that will earn value in a week.

ADP and Weekly Valuations

The 12-team weekly valuations for the 2018 season were then cross-matched against each player's preseason ADP in order to determine the typical weekly earnings over the course of the season for players of the various ADP ranges.

For example, both hitters and pitchers in the top 25 earned value in 19 of the 27 weeks on average. Yet hitters earned significantly more in weekly earnings over the course of the season ($272 to $214).

Total weekly earnings are also broken down to show the total earnings in positive earning weeks and the total losses in negative earning weeks. The thought here is that skilled fantasy owners may be able to foresee a negative week in which a player has a minor injury, has tough matchups, plays in tough ballparks, or has only five games scheduled. The owner can then bench the player, avoiding the losses.

Here are the hitter weekly results by preseason ADP:

Preseason ADP	Hitter Total Weekly Earnings	Hitter Positive Only Weekly Earnings	Hitter Negative Only Weekly Earnings	Hitter Number of Positive Weeks	Hitter Number of Negative Weeks	Hitter Weekly Earnings Over Next ADP Group
1-25	$272	$326	($54)	19	8	$129
26-50	$143	$227	($84)	16	11	$17
51-75	$126	$220	($94)	15	12	$38
76-100	$88	$183	($95)	15	13	($77)
101-125	$165	$244	($79)	17	10	N/A

Here are the pitcher weekly results by preseason ADP:

Preseason ADP	Pitcher Total Weekly Earnings	Pitcher Positive Only Weekly Earnings	Pitcher Negative Only Weekly Earnings	Pitcher Number of Positive Weeks	Pitcher Number of Negative Weeks	Pitcher Weekly Earnings over Next ADP Group
1-25	$214	$285	($72)	19	8	$122
26-50	$92	$199	($107)	15	12	$122
51-75	($30)	$128	($158)	12	15	($60)
76-100	$25	$153	($128)	13	14	($18)
101-125	($7)	$152	($159)	14	13	N/A

At first glance, it appears that selecting hitters in the top 25 is the optimal choice. They do earn more in terms of total weekly earnings. But a closer look shows the "Weekly Earnings over Next ADP Group" is very close for both groups. For those owners familiar with the principles of economics, this column represents the marginal productivity of one group over the next, which is generally how to make optimal decisions. This means the top pitchers are very comparable to the top hitters, despite what the pure weekly earnings show.

The weekly earnings for pitchers, both in total and in comparison to the next ADP group, plummet when moving down the table. It's downright ugly, to the point where avoiding these players looks ideal. In comparison, hitter values from ADPs 51-125 are generally positive. These measures seem to align with other findings in The Process, suggesting that it's generally a good strategy to invest in pitchers in the first handful of rounds and then go hitter-heavy in subsequent rounds.

What Does an Average Weekly Statistic Line Look Like?

Experienced fantasy owners have many years working with season-long valuations and preparing for auction drafts, giving them a lot of background context for what constitutes a $40 season-long valuation. That same history and familiarity do not exist for weekly valuations.

The tables that follow display the average weekly statistics required to earn a given weekly value in the 2018 season. This information may be helpful context both for making sense of the weekly lineup analysis in this book and for lineup-setting decisions in the future.

Here are the average weekly statistics for hitters in a 12-team league:

Weekly Value	G	PA	AB	H	AVG	R	HR	RBI	SB
$40+	6.1	27.4	23.9	10.5	0.440	7.1	3.4	8.5	1.3
$35-$40	6.2	27.2	23.9	9.6	0.399	6.3	2.8	7.2	1.1
$30-$35	6.0	25.9	22.8	8.9	0.390	5.8	2.5	6.3	0.7
$25-$30	5.9	25.5	22.6	8.4	0.374	5.3	2.1	5.9	0.6
$20-$25	5.6	23.8	21.0	7.5	0.357	4.5	1.6	5.0	0.7
$15-$20	5.6	22.9	20.3	6.9	0.339	4.0	1.4	4.3	0.5
$10-$15	5.4	21.9	19.6	6.2	0.317	3.4	1.0	3.5	0.5
$5-$10	5.1	19.9	17.7	5.2	0.295	2.8	0.8	2.7	0.3
$1-$5	4.8	18.3	16.4	4.4	0.267	2.2	0.5	2.1	0.3
$1	4.5	17.1	15.6	3.8	0.245	1.9	0.5	1.8	0.1

Here are the average weekly statistics for hitters in a 15-team league:

Weekly Value	G	PA	AB	H	AVG	R	HR	RBI	SB
$40+	6.2	27.7	24.1	10.4	0.432	7.1	3.5	8.6	1.1
$35-$40	6.1	26.7	23.5	9.4	0.401	6.2	2.5	6.6	1.3
$30-$35	6.0	25.7	22.8	8.8	0.384	5.5	2.4	6.5	0.6
$25-$30	5.9	25.2	22.2	8.2	0.368	5.0	1.9	5.6	0.6
$20-$25	5.6	23.3	20.6	7.1	0.345	4.3	1.5	4.6	0.6
$15-$20	5.6	22.8	20.3	6.7	0.331	3.8	1.2	4.0	0.5
$10-$15	5.3	21.1	18.8	5.7	0.305	3.1	0.9	3.1	0.4
$5-$10	5.0	19.1	17.0	4.7	0.277	2.4	0.6	2.3	0.3
$1-$5	4.6	17.1	15.3	3.8	0.247	1.8	0.4	1.6	0.2
$1	4.8	17.7	15.5	3.6	0.229	1.6	0.2	1.5	0.1

Notice how high the production is for hitters. It takes six games or more and a strong hot streak to reach a $30 week. Extrapolating the $30-$35 stat line in a 15-team league to a full 27-week season is the equivalent of 149 R, 65 HR, 176 RBI, 16 SB, .384 season. Obviously, that stat line is not sustainable and would earn well over $35 in season-long value.

The point is to be aware that these short-term explosions in value happen and they are more available on the waiver wire than an owner might have imagined. These valuable weeks might be captured by looking for ideal short-term circumstances; like seven games in a week, playing in good hitter's parks, and slated for weak pitcher matchups where the player has the platoon advantage.

Here are the average weekly statistics for pitchers in a 12-team league:

Weekly Value	GS	IP	W	SV	K	ERA	WHIP
$30+	1.8	12.7	1.6	0.0	14.1	0.97	0.66
$25-$30	1.4	10.4	1.2	0.4	11.2	1.18	0.76
$20-$25	1.2	8.6	1.0	0.3	9.7	1.18	0.71
$15-$20	1.0	7.5	0.9	0.3	7.9	1.22	0.78
$10-$15	0.8	6.2	0.8	0.3	6.4	1.46	0.85
$5-$10	0.6	5.2	0.6	0.4	5.1	1.71	0.92
$1-$5	0.5	4.4	0.3	0.2	4.5	2.01	0.93
$1	0.3	3.6	0.2	0.1	3.9	1.48	0.95

Here are the average weekly statistics for pitchers in a 15-team league:

Weekly Value	GS	IP	W	SV	K	ERA	WHIP
$30+	1.8	12.6	1.5	0.0	13.6	1.03	0.70
$25-$30	1.3	9.7	1.1	0.3	10.7	1.20	0.74
$20-$25	1.1	8.0	1.0	0.3	8.8	1.17	0.71
$15-$20	1.0	7.1	0.9	0.2	7.5	1.33	0.82
$10-$15	0.7	5.9	0.7	0.3	5.9	1.52	0.89
$5-$10	0.5	4.8	0.5	0.3	4.8	1.88	0.92
$1-$5	0.4	4.0	0.2	0.2	4.1	1.98	0.95
$1	0.3	3.2	0.1	0.2	2.8	1.71	0.85

These pitcher weeks are equally impressive, especially in terms of ratios. These tables suggest that focusing on pitchers with good matchups, despite only one start, are more valuable than chasing two starts that may hurt the season-long ratios. For instance, a $10-$20 pitcher appears to be one that goes six innings, has a strong chance to earn a win, strikes out a batter an inning, and gives up about one run. Moving further down the table, it appears strong relievers with a chance of a save earn more value than middling starters.

Skeptical owners might look at the pitcher values and say, "There's no way this value can be captured. If it were possible to average an ERA and WHIP around 1.00 with all pickups, of course I'd do that. Things are not that simple." This is a fair criticism. The difficulty in pitchers is to know if you're going to get the eight-inning gem or the three-inning blowup. There is still a learning opportunity here though. At least through the early-to-middle parts of the season, owners should be focusing on quality instead of quantity. The owner can later determine if it's advantageous to switch and focus on quantity of innings to pursue Wins and Strikeouts. It can be argued that there's too much of a mindset to blindly pursue two-start pitchers or high strikeout arms with ratio downside, despite what these values tell us.

FAAB Spending Trends

While the data shows most of the talent becomes available in the first four weeks of the season, owners seem to start out timidly when it comes to pursuing those players. The NFBC Main Event consisted of 34 and 28 15-team leagues in 2018 and 2019, respectively. Each team had a $1,000 FAAB budget. Over these two seasons, here are the average dollars spent per team, per week.

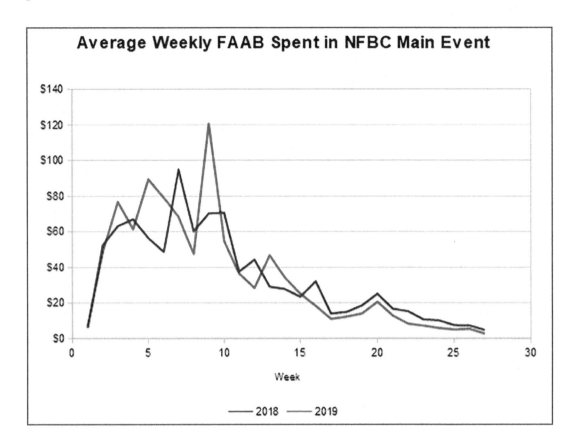

Note: The first week's bid was the weekend before the full season began.

As the chart demonstrates, most owners didn't spend on the emerging value. Instead, they waited for the second 4-week period to open their wallets more. From weeks 2 to 5, $238 was spent on average in 2018 and $276 in 2019. From weeks 6 to 9, $274 was spent in 2018 and $315 in 2019.

Looking at the percentage spent from the remaining budget makes the lack of early-season spending look even starker. For example, if $800 FAAB was left per team and on average $80 was spent, 10% (80/800) was spent. Here the average percentage of remaining budget spent each week.

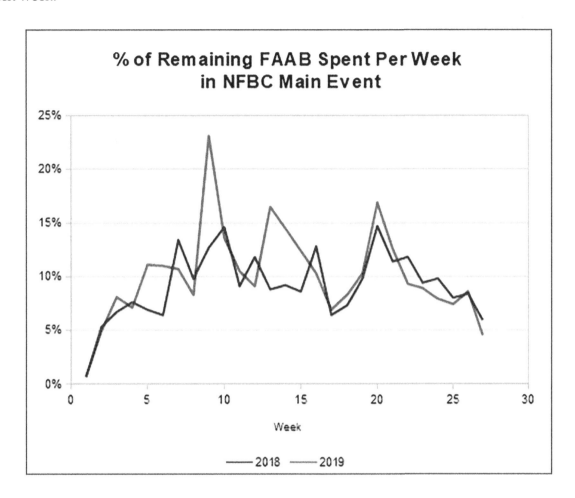

For the first four weeks, when most of the free agent talent shows up, owners spent 8% or less of their budget. Then the percentage stayed in the range of 9% to 14% for weeks.

It's tough to know the reasoning behind this lack of aggressiveness, but a few possible scenarios exist. First, around week eight or nine, the Super Two deadline passes when prospects can be called up and after which their arbitration is delayed a year. Owners may be hoarding FAAB in anticipation of these impact call-ups.

Second, owners are probably holding onto their below-replacement-level players with the hope of a rebound. Owners are maybe trusting their preseason analysis too much. After all, many in the fantasy-advice market preach for owners to exercise patience early in the season.

Finally, the bulge in spending may also be the result of owners panicking at around the six-week mark. Perhaps the early-season talent has slipped by competitors and owners have become desperate as they fall behind. No matter the reason, owners hold back on their early-season spending.

How Valuable Are Two-Start Pitchers?

Owners are bludgeoned to death by two-start pitcher blogs. How important are these double-dips? Are they worth all this attention? The short answer is a resounding "yes," while keeping in mind the previous observations that good ratios are needed to capture the very high-end values. The following table shows the average weekly earnings in one- and two-start weeks by different preseason pitcher rankings (according to ADP) in 12-team leagues:

Preseason Pitcher ADP	2018		2017	
	1-Start Weeks	2-Start Weeks	1-Start Weeks	2-Start Weeks
1 - 25	$1.45	$9.97	$0.79	$12.53
26 - 50	($1.27)	$3.58	($0.60)	$1.99
51 - 75	($2.35)	$1.90	($3.26)	$2.48
76 - 108	($2.62)	$2.58	($1.13)	$2.00

Here are the same results for 15-team leagues:

Preseason Pitcher ADP	2018	
	1-Start Weeks	2-Start Weeks
1 - 25	$3.21	$11.70
26 - 50	$0.05	$5.09
51 - 75	($1.00)	$3.37
76 - 135	($1.30)	$4.23

Here's the same data grouped by end of season (EoS) pitcher rankings (according to end of season yearly valuation) for 12-team leagues:

End-of-Season Rank	2018		2017	
	1-Start Weeks	2-Start Weeks	1-Start Weeks	2-Start Weeks
1 - 25	$3.07	$9.90	$3.40	$13.50
26 - 50	$0.66	$7.92	$1.90	$5.33
51 - 75	($0.23)	$4.78	($0.91)	$4.13
76 - 108	($0.63)	$3.37	($0.23)	$2.02

And for 15-team leagues:

End-of-Season Rank	2018	
	1-Start Weeks	2-Start Weeks
1 - 25	$4.45	$12.33
26 - 50	$2.37	$8.84
51 - 75	$0.51	$5.07
76 - 135	($0.60)	$4.67

Notice the average values drop significantly once below the top-25 (preseason or EoS) pitchers. The talent curve flattens greatly, so much so that there is not a significant difference between those drafted between 26-50 and those drafted after.

Maximizing the number of two-start weeks gives such a significant bump in counting stats that a two-start pitcher near the back of the draft is expected to outearn the typical 1-start week of even the 1st-25th ranked players.

In-Season Theory

Now that the in-season landscape has been laid and the owner understands how, where, and when value arises during the season, a discussion of some key in-season theory differences is needed. Much of the preseason preparations and decisions are done under certain assumptions that will gradually change as the season progresses.

The Split Changes During the Season

In the last edition of the book there were several pages on how the in-season split changes as the season progresses and how owners need to adjust. Looking back, the authors have concluded this section was useless. While the concept of a changing split may exist in theory, it's not actionable. The reality is that each team is so unique, and owners simply need to focus on their team's weaknesses and acquiring good players. We apologize for wasting anyone's time who read it last year. Sorry, and next year there will be no mention of its existence.

How Concept of Value Shifts During the Season in Roto Leagues

This book has spent plenty of time focusing on the concept of value, including how to formulate a projection and then run it through a valuation system to determine a player's projected earnings.

It's time to take a step back and think critically about what is happening. The dollar value gets calculated in March before a pitch is even thrown. Also, it's calculated before even one player has been drafted and with no consideration for the rest of the owner's team or its position in the projected standings. The preseason value calculation means little when it's based largely on the home runs a power hitter will have and a team is already projected for first place in the category with a 15-homer cushion.

In other words, valuations are a flimsy way of making decisions. They're the best objective tool available for making decisions, but they're still flimsy.

To add another layer of complexity, the owner's concept of value should change as the season goes along. In the preseason, the player's value is a theoretical value relative to every other player in the player pool. For example, this player is worth $20 based on everything we expect will happen and what we expect from other players and what owners are willing to pay.

As the season progresses, the owner's perception of value should gradually shift to become "this is the player's value *to my team*." It's no longer theoretical. Owners need to make decisions based on how their team and how the standings are affected by adding or dropping players. A player with a theoretical value of $10 in the league's context may have no value at all in a specific team's context.

Owners can argue in a draft-and-hold league or a league with limited trading activity that the value should move to "this is the player's value *to my team*" earlier in the season or even during the draft. It's difficult to adjust a team's category imbalance as the season progresses.

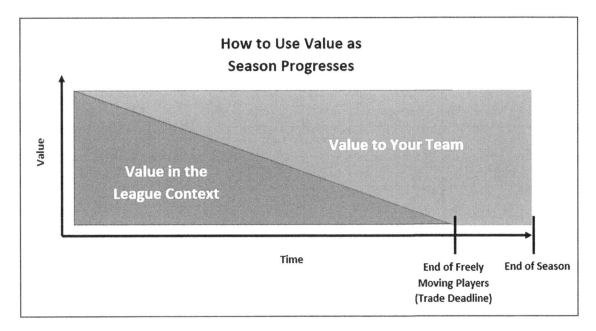

A stolen-base threat like Billy Hamilton (in his prime, not so much the terrible 2019 version) can help illustrate how the perception of value should change during the season. He shows a strong preseason projected value. His Stolen Base totals are many z-scores and SGPs above the category's average total. If an owner (Team No. 5) finds themselves in a set of standings like this, Hamilton's value is suddenly very limited *to their team:*

RNK	R	HR	RBI	SB	AVG	R PTS	HR PTS	RBI PTS	SB PTS	AVG PTS	HIT PTS
1	555	170	547	55	0.265	12.0	15.0	14.0	5.0	13.0	59.0
2	554	151	513	61	0.269	11.0	11.0	11.0	9.0	14.0	56.0
3	574	150	516	62	0.260	14.0	10.0	12.0	10.0	8.0	54.0
4	510	159	536	78	0.255	8.0	13.0	13.0	13.0	4.0	51.0
5	582	139	493	80	0.257	15.0	6.0	7.0	14.0	7.0	49.0
6	511	126	499	65	0.270	9.0	3.0	9.0	11.0	15.0	47.0
7	495	164	569	34	0.256	5.0	14.0	15.0	1.0	5.0	40.0
7	508	153	496	45	0.262	7.0	12.0	8.0	2.0	11.0	40.0
9	567	141	508	60	0.247	13.0	7.0	10.0	8.0	1.0	39.0
10	505	141	476	70	0.261	6.0	7.0	3.0	12.0	9.0	37.0
11	478	146	492	57	0.262	2.0	9.0	6.0	6.0	11.0	34.0
12	526	137	481	50	0.261	10.0	5.0	4.0	3.0	9.0	31.0
13	494	122	485	83	0.249	4.0	1.0	5.0	15.0	2.0	27.0
14	483	125	464	57	0.256	3.0	2.0	2.0	6.0	5.0	18.0
15	477	127	426	53	0.251	1.0	4.0	1.0	4.0	3.0	13.0

This owner has only one point available in stolen bases and little downside, but they're lacking in power and batting average. It's quite possible Hamilton's value, *to this team*, is negative. He's dead weight in the categories needed to move up in the standings.

Again, the days left in the season is an important consideration. If it's still only May then the standings could point to a Hamilton-like player being valuable, even as a team develops a stolen-base cushion. It's a long season and anything can happen. But as June and July pass by, the value proposition shifts and would dwindle for such a player on this team.

Beware of Blindness

Some owners do almost all their research in the offseason. They can squeeze in more research when their kids are in school and in bed at a reasonable time. When summer rolls around, kids stay up later, there's more running around with summer activities, and it becomes much harder to keep up with the never-ending news cycle. For this reason, some owners enjoy playing in draft-and-hold leagues that don't require much more than setting weekly or twice-weekly lineups. Those leagues go very deep into the player pool, often 50 rounds of a 15-team draft (750 players).

Because of this deep research that they do in the preseason, they've realized a blind spot for in-season players who develop out of nowhere. Max Muncy in 2018 is an example. This type of owner will miss on this player type every time. Muncy wasn't good or interesting enough to make it into the top-750 preseason players, but he came out of nowhere to hit 20 home runs in his first 63 games.

It's like a frog searching for grasshoppers to eat. The frog is sitting there looking for movement. If the grasshopper doesn't move, the frog would never see him. He's looking for a very specific thing: movement. Owners need to adjust this filter that says, "If I didn't know about Player X in the preseason, they couldn't possibly be worth my time."

It's likely all owners have some form of individual blindness. They need to figure out theirs and try to address it. This sounds obvious, but the above owner needs to adjust his filter so that if a player is promoted to the big leagues (especially a hitter), he has inherently become one of the top 750 players. If he were to begin a draft-and-hold league the day Muncy was promoted, he would have been in the top 750. A player like Muncy needs to be on the radar and cannot be dismissed.

Short-term Changes in Perception and Value

From the earlier discussions, a hitter's projection or skill level doesn't change just because of a handful of bad games, but the market's perceived value attached to the player can swing wildly because of a hot or cold start.

Owners can exploit this overreaction which takes place when a player is called up from the minor leagues. Assume a league allows an owner to make player pickups once a week via FAAB on Sunday night. A hypothetical prospect who is highly coveted is called up to the majors on a Tuesday night.

How different would those Sunday night bids be in these two scenarios:

1. Player hits a home run in his first at-bat and goes on to hit one other home run. The player's team wins five straight after his call-up and he's being covered on SportsCenter as saving the team's playoff hopes.

2. Player struggles in his first five games and hits .200 with no home runs, creating no national buzz.

Of course, it is a rhetorical question. The bids would be out of this world in the first scenario, but the player's RoS projection would still be nearly identical, regardless of the performance in his first five games. Owners would be able to bid a much lower amount in the second scenario.

Market forces are entirely the cause of this scenario. Owners could argue that the intrinsic value of the player is unchanged between the two scenarios. The wild swing we expect to see in price is simply due to the demand for the player.

Competing Motives in Decision-Making

As if decision-making wasn't complex enough, the issue is compounded by the fact that there are competing motivations owners use to make decisions. In many cases, the motivation is to find the player projected to be the most valuable player for the remainder of the season.

That framework often corresponds to identifying the player that will have the greatest effect on winning the league, but they're not necessarily the same. A player can be viewed as extremely valuable in the league's context (if he were dropped onto an average team), but if he only adds to categories in which a team is already relatively strong, his value to the team is limited.

Even more interesting and challenging to consider is the possibility that a player might not be valuable in most circumstances (therefore projecting for low value), but they could increase a team's winning chances if he hits his ceiling or highest percentile outcome. Examples are super-talented minor leaguers that might get called up, or players coming back from injury.

Players projected for earnings most often increase an owner's odds of winning. However, there are circumstances where it makes sense to pass over a $3 player for the one projected for -$5 in earnings that has the potential to possibly earn $25 in the perfect scenario. Owners can walk this fine line by asking, "which player increases the odds of me winning the league?" as opposed to "which player projects for the greatest value?"

The Los Angeles Dodgers have offered two recent examples of players that demonstrate this decision. Cody Bellinger and Walker Buehler, in the 2017 and 2018 seasons, respectively, were not projected to generate enough playing time to be highly impactful. Bellinger was seemingly blocked by Adrian Gonzalez at first base and Buehler was expected to make the big leagues, but nobody knew when. The Dodgers had a stable of starting pitcher options that could push Buehler's debut well into the season.

The median playing-time projections for Bellinger and Buehler would have shown them as negative earners. However, if the cards fell just right and they stumbled into full-time jobs early on, they had the talent to be potential league-winners. No projection system will be able to quantify value jump. It's up to the owner to make educated guesses and to build a portfolio of players that can protect against significant downside and still allow for the upside required to win.

Identifying Players to Add

The theory about valuations and splits is all well and good, but there is still something to be said for monitoring specific players and combing through statistics to uncover a diamond in the rough. How does an owner determine which players are more likely to explode in value? What statistics can help an owner more accurately determine who the early-season surprises are?

It bears reminding that rest-of-season projections are always going to be the best predictor, especially in the talent-based ratios (playing time is not guaranteed to be accurate). With that said, there is possibly an extreme payout to be had by identifying the exceptions to the rules earlier than one's opponents. The next segment will help owners focus on what's important and provide some shortcuts and safeguards to help make sure key free agents are not being missed.

In-Season Stats to Focus On

The best place to start for analyzing in-season changes is to go back to the Projections section of this book, especially for pitchers, to see if any of the talent-based components of the projection have changed. With pitchers, one should focus especially on velocity and pitch mix. These changes can immediately and significantly change a pitcher's talent level. FanGraphs player pages and BrooksBaseball.net are great resources for reviewing these details.

A velocity increase or decrease is a definite signal that talent level has changed for the better or worse, respectively. Be careful to not jump to conclusions about minor differences and avoid comparing last season's ending velocity to early-season velocities. Pitch speed tends to increase as the year progresses. But after taking those things into account, changes in velocity are actionable.

When reviewing pitch mix, look for new pitches, a reduction in usage of a terrible pitch, or a significant rebalancing of all pitch types. Any of these changes are likely to result in a better talent-level projection.

If both velocity and mix are constant and the pitcher's performance has been shaky, check their Zone Percentage at FanGraphs. Zone Percentage is simply the number of pitches thrown in the strike zone divided by total pitches thrown. A decline in this measure means the pitcher's command and control may be faltering. This could indicate a hidden injury or bad mechanics.

A newer factor to check is the pitcher's fastball spin rate. A spin rate change may point to a pitcher compensating for an injury. The best place to find a pitcher's spin rate is at the Pitch Tracking section on a pitcher's page at baseballsavant.mlb.com (change the filter from "Season" to "Month" or "Game" to see in-season detail).

As for hitters, their production can seem to change quite frequently, but only a few factors matter when trying to determine if a change is real. Most changes are simply noise.

The most critical area to assess is plate discipline, including walk rates and strikeout rates. An owner can dig a little past just walks and strikeouts and examine a hitter's inside- (Z-Swing%) and outside-the-strike-zone swing (O-Swing%) and contact rates (Z-Contact% and O-Contact%). All the plate discipline stats stabilize with minimal data points.

The reason a change in plate discipline is important is that it can lead to other changes, like a higher batting average (more contact) and power (better contact). The exact effects of better or worse plate discipline may vary for each hitter, but the difference can be substantial.

The next area to focus on is the newly available Statcast data and its relationship to pre-existing data. The first item is a hitter's power. While hitters used to gain power as they aged into their late 20s, this aging curve has changed. With all the advances in medicine and weight training, hitters are making it to the majors as strong and powerful as ever. Once in the major leagues, hitters rarely ever gain power, but they can certainly lose it.

When a hitter is struggling to hit home runs, the owner can do a quick dive into his power-related stats like Hard Hit%, Average Exit Velocity, Average Batted Ball Distance, and Barrels (the last three stats are also found at Baseball Savant). If all of these measures are down, the hitter may be playing through an undisclosed injury.

The next-most important batted-ball measure is the recently added Launch Angle, which correlates highly with ground-ball rate. Some people have gone as far as naming a podcast after it. A hitter can change his swing path to give batted balls more or less lift. The ideal launch angle is between 15 and 20 degrees, which will yield between a 32% to 42% ground-ball rate. Hitters who drop below this threshold don't give the ball enough loft for home runs and line drives. Hitters with too much loft hit too many easy-to-catch pop-ups.

The last power-related measure to check is the player's Pull Percentage. This statistic will give an indication of if the hitter is pulling every batted ball to get home runs over the shorter corner outfield fences. Pulling balls for home runs is how Jose Bautista went from a Quad-A talent to a 50-home run threat.

If a struggling hitter doesn't have underlying metrics that show a decline in power, owners can safely assume the hitter is just going through a spell of bad luck and some positive regression toward career norms will be expected. Likewise, if a player off to a hot start is demonstrating an across-the-board rise in skills, the power breakout is worth an investment.

Stolen Bases

Owners in need of Stolen Bases should consider looking ahead at matchups. Stolen Bases often come as much as a function of the opponent (a bad catcher or pitcher that is poor at holding on runners) as they do from the baserunner's own speed. This strategy is easier to use in leagues that allow daily moves or those leagues that allow swapping of hitters over a weekend (like the NFBC) when they're up against a team who has problems preventing steals.

Both FanGraphs and Baseball-Reference show Stolen Base and Caught Stealing numbers for catchers under the player's defensive statistics. Baseball-Reference even includes the Caught Stealing Percentage and the league-wide Caught Stealing Percentage for reference.

Lineup

Where a player hits in a lineup can create a noticeable difference in a player's counting stats as lineup position affects both the player's plate appearances and run-production opportunities. The following table shows the average difference in these statistics for the different spots in the lineup:

Lineup Spot	PA Diff	RBI/Runs
1	0	0.6
2	-17	0.8
3	-34	1.1
4	-50	1.2
5	-66	1.0
6	-84	1.1
7	-103	1.0
8	-122	1.0
9	-142	0.9

For each spot a player moves down, they'll lose 16-to-20 plate appearances over the course of a season. The difference can be seen when a bad-hitting speedster goes from leading off to batting last (e.g. Billy Hamilton in 2018). The lost plate appearances mean fewer chances to get on base and steal bases.

The next major factor to consider is the Runs-to-RBIs ratio. The value change is within the top four spots in the lineup, with the first two spots getting fewer RBI opportunities since they start the game with no one on base and weak hitters preceding them in later innings. The third and fourth hitters will have the good hitting leadoff hitters on base to drive in.

One final small lineup change that can occur and will have major implications is if a speedster on an NL team is moved to the eighth spot, in front of the pitcher. This move is a value killer. Teams don't like to have guys running with the pitcher hitting and prefer to use a sacrifice bunt to move the runner along.

Practical Tips for Determining Whom to Add

Not every free agent add can be researched for hours. Fantasy owners can't always be patrolling Twitter for beat writer tidbits that will lead to an amazing pickup.

When life gets in the way, or even as a simple safeguard to ensure an owner is not missing out on an obvious add, sorting the league's free-agent listing by two columns can help prevent a glaring mistake. First, sort by the change in percentage ownership. Most large league-hosting providers like ESPN, CBS, and Fantrax offer this column on the free agent listings. This will provide an owner with a list of the hottest pickups.

If the owner's league processes moves on a weekly basis, this information may not be available with enough lead time to be actionable. To work around this, the owner can register and set up a fake league at a website that allows daily transactions (e.g. CBS and Yahoo!). The ownership percentage changes will move faster on these sites and give a better sense of the market before most weekly FAAB leagues run on the weekend.

This is a great tool to uncover when a closer change has occurred on Saturday or Sunday. When it gets to be a summer weekend, it's easy to miss some news. Viewing the list of most-added players can help point an owner to where they need to focus their research.

Sorting by total ownership is another great tool. People make mistakes. Other owners may make a poor drop. Or maybe they're even forced to drop a player due to overwhelming injuries. Reviewing total ownership is an easy step to do each time before making a move and can help spot whether an unexpected player is available when an owner wouldn't otherwise be looking for him. This is especially helpful if an owner plays in multiple leagues and has a hard time keeping track of each league's players pool.

In deep leagues (AL- or NL-only, or more than 15-team mixed leagues), where playing time is critical, filtering the player statistics to show those from the past two weeks or 15 days (depending on the hosting site) can give owners a sense for who is playing and who is not. Be careful not to pick up someone who will quickly be losing playing time (because of someone returning from injury, for example), but this is another great place to start research.

Determining Whom to Drop

Releasing a player is just as much a skill as the decision about whom to add. Nobody talks about this, so there is little guidance on the topic, and it is very susceptible to cognitive biases such as loss aversion, sunk cost, and overvaluing one's own players (i.e. endowment effect).

Owners often have a weakness where they tend to overvalue their own players. This makes the simple act of adding a player from the waiver wire much more difficult, as owners are hesitant to drop a player, even if he's unlikely to be useful for weeks.

Owners can work around this bias in two ways. First, they can ask themselves in what kind of situations they would be comfortable using the player. Additionally, what would have to happen for them to be able to start the player. If after considering those two questions it's still going to be unlikely that they'd use the player, it becomes much easier to drop him.

The second way owners can combat the bias is to ask themselves, "Do I think someone else will even pick this player up?" This helps owners get comfortable with their decision to drop a player. Does an owner think his 16th-round draft pick who's hitting .180 six weeks into the season still has a chance to be a great late-round pick and will get scooped up? Possibly, but the reality is that more intriguing players are available and nobody's going to add him.

If owners struggle with cutting players, monitor the players dropped during the season. Do they frequently find that those players they've dropped are ignored by opposing managers and just end up going unrostered? It's probably a sign that the owner is making good decisions about whom to cut.

Negative Players

Major disappointments happen each season. Players selected in the third round or won for $20 at an auction sometimes do not perform. Even players with years of proven history suddenly hit a wall. If $20 of value is expected from a player and he ends up producing around $10 of value, there's not much to be done. An owner can continue to plug him into the lineup and try to market him to another team who thinks the player will turn the corner.

The decision about what to do with these players becomes extra challenging if there is something fundamentally wrong with the player.

There are two high-profile examples of players in recent seasons that fell into this situation.

- **Miguel Cabrera** was coming off a vintage 2016 season in which he hit 38 HR and drove in 108 runs with a .316 AVG. He was being selected at the tail end of the first round in 2017 drafts. He went on to struggle through 130 games in 2017, hitting only 16 HR with 60 RBI and a .249 AVG.

- **Matt Carpenter** had a subpar 2017 season by Matt Carpenter standards, hitting only .241. But he still managed 23 HR and scored 91 R. He was being selected in the mid-teen rounds of 2018 drafts. The hope was that 2017 was an outlier and Carpenter would get it together. After 44 games, Carpenter was hitting only .194 with 15 R, 3 HR, and 16 RBI. He was not even on pace for 60 R, 12 HR, and 64 RBI.

Cabrera never pulled out of the funk, while Carpenter went on to have an amazing run, finishing with a stat line of .257, 111 R, 36 HR, 81 RBI, and 4 SB (68 R, 28 HR, 52 RBI in June, July, and August).

What is an owner to do in this situation? Was there a tangible difference between Cabrera's and Carpenter's situations?

It's important to remember here that we're talking about players with track records of very good (or great) production. Cabrera and Carpenter had years of strong performances when they fell into these skids. When these downturns occur, owners know the sabermetrically responsible action is to trust the player's projections. It takes a lot more than 40 games to change a projection significantly enough to give up on previously talented players.

Injuries are the wild card. They're the outside factor for which projection systems cannot account. Carpenter supposedly played through shoulder pain in 2017, something many attributed to his career-low .241 average. Then Carpenter had shoulder and back problems when he arrived in 2018 for Spring Training.

Cabrera missed games due to groin, side, collarbone, and back injuries during the 2017 season, but he only landed on the IL once. The Tigers were facing a closing playoff window and Cabrera managed to play in 130 games, despite nagging injuries.

There is no right answer in these situations. With hints of injuries surrounding both players, benching them after 40-50 games of horrible performances could be warranted. Cutting a mid-round player like Carpenter might have made sense even removing hindsight. Consider the types of injuries associated with the player. Shoulders and backs are big problems.

Is there any difference between these situations? Carpenter never missed a game due to soreness or injury in his slow 2018 start. He missed games due to finger, quadriceps, hip, and shoulder injuries in 2017 (but never went on the IL). Perhaps this should have indicated that injuries were not the reason for his poor performance. We just mentioned that Cabrera missed quite a few games to nagging injuries in 2017.

The bottom line is, if there is a reason to believe there is an underlying injury, all bets are off. The RoS projections are not to be taken as gospel, especially if the injury continues to pop up and the player does not go on the IL. If there is no reason to believe the player is injured, the rest-of-season projections are the best resource available for deciding what to do with a player.

Sunk Costs

Sunk costs describe a situation where something's cost has already been incurred and cannot be recovered. The price paid or draft pick used to obtain a player is a sunk cost, as an owner cannot return the player and get the draft pick back.

Logically, the price paid for something in the past should not affect decisions about how to treat the object in the future. However, behavioral economic studies tell us that humans are not good at applying logic in these situations.

For example, assume $20 is paid for a player at auction. Part of the season goes by, and the player's situation changes, he's struggled some, and his rest-of-season projection values him being worth $5. Another owner offers a $7 player in exchange for the $5.

Should an owner take that deal? The $20 initial investment is irrelevant at this time and should not enter into the equation. If the best estimate places a player's worth at $5 and a $7 player is offered for him in trade, the best play is to take the deal. It's the logical action, but many of us would not make the deal. Many owners can't separate the player from the original $20 investment, so they turn down the $2 gain and just hope for the best. It isn't easy to do. The key is to be aware of this potential problem, so pitfalls are avoided. After all, trading a $5 player for a $7 player could tip the scales for an owner down the line.

It's also helpful to keep this bias in mind when trading with others. When trying to make a deal with another owner and they say something like, "but I paid $20 for him," consider taking that player out of the deal. Attempt to shift their thinking to the future by saying something like, "Yes, but they're only projected for $5 for the rest of the season, it's not possible to get that $20 back now." But that owner may be a victim of the sunk cost trap, and it's unlikely they can be talked out of it.

In-Season Tools

There are a variety of tools that can be used to alert owners of important information during the season and to help in lineup setting. It's been discussed that playing time changes lead to the swiftest adjustment in projected values. What follows are several in-season tools that can be used to alert owners a playing-time change has or is about to occur, as well as tools that can help in setting the optimal weekly lineup.

News Monitoring Tools

Being informed about recent MLB events is hugely important. This can be a challenge for those owners with hectic lives. They might be in a league that processes waivers or FAAB on a daily basis overnight. In those situations, having the diligence to scan through an updated news feed, like on the Rotoworld or MLBTradeRumors apps, can be a huge advantage.

The accounts seem to come and go, but there are specialty Twitter accounts that will alert followers to changes in closer roles for Major League teams. Likewise, many fantasy news providers, like the RotoGraphs section on FanGraphs, offer periodic bullpen reports that can help owners identify situations where and when a closer change is more likely to occur.

MLB Historic Lineup Monitoring Tools

When deciding whom to pick up, whom to cut, or even whom to start in a given week, it's important to be aware of how MLB teams are using their players. If an owner is busy or plays in multiple leagues, it can be a huge challenge to keep their lineups full of MLB starters.

RosterResource's full site offers a "Lineup Tracker[24]" that displays the notable IL activations for the past 10 days, the notable minor league promotions for the season, and perhaps most importantly, the last 10 lineups for each MLB team. The chart also shows if the MLB team faced a right- or left-handed pitcher each day. This is very helpful for spotting when a player has fallen into a platoon or is otherwise not playing every day. Owners also can see where the player is hitting in the lineup or if the player has recently missed time due to an injury. A more

---

[24] https://www.rosterresource.com/mlb-lineup-tracker/

truncated version of the lineup tool is available in the RosterResource pages on Fangraphs, where the lineup history goes back six days.

ARZ	Proj. Spot vs RHP	SUN 9/29 vsR	SAT 9/28 vsR	FRI 9/27 vsL	WED 9/25 vsR	TUE 9/24 vsR	MON 9/23 vsR	SUN 9/22 vsR	SAT 9/21 vsR	FRI 9/20 vsL	WED 9/18 vsR	Overall Rank
Jarrod Dyson	1	CF (7)	CF (1)			CF (8)	CF (1)		CF (8)		CF (8)	211
Josh Rojas	2	LF (5)	LF (2)	LF (6)	LF (6)	LF (5)	LF (2)	LF (2)	LF (5)	LF (2)	LF (2)	413
Eduardo Escobar	3	3B (3)	2B (3)	3B (3)		3B (3)	2B (3)	3B (3)	3B (3)	3B (3)	3B (3)	18
Christian Walker	4	1B (4)	1B (4)	1B (4)			1B (4)	1B (4)		1B (4)	1B (4)	82
Wilmer Flores	5	2B (1)		2B (2)	2B (3)			2B (5)		2B (5)		258
Adam Jones	6		RF (6)	RF (5)			RF (6)	RF (6)		RF (6)		142
Nick Ahmed	7	SS (2)	SS (7)	SS (7)	SS (7)	SS (7)	SS (7)	SS (7)	SS (6)	SS (7)	INJ	73
Alex Avila	8		C (8)			C (6)			C (7)		C (7)	331
Carson Kelly	Bench			C (8)			C (8)	C (8)		C (8)		191
Caleb Joseph	Bench	C (8)			C (8)							550
Kevin Cron	Bench				1B (5)							435
Jake Lamb	Bench		3B (5)		3B (4)	1B (4)	3B (5)		1B (4)		3B (5)	340
Domingo Leyba	Bench					2B (2)			2B (2)		SS (6)	534
Ildemaro Vargas	Bench											335
Abraham Almonte	Bench	INJ	INJ	INJ	RF (2)	RF (1)		CF (1)	RF (1)		RF (1)	480
Tim Locastro	Bench	RF (6)		CF (1)	CF (1)					CF (1)		339
Ketel Marte	INJ	INJ	INJ	INJ	INJ	INJ	INJ	INJ	INJ	INJ	INJ	13

Baseball-Reference offers its own batting order history[25] tracker for each team. While it doesn't mention call-up dates or IL information, Baseball-Reference's tracker shows all starting lineups for the entire season, longer than only the last 10 days visible at RosterResource.

MLB Starting Lineup Tools

With owners needing to get every advantage, having a reliable and timely source for seeing the daily starting lineups for MLB teams is an important tool. There are a number of important tips throughout this book that are dependent upon having good information about who is starting for an MLB team on a given day. While the lineups eventually come out on Twitter, they're not in a central location and it would be time consuming to continually check for them. Many websites make the data available as soon as it comes out. The authors prefer Fantasy Labs and Baseball Press, but many more exist.

---

[25]   https://www.baseball-reference.com/teams/ATL/2019-batting-orders.shtml

Projected Starting Pitcher Tools

Having a reliable place to check for projected starting pitchers offers peace of mind and is a huge time saver. There is enough news generated on a weekend of baseball that the last thing owners need to be doing is checking multiple sites to see which starters are slated to go in the upcoming week. The authors themselves use RotoWire's Projected Starters page. This feature is under the premium section of RotoWire, so it does require a subscription.

Weekly Projections and Lineup Setting Tools

While on the topic of premium services, the authors also both subscribe to Razzball's premium season-long fantasy baseball content and use the site's weekly projections as a significant input in determining free agents to pursue and which players to slot into the lineup. As mentioned in the projections area, Razzball's projections are based on Steamer, but they then take other short-term factors into consideration when arriving at a weekly projection. Things like the number of games, ball parks, and handedness of pitchers are all incorporated. All projections also include Razzball's own dollar value calculations for a variety of league sizes and types. This helps an owner make quick and reliable decisions. The authors could do all the work themselves each week, but for less than $1 per week, the time savings is huge.

Strategies During Different Stages of the Season

The strategies employed by an owner should change as the season progresses. An optimal early strategy is not necessarily optimal in the end game.

Early Season

The early stages of the season should mostly mirror the decision-making processes used in preparing for the draft, but with a heavy shift in focus to understanding incorrectly predicted playing-time situations. Owners should keep in mind that value appears early on. Be careful to properly weight preseason assumptions against the hard evidence of playing-time changes. Owners can detect mistakes in playing-time assessments by monitoring batting lineups, platoon situations, and early results. While putting a lot of stock in small samples can be a mistake, there will be playing-time situations that shake out according to who gets off to a hot start.

Owners should avoid putting too much stock into early-season standings. They're fun to monitor when leading, but they're a poor indicator of the season-long perspective. Instead of wasting time looking at the standings, be more productive by building a tool to use later in the season (next section), researching players, digesting the news, and looking for disgruntled owners frustrated by slow starts.

Mid-to-Late May

In May, two unofficial and undefined days occur: struggling hitters are frequently demoted, and the MLB Super Two deadline passes. Both are important dates to be aware of and anticipate.

Demotion of Struggling Hitters

Earlier in the book, it was noted that an OPS of around .635 was needed to keep a major league job. Here are the players who were demoted, released, or placed on waivers around mid-May of 2019 (a quarter of the way through the season) and their OPS at the time.

Name	OPS	Demotion
Justin Bour	.584	05/15/19
Jeimer Candelario	.573	05/16/19
Jake Cave	.615	05/13/19
Delino DeShields	.605	05/09/19
Wilmer Difo	.598	05/17/19
Garrett Hampson	.493	05/13/19
Teoscar Hernandez	.562	05/16/19
Kendrys Morales	.569	05/14/19
Mallex Smith	.502	04/30/19
Nick Williams	.493	05/19/19
Average	.559	05/13/19

Even the .635 OPS benchmark is too low for these 10 hitters. By mid-May, teams lose patience with struggling hitters and are forced to move on.

Super Two Deadline

First, here is MLB.com's explanation[26] of the Super Two deadline:

> *Players typically must accrue three years of Major League service time -- with one year of service time equaling 172 days on the 25-man roster or the Major League injured list -- to become eligible for salary arbitration. Super Two is a designation that allows a select group of players to become eligible for arbitration before reaching three years of service time.*

> *To qualify for the Super Two designation, players must rank in the top 22 percent, in terms of service time, among those who have amassed between two and three years in the Majors. Typically, this applies to players who have two years and at least 130 days of service time, although the specific cutoff date varies on a year-to-year basis.*

Translating this, there is a floating date where if called up before the date, players receive four years of arbitration instead of three, thereby saving the MLB team money. Historically, this date is thought to be around June 1st. In 2018, the date was May 7th, according to MLBTraderumors.[27]

> *Over the past decade, the Super Two cutoff level has ranged from a low of 2.122 (years of service time) to a high of 2.146. Last year's 2.134 cutoff lands smack dab in the middle. Players that were promoted on or before May 7th of this year were in line to accrue 146 days of service this season, thus putting them on track to clear all the bars we've seen in recent campaigns.*

Mid-May 2019 was when "FAABageddon" happened, with prospects like Austin Riley, Brendan Rodgers, Willie Calhoun, Oscar Mercado, and Nicky Lopez being called up during the same week. And according to MLBTraderumors[28], the date changed with a new low this past year.

> *A 2.115 cutoff would already be the lowest Super Two threshold in the past decade. The previous low points in that span came in 2010 and 2013 when the cutoff was 2.122. Last year, it settled at 2.134. If the threshold is any lower this season, others could also be impacted. Arizona's Luke Weaver (2.112) and Oakland's Matt Chapman (2.109) are the most notable names within reasonable distance of Hader's 2.115.*

---

[26]   http://m.mlb.com/glossary/transactions/super-two
[27]   https://www.mlbtraderumors.com/2019/05/prospect-promotions-super-two-timing.html
[28]   https://www.mlbtraderumors.com/2019/10/brewers-josh-hader-super-two-cutoff-arbitration.html

Understanding this rule is important and may tip off owners to who will get called up and who might be in line to stay in the minors longer. The Houston Astros' treatment of Kyle Tucker is a good example of this. Tucker was called up in July of 2018 and began accruing service time. He then started 2019 in the minors. Because Tucker had already accrued service time in 2018, the Astros couldn't call him up when players began to get called up near FAABageddon. He already had more service time than those players and would inherently qualify for the extra year of arbitration if called up at that time. The Astros were incentivized to keep him in the minors for at least another month, thus the call up of Yordan Alvarez instead.

While the official date is not set in advance, it hovers around mid-May to early-June, and owners can expect a huge number of prospect call ups during this time. Owners in leagues that allow speculative adds of minor leaguers (the NFBC does not) should consider trying to time this and attempt to add the notable rookies a week before the players are called up. This will be difficult to time precisely, but the savings in FAAB could be enormous.

Calculate Projected Standings

Instead of thinking about the actual standings, an owner can get a much better forecast of the season by calculating the projected end-of-season standings. This takes some skill with a spreadsheet and time to assign the owned players to each of the league's teams.

The projected standings are the sum of the current standings and the rest-of-season projections for the players of each team. Using Microsoft Excel or Google Sheets can help make these calculations more efficient. Research the SUMIF or SUMIFS spreadsheet functions to make this more practical.

The owner should not sweat if the projected standings show a middle-of-the-pack outlook in individual categories when viewed early in the season. Instead, they will want to look for glaring shortcomings that need correction and be on the lookout for potential breakout candidates that correspond to their team's weaknesses.

For example, if an owner determined they lacked home run power, this exercise may have made them more likely to gamble on a player like Max Muncy, or feel more confident in a decision to bypass the flavor-of-the-week pickup for a cheaper player off to a slow power start.

Mid-Season

Once into May, owners can begin to put more stock into the projected league standings and even begin to pay attention to deficiencies in the current year-to-date standings. If the projected league standings have not been calculated yet, mid-May is a perfect time to do that. The six-week mark is a significant enough portion of the season that minor blips in performance fade away and the standings start to stabilize.

The trade deadline falls into this part of the season. Owners should be monitoring players that stand to gain playing time at the trade deadline, especially for players that could address weaknesses in one's roster. Sometimes these can be predicted in advance. An example would be a speedy minor leaguer that could be promoted if a star is traded at the deadline, opening up a spot on the major league roster.

The owner should keep an eye on the actual standings to make sure things don't get out of balance and that they're not falling too far out of category races.

Attention tends to wane for many owners as the season reaches July, but the standings are far from finalized at this point. There are still many opportunities to make up ground. Early trades start to roll in before the deadline, blips in performance are not noticed as much as they are in April, MLB teams are starting to fall out of contention and shake up their lineups, football news and mock drafts are distracting others. The key point here is to maintain focus through the dog days.

Manually Calculate How Many Points Can Be Gained

The process of re-running a full-blown projected-standings recalculation is time-consuming. If the owner does not have the time for such an effort, they should periodically review their upward and downward standings mobility. Where can points be easily gained or lost? Where are problem areas developing? Where are dramatic measures needed? Reviewing the standings and answering these types of questions is necessary to maximize the chances of winning the league.

Take, for example, the standings below. Assume these are generated as of August 1st in a typical 15-team league. In this hypothetical scenario, this book's reader assumes they're managing the fifth-place team.

The manual standings review searches for teams in the proximity of being caught or falling behind in each category. The owner can do a simple tally of the points to be gained or lost in each category in order to better guide their lineup decisions, trades, and free agent targeting.

Note: Arrows have been added to the other teams' statistics that can be passed, or for which they could pass the fifth-place team..

RNK	Total	R	HR	RBI	SB	AVG	W	K	SV	ERA	WHIP
1	118.5	662	211	707	109↑	.261↑	64↑	967	56↑	3.82↓	1.203↑
2	112.0	722↓	189↑	660↓	75	.270	60↑	969	15	3.03	1.143
3	107.5	637	195↑	650↓	72	.262↑	52↓	1,033	68	3.23	1.108
4	96.5	770↑	193↑	664↑	86↓	.261↑	59↑	909↑	34↓	4.03	1.249
5	**96.0**	**740**	**176**	**661**	**93**	**.254**	**56**	**834**	**39**	**3.72**	**1.214**
6	92.5	702	206	678↑	71	.265	50↓	814↓	47↑	3.97	1.272
7	83.5	679	178↑	623	67	.262↑	64↑	919↑	30	3.87↓	1.236↓
8	76.0	671	201	664↑	61	.267	39	789↓	59	5.02	1.407
9	71.0	630	158	589	81↓	.257↑	65↑	898↑	42↑	4.24	1.233↓
10	70.0	663	214	745	43	.257↑	48↓	770	37↓	4.24	1.361
11	69.5	629	167↓	592	74	.256↑	51↓	918↑	59	3.74↓	1.250↓
12	67.0	652	156	623	80↓	.267	45	728	36↓	3.82↓	1.266
13	63.0	702	185↑	644↓	72	.257↑	45	807↓	30	4.00	1.283
14	46.5	668	184↑	607	89↓	.261↑	38	690	14	5.04	1.410
15	30.5	633	146	609	104↑	.249↓	37	685	13	5.10	1.430

For example, the team in question has 176 home runs. There are six teams within only 195 home runs or fewer that could be passed, while there is only one team within 10 home runs of jumping up from below. The owner has a dilemma though. There are nine teams within eight batting average points, so trades or acquisitions need to focus on the difficult-to-balance power and batting average categories, but the owner is aware and is not just blindly making decisions.

Mobility	Total	R	HR	RBI	SB	AVG	W	K	SV	ERA	WHIP
Up	+32	+1	+6	+3	+2	+9	+4	+3	+3	+0	+1
Down	-27	-1	-1	-3	-4	-1	-4	-3	-3	-4	-3

This owner also has some difficult decisions to make in regards to pitching. There is attainable upside in Wins and Strikeouts, but a heavy streaming strategy would have great ratio risk. More or less, the owner can only lose points in the pitching ratio categories.

This process is arbitrary and can be done with optimism to show that there is still hope. An owner could do a highly scientific calculation of what's likely to be attained with three months left versus only one month left, but this exercise is meant to be a quick analysis to guide decision making. It does not need extreme precision.

It is important to pay attention to the teams the owner will be leapfrogging within categories. Going back to the home run example, the second-, third-, and fourth-place teams are all ahead of this team in the standings. Passing those teams in the standings has double the impact because they will lose a point in the overall standings in addition to the extra point the owner gains.

One last factor to consider is that other owners may give up on the season. If it's determined that an owner has given up, it is much easier to catch them in a counting category, even if they have a sizeable lead.

Final Third of the Season

Once the final third of the season is reached, player valuation is entirely derived from their value to a team's context and place in the standings. Billy Hamilton may have 60 SB, but if a team is already in first place and 10 steals above the next team, Hamilton's value to his owner is probably negative. He can't help this owner gain any more points in the standings and he may cause the owner to lose points in the other offensive categories.

If an Owner Is Within Striking Distance

Owners shouldn't sweat it if they're not in first place but are still within striking distance of winning at the two-thirds mark. Similarly, if a league pays out money and an owner is close to a payout spot, they shouldn't pack it in just yet. This isn't a bad place to be.

The silver lining in these situations is that right around August 1st, summer is in full effect, other teams will have given up on the season, and the fantasy football hype reaches peak levels. Distractions are aplenty and folks may stop paying attention. This is an owner's chance to keep their eye on the prize, and they will hopefully have an easier path up the standings as teams drop out.

Not only are there distractions, but this time of the year involves heavy MLB roster fluctuations due to the trade deadline. Most owners are aware of the sexy sleepers in the preseason from the draft prep materials available at that time. The same high-upside players are around in late July and early August, and they can sneakily come into great amounts of playing time.

An owner might be able to get away with lower FAAB bids or even sneak an unexpected player through waivers because teams are not paying attention. A relentless strategy of monitoring rosters, lineups, and MLB news can really pay off.

If in First, Don't Let Up

Trailing teams might have an easy path to catch up as other owners stop paying attention. Also, an owner shouldn't just focus on where they can gain points. They should also make attempts to limit what they can lose and to block others from passing them. While perhaps more difficult to achieve than if working from lower in the standings, the leader still needs to grind out a few more points to maintain the lead.

Final Month of the Season

Think back to the graph that demonstrates how the theoretical value of a player decreases as the season progresses and how contextual value (relative to the owner's team) takes over. In the final month of the season, owners are clearly in the "Value To Their Own Team" zone. They should give almost no consideration to the value of players to other teams. Where this misconception comes into play is in deciding whom to cut from the team. If an owner has a 20-Save lead over the rest of the field with a month to go, they don't need a closer, or at least not as many as they have. They should get rid of them. Be aggressive and ruthless (while still being smart) in cutting players that don't provide contextual value. Figure out where points can be gained and attack the free agent list for players who can help in those categories. Speculate wildly. Winning the Saves category by 35 Saves gets no bonus points.

While owners need to be aggressive with their team, they need to take care not to help a team that can catch them in the standings. In the example above with Saves, the owner dropping the closer may need to make sure the teams right behind him cannot jump over him with the extra Saves. It might be best to make sure another active owner with the FAAB hammer can pick up the closers. A subtle tactic like a post on the league's message board saying "enjoy the Saves" may awaken an inactive team with plenty of FAAB to roster the free-agent closer.

The Point of "Nothing to Lose"

An owner can't win every season. In these times, there will come an inflection point after which their chances of winning will decrease significantly if drastic actions are not taken. This could be called the point of "Nothing to Lose." A good example of this would be a scenario where an owner faces considerable downside but only modest upside in pitching ratios. Perhaps they could easily lose five points in ERA and WHIP with a few bad starts, but unless something crazy happens, they can't gain much more than three points in the same categories.

If this owner is currently out of the money spots, it makes no sense to manage ratios. Shooting for upside is all that matters. Maximizing counting stats and hoping for luck on ratios is the best play. It doesn't mean starting an awful pitcher at Colorado for a couple of extra strikeouts, however. It still requires diligence and picking the best available streamers and two-start pitchers. It may even mean starting a viable streamer with two starts over a significantly higher-ranked pitcher with only one start.

An owner can identify the point where they need to take on more risk, and they can go all-in with crossed fingers

Free-Agent Acquisition Budget

Free-agent acquisition budget, or FAAB, is a method of blind auctioning players from the waiver wire. Depending on the league's settings, owners are given a budget (e.g. $100 or $1,000) for the season's free-agent pickups.

FAAB Procedure

While some people just wing their weekly FAAB bids, it's best to have a set of consistent procedures in place to best utilize the limited time available for each week's bids. The exact procedures can change over time if it's determined that some steps are not bearing fruit.

Here are some ideas to streamline the process:

- Keep a running list of potential targets in an online document or on a piece of paper. Add to this list during the week after reading available articles or listening to podcasts or the radio.

- Set an initial FAAB listing before the weekend. This provides three advantages. First, it saves the owner time so that on Sunday, they just need to incorporate the latest news into their bids and can enjoy the weekend. Second, the owner has a reasonable set of bids in place if unplanned things arise on Sunday. The other less obvious advantage is that the owner is less likely to be sucked into the hype of the latest call-up or potential closer news. By not having a list of well thought out names in place, owners will be much more likely to fall victim to primacy effect and overreact to what happens on Sunday.

- Follow the ownership trends from several websites to see who everyone is after or, more importantly, who isn't be sought after. They can be obtained cheaply. As mentioned earlier, the authors recommend CBS and Yahoo. CBS allows many of their leagues to make quick draw adds and keeps the trends available for the whole week. These two features allow owners to easily recall the early week adds and get an idea of the player's hype. Yahoo! only provides ownership trends from the last 24 hours. These will be the players in the news that day who will have recency bias baked into the price.

- Start by setting FAAB values in the deepest leagues and transitioning to the shallower ones. This way the owner has an idea of the deepest sleepers and can even consider picking up these players in their shallower formats.

- If the owner is in leagues of varying prize amounts, they might also consider first attacking and putting the most effort into the leagues with the most money on the line. As the season progresses, this order could be revised again to focus on the leagues with the highest win probabilities.

- Find a couple of reliable sources for the upcoming week's starting pitchers. Be wary of dated two-start sources, as rotation order changes all the time.

- Look ahead two weeks. Picking up a two-start pitcher or hitters going to Colorado a week early can help a team's budget.

- Once the bids are all entered, give them another once over. Make sure nothing stupid sticks out. An extra zero added to a bid could ruin an owner's season.

- About 30 minutes before FAAB is processed, give the news a quick review and make sure no players are headed to the IL or got demoted. It's tough to go a week with an empty roster spot, so be sure to review the news relating to one's own players. Late-breaking news about players not owned or owned by other teams can throw a significant wrench in FAAB plans and open the opportunity to get a great target for cheap.

- After FAAB is run for one week, start the running list of targets and notes for the next week. Make notes of needs not filled or desired players that ended up not rostered because they were further down the waiver wire preference.

There are countless little wrinkles and tips to incorporate into the process. The key is to develop and hone in on a repeatable and consistent process the owner can use every week. Take notes. Make a checklist. Be diligent. These are the behaviors that give owners an edge.

Understand the League's FAAB Rules

While most FAAB rules are uniform, there are two common variables within the rules that can affect how owners should allocate their FAAB resources.

First, consider if the league allows $0 acquisitions. This is especially important if the owner has a $100 budget and the rules do not allow $0 pickups. In this scenario, owners are limited to a maximum of 100 pickups during the year. That is not an issue in and of itself, but it can be especially problematic if an owner spends heavy early on and finds themselves with $5 left and eight weeks to go in the season. This would only allow them five total moves to utilize over those final eight weeks. September is a volatile time of year, with teams often benching veterans in order to give young rookies a chance to play. Owners would hate to be short on acquisitions when they need to hold off a charging competitor or gain ground in the standings.

The next variable is the Vickrey auction method. This method of auctioning awards a player to the highest bidder, but instead of charging them the full auction bid price, the transaction costs only $1 more than the next highest bid. This seems to be the exception more than the rule when it comes to auctions, but it is very important to note.

Should Owners Spend Early or Hoard for Later

In addition to the previous demonstration that the surprise earners appear earlier in the season, there is a theoretical reason owners should spend FAAB earlier, too. In a league that drafts early and allows preseason waiver moves, the owner can potentially gain 27 weeks of player ownership. If an owner makes a move one week into the season, he can benefit for 26 weeks. Two weeks into the season yields 25 weeks of benefits. A move made before the final week can only benefit a team for one week, and so on.

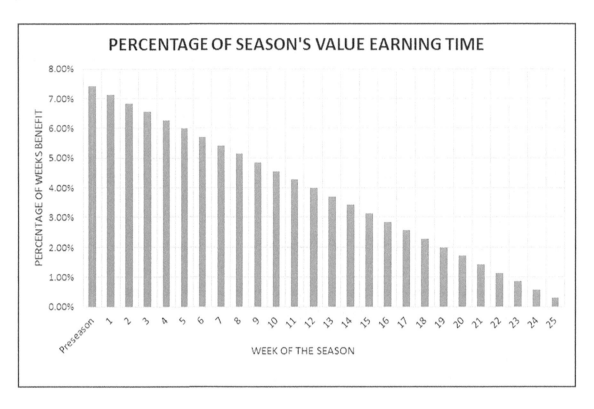

The bottom line is that players acquired early in the season give owners more time to reap the benefits of owning these players, and therefore are more valuable. Throw in the fact that better-earning players tend to appear early in the year, and it's a no-brainer that FAAB spending should occur early.

Depending on the league, some owners may be trying to look good and to avoid being seen as overpaying. These owners will often miss out on their targets but justify the results by saying at least they didn't overpay. Remember, the key is to win the valuable players, not to "not look bad" while losing.

There will be increased competition for players early in the season when attention levels are high, but strategies that follow can help to minimize unnecessary spending.

Bidding Theory

Several of the topics and concepts already discussed in this book must be woven together to understand the theory behind FAAB bidding. For the leagues that set weekly lineups, the results of the weekly valuation analysis earlier in the in-season management section must be understood. The topic of risk and adjusting a projection for the various types of risk (e.g. Sucking Risk) is also highly relevant. An owner needs to be able to recognize and adjust those players' values who are not expected to retain roles for the remainder of the season (many players pop up in relevance but will experience only a short-lived bump in playing time).

While the same concepts of preseason valuations apply to in-season bidding, the difference is that decisions are able to be made each week. When this process is performed during the preseason, it's treated as if owners are locked into the lineup for the remainder of the season. But it's likely a skilled owner that can spot a player who will outperform a replacement-level player's stats for a short period of time. If an owner can string together a series of these temporarily valuable players, they can out-earn a player that looks valuable from the preseason point of view.

It's already been demonstrated that valuations can be calculated on a weekly basis. In shallower leagues (10- and 12-team), thinking in this manner can be very helpful. Owners should regularly be looking for those players that temporarily project to outperform replacement level (e.g. hitters with a series in Coors). In 15-team and NL- or AL-only leagues, the challenge is a bit more difficult, but it may still be relevant.

Once an owner realizes that the weekly mindset can be helpful, the next step in understanding FAAB bidding theory is to realize that there are only 25 or 26 bidding periods for the entire season. Each week, there will be several impactful players that rise above replacement-level expectations that owners will bid on.

Ideally, a FAAB bid would be calculated as follows:

$$\left(\frac{\text{Player X's Projected Positive Weekly Values}}{\text{Total Positive Weekly Value to Enter League Via Waivers all Season}} \right) * \text{Total League FAAB Allowance}$$

The player's percentage of total positive value to enter the league via the FAAB process for the entire season is multiplied by the league's total FAAB allowance for the year.

While this is neat in theory, it's remarkably difficult to use in practice. Annual projections have enough variability. Trying to use weekly valuations will be even more volatile. Further, this analysis assumes owners could make perfect decisions about when to start these acquired players. Often players are added after they have their only positive earning weeks of the season, only to be started after they've dropped below replacement level and end up costing the owner value.

Another issue with this formula is that it still is using the season-long perspective of value. It's not considering the value *to the owner's team*. Owners should try to maximize theoretical value early in the season and then gradually shift that perception of value, so they are pursuing value to the owner's team by the league's trading deadline.

While it has weaknesses, this is the theoretical framework to be used if an owner is trying to estimate a FAAB bid. Although it will be imprecise, it's a valuable thought exercise. An owner should ask themselves questions like, "What other value do I expect to come into the league this year? Will there be other players like this that come along? If so, how many?"

Asking questions like this can help an owner determine if the player is a truly special source of value or if this is simply going to be one of many possibilities to capture a player like this via FAAB. This exercise should help the owner to determine what category, from the next section, of player they're bidding on.

Specific Bidding Strategies

FAAB Binning Strategy

When adding players there are three general categories in which to bucket them:

1. Triage - Get a warm body in each roster spot

2. Tactical - Short-term or weekly add in order to roster the player

3. Strategic - Difference-makers who the owner hopes to start every week

Many owners, including the authors at times, sort of just wing it with their FAAB budget during the season, failing to consider where the desired player falls in the bins above. A more sophisticated approach is to consider each player target and what bin category they fall into, then bid accordingly. There are circumstances where each category of player is needed.

To stay disciplined throughout the year, an owner could set hard spending limits on how they will allocate their FAAB across these three categories of players. An example could be to budget $20 (2%) per week of a $1,000 budget to tactical and triage players. Having spent $540 (27 weeks * $20), the owner would then have $460 left for strategic adds. If needed, they can steal resources from future periods and the amounts allocated for upcoming tactical and strategic budgets.

For example, assume an owner needs a hitter and pitcher to fill in for two injured players. It seems like it'll take $40 to win a possible longer-term valuable pitcher. If $5 of the $20 weekly budget is spent on a hitter replacement, The remaining $15 of the weekly tactical budget can be applied toward that $40 FAAB pitcher, leaving $25 to come from the strategic budget to get the pitcher.

It may be tough for an owner to stay out of the tactical budget as the season goes on, but as other teams start to run out of money, having that solid reserve set aside makes the top free agents more attainable. Also, having the FAAB hammer can help over the last month of the season when an owner needs to focus on specific stats to move up in the rankings.

Group Players Cost into Categories

FAABing is an art more than a science. Knowing how much to bid comes down to a mix of numbers (projecting the player's worth), feel (judging the market), and experience. Experience is an underappreciated skill here. The more FAAB bidding periods an owner has been through, the better they'll be able to judge the market and understand approximately what it will take to win a player.

Fortunately, there are certain classes or categories of free agents for which experience doesn't come into play. At a high level, there are three categories of costs for fantasy free agents: minimum-bid players, bank breakers, and in-between players. Here is a quick synopsis of each category with more details later.

A minimum-bid player is one that is unlikely to be eyed by anyone else in the league. It may be that the owner has experienced injuries and just needs a warm body to slot into their lineup. They don't have a strong preference for the free agent to add, so there's no sense in bidding much more than the league's minimum bid ($1 or $0).

The bank breakers are players on the waiver wire who are the main flavor of the week, the big-name player on whom most teams in the league will be bidding. He could be a minor league call-up, a newly appointed closer, or a pretty good player that was cut by an opposing team the previous week.

The in-between players are a danger zone. This is the area where an owner might bid $100 only to find out the next-closest competitor only bid $30.

Even those owners new to FAAB easily should be able to classify the week's free agents into these three major buckets. This is the first major step toward formulating a bid on a player.

These three cost groups (minimum, in-between, and bank breaker) seem to line up with the three binned groups discussed the previous section (triage, tactical, and strategic), but depending on the league setup, this is not necessarily the case. In a deep AL-Only league with just a $100 budget and no $0 bids, there really is not a tactical class of player. Any player of note is already owned in such a league, and teams are just bidding on rookie call-ups (strategic) and trying to fill injured spots (triage). In this league, triage and tactical might only be pursued with the minimum bid grouping, with strategic adds requiring judgment about whether to utilize an in-between or bank breaker bid.

Before diving into the bidding strategies, the following charts of NFBC 2019 and 2018 bidding activity offer insight into the bidding frequency and the total amount bid on these player types. These first charts demonstrate that bank breakers appear in the first half of the season, while the number of $1 winning bids increases steadily as the season progresses. Note the number of teams in the NFBC Main Event increased from 510 teams in 2018 to 570 teams in 2019, causing the magnitude of transactions and spending to change, but the trends in activity and spending levels can still be observed.

Here's the volume of FAAB transactions for each week of the 2019 season:

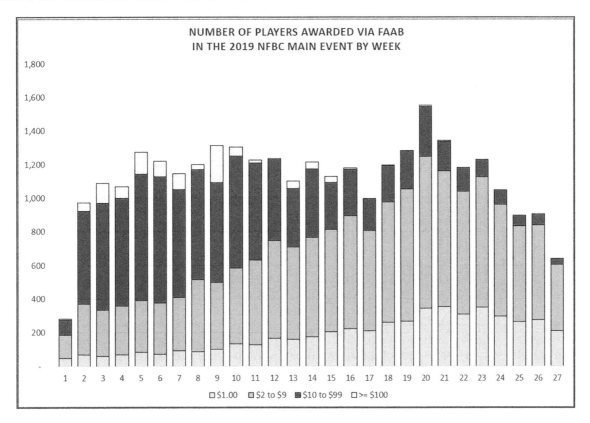

Here's the volume of transactions for each week of the 2018 season:

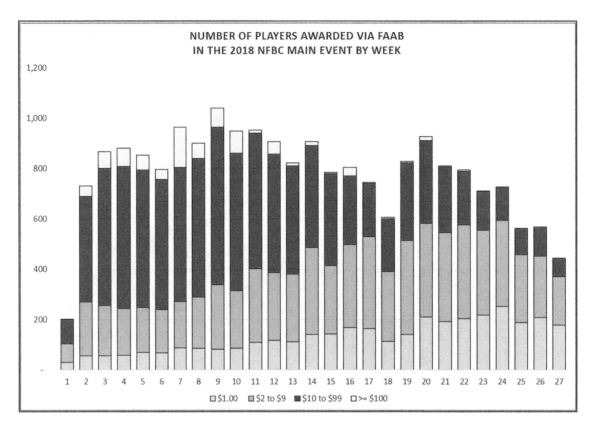

What might be surprising is the total dollar value spent on these different categories of players. The $1 bids hardly even register on the graph. The huge bids are generally within the first 10 weeks of the season. Finally, the players between those categories represent a significant portion of the total spending. Owners need to carefully consider how to spend money on those in that middle category.

Here's the total spending across all NFBC Main Event leagues for each week of the 2019 season:

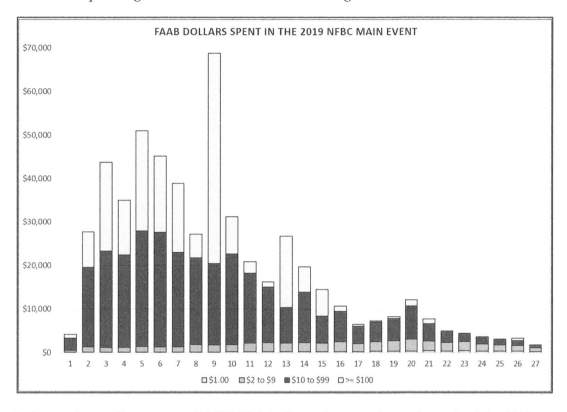

Here's the total spending across all NFBC Main Event leagues for each week of the 2018 season:

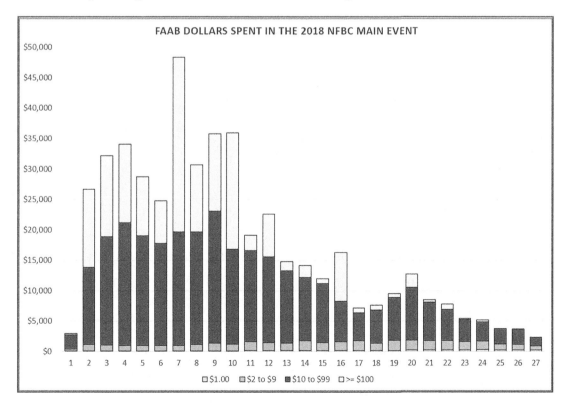

The Bidding Bubble Theory

Bids start out conservative as no one wants to look the fool and teams don't know their needs, they just drafted the best team possible. About a month in, the winners and losers start sorting themselves out. The losers are desperate (for good reason) and start spending like crazy. Then the spending gets even worse as the ones who lose out on FAAB double down and bid even higher until they have no money, and then everything settles down.

Minimum-Bid Players

There is no sense spending much time formulating bids on these players. These players cannot be very impactful and there will be little or no competition in bidding for them. An example would be an injury-replacement catcher in a two-catcher league. The waiver wire catcher will have minimal talent. Further, there will be little differentiation between the ones on the waiver wire. An owner shouldn't spend $5 on Player A just to find out that Player B could have been won for a $1 bid.

When entering bids for these players, an owner should enter several of them, all at the lowest price at which they expect to win one of the players. For example, the owner might rank the players involved as Player A first, Player B second, then Player C third, but really the difference between them is minimal. The owner should enter a $1 bid for Player A, a separate $1 bid for Player B, and a final $1 bid for Player C. That way, if Player A or B are bid up for $2 or more, the owner will still be satisfied with Player C for only $1.

Bank Breakers

The bank breaker class of player appears due to an unforeseen and often overnight shift in the player's playing-time projection. Whether it's a high-profile call-up or a reliever inheriting a closer role, these players will be sought after by most owners in the league. It's up to the owner to ask some critical questions.

How much value will this player provide on a weekly basis? How much will winning the bidding process increase the owner's chances of winning the league? How likely is it that this player will retain the job? How many other players of this caliber will become available during the rest of the season?

These questions are designed to uncover the value of the player while also considering risk and opportunity cost (what other options might be available if the player is passed on). These are the same themes an owner should consider during the draft.

Lastly, the owner should ask what other owners are likely to bid on the player. This is the cost component of the decision-making process. The owner can obtain this information by drawing on history and experience of what similar types of players have gone for or do research by reading the various FAAB bidding articles that tend to pop up online on the weekends.

Once the owner understands the value and cost components related to the player, he can make an informed decision about if the investment is worth the price.

In-Between Players

Percentagewise, the in-between players can produce the greatest amount of overbidding. An owner might bid $75 on a player that the next-highest bid for is $20, or nearly quadruple the price that was needed. The same general process used for the bank breakers should be used with these players. The key difference, however, is that owners should remind themselves that these players come with a significantly lower opportunity cost. Missing out on one of these players is not likely to be the end of the world. There will be many similar options that come along the next week. In fact, there are probably very similar options available the same week.

It's very easy to get caught up in the competitiveness and urgency of FAAB bidding. It's okay to continually bump up a bid for fear of losing a player, just be sure to consider the alternative options. Would an owner rather have Player A for $75? Or is spending $10 on Player B more prudent?

One way to get an understanding of how a league's bidding pattern may play out is to track how much a player's ownership jumped from a hosting website which allows a daily waiver wire for some of its leagues (e.g. Yahoo or CBS). The ownership jump from those leagues with daily moves can be correlated to the league's actual bids to get a rough estimate of a player's FAAB price.

Find More Than One Target

Often the result of waiver wire research is identifying a single target that brings up the emotion of "I have to get this player. This one player." Several different cognitive biases are coming into play. Owners are likely overvaluing recent performance and using a very narrow decision-making frame. An owner is much more likely to overbid in a situation like this.

To combat this, find more than one free agent add and then assign bids. The owner can pick the player they feel better about. Instead of overpaying for this week's hot item at $200, consider the backup option at a price of only $10.

Put in More Bids than Necessary

When an owner has truly obvious drops that can be made or needs to fill an empty position, extra bids should be entered to ensure at least a $1 triage player is won. Assume a scenario where an owner is decimated by injuries and they must replace three injured players. They should not stop at identifying only three possible replacements. Other owners are likely pursuing the same free agents, so the owner should go overboard and enter bids for a long string of players.

If an owner really needs the roster spots filled (because the player has to start), they may need to have seven or eight targets. Starting a mildly effective middle reliever is better than taking a zero all week because they didn't have enough active pitchers.

The Balancing Act of Player Valuation

When acquiring players, owners need to strike a balance between maximizing short-term value and long-term value. An owner that maximizes short-term value over long-term value find themselves short on players with strong season-long values and scrambling on the waiver wire all season. The owner that maximizes long-term value will fall behind the teams better able to capitalize on short-term and mid-term plays. The key is to find a nice middle ground.

Three inputs to consider in this balancing act are talent, playing time, and opponents (including teams, schedule, parks). All three of the pillars need to be maximized as much as possible each week, but they should be ranked as follows when considering new moves.

1. Talent - Good players find playing time. They can become great short- and long-term values. This should be prioritized over all other categories.

2. Playing time - Counting stats are key and they can't be accumulated from the bench or minors. Players receiving solid playing time or in line for more playing time are usually strong sources of value, even if they're only average players.

3. Opponents - Once good, talented players are on the diamond, this is where owners can then start slicing, dicing, and squeezing every last stat from their lineup. This is the trait that is the most fleeting and least worth investing in. It may only be a quick three-game series in Colorado for a hitter or a trip to San Francisco for a pitcher.

The key is to not drop talented players because they may be missing some time in the short-term or have a bad schedule. Later on during the season, it'll take a ton of resources to reacquire this talent. Bad players with a favorable schedule are always cheaper and easier to acquire.

Mixed League vs. Only League FAAB

When playing in AL- or NL-Only leagues, the trade deadline heavily influences how FAAB is spent. With few impactful players leaving and joining the league's player pool, owners can't treat FAAB the same as in mixed leagues.

The first and most important factor is to learn the league rules for players changing leagues. In many instances, the owners just lose their players traded out of the league and must bid on the entering players. Some leagues allow owners to keep accumulating stats from the players leaving the MLB league. Fewer still don't allow the new players to be added as part of the player pool. As always, make sure to know the league rules.

In most Only leagues, all regularly playing real talent is owned and few if any choices remain on the waiver wire. The chance to acquire impactful talent is hugely important.

Don't be afraid to go in heavy for a rookie that appears early in the season. Most of the impactful rookies will be called up in mid-April or by early May. Most of these call-ups are expected and the player is already owned, but sometimes contending major league teams are forced to turn to a rookie earlier than expected (e.g. Juan Soto in 2018) and the bidding may seem irrational. But in these instances, jump right in. While the rookie may not be as talented as the unknown players moved at the trade deadline, they will accumulate stats for an extra two months. The time these players earn value should be a huge consideration in these instances.

About a month before the trade MLB deadline, the owner should know all their competitors' FAAB balances and needs. Many owners will zero in on the last few days in July as the time to start spending their hoarded FAAB, but that may not be early enough. Major league teams continue to raise the white flag earlier each season, so some trades are happening weeks before the trade deadline. Around July 1st, an owner needs to see where they rank in remaining FAAB, knowing they'll get the nth player coming over and how close they are to the owners above and below them.

While an owner has no control in moving up (assuming FAAB cannot be traded), they can control moving down in available FAAB. If the owner has one of the top FAAB totals and is therefore guaranteed one of the top talents, they should not spend an amount that would force them below the next team. While sometimes that talent is underwhelming, it's likely better than anything else on the wire.

A subtler tactic is to follow minor league promotions that shake out from trades. The MLB teams giving up on the season will often promote minor leaguers into the cleared roster spots. Cheaply pick up any promoted starter, almost regardless of their minor league track record. Bench the player and find out if they are good later. Viable MLB starters seem to materialize out of nowhere (e.g. Dereck Rodriguez) when they gain access to new coaches, new pitching environments, and major league catchers. In the time this player remains on the owner's bench, they can verify if the player is worth starting before his price has skyrocketed or he is already owned. In these situations, it's best to be a week early than right on time.

Is it Optimal to Hoard FAAB in Only Leagues?

The last section suggested that owners should not be afraid to jump in early on potential starters that materialize in Only leagues. Specific strategies were given for managing a FAAB balance if the owner decided to hoard FAAB for the trade deadline, but what is the optimal play?

The first consideration for this question is the time period from which the owner can capture a player's earnings. A player projected to earn $30 over the course of the season who is obtained at the July 31st MLB trade deadline converts to just $10 of earnings over the season's last two months.

The above example is the dream scenario for hoarding FAAB to win a $30 player at the deadline, yet it is the equivalent of earning $10 of extra earnings over the owner's drafted alternatives. The probability of the owner being able to secure such a $30 player needs to be considered. For instance, assume these hypothetical scenarios:

Description of Event	Likelihood
The owner drafts a good enough team to be in contention so he can bypass the need to make a significant FAAB bid early in the season	65%
The owner avoids injuries and the need to spend FAAB to address the problem	60%
A $30 player switches leagues and becomes available at the trade deadline	75%
The owner has the highest available FAAB balance (no other owner has been as fortunate)	80%

Those likelihoods are made up and can be adjusted for what the owner deems correct. These numbers are likely too optimistic, and yet they imply a combined likelihood of only 23% (65% * 60% * 75% * 80% = 23.4%) that an owner would be able to secure the $30 player. Extending that probability of winning the $30 player, the player's projected value ends up at $2.34 ($10 of projected value * 23.4%). And that doesn't even include the possibility that the owner goes for the $30 player at the deadline only to find out that the $40 player surfaces the week after or the chance that the player doesn't fit well into the owner's lineup.

The owner should pursue players that arise early in the season. This illustration of probability demonstrates the bleak chances an owner has of landing the big fish that switches leagues. The more prudent strategy is to be aggressive early and capture as much value as possible. It's tough to find the perfect balance of bypassing the known for a gamble on the unknown. Good luck.

Know the Hosting Site's FAAB System

A good example of this is that in the past, ESPN has automatically assigned priority to claims in descending order by the amount bid on each player. A bid on a player for $20 would be processed before a $1 bid on another player.

On the contrary, a site like Fantrax would allow an owner to prioritize a $1 bid on a player over a $20 bid on a player.

Understanding these differences is important, especially in scenarios where an owner would rather have Player X for $1 than Player Y for $20, even if they think Player Y might be the superior player (so they can save the $19 for a later time).

Understand the Effect of $0 or $1 Bid Minimums

It is critical that an owner knows their league rules and whether $0 bids are allowed, especially at the end of the season. In leagues that require a $1 bid minimum, owners should pace spending to leave at least $1 per week remaining in the season in their remaining budget. This will allow for at least one transaction per week, which may be necessary to fend off an opponent or to make a charge down the stretch.

When $0 bids are allowed, an owner can allow their remaining budget to run out well before the end of the season. They'll miss out on significant or moderate available options but can still make transactions to replace injured players or to speculate on talented players in advance of other teams.

Bid Proactively Instead of Reactively

The most effective way to save money in bidding is to have a proactive mindset instead of a reactive mindset. A reactive mindset will be distracted by "the hot flavor of the day" that is likely coming off of a strong week or is in the news, whereas a proactive mindset is looking a week or two into the future for players that can be purchased for pennies on the dollar.

Many times, there is writing on the wall when a closer is about to change, or if a struggling player will be sent to the bench, or if a talented minor leaguer may only be a week or two from getting the call-up. The likelihood of these events happening may only be 10%-30%, but the players involved can likely be purchased for minimum bids. On the other hand, wait for the actual benching or promotion to occur and an owner can expect to spend much more of their budget to obtain a trendy pick.

Bidding on Closers When the Replacement is Known

When a closer loses his job via injury or non-productiveness and a skilled replacement is available, owners should be ready to open their wallets, especially the owner who just lost a closer. Historically, these bids have been extremely aggressive, especially when everyone has a near-full FAAB allocation.

First, an owner must understand how long the closer role has been lost. Even if the closer in question has suffered a major injury, the replacement may only be a couple-month rental. Are the old and new closers near the same talent level, so if the new one falters, could the old one get his job back? Come up with a reasonable estimate of a time frame for the new closer to keep the role.

The next step comes down to determining the maximum amount of FAAB an owner is willing to spend. Early in the book, 5% was said to be the minimum FAAB needed to roster a potential closer, with the cost only going up from there.

Two bidding strategies need to be implemented: crazy-all-in and keeping honest. With the crazy-all-in approach, a minimum 15% bid is used, with possibly more, to have a chance at winning the pitcher. It's likely some FAAB will be wasted but at least the owner will end up with the closer.

Otherwise, owners need to go with a bid which doesn't cut too much into the overall budget but isn't the minimum. These bids will likely be crushed early in the season, but they may pick up a closer or two as the summer progresses.

Bidding on Closers When the Replacement is Not Known

Normally, this case is the most frequent scenario. A middling non-contender trades away an established closer like Fernando Rodney and the owners are left with three or four closing candidates, or Roberto Osuna finds himself in legal trouble and therefore a club is left to choose from three below-average arms for their next closer.

MLB managers often are very slow to name a designated closer in these situations. There is little benefit to doing so, and they typically say something about a committee or playing the matchups.

The fantasy baseball community will likely focus on the lead candidate. The buzz will build and a consensus will be formed. The anointed replacement will generally be the most dominant reliever or the "sexiest" name. This strategy is not how major league managers or GMs think, as they have different incentives.

General managers are incentivized to keep a young dominant reliever from the closer's role to lower his future contract, as saves mean money in arbitration. Managers might want the most dominant reliever to be on call for the higher leverage situations, not just the clean slate of the ninth inning.

Owners can benefit from this inefficiency. Attention and FAAB will be focused on the consensus name, and the community may incorrectly assess the likelihood that the agreed upon player wins the role. This means an owner can swoop in with lower bids and take the other candidates. As previously mentioned, closer bids are enormous. The best use of an owner's FAAB, if they are not in absolutely dire straits for saves, is to go after the name other owners are likely to overlook. Instead of $200 bids for a closer, an owner might easily end up with a closer for less than $10 (assuming a $1000 budget).

Other times, an MLB team's bullpen is a complete mess with no one obvious choice. This usually happens at the trade deadline when a non-contender sells off everyone decent and is left with several scrubs. In this situation, it pays to cheaply gamble. Put in minimum bids on each of the candidates and see if anyone sneaks through the FAAB process. Likely the gamble will fail, but no significant resources were lost. But if it does hit, jackpot.

Strategic FAAB Use Without the Hammer

While it may not be the best use of the resource, having the most remaining FAAB (the "hammer") as the MLB trade deadline approaches can be a significant advantage, especially in Only leagues. Assume an owner freely used FAAB during the season and they have a low percentage of their budget remaining (say 30%). At this later point in the season with a smaller budget left to churn a roster's last few players, this owner won't be winning any high-profile players.

If a league allows the trading of FAAB, this could be an owner's chance to turn the small into something valuable. One owner with FAAB to trade can pitch to teams that they could have the "hammer"… for a price.

Hopefully, some high-profile MLB trades occur a few days before the deadline. Use these trades to say, "I'll trade $200 of my remaining $300 for Player X. My $200 will give you $1,100. You'll have the most FAAB in the league and will be guaranteed to get Player Y. And if someone even better comes along and is traded by the end of the week, you could get him instead."

It's difficult to say what an owner can get for such a trade. The better the player that's available, the better the leverage. For example, Manny Machado was traded into the NL in 2018 and J.D. Martinez was traded into the NL in 2017. An owner may be able to use only $200 of FAAB and convert it into a solid player for their team, likely a more meaningful player than what they might turn up by streaming and speculating with that $200.

Keeping Honest Bids

If an owner has been following the recommendations from this book so far, they've spent a heavier-than-normal amount in early spending. As the season goes on, they may feel they do not have the ability to competitively bid on the new talent. However, the owner should keep in mind that some competitors don't even put in bids in all weeks. This can happen especially in weeks with several obvious targets. The competitors may only bid on three of the four obvious candidates, increasing the likelihood that a player slips through the cracks.

Any player who can make the owner's team better should be bid on. The owner may stumble into some luck and find great bargains, but this also lets other owners know they need to keep spending their FAAB.

Waiver Wire Priority

Many of the concepts that apply to FAAB can also be applied to waiver wire priority, with the key difference being owners are expending a different resource. Instead of spending FAAB dollars, owners are spending their waiver priority spot.

One subtle point to consider is how the waiver wire priority cycles in an owner's league. In many rotisserie leagues, an owner simply falls to the bottom of the priority listing any time they pick up a player from waivers. In a weekly head-to-head league, there's the possibility that priority is reset each week to the inverse order of the league's standings. This rule gives the league's worst team the first priority each week. In such a league, owners should give zero consideration to using their waiver priority.

Assuming the league settings are of the type that ignores the standings, an owner is generally going to be better off making moves without considering the loss of waiver priority. The reason for this is that outside of a few specific times of the season, it's fairly unpredictable about when a deeply valuable player will come along.

If there is an argument for preserving a high waiver priority, it would only make sense to do so at one of these special times of the season when a valuable player may surface. Those times are about two weeks into the season, the Super Two Deadline (late-May or early-June), and the major league trade deadline.

If a minor leaguer is called up two weeks into the season as opposed to the first game of the season, the major league team can control the player for an additional year. This is when Kris Bryant was called up in 2015 and when many expected Ronald Acuna to be promoted in 2018. The Super Two Deadline fluctuates from year-to-year but allows a major league team to hold a player's salary down an additional season by avoiding arbitration. Prospect promotions, especially for impact players, will tend to be more concentrated around these dates.

The major league trade deadline is a tumultuous time when player roles and playing-time estimates can fluctuate wildly. Delaying a move, especially an insignificant one, in order to retain top waiver priority near these dates would be wise.

Other In-Season Strategies

Punting Categories

Consider punting a category once they have time to stabilize a couple of months into the season. If an owner can see it might make sense to punt stolen bases, batting average, or saves at that time, it might be in their best interest to do so.

Owners do have to be careful about punting correlated categories like Home Runs (tied to Runs and RBI), and Wins and Strikeouts (correlated because they're starting pitcher volume categories).

Think Ahead, Use Roster Spots for the Future

There's a cheesy quote Wayne Gretzky's father is credited with often reminding Wayne: "Skate to where the puck is going to be, not where it's been." As corny as it may be, it is relevant to in-season team management. Most advice owners seek online about who to pick up is reactionary. A player gets hurt, is officially benched, ousted from their closer role, or sent to the minors. To claim such a player means a manager would be fighting against all the other managers.

But if an owner applies the Gretzky quote, they can predict these situations before an official announcement. They can't predict injury, but they often can see a benching or demotion looming.

So instead of being reactionary and waiting for official announcements, expand the decision-making horizon out into the future. The trade deadline can be a great example. Heading into the 2018 trade deadline, rumors were swirling that several teams would be trading their closers (the Texas Rangers and Keone Kela, Baltimore Orioles and Brad Brach, San Diego Padres and Brad Hand, and Minnesota Twins and Fernando Rodney). These rumors started well before the deadline. There was a definite opportunity to speculate and snag the next-in-line reliever a week or two in advance and with little competition for the player. Things were less eventful in 2019, but both Shane Greene and Mark Melancon were traded to Atlanta. Greene's trade freed up a spot in Detroit and Melancon went from not really being in line for saves in San Francisco to being considered for the closer's role in Atlanta.

In the 2018 NFBC Main Event, 14 owners gambled the week before Kela was traded by grabbing Jose Leclerc for an average bid of $7. The week after Leclerc got the job, his average price jumped to $53.

Beyond just closers, owners can also set a two-week time horizon for considering streaming pitcher options. Most owners will be focusing on just the upcoming week by grabbing those immediate two-start pitchers or hitters visiting Colorado. Every website publishes a two-start preview. Even below-average owners know to look for players visiting the Rockies. This just means added competition for bids and more FAAB required to win these players.

Instead, an owner can look two weeks out and pick up projected two-start pitchers for next to nothing. This strategy takes some effort and is not 100% reliable given increased days off and higher IL turnover messing up rotations. Fortunately, there are some sources, like the aforementioned RotoWire starting pitcher schedule, that do a very reliable job of estimating and updating these projected starters for changes.

Protect Team Ratios

Owners shouldn't be afraid to start slow in pitching counting categories. Don't take unnecessary risks with ratios early in the year. There are a few good reasons for this. First, by taking a wait-and-see approach, owners can learn more about matchups and pitcher performance. Heading into 2018, teams like Kansas City could have easily been predicted to struggle offensively, but we didn't really anticipate significant struggles for Baltimore and Seattle. Other teams, like the Athletics, were relatively surprising on offense. We often don't know as much as we think we know.

Another reason to take it slow is to not get caught up in competition for streamers early on. Many teams in the league will come out competing for streamers early in the season when the matchups aren't understood. This can be a perfect time to focus more on the talent that might only have one start in a given week. The data shows that unexpected pitchers materialize early in the season, so while others are mainly just focused on opponent matchups, the owner can invest in pitchers who show changes in talent. Fish where others aren't fishing.

As the season wears on, teams will begin to lose interest and drop out of the race. Owners should be able to make up ground by streaming and gaining in counting stats (W and Ks) as teams stop paying attention.

Lineup Setting

The Scoring System

The two scoring systems, points and rotisserie, require different approaches to in-season player evaluations, but some ideas overlap.

Overlap

Each week an owner must handle the tactical (short-term) and strategic (long-term) roster construction. The tactical comes down to filling up a roster with healthy starters after dealing with injuries and demotions. The strategic approach involves rostering the best players to win beyond the upcoming week. Many times, the two goals clash as owners must weigh their short-term and long-term goals.

In weekly transaction leagues, a team's bench spots (non-starters) are part of the team's long-term strategy containing injured players, prospects, and pitchers with good future matchups (or horrible matchups that week).

Using a bench for future moves is a little tougher in daily transaction leagues where hitters can fill in on off days or pitchers can be streamed. It's more difficult to balance the different needs in these leagues.

Streaming Pitcher Slot(s)

In the draft or auction phase, most owners drafted a couple of replacement-level pitchers. Additionally, pitchers often get injured. There are going to be openings for pitchers to be added.

Many owners always have one pitching slot open to stream in a pitcher for wins and strikeouts. These owners normally acquired a couple of top-20 starters so they can absorb a hit to their ratios.

In recent seasons, there has been a decline in quality available starters. Instead of streaming starters, owners are forced to use a middle reliever. Ideally, the reliever would have the chance for Saves, but he could be a multi-inning specialist who helps an owner with ratios and gives comparable strikeout numbers to some starters. This strategy may not be useable in points leagues where innings are a key scoring factor.

As the league quality increases and owners get savvier, they will no longer be focusing on this week's two-start pitchers. Instead, they'll acquire next week's guys who are usually throwing on Wednesday or Thursday for the current week. If a roster is being correctly managed, the owner will have several two-start options each week.

What to Consider for Weekly Lineups

The games an owner expects a player to play is the single biggest factor to consider when determining who to pick up and start in a given week. If an owner is having a hard time deciding between a player they project for five games and one projected for seven games, odds favor the player with seven games.

To illustrate, examine these three hypothetical stat lines:

	GP	R	HR	RBI	SB
Player A	155	90	24	90	12
Player B	155	75	20	75	10
Player C	155	64	17	64	9

Player A has the makings of a top-round pick, whereas Player C might be a free agent in many league types. Yet these players project out the same in a week in which Player A has five games, Player B has six, and Player C has seven:

	GP	R	HR	RBI	SB
Player A	5	2.9	0.8	2.9	0.4
Player B	6	2.9	0.8	2.9	0.4
Player C	7	2.9	0.8	2.9	0.4

Granted, there are other factors like platoon splits and park factors that owners could consider in a deeper analysis, but the point to drive home here is how much playing time matters in weekly lineup decisions.

An owner should be working with weekly projections and projected dollar values when making lineup-setting decisions for hitters. The following table can assist in determining who to start in situations where this information is not available. This table represents the expected amount of earnings lost if a hitter misses a game in a 7-game, 4-game, or 3-game lineup period.

The owner must first have a sense of where the player fits in the range of season-long values. For example, in a situation where an owner can make lineup changes for a Friday-Sunday period (3-game period), assume Mike Trout has a known off day on Friday. Trout, a $40+ season-long earner, loses $9 of value for sitting out one of those three games (the hitter becomes a $30-$35 hitter).

Season-long Valuation	12-team League			15-team League		
	7 Games	4 Games	3 Games	7 Games	4 Games	3 Games
$40+	$5	$7	$9	$5	$7	$9
$35-$40	$4	$6	$8	$4	$6	$8
$30-$35	$4	$6	$8	$4	$6	$7
$25-$30	$4	$5	$8	$3	$5	$7
$20-$25	$3	$5	$7	$3	$5	$7
$15-$20	$3	$5	$7	$3	$5	$7
$10-$15	$3	$5	$7	$3	$5	$7
$5-$10	$3	$5	$7	$3	$4	$6
$1-$5	$3	$5	$6	$2	$4	$6

The next table does require the owner to have a weekly projection and projected dollar value. This table can then be used to make manual adjustments when it becomes known that a player will miss a game. The weekly projection being used should already have a projection for the number of games played, but if news comes out before lineups lock that a player is getting an off day, this table can be used to quickly adjust the valuation on the fly. In general, a hitter drops one valuation tier for missing a game in a 7-game lineup period and drops two tiers for missing a game in a 3- or 4-game lineup period.

Using Trout again as an example, if he has a $40 projection for the week and he is known to have an off day on a Friday, he loses $13 of value by sitting out one game of the weekend.

Weekly Valuation	12-team League			15-team League		
	7 Games	4 Games	3 Games	7 Games	4 Games	3 Games
$40+	$8	$10	$13	$8	$10	$13
$35-$40	$7	$9	$12	$6	$9	$11
$30-$35	$6	$8	$11	$6	$8	$11
$25-$30	$5	$7	$10	$5	$7	$10
$20-$25	$5	$7	$9	$4	$6	$9
$15-$20	$4	$6	$8	$4	$6	$8
$10-$15	$3	$5	$7	$3	$5	$6
$5-$10	$3	$4	$6	$2	$4	$5
$1-$5	$2	$4	$5	$2	$3	$4

Lineup Setting Strategies

When setting the hitter lineup, pay very close attention to the actual MLB lineups that come out on Monday. Be sure to check those and incorporate them into the decision-making process. This is important to check for all players on the roster, not just those where the owner is monitoring for an injury. This simple lineup-checking process is likely a way to add 10-20 games to an owner's team over the course of the season.

An owner should attempt to have enough positional flexibility to bench any player on the team. This will help significantly to shuffle players not starting, when a given player is scheduled for a small number of games, or when it is unknown if they will lose time to an injury. This sounds harder than it is. Something like a 1B/OF, 2B/3B, and 2B/SS will do the trick and help pile up the games played.

All else equal, and if two players are not starting, the next level tiebreaker is to use a National League bat. Even if the player sits for a game, there is a good chance he'll pinch hit, with teams using shorter and shorter benches.

Utility Advantage

This is an advanced tip that can make adjusting the lineup much easier when unexpected news comes out that a player is not playing. By following this tip, it's also more likely an owner can fill a lineup hole with a starting player. First, set the optimal lineup by getting the desired starters into place. From this determined lineup, attempt to shuffle players around by putting any of the following players into the Utility spot and then Middle and Corner Infield spots:

1. Players with multi-position eligibility (as many as possible)

2. Players with the latest (west-coast game) or a Tuesday start

3. Players with a medical issue that could cause him to miss time

Assume news comes out that the owner's second baseman is not playing on Monday. The multi-position Utility bat might be able to be moved to cover for the second baseman, and then any bench player can be slotted into the UTIL spot. Similarly, if it gets to be Tuesday and it's learned the UTIL player will not be starting, perhaps the owner will have another hitter on the bench with a Tuesday start that can be inserted. If that original UTIL player was already put at 2B, there's a much lower likelihood of having a 2B with their first game on Tuesday.

Injuries

It can be a risk to start a player if there is any uncertainty about his injury status. It's not uncommon for a player to leave a game early on Friday and sit out Saturday and Sunday. Owners can read the news regarding the player on Monday and see something like, "Player X is expected to avoid the IL and return to action this week."

Upon seeing news like this, owners should immediately begin looking for other options to place in the lineup over Player X. As the illustration above shows, even a top-round talent is quickly the equal of lesser players in a week where he doesn't play six or seven games. Even if Player X's team is scheduled for seven games, an owner would adjust the projection for this player down significantly unless they had concrete news he was in Monday's starting lineup.

Further, there's a very legitimate chance the player doesn't improve and hits the IL mid-week, leaving the owner with a zero. Instead of taking the chance, owners may be able to get close to his projections that week by finding a lesser talent scheduled for a full week of games.

Two-start Pitchers

The value of two-start pitchers was illustrated earlier in this book. The following table illustrates more specifically how much the doubling of statistics matters, as well as how valuable a win is. These values were calculated from a weekly point of view.

Scenario	IP	W	H+BB	ER	K	Value	Rank
One Start (1W)	7	1	6	1	4	$10.29	35
One Start (0W)	7	0	6	1	4	$3.16	82
Two Starts (2W)	14	2	12	2	8	$27.95	6
Two Starts (1W)	14	1	12	2	8	$21.20	11
Two Starts (0W)	14	0	12	2	8	$14.14	25

In that same week, here's what the values of a pitcher with below-average statistics would look like:

Scenario	IP	W	H+BB	ER	K	Value	Rank
One Start (1W)	6	1	8	4	4	($1.02)	142
One Start (0W)	6	0	8	4	4	($8.04)	<300
Two Starts (2W)	12	2	16	8	8	$5.48	62
Two Starts (1W)	12	1	16	8	8	($1.41)	147
Two Starts (0W)	12	0	16	8	8	($8.43)	<300

Two-start pitchers are extremely valuable. Even if they don't have a strong start, if they should manage to squeak out just one win, it hides a lot of other damage. If an owner is willing to do a little bit of homework, they can use a site like FanGraphs or Baseball-Reference to look up MLB team split information for each two-start pitcher's opponents to gauge the matchup's quality. Using team-split measures for stats like wOBA, OPS, and K% against the handedness of pitcher might add great insight into the opponent's strength.

If FAAB is involved, an owner can use the tables above to estimate the pitcher's earnings for the week and then formulate a FAAB bid based on those projections.

243

Most league hosting sites offer a way to view a list of two-start pitchers for the coming period or a method of filtering the free agent list by those scheduled for two turns. Owners should monitor the accuracy of this information and perhaps verify on at least one other site that the player is in fact scheduled for two. Also, beware of weather problems, injury situations, and minor league activity that could push a start into the next week.

What to Consider for Daily Lineups

If this book was written over five years ago, this section may have been pages long. Even when knowing what factors to consider, maximizing daily lineups has historically been time-consuming. There was a huge edge to those owners who spent the time looking at factors like lefty-righty splits and the weather.

Collecting this player information is so much easier with the proliferation of daily fantasy sports (DFS). While DFS participants work under a salary cap, season-long owners just need to find who is projected to perform the best in a given day. While many DFS projections are behind paywalls, FanGraphs provides two free ones (SaberSim and RotoQL). The daily projections have simplified what used to be a huge task. Thank you, gamblers.

Innings Limits

Certain league hosting sites, like ESPN and Yahoo, have historically used innings pitched limitations, which owners can take advantage at the season's end. This strategy only applies to leagues where there is an innings or games started limit. Assume the league has a rule that says a team cannot exceed 1,400 innings pitched or 200 games started. On a site like ESPN, owners can slowly position themselves to have something like 1,395 innings heading into the last week, then load up a full roster of starters who all start on the same day.

Because ESPN can't logistically determine what pitcher in what game is truly the 1,400th inning pitched, they count all pitching stats on the day which exceeds the 1,400 limit. If done properly, this could realistically net an owner 30-40 extra innings pitched and possibly get them 30-40 more strikeouts.

Deciding when to pull off this coup can take a little balancing. If an owner moves too early, they alert or remind the entire league of the strategy and other contenders can pull it off also. If fewer days are left, the alerted owners will be fighting over a smaller starter pool preventing anyone from really loading up.

If an owner waits too long into the final week, they'll also run into their own issues. First, it is possible other owners are already aware of the loophole and several teams could be fighting for pitchers on those last couple of days. Also, as the season winds down, starters get shut down, have starts skipped, and throw fewer innings.

Pick a day before the weekend, probably Wednesday or Friday (there's usually a small slate on Thursday) to pull it off.

Trading

Trading should be viewed as another means of acquiring players, but it, unfortunately, comes with more baggage. From a high level, the decision to offer or accept a trade comes down to the same principles discussed earlier in this book: projections, value, risk, and in-season decision management. The difficulty with trading involves much higher stakes than other decisions. High-value players might be involved, and the situation is intensified by the perception that trades are not a zero-sum game. One owner wins while the other owner loses.

Much has been written about how to properly offer a trade. Outside of a couple of basics, these etiquette aspects of trading are outside the scope of this book. The golden rule is all an owner needs to keep in mind: Don't be a jerk. Beyond that, the owner would ideally download a set of RoS projections and calculate a fresh set of valuations using those statistics that would then be used to decide on the trade.

The further into the season the offer is, the more previously mentioned in-season management tactics apply. The calculation of value should shift from the theoretical value in the league's context toward the value to the owner's team and his chances of winning the league.

Given most leagues have some continuing set of owners, attempting to rip off one of those owners is a poor long-term proposition. This means an owner should try to formulate offers that include a similar set of theoretical values, ones that both parties of the trade could perceive as increasing their chances of winning the league.

Although it sounds simple, aligning theoretical values for two different owners can be difficult, mostly because of playing time and other perceived risks.

The owner may even consider a theoretical loss in value to increase their chances of winning the league. A practical example might be to trade a $10 outfielder for a $9 second baseman, where the owner has an $8 outfielder on his bench and a $5 second basemen in his starting lineup. This example illustrates that changing perspective can help analyze a trade offer.

Trading is highly susceptible to cognitive biases. Owners will often overvalue players they have drafted. The natural inclination of many owners receiving a trade offer is to think, "No way. My players are way more valuable." This mindset is detrimental. Obtaining an updated set of projections and valuations can help add objectivity to the decision-making process and help the owner recognize situations that could more subtly help his chances of winning.

Notice that the original cost to acquire the players involved in the trade should not be a factor in the decision process. The fact that a second-round pick, $30 in an auction, or $200 of FAAB was spent on a player is irrelevant in a trade, but these facts will be used by others in negotiations.

If an opposing owner is really locked onto pre-season costs, this can be used as an advantage. The opposing owner may be interested in trading for an 8th-round pick that has fallen into a platoon situation, given his preseason valuation, despite the new circumstances. That same owner may be more likely to give up one of his valuable reserve-round pick-ups or an in-season free-agent acquisition given that he spent little on these players and has the possibility of adding an early-round pick in return.

Being able to identify a willing trade partner and knowing who other owners will be interested in trading for are challenges. During the draft or auction, an owner should track the players on his final roster that another owner wanted or was upset they missed out on. If the owner wanted them in the preseason, they'll likely still want them during the season. This other owner's desire for the player can be something to help break the ice in trade talks or be something to exploit.

Prospects won during the FAAB bidding cycle also make great trade pieces. If an owner just outbids another, the losing owner may be up for a trade. If the prospect isn't needed by the winning owner, he can be put up on the trade block and marketed to the highest bidder. There are those owners that just love their prospects and would offer the world in a competitive bidding situation.

Certain owners may avoid trading due to its frustrating and annoying nature. Completely writing off the possibility of trading closes the doors to many options of improving an owner's team. Outside of great luck, it's impossible for an owner to acquire large chunks of stolen bases, home runs, and quality starting pitching in-season, but trading gives an owner access to these possibilities for a fair price.

Wrap Up Last Season

Start Thinking About Next Season

When the season ends, take a breather. For owners who fought the whole season need a break. After a week or two, owners need to sit down for about an hour and reflect on the season to get a retrospective of the past season to help for the next one.

League Notes

While the league tendencies are still fresh, it's best to spend a few minutes on each league and write them down at the season's end. This helps to free the mind for other information, especially as the number of leagues the owner is in increases. These league tendencies and biases can be utilized next season to give owners an advantage. This can be something as simple as noting that half the owners quit once football got going.

It's advisable for the owner to write down notes on every league, even if they don't plan on participating in it next year. The reason for not being in a league may be just as important as being in one. These don't have to be detailed at all, but overarching ideas could include "this league doesn't trade," or "half the owners quit once football started," or "pitching is tough to find on the waiver wire."

Some websites claim to keep all the league histories, but don't trust them. Several times in the past a major hosting service had its league records erased. With that in mind, there are four items to keep track of once a league is over:

1. Final league standings, including the individual category totals

2. FAAB usage throughout the season

3. Owners who made trades and if they're likely to make more in the future

4. Top players on the waiver wire to help set the league replacement level

Analyze the Unexpected

Before looking ahead to the next season, owners should take some time and examine where the entire industry missed. Why did a player over or underperform expectations, and was there a way to target similar players in the future? Or was it all luck? Look for consistent biases and it may point to a player subset to target in seasons going forward.

Offseason News Collection

Owners should start collecting relevant news or resources as they read it in an easily accessible spreadsheet. The key here is to keep the information actionable. With any news, owners need to ask, "Will this information change the player's talent or playing-time projection?" If no, move on. If yes, adjust the player's projection once next year's prep begins.

Here's some information to collect:

- Injuries, chronic vs. temporary. Also, the return times for these injuries.
- Changes to pitches or swing path, especially those done late in the season.
- Prospect lists - which prospects need to be on radars.

Consider Major League Baseball Trends

With the increasing use of analytics, new Statcast data, and developing sabermetric ideas, the landscape of the major leagues is changing. Owners should consider the trends observed in the most recent season and determine if they could influence fantasy teams.

For example, several major league teams began using "openers" in the 2018 season. Similarly, there seems to be a trend toward more closers-by-committee, which will lower the saves captured by fantasy owners. If these trends spread, it may become more difficult to predict usage patterns and to extract pitching wins and saves from those teams. Determining how to project those pitchers and disagreeing with major systems, like Steamer, may be an advantage.

Other trends include the decline in stolen bases, the increase in strikeouts, rising home run totals, and more frequent injured list usage. Owners should develop thoughts about if these trends will continue, and then when projections become available, verify the projection system to reflect the owner's beliefs. The availability or decline in the availability of certain statistics will then have an effect on fantasy leagues. If a given statistic will be harder to acquire in-season, the owner should adjust projections accordingly and consider what players will be affected by these changes.

Studying Success Factors and Winning Owners

The suggestions in this book come from observations, analysis, and critical thinking about the best ways to play fantasy baseball. Every effort has been made to incorporate hard data and tangible evidence of the strategies proposed, but are these suggestions performed by successful owners?

In order to further verify the authors' own suggestions and to search for other contributing success factors, the following research was performed on the 2018 NFBC Main Event final standings data and all FAAB drops and adds. The NFBC Main Event is an incredible laboratory to study given the breadth of the competition (34 leagues, 510 teams) and the high-stakes league buy-in ($1,700).

The format of this competition awards owners both for winning their individual league and for performing well in an overall competition that spans across all 510 teams. The following research aims to understand what leads to success in the individual league context as well as in the top of the overall competition.

Single Versus Multiple Team Ownership

Given the largest available prize pools of all premium fantasy baseball contests, like $150,000 to the Main Event Champion, the NFBC draws the best owners. While obviously limited to one team in a given league, these owners are allowed to enter multiple teams into the larger overall competitions. Is it possible with owners of only one team to compete with the multi-entry competitors? How do these multi-entry owners fare?

Not surprisingly, the results in 2018 did show an advantage to those with multiple teams. Those willing to pay for multiple $1,700 entries are likely skilled and confident enough in those skills to pay that amount of money. The results are not striking, though. Owners of multiple teams appear to finish slightly better than the league finish of eighth that a perfectly average team should expect. Owners of just one team perform somewhat worse than that. The following table displays the overall averages across the 34 leagues and 510 Main Event teams.

Owner Type	Average League Finish	Average Overall Finish
Single Team	8.7	282
Multiple Team	7.4	233

While the averages show an advantage in skill level, that is not surprising. Better owners will be likely to enter more times when allowed.

It's not all doom and gloom for single-entry new owners. In terms of raw count, the owners of just one team finished first in 13 of the 34 leagues and finished in second another 12 times. This represents about 10% of the single-owner teams (25 / 239 teams). Multiple-team owners do win at a higher rate, though. For example, owners of two teams won 10 of the 34 leagues and finished second nine times. This was good for 14% of the two-team owners (19 / 132 teams).

The most eye-catching number below is the number of owners of one team that finish in the bottom three. Sixty-three of the 239 single-team owners finished in the bottom three spots, or 26% of those teams, whereas only 15% (20 / 132 teams) of two-team owners did. Again, this is not wholly surprising or discouraging. A learning curve is likely to be involved in playing at these stakes.

League Finish by Number of Teams Owned										
Number of Teams	Owner Count	Team Count	1-2 League	3-4 League	5-6 League	7-8 League	9-10 League	11-12 League	13-15 League
1	239	239	25	32	23	29	33	34	63
2	66	132	19	12	20	24	15	22	20
3	19	57	14	11	10	7	5	5	5
4	7	28	4	5	8	3	3	0	5
5	7	35	3	3	6	4	9	5	5
6	2	12	0	4	1	0	3	2	2
7	1	7	3	1	0	1	0	0	2

The level of success in the overall competition is similar to that of individual leagues.

Teams Owned	Owner Count	Team Count	1-75 Overall	76-150 Overall	151-225 Overall	226-300 Overall	301-375 Overall	376-450 Overall	450+ Overall
Overall Finish by Number of Teams Owned									
1	239	239	27	36	24	35	36	40	41
2	66	132	22	14	20	25	23	19	9
3	19	57	15	11	13	6	2	5	5
4	7	28	3	8	8	0	4	4	1
5	7	35	4	5	6	7	7	4	2
6	2	12	1	0	4	1	3	2	1
7	1	7	3	1	0	1	0	1	1

Breaking down the top ten in the 2018 Main Event, the third, fifth, and ninth place teams were owners of just one team, while the rest of the top ten were owners of multiple teams.

The data shows owners able to afford or interested in only running one team can compete, but there is an apparent learning curve. Those owners aspiring to test their skill at this high level can draw some comfort from the many different price points in the NFBC family of contests. There are buy-ins starting at $50 and going up from there.

Draft Position

Another interesting aspect of the NFBC competitions is the Kentucky Derby style used for owners to select their desired draft position. The owner that "wins the draft lottery" doesn't necessarily get the first pick. Instead, that owner gets first pick of their desired draft slot. Should owners choose a higher pick? Or there is a common train of thought that it's better to pick toward the end of the first round in order to secure a better player in the second round. Is there validity to this?

It turns out that there was a general advantage to picking first in 2018. Picking first led to the best average league rank and the most teams ranked inside the top 75 overall. This was not an advantage that couldn't be overcome, though. There also isn't a continuous and steady drop off in top league or overall finishes. Owners from several other draft slots had first- or second-place finishes and similar finishes in the overall rankings.

A small sample-size caveat (this is one year of results) is probably warranted here, but the idea that picking toward the back end of the first round is advantageous does not prove out. Keeping in mind that the expected finish in a 15-team league is 8th place, picking 10th or later resulted in below average results.

Results by Draft Pick				
Draft Pick	League Rank	1st & 2nd Place Finishes	Overall Rank	1-75 Overall Rank
1	6.03	7	195	9
2	7.82	2	247	5
3	7.71	5	241	5
4	7.94	3	254	4
5	7.47	6	249	4
6	8.76	4	277	4
7	6.65	7	218	7
8	7.12	7	220	8
9	6.21	5	193	6
10	8.56	4	257	5
11	8.88	4	286	6
12	8.38	7	275	5
13	9.71	1	306	2
14	9.12	2	301	1
15	9.65	4	314	4

Playing Time Versus Skills

Maximizing playing time and the tactics to do so are a focus of *The Process*. Can this be observed in league standings? And if so, to what extent? What drives success more, more playing time or better players? Please note that in the following section, the word "skill" takes a slightly different meaning than elsewhere in this book. Here it's meant to convey "per playing time" measures like "runs per at-bat" or "strikeouts per inning pitched," even though some of those measures are not indicative of skill and are somewhat indicative of the player's team and context.

Hitter Playing Time and Skill Analysis

The following tables show the correlation of team at-bats and team skills (R/AB, HR/AB, RBI/AB, SB/AB) to the rotisserie points scored in the offensive counting categories, or R, HR, RBI, and SB. Correlation is a measure of how related or dependent two variables are and is scored on a scale of -1 to 1. A positive correlation, like those in the following table, indicates that as one variable (playing time or skill) increases, the other variable being measured also increases (points in the R or SB categories). A negative correlation indicates that as one variable increases, the other decreases.

The data clearly demonstrates a strong correlation between playing time and skill and success in the R, HR, and RBI categories. Interestingly, performance in the Stolen Base category is significantly less dependent upon playing time and is extremely well correlated to the skill component. In general, the skill component is noticeably more important than simply gathering playing time.

Individual League Results - Hitter Correlations		
Category	Playing Time (AB) Correlation	Skill (Stats Per AB) Correlation
R League Points	0.719	0.708
HR League Points	0.531	0.840
RBI League Points	0.661	0.720
SB League Points	0.317	0.920

Overall Competition Results - Hitter Correlations		
Category	Playing Time (AB) Correlation	Skill (Stats Per AB) Correlation
R Overall Points	0.743	0.728
HR Overall Points	0.537	0.874
RBI Overall Points	0.680	0.750
SB Overall Points	0.313	0.956

Knowing that both playing time and accumulating more skilled players are success factors isn't groundbreaking analysis. Just how much difference in skill level is required to move up in league and overall standings? To answer this question, the final standings were bucketed into tiers and then converted to a "per at bat" scale.

Successful owners do accumulate more at-bats, often several hundred more than lower-ranking owners. When the skill level "per at-bat" statistics are analyzed, it seems like there isn't much of a discernible difference between managers in this regard. The difference between owners is measured in thousandths of decimal places. For example, there is roughly a 0.007 difference in RBI/AB from the top league finishers to the bottom finishers. However, when this difference is multiplied by a 7,200 AB base, it yields a difference of about 50 RBI over the course of the season. This is where the work spent on player evaluation, MLB team context, and identifying changes in player skill level become apparent.

The results of the same analysis on the overall standings is similar. The tables that follow demonstrate what it takes for an owner to elevate from being a league winner to someone that competes for the overall prizes. Both the playing time and skill level measures increase across the board.

Individual League Results - Hitter Counting Stats					
League Finish	AB	R	HR	RBI	SB
1-2	7,411	1,059	297	1,016	130
3-4	7,424	1,040	288	1,005	120
5-6	7,271	1,016	283	976	116
7-8	7,197	1,003	270	951	119
9-10	7,117	981	268	938	114
11-12	7,053	960	259	920	109
13-15	6,789	923	246	884	102

Overall Competition Results - Hitter Counting Stats					
Overall Finish	AB	R	HR	RBI	SB
1-25	7,484	1,096	312	1,039	139

Here are the per at bat skill components:

Individual League Results - Hitter Per At Bat Stats					
League Finish	AB	R/AB	HR/AB	RBI/ AB	SB/AB
1-2	7,411	0.143	0.040	0.137	0.018
3-4	7,424	0.140	0.039	0.135	0.016
5-6	7,271	0.140	0.039	0.134	0.016
7-8	7,197	0.139	0.038	0.132	0.017
9-10	7,117	0.138	0.038	0.132	0.016
11-12	7,053	0.136	0.037	0.131	0.015
13-15	6,789	0.136	0.036	0.130	0.015

Overall Competition Results - Hitter Per At Bat Stats					
Overall Finish	AB	R/AB	HR/AB	RBI/ AB	SB/AB
1-25	7,484	0.146	0.042	0.139	0.019

Pitcher Playing Time and Skill Analysis

The tables below demonstrate the correlation of pitching playing time to the standard rotisserie pitching categories. The pitching data is quite different than the results of the hitting categories. Interestingly, those stats most owners would likely consider "luck-based," Wins and Saves, show a stronger correlation with skill level than just raw playing time. Saves display a negative correlation with playing time. This makes sense. Owners can't just accumulate Saves by maximizing innings pitched. The way to maximize Strikeouts is focus more on innings (two-start pitchers) than straight skill level.

Individual League Results - Pitcher Correlations		
Category	Playing Time (IP) Correlation	Skill (Stats Per IP) Correlation
W League Points	0.660	0.754
K League Points	0.674	0.490
SV League Points	-0.296	0.927

Overall Competition Results - Pitcher Correlations		
Category	Playing Time (IP) Correlation	Skill (Stats Per IP) Correlation
W League Points	0.687	0.780
K League Points	0.705	0.497
SV League Points	-0.325	0.954

The effect of simply accumulating raw playing time (innings pitched) on pitchers is not as severe for pitchers. There is only roughly a 20 IP drop-off from each tier to the next. The analysis shows that more successful owners do perform better in the "skill" metrics wins per inning pitched and strikeouts per inning pitched; however, Saves do not follow this same pattern as cleanly. The top-tier teams do accumulate more saves per inning pitched, meaning they probably have more active roster spots occupied by Save-earning players, but the obvious pattern stops there.

Individual League Results - Pitcher Counting Stats				
League Finish	IP	W	K	SV
1-2	1,389	92	1,449	68
3-4	1,373	88	1,380	67
5-6	1,370	86	1,366	60
7-8	1,350	84	1,342	60
9-10	1,358	84	1,330	52
11-12	1,315	80	1,292	55
13-15	1,271	76	1,238	55

Overall Competition Results - Pitcher Counting Stats				
Overall Finish	IP	W	K	SV
1-25	1,380	94	1,451	74

Here are the per at bat skill components:

Individual League Results - Pitcher Per Inning Pitched Stats				
League Finish	IP	W/IP	K/IP	SV/IP
1-2	1,389	0.067	1.044	0.049
3-4	1,373	0.064	1.007	0.050
5-6	1,370	0.063	0.999	0.044
7-8	1,350	0.062	0.995	0.045
9-10	1,358	0.062	0.982	0.039
11-12	1,315	0.061	0.984	0.043
13-15	1,271	0.060	0.976	0.044

Overall Competition Results - Pitcher Per Inning Pitched Stats				
Overall Finish	IP	W/IP	K/IP	SV/IP
1-25	1,380	0.068	1.051	0.054

Free Agent Transactions

This section seeks to provide insights into winning owners' free agent bidding behaviors. Topics like the frequency of moves, allocation between hitting and pitching moves, bid amounts, closer speculation, two-start pitcher usage, and drop decisions are just some of the topics explored.

Transaction Counts and Frequency

It is a common belief that accumulating playing time and aggressive pursuit of free agents helps to win leagues. Striking early in the season in order to secure impact free agents for longer chunks of the season is our recommendation, but does an analysis of actual transactions support this philosophy? Sort of.

The tables below clearly show that higher finishing teams made more acquisitions over the course of the season. The disparity becomes more pronounced as the season progresses. One interpretation of this is that more transactions lead to better finishes.

Keeping in mind that correlation does not equal causation, be careful with that assumption. There is another interpretation of this data that the authors of this book wish to research in the future. Notice in the first two months of the season, Weeks 1-4 and 5-8, the top-performing owners are slightly less active than other owners in the top half of the standings.

This seems to indicate that the top half of the owners are more aggressive. But perhaps those that rise to the very top are simply luckier than those that finish third through sixth. They know to be aggressive, but they still make slightly fewer pickups than other successful managers in those first two months.

Average Monthly Transactions by League Finish								
League Finish	Total Moves	Moves Weeks 1-4	Moves Weeks 5-8	Moves Weeks 9-12	Moves Weeks 13-16	Moves Weeks 17-20	Moves Weeks 21-24	Moves Weeks 25-27
1-2	51	5.4	6.8	8.5	7.4	7.9	8.6	6.3
3-4	48	5.3	6.9	7.6	7.1	7.4	7.8	5.5
5-6	47	5.7	7.4	8.0	6.9	7.7	7.7	4.0
7-8	43	4.9	6.9	7.9	6.6	6.9	6.5	3.0
9-10	40	5.2	7.2	7.5	6.6	5.7	5.8	1.9
11-12	45	4.8	6.7	7.2	6.0	4.7	4.1	1.2
13-15	28	5.2	6.1	6.1	4.9	3.1	2.5	0.6

Average Monthly Transactions by Overall Finish								
Overall Finish	Total Moves	Moves Weeks 1-4	Moves Weeks 5-8	Moves Weeks 9-12	Moves Weeks 13-16	Moves Weeks 17-20	Moves Weeks 21-24	Moves Weeks 25-27
1-25	57.5	6.3	7.0	9.5	8.4	8.5	10.0	7.7

It is very apparent that by the end of the season, those owners at the lower end of the standings stop paying attention. Transaction frequency plummets relative to the top teams as the season reaches the last two to three months of the season. In fact, the top owners reach their highest levels of activity in those final two-to-three months.

In order to compete for a league prize or in the overall, a late flurry of activity in the final months may be necessary. This strongly supports the tactic suggested earlier in the book about reserving at least a portion of FAAB for the end of the season. Not only will this allow for a late push up the standings, but the owner will face significantly less competition for those bids, as many teams will be making less than one acquisition per week by that time.

Budget Allocation, Spending by Month

The top finishing owners didn't make more pickups in the first month. In fact, they made fewer moves than several other owner groups. Those best-finishing owners did spend more in total, however, perhaps indicating that aggressive early-season pursuit of players is a trait of those successful owners.

The successful owners held a budget of $150-$200 for the final 11 weeks of the season, or about $20, $15, and $10 per week in the final three months of the season, respectively.

Monthly FAAB Spending by League Finish								
League Finish	Total Spent	Spent Weeks 1-4	Spent Weeks 5-8	Spent Weeks 9-12	Spent Weeks 13-16	Spent Weeks 17-20	Spent Weeks 21-24	Spent Weeks 25-27
1-2	$981	$205	$252	$244	$119	$79	$56	$27
3-4	$956	$179	$231	$231	$120	$96	$69	$29
5-6	$943	$201	$269	$232	$85	$77	$51	$29
7-8	$947	$185	$245	$225	$122	$83	$60	$27
9-10	$894	$162	$264	$213	$108	$77	$57	$13
11-12	$906	$162	$256	$258	$104	$62	$53	$11
13-15	$821	$201	$272	$165	$110	$40	$30	$3

Monthly FAAB Spending by Overall Finish								
Overall Finish	Total Spent	Spent Weeks 1-4	Spent Weeks 5-8	Spent Weeks 9-12	Spent Weeks 13-16	Spent Weeks 17-20	Spent Weeks 21-24	Spent Weeks 25-27
1-25	$998	$194	$240	$253	$130	$83	$70	$28

Spending Per Transaction, by Month

Dividing total monthly spending by the number of transactions in a given month yields the average bid throughout each month of the season. Owners at all levels of success are following the principles of spending more, even on a transaction level, early in the season, when more value can be obtained.

It is notable that the best performing owners are the highest or near-highest bidders in the first month of the season and then move toward becoming at or near the lowest bidders in most other months. This suggests that in addition to high levels of volume, the best owners also spend FAAB resources more efficiently. The very worst-performing owners tend to be at or near the highest average bid in each month.

This information is also very helpful for establishing a budget in the final months of the season. It's clear to see that minimal bids can be successful at winning players in those months.

Average Bid Each Month by League Finish							
League Finish	Avg Bid Weeks 1-4	Avg Bid Weeks 5-8	Avg Bid Weeks 9-12	Avg Bid Weeks 13-16	Avg Bid Weeks 17-20	Avg Bid Weeks 21-24	Avg Bid Weeks 25-27
1-2	$38	$37	$29	$16	$10	$7	$4
3-4	$34	$33	$31	$17	$13	$9	$5
5-6	$35	$36	$29	$12	$10	$7	$7
7-8	$38	$35	$28	$18	$12	$9	$9
9-10	$31	$37	$29	$16	$14	$10	$7
11-12	$33	$39	$36	$17	$13	$13	$9
13-15	$39	$45	$27	$22	$13	$12	$5

Average Bid Each Month by Overall Finish							
Overall Finish	Avg Bid Weeks 1-4	Avg Bid Weeks 5-8	Avg Bid Weeks 9-12	Avg Bid Weeks 13-16	Avg Bid Weeks 17-20	Avg Bid Weeks 21-24	Avg Bid Weeks 25-27
1-25	$31	$34	$27	$16	$10	$7	$4

Bid Sizes

The issue with using averages to evaluate a bidding strategy is that the disbursement of the bidding across owner skill-level may be different. For example, Owner A, who wins two players at $200 each, has the same average bid as Owner B that wins a player at $399 and $1. The ideas of "minimum-bid," "bank breaker," and "in-between" players were introduced in the Free-

Agent Acquisition Budget section of the book. The following tables demonstrate how owners of different success levels adhere to that bucketing strategy.

There's not an easily discernible trend in the $50-$99 or $100+ bid ranges. The more successful owners are noticeably more active in the $1 and $2-$9 ranges. This is where their higher levels of activity occur. There are two reasons that might contribute to the activity in these price ranges. First, the best owners are likely more comfortable owning players that others are not (more on this later). Second, these owners may be more efficient at recognizing when bidding competition will be lower on a player. For instance, it was demonstrated a few pages ago that the top owners are active through the end of the season when FAAB budgets are lower and much of the competition has stopped bidding.

Count of Bid Sizes by League Finish					
League Finish	$1 Moves	$2-$9 Moves	$10-$49 Moves	$50-$99 Moves	$100+ Moves
1-2	9.1	19.7	17.6	2.7	2.5
3-4	8.2	17.0	18.3	2.6	2.2
5-6	8.4	18.1	16.6	2.7	2.2
7-8	7.5	14.4	16.7	2.5	2.5
9-10	6.9	12.2	16.2	3.1	1.9
11-12	4.0	11.5	14.6	2.7	2.6
13-15	4.5	7.6	12.3	2.2	2.6

Count of Bid Sizes by Overall Finish					
Overall Finish	$1 Moves	$2-$9 Moves	$10-$49 Moves	$50-$99 Moves	$100+ Moves
1-25	9.8	23.4	19.9	3.0	2.0

Hitting and Pitching Bid Allocation

Much is made of the hitter-pitcher split in valuing players and in progressing through a draft. The tables below seek to find out how better owners allocate transactions and FAAB in-season. For comparison purposes to the information below, there were 10,681 hitters added for a total of $223,372 and 10,383 pitchers added for a total of $249,085 across all the Main Event leagues in 2018. This works out to a 51-49 hitter-pitcher split in terms of transaction count and a 47-53 split in terms of the dollar spent. The average winning bid was $20.91 and $23.99 for hitters and pitchers, respectively.

No individual ownership bucket deviates noticeably from these general split allocations. It does appear that the top half of finishers devote slightly more moves and spending to pitchers than the bottom half of finishers.

Given the NFBC roster setup of 14 hitters and 9 pitchers, all things equal, an owner would expect 61% of transactions to involve hitters and 39% pitchers (14 / (14 + 9)). It is interesting that nearly the same quantity of transactions target pitchers as hitters. This speaks to the significance of turnover for pitchers during the season. The fact that the spending split of 47-53 moves even more toward pitchers really demonstrates the relative competition for pitchers during the season.

Hitter-Pitcher Transaction Allocation by League Finish								
League Finish	Total Moves	H Moves	P Moves	% H Moves	% P Moves	Total Spent	% Spent H	% Spent P
1-2	50.8	26.5	24.4	52%	48%	$981	47%	53%
3-4	47.6	24.0	23.7	50%	50%	$956	47%	53%
5-6	47.4	22.7	24.7	48%	52%	$943	45%	55%
7-8	42.7	21.3	21.4	50%	50%	$947	47%	53%
9-10	39.9	20.3	19.6	51%	49%	$894	48%	52%
11-12	34.6	18.1	16.5	52%	48%	$906	48%	52%
13-15	28.4	14.8	13.7	52%	48%	$821	50%	50%

Hitter-Pitcher Transaction Allocation by Overall Finish								
Overall Finish	Total Moves	H Moves	P Moves	% H Moves	% P Moves	Total Spent	% Spent H	% Spent P
1-25	57.5	29.2	28.2	51%	49%	$998	44%	56%

Acquiring Hitter Playing Time

This analysis seeks to determine if more successful owners do acquire more hitter playing time with their transactions during the course of the year. To do this, each individual player acquisition was matched up against the actual number of games played by the player in the following week.

Note that the average games played in the following week does not differ across the spectrum of owner success; nearly all owners average around 4.6 games played by the players picked up. More successful owners are more active, so it stands to reason they would acquire more total games played and have more transactions within each of the games played columns. To help interpret the following table, the 3.3 in the 7GP column for teams that finished first or second means those teams averaged 3.3 hitter pickups that played in seven games the week after their acquisition.

Count of Games Played Week Following Acquisition by League Finish											
League Finish	Hitter Moves	GP in Next Week	Avg GP Next Week	7 GP	6 GP	5 GP	4 GP	3 GP	2 GP	1 GP	0 GP
1-2	26.5	123	4.6	3.3	7.2	6.0	4.1	1.8	1.2	0.6	2.1
3-4	24.0	109	4.6	2.7	6.2	5.7	3.3	2.1	1.2	0.5	2.1
5-6	22.7	105	4.7	2.4	6.4	4.8	3.9	2.2	0.9	0.3	1.6
7-8	21.3	99	4.6	2.3	5.9	4.9	3.3	1.8	0.9	0.5	1.5
9-10	20.3	93	4.5	2.1	5.6	4.5	3.3	1.7	1.1	0.4	1.5
11-12	18.1	83	4.6	1.7	5.4	3.7	3.3	1.4	0.9	0.3	1.3
13-15	14.8	67	4.6	1.4	4.2	3.1	2.6	1.3	0.8	0.2	1.1

Count of Games Played Week Following Acquisition by Overall Finish											
Overall Finish	Hitter Moves	GP in Next Week	Avg GP Next Week	7 GP	6 GP	5 GP	4 GP	3 GP	2 GP	1 GP	0 GP
1-25	29.2	138	4.7	3.7	8.3	6.6	4.5	1.8	1.5	0.8	1.9

It's difficult to tease from the tables above if successful owners are better at identifying players likely to play in six or seven games, or if they're simply more active. To determine the effect, the tables above have been converted into percentages of all the owners' additions. For example, 12.7% of all hitter moves for owners that finished in the top two involved players that played in seven games the following week.

This table does well to illustrate how averages can mask trends in the underlying data. Notice that the top-performing owners focused more of their acquisitions on players that played seven games the following week, and they are also among the highest allocation in acquiring players that didn't play any games or only played one game the subsequent week. This is likely an indication that those owners are maximizing games played for the current week and they're also looking further ahead on the horizon and identifying players that may not play in the current week but might be returning from injury or are otherwise expected to play in the future.

Percentage of Games Played Week Following Acquisition by League Finish								
League Finish	7GP Pct	6GP Pct	5GP Pct	4GP Pct	3GP Pct	2GP Pct	1GP Pct	0GP Pct
1-2	12.7%	27.2%	23.0%	15.6%	6.7%	4.5%	2.4%	7.9%
3-4	11.5%	26.0%	23.9%	14.0%	8.8%	5.1%	1.9%	8.7%
5-6	10.8%	28.4%	21.3%	17.5%	9.6%	4.1%	1.4%	6.9%
7-8	11.1%	27.8%	23.4%	15.6%	8.7%	4.2%	2.2%	7.2%
9-10	10.2%	27.9%	22.6%	16.1%	8.3%	5.5%	1.8%	7.6%
11-12	9.6%	29.9%	20.8%	18.2%	7.5%	5.1%	1.8%	7.1%
13-15	9.5%	28.6%	21.0%	18.0%	8.6%	5.6%	1.5%	7.2%

Percentage of Games Played Week Following Acquisition by Overall Finish								
Overall Finish	7GP Pct	6GP Pct	5GP Pct	4GP Pct	3GP Pct	2GP Pct	1GP Pct	0GP Pct
1-25	12.8%	28.5%	22.9%	15.6%	6.1%	5.1%	2.6%	6.5%

Acquiring Stolen Bases

The decline in stolen bases across the major league landscape is a growing area of concern for fantasy baseball owners. The strategies to acquire stolen bases in the draft and during the season are a major area of focus. To identify the strategies used, all transactions that involved players that stole 10 bases or more during the season are summarized below.

It does not appear there is a silver bullet strategy to acquiring stolen bases. Again, better-performing owners simply display a greater volume of transactions in pursuing stolen bases. There is no obvious trend in the percent of moves; all owner categories use 7-8% of hitter-focused moves on stolen base threats. However, these owners again demonstrate greater efficiency in the form of lower average bids to secure these players.

Stolen Base Acquisitions by League Finish				
League Finish	Moves on Stolen Bases	Percent of Hitter Moves	FAAB Spent on Stolen Bases	FAAB Spent per Stolen Base Transaction
1-2	4.1	8.0%	$70	$17.1
3-4	3.5	7.3%	$69	$19.7
5-6	3.3	7.0%	$58	$17.6
7-8	3.1	7.3%	$63	$20.3
9-10	3.2	8.0%	$64	$20.0
11-12	2.7	7.8%	$59	$21.9
13-15	2.3	7.9%	$62	$27.0

Stolen Base Acquisitions by Overall Finish				
Overall Finish	Moves on Stolen Bases	Percent of Hitter Moves	FAAB Spent on Stolen Bases	FAAB Spent per Stolen Base Transaction
1-25	4.8	8.4%	$64	$13.3

Acquiring Two-start Pitchers

The analysis of transactions involving two-start pitchers for an upcoming week was surprising on two levels. Most notably, the quantity of player additions that had two starts the very next week looks inaccurate. More than three-to-four transactions per team should be expected throughout the season, yet after checking the analysis multiple times, the numbers are accurate. Keep in mind the Main Event is a 15-team league where two-start pitchers are more likely to be owned. Recent MLB trends, rules and policy changes like the use of openers, the 10-day injured-list rule changes, and recent MLB schedule changes make it more difficult to predict who will ultimately receive two starts in a given week. The numbers below only reflect those pitchers that were added and did ultimately start two games. There are surely many transactions involving pitchers projected for two starts who did not make both.

The other surprising observation is that most successful owners make among the lowest percentage of two-start transactions! They are in the top half in terms of volume, but noticeably less than other owner buckets in terms of percentage. Notice that to compete for the overall title, owners must ramp up the pursuit of two-start pitchers and be among the most active in the category.

When it comes to the amount spent on two-start pitchers, the best owners are again the most efficient bidders. It's very eye-opening to see the top owners spend roughly half the amount as the bottom owners do on each two-start pitcher bid.

Two-start Pitcher Acquisitions by League Finish				
League Finish	Moves on Two-start Pitchers	Percent of Pitcher Moves	FAAB Spent on Two-start Pitchers	FAAB Spent per Two-start Transaction
1-2	3.0	12.5%	$47	$15.7
3-4	3.6	15.2%	$63	$17.5
5-6	3.8	15.2%	$58	$15.3
7-8	3.5	16.2%	$57	$16.3
9-10	2.9	14.6%	$74	$25.5
11-12	2.1	12.6%	$50	$23.8
13-15	2.0	14.3%	$56	$28.0

Two-start Pitcher Acquisitions by Overall Finish				
Overall Finish	Moves on Two-start Pitchers	Percent of Pitcher Moves	FAAB Spent on Two Start Pitchers	FAAB Spent per Two Start Transaction
1-25	3.6	12.9%	$47	$13.1

Acquiring Closers

The strategy for acquiring closers is another source of disagreement among fantasy baseball owners, with one side arguing not to invest in closers at the draft due to their uncertain nature and the other side arguing they'd rather invest draft capital than waste significant FAAB resources during the season.

The results of the study on this topic earlier in the book were not conclusive, but we can see from the results below that successful owners are highly aggressive in the pursuit of Saves during the season. They're not deterred by this arguably high price. The best owners make the most moves, the highest percentage of their moves pursuing closers, and expend the most FAAB, all while being more efficient per transaction than most other owner groups. They make more moves more cheaply. They don't avoid the theoretically high cost of saves, they manage it.

The lack of specific draft results to pair into this analysis is unfortunate. It would be great to see how successful owners chose to invest during the draft. The authors suspect this aggressive pursuit of closers via FAAB is in part because the top owners elected to invest less at the draft, however, that specific research will have to wait for a future edition of *The Process.*

Closer Acquisitions by League Finish				
League Finish	**Moves on Closer Speculation**	**Percent of Pitcher Moves**	**FAAB Spent on Closers**	**FAAB Spent per Closer Transaction**
1-2	9.1	37.5%	$263	$28.9
3-4	8.4	35.3%	$236	$28.1
5-6	6.9	28.1%	$214	$31.0
7-8	7.5	35.3%	$259	$34.5
9-10	6.3	32.3%	$182	$28.9
11-12	5.7	34.5%	$206	$36.1
13-15	3.6	26.6%	$139	$38.6

Closer Acquisitions by Overall Finish				
Overall Finish	**Moves on Closer Speculation**	**Percent of Pitcher Moves**	**FAAB Spent on Closers**	**FAAB Spent per Closer Transaction**
1-25	10.3	36.5%	$250	$24.3

Pitcher Transactions by Month

The following table illustrates how the average closer, starting pitcher, two-start pitcher, and hybrid pitcher bids and volumes changed over the course of the season. For reference, a hybrid pitcher was a player that did not fit neatly into the closer speculation or starting pitcher categories. These were generally multi-inning relievers, openers, strong relievers far from closing, or other undefined roles, For 2018, these were players like Chad Green, Collin McHugh, and Seth Lugo.

This analysis may help provide context on what to bid on the different pitcher types at different points in the season. Keep in mind that averages can be very misleading. The average closer bid likely includes extremely high bids on those thought to be assuming a role and very low bids for the "forgotten guy" that may be next in line.

Pitcher Transactions by Month								
Month	Closer Bids per League	Average Closer Bid	Starting Pitcher Bids per League	Average Starting Pitcher Bid	Two-start Pitcher Bids per League	Average Two-start Pitcher Bid	Hybrid Bids per League	Average Hybrid Bid
1	13	$63.6	23	$29.3	5	$29.5	1	$15.6
2	15	$40.0	32	$47.0	8	$40.0	2	$21.5
3	19	$46.1	34	$22.0	8	$20.9	3	$22.2
4	17	$19.5	31	$15.8	7	$16.1	3	$10.0
5	17	$18.4	25	$9.7	4	$11.1	3	$8.3
6	13	$12.8	30	$8.3	7	$7.8	2	$7.2
7	6	$7.7	17	$5.4	4	$6.0	0	$5.1

Effectiveness of Transactions

Having looked at the types of moves successful owners make, the next dimension to analyze them on is the amount of value acquired by making these moves. Looking at each move and determining the season-long and weekly earnings or losses the added player experienced can bring out the skill level behind these decisions. Performing the same analysis on dropped players will illustrate how well owners are at determining which players to move on from.

To perform this analysis, the authors joined the acquisition data for each NFBC Main Event team with the following pieces of valuation data:

- Season-long earnings or loss

- Cumulative weekly earnings or loss for the season

- Weekly earnings or loss in the week following the transaction

Before proceeding with the analysis, there are a few key points to understand about player value and proper decision-making. Consider the scenario of a player that comes into a starting role due to an injury on his MLB team. Assume the player is thrust into the starting role in the middle of the season for a total of six weeks. During those six weeks, he is a slightly-above-average fantasy player. After those six weeks, the MLB team's incumbent starter returns from injury and the player in question returns to a bench role.

It is very likely that the player in this scenario will have a negative season-long value. He only played as a full-time player for a six-week period. Yet during those six weeks, he was likely a positive weekly earner due to being above-average and being in a full-time role. It's easy to see that this player would be "ownable" in a 15-team rotisserie league. He'd be an intriguing in-season free-agent target.

Consider how the values for this player would appear when attempting to evaluate a fantasy owner. This player would show up as a negative season-long value, likely a negative weekly earner across the full spectrum of the season, but a solid contributor if the focus was just on the six-week period in which he had a full-time job. Understanding the nuance of this scenario will be helpful in interpreting the tables that follow.

Season-long Earnings and Losses - Adds

Given injuries and other scenarios where MLB players move into and out of starting roles, many players temporarily become weekly earners, but it is very difficult for these types of players to earn season-long value. For this reason, even the most skilled owners are shown as having acquired negative season-long earnings.

More information can be gleaned by separating out those players that were positive earners over the course of the season. For example, an owner may have speculated on Player A, Player B, and Player C that each earned $20, -$15, and -$10, respectively, in season-long valuations. This would display a total of -$5 acquired in season-long value. However, this aggregated look is not helpful. A skilled owner would have held onto Player A and quickly dropped Player B and Player C, so the full negative values were not incurred by the team.

The following table displays the aggregated season-long earnings and then extracts out the positive and negative earners. The top owners make the most transactions, leading to them displaying the largest season-long loss in aggregate; however, their positive and negative values are the most extreme. This suggests they find the most season-long value by churning through more transactions. They likely identify and drop the negative earners well before the full extent of the loss is incurred. It's also interesting to note that the better owners have among the highest average earnings per positive transaction and among the lowest average loss per negative transaction. Their wins are bigger and their losses are smaller.

Season-long Earnings (Loss) of Acquisitions by League Finish						
League Finish	Season-long Earnings (Loss) Added	Season-long Earnings (Loss) Per Add	Positive Season-long Earnings Added	Season-long Earnings Per Positive Add	Negative Season-long Loss Added	Season-long Loss Per Negative Add
1-2	($122)	($2.41)	$109	$5.78	($232)	($7.25)
3-4	($101)	($2.12)	$112	$6.15	($213)	($7.26)
5-6	($119)	($2.51)	$99	$5.52	($217)	($7.35)
7-8	($91)	($2.12)	$94	$5.52	($185)	($7.22)
9-10	($100)	($2.52)	$83	$5.66	($184)	($7.32)
11-12	($87)	($2.52)	$73	$5.51	($160)	($7.45)
13-15	($81)	($2.85)	$57	$5.43	($138)	($7.73)

Season-long Earnings (Loss) of Acquisitions by Overall Finish						
Overall Finish	Season-long Earnings (Loss) Added	Season-long Earnings (Loss) Per Add	Positive Season-long Earnings Added	Season-long Earnings Per Positive Add	Negative Season-long Loss Added	Season-long Loss Per Negative Add
1-25	($152)	($2.64)	$122	$6.09	($274)	($7.32)

Season-long Earnings and Losses - Drops

An analysis of players dropped shows similar characteristics. All owners drop a significant amount of losses during the season. It is particularly interesting, however, that the best-performing owners drop the highest amount of positive season-long earnings, both in total and on a per transaction basis. Given that these are the most skilled owners, it seems unlikely that this is a mistake, that these owners are accidentally dropping good players. Rather, this likely indicates an aggressiveness in being willing to move on from a player that may have performed well for a significant chunk of the season, but that the owner now believes will be less productive moving forward.

Similarly, these could indicate situations where the owner drafted a stacked team and has decided to let go of a long-term $2 player. It's very possible the better teams had superior drafts and they can afford to let go of some lower positive-earning players to pursue those with higher potential rewards or to play matchups. It's much easier to justify the drop of a positive earner if the team is so strong the player doesn't regularly make the starting lineup. It could also demonstrate these owners are playing an aggressive weekly game with a portion of their roster and streaming through the best short-term options that can be started over otherwise strong season-long players.

Season-long Earnings (Loss) of Drops by League Finish						
League Finish	Season-long Earnings (Loss) Dropped	Season-long Earnings (Loss) Per Drop	Positive Season-long Earnings Dropped	Season-long Earnings Per Positive Drop	Negative Season-long Loss Dropped	Season-long Loss Per Negative Drop
1-2	($155)	($3.05)	$98	$5.50	($253)	($7.68)
3-4	($140)	($2.95)	$96	$5.72	($236)	($7.62)
5-6	($165)	($3.48)	$84	$5.40	($249)	($7.81)
7-8	($137)	($3.21)	$77	$5.29	($215)	($7.65)
9-10	($145)	($3.64)	$66	$5.39	($212)	($7.70)
11-12	($153)	($4.42)	$49	$4.96	($202)	($8.14)
13-15	($129)	($4.53)	$42	$5.25	($170)	($8.30)

Season-long Earnings (Loss) of Drops by Overall Finish						
Overall Finish	Season-long Earnings (Loss) Dropped	Season-long Earnings (Loss) Per Drop	Positive Season-long Earnings Dropped	Season-long Earnings Per Positive Drop	Negative Season-long Loss Dropped	Season-long Loss Per Negative Drop
1-25	($172)	($2.99)	$115	$5.83	($288)	($7.64)

Weekly Earnings and Losses - Adds

Moving from season-long valuation analysis to a weekly analysis is a bit odd. Fantasy owners are generally used to what a $40 annual hitter valuation means but converting a performance like that into 26 or 27 individual weekly values results in different numbers. For example, Mookie Betts earned $43 in 2018 with his .346, 129 R, 32 HR, 80 RBI, 30 SB season. That translated into $526 of weekly earnings or roughly $19.50 per week across the 27-week season.

The analysis below sums up all the weekly earnings for players added in the 2018 NFBC Main Event. Like above, those totals are then extracted into positive and negative only weeks in order to better illustrate that a negative player across the course of the season can still have an extended period of positive-earning weeks.

The top owners have the lowest average positive weekly earnings and among the largest average negative weekly loss per add. This is not necessarily what one would expect and it's not what the season-long data showed. Recall that the top owners displayed the highest season-long earnings per add and the lowest season-long losses per add. Those same top owners do display the most total positive weekly earnings.

		Weekly Earnings (Loss) Added	Average Weekly (Loss)Per Add	Positive Weekly Earnings Added	Positive Weekly Earnings per Add	Negative Weekly Earnings Added	Negative Weekly (Loss) per Add
Weekly Earnings (Loss) of Acquisitions by League Finish							
League Finish	Total Moves	Weekly Earnings (Loss) Added	Average Weekly (Loss)Per Add	Positive Weekly Earnings Added	Positive Weekly Earnings per Add	Negative Weekly Earnings Added	Negative Weekly (Loss) per Add
1-2	50.8	($2,149)	($42.30)	$4,671	$91.95	($6,820)	($134.25)
3-4	47.6	($1,906)	($40.04)	$4,496	$94.45	($6,403)	($134.52)
5-6	47.4	($1,999)	($42.17)	$4,399	$92.81	($6,398)	($134.98)
7-8	42.7	($1,546)	($36.21)	$4,064	$95.18	($5,609)	($131.36)
9-10	39.9	($1,614)	($40.45)	$3,702	$92.78	($5,317)	($133.26)
11-12	34.6	($1,309)	($37.83)	$3,244	$93.76	($4,553)	($131.59)
13-15	28.4	($1,073)	($37.78)	$2,707	$95.32	($3,780)	($133.10)

		Weekly Earnings (Loss) Added	Average Weekly (Loss) Per Add	Positive Weekly Earnings Added	Positive Weekly Earnings per Add	Negative Weekly Earnings Added	Negative Weekly (Loss) per Add
Weekly Earnings (Loss) of Acquisitions by Overall Finish							
Overall Finish	Total Moves	Weekly Earnings (Loss) Added	Average Weekly (Loss) Per Add	Positive Weekly Earnings Added	Positive Weekly Earnings per Add	Negative Weekly Earnings Added	Negative Weekly (Loss) per Add
1-25	57.5	($2,727)	($47.43)	$5,157	$89.69	($7,883)	($137.10)

Weekly Earnings and Losses - Drops

Using this same concept of positive and negative weekly earnings to look at the players dropped, there is more evidence of the aggressiveness exhibited by top owners. These top owners drop players with higher average positive weekly earnings and the lowest average negative losses. This suggests both that they are capable of finding better players and that they're more willing to move on from those good players when they fall out of value. Better owners seem to truly subscribe to the theory of weekly value and it may be driving their success.

Weekly Earnings (Loss) of Drops by League Finish							
League Finish	Total Moves	Weekly Earnings (Loss) Dropped	Weekly Earnings (Loss) Per Drop	Positive Weekly Earnings Dropped	Weekly Earnings Per Positive Drop	Negative Weekly Loss Dropped	Weekly Loss Per Negative Drop
1-2	50.8	($2,391)	($47.07)	$4,470	$87.99	($6,861)	($135.06)
3-4	47.6	($2,239)	($47.04)	$4,253	$89.35	($6,493)	($136.41)
5-6	47.4	($2,522)	($53.21)	$4,044	$85.32	($6,566)	($138.52)
7-8	42.7	($2,088)	($48.90)	$3,724	$87.21	($5,812)	($136.11)
9-10	39.9	($2,168)	($54.34)	$3,332	$83.51	($5,500)	($137.84)
11-12	34.6	($2,143)	($61.94)	$2,734	$79.02	($4,877)	($140.95)
13-15	28.4	($1,766)	($62.18)	$2,297	$80.88	($4,062)	($143.03)

Weekly Earnings (Loss) of Drops by Overall Finish							
Overall Finish	Total Moves	Weekly Earnings (Loss) Dropped	Weekly Earnings (Loss) Per Drop	Positive Weekly Earnings Dropped	Weekly Earnings Per Drop	Negative Weekly Loss Dropped	Weekly Loss Per Drop
1-25	57.5	($2,731)	($47.50)	$5,083	$88.40	($7,814)	($135.89)

275

Weekly Earnings and Losses - Net for Adds and Drops

These next tables show the net positive earnings added with the positive earnings dropped, and they do the same for the negative transactions. It's worth reiterating that these are the total amounts gained and lost by the players added and dropped across the entire season. It isn't known exactly when those gains or losses were on fantasy teams but note that the top teams have the lowest positive net earnings ($201) and the smallest amount of net losses (-$41). This is what an owner would expect to observe for an owner that was tightly and efficiently adding and dropping players all season long. If most players added are short-term plays and are perfectly expendable, the amount of gains or losses added and dropped would be nearly the same. Add a player for two weeks, capture his positive weeks, recognize losses are coming, drop the player. Rinse, wash, repeat.

Another contributing factor or plausible explanation for this is that better teams experienced better drafts. A player with high weekly earnings acquired during the draft would not hit the positive weekly earnings added column, but would hit the positive weekly earnings dropped column, if let go. Similarly, owners with poor drafts would have lower negative weekly earnings added and more negative weekly losses to drop. There is a cyclical effect here, in that those owners with poor drafts would also be less likely to drop the positive earners they added because they need to retain those players to backfill for missed draft picks. Owners with good drafts and good weekly pickups will reach a point where they must decide between the good players on their team and the good free agents available. The authors hope to get to the bottom of this in future editions of *The Process* by pairing draft analysis with weekly transactions.

	Net Weekly Earnings (Loss) of Drops by League Finish					
League Finish	Positive Weekly Earnings Added	Positive Weekly Earnings Dropped	Net Positive Weekly Earnings	Negative Weekly Earnings Added	Negative Weekly Loss Dropped	Net Negative Weekly Earnings
1-2	$4,671	$4,470	$201	($6,820)	($6,861)	($41)
3-4	$4,496	$4,253	$243	($6,403)	($6,493)	($90)
5-6	$4,399	$4,044	$355	($6,398)	($6,566)	($168)
7-8	$4,064	$3,724	$340	($5,609)	($5,812)	($203)
9-10	$3,702	$3,332	$370	($5,317)	($5,500)	($184)
11-12	$3,244	$2,734	$510	($4,553)	($4,877)	($324)
13-15	$2,707	$2,297	$411	($3,780)	($4,062)	($282)

The very best of the best owners tighten this process even further. The authors are not certain what to make of the fact that these top teams add more losses than they drop, but we believe it may be due to these owners being significantly more active all the way to the end of the season. MLB players that don't become positive earners until September likely have enormous amounts of losses incurred in previous months. Adding such a player and holding him until the end of the season would distort these negative weekly columns, such as those below.

Net Weekly Earnings (Loss) of Drops by Overall Finish						
League Finish	Positive Weekly Earnings Added	Positive Weekly Earnings Dropped	Net Positive Weekly Earnings	Negative Weekly Earnings Added	Negative Weekly Loss Dropped	Net Negative Weekly Earnings
1-25	$5,157	$5,083	$74	($7,883)	($7,814)	$69

Next Week's Earnings and Losses

The last several analyses covered the cumulative weekly earnings and losses over the course of the 27-week 2018 season. Another measure of transactions to review is the amount of value earned in the week immediately after a player was added.

The same strategy of separating total weekly earnings into positive- and negative-only earnings is used; however, the total and average of next week's earnings is much more meaningful in this regard. These columns are a direct measure of the success of an owner's player acquisitions, especially those added for only short-term time horizons.

The top owners are slightly better in every measure of this analysis. They add more net earnings, net more earnings per transaction, average among the most positive earnings per add and among the lowest losses per add. Perhaps not surprisingly, these owners are better at identifying short-term value.

With that said, it's still a bit comforting to see that nobody is perfect. Even these owners still end up adding a significant amount of losses in the week immediately after acquisition. Let this serve as a reminder that it's tough to predict baseball (or maybe even cognitive biases and mistakes in judgment ail us all).

League Finish	Earnings (Loss) in Week Following Transaction by League Finish					
	Next Week's Net Earnings	Next Week's Net Earnings per Add	Positive Next Week's Earnings	Next Week's Earnings Per Positive Add	Negative Next Week's Loss	Next Week's Loss Per Negative Add
1-2	$32.75	$0.64	$244.10	$10.20	($211.35)	($7.86)
3-4	$23.81	$0.50	$230.05	$10.21	($206.24)	($8.21)
5-6	$14.47	$0.31	$218.67	$9.80	($204.21)	($8.14)
7-8	$23.97	$0.56	$199.80	$9.91	($175.84)	($7.80)
9-10	$19.58	$0.49	$189.75	$10.36	($170.17)	($7.89)
11-12	($2.30)	($0.07)	$147.46	$9.31	($149.75)	($7.97)
13-15	$1.67	$0.06	$123.39	$9.46	($121.72)	($7.91)

It is remarkable to see just how much better those competing for the overall championship are at identifying short-term gains and limiting losses. They add nearly twice as much net earnings in the week following an acquisition.

Overall Finish	Earnings (Loss) in Week Following Transaction by Overall Finish					
	Next Week's Net Earnings	Next Week's Net Earnings per Add	Positive Next Week's Earnings	Next Week's Earnings Per Positive Add	Negative Next Week's Loss	Next Week's Loss Per Negative Add
1-25	$62.78	$1.09	$294.28	$10.90	($231.50)	($7.71)

Conclusion

These last segments analyzing the behaviors of the best owners was a bit tedious and mostly served to confirm what many owners already suspected. But that's what *The Process* is all about: Making decisions based on facts and not guesses wherever possible, seeking to continually improve by observing and learning from the behaviors of others, and monitoring trends in owners' actions and seeking to determine if they contribute to success. This study demonstrated that the ideas provided by this book are sound and verifiable at the highest levels of fantasy baseball competition.

Until next year...

Reference Material

The following appendices are included for reference:

- Appendix A – Steamer 600 Hitters
- Appendix B – Steamer 180 Starting Pitchers
- Appendix C – Steamer 60 Relievers
- Appendix D – Steamer Hitter OPS Splits
- Appendix E – Pitcher pERA Values, 2017 and 2019 Ball
- Appendix F – Pitcher pERA Values, 2016 and 2018 Ball
- Appendix G – Large Salaries
- Appendix H – Standings Gain Points for Different League Types
- Appendix I – Average League Standings

Name	POS	AB	R	HR	RBI	SB	AVG	OBP	SLG	OPS	K%	BB%	15-tm Mixed, Std.	15-tm Mixed, OBP	15-tm Draft & Hold	12-tm Mixed, Std.	12-tm, AL OBP	12-tm, NL OBP	12-tm, AL Std.	12-tm, NL Std.
Christian Yelich	OF	510	98	32	89	20	.301	.396	.562	.957	20.7%	12.7%	24.9	8.6	22.5	18.3	15.0	28.6	17.6	17.8
Ronald Acuna Jr.	CF	523	95	32	82	26	.281	.361	.522	.883	24.4%	10.2%	24.6	8.1	22.2	18.0	15.2	32.3	17.7	17.2
Mike Trout	OF	470	102	39	96	12	.294	.437	.605	1.041	20.4%	18.7%	24.2	8.8	21.9	17.9	14.5	23.8	16.7	17.1
Trea Turner	SS	537	91	19	67	34	.289	.352	.468	.820	18.6%	8.3%	23.8	6.2	21.4	17.2	14.7	36.4	17.6	17.0
Cody Bellinger	CF	509	93	38	105	11	.285	.384	.579	.963	18.2%	13.5%	23.7	8.3	21.5	17.6	14.2	22.9	16.3	16.4
Trevor Story	SS	536	85	33	98	18	.278	.345	.537	.882	26.5%	8.7%	23.0	6.9	20.8	17.0	14.0	26.4	16.3	15.8
Francisco Lindor	SS	536	95	30	84	18	.287	.352	.527	.879	14.4%	8.5%	23.0	6.6	20.8	16.9	13.8	26.5	16.3	16.3
Adalberto Mondesi	SS	559	72	17	69	45	.250	.288	.420	.709	27.2%	4.8%	23.0	4.9	20.4	16.4	15.0	43.0	17.6	15.3
Jose Ramirez	3B	523	87	28	92	22	.276	.360	.518	.878	13.1%	11.1%	22.8	6.5	20.6	16.7	14.0	28.5	16.3	15.7
Mookie Betts	RF	511	103	28	82	16	.295	.389	.539	.928	14.4%	12.6%	22.8	6.6	20.6	16.7	13.5	25.1	16.0	16.4
Giancarlo Stanton	LF	521	99	47	112	3	.266	.354	.586	.939	29.4%	11.0%	22.5	8.1	20.5	16.9	13.5	17.1	15.2	15.1
Luis Robert	OF	554	79	29	86	24	.273	.317	.499	.816	26.1%	4.9%	22.4	5.4	20.2	16.4	13.7	29.1	16.2	15.3
J.D. Martinez	DH	527	94	36	108	2	.300	.377	.572	.949	22.8%	10.6%	22.2	6.9	20.2	16.6	12.8	16.4	15.0	15.8
Nolan Arenado	3B	529	91	36	103	3	.295	.369	.568	.938	16.2%	10.2%	21.6	6.0	19.6	16.1	12.4	16.3	14.6	15.2
Rafael Devers	3B	544	86	29	97	9	.297	.353	.540	.893	17.8%	7.6%	21.4	5.1	19.4	15.8	12.3	19.3	14.8	15.2
Juan Soto	LF	495	93	31	95	8	.290	.405	.550	.954	18.9%	15.8%	21.3	5.6	19.3	15.8	12.6	19.6	14.7	15.0
Starling Marte	CF	549	79	20	73	25	.285	.335	.464	.799	17.9%	5.3%	21.1	3.4	19.0	15.3	12.7	28.8	15.4	14.9
Yordan Alvarez	DH	516	95	38	100	4	.274	.365	.550	.915	24.4%	12.0%	20.7	5.5	18.7	15.5	12.1	16.3	14.0	14.1
Freddie Freeman	1B	515	90	30	94	6	.292	.384	.538	.922	19.0%	12.2%	20.4	4.4	18.5	15.1	11.8	17.3	14.0	14.4
Shohei Ohtani	DH	533	80	29	88	13	.278	.348	.511	.859	25.8%	9.2%	20.3	3.7	18.4	15.0	12.1	21.7	14.4	14.0
Bryce Harper	RF	492	92	36	92	10	.258	.382	.537	.919	24.9%	16.2%	20.3	4.9	18.4	15.1	12.1	20.1	14.1	13.6
Nelson Cruz	DH	525	90	37	105	1	.280	.361	.542	.903	24.6%	10.0%	20.3	5.0	18.4	15.2	11.8	14.5	13.7	14.0
Alex Bregman	3B	499	99	29	90	6	.285	.395	.537	.932	12.8%	14.2%	20.2	4.6	18.3	15.0	11.8	17.5	13.8	14.2
Byron Buxton	OF	545	79	21	79	25	.258	.314	.455	.769	25.8%	6.8%	20.2	3.1	18.0	14.6	12.5	28.9	14.8	13.5
Javier Baez	SS	558	77	30	91	14	.270	.310	.500	.809	26.8%	5.1%	20.0	3.4	18.0	14.7	11.9	21.6	14.2	13.6
Kyle Tucker	LF	537	83	29	85	20	.245	.313	.463	.776	24.2%	8.1%	19.9	3.5	17.8	14.6	12.4	25.9	14.3	12.9
Jose Altuve	2B	536	87	22	85	11	.294	.359	.483	.842	14.8%	8.5%	19.7	3.0	17.8	14.5	11.3	19.7	13.8	14.1
Jonathan Villar	2B	535	76	18	64	30	.260	.329	.419	.748	25.4%	8.8%	19.7	1.8	17.6	14.2	12.2	31.2	14.7	13.3
Austin Meadows	RF	536	82	27	83	14	.270	.336	.491	.827	20.4%	8.2%	19.4	2.8	17.5	14.3	11.6	21.6	13.8	13.3
Gleyber Torres	2B	535	85	33	93	7	.270	.338	.504	.842	20.6%	8.7%	19.3	3.4	17.5	14.4	11.3	17.1	13.4	13.1
Charlie Blackmon	RF	537	93	27	75	7	.293	.355	.517	.873	18.3%	7.7%	19.3	2.6	17.5	14.3	10.9	17.4	13.4	14.0
Yasiel Puig	RF	535	78	27	84	16	.264	.332	.471	.803	20.6%	8.7%	19.2	2.5	17.2	14.1	11.5	22.4	13.7	12.9
George Springer	CF	515	99	31	80	7	.272	.363	.506	.870	19.9%	11.5%	19.2	3.3	17.3	14.2	11.2	17.5	13.3	13.3
Aaron Judge	RF	496	95	36	91	6	.252	.371	.520	.891	30.8%	15.2%	19.2	4.0	17.3	14.3	11.5	16.8	13.1	12.7
Bo Bichette	SS	546	75	20	75	20	.272	.325	.458	.783	20.4%	6.9%	19.1	1.7	17.1	13.9	11.4	25.1	13.9	13.1
Jarren Duran	OF	552	72	9	65	28	.281	.327	.408	.735	23.3%	5.7%	19.1	0.7	17.0	13.7	11.5	29.7	14.2	13.4
Fernando Tatis Jr.	SS	537	72	26	78	19	.260	.326	.470	.796	27.4%	8.0%	19.0	1.9	17.1	13.9	11.5	24.4	13.8	12.7
Anthony Rizzo	1B	505	88	28	89	5	.282	.387	.518	.905	14.1%	11.7%	19.0	2.9	17.1	14.1	11.0	16.1	13.0	13.2
Ozzie Albies	2B	542	85	22	75	13	.285	.342	.486	.829	15.4%	7.4%	18.9	1.9	17.1	13.9	10.9	20.4	13.4	13.4
Victor Robles	CF	538	75	16	67	27	.260	.324	.418	.743	21.0%	6.4%	18.9	1.2	16.9	13.6	11.7	29.1	14.1	12.8
Anthony Rendon	3B	515	86	25	89	4	.295	.386	.520	.905	14.2%	11.8%	18.8	2.5	17.0	14.0	10.6	15.0	12.9	13.4
Tommy Pham	LF	513	83	22	74	17	.268	.364	.457	.821	21.9%	12.1%	18.8	1.9	16.9	13.7	11.3	23.1	13.5	12.9
Keston Hiura	2B	542	76	28	84	12	.269	.328	.491	.819	26.5%	6.8%	18.8	2.0	16.9	13.8	11.1	20.1	13.3	12.7
Carlos Correa	SS	522	88	31	99	3	.271	.357	.514	.871	21.6%	11.4%	18.7	3.2	16.9	14.0	10.9	14.4	12.7	12.7
Eddie Rosario	LF	561	82	28	91	5	.283	.319	.498	.816	16.5%	5.0%	18.7	2.3	17.0	13.9	10.6	15.4	12.9	13.1
Manny Machado	3B	534	83	33	88	6	.270	.341	.511	.852	17.7%	9.4%	18.7	2.5	16.9	13.9	10.9	16.3	13.0	12.7
Joc Pederson	RF	518	89	37	94	4	.254	.344	.533	.878	21.0%	10.5%	18.7	3.3	16.9	14.0	11.1	15.1	12.8	12.3
Joey Gallo	DH	500	86	41	94	7	.228	.345	.523	.868	35.3%	14.4%	18.4	3.3	16.6	13.8	11.4	17.5	12.8	11.5
Kyle Schwarber	LF	511	86	37	94	5	.251	.352	.523	.875	26.5%	12.8%	18.4	2.9	16.6	13.8	11.0	15.5	12.7	12.0
Xander Bogaerts	SS	527	85	23	87	5	.290	.367	.495	.862	17.6%	10.2%	18.4	1.9	16.6	13.6	10.4	15.7	12.7	13.1
Marcell Ozuna	LF	537	77	29	92	7	.275	.343	.490	.832	20.2%	9.1%	18.4	2.0	16.6	13.7	10.6	16.3	12.8	12.6
Ryan Braun	LF	543	78	28	87	10	.267	.327	.484	.811	20.5%	7.5%	18.4	1.9	16.6	13.6	10.8	18.5	13.0	12.4
Eloy Jimenez	LF	549	80	34	91	2	.277	.326	.516	.843	22.7%	6.3%	18.2	2.0	16.5	13.6	10.3	13.2	12.5	12.5
Yuli Gurriel	1B	554	80	24	91	5	.287	.332	.487	.819	12.2%	5.5%	18.2	1.7	16.4	13.5	10.2	14.9	12.5	12.8
Mike Moustakas	3B	539	83	36	94	3	.262	.328	.515	.843	17.4%	8.2%	18.2	2.4	16.4	13.6	10.5	13.9	12.5	12.1
Mallex Smith	CF	535	64	7	50	39	.248	.316	.358	.674	22.1%	8.1%	18.0	-0.8	15.9	12.7	11.6	36.1	14.2	11.9
Gary Sanchez	C	527	87	40	100	2	.241	.323	.512	.835	25.6%	9.5%	18.0	2.9	16.2	13.5	10.7	13.7	12.2	11.4
Franmil Reyes	DH	535	83	37	96	1	.258	.328	.511	.839	25.9%	9.1%	17.9	2.3	16.2	13.4	10.4	13.0	12.2	11.8
Howie Kendrick	1B	544	79	19	79	6	.304	.359	.476	.835	16.1%	6.9%	17.8	0.5	16.1	13.1	9.7	15.1	12.4	13.1
Ramon Laureano	RF	538	78	23	76	15	.262	.326	.453	.779	25.0%	7.5%	17.8	0.8	15.9	13.0	10.6	20.9	12.8	12.0
Garrett Hampson	2B	543	66	11	63	27	.269	.326	.400	.726	21.1%	7.5%	17.8	-0.6	15.8	12.7	10.8	28.0	13.4	12.2
Miguel Sano	3B	521	87	38	99	1	.245	.336	.515	.851	34.8%	11.6%	17.8	2.6	16.0	13.3	10.5	13.2	12.0	11.4
Peter Alonso	1B	518	83	39	94	2	.250	.341	.524	.868	25.3%	11.7%	17.7	2.2	16.0	13.3	12.1	13.3	12.1	11.5
Josh Rojas	LF	532	67	16	67	23	.262	.335	.430	.765	19.9%	9.3%	17.7	-0.3	15.8	12.8	10.7	26.1	13.2	11.9
Edwin Encarnacion	DH	517	86	37	99	2	.244	.340	.500	.840	23.1%	11.7%	17.6	2.5	15.9	13.2	10.5	13.2	11.9	11.2
Tim Anderson	SS	563	70	20	70	17	.274	.307	.438	.744	22.4%	4.0%	17.6	-0.2	15.8	12.8	10.2	21.6	12.8	12.2
Kris Bryant	3B	507	90	28	81	4	.272	.375	.504	.878	22.5%	12.0%	17.5	1.4	15.8	13.0	10.0	14.5	12.0	12.0
Vladimir Guerrero Jr.	3B	533	80	24	81	3	.292	.360	.495	.855	15.8%	9.0%	17.5	0.6	15.8	12.9	9.6	13.6	12.1	12.5
Paul Goldschmidt	1B	513	83	28	84	5	.271	.368	.491	.859	23.9%	12.6%	17.4	1.2	15.7	12.9	10.0	14.8	12.1	11.9
Matt Olson	1B	520	85	35	94	1	.253	.342	.510	.852	24.6%	10.6%	17.4	1.9	15.7	13.0	10.2	12.8	11.8	11.3

Name	POS	AB	R	HR	RBI	SB	AVG	OBP	SLG	OPS	K%	BB%	15-tm Mixed, Std.	15-tm Mixed, OBP	15-tm Draft & Hold	12-tm Mixed, Std.	12-tm AL, OBP	12-tm NL, OBP	12-tm AL Std.	12-tm NL Std.
C.J. Cron	1B	542	83	32	92	2	.263	.325	.497	.821	23.3%	6.6%	17.3	1.5	15.7	12.9	10.0	12.9	11.8	11.6
Whit Merrifield	2B	544	76	12	58	20	.281	.336	.424	.760	16.6%	6.9%	17.3	-0.8	15.5	12.5	10.1	23.8	12.8	12.3
Ketel Marte	SS	537	74	20	77	8	.292	.356	.490	.846	14.0%	8.5%	17.3	-0.1	15.6	12.7	9.7	16.1	12.2	12.4
Alonzo Harris	2b	540	68	22	71	23	.237	.302	.411	.713	23.7%	7.8%	17.3	-0.1	15.4	12.5	10.8	26.0	12.9	11.0
Randy Arozarena	OF	537	68	17	69	20	.265	.330	.427	.757	21.1%	7.1%	17.3	-0.5	15.4	12.5	10.3	23.8	12.8	11.7
Michael Brantley	LF	540	85	19	80	5	.287	.348	.462	.810	11.7%	7.9%	17.1	0.4	15.4	12.6	9.5	14.6	11.9	12.2
David Dahl	OF	546	76	23	81	9	.271	.327	.473	.799	26.0%	7.0%	17.1	0.2	15.4	12.6	9.9	17.0	12.1	11.7
Andrew Benintendi	LF	525	86	17	73	12	.272	.352	.453	.805	19.5%	10.3%	17.1	0.2	15.3	12.5	10.0	18.9	12.1	11.9
Yoan Moncada	3B	530	80	24	71	11	.265	.339	.470	.809	27.5%	9.5%	17.1	0.2	15.4	12.6	10.0	18.3	12.2	11.6
Jose Abreu	1B	545	77	29	89	2	.274	.331	.493	.825	21.2%	6.4%	17.1	0.7	15.5	12.7	9.6	12.9	11.8	11.7
Lourdes Gurriel Jr.	LF	556	77	26	80	9	.263	.305	.466	.771	23.1%	4.8%	17.1	0.3	15.4	12.6	9.9	16.8	12.1	11.5
Josh Donaldson	3B	501	91	31	81	4	.256	.368	.495	.863	23.9%	14.3%	17.1	1.3	15.4	12.7	10.0	14.4	11.7	11.4
Marcus Semien	SS	526	84	22	73	10	.268	.346	.462	.807	16.4%	10.3%	17.1	0.3	15.3	12.5	9.9	17.9	12.1	11.7
Khris Davis	DH	531	83	37	99	1	.241	.320	.495	.815	28.1%	9.5%	17.0	1.7	15.3	12.7	10.0	12.2	11.5	10.7
Rougned Odor	2B	539	75	29	81	14	.233	.300	.452	.752	27.1%	7.6%	16.9	0.5	15.1	12.4	10.4	20.2	12.2	10.6
Nick Madrigal	2b	549	64	6	57	24	.284	.333	.385	.718	6.1%	6.0%	16.9	-2.0	13.1	12.1	11.9	25.9	12.8	12.0
Yoenis Cespedes	OF	539	79	32	87	5	.253	.319	.485	.804	26.2%	8.2%	16.9	0.7	15.2	12.6	9.9	14.5	11.7	11.0
Jorge Soler	DH	517	81	32	87	4	.256	.348	.498	.846	26.8%	11.3%	16.9	0.9	15.2	12.6	9.8	13.7	11.6	11.1
Danny Santana	3B	554	70	20	72	20	.247	.293	.425	.717	27.7%	5.4%	16.9	-0.6	15.0	12.2	10.3	23.4	12.4	10.9
Justin Turner	3B	522	84	25	82	2	.279	.363	.483	.846	15.7%	9.5%	16.8	0.4	15.2	12.5	9.4	12.9	11.6	11.7
Amed Rosario	SS	555	68	14	64	19	.274	.316	.420	.736	18.0%	5.4%	16.8	-1.3	15.0	12.2	9.8	22.7	12.5	11.7
Matt Chapman	3B	522	85	31	88	2	.255	.341	.505	.847	23.5%	10.4%	16.8	1.0	15.2	12.5	9.8	13.1	11.5	11.1
Max Kepler	CF	524	82	28	86	5	.258	.341	.484	.825	17.1%	10.4%	16.8	0.7	15.1	12.5	9.8	14.6	11.6	11.1
Vance Vizcaino	OF	546	64	13	62	25	.258	.313	.392	.705	26.0%	6.9%	16.8	-1.5	14.9	12.0	10.2	26.6	12.7	11.2
Aristides Aquino	RF	548	73	35	87	8	.239	.293	.477	.770	28.0%	6.4%	16.8	0.6	15.1	12.5	10.1	16.2	11.8	10.5
Lorenzo Cain	CF	532	77	14	60	17	.275	.347	.412	.759	17.2%	9.0%	16.8	-1.1	15.0	12.1	9.8	21.8	12.3	11.8
Sam Hilliard	LF	544	70	23	74	17	.247	.305	.433	.738	30.4%	7.4%	16.8	-0.5	15.0	12.2	10.2	21.9	12.3	10.8
Oscar Mercado	CF	544	69	15	67	22	.254	.311	.398	.709	19.4%	6.8%	16.7	-1.1	14.8	12.0	10.2	24.8	12.5	11.0
Josh Bell	1B	514	79	27	86	2	.273	.368	.499	.867	18.9%	12.7%	16.7	0.3	15.1	12.4	9.5	12.8	11.5	11.4
Daulton Varsho	C	544	67	20	71	15	.266	.323	.440	.764	17.4%	6.8%	16.6	-1.0	14.9	12.1	9.7	20.3	12.1	11.2
J.T. Realmuto	C	543	76	25	80	6	.268	.327	.473	.801	20.9%	7.1%	16.6	-0.2	15.0	12.3	9.5	15.1	11.7	11.3
Willians Astudillo	1B	565	73	19	78	5	.293	.323	.450	.773	6.5%	3.1%	16.6	-0.9	15.0	12.2	9.0	14.1	11.6	11.9
Ian Desmond	LF	543	73	23	79	10	.262	.322	.455	.777	24.7%	7.5%	16.6	-0.4	14.9	12.1	9.7	17.4	11.8	11.1
Daniel Murphy	1B	547	77	22	82	3	.287	.340	.482	.821	15.2%	7.0%	16.6	-0.3	15.0	12.3	9.1	12.7	11.5	11.7
Daniel Johnson	OF	547	73	19	74	14	.263	.316	.436	.752	23.4%	6.3%	16.6	-0.7	14.8	12.1	9.7	19.6	12.0	11.2
Nicholas Castellanos	RF	546	79	26	86	3	.271	.328	.490	.817	22.6%	7.1%	16.5	0.1	14.9	12.3	9.3	12.9	11.4	11.3
Michael Conforto	RF	506	83	30	82	5	.250	.357	.486	.842	23.8%	13.0%	16.5	0.5	14.9	12.3	9.7	14.7	11.5	10.8
Austin Hays	CF	557	72	25	77	11	.256	.296	.450	.746	21.5%	4.8%	16.5	-0.5	14.8	12.1	9.7	17.8	11.8	10.9
Eugenio Suarez	3B	518	78	32	88	3	.251	.344	.489	.833	26.5%	11.2%	16.5	0.5	14.9	12.3	9.6	13.2	11.4	10.7
Nomar Mazara	RF	542	76	27	86	4	.267	.329	.472	.801	21.4%	7.6%	16.5	-0.1	14.8	12.2	9.5	13.4	11.4	11.1
Evan Gattis	DH	542	74	33	91	3	.250	.311	.485	.797	21.8%	7.4%	16.4	0.3	14.8	12.3	9.6	13.0	11.3	10.5
Elvis Andrus	SS	550	68	13	65	20	.266	.317	.401	.718	15.4%	6.4%	16.4	-1.7	14.6	11.8	9.7	23.1	12.2	11.2
Luis Castro	3b	534	73	20	75	8	.279	.347	.457	.804	21.0%	7.9%	16.4	-0.9	14.8	12.1	9.3	16.0	11.6	11.4
Andrew McCutchen	OF	512	82	27	77	7	.255	.354	.467	.821	22.6%	12.5%	16.4	0.0	14.7	12.1	9.6	15.9	11.5	10.9
Jonathan Schoop	2B	556	78	28	88	2	.264	.307	.477	.784	23.3%	4.7%	16.4	0.0	14.7	12.2	9.3	12.4	11.3	10.9
Willie Calhoun	LF	539	77	27	83	3	.271	.333	.479	.811	15.1%	7.9%	16.4	-0.3	14.8	12.2	9.2	12.6	11.3	11.1
Jeff McNeil	RF	540	77	18	70	8	.286	.345	.458	.803	13.4%	6.4%	16.3	-1.1	14.7	12.0	9.1	15.5	11.6	11.7
Didi Gregorius	SS	553	76	25	86	6	.261	.310	.456	.766	14.1%	5.9%	16.3	-0.3	14.7	12.1	9.4	14.5	11.4	10.8
Mike Ford	1B	522	83	31	86	2	.252	.337	.478	.815	19.3%	10.4%	16.2	0.4	14.6	12.1	9.4	12.5	11.1	10.6
Rhys Hoskins	1B	495	88	32	83	3	.241	.364	.496	.860	23.3%	15.1%	16.2	0.6	14.6	12.1	9.7	13.6	11.2	10.4
Jean Segura	SS	551	78	14	59	12	.286	.333	.430	.763	12.5%	5.7%	16.2	-1.7	14.6	11.8	9.0	18.1	11.7	11.7
Maikel Franco	3B	540	75	31	89	1	.260	.324	.486	.809	15.0%	8.4%	16.1	-0.1	14.6	12.1	9.2	11.7	11.1	10.6
Randal Grichuk	RF	549	78	33	89	3	.244	.297	.495	.792	26.9%	6.3%	16.1	0.2	14.5	12.0	9.4	13.1	11.1	10.2
Miguel Andujar	3b	558	75	25	86	4	.266	.307	.465	.772	17.2%	5.0%	16.1	-0.5	14.5	11.9	9.1	13.1	11.2	10.8
Tommy Edman	3B	552	65	13	67	17	.273	.320	.418	.738	16.8%	5.7%	16.1	-2.1	14.4	11.6	9.3	20.9	11.9	11.1
Yonathan Daza	CF	559	65	9	65	13	.299	.335	.422	.756	15.8%	4.7%	16.1	-2.5	14.4	11.6	8.8	18.4	11.7	11.8
Adam Eaton	RF	520	84	14	59	12	.281	.365	.430	.795	17.3%	10.0%	16.0	-1.5	14.4	11.6	9.1	18.2	11.5	11.5
Wilmer Flores	2B	549	72	23	82	2	.286	.336	.479	.815	12.1%	6.2%	16.0	-1.1	14.5	11.9	8.7	11.5	11.1	11.2
Delino DeShields	CF	525	70	9	49	31	.239	.323	.348	.671	23.9%	10.3%	16.0	-2.3	14.1	11.3	10.1	30.0	12.4	10.4
A.J. Pollock	LF	542	77	24	77	10	.252	.314	.445	.758	21.1%	7.0%	16.0	-0.8	14.3	11.8	9.4	16.9	11.4	10.5
Carlos Santana	1B	498	86	27	81	3	.258	.374	.478	.853	15.7%	15.1%	16.0	0.0	14.4	11.9	9.2	12.9	11.0	10.6
Trey Mancini	RF	537	78	27	81	1	.271	.337	.482	.819	22.5%	8.2%	16.0	-0.6	14.4	11.9	8.9	11.6	11.0	10.9
Dee Gordon	2B	561	64	5	46	28	.272	.306	.357	.664	14.7%	3.8%	15.9	-3.3	14.1	11.3	10.1	27.2	12.3	11.2
Ryan Zimmerman	1B	540	75	27	89	2	.261	.326	.471	.797	21.2%	8.1%	15.9	-0.4	14.3	11.8	9.0	11.9	10.9	10.5
Alex Verdugo	OF	542	73	19	75	7	.280	.338	.448	.786	14.1%	7.5%	15.9	-1.4	14.3	11.7	8.8	14.6	11.2	11.1
Paul DeJong	SS	536	73	27	83	7	.251	.321	.461	.781	23.5%	8.0%	15.8	-0.7	14.2	11.7	9.2	14.8	11.1	10.2
Nick Solak	3B	532	74	22	74	8	.267	.338	.443	.782	21.8%	8.7%	15.8	-1.3	14.2	11.6	9.0	15.6	11.2	10.7
Jorge Polanco	SS	539	78	17	75	7	.279	.342	.449	.792	16.5%	8.3%	15.8	-1.4	14.2	11.6	8.8	14.7	11.1	11.1
Ryan McMahon	2B	533	73	23	79	6	.266	.336	.458	.794	26.5%	9.1%	15.7	-1.2	14.1	11.6	9.0	14.5	11.1	10.6
Corey Seager	SS	532	86	22	73	2	.276	.347	.474	.821	18.1%	9.1%	15.7	-1.0	14.2	11.6	8.7	12.1	10.9	11.0

Name	POS	AB	R	HR	RBI	SB	AVG	OBP	SLG	OPS	K%	BB%	15-tm Mixed, Std.	15-tm Mixed, OBP	15-tm Draft & Hold	12-tm Mixed, Std.	12-tm, AL, OBP	12-tm, NL, OBP	12-tm, AL Std.	12-tm, NL Std.
Nick Senzel	OF	540	66	18	69	16	.256	.319	.429	.748	24.1%	7.9%	15.7	-2.0	14.0	11.4	9.3	20.1	11.5	10.4
Avisail Garcia	DH	547	71	22	79	8	.262	.317	.438	.755	24.1%	6.4%	15.7	-1.3	14.1	11.6	9.0	15.2	11.1	10.4
Roman Quinn	CF	537	65	13	59	26	.238	.306	.372	.678	26.9%	8.2%	15.7	-2.4	13.8	11.2	9.8	26.8	12.0	10.0
Michael A. Taylor	CF	545	65	17	67	23	.234	.293	.386	.680	31.3%	7.3%	15.6	-2.1	13.8	11.2	9.7	24.4	11.8	9.7
Tyler Naquin	OF	548	71	19	75	8	.271	.322	.441	.763	24.0%	6.4%	15.6	-1.7	14.0	11.4	8.8	15.0	11.0	10.6
DJ LeMahieu	1B	540	82	17	67	5	.283	.343	.431	.774	14.6%	7.8%	15.5	-1.7	14.0	11.4	8.5	13.8	10.9	11.1
Hunter Pence	DH	546	71	22	75	8	.265	.321	.441	.763	23.3%	7.1%	15.5	-1.7	13.9	11.4	8.8	15.0	11.0	10.5
Kevin Kiermaier	CF	541	73	18	65	19	.238	.301	.406	.706	23.1%	7.2%	15.5	-1.9	13.8	11.2	9.5	22.5	11.5	9.9
Alex Kirilloff	OF	554	73	17	73	8	.276	.320	.431	.751	19.0%	5.4%	15.5	-2.0	13.9	11.3	8.6	15.2	11.0	10.7
Corey Dickerson	RF	554	75	24	79	4	.265	.310	.471	.781	21.5%	5.7%	15.5	-1.4	13.9	11.4	8.7	13.0	10.8	10.4
Jordan Luplow	LF	524	77	23	75	9	.248	.332	.443	.775	22.4%	10.2%	15.5	-1.2	13.8	11.4	9.1	16.2	11.0	10.0
Roberto Ramos	1B	535	74	27	81	3	.261	.329	.470	.799	29.1%	8.6%	15.4	-1.2	13.9	11.5	8.7	12.0	10.7	10.2
Trent Grisham	RF	519	73	23	74	10	.250	.340	.445	.785	21.3%	11.4%	15.4	-1.5	13.8	11.3	9.1	16.8	11.1	10.0
Kevin Cron	DH	535	73	32	84	3	.245	.315	.480	.795	27.7%	8.3%	15.4	-0.9	13.9	11.5	8.9	12.3	10.7	9.8
Manuel Margot	CF	541	67	16	60	20	.249	.310	.404	.714	18.7%	7.7%	15.4	-2.5	13.7	11.1	9.3	22.5	11.6	10.1
Jarrod Dyson	CF	529	61	9	52	30	.238	.316	.349	.665	18.5%	9.3%	15.4	-3.2	13.5	10.9	9.7	28.7	12.0	9.8
Steven Souza Jr.	OF	522	73	25	77	10	.242	.329	.448	.778	29.5%	10.6%	15.4	-1.3	13.7	11.3	9.2	16.6	11.0	9.7
Raimel Tapia	CF	557	67	12	66	14	.276	.315	.415	.730	21.3%	5.2%	15.4	-2.7	13.7	11.1	8.7	18.7	11.3	10.7
Kevin Newman	SS	551	58	9	62	18	.281	.327	.398	.724	13.1%	5.7%	15.3	-3.4	13.7	11.1	8.7	20.5	11.5	10.8
Lane Thomas	OF	540	67	21	71	15	.243	.307	.420	.727	26.2%	7.7%	15.3	-2.0	13.6	11.2	9.2	19.4	11.2	9.7
D.J. Stewart	RF	525	72	23	72	10	.250	.332	.434	.767	21.8%	9.8%	15.3	-1.7	13.7	11.2	9.0	16.8	11.0	9.9
Gavin Lux	2B	540	70	19	72	10	.264	.326	.433	.759	20.7%	8.2%	15.3	-2.1	13.7	11.2	8.8	16.3	11.0	10.3
Josh VanMeter	LF	533	67	20	69	14	.249	.322	.425	.747	20.7%	9.2%	15.3	-2.2	13.6	11.1	9.1	19.1	11.2	9.9
Rusney Castillo	OF	559	69	14	71	10	.279	.316	.411	.727	17.0%	4.5%	15.3	-2.5	13.7	11.1	8.5	15.8	11.0	10.7
Bobby Dalbec	3b	531	78	28	82	6	.239	.315	.448	.762	30.1%	8.7%	15.2	-1.0	13.6	11.3	9.0	14.1	10.7	9.6
Eric Thames	1B	515	82	30	77	6	.232	.328	.464	.792	30.8%	11.3%	15.2	-0.8	13.6	11.3	9.1	14.5	10.7	9.5
Kurt Suzuki	C	543	72	25	85	2	.265	.324	.455	.779	13.1%	6.1%	15.2	-1.4	13.7	11.3	8.5	11.4	10.5	10.1
Josh Reddick	RF	543	76	20	77	6	.266	.326	.430	.756	14.6%	8.1%	15.2	-1.7	13.6	11.2	8.6	13.7	10.7	10.3
Austin Riley	LF	546	73	30	85	3	.247	.303	.467	.769	29.2%	6.6%	15.2	-1.2	13.6	11.3	8.7	11.9	10.5	9.6
Aaron Hicks	OF	511	81	25	76	8	.238	.341	.438	.778	23.0%	13.0%	15.2	-1.1	13.5	11.2	9.1	15.3	10.7	9.6
David Peralta	OF	539	77	21	72	3	.277	.339	.468	.807	20.3%	7.8%	15.1	-2.0	13.7	11.2	8.3	11.9	10.6	10.6
Wil Myers	CF	528	72	23	68	16	.228	.310	.412	.722	31.1%	10.1%	15.1	-1.9	13.4	11.0	9.4	20.5	11.1	9.3
Max Muncy	1B	500	81	29	80	4	.239	.354	.463	.817	26.2%	14.2%	15.1	-0.8	13.6	11.2	8.9	12.9	10.5	9.6
Salvador Perez	C	561	71	29	88	2	.249	.288	.460	.749	20.8%	4.0%	15.1	-1.3	13.6	11.3	8.6	11.6	10.5	9.6
Jay Bruce	LF	541	74	33	90	3	.232	.298	.469	.767	24.7%	8.3%	15.1	-0.8	13.6	11.3	9.0	12.2	10.5	9.2
Kolten Wong	2B	524	65	13	64	17	.264	.345	.405	.750	15.6%	8.9%	15.1	-2.9	13.5	10.9	8.8	20.2	11.2	10.2
Victor Reyes	LF	562	62	11	62	17	.271	.305	.396	.701	19.1%	4.5%	15.1	-3.3	13.4	10.9	8.6	20.1	11.2	10.4
Jarred Kelenic	OF	548	67	21	71	13	.245	.299	.421	.720	24.2%	6.5%	15.1	-2.3	13.4	11.0	8.9	18.2	11.0	9.6
Yasmani Grandal	C	500	77	28	82	4	.243	.359	.468	.827	23.5%	14.8%	15.0	-1.1	13.5	11.2	8.8	12.7	10.5	9.6
Mitch Moreland	1B	532	78	26	87	2	.249	.324	.464	.788	23.2%	9.5%	15.0	-1.1	13.5	11.2	8.7	11.7	10.3	9.6
Matt Adams	1B	544	74	31	90	2	.239	.299	.462	.760	28.5%	7.3%	15.0	-0.9	13.5	11.2	8.8	11.4	10.4	9.3
Anthony Santander	LF	554	71	24	77	5	.259	.304	.449	.753	19.9%	5.4%	15.0	-2.0	13.5	11.1	8.5	13.4	10.6	9.9
Bryan Reynolds	LF	538	68	17	70	6	.286	.348	.448	.797	21.2%	8.1%	15.0	-2.7	13.5	11.0	8.2	13.5	10.7	10.7
Ian Happ	2B	518	74	26	77	9	.237	.330	.440	.770	29.2%	11.6%	15.0	-1.5	13.4	11.1	9.0	15.8	10.7	9.4
Colton Welker	3b	549	69	17	72	4	.288	.337	.445	.782	18.7%	6.4%	15.0	-2.6	13.5	11.1	8.1	12.5	10.6	10.7
Brian Dozier	2B	520	83	25	70	8	.241	.331	.440	.770	21.5%	11.0%	15.0	-1.5	13.4	11.0	8.9	15.5	10.6	9.6
Hunter Renfroe	RF	545	72	33	87	4	.232	.293	.463	.756	28.8%	7.3%	15.0	-1.1	13.5	11.2	8.9	12.9	10.5	9.1
Brett Gardner	CF	526	84	20	64	12	.245	.326	.419	.745	19.5%	9.8%	15.0	-1.9	13.4	10.9	8.9	17.6	10.8	9.8
Dylan Carlson	OF	536	67	19	70	13	.252	.320	.424	.745	21.5%	8.3%	15.0	-2.5	13.3	10.9	8.8	17.8	10.9	9.8
J.D. Davis	LF	538	70	25	80	3	.262	.327	.457	.784	23.1%	8.3%	14.9	-1.9	13.4	11.1	8.4	12.0	10.5	9.9
Rowdy Tellez	1B	538	74	27	81	4	.248	.315	.457	.772	24.6%	8.1%	14.9	-1.5	13.4	11.1	8.6	12.6	10.4	9.6
Jose Peraza	2B	555	66	12	57	16	.271	.310	.392	.706	13.4%	4.7%	14.9	-3.5	13.3	10.7	8.5	19.7	11.1	10.3
Brendan Rodgers	SS	551	69	19	74	5	.276	.324	.444	.768	21.1%	5.5%	14.9	-2.6	13.4	11.0	8.2	12.9	10.5	10.3
Cameron Maybin	LF	525	73	15	62	18	.243	.326	.378	.704	24.3%	10.4%	14.9	-2.6	13.2	10.7	9.0	21.4	11.1	9.6
Gregory Polanco	OF	532	72	22	75	9	.246	.322	.440	.761	23.1%	9.5%	14.9	-2.0	13.3	10.9	8.8	16.0	10.7	9.5
Michael Chavis	2B	540	76	26	81	4	.245	.309	.444	.753	28.4%	7.5%	14.9	-1.5	13.3	11.0	8.6	12.8	10.4	9.5
Tyler Nevin	3b	539	70	17	71	6	.281	.343	.439	.782	17.6%	8.1%	14.9	-2.7	13.3	10.9	8.1	13.3	10.5	10.4
Aledmys Diaz	SS	543	76	21	78	5	.258	.317	.437	.753	15.4%	7.1%	14.8	-1.9	13.3	10.9	8.4	13.3	10.4	9.8
Tyler O'Neill	DH	545	71	29	83	6	.235	.294	.443	.736	32.0%	7.2%	14.8	-1.6	13.3	11.0	8.8	13.8	10.5	9.1
Mark Canha	CF	517	79	25	78	4	.249	.341	.456	.797	23.3%	10.1%	14.8	-1.5	13.3	11.0	8.6	12.8	10.3	9.6
Jake Bauers	LF	520	73	20	72	12	.241	.332	.414	.746	24.5%	11.4%	14.8	-2.1	13.2	10.8	8.9	17.9	10.7	9.4
Alec Bohm	3b	543	69	22	75	5	.264	.322	.447	.769	17.5%	7.4%	14.8	-2.3	13.3	10.9	8.3	13.1	10.5	9.9
Jesse Winker	LF	517	75	20	68	4	.277	.366	.455	.821	16.1%	11.2%	14.8	-2.4	13.3	10.9	8.1	12.2	10.4	10.4
Jake Fraley	OF	548	65	17	66	17	.242	.296	.403	.699	23.8%	6.1%	14.8	-2.9	13.1	10.7	8.9	20.7	11.0	9.4
Drew Weeks	OF	548	68	20	72	10	.257	.310	.428	.737	22.1%	6.1%	14.8	-2.6	13.2	10.8	8.5	16.0	10.7	9.7
Ryan Mountcastle	SS	563	70	23	77	3	.268	.302	.449	.751	23.1%	4.0%	14.8	-2.4	13.3	10.9	8.1	11.7	10.4	10.0
Yadiel Hernandez	OF	536	70	21	74	6	.265	.332	.430	.762	24.4%	8.8%	14.8	-2.4	13.3	10.9	8.3	13.6	10.5	9.9
Willson Contreras	C	524	73	23	81	4	.256	.340	.453	.793	23.8%	10.0%	14.8	-1.8	13.3	11.0	8.5	12.6	10.3	9.6
Travis Jones	OF	539	63	11	59	21	.252	.317	.373	.690	24.8%	6.7%	14.8	-3.5	13.1	10.6	8.9	22.6	11.2	9.7
Stephen Piscotty	RF	534	76	23	79	3	.260	.331	.455	.786	21.3%	8.5%	14.8	-1.9	13.2	10.9	8.3	11.8	10.3	9.8

Name	POS	AB	R	HR	RBI	SB	AVG	OBP	SLG	OPS	K%	BB%	15-tm Mixed, Std.	15-tm Mixed, OBP	15-tm Draft & Hold	12-tm Mixed, Std.	12-tm, AL, OBP	12-tm, NL, OBP	12-tm, AL, Std.	12-tm, NL, Std.
Ender Inciarte	CF	537	72	10	54	18	.263	.328	.381	.709	15.5%	8.2%	14.8	-3.4	13.1	10.6	8.6	20.8	11.0	10.1
Billy Hamilton	CF	540	64	5	45	34	.227	.291	.310	.601	23.7%	8.0%	14.8	-3.9	12.9	10.3	9.5	31.1	11.8	9.2
Shin-Soo Choo	DH	509	82	20	63	9	.254	.355	.427	.782	24.7%	11.9%	14.7	-2.2	13.2	10.8	8.5	15.6	10.5	9.8
Clint Frazier	LF	541	77	24	77	7	.244	.307	.436	.743	25.7%	7.4%	14.7	-1.9	13.2	10.9	8.6	14.4	10.4	9.4
Brent Rooker	OF	537	77	26	80	4	.244	.313	.447	.760	31.2%	7.9%	14.7	-1.7	13.2	10.9	8.5	12.8	10.3	9.4
Jackie Bradley Jr.	CF	524	76	20	73	11	.239	.324	.423	.747	26.2%	9.6%	14.7	-2.0	13.1	10.8	8.8	17.1	10.6	9.3
Brandon Lowe	2B	532	73	24	77	7	.246	.320	.443	.763	27.4%	8.9%	14.7	-2.0	13.1	10.8	8.6	14.3	10.4	9.4
Derek Fisher	DH	524	73	23	70	14	.227	.313	.412	.724	31.4%	10.3%	14.7	-2.2	13.0	10.7	9.0	18.8	10.7	9.0
Matt Beaty	DH	547	70	19	74	5	.271	.323	.439	.762	14.4%	6.2%	14.7	-2.7	13.2	10.8	8.1	13.0	10.4	10.0
Jose Martinez	RF	537	72	18	73	4	.278	.345	.436	.781	20.5%	8.9%	14.7	-2.7	13.2	10.8	8.0	12.1	10.3	10.2
Justin Upton	OF	526	73	29	81	5	.237	.322	.448	.770	30.4%	10.4%	14.7	-1.7	13.1	10.9	8.6	13.3	10.3	9.1
Ronny Rodriguez	2B	564	65	21	73	10	.255	.289	.431	.720	23.1%	4.3%	14.6	-2.8	13.1	10.7	8.4	15.5	10.6	9.6
Vince Fernandez	OF	534	72	25	77	6	.247	.318	.451	.769	30.6%	8.6%	14.6	-2.1	13.1	10.8	8.5	13.8	10.4	9.4
Mitch Garver	C	527	78	25	81	2	.252	.331	.460	.791	24.1%	9.9%	14.6	-1.7	13.1	10.9	8.3	11.2	10.1	9.5
Luis Arraez	2B	541	72	6	62	6	.308	.365	.408	.773	8.7%	7.9%	14.6	-3.7	13.1	10.6	7.6	13.3	10.4	11.1
Justin Smoak	1B	507	80	29	84	1	.238	.347	.465	.812	23.5%	13.6%	14.6	-1.3	13.1	10.9	8.5	10.9	10.0	9.1
Bobby Bradley	1B	539	77	32	86	2	.229	.296	.461	.757	32.4%	8.0%	14.5	-1.3	13.0	10.9	8.6	11.4	10.1	8.8
Jacob Robson	RF	537	63	13	59	19	.250	.318	.381	.698	27.3%	8.5%	14.5	-3.6	12.9	10.5	8.7	21.5	11.0	9.5
Nathaniel Lowe	1B	524	76	24	77	2	.261	.342	.451	.793	23.3%	10.4%	14.5	-2.1	13.1	10.8	8.1	11.2	10.1	9.7
Christian Walker	1B	529	71	25	77	6	.246	.323	.449	.772	26.6%	9.3%	14.5	-2.2	13.0	10.7	8.4	13.5	10.3	9.2
Eduardo Nunez	SS	565	63	15	66	12	.267	.299	.406	.704	14.7%	3.8%	14.5	-3.6	13.0	10.5	8.2	16.8	10.6	9.9
Teoscar Hernandez	CF	536	75	27	76	8	.228	.300	.439	.739	31.0%	8.8%	14.5	-2.0	12.9	10.7	8.7	15.3	10.3	8.8
Yermin Mercedes	C	542	71	24	76	3	.258	.317	.443	.761	21.0%	7.4%	14.5	-2.4	13.0	10.7	8.1	11.9	10.2	9.5
Greg Allen	LF	539	66	9	57	22	.245	.309	.359	.668	22.0%	6.4%	14.5	-3.7	12.7	10.3	8.8	23.4	11.0	9.3
Joey Votto	1B	501	77	20	72	3	.268	.380	.448	.828	14.5%	14.5%	14.4	-2.4	13.0	10.7	8.1	11.9	10.1	9.8
Logan Morrison	DH	529	74	32	87	2	.228	.310	.458	.768	24.2%	9.5%	14.4	-1.5	12.9	10.8	8.6	11.4	10.0	8.7
Wilson Ramos	C	544	68	22	79	1	.272	.330	.443	.773	15.8%	7.7%	14.4	-2.7	13.0	10.7	7.9	10.3	10.0	9.8
Jurickson Profar	2B	527	76	20	73	8	.248	.329	.427	.756	14.6%	9.5%	14.4	-2.4	12.9	10.6	8.4	15.1	10.3	9.3
Mauricio Dubon	2B	559	59	15	64	14	.264	.303	.399	.702	15.7%	4.8%	14.4	-3.8	12.9	10.5	8.2	17.9	10.7	9.7
Junior Lake	OF	529	69	17	66	16	.240	.318	.396	.715	25.4%	9.7%	14.4	-3.0	12.8	10.4	8.7	19.4	10.6	9.1
Odubel Herrera	OF	542	71	19	71	8	.258	.319	.427	.746	22.3%	7.5%	14.4	-2.9	12.9	10.6	8.4	14.5	10.3	9.5
Mark Trumbo	1B	547	72	30	85	2	.240	.298	.451	.749	26.0%	7.3%	14.4	-1.9	12.9	10.7	8.3	10.8	10.0	8.9
Marwin Gonzalez	1B	538	74	20	76	3	.267	.332	.440	.772	21.4%	8.0%	14.4	-2.6	12.9	10.6	7.9	11.5	10.0	9.7
Justin Bour	1B	521	74	29	82	3	.238	.329	.453	.781	26.5%	11.5%	14.4	-1.8	12.9	10.7	8.4	11.5	10.0	8.9
Chris Carter	1B	516	81	36	89	2	.207	.307	.457	.764	37.8%	11.7%	14.4	-0.9	12.8	10.8	8.8	11.6	9.9	8.1
Harrison Bader	CF	527	66	20	68	14	.237	.318	.404	.722	28.3%	8.9%	14.4	-3.0	12.7	10.5	8.7	18.5	10.6	9.0
Scott Kingery	3B	548	63	19	70	15	.238	.293	.406	.699	26.9%	6.4%	14.3	-3.2	12.7	10.4	8.6	18.6	10.6	8.9
Jose Fernandez	1B	550	67	20	74	4	.271	.321	.435	.756	13.8%	6.0%	14.3	-3.1	12.8	10.6	7.8	11.9	10.1	9.7
Eduardo Escobar	3B	543	70	23	78	4	.256	.316	.459	.775	19.8%	7.5%	14.3	-2.6	12.8	10.6	8.1	12.0	10.0	9.3
Kevin Pillar	CF	559	62	16	67	13	.259	.298	.412	.710	16.0%	4.3%	14.3	-3.7	12.7	10.4	8.2	17.1	10.5	9.4
Phillip Ervin	CF	533	64	17	66	15	.241	.315	.407	.722	24.1%	8.5%	14.3	-3.3	12.7	10.4	8.6	19.1	10.6	9.0
Cavan Biggio	2B	504	74	20	67	13	.233	.344	.409	.753	26.0%	13.9%	14.3	-2.6	12.7	10.4	8.7	17.9	10.4	8.9
Tim Locastro	CF	535	59	10	58	22	.248	.319	.372	.690	19.2%	8.6%	14.3	-4.1	12.6	10.2	8.6	23.0	10.9	9.2
Yonder Alonso	DH	526	73	23	79	2	.260	.341	.447	.788	21.3%	10.5%	14.3	-2.4	12.8	10.6	8.0	10.8	9.9	9.4
Jason Martin	OF	548	63	17	67	13	.254	.307	.411	.718	21.9%	6.8%	14.2	-3.6	12.7	10.3	8.2	17.2	10.5	9.3
Tony Kemp	DH	533	66	9	60	16	.264	.333	.379	.713	14.6%	8.6%	14.2	-3.9	12.6	10.2	8.2	19.2	10.6	9.6
Tommy Joseph	1B	550	73	26	85	2	.245	.298	.441	.740	25.5%	6.4%	14.2	-2.1	12.7	10.6	8.1	11.1	9.8	8.9
Cedric Mullins II	CF	545	69	14	55	20	.238	.294	.375	.669	17.9%	6.8%	14.2	-3.7	12.6	10.2	8.6	22.0	10.8	9.0
Seth Beer	OF	540	68	24	75	3	.261	.323	.449	.773	23.2%	6.4%	14.2	-2.9	12.8	10.5	7.9	11.3	10.0	9.4
Asdrubal Cabrera	2B	536	77	20	73	3	.264	.333	.438	.770	19.8%	8.7%	14.2	-2.7	12.7	10.5	7.9	11.5	9.9	9.6
Ian Miller	CF	547	63	6	53	26	.241	.296	.332	.628	21.3%	6.5%	14.2	-4.3	12.5	10.0	8.8	25.5	11.0	9.1
Eric Hosmer	1B	540	70	22	75	3	.262	.326	.437	.764	22.2%	8.5%	14.2	-2.9	12.7	10.5	7.9	11.5	10.0	9.4
Hernan Perez	DH	558	64	18	70	13	.247	.288	.399	.687	22.6%	5.4%	14.2	-3.4	12.6	10.3	8.3	17.3	10.4	9.0
Devon Travis	2b	557	71	17	69	8	.259	.300	.424	.725	18.2%	4.7%	14.2	-3.3	12.6	10.4	8.0	14.5	10.2	9.4
Franklin Barreto	2B	545	70	21	72	11	.237	.295	.410	.705	30.5%	6.7%	14.1	-2.9	12.6	10.3	8.4	16.4	10.2	8.8
Tim Lopes	LF	545	59	9	55	23	.247	.304	.355	.659	21.0%	7.1%	14.1	-4.4	12.4	10.1	8.5	23.6	10.9	9.1
Jung Ho Kang	3B	541	71	28	83	3	.238	.303	.447	.750	27.7%	7.7%	14.1	-2.3	12.6	10.5	8.2	11.7	9.9	8.7
Mitch Haniger	OF	524	73	23	72	6	.246	.331	.441	.772	25.1%	9.9%	14.1	-2.7	12.6	10.4	8.2	13.5	10.0	9.0
Jake Marisnick	CF	544	72	21	71	15	.218	.278	.391	.669	31.9%	6.2%	14.1	-2.7	12.5	10.3	8.8	19.4	10.4	8.3
Domingo Santana	DH	522	71	23	72	8	.241	.328	.427	.755	31.9%	10.9%	14.1	-2.8	12.6	10.4	8.3	14.6	10.1	8.9
Adam Duvall	RF	540	72	29	87	2	.231	.298	.453	.751	26.4%	7.5%	14.1	-2.0	12.6	10.5	8.3	11.3	9.7	8.4
Travis Shaw	DH	517	73	28	82	4	.231	.329	.442	.771	25.4%	12.0%	14.0	-2.1	12.6	10.5	8.3	12.1	9.8	8.5
Luke Voit	DH	518	78	25	78	1	.248	.340	.442	.782	26.4%	10.9%	14.0	-2.3	12.6	10.4	8.0	10.7	9.7	9.0
Christian Vazquez	C	550	71	17	73	6	.260	.309	.413	.723	18.8%	6.2%	14.0	-3.2	12.5	10.3	7.9	13.4	10.0	9.3
Jedd Gyorko	DH	532	71	26	79	5	.239	.314	.429	.743	23.1%	9.4%	14.0	-2.5	12.5	10.4	8.2	12.6	9.9	8.7
Bradley Zimmer	CF	534	69	17	64	17	.229	.301	.381	.682	31.9%	8.4%	14.0	-3.4	12.4	10.1	8.6	20.4	10.5	8.6
Jon Berti	SS	534	57	11	53	24	.240	.311	.358	.670	22.4%	8.1%	14.0	-4.5	12.4	10.0	8.4	24.2	10.9	8.9
Dwight Smith Jr.	LF	538	69	19	68	8	.257	.322	.420	.742	19.9%	8.0%	14.0	-3.4	12.5	10.3	7.9	14.3	10.1	9.2
Andrew Velazquez	2B	554	65	13	63	18	.240	.287	.374	.661	26.3%	5.6%	14.0	-3.9	12.4	10.1	8.4	20.5	10.5	8.8
Giovanny Urshela	3B	554	73	19	74	3	.266	.310	.425	.735	18.0%	5.2%	14.0	-3.1	12.5	10.3	7.6	11.1	9.8	9.4

Name	POS	AB	R	HR	RBI	SB	AVG	OBP	SLG	OPS	K%	BB%	15-tm Mixed, Std.	15-tm Mixed, OBP	15-tm Draft & Hold	12-tm Mixed, Std.	12-tm, AL, OBP	12-tm, NL, OBP	12-tm, AL, Std.	12-tm, NL, Std.
Robinson Cano	2B	547	72	20	76	1	.268	.325	.443	.768	16.1%	7.0%	14.0	-3.1	12.6	10.4	7.6	10.0	9.7	9.5
Reynaldo Rodriguez	1B	545	67	24	74	8	.240	.298	.426	.723	24.3%	6.9%	14.0	-3.0	12.5	10.3	8.2	14.5	10.1	8.7
Enrique Hernandez	2B	528	74	24	77	4	.244	.323	.440	.762	20.2%	9.8%	14.0	-2.6	12.5	10.3	8.1	12.3	9.8	8.9
Noel Cuevas	RF	552	65	13	67	9	.270	.316	.407	.723	21.1%	5.7%	14.0	-4.0	12.5	10.2	7.7	14.9	10.1	9.5
Andrelton Simmons	SS	550	63	12	63	10	.276	.326	.400	.726	9.4%	6.5%	14.0	-4.3	12.5	10.1	7.7	15.4	10.2	9.7
Renato Nunez	DH	540	70	28	79	2	.245	.309	.448	.757	24.6%	7.5%	13.9	-2.7	12.5	10.4	7.9	10.8	9.7	8.8
Balbino Fuenmayor	3b	558	66	22	75	3	.262	.303	.435	.738	22.8%	4.8%	13.9	-3.4	12.5	10.3	7.6	11.0	9.8	9.2
Carlos Gomez	RF	536	65	20	68	15	.230	.301	.397	.698	28.1%	6.4%	13.9	-3.4	12.3	10.1	8.5	18.6	10.3	8.4
Yairo Munoz	DH	551	60	14	64	15	.253	.302	.384	.687	20.0%	5.9%	13.9	-4.2	12.3	10.0	8.1	18.5	10.4	9.0
Nick Dini	C	548	66	18	69	10	.251	.304	.408	.711	19.6%	5.8%	13.9	-3.6	12.4	10.1	8.0	15.3	10.1	9.0
Ka'ai Tom	OF	536	71	19	71	9	.247	.315	.417	.733	25.3%	8.2%	13.9	-3.3	12.3	10.1	8.0	14.7	10.0	8.9
Greg Bird	1B	523	77	29	82	3	.225	.314	.445	.759	26.7%	10.5%	13.8	-2.1	12.4	10.3	8.2	11.6	9.6	8.3
David Freese	1B	529	73	22	78	2	.256	.334	.436	.770	25.5%	9.1%	13.8	-2.9	12.4	10.3	7.8	10.5	9.6	9.0
Hanser Alberto	3B	567	64	12	66	6	.285	.313	.407	.721	9.8%	3.4%	13.8	-4.3	12.4	10.1	7.3	12.4	9.9	9.9
Scott Heineman	CF	539	66	14	63	12	.257	.321	.394	.715	24.9%	7.7%	13.8	-4.0	12.3	10.0	8.0	16.9	10.2	9.1
Nico Hoerner	SS	552	65	13	67	9	.269	.315	.411	.726	12.6%	5.6%	13.8	-4.1	12.3	10.1	7.6	14.5	10.0	9.4
Albert Pujols	DH	548	68	25	81	2	.249	.306	.429	.735	14.6%	7.1%	13.8	-3.0	12.4	10.3	7.8	10.7	9.6	8.8
Daniel Palka	LF	535	72	31	82	3	.226	.301	.442	.743	30.2%	9.3%	13.8	-2.4	12.3	10.3	8.1	11.4	9.6	8.2
Nick Markakis	LF	532	71	14	74	2	.281	.355	.428	.782	14.1%	9.8%	13.8	-3.6	12.3	10.1	7.3	10.2	9.6	9.6
Matt Kemp	OF	555	68	25	81	2	.251	.298	.437	.734	25.3%	6.0%	13.7	-3.0	12.3	10.2	7.7	10.3	9.6	8.8
Miguel Cabrera	DH	533	69	19	74	1	.274	.347	.436	.783	20.8%	9.6%	13.7	-3.5	12.4	10.2	7.4	9.7	9.6	9.4
Kendrys Morales	1B	532	70	24	79	2	.249	.325	.433	.758	20.4%	9.2%	13.7	-3.0	12.3	10.2	7.8	10.8	9.6	8.7
Dansby Swanson	SS	532	66	17	69	10	.251	.323	.412	.735	22.2%	9.2%	13.7	-3.7	12.2	10.0	7.9	15.4	10.0	8.8
Mike Tauchman	OF	531	72	16	67	11	.245	.319	.395	.714	22.6%	9.3%	13.7	-3.6	12.1	10.0	8.0	16.1	9.9	8.8
Abraham Toro	3B	534	75	18	73	6	.251	.322	.418	.740	19.5%	8.4%	13.7	-3.2	12.2	10.0	7.8	13.0	9.7	8.9
Sean Murphy	C	540	74	22	76	4	.245	.308	.431	.739	22.0%	7.5%	13.7	-3.0	12.2	10.1	7.8	11.9	9.6	8.7
Chas McCormick	OF	532	72	14	65	13	.243	.317	.379	.696	17.4%	8.9%	13.7	-3.7	12.1	9.9	8.1	17.4	10.0	8.7
Ji-Man Choi	1B	513	74	22	75	4	.245	.344	.435	.779	24.9%	12.3%	13.6	-3.0	12.2	10.1	7.9	11.9	9.6	8.7
Moises Sierra	OF	535	64	14	66	11	.259	.328	.390	.717	23.2%	8.2%	13.6	-4.2	12.1	9.9	7.8	15.8	10.0	9.0
Mitch Longo	OF	549	66	12	63	13	.256	.307	.387	.695	22.2%	6.2%	13.6	-4.2	12.1	9.9	7.8	16.9	10.0	9.0
Jose Osuna	RF	548	67	18	73	4	.263	.316	.436	.752	19.1%	6.6%	13.6	-3.7	12.2	10.0	7.5	11.8	9.7	9.1
Josh Naylor	LF	537	66	20	70	4	.264	.330	.424	.763	17.5%	8.5%	13.6	-3.8	12.2	10.0	7.5	11.6	9.7	9.1
Colby Rasmus	OF	537	69	28	80	5	.227	.298	.434	.731	31.8%	8.4%	13.6	-2.8	12.1	10.1	8.1	12.7	9.6	8.1
Alex Dickerson	LF	539	66	17	72	4	.269	.332	.441	.773	21.1%	7.7%	13.6	-3.9	12.2	10.0	7.4	11.4	9.6	9.2
Rafael Ortega	DH	538	68	13	59	14	.250	.315	.382	.698	19.6%	8.4%	13.6	-4.2	12.0	9.8	7.9	18.0	10.1	8.9
Ryan LaMarre	CF	544	66	11	61	15	.250	.308	.376	.684	29.7%	6.7%	13.6	-4.4	12.0	9.8	7.9	18.6	10.1	8.8
Austin Dean	LF	548	62	20	70	6	.262	.316	.434	.749	20.5%	6.6%	13.6	-4.1	12.1	10.0	7.5	12.4	9.7	9.0
Kyle Seager	3B	538	69	26	79	3	.241	.310	.442	.752	20.3%	8.3%	13.6	-3.1	12.1	10.1	7.8	11.2	9.5	8.4
Ryon Healy	3b	555	66	26	78	2	.250	.296	.443	.739	23.0%	5.6%	13.6	-3.3	12.2	10.1	7.6	10.1	9.5	8.6
Ty France	2B	539	67	22	72	3	.260	.324	.439	.763	19.0%	6.1%	13.6	-3.7	12.2	10.0	7.5	10.9	9.6	9.0
Trey Harris	OF	552	65	15	69	7	.268	.315	.415	.730	20.1%	5.4%	13.5	-4.2	12.1	9.9	7.4	12.9	9.7	9.2
Jason Kipnis	2b	537	73	18	69	7	.249	.317	.417	.734	19.1%	8.4%	13.5	-3.6	12.1	9.9	7.7	13.6	9.7	8.8
Pablo Reyes	DH	545	64	14	61	13	.253	.310	.394	.704	20.0%	7.0%	13.5	-4.4	12.0	9.8	7.8	17.1	10.0	8.8
Mikie Mahtook	CF	539	66	20	68	11	.236	.302	.408	.711	26.8%	7.7%	13.5	-3.8	12.0	9.9	8.0	16.0	9.9	8.3
Jason Heyward	CF	526	70	16	68	7	.260	.340	.415	.756	16.7%	10.3%	13.5	-3.8	12.1	9.9	7.6	13.2	9.7	9.0
Rajai Davis	CF	555	59	11	54	25	.226	.272	.340	.612	25.2%	5.1%	13.5	-4.8	11.8	9.6	8.4	24.3	10.5	8.1
Brian O'Grady	CF	533	65	24	70	12	.220	.296	.407	.704	30.6%	9.0%	13.5	-3.5	11.9	9.9	8.3	16.9	9.9	7.9
Danny Mendick	3B	537	65	16	63	13	.243	.310	.383	.693	20.2%	8.2%	13.5	-4.2	11.9	9.8	7.9	17.3	10.0	8.5
Evan Longoria	3B	547	68	22	76	3	.251	.309	.437	.746	21.0%	6.8%	13.5	-3.5	12.0	10.0	7.5	11.1	9.5	8.6
Gerardo Parra	DH	550	63	13	67	11	.254	.306	.387	.693	19.6%	6.0%	13.5	-4.3	11.9	9.8	7.7	16.0	9.9	8.8
Tyler Austin	1B	531	69	29	79	6	.219	.298	.432	.730	34.1%	9.5%	13.5	-2.9	12.0	10.0	8.1	13.2	9.6	7.8
Alejandro De Aza	OF	535	73	15	66	8	.254	.323	.402	.725	22.0%	8.2%	13.4	-3.9	12.0	9.8	7.6	14.3	9.7	8.9
Willy Adames	SS	534	68	18	69	7	.254	.324	.411	.735	24.3%	9.0%	13.4	-3.9	12.0	9.9	7.6	13.3	9.6	8.8
Will Smith	C	530	72	29	79	4	.223	.302	.435	.738	25.1%	8.9%	13.4	-2.8	12.0	10.0	8.0	11.8	9.4	7.9
Drew Ferguson	OF	521	71	12	61	17	.233	.322	.363	.686	26.8%	10.4%	13.4	-4.0	11.8	9.7	8.2	19.6	10.0	8.4
Denard Span	LF	535	72	16	61	10	.251	.321	.405	.725	17.2%	8.5%	13.4	-4.1	11.9	9.8	7.7	15.4	9.8	8.8
Matt Carpenter	3B	500	84	23	64	5	.236	.351	.438	.789	25.0%	14.0%	13.4	-3.1	12.0	9.9	7.9	12.9	9.5	8.5
Yusniel Diaz	OF	536	68	18	67	9	.251	.319	.408	.727	21.2%	8.6%	13.4	-4.0	12.0	9.8	7.7	14.4	9.7	8.7
Christian Villanueva	3b	545	68	26	80	4	.234	.295	.426	.720	26.6%	6.7%	13.4	-3.2	12.0	10.0	7.8	11.8	9.5	8.1
Chad Pinder	LF	544	73	22	73	3	.249	.307	.426	.733	25.5%	6.5%	13.4	-3.5	12.0	9.9	7.5	11.2	9.4	8.6
Johan Camargo	SS	545	67	18	75	2	.266	.322	.432	.754	19.6%	7.1%	13.4	-3.9	12.0	9.9	7.3	10.4	9.4	9.0
Trevor Larnach	OF	542	72	16	69	4	.265	.324	.414	.738	24.1%	7.4%	13.4	-3.9	12.0	9.8	7.3	11.5	9.5	9.0
Travis Demeritte	RF	533	70	23	72	6	.238	.311	.432	.743	28.8%	9.0%	13.4	-3.5	11.9	9.9	7.8	13.1	9.6	8.3
Brian Mundell	1B	542	68	14	68	2	.281	.339	.430	.769	19.9%	7.6%	13.4	-4.3	12.0	9.8	7.0	10.3	9.4	9.4
Jake Cave	LF	542	71	18	72	5	.255	.315	.422	.737	28.9%	7.1%	13.4	-3.8	11.9	9.8	7.5	11.9	9.5	8.7
Taylor Ward	LF	524	66	21	68	9	.241	.325	.405	.730	26.0%	10.2%	13.3	-3.9	11.9	9.8	7.8	14.6	9.7	8.4
Pedro Alvarez	3b	542	69	28	80	3	.231	.294	.437	.730	28.3%	7.6%	13.3	-3.1	11.9	9.9	7.8	11.0	9.4	8.0
Yadier Molina	C	553	65	17	70	6	.262	.309	.407	.717	15.0%	5.5%	13.3	-4.2	11.9	9.8	7.3	12.4	9.5	8.8
Jose Pirela	LF	549	68	20	71	6	.252	.305	.420	.724	22.6%	6.5%	13.3	-3.9	11.9	9.8	7.5	12.4	9.5	8.6
Hanley Ramirez	SS	536	69	24	77	5	.238	.310	.417	.727	22.9%	8.5%	13.3	-3.4	11.9	9.8	7.7	12.0	9.4	8.2

Name	POS	AB	R	HR	RBI	SB	AVG	OBP	SLG	OPS	K%	BB%	15-tm Mixed, Std.	15-tm Mixed, OBP	15-tm Draft & Hold	12-tm Mixed, Std.	12-tm, AL, OBP	12-tm, NL, OBP	12-tm, AL, Std.	12-tm, NL, Std.
Tommy La Stella	2B	540	68	17	68	3	.272	.333	.422	.754	12.9%	7.6%	13.3	-4.2	11.9	9.8	7.1	10.5	9.4	9.1
Matt Joyce	RF	508	79	22	70	3	.243	.347	.430	.777	21.8%	13.3%	13.3	-3.2	11.9	9.8	7.6	11.3	9.3	8.5
Dylan Moore	3B	538	61	15	59	21	.220	.289	.360	.649	25.0%	7.4%	13.3	-4.6	11.7	9.5	8.4	22.2	10.2	7.8
Danny Valencia	3b	542	67	21	74	4	.250	.313	.423	.735	24.3%	7.8%	13.3	-3.8	11.9	9.8	7.5	11.5	9.4	8.5
Pat Valaika	2B	555	67	21	75	5	.247	.291	.424	.715	26.5%	5.5%	13.3	-3.8	11.8	9.8	7.5	12.1	9.4	8.4
Magneuris Sierra	CF	560	49	6	51	24	.253	.290	.347	.637	18.7%	4.5%	13.3	-6.0	11.7	9.4	7.9	22.9	10.5	8.7
Brandon Belt	1B	508	72	19	69	5	.252	.357	.437	.793	21.9%	13.4%	13.3	-3.7	11.8	9.8	7.5	12.1	9.4	8.6
Mason Williams	CF	549	63	13	63	9	.267	.317	.391	.708	19.9%	6.7%	13.2	-4.8	11.8	9.6	7.3	14.1	9.7	9.0
Alex Guerrero	2b	548	67	24	75	5	.238	.293	.425	.718	23.6%	5.7%	13.2	-3.7	11.8	9.8	7.6	12.1	9.4	8.1
Shed Long	LF	541	65	17	66	11	.245	.308	.401	.709	24.4%	7.8%	13.2	-4.3	11.8	9.6	7.7	15.4	9.7	8.4
Anthony Alford	CF	540	62	11	55	23	.223	.289	.345	.634	29.9%	7.2%	13.2	-4.9	11.6	9.4	8.3	23.1	10.2	7.9
Adam Jones	RF	554	69	20	69	3	.260	.306	.422	.729	18.9%	5.3%	13.2	-4.2	11.8	9.7	7.2	10.9	9.4	8.8
Michael Brosseau	2B	546	68	18	70	6	.251	.306	.409	.715	22.2%	6.1%	13.2	-4.1	11.7	9.7	7.5	12.9	9.5	8.5
Hunter Dozier	3B	536	68	20	74	4	.249	.319	.440	.759	27.0%	8.8%	13.2	-3.8	11.8	9.7	7.4	11.5	9.3	8.4
Adam Frazier	2B	537	70	10	57	8	.275	.339	.409	.748	13.4%	7.7%	13.2	-4.9	11.8	9.6	7.1	13.5	9.6	9.3
Brian McCann	C	530	68	24	78	2	.243	.321	.424	.745	17.8%	9.2%	13.2	-3.5	11.8	9.8	7.5	10.2	9.2	8.2
Cristian Pache	OF	553	63	14	66	10	.254	.300	.399	.699	23.5%	5.9%	13.2	-4.6	11.7	9.6	7.5	15.1	9.6	8.5
Troy Stokes Jr.	LF	531	65	18	64	14	.230	.306	.391	.697	24.8%	8.8%	13.2	-4.3	11.6	9.5	7.9	17.5	9.8	8.0
Jefry Marte	1B	541	66	24	76	6	.233	.299	.422	.721	22.7%	7.5%	13.1	-3.7	11.7	9.7	7.7	12.6	9.4	7.9
Sam Travis	1B	541	70	16	70	6	.255	.317	.400	.716	24.2%	7.8%	13.1	-4.2	11.7	9.6	7.4	12.7	9.4	8.6
Alan Trejo	SS	559	63	15	67	6	.265	.303	.406	.709	21.1%	4.6%	13.1	-4.7	11.7	9.6	7.2	12.6	9.5	8.8
Brad Miller	LF	526	71	26	75	5	.227	.312	.430	.742	28.9%	10.4%	13.1	-3.4	11.7	9.7	7.8	12.4	9.3	7.8
Niko Goodrum	RF	539	65	17	66	12	.238	.306	.400	.707	27.5%	8.4%	13.1	-4.4	11.6	9.5	7.7	16.3	9.7	8.1
Todd Frazier	3B	522	70	26	78	4	.225	.316	.426	.742	22.7%	10.0%	13.1	-3.2	11.7	9.7	7.8	11.8	9.2	7.7
Robel Garcia	2B	539	69	27	77	6	.224	.291	.426	.717	34.6%	7.8%	13.1	-3.4	11.7	9.7	7.8	12.6	9.3	7.7
Orlando Arcia	SS	544	60	16	66	11	.249	.306	.391	.697	19.3%	7.4%	13.1	-4.7	11.6	9.5	7.5	15.4	9.6	8.4
Mark Payton	OF	540	69	17	68	8	.243	.307	.398	.705	22.0%	8.0%	13.1	-4.2	11.6	9.6	7.6	14.1	9.4	8.3
Luke Raley	OF	546	70	18	70	6	.248	.303	.404	.708	27.0%	5.6%	13.1	-4.1	11.6	9.6	7.4	12.7	9.4	8.4
Monte Harrison	CF	545	57	17	60	19	.224	.283	.369	.652	31.8%	6.5%	13.1	-4.9	11.5	9.4	8.1	20.7	10.0	7.7
Nick Williams	LF	548	67	24	77	4	.241	.296	.426	.722	29.1%	5.9%	13.1	-3.8	11.7	9.7	7.5	11.1	9.2	8.1
Billy McKinney	RF	536	77	23	69	5	.237	.307	.435	.742	23.6%	8.4%	13.1	-3.7	11.6	9.6	7.5	11.9	9.2	8.1
Cesar Hernandez	2B	524	75	12	51	10	.265	.345	.387	.733	17.8%	10.3%	13.0	-4.9	11.6	9.4	7.2	14.9	9.6	9.0
Yandy Diaz	1B	520	69	13	65	5	.272	.360	.406	.765	19.1%	11.6%	13.0	-4.6	11.7	9.5	7.1	11.6	9.3	9.0
Drew Waters	OF	554	62	12	64	11	.257	.303	.394	.697	28.7%	5.6%	13.0	-5.0	11.6	9.4	7.4	15.7	9.6	8.6
Josh Palacios	OF	538	65	12	60	14	.247	.313	.377	.690	23.3%	8.1%	13.0	-4.8	11.5	9.4	7.6	17.2	9.7	8.4
T.J. Rivera	2b	557	63	11	66	6	.276	.317	.395	.713	18.1%	4.6%	13.0	-5.0	11.6	9.5	6.9	12.2	9.4	9.1
Melky Cabrera	LF	555	64	14	68	3	.278	.322	.417	.739	12.8%	5.7%	13.0	-4.8	11.7	9.6	6.8	10.4	9.3	9.1
Albert Almora Jr.	CF	556	67	15	66	5	.264	.305	.407	.713	17.7%	5.3%	13.0	-4.7	11.6	9.5	7.1	12.0	9.3	8.7
Travis d'Arnaud	C	542	69	22	75	2	.247	.308	.423	.731	20.8%	7.5%	13.0	-3.9	11.6	9.6	7.3	10.3	9.1	8.2
Starlin Castro	3B	557	63	17	68	4	.268	.311	.421	.732	18.0%	5.5%	13.0	-4.8	11.6	9.5	6.9	10.7	9.3	8.8
Zander Wiel	1B	547	72	20	73	5	.241	.297	.421	.717	28.1%	6.4%	13.0	-3.9	11.5	9.6	7.4	11.8	9.2	8.1
Joey Wendle	3B	550	64	10	60	13	.255	.307	.377	.684	19.1%	5.6%	13.0	-5.1	11.4	9.3	7.4	16.9	9.7	8.5
Jesus Aguilar	1B	528	72	26	79	1	.235	.317	.427	.744	25.9%	9.9%	13.0	-3.4	11.6	9.6	7.4	9.4	9.0	7.9
Addison Russell	SS	534	67	20	74	5	.245	.317	.418	.736	22.7%	8.7%	12.9	-4.1	11.5	9.5	7.4	11.8	9.2	8.1
Kelvin Gutierrez	3b	547	63	12	61	12	.255	.310	.383	.692	24.8%	6.7%	12.9	-5.1	11.5	9.4	7.3	15.7	9.6	8.5
Jaylin Davis	RF	541	63	21	68	8	.240	.304	.409	.713	28.2%	7.5%	12.9	-4.5	11.5	9.5	7.5	13.6	9.4	8.0
David Wright	3b	529	71	20	66	7	.238	.317	.407	.724	27.2%	9.6%	12.9	-4.2	11.5	9.5	7.5	13.6	9.3	8.0
Andrew Toles	OF	555	66	17	68	7	.249	.294	.403	.697	24.1%	5.2%	12.9	-4.6	11.5	9.4	7.3	13.3	9.3	8.3
Andy Ibanez	2b	543	66	15	65	7	.259	.317	.396	.713	18.8%	7.2%	12.9	-4.8	11.5	9.4	7.2	13.2	9.4	8.6
Danny Jansen	C	529	71	21	72	3	.247	.323	.425	.748	18.1%	8.8%	12.9	-4.0	11.5	9.5	7.3	10.9	9.1	8.2
Breyvic Valera	2B	540	65	11	60	10	.260	.322	.383	.705	12.6%	7.9%	12.9	-5.1	11.4	9.3	7.2	15.1	9.5	8.6
Ronnier Mustelier	3b	543	64	14	64	5	.271	.329	.404	.734	14.9%	7.4%	12.9	-5.0	11.5	9.4	6.9	11.8	9.3	8.8
Lucas Duda	1b	531	71	29	81	2	.223	.303	.436	.739	30.1%	9.1%	12.9	-3.3	11.5	9.6	7.6	10.2	9.0	7.5
Francisco Mejia	C	550	66	20	71	4	.254	.304	.424	.728	20.3%	5.7%	12.9	-4.5	11.5	9.5	7.1	10.9	9.2	8.4
Carter Kieboom	SS	531	68	16	68	5	.258	.332	.408	.739	23.6%	9.2%	12.9	-4.5	11.5	9.4	7.1	11.9	9.2	8.5
Frank Schwindel	1B	562	65	20	72	3	.257	.292	.424	.716	17.4%	4.2%	12.9	-4.5	11.5	9.5	7.0	10.2	9.1	8.4
Chris Marrero	OF	543	69	18	71	8	.237	.297	.396	.693	25.6%	7.0%	12.9	-4.2	11.4	9.4	7.5	13.8	9.3	7.9
Cory Spangenberg	DH	546	61	14	63	15	.235	.292	.373	.665	31.9%	6.8%	12.9	-5.0	11.3	9.3	7.7	18.0	9.7	7.9
Willi Castro	SS	552	61	12	61	12	.255	.303	.388	.691	22.0%	5.3%	12.8	-5.3	11.4	9.3	7.3	15.8	9.5	8.4
Luis Rengifo	2b	534	63	12	59	14	.247	.319	.377	.696	20.1%	8.7%	12.8	-5.2	11.3	9.2	7.5	17.3	9.6	8.2
Scooter Gennett	2B	552	67	18	71	3	.259	.309	.415	.723	22.0%	6.0%	12.8	-4.5	11.5	9.4	7.0	10.6	9.1	8.4
Tyler Wade	LF	541	64	9	57	18	.237	.300	.346	.647	24.4%	7.6%	12.8	-5.2	11.3	9.2	7.7	20.0	9.7	8.0
Colin Moran	3B	542	63	17	72	2	.266	.326	.420	.746	21.1%	7.6%	12.8	-4.7	11.5	9.5	6.9	9.8	9.1	8.6
Ronald Guzman	1B	528	69	21	71	4	.244	.323	.420	.743	25.7%	9.4%	12.8	-4.2	11.4	9.4	7.3	11.2	9.1	8.1
Kole Calhoun	RF	522	73	23	68	5	.234	.322	.420	.742	24.2%	10.6%	12.8	-4.0	11.4	9.4	7.4	11.8	9.1	7.9
Nicky Delmonico	OF	530	68	20	71	5	.242	.320	.418	.738	23.8%	9.3%	12.8	-4.3	11.3	9.4	7.3	12.0	9.1	8.0
Leury Garcia	CF	559	61	10	56	13	.259	.298	.371	.669	22.9%	4.2%	12.7	-5.7	11.3	9.2	7.1	16.3	9.6	8.5
Brian Anderson	3b	529	68	18	66	4	.256	.334	.424	.759	21.6%	8.9%	12.7	-4.6	11.4	9.4	7.0	11.2	9.1	8.4
Marco Hernandez	2B	558	66	8	62	10	.265	.305	.380	.685	22.5%	4.4%	12.7	-5.3	11.3	9.2	7.0	14.4	9.3	8.6
Pablo Sandoval	3b	549	63	23	75	3	.247	.300	.428	.728	22.4%	6.6%	12.7	-4.4	11.4	9.4	7.1	10.3	9.0	8.0

Appendix B - Steamer 180 Starting Pitchers

Name	GS	W	K	ERA	WHIP	SV	K/9	K%	BB/9	BB%	GB%	FBv	15-tm Mixed, Std.	15-tm Mixed, OBP	15-tm Mixed, Draft & Hold	12-tm Mixed, Std.	12-tm, AL, OBP	12-tm, NL, OBP	12-tm, AL, Std.	12-tm, NL, Std.
Gerrit Cole	29	16	252	3.08	1.02	0	12.6	35.0%	2.5	6.9%	40.8%	97.1	24.0	26.8	21.0	17.3	16.6	33.5	16.0	32.1
Chris Sale	32	15	239	3.19	1.02	0	11.9	32.9%	2.1	5.8%	41.2%	93.1	22.9	25.6	20.1	16.5	16.0	31.8	15.4	31.3
Max Scherzer	28	14	239	3.27	1.04	0	12.0	32.8%	2.2	6.1%	36.7%	94.7	22.0	24.8	19.2	15.8	15.2	30.4	14.8	30.7
Justin Verlander	28	15	234	3.47	1.04	0	11.7	32.2%	2.1	5.8%	33.9%	94.4	21.6	24.3	18.8	15.5	15.1	29.3	14.5	30.3
Jacob deGrom	28	13	227	3.12	1.06	0	11.4	31.2%	2.2	5.9%	45.4%	96.7	21.2	23.8	18.5	15.2	14.6	29.8	14.2	30.2
Blake Snell	32	15	226	3.40	1.18	0	11.3	30.3%	3.4	9.0%	42.2%	95.4	19.0	21.8	16.3	13.6	13.2	26.1	12.9	28.5
Walker Buehler	30	14	208	3.48	1.14	0	10.4	28.1%	2.4	6.6%	46.6%	96.5	18.6	21.1	16.1	13.3	13.2	25.5	12.7	28.3
Jack Flaherty	30	12	216	3.58	1.16	0	10.8	28.9%	2.9	7.7%	41.8%	93.8	17.8	20.7	15.4	12.8	12.5	24.2	12.2	27.7
Stephen Strasburg	29	13	206	3.57	1.17	0	10.3	27.6%	2.6	6.9%	46.6%	93.8	17.7	20.3	15.2	12.7	12.6	24.1	12.1	27.6
Charlie Morton	30	13	208	3.47	1.18	0	10.4	27.9%	3.0	8.0%	48.5%	94.3	17.7	20.3	15.2	12.6	12.5	24.3	12.0	27.6
Mike Clevinger	29	13	218	3.66	1.19	0	10.9	29.1%	3.1	8.2%	41.0%	95.0	17.6	20.5	15.1	12.6	12.4	23.7	12.0	27.5
James Paxton	31	14	210	3.83	1.18	0	10.5	28.3%	2.9	7.8%	41.0%	95.2	17.3	20.1	14.8	12.4	12.4	22.8	11.9	27.2
Tyler Glasnow	32	13	224	3.69	1.22	0	11.2	29.7%	3.6	9.6%	44.8%	97.2	17.3	20.4	14.7	12.4	12.2	23.1	11.8	27.2
Shane Bieber	29	13	194	3.70	1.13	0	9.7	26.2%	1.8	4.9%	45.1%	92.9	17.1	19.5	14.8	12.3	12.3	23.0	11.8	27.2
Patrick Corbin	30	13	204	3.56	1.22	0	10.2	27.1%	3.0	7.9%	48.7%	91.9	17.0	19.6	14.6	12.2	12.1	23.2	11.6	27.1
Dinelson Lamet	32	12	228	3.74	1.22	0	11.4	30.1%	3.5	9.3%	41.5%	95.9	16.9	20.2	14.3	12.0	11.8	22.5	11.5	26.9
Clayton Kershaw	29	13	184	3.56	1.16	0	9.2	24.6%	2.1	5.5%	47.9%	90.2	16.8	18.9	14.6	12.1	12.1	23.1	11.6	27.1
Yu Darvish	31	13	217	3.88	1.20	0	10.8	29.0%	3.0	8.0%	43.9%	93.9	16.8	19.8	14.3	12.0	12.0	22.0	11.5	26.8
Rich Hill	33	14	203	3.79	1.19	0	10.1	26.9%	2.9	7.8%	42.3%	89.8	16.8	19.4	14.4	12.0	12.1	22.3	11.6	26.9
Shohei Ohtani	32	11	219	3.79	1.23	0	10.9	28.9%	3.6	9.4%	41.7%	96.5	16.0	19.2	13.6	11.4	11.2	21.2	11.0	26.3
Luis Severino	31	13	194	3.96	1.21	0	9.7	25.9%	2.7	7.1%	45.4%	96.0	15.8	18.4	13.4	11.3	11.6	20.5	10.9	26.1
Chris Paddack	32	12	194	3.88	1.17	0	9.7	25.9%	2.3	6.1%	41.4%	93.8	15.6	18.2	13.3	11.1	11.2	20.6	10.8	26.1
Trevor Bauer	29	11	216	3.85	1.23	0	10.8	28.4%	3.3	8.7%	44.7%	94.2	15.6	18.8	13.2	11.1	10.9	20.5	10.7	26.0
Lance McCullers Jr.	31	14	194	3.78	1.29	0	9.7	25.6%	3.5	9.3%	51.9%	94.4	15.5	18.0	13.1	11.1	11.3	20.6	10.7	26.0
Luis Castillo	31	11	205	3.79	1.24	0	10.2	27.0%	3.2	8.5%	49.8%	96.4	15.3	18.2	13.0	10.9	10.8	20.4	10.6	25.8
Brendan McKay	33	13	196	3.95	1.23	0	9.8	25.9%	3.0	7.8%	39.7%	93.5	15.2	17.9	12.9	10.8	11.0	19.8	10.5	25.7
Hyun-Jin Ryu	30	13	167	3.74	1.19	0	8.4	22.3%	1.9	5.2%	49.7%	90.5	15.1	17.1	13.1	10.8	11.2	20.4	10.5	25.9
Corey Kluber	30	12	187	3.99	1.19	0	9.4	24.9%	2.2	5.9%	43.4%	91.7	15.0	17.6	12.8	10.7	11.0	19.5	10.5	25.7
Aaron Nola	29	12	201	3.85	1.25	0	10.1	26.4%	3.1	8.0%	49.5%	93.0	15.0	17.9	12.7	10.7	10.7	19.9	10.4	25.6
Max Fried	33	13	184	3.66	1.30	0	9.2	24.1%	3.3	8.7%	53.7%	93.6	14.8	17.2	12.6	10.6	10.9	20.2	10.3	25.6
Brandon Woodruff	30	12	202	3.97	1.25	0	10.1	26.4%	2.9	7.6%	46.6%	96.4	14.8	17.8	12.5	10.6	10.7	19.2	10.3	25.5
Kevin Gausman	7	9	198	3.84	1.18	0	9.9	26.4%	2.3	6.2%	45.4%	94.1	14.7	17.6	12.6	10.5	10.3	19.6	10.2	25.5
Noah Syndergaard	29	12	184	3.90	1.21	0	9.2	24.5%	2.4	6.4%	48.7%	97.4	14.6	17.1	12.4	10.4	10.6	19.2	10.2	25.4
Andrew Heaney	30	11	195	4.07	1.20	0	9.7	25.9%	2.6	6.9%	39.6%	92.2	14.3	17.2	12.1	10.2	10.3	18.4	10.0	25.1
David Price	32	13	185	4.15	1.26	0	9.2	24.1%	2.7	7.1%	41.0%	91.7	14.1	16.7	11.8	10.0	10.5	17.8	9.9	24.9
Robbie Ray	32	11	223	4.12	1.32	0	11.1	28.8%	4.1	10.6%	40.7%	92.0	14.1	17.7	11.6	10.0	10.0	17.8	9.8	24.8
Framber Valdez	16	12	192	3.62	1.35	0	9.6	25.1%	4.3	11.3%	56.8%	93.2	14.1	16.7	11.8	10.0	10.1	19.2	9.7	25.0
Sonny Gray	31	11	197	3.87	1.29	0	9.9	25.7%	3.4	9.0%	51.4%	93.0	14.0	16.9	11.8	9.9	10.0	18.5	9.7	24.9
Lance Lynn	30	11	196	4.04	1.27	0	9.8	25.7%	3.1	8.2%	42.8%	94.1	13.9	16.8	11.6	9.8	10.0	17.8	9.7	24.8
Lucas Sims	14	9	223	4.20	1.26	0	11.1	29.0%	3.8	10.0%	36.2%	93.6	13.8	17.5	11.4	9.8	9.6	17.3	9.6	24.6
Jose Urquidy	23	12	184	4.30	1.21	0	9.2	24.4%	2.3	6.2%	38.5%	93.3	13.8	16.5	11.6	9.8	10.3	17.1	9.7	24.7
German Marquez	31	12	188	4.16	1.25	0	9.4	24.8%	2.4	6.3%	47.3%	95.4	13.8	16.5	11.6	9.8	10.2	17.4	9.7	24.7
Brent Honeywell	32	12	188	4.17	1.26	0	9.4	24.7%	2.9	7.6%	41.5%	\N	13.5	16.3	11.4	9.6	10.0	17.1	9.5	24.5
Adrian Morejon	16	10	199	3.84	1.30	0	10.0	25.9%	3.7	9.7%	45.1%	96.4	13.5	16.6	11.3	9.6	9.5	17.9	9.4	24.6
Zack Wheeler	30	11	181	4.06	1.24	0	9.0	23.8%	2.6	6.9%	44.5%	96.3	13.5	16.1	11.4	9.6	9.9	17.4	9.5	24.5
Matthew Boyd	30	10	199	4.31	1.21	0	9.9	26.3%	2.7	7.1%	34.6%	92.1	13.5	16.6	11.3	9.6	9.7	16.6	9.5	24.4
Eduardo Rodriguez	30	13	189	4.18	1.31	0	9.4	24.4%	3.3	8.5%	42.0%	93.0	13.4	16.2	11.1	9.5	10.0	16.8	9.4	24.4
Garrett Richards	34	12	188	3.88	1.32	0	9.4	24.4%	3.6	9.4%	50.6%	94.7	13.3	16.2	11.0	9.5	9.7	17.6	9.4	24.5
Zac Gallen	32	11	198	4.21	1.28	0	9.9	25.8%	3.2	8.4%	41.5%	92.7	13.2	16.3	10.9	9.3	9.6	16.4	9.3	24.2
Lewis Thorpe	10	10	194	4.19	1.25	0	9.7	25.5%	2.9	7.7%	38.0%	91.2	13.1	16.2	11.0	9.3	9.5	16.5	9.2	24.2
Kyle McGowin	8	10	185	4.06	1.25	0	9.2	24.3%	2.8	7.4%	43.5%	90.7	13.0	15.8	10.9	9.2	9.4	16.7	9.2	24.2
Nathan Eovaldi	33	13	173	4.23	1.30	0	8.7	22.6%	2.9	7.6%	45.0%	97.1	12.8	15.3	10.7	9.1	9.8	15.9	9.1	24.0
Zack Greinke	29	13	163	4.29	1.25	0	8.1	21.4%	2.1	5.4%	43.4%	89.9	12.8	15.0	10.8	9.1	9.8	15.8	9.1	24.0
Frankie Montas	32	13	170	4.17	1.29	0	8.5	22.3%	2.9	7.7%	46.2%	96.5	12.7	15.1	10.6	9.0	9.6	16.0	9.0	24.0
Nik Turley	17	10	195	4.08	1.30	0	9.8	25.3%	3.4	8.8%	40.9%	94.4	12.6	15.7	10.5	8.9	9.0	16.1	8.9	23.9
Madison Bumgarner	29	10	173	4.12	1.23	0	8.6	22.7%	2.3	6.1%	39.6%	91.0	12.6	15.2	10.7	8.9	9.4	16.1	8.9	24.0
Lucas Giolito	32	11	202	4.37	1.30	0	10.1	26.3%	3.7	9.5%	40.6%	94.2	12.6	15.9	10.3	8.9	9.2	15.2	8.9	23.7
Adrian Houser	19	11	183	4.06	1.30	0	9.1	23.7%	2.9	7.6%	51.0%	94.4	12.5	15.3	10.5	8.9	9.2	16.1	8.9	23.9
Jon Gray	32	12	187	4.29	1.32	0	9.3	24.3%	3.0	7.8%	48.0%	95.9	12.5	15.4	10.3	8.9	9.4	15.4	8.9	23.7
Luke Weaver	33	11	186	4.26	1.28	0	9.3	24.2%	2.8	7.4%	42.9%	94.0	12.5	15.4	10.4	8.8	9.2	15.5	8.9	23.8
Nick Pivetta	23	11	195	4.29	1.29	0	9.8	25.5%	3.3	8.5%	45.2%	94.6	12.5	15.7	10.3	8.8	9.1	15.3	8.8	23.7
Chris Archer	32	11	194	4.26	1.32	0	9.7	25.2%	3.2	8.4%	43.9%	94.0	12.4	15.5	10.2	8.7	9.1	15.3	8.8	23.6
Erik Swanson	14	9	169	4.65	1.28	9	8.5	22.2%	2.7	7.2%	37.0%	93.1	12.0	15.7	9.9	8.5	9.5	12.2	9.2	23.0
Mitch Keller	33	11	189	4.25	1.34	0	9.4	24.3%	3.4	8.8%	45.1%	95.1	12.0	15.0	9.8	8.5	8.9	14.8	8.5	23.4
Jake Odorizzi	32	12	189	4.63	1.31	0	9.5	24.4%	3.2	8.2%	33.8%	92.7	11.9	15.0	9.7	8.4	9.1	13.6	8.5	23.2
Wilmer Font	16	10	195	4.54	1.27	0	9.7	25.4%	3.0	7.9%	37.1%	94.7	11.9	15.2	9.7	8.4	8.7	13.9	8.5	23.2
MacKenzie Gore	32	11	186	4.27	1.33	0	9.3	24.0%	3.6	9.2%	41.2%	\N	11.8	14.8	9.7	8.3	8.7	14.5	8.4	23.2
Bryse Wilson	28	12	172	4.32	1.31	0	8.6	22.3%	2.9	7.5%	45.0%	95.0	11.7	14.4	9.7	8.3	8.9	14.3	8.4	23.2
Collin McHugh	17	11	182	4.42	1.31	0	9.1	23.7%	3.3	8.5%	40.1%	90.4	11.7	14.6	9.6	8.2	8.8	13.9	8.4	23.1
Conner Menez	21	10	196	4.15	1.36	0	9.8	25.0%	4.3	11.1%	40.0%	91.1	11.7	14.9	9.5	8.2	8.4	14.7	8.3	23.2

Name	GS	W	K	ERA	WHIP	SV	K/9	K%	BB/9	BB%	GB%	FBv	15-tm Mixed, Std.	15-tm Mixed, OBP	15-tm Draft & Hold	12-tm Mixed, Std.	12-tm, AL OBP	12-tm, NL OBP	12-tm, AL Std.	12-tm, NL Std.
Tyler Mahle	27	10	184	4.39	1.29	0	9.2	23.9%	2.8	7.4%	44.8%	93.5	11.6	14.7	9.6	8.2	8.6	14.0	8.3	23.1
Marcus Stroman	31	12	155	3.90	1.35	0	7.8	20.2%	3.0	7.7%	57.6%	92.2	11.6	13.7	9.7	8.2	8.8	15.4	8.3	23.3
Jordan Montgomery	16	11	181	4.44	1.30	0	9.1	23.7%	3.0	7.9%	40.2%	91.8	11.6	14.5	9.5	8.2	8.7	13.8	8.3	23.1
Anthony DeSclafani	32	10	179	4.45	1.28	0	8.9	23.4%	2.6	6.8%	43.0%	94.4	11.5	14.5	9.5	8.1	8.7	13.8	8.3	23.1
Miles Mikolas	30	11	145	4.17	1.24	0	7.3	19.1%	1.7	4.5%	48.7%	93.5	11.5	13.5	9.8	8.2	8.9	14.6	8.3	23.2
Mike Soroka	30	12	155	4.18	1.31	0	7.8	20.2%	2.5	6.5%	50.7%	92.3	11.5	13.7	9.6	8.1	8.8	14.4	8.2	23.1
Griffin Canning	31	10	183	4.42	1.29	0	9.2	23.7%	3.1	8.0%	40.1%	93.8	11.4	14.5	9.4	8.1	8.5	13.7	8.2	23.0
Jameson Taillon	32	11	167	4.24	1.30	0	8.4	21.8%	2.4	6.3%	47.7%	95.0	11.4	14.0	9.5	8.1	8.6	14.2	8.2	23.1
Steven Matz	33	11	174	4.37	1.32	0	8.7	22.5%	3.0	7.7%	46.7%	93.4	11.4	14.2	9.4	8.0	8.6	13.8	8.2	23.0
Jose Berrios	29	12	173	4.55	1.30	0	8.7	22.5%	2.7	7.0%	40.9%	92.8	11.3	14.1	9.3	8.0	8.7	13.2	8.2	22.9
Domingo German	30	12	183	4.73	1.31	0	9.1	23.7%	3.0	7.9%	39.9%	93.3	11.2	14.3	9.1	7.9	8.7	12.5	8.1	22.7
Masahiro Tanaka	30	12	158	4.52	1.28	0	7.9	20.7%	2.2	5.6%	46.5%	91.2	11.2	13.6	9.3	7.9	8.8	13.1	8.1	22.8
Kyle Hendricks	30	12	152	4.35	1.28	0	7.6	19.9%	2.1	5.5%	45.8%	86.7	11.1	13.3	9.2	7.8	8.6	13.5	8.0	22.8
Joe Ryan	31	11	182	4.64	1.30	0	9.1	23.6%	3.2	8.2%	35.0%	\N	11.1	14.2	9.0	7.8	8.4	12.6	8.0	22.6
Jose Quintana	31	12	162	4.34	1.33	0	8.1	21.0%	2.8	7.2%	45.4%	91.3	11.0	13.5	9.0	7.7	8.5	13.3	7.9	22.7
Kyle Gibson	29	12	166	4.32	1.37	0	8.3	21.4%	3.2	8.1%	50.8%	93.1	10.9	13.5	8.9	7.7	8.5	13.2	7.9	22.7
Tony Gonsolin	22	11	179	4.54	1.33	0	9.0	23.1%	3.5	8.9%	39.7%	93.4	10.8	13.9	8.8	7.6	8.3	12.6	7.8	22.5
Michael Pineda	32	12	166	4.68	1.29	0	8.3	21.6%	2.2	5.7%	42.1%	92.4	10.8	13.5	8.9	7.6	8.5	12.2	7.9	22.5
Austin Gomber	24	11	173	4.31	1.34	0	8.6	22.2%	3.5	9.0%	41.1%	92.1	10.8	13.6	8.8	7.6	8.2	13.2	7.8	22.6
Johnny Cueto	31	10	155	4.19	1.30	0	7.7	20.0%	2.6	6.8%	44.9%	90.9	10.8	13.2	9.0	7.6	8.2	13.6	7.8	22.7
Joe Musgrove	30	10	162	4.35	1.30	0	8.1	21.1%	2.3	6.1%	44.5%	92.8	10.7	13.3	8.9	7.6	8.2	13.0	7.8	22.6
Alex Meyer	32	10	184	4.40	1.36	0	9.2	23.8%	3.9	10.1%	43.0%	95.0	10.7	13.8	8.6	7.5	8.0	12.8	7.7	22.4
Cole Hamels	32	12	175	4.46	1.37	0	8.7	22.3%	3.4	8.8%	47.4%	91.2	10.7	13.5	8.6	7.5	8.2	12.5	7.7	22.4
Dallas Keuchel	29	12	143	4.01	1.37	0	7.2	18.3%	2.8	7.2%	57.5%	88.3	10.6	12.6	8.8	7.5	8.3	13.8	7.7	22.6
Kyle Wright	27	11	174	4.40	1.37	0	8.7	22.2%	3.5	8.9%	48.3%	94.2	10.6	13.4	8.5	7.4	8.1	12.6	7.6	22.4
Daulton Jefferies	28	11	158	4.58	1.29	0	7.9	20.6%	2.5	6.5%	40.7%	\N	10.5	13.1	8.7	7.4	8.3	12.1	7.7	22.4
Joey Lucchesi	31	10	173	4.35	1.35	0	8.7	22.2%	3.2	8.2%	45.4%	89.9	10.5	13.4	8.6	7.4	8.0	12.7	7.6	22.4
Pablo Lopez	32	10	154	4.19	1.30	0	7.7	20.0%	2.6	6.8%	48.5%	93.4	10.5	12.9	8.7	7.4	7.9	13.2	7.6	22.5
Tyler Chatwood	9	10	188	4.08	1.45	0	9.4	23.8%	4.7	11.9%	53.2%	96.4	10.5	13.6	8.4	7.3	7.6	13.3	7.5	22.4
Mitchell White	31	12	165	4.49	1.35	0	8.2	21.2%	3.2	8.3%	46.1%	\N	10.4	13.1	8.5	7.3	8.2	12.2	7.6	22.3
Vince Velasquez	35	11	187	4.82	1.34	0	9.4	24.0%	3.4	8.7%	38.1%	93.7	10.4	13.7	8.2	7.3	8.0	11.1	7.6	22.0
Caleb Smith	31	9	190	4.60	1.32	0	9.5	24.2%	3.5	9.0%	32.0%	91.2	10.3	13.7	8.3	7.2	7.6	11.8	7.5	22.1
Alex Wood	30	10	162	4.33	1.34	0	8.1	20.9%	2.9	7.4%	48.8%	89.6	10.3	12.9	8.4	7.2	7.9	12.5	7.5	22.2
Andrew Cashner	4	10	155	4.48	1.35	5	7.7	19.8%	2.8	7.2%	44.1%	94.1	10.3	13.2	8.3	7.2	8.2	11.2	7.8	22.0
Felix Pena	9	9	177	4.41	1.31	0	8.9	22.9%	3.1	8.1%	41.7%	91.6	10.3	13.3	8.4	7.2	7.6	12.2	7.4	22.2
J.A. Happ	32	12	166	4.74	1.34	0	8.3	21.5%	3.0	7.7%	41.3%	91.3	10.2	13.0	8.2	7.2	8.1	11.2	7.5	22.0
Eric Lauer	32	10	166	4.42	1.35	0	8.3	21.4%	3.2	8.4%	41.3%	91.9	10.1	12.9	8.2	7.1	7.8	12.0	7.4	22.1
Cody Anderson	13	10	170	4.49	1.32	0	8.5	22.0%	3.1	7.9%	42.5%	95.0	10.1	13.0	8.2	7.1	7.7	11.8	7.4	22.1
Hector Noesi	26	9	169	4.44	1.30	0	8.4	21.9%	2.9	7.6%	39.9%	92.8	10.1	13.0	8.3	7.1	7.6	12.0	7.4	22.1
Drew Rasmussen	30	11	184	4.60	1.39	0	9.2	23.4%	3.7	9.4%	45.5%	\N	10.1	13.3	8.0	7.0	7.7	11.4	7.3	21.9
Joseph Palumbo	31	11	193	4.68	1.40	0	9.6	24.4%	4.1	10.3%	39.2%	93.6	10.0	13.5	7.9	7.0	7.6	11.0	7.3	21.8
Mike Minor	29	10	169	4.61	1.32	0	8.4	21.8%	2.8	7.2%	38.3%	92.1	10.0	12.9	8.1	7.0	7.7	11.3	7.3	21.9
Tsuyoshi Wada	31	11	159	4.55	1.32	0	7.9	20.5%	2.6	6.8%	42.9%	87.4	9.9	12.5	8.1	7.0	7.8	11.4	7.3	21.9
Corbin Martin	32	10	181	4.53	1.38	0	9.1	23.1%	3.8	9.6%	44.8%	95.2	9.9	13.1	7.8	6.9	7.5	11.3	7.2	21.8
Logan Webb	32	10	157	4.20	1.38	0	7.9	20.1%	3.6	9.1%	50.5%	92.6	9.8	12.3	8.0	6.9	7.5	12.2	7.1	22.0
CC Sabathia	23	11	169	4.69	1.35	0	8.5	21.7%	3.0	7.8%	44.3%	89.1	9.8	12.7	7.8	6.9	7.7	10.8	7.2	21.7
Daniel Ponce de Leo	22	10	187	4.60	1.39	0	9.4	23.6%	4.2	10.7%	37.2%	93.0	9.8	13.2	7.7	6.8	7.4	11.0	7.1	21.7
Spencer Howard	32	10	184	4.73	1.38	0	9.2	23.5%	3.8	9.7%	43.0%	\N	9.7	13.0	7.6	6.8	7.5	10.5	7.1	21.6
Sean Manaea	29	11	149	4.58	1.33	0	7.4	19.3%	2.6	6.9%	42.9%	89.6	9.7	12.0	7.9	6.8	7.8	11.0	7.1	21.8
Bailey Ober	31	11	159	4.86	1.31	0	7.9	20.6%	2.4	6.3%	38.5%	\N	9.7	12.4	7.8	6.8	7.8	10.2	7.2	21.6
Andrew Suarez	12	9	149	4.13	1.33	0	7.4	19.2%	2.8	7.3%	48.3%	92.2	9.7	12.0	8.0	6.8	7.3	12.4	7.1	21.9
David Peterson	32	11	154	4.24	1.40	0	7.7	19.6%	3.5	8.8%	52.9%	\N	9.7	12.1	7.8	6.8	7.6	11.9	7.1	21.8
Adam Wainwright	32	11	155	4.41	1.37	0	7.8	19.8%	3.1	8.0%	48.0%	89.7	9.6	12.1	7.8	6.7	7.6	11.4	7.1	21.8
Ryan Yarbrough	31	11	146	4.52	1.32	0	7.3	18.9%	2.5	6.5%	42.8%	87.7	9.6	11.9	7.8	6.7	7.7	11.1	7.1	21.8
Drew Smyly	33	10	192	5.01	1.36	0	9.6	24.5%	3.4	8.8%	36.6%	91.4	9.5	13.2	7.4	6.6	7.4	9.5	7.0	21.4
Tyler Beede	33	10	174	4.46	1.40	0	8.7	22.0%	4.0	10.2%	44.6%	94.1	9.5	12.5	7.5	6.6	7.3	11.1	7.0	21.6
Tarik Skubal	32	10	178	4.67	1.36	0	8.9	22.8%	3.6	9.1%	39.0%	\N	9.5	12.7	7.5	6.6	7.2	10.4	7.0	21.5
Mike Foltynewicz	31	11	168	4.78	1.36	0	8.4	21.5%	3.1	7.9%	40.2%	94.6	9.4	12.4	7.5	6.6	7.5	10.1	7.0	21.5
Josiah Gray	31	11	160	4.82	1.33	0	8.0	20.6%	3.0	7.7%	39.5%	\N	9.4	12.2	7.5	6.6	7.6	9.9	7.0	21.4
Andrew Albers	24	10	152	4.56	1.32	0	7.6	19.7%	2.5	6.5%	43.7%	87.0	9.3	11.9	7.6	6.5	7.4	10.7	6.9	21.5
Jordan Lyles	32	11	177	4.80	1.38	0	8.8	22.5%	3.3	8.3%	43.1%	92.4	9.3	12.5	7.3	6.5	7.3	9.8	6.9	21.3
Taylor Widener	32	10	183	4.81	1.37	0	9.2	23.3%	3.6	9.3%	37.0%	\N	9.2	12.7	7.2	6.4	7.1	9.7	6.8	21.3
Victor Gonzalez	23	11	154	4.46	1.38	0	7.7	19.6%	3.4	8.8%	46.1%	\N	9.2	11.8	7.4	6.5	7.3	10.7	6.8	21.5
Michael Kopech	32	10	201	4.89	1.42	0	10.0	25.4%	4.5	11.5%	37.9%	95.1	9.2	13.1	7.1	6.4	7.0	9.4	6.8	21.2
Patrick Sandoval	32	10	168	4.45	1.40	0	8.4	21.5%	4.0	10.2%	44.8%	92.6	9.2	12.1	7.3	6.4	7.1	10.7	6.8	21.4
Dylan Cease	31	10	186	4.63	1.43	0	9.3	23.5%	4.4	11.2%	45.7%	96.4	9.2	12.6	7.1	6.4	7.0	10.1	6.7	21.3
Markus Solbach	31	11	148	4.70	1.34	0	7.4	19.1%	2.6	6.8%	45.3%	\N	9.2	11.6	7.4	6.4	7.5	10.0	6.8	21.4
Tyler Ivey	30	12	168	4.86	1.40	0	8.4	21.4%	3.6	9.2%	41.7%	\N	9.2	12.1	7.2	6.4	7.4	9.4	6.8	21.2
Jon Duplantier	14	9	183	4.44	1.43	0	9.2	23.2%	4.4	11.0%	46.6%	91.9	9.0	12.4	7.0	6.3	6.7	10.5	6.6	21.3
Michael Fulmer	32	10	155	4.57	1.34	0	7.7	20.0%	2.8	7.2%	46.0%	95.7	9.0	11.7	7.2	6.3	7.1	10.2	6.7	21.3

Name	GS	W	K	ERA	WHIP	SV	K/9	K%	BB/9	BB%	GB%	FBv	15-tm Mixed, Std.	15-tm Mixed, OBP	15-tm Draft & Hold	12-tm Mixed, Std.	12-tm, AL OBP	12-tm, NL OBP	12-tm, AL Std	12-tm, NL Std
Ian Anderson	32	11	184	4.72	1.47	0	9.2	23.0%	4.6	11.5%	43.9%	\N	8.9	12.3	6.8	6.2	7.0	9.5	6.6	21.1
Gio Gonzalez	33	11	165	4.58	1.43	0	8.3	20.8%	3.6	9.0%	46.7%	89.0	8.9	11.8	7.0	6.2	7.1	9.9	6.6	21.2
Connor Seabold	31	10	164	4.81	1.35	0	8.2	21.0%	3.0	7.7%	43.6%	\N	8.9	11.9	7.1	6.2	7.1	9.4	6.7	21.1
Joe Ross	22	11	156	4.66	1.37	0	7.8	20.0%	3.1	7.8%	43.9%	94.0	8.8	11.6	7.0	6.2	7.1	9.7	6.6	21.1
Jonathan Albaladejo	31	10	147	4.66	1.33	0	7.3	19.0%	2.4	6.1%	45.7%	\N	8.8	11.3	7.1	6.2	7.1	9.8	6.6	21.2
Jon Lester	31	11	163	4.76	1.38	0	8.1	20.6%	3.0	7.5%	44.1%	90.2	8.8	11.7	6.9	6.1	7.1	9.4	6.6	21.1
Rick Porcello	30	11	150	4.93	1.33	0	7.5	19.3%	2.3	5.8%	40.1%	90.1	8.8	11.4	7.0	6.2	7.3	8.9	6.7	21.0
Elieser Hernandez	31	9	173	4.79	1.34	0	8.6	22.0%	3.3	8.5%	35.5%	90.2	8.8	12.0	6.9	6.1	6.8	9.3	6.6	21.0
Chris Mazza	10	9	147	4.34	1.36	0	7.3	18.8%	2.8	7.2%	51.1%	91.3	8.8	11.2	7.1	6.1	6.8	10.6	6.5	21.2
Spencer Turnbull	34	10	163	4.63	1.39	0	8.2	20.9%	3.4	8.8%	47.1%	93.7	8.8	11.7	6.9	6.1	6.9	9.7	6.5	21.1
Kent Emanuel	20	11	142	4.53	1.38	0	7.1	18.2%	3.0	7.6%	48.2%	\N	8.7	11.1	7.0	6.1	7.2	10.0	6.6	21.1
Chad Kuhl	32	10	171	4.71	1.40	0	8.5	21.8%	3.3	8.5%	41.7%	95.2	8.7	11.8	6.8	6.0	6.8	9.3	6.5	21.0
Artie Lewicki	11	9	158	4.58	1.33	0	7.9	20.4%	2.8	7.3%	43.2%	91.4	8.7	11.5	7.0	6.0	6.7	9.8	6.5	21.1
Trevor Cahill	16	9	162	4.51	1.37	0	8.1	20.8%	3.3	8.5%	49.0%	91.7	8.7	11.6	6.9	6.0	6.7	9.9	6.4	21.1
Luis Patino	31	10	176	4.71	1.41	0	8.8	22.2%	4.0	10.2%	41.0%	\N	8.6	11.9	6.7	6.0	6.7	9.2	6.4	20.9
Pedro Avila	32	10	168	4.61	1.41	0	8.4	21.3%	3.9	9.8%	45.0%	93.8	8.6	11.7	6.7	6.0	6.8	9.5	6.4	21.0
Mike Kickham	25	9	150	4.34	1.37	0	7.5	19.2%	3.2	8.1%	47.8%	\N	8.6	11.1	6.9	6.0	6.6	10.4	6.4	21.1
Alec Mills	23	10	160	4.78	1.37	0	8.0	20.4%	3.1	7.9%	42.6%	90.0	8.5	11.4	6.7	5.9	6.9	9.0	6.4	20.9
Forrest Whitley	30	12	185	5.01	1.47	0	9.3	23.2%	4.7	11.8%	39.2%	\N	8.5	12.0	6.4	5.9	6.9	8.1	6.4	20.6
Jakob Junis	32	10	159	4.83	1.34	0	7.9	20.4%	2.7	7.0%	41.9%	91.4	8.5	11.4	6.7	5.9	6.8	8.8	6.4	20.8
Brett Conine	28	12	154	4.79	1.41	0	7.7	19.7%	3.4	8.7%	46.9%	\N	8.5	11.2	6.6	5.9	7.0	8.8	6.4	20.8
Brett Kennedy	32	10	154	4.66	1.36	0	7.7	19.7%	3.0	7.7%	45.4%	91.2	8.5	11.2	6.7	5.9	6.8	9.2	6.4	20.9
Jeffrey Passantino	19	10	162	4.87	1.35	0	8.1	20.8%	2.9	7.5%	38.7%	\N	8.4	11.4	6.6	5.9	6.8	8.6	6.4	20.8
Sean Hjelle	32	10	136	4.27	1.39	0	6.8	17.4%	3.1	8.0%	54.0%	\N	8.4	10.6	6.8	5.9	6.8	10.3	6.3	21.0
Walker Lockett	19	10	144	4.58	1.34	0	7.2	18.4%	2.4	6.2%	47.6%	92.6	8.4	10.9	6.8	5.9	6.8	9.5	6.3	20.9
Matt Lujan	30	10	142	4.45	1.37	0	7.1	18.1%	3.0	7.6%	45.0%	\N	8.4	10.8	6.7	5.8	6.7	9.8	6.3	20.9
Scott Snodgress	16	10	175	4.57	1.45	0	8.7	22.0%	4.3	10.8%	45.0%	\N	8.4	11.6	6.4	5.8	6.5	9.3	6.2	20.8
Homer Bailey	33	12	144	4.81	1.37	0	7.2	18.6%	2.9	7.5%	43.3%	92.9	8.4	10.8	6.6	5.8	7.0	8.7	6.3	20.8
Ben Holmes	32	11	154	4.75	1.41	0	7.7	19.5%	3.6	9.2%	42.3%	\N	8.3	11.0	6.5	5.8	6.9	8.8	6.3	20.7
Logan Gilbert	32	9	165	4.86	1.35	0	8.3	21.2%	3.2	8.2%	38.4%	\N	8.3	11.4	6.5	5.8	6.6	8.5	6.3	20.7
Edgar Olmos	14	10	162	4.53	1.41	0	8.1	20.5%	3.8	9.6%	45.6%	91.7	8.3	11.2	6.5	5.8	6.5	9.4	6.2	20.8
Nate Pearson	32	10	167	5.02	1.36	0	8.4	21.4%	3.1	7.9%	38.5%	\N	8.3	11.5	6.4	5.8	6.7	8.0	6.3	20.6
Kevin Smith	32	10	165	4.69	1.43	0	8.2	20.8%	3.9	9.8%	43.2%	\N	8.3	11.3	6.4	5.7	6.6	8.9	6.2	20.7
Taijuan Walker	32	10	163	4.81	1.38	0	8.1	20.7%	3.0	7.7%	43.9%	92.9	8.3	11.3	6.5	5.7	6.6	8.5	6.2	20.7
Deivi Garcia	30	11	188	5.15	1.44	0	9.4	23.7%	4.4	11.1%	38.3%	\N	8.3	11.9	6.1	5.7	6.7	7.4	6.2	20.4
Nick Margevicius	21	9	140	4.59	1.33	0	7.0	18.1%	2.5	6.5%	43.5%	88.7	8.3	10.7	6.7	5.8	6.7	9.3	6.3	20.8
Steven Fuentes	24	11	151	4.55	1.43	0	7.5	19.1%	3.6	9.2%	49.5%	\N	8.3	10.9	6.5	5.7	6.7	9.2	6.2	20.8
Kendall Graveman	32	11	144	4.62	1.40	0	7.2	18.2%	2.8	7.1%	51.3%	93.6	8.3	10.7	6.5	5.7	6.8	9.1	6.2	20.8
Tylor Megill	26	10	172	4.72	1.43	0	8.6	21.7%	4.0	10.1%	44.7%	\N	8.2	11.4	6.3	5.7	6.5	8.7	6.2	20.6
Nathan Karns	24	10	167	4.82	1.39	0	8.4	21.3%	3.4	8.7%	43.2%	91.6	8.2	11.4	6.4	5.7	6.6	8.4	6.2	20.6
Cal Quantrill	33	10	150	4.69	1.37	0	7.5	19.1%	2.9	7.5%	45.2%	94.1	8.2	10.9	6.5	5.7	6.7	8.9	6.2	20.7
Aaron Civale	32	11	140	4.86	1.33	0	7.0	18.1%	2.3	6.0%	42.5%	92.3	8.2	10.6	6.5	5.7	6.9	8.4	6.3	20.7
Danny Duffy	30	10	156	4.76	1.36	0	7.8	20.1%	3.1	8.1%	37.3%	92.3	8.2	11.1	6.4	5.7	6.6	8.6	6.2	20.7
Wade Miley	34	13	145	4.70	1.45	0	7.3	18.2%	3.5	8.7%	49.3%	90.0	8.2	10.6	6.3	5.7	7.0	8.7	6.2	20.6
Carlos Rodon	32	10	169	4.82	1.41	0	8.5	21.7%	3.9	10.0%	42.8%	92.1	8.1	11.3	6.2	5.6	6.5	8.3	6.1	20.5
Merrill Kelly	31	9	162	4.80	1.38	0	8.1	20.6%	3.0	7.5%	43.1%	91.8	8.1	11.1	6.3	5.6	6.5	8.4	6.1	20.6
Jordan Yamamoto	32	9	169	4.73	1.40	0	8.5	21.4%	3.8	9.6%	41.3%	91.4	8.1	11.3	6.2	5.6	6.3	8.5	6.1	20.5
Matt Shoemaker	32	10	160	5.04	1.36	0	8.0	20.4%	2.7	6.9%	39.9%	90.9	7.9	11.0	6.1	5.5	6.5	7.4	6.6	20.3
Jeff Samardzija	31	9	145	4.75	1.34	0	7.2	18.6%	2.7	6.8%	39.9%	91.7	7.8	10.6	6.1	5.4	6.3	8.2	5.9	20.4
Tanner Roark	32	11	146	4.97	1.38	0	7.3	18.6%	2.9	7.3%	40.6%	91.7	7.7	10.4	6.0	5.4	6.6	7.4	6.0	20.3
Sixto Sanchez	32	9	140	4.54	1.37	0	7.0	17.9%	2.8	7.2%	47.8%	\N	7.7	10.2	6.1	5.4	6.2	8.7	5.9	20.5
Jesse Hahn	12	9	150	4.48	1.41	0	7.5	19.3%	3.6	9.2%	48.0%	94.4	7.7	10.4	6.0	5.3	6.1	8.7	5.8	20.4
Dylan Bundy	31	9	171	5.13	1.37	0	8.5	22.0%	3.1	8.0%	37.5%	91.3	7.7	11.0	5.8	5.3	6.2	6.8	5.9	20.1
Jake Arrieta	32	10	150	4.77	1.41	0	7.5	19.1%	3.3	8.4%	50.5%	92.4	7.6	10.4	5.9	5.3	6.3	7.9	5.9	20.3
Alex Young	32	10	156	4.73	1.42	0	7.8	19.7%	3.5	8.7%	45.1%	88.8	7.6	10.5	5.8	5.3	6.2	7.9	5.8	20.2
Logan Allen	25	10	159	4.84	1.43	0	7.9	20.0%	3.8	9.6%	42.1%	92.5	7.6	10.6	5.8	5.2	6.3	7.6	5.8	20.2
Chase Anderson	33	10	167	5.16	1.38	0	8.3	21.1%	3.1	7.8%	37.1%	93.1	7.6	10.9	5.7	5.2	6.3	6.6	5.8	20.0
Zack Godley	13	9	159	4.66	1.43	0	7.9	20.1%	3.6	9.2%	47.1%	89.8	7.6	10.5	5.8	5.2	6.0	8.1	5.8	20.2
Anibal Sanchez	32	11	156	5.06	1.40	0	7.8	19.8%	3.1	7.9%	40.8%	90.2	7.6	10.5	5.7	5.2	6.4	6.9	5.8	20.1
Justin Dunn	24	9	170	4.91	1.41	0	8.5	21.6%	3.8	9.7%	40.0%	92.4	7.5	10.8	5.7	5.2	6.0	7.3	5.7	20.1
Daniel Norris	34	10	155	4.93	1.39	0	7.8	19.9%	3.1	7.9%	40.6%	90.9	7.4	10.4	5.7	5.1	6.1	7.1	5.7	20.0
Marco Gonzales	30	9	136	4.68	1.36	0	6.8	17.4%	2.5	6.5%	43.4%	89.0	7.3	9.8	5.8	5.1	6.1	7.8	5.7	20.1
Cole Irvin	17	9	142	4.87	1.34	0	7.1	18.2%	2.4	6.0%	43.5%	89.2	7.3	10.0	5.7	5.0	6.1	7.2	5.7	20.1
Yusei Kikuchi	32	9	146	4.79	1.38	0	7.3	18.8%	3.1	7.9%	44.0%	92.2	7.3	10.0	5.6	5.0	6.0	7.3	5.6	20.0
Reynaldo Lopez	30	9	163	5.10	1.38	0	8.2	20.9%	3.4	8.6%	35.1%	95.6	7.2	10.4	5.4	4.9	5.9	6.4	5.6	19.8
Trent Thornton	32	10	159	5.13	1.39	0	7.9	20.2%	3.1	7.9%	39.6%	92.7	7.2	10.3	5.4	4.9	6.1	6.3	5.6	19.8
Jose Suarez	34	10	160	4.93	1.43	0	8.0	20.1%	3.8	9.7%	40.4%	91.6	7.1	10.2	5.3	4.9	5.9	6.7	5.5	19.8
Mike Leake	29	9	124	4.71	1.34	0	6.2	16.0%	1.7	4.3%	49.8%	88.3	7.0	9.2	5.5	4.8	5.9	7.3	5.5	19.9
Tyler Alexander	27	9	137	4.96	1.33	0	6.9	17.7%	2.1	5.5%	40.0%	90.4	6.9	9.5	5.4	4.7	5.8	6.4	5.4	19.7
John Lackey	31	10	152	5.15	1.38	0	7.6	19.3%	2.8	7.1%	40.7%	90.3	6.8	9.8	5.1	4.7	5.9	5.8	5.4	19.6

Name	GS	W	K	ERA	WHIP	SV	K/9	K%	BB/9	BB%	GB%	FBv	15-tm Mixed, Std.	15-tm Mixed, OBP	15-tm Draft & Hold	12-tm Mixed, Std.	12-tm, AL, OBP	12-tm, NL, OBP	12-tm, AL Std.	12-tm, NL Std.
Dakota Hudson	32	11	138	4.51	1.50	0	6.9	17.3%	4.1	10.2%	55.5%	93.4	6.8	9.3	5.1	4.7	5.8	7.5	5.3	19.8
Zach Eflin	32	10	148	5.10	1.39	0	7.4	18.8%	2.7	6.9%	43.5%	93.5	6.8	9.6	5.1	4.6	5.8	5.8	5.3	19.5
Zach Plesac	31	10	147	5.13	1.39	0	7.3	18.6%	2.9	7.5%	39.2%	93.6	6.8	9.6	5.0	4.6	5.9	5.7	5.3	19.5
Martin Perez	32	12	138	4.84	1.47	0	6.9	17.3%	3.3	8.3%	49.2%	93.6	6.7	9.2	5.0	4.6	6.0	6.4	5.3	19.6
Thomas Pannone	21	9	165	5.25	1.40	0	8.3	20.8%	3.4	8.5%	33.1%	89.0	6.7	10.1	4.9	4.6	5.6	5.3	5.3	19.4
Dereck Rodriguez	31	9	138	4.82	1.40	0	6.9	17.5%	3.1	7.7%	46.7%	90.3	6.6	9.2	5.1	4.6	5.7	6.5	5.2	19.6
Enyel De Los Santos	27	9	162	5.14	1.42	0	8.1	20.5%	3.7	9.2%	41.6%	93.5	6.6	9.9	4.8	4.5	5.6	5.4	5.2	19.4
Jhoulys Chacin	34	12	145	5.16	1.45	0	7.2	18.2%	3.4	8.6%	41.0%	89.9	6.6	9.3	4.8	4.5	5.9	5.3	5.2	19.4
Mike Fiers	31	10	139	5.20	1.39	0	6.9	17.6%	2.8	7.0%	40.0%	90.1	6.4	9.1	4.7	4.3	5.7	5.0	5.1	19.2
Taylor Clarke	26	9	154	5.10	1.41	0	7.7	19.4%	3.3	8.3%	39.7%	93.5	6.3	9.4	4.6	4.3	5.4	5.2	5.0	19.2
Brett Anderson	32	11	106	4.67	1.43	0	5.3	13.6%	2.6	6.6%	53.2%	90.3	6.2	8.0	4.8	4.3	5.8	6.4	5.0	19.4
Julio Teheran	32	10	163	5.25	1.47	0	8.2	20.2%	3.9	9.6%	38.9%	89.4	6.1	9.5	4.3	4.2	5.4	4.5	5.0	19.0
Kyle Freeland	33	11	150	5.07	1.48	0	7.5	18.7%	3.4	8.4%	46.7%	92.0	6.1	9.1	4.3	4.1	5.4	5.0	4.9	19.1
Sandy Alcantara	29	8	149	4.77	1.45	0	7.5	18.8%	3.9	9.7%	45.4%	95.5	6.1	9.0	4.4	4.1	5.0	5.8	4.8	19.2
Justus Sheffield	32	9	156	4.87	1.50	0	7.8	19.6%	4.4	11.1%	45.1%	92.7	6.0	9.1	4.2	4.0	5.1	5.4	4.8	19.0
Edinson Volquez	11	9	159	4.93	1.48	0	8.0	20.0%	3.9	9.8%	45.3%	94.0	5.9	9.2	4.2	4.0	5.0	5.1	4.7	19.0
Wade LeBlanc	14	8	140	5.01	1.38	0	7.0	17.8%	2.6	6.6%	39.2%	86.4	5.9	8.7	4.4	4.0	5.1	5.0	4.8	19.0
Jeff Hoffman	33	10	167	5.38	1.48	0	8.3	20.8%	3.8	9.5%	41.6%	93.4	5.8	9.3	4.0	3.9	5.2	3.7	4.7	18.7
Ronald Bolanos	32	9	158	4.94	1.51	0	7.9	19.6%	4.6	11.3%	45.9%	94.2	5.8	9.0	4.1	3.9	5.0	5.0	4.7	18.9
Jaime Barria	32	9	148	5.31	1.38	0	7.4	18.8%	2.9	7.2%	33.4%	91.6	5.8	8.9	4.2	3.9	5.2	4.0	4.8	18.8
Jorge Lopez	32	9	143	5.03	1.45	0	7.2	18.1%	3.5	8.7%	45.3%	94.1	5.8	8.7	4.2	3.9	5.1	4.8	4.7	18.9
Hector Velazquez	29	11	137	5.16	1.48	0	6.8	17.1%	3.7	9.2%	43.2%	91.5	5.5	8.2	3.9	3.7	5.3	4.0	4.6	18.7
Jason Vargas	32	9	150	5.31	1.44	0	7.5	18.8%	3.4	8.4%	40.4%	84.0	5.5	8.6	3.8	3.7	5.0	3.5	4.5	18.5
Steven Brault	32	10	152	4.93	1.53	0	7.6	18.9%	4.4	11.0%	45.4%	91.8	5.4	8.5	3.7	3.6	4.8	4.5	4.4	18.6
Alex McRae	15	9	146	4.91	1.48	0	7.3	18.3%	3.6	9.0%	46.9%	92.4	5.4	8.4	3.8	3.6	4.7	4.6	4.4	18.6
Trevor Williams	31	9	143	5.13	1.44	0	7.1	17.9%	2.9	7.3%	41.2%	91.1	5.4	8.3	3.8	3.6	4.8	3.9	4.4	18.6
Kolby Allard	32	10	143	5.11	1.48	0	7.2	18.1%	3.7	9.2%	42.3%	91.9	5.3	8.3	3.7	3.6	4.9	3.9	4.4	18.5
Tommy Milone	31	9	140	5.31	1.38	0	7.0	17.9%	2.6	6.5%	36.1%	87.0	5.2	8.2	3.7	3.5	4.8	3.3	4.4	18.4
Dillon Peters	33	9	131	5.03	1.45	0	6.6	16.6%	3.3	8.4%	43.8%	90.6	5.1	7.8	3.6	3.4	4.8	3.9	4.3	18.5
John Means	31	9	140	5.41	1.39	0	7.0	17.7%	2.6	6.5%	33.6%	91.7	5.0	8.0	3.5	3.4	4.7	2.7	4.3	18.3
Nick Tropeano	32	8	151	5.33	1.44	0	7.5	19.0%	3.5	8.9%	36.4%	90.0	5.0	8.2	3.3	3.3	4.5	2.8	4.2	18.2
Felix Hernandez	33	9	142	5.21	1.46	0	7.1	17.8%	3.3	8.2%	47.0%	89.4	4.8	7.8	3.2	3.2	4.5	2.9	4.1	18.1
Manny Banuelos	22	9	165	5.25	1.53	0	8.3	20.6%	4.7	11.6%	40.6%	92.1	4.8	8.4	3.0	3.1	4.2	2.7	4.0	18.0
Robert Dugger	32	8	140	5.15	1.44	0	7.0	17.5%	3.5	8.6%	40.5%	89.6	4.7	7.7	3.2	3.1	4.3	3.1	4.0	18.1
Mike Montgomery	32	9	125	4.93	1.49	0	6.2	15.7%	3.5	8.8%	49.5%	91.6	4.7	7.2	3.2	3.1	4.5	3.6	4.0	18.2
Dario Agrazal	32	9	120	5.18	1.42	0	6.0	15.2%	2.2	5.7%	45.1%	90.9	4.6	7.1	3.2	3.1	4.6	2.9	4.0	18.1
Sean Reid-Foley	33	9	170	5.45	1.55	0	8.5	20.9%	5.0	12.2%	41.0%	92.3	4.6	8.3	2.7	3.0	4.3	1.8	3.9	17.8
Adrian Sampson	22	8	138	5.42	1.41	0	6.9	17.3%	2.5	6.3%	39.5%	92.1	4.5	7.5	3.0	3.0	4.4	2.1	4.0	17.9
Anthony Kay	32	9	156	5.46	1.50	0	7.8	19.4%	4.2	10.4%	37.6%	93.6	4.5	7.9	2.8	2.9	4.3	1.8	3.9	17.8
Brian Johnson	33	11	142	5.45	1.51	0	7.1	17.5%	3.8	9.5%	38.2%	88.4	4.5	7.5	2.8	3.0	4.6	1.8	3.9	17.8
Adam Plutko	31	9	140	5.76	1.41	0	7.0	17.7%	2.7	6.9%	30.7%	90.9	4.1	7.3	2.6	2.7	4.3	0.6	3.8	17.5
Jordan Zimmermann	32	8	127	5.43	1.40	0	6.4	16.2%	2.2	5.7%	39.5%	90.3	4.1	6.9	2.7	2.7	4.2	1.5	3.7	17.6
Drew VerHagen	32	9	138	5.27	1.48	0	6.9	17.3%	3.6	9.0%	45.0%	92.9	4.1	7.1	2.5	2.6	4.0	1.9	3.6	17.6
Jacob Waguespack	30	9	142	5.37	1.50	0	7.1	17.8%	3.8	9.5%	44.1%	91.2	4.1	7.2	2.5	2.6	4.1	1.5	3.6	17.5
Clay Buchholz	30	9	131	5.42	1.44	0	6.6	16.5%	2.8	7.0%	41.0%	89.8	4.0	6.9	2.6	2.6	4.1	1.4	3.7	17.6
Ervin Santana	32	9	129	5.38	1.46	0	6.5	16.2%	3.1	7.7%	40.2%	90.3	3.9	6.8	2.5	2.6	4.1	1.4	3.6	17.5
Brock Burke	33	9	140	5.36	1.51	0	7.0	17.4%	3.8	9.5%	41.2%	91.3	3.9	7.0	2.3	2.5	4.0	1.4	3.5	17.5
Zach Davies	32	9	129	5.37	1.49	0	6.5	15.9%	2.8	7.0%	45.6%	88.6	3.7	6.6	2.2	2.4	4.0	1.1	3.4	17.4
Asher Wojciechowski	32	8	158	5.90	1.44	0	7.9	19.8%	3.4	8.6%	29.1%	91.2	3.6	7.4	2.0	2.3	3.7	-0.6	3.4	17.0
Hector Santiago	25	8	162	5.60	1.52	0	8.1	20.1%	4.6	11.5%	32.2%	92.7	3.6	7.3	1.9	2.2	3.6	0.2	3.3	17.1
Chi Chi Gonzalez	31	10	142	5.44	1.55	0	7.1	17.5%	3.9	9.5%	47.3%	92.1	3.5	6.7	1.8	2.2	3.8	0.5	3.2	17.1
Peter Lambert	33	10	128	5.51	1.50	0	6.4	15.9%	2.9	7.3%	46.2%	92.4	3.3	6.2	1.8	2.1	3.8	0.2	3.2	17.0
Ivan Nova	31	8	119	5.44	1.44	0	5.9	15.1%	2.3	5.9%	46.0%	92.3	3.3	6.0	2.0	2.1	3.7	0.5	3.2	17.1
Rico Garcia	32	9	148	5.66	1.53	0	7.4	18.2%	3.8	9.3%	41.9%	89.8	3.3	6.7	1.6	2.0	3.6	-0.4	3.1	16.8
Miguel Gonzalez	30	9	122	5.49	1.45	0	6.1	15.3%	2.8	7.0%	39.8%	90.0	3.2	6.0	1.8	2.0	3.6	0.2	3.1	17.0
James Marvel	32	9	125	5.32	1.50	0	6.3	15.6%	3.2	8.0%	45.6%	90.3	3.2	6.0	1.8	2.0	3.6	0.6	3.1	17.0
Ariel Jurado	32	9	113	5.40	1.49	0	5.6	14.1%	2.7	6.9%	46.8%	91.9	2.8	5.3	1.4	1.7	3.4	-0.1	2.8	16.7
Chandler Shepherd	31	8	136	5.67	1.49	0	6.8	17.0%	3.4	8.6%	40.6%	91.9	2.7	5.9	1.2	1.6	3.2	-1.1	2.8	16.5
Jefry Rodriguez	32	10	135	5.50	1.57	0	6.8	16.7%	4.5	11.2%	44.4%	93.8	2.7	5.8	1.1	1.6	3.3	-0.7	2.8	16.5
Marco Estrada	31	8	136	5.81	1.48	0	6.8	16.7%	3.4	8.5%	30.0%	87.8	2.5	5.8	1.0	1.5	3.1	-1.7	2.7	16.3
Danny Salazar	15	9	129	5.56	1.53	0	6.4	16.0%	3.7	9.2%	41.8%	86.7	2.3	5.4	0.9	1.3	3.0	-1.2	2.5	16.3
Gabriel Ynoa	23	8	122	5.65	1.48	0	6.1	15.4%	2.7	6.8%	42.5%	93.6	2.2	5.2	0.9	1.3	3.0	-1.5	2.5	16.2
Keegan Akin	32	8	162	5.83	1.58	0	8.1	19.8%	4.9	12.1%	33.0%	\N	2.2	6.2	0.5	1.2	2.7	-2.3	2.4	16.0
Antonio Senzatela	31	9	122	5.49	1.57	0	6.1	15.0%	3.5	8.6%	50.2%	93.5	2.1	5.0	0.7	1.2	3.0	-1.3	2.4	16.2
T.J. Zeuch	32	9	112	5.44	1.55	0	5.6	13.8%	3.4	8.4%	50.9%	91.5	2.0	4.6	0.6	1.1	2.9	-1.3	2.3	16.1
David Hess	33	8	146	6.03	1.51	0	7.3	18.2%	3.6	8.9%	34.5%	92.9	1.9	5.5	0.3	1.0	2.7	-3.2	2.3	15.8
Ross Detwiler	32	9	120	5.53	1.54	0	6.0	14.9%	3.7	9.2%	44.8%	91.1	1.8	4.7	0.4	1.0	2.7	-1.8	2.2	16.0
Carson Fulmer	20	8	165	5.75	1.62	0	8.2	20.0%	5.5	13.3%	39.2%	94.1	1.8	5.9	0.1	0.9	2.4	-2.6	2.1	15.7
Aaron Brooks	34	9	122	5.75	1.51	0	6.1	15.2%	3.0	7.5%	44.2%	91.5	1.8	4.8	0.4	1.0	2.8	-2.4	2.2	15.9
Glenn Sparkman	32	8	110	5.72	1.50	0	5.5	13.7%	2.8	7.0%	40.4%	93.1	1.2	4.0	0.0	0.5	2.4	-3.0	1.9	15.5

Name	GS	W	K	ERA	WHIP	SV	K/9	K%	BB/9	BB%	GB%	FBV	15-tm Mixed, Std.	15-tm Mixed, OBP	15-tm Draft & Hold	12-tm Mixed, Std.	12-tm, AL, OBP	12-tm, NL, OBP	12-tm, AL, Std.	12-tm, NL, Std.
Josh Hader	0	4	99	2.89	1.02	23	14.8	40.7%	3.4	9.4%	33.5%	95.5	18.2	21.0	16.4	13.3	13.8	23.0	14.1	27.8
Edwin Diaz	0	3	90	2.90	1.05	23	13.5	37.2%	3.2	8.8%	42.5%	97.6	17.3	20.0	15.6	12.6	13.2	21.9	13.5	27.2
Kirby Yates	0	3	82	3.20	1.08	29	12.4	33.3%	2.8	7.6%	41.9%	93.5	17.3	20.2	15.5	12.6	13.7	19.9	14.0	26.8
Will Smith	0	3	77	3.14	1.14	33	11.6	31.2%	3.2	8.7%	42.4%	92.3	17.3	20.3	15.4	12.6	13.9	19.4	14.2	26.7
Aroldis Chapman	0	4	87	2.98	1.12	27	13.1	35.8%	3.9	10.6%	43.6%	98.3	17.2	20.1	15.4	12.6	13.5	20.8	13.8	26.9
Liam Hendriks	0	4	79	3.15	1.07	24	11.9	32.7%	2.8	7.6%	38.2%	96.4	16.1	18.7	14.5	11.7	12.7	19.5	12.9	26.3
Craig Kimbrel	0	3	84	3.57	1.19	31	12.6	33.5%	3.9	10.4%	38.1%	96.2	15.4	18.8	13.5	11.3	12.7	16.1	12.9	25.3
Kenley Jansen	0	3	69	3.87	1.13	32	6.8	27.9%	2.5	6.6%	36.9%	93.0	14.9	18.0	13.1	10.9	12.6	14.5	12.7	24.9
Brad Hand	0	3	74	3.69	1.19	30	11.1	29.6%	3.3	8.7%	40.2%	92.6	14.5	17.6	12.7	10.6	12.1	14.7	12.3	24.7
Ken Giles	0	3	76	3.57	1.16	27	11.4	30.5%	2.9	7.9%	41.6%	96.6	14.3	17.2	12.7	10.4	11.8	15.5	11.9	24.7
Roberto Osuna	0	3	70	3.65	1.13	27	10.5	28.3%	2.4	6.5%	40.0%	96.6	14.3	17.0	12.7	10.4	11.8	15.2	11.9	24.7
Emilio Pagan	0	3	75	3.69	1.11	24	11.3	30.4%	2.7	7.2%	31.8%	95.4	14.0	16.8	12.5	10.2	11.5	15.2	11.6	24.6
Hector Neris	0	3	76	3.87	1.20	28	11.4	30.2%	3.3	8.7%	40.5%	94.6	13.4	16.6	11.7	9.8	11.4	13.2	11.5	24.0
Taylor Rogers	0	3	72	3.46	1.17	23	10.8	28.9%	2.6	7.0%	46.5%	94.8	13.3	15.9	11.9	9.7	10.9	15.3	11.0	24.3
Raisel Iglesias	0	3	72	3.82	1.20	27	10.8	28.8%	3.2	8.4%	40.8%	95.4	13.0	16.0	11.4	9.5	11.0	13.0	11.2	23.7
Carlos Martinez	0	3	64	3.54	1.24	26	9.7	25.5%	3.1	8.2%	49.7%	94.5	12.8	15.4	11.2	9.3	10.8	13.6	10.9	23.7
Brandon Workman	0	3	73	3.84	1.31	29	10.9	28.2%	4.1	10.6%	43.6%	92.9	12.1	15.2	10.4	8.8	10.5	11.4	10.7	23.0
Jose Leclerc	0	3	83	3.72	1.28	24	12.4	32.3%	4.7	12.1%	36.1%	96.4	11.9	14.9	10.3	8.6	9.9	12.4	10.2	23.0
Keone Kela	0	3	73	3.71	1.24	22	11.0	29.1%	3.5	9.4%	41.1%	96.4	11.4	14.1	9.9	8.2	9.5	12.2	9.7	22.8
Archie Bradley	0	3	67	3.93	1.31	28	10.0	25.9%	3.5	9.1%	46.7%	95.4	11.4	14.4	9.7	8.2	10.0	10.3	10.2	22.5
Carlos Carrasco	0	4	77	2.98	1.01	0	11.5	31.9%	1.7	4.6%	45.1%	94.0	10.9	12.1	10.2	7.8	7.7	17.8	7.9	23.6
Mark Melancon	0	3	56	3.76	1.30	26	8.4	21.9%	2.7	7.1%	54.0%	91.9	10.9	13.4	9.4	7.9	9.6	10.7	9.7	22.3
Ian Kennedy	0	3	62	4.37	1.26	28	9.3	24.4%	2.7	7.1%	35.6%	92.6	10.7	13.7	9.1	7.8	9.8	8.2	9.8	21.9
Seth Lugo	0	3	69	3.53	1.15	12	10.4	27.9%	2.4	6.4%	44.0%	93.7	10.5	12.5	9.4	7.5	8.3	13.3	8.5	22.6
Felipe Vazquez	0	3	82	2.90	1.10	0	12.3	33.6%	3.0	8.1%	45.2%	98.5	10.1	11.5	9.4	7.2	7.0	17.0	7.3	23.0
Nick Anderson	0	3	83	3.23	1.08	1	12.4	33.9%	3.0	8.1%	35.4%	96.0	10.0	11.6	9.2	7.1	7.2	15.6	7.4	22.8
Jose Urena	2	3	53	4.07	1.28	24	8.0	20.8%	2.5	6.5%	47.0%	96.3	9.5	12.0	8.2	6.9	8.7	8.4	8.8	21.3
Kenta Maeda	0	3	75	3.31	1.09	2	11.2	30.5%	2.4	6.5%	41.9%	92.8	9.4	10.9	8.7	6.7	6.9	14.6	7.1	22.4
Chad Green	0	4	81	3.41	1.06	0	12.1	33.3%	2.6	7.2%	37.1%	97.2	9.3	10.8	8.5	6.6	6.7	14.4	6.9	22.3
Alex Colome	0	3	59	4.32	1.35	28	8.9	23.0%	3.4	8.9%	44.7%	94.4	9.3	12.3	7.8	6.7	8.8	6.6	8.9	20.9
Joe Jimenez	0	3	70	4.18	1.27	20	10.5	27.6%	3.6	9.4%	35.8%	95.0	9.3	12.0	7.9	6.7	8.2	8.4	8.3	21.2
Sean Doolittle	0	3	67	4.05	1.20	15	10.0	26.5%	2.7	7.1%	32.7%	93.3	9.1	11.4	8.0	6.5	7.8	9.6	7.9	21.4
Hansel Robles	0	3	65	4.25	1.28	20	9.7	25.3%	3.4	8.8%	36.8%	96.4	8.6	11.3	7.3	6.1	7.8	7.3	7.9	20.7
Mychal Givens	0	3	71	4.03	1.27	16	10.6	27.9%	3.7	9.8%	39.5%	95.3	8.5	11.1	7.4	6.1	7.4	8.7	7.5	20.9
Ryan Pressly	0	4	72	3.37	1.15	2	10.8	29.4%	2.9	7.8%	47.1%	95.2	8.3	9.7	7.5	5.8	6.2	13.0	6.3	21.5
Matt Barnes	0	4	83	3.32	1.22	2	12.4	32.8%	4.1	10.8%	45.3%	96.6	8.0	9.7	7.2	5.6	5.9	12.6	6.1	21.3
Joshua James	0	4	83	3.40	1.18	0	12.5	33.4%	3.9	10.5%	40.7%	97.3	7.9	9.6	7.2	5.6	5.8	12.7	6.0	21.3
Chris Martin	0	3	68	3.38	1.12	0	10.1	27.4%	1.9	5.3%	48.2%	95.4	7.9	9.2	7.3	5.6	5.9	12.8	6.0	21.4
Diego Castillo	0	3	73	3.25	1.17	0	11.0	29.7%	3.3	8.8%	47.1%	99.0	7.9	9.2	7.2	5.5	5.7	13.1	5.9	21.3
Corey Knebel	0	3	85	3.39	1.18	0	12.7	33.7%	3.8	10.0%	43.3%	96.7	7.8	9.6	7.1	5.5	5.7	12.6	5.9	21.2
Anthony Bass	0	3	57	4.14	1.31	19	8.6	22.4%	3.1	8.1%	46.7%	95.2	7.8	10.3	6.7	5.6	7.2	7.0	7.3	20.3
Colin Poche	0	3	81	3.62	1.16	1	12.1	32.3%	3.6	9.6%	30.7%	93.2	7.7	9.5	7.0	5.4	5.8	11.6	6.0	21.0
Freddy Peralta	0	3	84	3.52	1.17	0	12.6	33.7%	3.7	9.9%	37.1%	93.2	7.6	9.4	6.9	5.3	5.6	12.0	5.8	21.1
Jesus Luzardo	0	3	70	3.39	1.16	0	10.5	28.2%	2.9	7.7%	44.0%	96.0	7.6	8.9	6.9	5.3	5.6	12.3	5.8	21.1
Dellin Betances	0	3	82	3.45	1.19	0	12.2	32.7%	4.0	10.7%	46.0%	96.1	7.5	9.2	6.8	5.3	5.5	12.0	5.7	21.0
Ross Stripling	0	3	64	3.43	1.13	0	9.6	25.9%	2.0	5.3%	46.1%	91.0	7.5	8.7	6.9	5.3	5.6	12.1	5.8	21.1
Oliver Drake	0	3	71	3.43	1.21	2	10.6	28.2%	3.3	8.7%	46.8%	93.4	7.2	8.7	6.5	5.1	5.5	11.4	5.7	20.8
Ryne Stanek	0	3	77	3.56	1.22	3	11.5	30.4%	3.8	10.0%	38.2%	97.9	7.2	9.0	6.4	5.1	5.5	10.7	5.7	20.6
Ty Buttrey	0	3	68	3.61	1.22	5	10.2	27.2%	3.3	8.8%	45.0%	97.0	7.2	8.9	6.4	5.1	5.7	10.3	5.9	20.6
Giovanny Gallegos	0	3	71	3.67	1.16	1	10.7	28.5%	2.7	7.1%	37.8%	93.5	7.1	8.7	6.4	5.0	5.4	10.7	5.6	20.6
Drew Pomeranz	0	3	77	3.60	1.20	1	11.6	30.6%	3.2	8.6%	43.2%	92.3	7.1	8.8	6.3	4.9	5.3	10.8	5.5	20.6
Andrew Kittredge	0	3	67	3.45	1.17	0	10.1	27.2%	2.7	7.2%	46.2%	95.2	7.0	8.4	6.4	4.9	5.3	11.4	5.4	20.7
Julio Urias	0	3	72	3.44	1.20	0	10.9	28.4%	3.8	9.1%	43.3%	95.7	7.0	8.5	6.4	4.9	5.2	11.4	5.4	20.7
Tommy Kahnle	0	3	76	3.58	1.21	0	11.4	30.4%	3.6	9.6%	44.6%	96.2	6.7	8.3	6.0	4.7	5.1	10.6	5.2	20.4
Jairo Diaz	0	3	64	4.19	1.36	16	9.5	24.5%	3.7	9.4%	49.2%	96.6	6.7	9.2	5.6	4.8	6.3	5.9	6.4	19.6
Dustin May	0	3	60	3.55	1.17	0	8.9	23.9%	2.3	6.1%	51.5%	96.1	6.4	7.6	5.9	4.5	5.0	10.4	5.1	20.3
A.J. Puk	0	3	74	3.57	1.24	1	11.1	29.3%	3.9	10.2%	41.3%	96.3	6.4	8.0	5.7	4.5	4.9	10.1	5.1	20.2
Caleb Ferguson	0	3	75	3.55	1.23	0	11.2	29.5%	3.8	10.0%	44.0%	94.7	6.4	8.0	5.7	4.4	4.8	10.3	5.0	20.2
Daniel Hudson	0	3	62	4.34	1.35	16	9.3	23.9%	3.8	9.8%	41.0%	96.2	6.4	8.9	5.3	4.5	6.1	5.0	6.2	19.3
Chris Bassitt	0	3	64	3.70	1.17	0	9.6	25.9%	2.6	6.9%	42.6%	94.0	6.4	7.7	5.8	4.4	5.0	9.9	5.1	20.2
Jose Castillo	0	3	77	3.55	1.24	0	11.6	30.3%	4.0	10.4%	40.9%	94.8	6.3	7.9	5.6	4.3	4.7	10.1	4.9	20.1
Andrew Miller	0	3	71	3.60	1.23	1	10.7	28.2%	3.5	9.3%	44.8%	92.1	6.2	7.8	5.6	4.3	4.8	9.8	4.9	20.0
Andres Munoz	0	3	80	3.40	1.28	0	11.9	31.2%	4.6	12.1%	47.1%	99.7	6.2	7.9	5.5	4.3	4.6	10.4	4.8	20.1
Jonathan Loaisiga	0	3	72	3.74	1.20	0	10.8	29.0%	3.2	8.7%	44.1%	97.3	6.2	7.8	5.6	4.3	4.8	9.5	4.9	20.0
Yonny Chirinos	0	3	60	3.67	1.17	0	8.9	24.0%	2.0	5.4%	45.4%	94.4	6.2	7.4	5.7	4.3	4.8	9.8	4.9	20.1
Ray Black	0	3	82	3.76	1.23	0	12.4	32.5%	4.0	10.4%	38.2%	97.9	6.2	8.0	5.4	4.3	4.7	9.4	4.9	19.9
Luke Jackson	0	3	73	3.51	1.25	0	10.9	28.8%	3.6	9.4%	48.7%	96.0	6.2	7.7	5.5	4.3	4.6	10.1	4.8	20.0
Joe Kelly	0	3	68	3.41	1.25	0	10.2	26.8%	3.6	9.5%	52.8%	98.0	6.2	7.5	5.5	4.3	4.6	10.4	4.8	20.1
Matt Strahm	0	3	67	3.78	1.17	0	10.0	26.7%	2.5	6.6%	39.4%	91.8	6.1	7.6	5.5	4.2	4.7	9.3	4.9	19.9
David Robertson	0	3	77	3.70	1.23	0	11.5	30.3%	3.7	9.7%	44.8%	92.9	6.0	7.7	5.3	4.1	4.6	9.3	4.8	19.8

Name	GS	W	K	ERA	WHIP	SV	K/9	K%	BB/9	BB%	GB%	FBv	15-tm Mixed Std.	15-tm Mixed OBP	15-tm Draft & Hold	12-tm Mixed Std.	12-tm AL OBP	12-tm NL OBP	12-tm AL Std.	12-tm NL Std.
Brad Wieck	0	3	79	3.72	1.25	0	11.9	31.1%	4.0	10.4%	38.5%	93.7	5.9	7.7	5.2	4.1	4.5	9.2	4.7	19.8
James Karinchak	0	3	84	3.60	1.29	0	12.6	32.7%	4.8	12.6%	40.3%	96.8	5.9	7.8	5.2	4.1	4.4	9.5	4.7	19.8
Peter Fairbanks	0	3	72	3.61	1.24	0	10.8	28.7%	3.7	9.7%	44.0%	97.3	5.9	7.5	5.3	4.1	4.5	9.5	4.7	19.8
Kevin Gausman	2	3	66	3.84	1.18	0	9.9	26.4%	2.3	6.2%	45.4%	94.1	5.9	7.3	5.3	4.1	4.6	8.8	4.7	19.8
Andrew Chafin	0	3	69	3.55	1.28	2	10.3	26.9%	3.7	9.7%	49.7%	93.3	5.8	7.4	5.1	4.0	4.5	9.2	4.7	19.7
Tyler Duffey	0	3	68	3.85	1.21	0	10.2	27.1%	2.6	6.9%	43.6%	94.0	5.7	7.2	5.1	3.9	4.5	8.5	4.6	19.6
Kevin Ginkel	0	3	73	3.93	1.26	3	11.0	28.7%	3.7	9.7%	39.7%	93.1	5.6	7.6	4.9	3.9	4.6	7.6	4.8	19.4
Austin Voth	0	3	64	3.82	1.20	0	9.6	25.7%	2.7	7.1%	41.3%	93.1	5.6	7.0	5.0	3.9	4.5	8.5	4.6	19.6
Brad Peacock	0	3	72	3.93	1.22	0	10.8	28.4%	3.1	8.2%	39.8%	92.8	5.4	7.1	4.8	3.7	4.3	7.9	4.4	19.4
Seranthony Domingu	0	3	74	3.70	1.27	0	11.1	29.1%	3.9	10.2%	48.1%	97.6	5.4	7.1	4.7	3.7	4.2	8.6	4.4	19.4
Corbin Burnes	0	3	69	3.81	1.23	0	10.3	27.2%	3.1	8.1%	46.6%	95.6	5.4	7.0	4.8	3.7	4.3	8.3	4.4	19.4
JT Chargois	0	3	67	3.59	1.28	0	10.1	26.4%	3.7	9.6%	51.9%	96.0	5.3	6.8	4.7	3.6	4.2	8.8	4.3	19.4
Jake Diekman	0	3	72	3.54	1.31	0	10.9	28.4%	4.6	12.0%	46.8%	95.7	5.3	6.9	4.6	3.6	4.1	8.9	4.3	19.4
Shaun Anderson	0	3	54	3.85	1.26	4	8.1	21.4%	2.7	7.1%	46.4%	92.9	5.3	6.8	4.7	3.7	4.5	7.2	4.7	19.2
Jordan Hicks	0	3	70	3.44	1.32	0	10.4	27.2%	4.3	11.2%	54.0%	101.1	5.3	6.8	4.6	3.6	4.0	9.1	4.3	19.4
Lance McCullers Jr.	10	5	65	3.78	1.29	0	9.7	25.6%	3.5	9.3%	51.9%	94.4	5.3	6.7	4.6	3.6	4.4	8.1	4.3	19.3
Sam Selman	0	3	74	3.61	1.30	0	11.2	28.9%	4.5	11.7%	40.9%	89.6	5.2	6.9	4.6	3.6	4.0	8.6	4.3	19.3
Justin Wilson	0	3	72	3.66	1.29	0	10.9	28.5%	4.1	10.9%	45.0%	94.8	5.2	6.8	4.5	3.5	4.0	8.4	4.2	19.3
Brandon Morrow	0	3	66	3.76	1.25	0	9.9	25.9%	3.1	8.1%	46.9%	97.2	5.2	6.6	4.6	3.5	4.1	8.1	4.3	19.3
Amir Garrett	0	3	74	3.82	1.28	1	11.2	29.3%	4.1	10.7%	44.9%	95.0	5.2	6.9	4.5	3.5	4.1	7.7	4.3	19.2
Will Harris	0	3	61	3.81	1.25	0	9.2	24.4%	2.8	7.3%	50.0%	91.9	5.0	6.3	4.4	3.4	4.0	7.7	4.1	19.1
Trevor Megill	0	3	68	3.79	1.26	0	10.2	26.8%	3.5	9.1%	44.3%	\N	4.9	6.5	4.3	3.3	3.9	7.7	4.1	19.1
Joakim Soria	0	3	64	3.89	1.24	0	9.6	25.2%	3.0	8.0%	42.3%	92.6	4.9	6.4	4.3	3.3	4.0	7.4	4.1	19.1
Dennis Santana	0	3	67	3.80	1.27	0	10.1	26.3%	3.7	9.5%	46.8%	93.2	4.9	6.4	4.3	3.3	3.9	7.6	4.1	19.0
Carlos Estevez	0	3	67	4.31	1.32	7	10.0	25.9%	3.5	9.0%	42.2%	97.8	4.8	7.0	4.0	3.3	4.5	4.7	4.6	18.5
Aaron Loup	0	3	64	3.63	1.29	0	9.6	24.9%	3.5	9.1%	51.1%	91.7	4.8	6.2	4.2	3.2	3.8	7.9	4.0	19.0
Brent Suter	0	3	59	4.02	1.20	0	8.9	23.5%	2.0	5.2%	42.3%	87.0	4.8	6.2	4.2	3.2	4.0	6.9	4.0	18.9
Trey Wingenter	0	3	76	3.79	1.30	0	11.4	29.5%	4.4	11.4%	42.9%	96.2	4.8	6.5	4.1	3.2	3.7	7.4	4.0	18.9
Sean Newcomb	0	3	68	3.80	1.29	0	10.2	26.6%	3.6	9.4%	44.2%	94.0	4.7	6.3	4.1	3.2	3.8	7.3	3.9	18.9
Aaron Bummer	0	3	61	3.58	1.34	2	9.1	23.9%	4.0	10.4%	56.6%	95.4	4.7	6.1	4.0	3.2	3.9	7.6	4.1	18.9
Trevor Richards	0	3	64	3.99	1.23	0	9.6	25.2%	2.8	7.4%	38.1%	91.5	4.7	6.2	4.1	3.2	3.9	6.8	4.0	18.8
Bobby Wahl	0	3	76	3.97	1.28	0	11.4	29.6%	3.9	10.3%	40.2%	94.8	4.7	6.5	4.0	3.1	3.8	6.8	3.9	18.8
Noe Ramirez	0	3	63	4.26	1.28	5	9.4	24.5%	3.2	8.2%	40.0%	89.8	4.6	6.6	3.9	3.2	4.3	5.0	4.4	18.5
Rowan Wick	0	3	64	4.20	1.38	9	9.5	24.4%	4.2	10.8%	46.3%	95.8	4.5	6.7	3.7	3.1	4.4	4.3	4.5	18.3
Fernando Abad	0	3	59	3.78	1.26	0	8.8	23.2%	2.9	7.7%	44.4%	92.9	4.5	5.9	4.0	3.1	3.7	7.3	3.9	18.8
Reyes Moronta	0	3	73	3.76	1.31	0	10.9	28.4%	4.6	11.9%	40.3%	97.1	4.5	6.2	3.9	3.0	3.6	7.2	3.8	18.8
Jose Urquidy	8	4	61	4.30	1.21	0	9.2	24.4%	2.3	6.2%	38.5%	93.3	4.5	6.0	3.9	3.1	4.0	5.7	3.9	18.6
Zack Britton	0	3	57	3.38	1.39	2	8.5	22.2%	4.2	10.9%	63.4%	94.4	4.5	5.8	3.9	3.0	3.7	8.0	3.9	18.9
Framber Valdez	5	4	64	3.62	1.35	0	9.6	25.4%	4.3	11.3%	56.8%	93.2	4.5	5.9	3.9	3.0	3.7	7.6	3.8	18.8
Casey Sadler	0	3	57	3.95	1.24	0	8.5	22.4%	2.4	6.4%	47.8%	95.0	4.4	5.8	3.9	3.0	3.8	6.7	3.8	18.7
Adrian Morejon	5	3	66	3.84	1.30	0	10.0	25.9%	3.7	9.7%	45.1%	96.4	4.4	6.0	3.8	3.0	3.7	6.9	3.8	18.7
A.J. Minter	0	3	70	3.89	1.30	0	10.5	27.2%	3.8	10.0%	41.4%	96.1	4.4	6.1	3.8	3.0	3.6	6.7	3.8	18.7
Drew Gagnon	0	3	59	4.04	1.23	0	8.9	23.5%	2.4	6.5%	44.4%	92.5	4.4	5.8	3.9	3.0	3.7	6.4	3.8	18.7
Trevor Gott	0	3	62	3.73	1.29	0	9.3	24.1%	3.5	8.9%	48.1%	94.4	4.4	5.8	3.8	2.9	3.6	7.2	3.7	18.7
Rafael Montero	0	3	66	4.18	1.31	4	9.9	25.6%	3.5	9.0%	42.1%	94.7	4.4	6.3	3.6	2.9	4.0	5.0	4.1	18.4
Cody Reed	0	3	66	3.80	1.29	0	9.8	25.8%	3.6	9.4%	50.9%	92.7	4.4	5.9	3.8	2.9	3.6	6.9	3.7	18.7
Buck Farmer	0	3	61	4.38	1.34	9	9.2	23.7%	3.5	8.9%	41.6%	94.9	4.3	6.5	3.5	3.0	4.3	3.6	4.4	18.1
Adam Kolarek	0	3	51	3.58	1.30	0	7.7	20.1%	2.9	7.5%	58.2%	88.9	4.3	5.4	3.9	2.9	3.6	7.6	3.7	18.8
Robert Stephenson	0	3	75	4.06	1.28	0	11.2	29.3%	4.0	10.4%	37.2%	94.2	4.3	6.2	3.7	2.9	3.6	6.1	3.7	18.5
Kyle McGowin	3	3	62	4.06	1.25	0	9.2	24.3%	2.8	7.4%	43.5%	90.7	4.3	5.8	3.8	2.9	3.7	6.2	3.8	18.6
Nick Burdi	0	3	72	3.91	1.30	0	10.8	28.0%	3.8	9.7%	42.0%	97.4	4.3	6.0	3.7	2.9	3.5	6.5	3.7	18.6
Jimmy Nelson	0	3	67	3.99	1.27	0	10.0	26.1%	3.3	8.5%	47.2%	92.6	4.3	5.9	3.7	2.9	3.6	6.3	3.7	18.6
Robert Stock	0	3	68	3.71	1.33	0	10.2	26.2%	4.0	10.4%	49.2%	97.7	4.3	5.9	3.7	2.9	3.5	7.1	3.7	18.6
Robbie Erlin	0	3	54	3.89	1.25	0	8.1	21.4%	2.2	5.8%	47.6%	91.0	4.3	5.5	3.8	2.9	3.6	6.6	3.7	18.6
Lucas Sims	5	3	74	4.20	1.26	0	11.1	29.0%	3.8	10.0%	36.2%	93.6	4.2	6.1	3.6	2.8	3.6	5.6	3.7	18.4
Alex Reyes	0	3	73	3.85	1.33	0	11.0	28.3%	4.5	11.6%	41.1%	95.9	4.2	6.0	3.6	2.8	3.4	6.6	3.6	18.5
Tony Watson	0	3	55	3.87	1.26	0	8.3	21.8%	2.8	7.3%	44.9%	93.0	4.2	5.5	3.7	2.8	3.6	6.6	3.7	18.6
Richard Rodriguez	0	3	62	4.39	1.31	7	9.3	24.1%	3.2	8.2%	37.6%	93.2	4.2	6.2	3.4	2.9	4.1	3.8	4.2	18.1
Oliver Perez	0	3	65	4.08	1.26	0	9.8	25.5%	3.2	8.3%	39.0%	91.6	4.2	5.8	3.6	2.8	3.6	6.0	3.7	18.5
David Bednar	0	3	67	3.98	1.32	2	10.1	26.0%	3.9	10.1%	43.9%	95.0	4.2	6.0	3.5	2.8	3.6	5.8	3.8	18.4
Zach McAllister	0	3	63	4.09	1.25	0	9.4	24.7%	2.9	7.5%	42.7%	94.9	4.2	5.7	3.6	2.8	3.6	5.9	3.7	18.5
Scott Alexander	0	3	53	3.43	1.35	0	8.0	20.8%	3.6	9.3%	61.9%	93.0	4.2	5.3	3.7	2.8	3.4	7.8	3.6	18.7
Grant Dayton	0	3	67	4.09	1.26	0	10.0	26.3%	3.3	8.5%	38.0%	90.8	4.2	5.8	3.6	2.8	3.6	5.9	3.7	18.4
Steven Okert	0	3	63	4.01	1.26	0	9.4	24.6%	3.3	8.6%	35.6%	91.3	4.2	5.7	3.6	2.8	3.5	6.1	3.6	18.5
Shane Greene	0	3	61	4.08	1.30	3	9.2	23.7%	3.0	7.9%	45.7%	92.3	4.2	5.8	3.5	2.8	3.7	5.3	3.8	18.3
Ryan Madson	0	3	61	4.00	1.26	0	9.1	24.0%	2.8	7.5%	47.0%	95.1	4.1	5.6	3.6	2.8	3.5	6.1	3.6	18.5
Lewis Thorpe	3	3	65	4.19	1.25	0	9.7	25.5%	2.9	7.7%	38.0%	91.2	4.1	5.7	3.5	2.7	3.6	5.5	3.6	18.4
Chris Flexen	0	3	64	4.00	1.27	0	9.6	25.1%	3.1	8.2%	44.1%	93.6	4.1	5.6	3.5	2.7	3.5	6.0	3.6	18.4
John Brebbia	0	3	66	4.22	1.24	0	9.9	25.9%	3.1	8.1%	31.8%	93.2	4.0	5.7	3.5	2.7	3.5	5.3	3.6	18.3
Craig Stammen	0	3	59	3.95	1.27	0	8.8	23.0%	2.6	6.7%	48.6%	92.9	4.0	5.4	3.5	2.7	3.4	6.1	3.5	18.4

Name	GS	W	K	ERA	WHIP	SV	K/9	K%	BB/9	BB%	GB%	FBv	15-tm Mixed, Std	15-tm Mixed, OBP	15-tm Draft & Hold	12-tm Mixed, Std	12-tm, AL OBP	12-tm, NL OBP	12-tm, AL Std	12-tm, NL Std
Deolis Guerra	0	3	63	4.11	1.25	0	9.4	24.7%	2.9	7.6%	41.9%	91.6	4.0	5.6	3.5	2.7	3.5	5.6	3.6	18.3
Trevor May	0	3	71	4.15	1.28	0	10.7	27.8%	3.6	9.5%	37.8%	95.4	4.0	5.8	3.4	2.7	3.4	5.5	3.5	18.3
Josh Taylor	0	3	66	3.91	1.32	0	9.9	25.8%	3.9	10.0%	43.4%	94.7	4.0	5.6	3.4	2.7	3.4	6.1	3.5	18.4
Dillon Maples	0	3	82	3.52	1.45	0	12.4	31.4%	6.5	16.4%	52.4%	96.4	4.0	5.9	3.2	2.6	3.1	7.1	3.4	18.4
Genesis Cabrera	0	3	66	4.01	1.29	0	9.9	25.7%	3.7	9.6%	38.4%	96.5	4.0	5.6	3.4	2.6	3.4	5.9	3.5	18.3
Matt Andriese	0	3	61	4.02	1.27	0	9.2	24.2%	2.8	7.5%	46.8%	92.2	4.0	5.5	3.4	2.6	3.4	5.8	3.5	18.3
Rubby de la Rosa	0	3	68	4.08	1.28	0	10.1	26.4%	3.4	9.0%	44.1%	94.9	3.9	5.6	3.3	2.6	3.4	5.5	3.5	18.3
Josh Sborz	0	3	64	4.07	1.29	0	9.6	25.0%	3.4	8.8%	43.1%	95.2	3.8	5.4	3.3	2.5	3.3	5.5	3.4	18.2
Jay Jackson	0	3	72	4.12	1.30	0	10.8	27.8%	3.7	9.5%	42.1%	94.4	3.8	5.6	3.2	2.5	3.3	5.3	3.4	18.2
Austin Pruitt	0	3	54	4.02	1.26	0	8.2	21.4%	2.3	6.0%	47.1%	92.1	3.8	5.1	3.3	2.5	3.4	5.7	3.4	18.3
Sam Delaplane	0	3	70	4.00	1.31	0	10.4	27.2%	4.1	10.6%	41.8%	\N	3.8	5.5	3.2	2.5	3.2	5.6	3.4	18.2
Darren O'Day	0	3	67	4.15	1.28	0	10.0	25.8%	3.3	8.5%	40.4%	86.6	3.8	5.4	3.2	2.5	3.3	5.2	3.4	18.1
Adrian Houser	6	4	61	4.06	1.30	0	9.1	23.7%	2.9	7.6%	51.0%	94.4	3.8	5.3	3.2	2.5	3.4	5.4	3.4	18.2
Drew Steckenrider	0	3	67	4.05	1.29	0	10.1	26.2%	3.7	9.5%	39.0%	94.8	3.8	5.4	3.2	2.5	3.2	5.5	3.4	18.2
Blake Treinen	0	3	60	3.85	1.33	0	9.0	23.7%	3.8	9.9%	50.2%	96.3	3.7	5.1	3.2	2.4	3.2	6.0	3.3	18.2
Nik Turley	6	3	65	4.08	1.30	0	9.8	25.3%	3.4	8.8%	40.9%	92.4	3.7	5.3	3.1	2.4	3.3	5.3	3.3	18.1
Michael Feliz	0	3	71	4.18	1.33	2	10.6	27.4%	3.9	10.1%	38.5%	94.9	3.7	5.6	3.0	2.4	3.3	4.6	3.5	18.0
Chris Devenski	0	3	65	4.33	1.25	0	9.7	25.4%	2.9	7.7%	36.2%	94.5	3.7	5.4	3.1	2.4	3.4	4.6	3.4	18.0
Corey Oswalt	0	3	59	4.16	1.26	0	8.8	23.0%	2.5	6.6%	44.1%	91.5	3.7	5.2	3.2	2.4	3.3	5.1	3.4	18.1
Zac Grotz	0	3	56	3.95	1.28	0	8.5	22.2%	2.8	7.4%	49.9%	92.8	3.7	5.0	3.2	2.4	3.2	5.6	3.3	18.2
Rogelio Armenteros	0	3	64	4.28	1.27	0	9.6	25.3%	3.2	8.3%	37.7%	91.1	3.6	5.3	3.0	2.4	3.3	4.6	3.3	18.0
Ryan Helsley	0	3	66	4.06	1.31	0	9.9	25.6%	3.8	9.8%	40.4%	97.7	3.6	5.2	3.0	2.4	3.1	5.2	3.3	18.0
Gerardo Reyes	0	3	71	4.02	1.33	0	10.7	27.4%	4.3	11.1%	40.8%	96.6	3.6	5.4	3.0	2.3	3.1	5.3	3.2	18.0
Michael Wacha	0	3	57	4.00	1.29	0	8.6	22.4%	2.9	7.5%	47.2%	93.7	3.6	5.0	3.1	2.4	3.2	5.4	3.3	18.1
Tanner Rainey	0	3	80	3.79	1.42	0	12.0	30.4%	5.9	14.9%	44.3%	97.6	3.6	5.5	2.8	2.3	2.9	5.8	3.2	18.0
Tanner Scott	0	3	73	3.84	1.38	0	10.9	28.2%	4.8	12.4%	48.4%	96.2	3.5	5.3	2.9	2.3	3.0	5.7	3.2	18.1
Michael Lorenzen	0	3	60	4.18	1.34	4	9.0	23.2%	3.4	8.8%	49.3%	96.0	3.5	5.3	2.9	2.3	3.4	4.1	3.5	17.8
Mike Zagurski	0	3	68	4.09	1.31	0	10.1	26.3%	3.7	9.7%	39.9%	93.0	3.5	5.2	2.9	2.3	3.1	5.0	3.2	18.0
Kevin Quackenbush	0	3	63	4.25	1.27	0	9.5	24.7%	3.0	7.8%	40.3%	90.1	3.5	5.2	3.0	2.3	3.2	4.6	3.3	17.9
Shea Spitzbarth	0	3	64	4.09	1.30	0	9.5	24.8%	3.6	9.4%	43.3%	\N	3.5	5.1	2.9	2.3	3.1	5.0	3.2	18.0
Emmanuel Clase	0	3	62	4.04	1.35	2	9.3	24.2%	3.6	9.5%	49.0%	99.7	3.5	5.2	2.9	2.3	3.2	4.7	3.4	17.9
Scott Barlow	0	3	66	4.17	1.33	2	9.9	25.7%	4.1	10.6%	39.1%	94.1	3.5	5.3	2.8	2.3	3.2	4.4	3.3	17.8
Jeurys Familia	0	3	64	3.91	1.38	2	9.6	24.9%	4.3	11.2%	50.9%	95.7	3.4	5.1	2.8	2.3	3.1	5.1	3.3	17.9
Jaime Schultz	0	3	69	4.05	1.34	0	10.3	26.7%	4.4	11.3%	42.5%	95.4	3.4	5.2	2.8	2.2	3.0	5.0	3.2	17.9
Ryan Brasier	0	3	63	4.27	1.27	0	9.4	24.4%	3.0	7.9%	37.5%	96.0	3.4	5.1	2.9	2.2	3.2	4.4	3.2	17.9
Anthony Banda	0	3	61	4.08	1.30	0	9.2	24.0%	3.4	8.9%	40.5%	93.7	3.4	5.0	2.9	2.2	3.1	4.9	3.2	17.9
Nick Pivetta	8	4	65	4.29	1.29	0	9.8	25.5%	3.3	8.5%	45.2%	94.6	3.4	5.1	2.8	2.2	3.2	4.3	3.2	17.8
C.C. Lee	0	3	67	4.10	1.32	0	10.0	25.9%	3.8	9.8%	43.2%	92.0	3.4	5.1	2.8	2.2	3.0	4.8	3.1	17.9
Danny Hultzen	0	3	68	3.99	1.35	0	10.3	26.4%	4.2	10.9%	44.9%	93.0	3.4	5.1	2.7	2.2	2.9	5.1	3.1	17.9
Caleb Thielbar	0	3	58	4.23	1.27	0	8.7	22.6%	2.6	6.8%	40.4%	89.1	3.3	4.8	2.8	2.2	3.1	4.4	3.1	17.8
Jamie Callahan	0	3	62	4.03	1.31	0	9.3	23.9%	3.6	9.3%	42.6%	95.4	3.3	4.9	2.8	2.2	3.0	4.9	3.1	17.9
Wander Suero	0	3	62	4.12	1.31	0	9.3	24.0%	3.4	8.9%	42.7%	91.8	3.3	4.8	2.7	2.1	3.0	4.6	3.1	17.8
Boone Logan	0	3	69	4.03	1.35	0	10.4	26.8%	4.3	11.0%	43.1%	93.4	3.3	5.0	2.6	2.1	2.9	4.8	3.0	17.8
Andrew Robinson	0	3	63	4.20	1.30	0	9.4	24.4%	3.3	8.7%	42.3%	\N	3.3	4.9	2.7	2.1	3.0	4.4	3.1	17.8
Luis Perdomo	0	3	54	3.94	1.31	0	8.1	20.9%	2.6	6.8%	53.3%	94.5	3.2	4.6	2.8	2.1	2.9	5.1	3.1	17.9
Pedro Baez	0	3	62	4.27	1.29	0	9.3	24.2%	3.4	8.9%	37.7%	95.7	3.2	4.9	2.7	2.1	3.0	4.2	3.1	17.7
Adbert Alzolay	0	3	69	4.30	1.30	0	10.3	26.7%	3.7	9.6%	36.7%	95.0	3.2	5.0	2.6	2.1	3.0	4.0	3.1	17.7
Jon Gray	11	4	62	4.29	1.32	0	9.3	24.3%	3.0	7.8%	48.0%	95.9	3.2	4.8	2.6	2.1	3.1	4.0	3.1	17.7
Tony Cingrani	0	3	62	4.00	1.34	0	9.3	24.0%	3.8	9.8%	42.9%	93.2	3.2	4.8	2.6	2.1	2.9	4.8	3.0	17.8
Chaz Roe	0	3	65	4.06	1.34	0	9.8	25.2%	4.0	10.2%	45.0%	91.9	3.2	4.8	2.6	2.1	2.9	4.7	3.0	17.8
Darwinzon Hernande	0	3	76	4.01	1.43	2	11.4	28.9%	5.8	14.7%	41.0%	95.1	3.2	5.2	2.4	2.0	2.9	4.4	3.1	17.6
John Gant	0	3	59	3.99	1.33	0	8.9	23.1%	3.6	9.4%	46.3%	94.1	3.2	4.7	2.6	2.1	2.9	4.9	3.0	17.8
Dylan Floro	0	3	53	3.98	1.32	0	7.9	20.5%	2.9	7.6%	51.9%	93.0	3.1	4.4	2.7	2.0	2.9	4.9	3.0	17.8
Ranger Suarez	0	3	55	4.04	1.31	0	8.2	21.5%	2.9	7.5%	51.0%	92.4	3.1	4.5	2.7	2.0	2.9	4.7	3.0	17.8
Jake Faria	0	3	68	4.26	1.31	0	10.2	26.2%	3.6	9.2%	40.7%	92.6	3.1	4.9	2.5	2.0	2.9	4.0	3.0	17.6
Blake Parker	0	3	65	4.40	1.30	2	9.7	25.1%	3.3	8.4%	43.0%	91.6	3.1	5.0	2.5	2.0	3.1	3.3	3.1	17.5
Tim Hill	0	3	52	3.96	1.35	2	7.8	20.3%	3.3	8.7%	51.9%	89.9	3.1	4.5	2.6	2.0	3.0	4.5	3.1	17.7
Hoby Milner	0	3	60	4.14	1.31	0	9.1	23.5%	3.4	8.9%	41.3%	87.4	3.1	4.6	2.5	2.0	2.9	4.3	3.0	17.7
Adam Ottavino	0	3	73	4.32	1.36	2	11.0	28.4%	4.7	12.1%	40.5%	93.5	3.1	5.1	2.4	2.0	2.9	3.4	3.1	17.5
Enderson Franco	0	3	56	4.24	1.27	0	8.4	21.8%	2.8	7.4%	38.7%	95.5	3.0	4.5	2.6	2.0	2.9	4.0	3.0	17.6
Matt Wisler	0	3	58	4.40	1.25	0	8.7	22.8%	2.4	6.4%	37.7%	93.2	3.0	4.6	2.5	1.9	2.9	3.5	3.0	17.6
Matt Magill	0	3	65	4.27	1.30	0	9.7	25.3%	3.5	9.2%	39.0%	95.1	3.0	4.7	2.5	1.9	2.8	3.9	2.9	17.6
Huascar Ynoa	0	3	67	4.10	1.35	0	10.0	25.6%	4.0	10.1%	45.4%	97.4	3.0	4.7	2.4	1.9	2.8	4.3	2.9	17.6
Steven Wilson	0	3	67	4.08	1.35	0	10.1	25.8%	4.1	10.6%	43.7%	\N	3.0	4.7	2.4	1.9	2.7	4.3	2.9	17.6
Michel Baez	0	3	65	4.21	1.32	0	9.8	25.2%	3.8	9.6%	39.8%	96.1	3.0	4.7	2.4	1.9	2.8	4.0	2.9	17.6
Travis Radke	0	3	56	3.91	1.35	0	8.4	21.6%	3.4	8.7%	50.9%	\N	3.0	4.4	2.5	1.9	2.7	4.9	2.9	17.7
Joe Smith	0	3	57	4.22	1.30	0	8.5	22.1%	2.8	7.4%	46.1%	87.4	3.0	4.4	2.5	1.9	2.9	4.0	2.9	17.6
Tyler Mahle	9	3	61	4.39	1.29	0	9.2	23.9%	2.8	7.4%	44.8%	93.5	3.0	4.6	2.4	1.9	2.9	3.5	2.9	17.5
Bryse Wilson	9	4	57	4.32	1.31	0	8.6	22.3%	2.9	7.5%	45.0%	95.0	3.0	4.5	2.4	1.9	3.0	3.6	2.9	17.5
Juan Nicasio	0	3	62	4.25	1.30	0	9.2	23.9%	3.1	8.0%	45.1%	93.5	2.9	4.6	2.4	1.9	2.8	3.8	2.9	17.5

Name	GS	W	K	ERA	WHIP	SV	K/9	K%	BB/9	BB%	GB%	FBv	15-tm Mixed, Std.	15-tm Mixed, OBP	15-tm Draft & Hold	12-tm Mixed, Std.	12-tm, AL, OBP	12-tm, NL, OBP	12-tm, AL Std.	12-tm, NL Std.
Kyle Keller	0	3	66	4.09	1.34	0	9.9	25.4%	4.2	10.7%	41.0%	94.4	2.9	4.7	2.4	1.9	2.7	4.3	2.8	17.6
Jose Alvarez	0	3	57	4.10	1.32	0	8.6	22.3%	3.1	8.0%	47.8%	91.4	2.9	4.4	2.4	1.9	2.8	4.3	2.9	17.6
Tommy Hunter	0	3	57	4.23	1.29	0	8.5	22.3%	2.8	7.2%	47.7%	94.2	2.9	4.4	2.4	1.9	2.8	3.9	2.9	17.6
Hunter Harvey	0	3	62	4.68	1.36	7	9.3	23.9%	3.6	9.3%	39.3%	98.1	2.9	5.2	2.1	1.9	3.4	1.2	3.4	17.1
Wilmer Font	5	3	65	4.54	1.27	0	9.7	25.4%	3.0	7.9%	37.1%	94.7	2.9	4.7	2.3	1.9	2.9	3.0	2.9	17.4
Jeff Brigham	0	3	62	4.27	1.29	0	9.3	24.2%	3.4	8.8%	37.0%	94.3	2.9	4.6	2.4	1.8	2.7	3.7	2.9	17.5
Luis Garcia	0	3	59	4.11	1.35	2	8.9	22.9%	3.8	9.7%	48.1%	97.4	2.9	4.5	2.3	1.8	2.8	3.9	2.9	17.5
Cionel Perez	0	3	62	4.13	1.35	0	9.4	24.2%	3.8	9.8%	45.7%	95.2	2.9	4.5	2.3	1.8	2.7	4.1	2.8	17.5
Brett Martin	0	3	58	4.04	1.34	0	8.7	22.6%	3.3	8.6%	48.1%	93.8	2.9	4.3	2.3	1.8	2.7	4.3	2.8	17.6
Chad Sobotka	0	3	70	4.12	1.37	0	10.5	26.9%	4.5	11.5%	44.2%	96.2	2.8	4.7	2.2	1.8	2.6	4.0	2.8	17.5
Joel Payamps	0	3	56	4.32	1.27	0	8.4	21.9%	2.5	6.5%	42.5%	92.7	2.8	4.4	2.4	1.8	2.8	3.5	2.9	17.5
Touki Toussaint	0	3	67	4.13	1.36	0	10.1	25.7%	4.2	10.6%	43.7%	93.2	2.8	4.6	2.2	1.8	2.6	4.0	2.8	17.5
Griffin Canning	10	3	61	4.42	1.29	0	9.2	23.7%	3.1	8.0%	40.1%	93.8	2.8	4.5	2.3	1.8	2.8	3.2	2.8	17.4
Ben Taylor	0	3	65	4.30	1.31	0	9.8	25.4%	3.5	9.0%	40.5%	93.0	2.8	4.6	2.3	1.8	2.7	3.5	2.8	17.4
Jose De Leon	0	3	69	4.26	1.34	0	10.3	26.5%	4.2	10.7%	38.0%	92.1	2.8	4.6	2.2	1.8	2.7	3.6	2.8	17.4
Silvino Bracho	0	3	67	4.36	1.30	0	10.0	26.0%	3.6	9.4%	36.9%	92.9	2.8	4.6	2.2	1.8	2.7	3.3	2.8	17.4
Conner Menez	7	3	65	4.15	1.36	0	9.8	25.0%	4.3	11.1%	40.0%	91.1	2.8	4.5	2.2	1.8	2.7	3.9	2.8	17.4
Brad Brach	0	3	63	4.10	1.35	0	9.5	24.5%	3.9	10.1%	44.9%	93.9	2.8	4.4	2.2	1.8	2.6	4.1	2.8	17.5
JT Brubaker	0	3	56	4.11	1.32	0	8.5	21.9%	2.9	7.6%	48.2%	\N	2.8	4.3	2.3	1.8	2.7	4.1	2.8	17.5
Reymin Guduan	0	3	67	3.92	1.40	0	10.0	25.7%	4.6	11.8%	49.0%	95.8	2.8	4.5	2.2	1.8	2.5	4.5	2.7	17.5
Jordan Montgomery	5	4	60	4.44	1.30	0	9.1	23.7%	3.0	7.9%	40.2%	91.8	2.8	4.4	2.2	1.8	2.9	3.1	2.8	17.4
Victor Arano	0	3	66	4.38	1.31	0	9.9	25.6%	3.4	8.9%	40.6%	93.7	2.8	4.6	2.2	1.7	2.7	3.2	2.8	17.3
Addison Russ	0	3	66	4.25	1.33	0	9.9	25.4%	3.8	9.8%	45.0%	\N	2.7	4.5	2.2	1.7	2.6	3.6	2.7	17.4
Tim Mayza	0	3	65	4.14	1.35	0	9.8	25.2%	4.0	10.2%	44.9%	94.2	2.7	4.5	2.2	1.7	2.6	3.8	2.7	17.4
Derek Holland	0	3	65	4.25	1.33	0	9.8	25.1%	3.6	9.2%	41.3%	92.7	2.7	4.5	2.2	1.7	2.6	3.5	2.7	17.4
Yimi Garcia	0	3	60	4.57	1.26	0	9.1	23.5%	2.6	6.7%	35.0%	94.0	2.7	4.4	2.2	1.7	2.8	2.7	2.8	17.3
Erik Swanson	5	3	56	4.65	1.28	3	8.5	22.2%	2.7	7.2%	37.0%	93.1	2.7	4.5	2.1	1.7	3.0	1.9	3.0	17.1
Cory Burns	0	3	63	4.04	1.37	0	9.4	24.3%	4.0	10.2%	49.1%	\N	2.7	4.3	2.2	1.7	2.6	4.1	2.7	17.4
Collin McHugh	6	4	61	4.42	1.31	0	9.1	23.7%	3.3	8.5%	40.1%	90.4	2.7	4.4	2.2	1.7	2.8	3.0	2.8	17.3
Jimmie Sherfy	0	3	68	4.32	1.32	0	10.2	26.2%	3.8	9.8%	37.9%	91.9	2.7	4.6	2.1	1.7	2.6	3.3	2.7	17.3
Dan Altavilla	0	3	71	4.18	1.36	0	10.6	27.3%	4.6	11.9%	39.9%	96.6	2.7	4.6	2.1	1.7	2.5	3.7	2.7	17.4
Brian Moran	0	3	61	4.07	1.35	0	9.1	23.4%	3.9	10.0%	43.9%	84.1	2.7	4.3	2.2	1.7	2.5	4.0	2.7	17.4
Trevor Bettencourt	0	3	64	4.23	1.33	0	9.6	24.7%	3.6	9.4%	47.0%	\N	2.7	4.4	2.1	1.7	2.6	3.6	2.7	17.3
Connor Brogdon	0	3	68	4.41	1.31	0	10.3	26.4%	3.8	9.9%	38.7%	\N	2.7	4.6	2.1	1.7	2.6	3.0	2.7	17.3
Rob Zastryzny	0	3	54	4.12	1.33	0	8.1	21.1%	3.2	8.3%	47.1%	89.0	2.7	4.1	2.2	1.7	2.6	3.8	2.7	17.4
Adalberto Mejia	0	3	59	4.20	1.32	0	8.8	22.9%	3.5	8.9%	39.7%	92.8	2.6	4.2	2.1	1.7	2.6	3.6	2.7	17.3
Angel Sanchez	0	3	60	4.26	1.32	0	9.0	23.4%	3.2	8.3%	44.9%	94.3	2.6	4.2	2.1	1.6	2.6	3.4	2.7	17.3
Taylor Cole	0	3	59	4.08	1.35	0	8.8	22.7%	3.6	9.3%	47.0%	93.7	2.6	4.2	2.1	1.6	2.5	3.9	2.7	17.4
Matt Hall	0	3	61	4.15	1.34	0	9.1	23.5%	3.5	9.1%	45.1%	90.0	2.6	4.2	2.1	1.6	2.5	3.7	2.7	17.3
Dominic Leone	0	3	64	4.24	1.34	0	9.7	24.9%	3.8	9.9%	40.0%	94.3	2.6	4.3	2.1	1.6	2.6	3.4	2.7	17.3
Sal Romano	0	3	59	4.26	1.31	0	8.8	22.9%	3.0	7.9%	46.5%	94.9	2.6	4.2	2.1	1.6	2.6	3.4	2.7	17.3
David Paulino	0	3	62	4.37	1.31	0	9.4	24.2%	3.3	8.4%	40.0%	93.3	2.6	4.3	2.1	1.6	2.6	3.0	2.7	17.2
Daniel Zamora	0	3	62	4.15	1.35	0	9.3	23.9%	3.8	9.8%	44.6%	88.5	2.6	4.2	2.0	1.6	2.5	3.6	2.6	17.3
Burch Smith	0	3	63	4.17	1.35	0	9.5	24.3%	4.0	10.2%	40.9%	92.6	2.6	4.2	2.0	1.6	2.5	3.5	2.6	17.3
Stefan Crichton	0	3	57	4.13	1.34	0	8.6	22.3%	3.2	8.4%	49.9%	92.6	2.6	4.1	2.1	1.6	2.5	3.7	2.6	17.3
Wei-Yin Chen	0	3	55	4.32	1.29	0	8.3	21.5%	2.6	6.8%	39.6%	93.1	2.6	4.1	2.1	1.6	2.6	3.2	2.7	17.3
Sam Coonrod	0	3	60	4.06	1.36	0	9.0	23.2%	4.2	10.7%	45.1%	96.2	2.6	4.1	2.0	1.6	2.5	3.9	2.6	17.3
Jace Fry	0	3	68	3.96	1.41	0	10.2	26.3%	5.0	12.7%	49.1%	92.5	2.5	4.3	1.9	1.6	2.4	4.1	2.6	17.3
Josh A. Smith	0	3	57	4.54	1.27	0	8.6	22.3%	2.4	6.3%	37.4%	92.2	2.5	4.2	2.1	1.6	2.7	2.5	2.7	17.2
Brusdar Graterol	0	3	62	4.22	1.35	0	9.2	23.8%	3.6	9.2%	46.5%	98.6	2.5	4.2	2.0	1.6	2.5	3.4	2.6	17.2
Robert Gsellman	0	3	57	4.17	1.33	0	8.6	22.1%	3.1	8.1%	47.9%	94.9	2.5	4.0	2.0	1.6	2.5	3.5	2.6	17.3
Derek Law	0	3	60	4.51	1.40	6	9.0	22.8%	3.9	10.0%	44.4%	94.0	2.5	4.6	1.8	1.6	3.0	1.4	3.1	16.9
Hector Rondon	0	3	59	4.35	1.32	0	8.9	23.2%	3.1	8.1%	45.1%	96.1	2.5	4.1	2.0	1.6	2.6	3.0	2.6	17.2
Fabio Castillo	0	3	65	4.40	1.32	0	9.8	25.2%	3.5	9.1%	38.1%	95.7	2.5	4.3	2.0	1.6	2.5	2.8	2.6	17.2
Patrick Ruotolo	0	3	64	4.18	1.35	0	9.7	24.7%	4.2	10.8%	39.2%	\N	2.5	4.2	2.0	1.6	2.4	3.4	2.6	17.2
Carl Edwards Jr.	0	3	68	4.19	1.37	0	10.3	26.3%	4.5	11.7%	41.4%	93.7	2.5	4.3	1.9	1.5	2.4	3.4	2.6	17.2
Austin Davis	0	3	67	4.31	1.34	0	10.1	26.0%	4.1	10.4%	42.1%	94.2	2.5	4.3	1.9	1.5	2.5	3.0	2.6	17.2
David Phelps	0	3	63	4.30	1.38	2	9.5	24.3%	4.0	10.2%	43.3%	92.0	2.5	4.3	1.8	1.5	2.6	2.7	2.7	17.1
James Hoyt	0	3	62	4.29	1.34	0	9.4	24.2%	3.6	9.2%	44.7%	93.7	2.5	4.2	1.9	1.5	2.5	3.1	2.6	17.2
J.P. Feyereisen	0	3	71	4.30	1.36	0	10.7	27.3%	4.5	11.5%	39.3%	\N	2.5	4.4	1.8	1.5	2.4	3.0	2.6	17.1
Sam Wolff	0	3	63	4.21	1.35	0	9.4	24.2%	4.0	10.3%	39.3%	\N	2.5	4.1	1.9	1.5	2.4	3.3	2.6	17.2
Christian Jones	0	3	58	3.97	1.38	0	8.8	22.4%	4.0	10.2%	47.5%	\N	2.4	3.9	1.9	1.5	2.3	3.9	2.5	17.3
Sam Tuivailala	0	3	54	4.69	1.39	9	8.1	20.7%	3.5	9.1%	41.8%	93.4	2.4	4.6	1.7	1.5	3.2	0.3	3.2	16.7
Bryan Abreu	0	3	72	4.24	1.39	0	10.8	27.4%	4.9	12.4%	41.3%	94.7	2.4	4.4	1.8	1.5	2.4	3.1	2.5	17.1
Tony Barnette	0	3	58	4.28	1.33	0	8.7	22.3%	3.1	7.9%	45.8%	91.6	2.4	4.0	1.9	1.5	2.5	3.1	2.6	17.2
Bradley Roney	0	3	68	4.23	1.37	0	10.2	25.9%	4.2	10.8%	42.9%	\N	2.4	4.2	1.8	1.5	2.4	3.2	2.5	17.1
Miguel Diaz	0	3	65	4.22	1.36	0	9.7	25.0%	4.1	10.6%	42.7%	95.0	2.4	4.1	1.8	1.5	2.4	3.2	2.5	17.1
Andrew Suarez	4	3	50	4.13	1.33	0	7.4	19.2%	2.8	7.3%	48.3%	92.2	2.4	3.7	1.9	1.5	2.5	3.5	2.5	17.2
Lou Trivino	0	3	60	4.20	1.36	0	9.0	23.4%	3.9	10.2%	45.1%	97.1	2.4	4.0	1.8	1.5	2.4	3.2	2.5	17.1
Michael Tonkin	0	3	65	4.34	1.34	0	9.8	25.1%	3.7	9.6%	42.3%	93.5	2.4	4.2	1.8	1.4	2.4	2.8	2.5	17.1

Note: Splits of .635 or below (Sucking Risk) are shown in bold.

NAME	Bats	OPS vs LHP	OPS vs RHP	Diff
Joc Pederson	L	.721	.910	.189
Kyle Schwarber	L	.739	.912	.173
Justin Bour	L	.651	.815	.164
Logan Morrison	L	**.647**	.803	.156
Michael Conforto	L	.727	.878	.151
Travis Shaw	L	.660	.806	.146
Lucas Duda	L	**.627**	.773	.145
Shohei Ohtani	L	.755	.899	.144
Daniel Palka	L	**.635**	.772	.138
Derek Dietrich	L	**.638**	.775	.137
Giancarlo Stanton	R	1.043	.906	.137
Cory Spangenberg	L	**.563**	.698	.135
Jake Lamb	L	.656	.790	.134
Corey Dickerson	L	.679	.813	.134
Christian Yelich	L	.860	.994	.134
Freddie Freeman	L	.828	.960	.133
Carlos Gonzalez	L	**.617**	.748	.131
David Peralta	L	.711	.841	.131
Juan Soto	L	.862	.990	.128
Eric Thames	L	.686	.814	.128
Eddie Rosario	L	.725	.851	.127
Daniel Vogelbach	L	.682	.808	.126
Bobby Bradley	L	.662	.787	.125
Nomar Mazara	L	.710	.835	.125
Matt Olson	L	.759	.883	.124
Eric Hosmer	L	.678	.801	.123
Rafael Devers	L	.802	.925	.123
Jason Heyward	L	.663	.786	.122
Gregory Polanco	L	.670	.790	.121
Mitch Moreland	L	.693	.813	.120
Edwin Rios	L	**.616**	.736	.120
Matt Joyce	L	.674	.794	.120
Nick Williams	L	**.629**	.749	.120
Brad Miller	L	**.647**	.768	.120
Ryan O'Hearn	L	.653	.773	.120
Jesse Winker	L	.726	.845	.120
Bryce Harper	L	.834	.953	.119
Zack Collins	L	**.643**	.761	.119
Shin-Soo Choo	L	.698	.816	.118
A.J. Reed	L	**.582**	.698	.116
Scooter Gennett	L	**.635**	.748	.113
Brian O'Grady	L	**.618**	.730	.113
Michael Brantley	L	.730	.843	.112
Jackie Bradley Jr.	L	.667	.778	.112
Ji-Man Choi	L	.687	.799	.112
Yordan Alvarez	L	.835	.946	.111
Alex Avila	L	**.622**	.733	.111
Nicky Delmonico	L	.651	.762	.111
Matt Skole	L	**.577**	.688	.111
David Dahl	L	.717	.827	.110
Max Kepler	L	.743	.853	.110
Brandon Nimmo	L	.667	.777	.110
Brett Gardner	L	.665	.774	.109
Brandon Lowe	L	.679	.788	.109
Daniel Murphy	L	.741	.850	.109
Joey Votto	L	.751	.859	.109
Matt Adams	L	.672	.780	.108
Trent Grisham	L	.703	.810	.108
Brett Phillips	L	**.583**	.690	.107

Note: Splits of .635 or below (Sucking Risk) are shown in bold.

NAME	Bats	OPS vs LHP	OPS vs RHP	Diff
Chance Sisco	L	**.635**	.742	.107
Robinson Cano	L	.695	.801	.106
Andrew Benintendi	L	.728	.834	.106
Ryan Flaherty	L	**.601**	.706	.105
Hunter Renfroe	R	.830	.725	.105
Josh VanMeter	L	.664	.768	.105
Sam Hilliard	L	.659	.763	.104
Cody Bellinger	L	.891	.995	.104
Socrates Brito	L	**.607**	.711	.104
Dom Nunez	L	**.617**	.721	.104
Matt Carpenter	L	.713	.817	.104
Max Muncy	L	.735	.839	.103
Mike Gerber	L	**.591**	.694	.103
Colin Moran	L	.667	.770	.103
Jay Bruce	L	.692	.795	.103
Nick Markakis	L	.709	.811	.102
Yonder Alonso	L	.708	.809	.102
Jason Kipnis	L	.665	.766	.102
Jake Cave	L	.659	.761	.101
Corey Seager	L	.753	.854	.101
Austin Allen	L	**.609**	.709	.101
Cavan Biggio	L	.680	.781	.101
Gavin Lux	L	.682	.782	.100
Joey Gallo	L	.793	.893	.100
Seth Brown	L	**.607**	.706	.100
Jason Castro	L	**.636**	.735	.100
Brandon Belt	L	.723	.823	.100
Austin Meadows	L	.757	.856	.099
Odubel Herrera	L	.671	.770	.099
Kyle Tucker	L	.701	.800	.099
D.J. Stewart	L	.691	.789	.098
Dwight Smith Jr.	L	.669	.767	.098
Anthony Rizzo	L	.833	.931	.098
Curtis Granderson	L	**.606**	.704	.098
Jared Walsh	L	.661	.759	.098
Ronald Guzman	L	.669	.767	.098
Jake Fraley	L	**.625**	.722	.097
Willie Calhoun	L	.740	.837	.097
Josh Reddick	L	.682	.779	.097
Raimel Tapia	L	.657	.754	.097
Christin Stewart	L	.679	.776	.097
Chris Davis	L	**.597**	.694	.097
Mason Williams	L	**.635**	.731	.096
Rowdy Tellez	L	.701	.797	.096
Billy McKinney	L	.667	.764	.096
Dominic Smith	L	**.638**	.733	.095
J.P. Crawford	L	**.617**	.712	.095
Adam Eaton	L	.720	.815	.095
Kevin Kiermaier	L	**.638**	.733	.095
Didi Gregorius	L	.697	.791	.094
Nick Martini	L	**.610**	.704	.094
Steven Duggar	L	**.596**	.689	.094
Matt Beaty	L	.688	.781	.094
Isan Diaz	L	**.636**	.730	.093
Nathaniel Lowe	L	.721	.814	.093
Jason Martin	L	**.646**	.739	.093
J.D. Martinez	R	1.019	.926	.093
Rafael Ortega	L	**.625**	.718	.093
Stephen Vogt	L	**.638**	.730	.092

Note: Splits of .635 or below (Sucking Risk) are shown in bold.

NAME	Bats	OPS vs LHP	OPS vs RHP	Diff
Jace Peterson	L	**.620**	.712	.092
Rio Ruiz	L	**.644**	.736	.092
Gerardo Parra	L	**.623**	.715	.091
Michael Perez	L	**.590**	.681	.091
Josh Rojas	L	.695	.786	.091
Aaron Judge	R	.957	.866	.091
Adam Haseley	L	**.641**	.732	.091
Charlie Blackmon	L	.811	.900	.090
Greg Garcia	L	**.612**	.702	.090
Paul Goldschmidt	R	.927	.838	.090
Nolan Arenado	R	1.002	.913	.089
Leonys Martin	L	**.603**	.692	.089
Travis Jankowski	L	**.569**	.658	.089
Jeff McNeil	L	.737	.826	.089
Josh Naylor	L	.695	.783	.088
Rougned Odor	L	.691	.779	.088
Beau Taylor	L	**.547**	**.635**	.087
Rhys Hoskins	R	.923	.836	.087
Adam Frazier	L	.679	.766	.087
Jake Bauers	L	.683	.769	.086
Andrew Stevenson	L	**.585**	.671	.086
Kevin Kramer	L	**.591**	.677	.086
Matt Thaiss	L	**.645**	.731	.086
Mike Tauchman	L	.651	.736	.085
Nelson Cruz	R	.963	.878	.085
Omar Narvaez	L	.657	.742	.085
LaMonte Wade	L	.660	.745	.085
Brian Goodwin	L	**.622**	.707	.085
Reese McGuire	L	**.618**	.703	.085
Tyler Austin	R	.784	.699	.085
Brock Holt	L	.654	.739	.084
Alex Verdugo	L	.722	.806	.084
Tyler Wade	L	**.582**	.666	.084
Tzu-Wei Lin	L	**.592**	.675	.083
Alex Dickerson	L	.708	.790	.083
Miguel Sano	R	.912	.829	.083
Ben Gamel	L	.656	.738	.082
Ryan Goins	L	**.569**	.652	.082
Javier Baez	R	.871	.789	.082
Kolten Wong	L	.688	.769	.081
Ian Desmond	R	.834	.753	.081
Ryan Braun	R	.868	.787	.081
Ryan McMahon	L	.733	.813	.080
Joey Wendle	L	**.621**	.701	.080
Alex Gordon	L	.680	.759	.079
Tyler Naquin	L	.699	.777	.079
Ender Inciarte	L	.651	.729	.078
Brian McCann	L	.685	.762	.077
Harold Castro	L	**.589**	.666	.077
Chris Iannetta	R	.757	.681	.076
Greg Bird	L	.700	.776	.076
Mike Moustakas	L	.787	.863	.076
Nicholas Castellanos	R	.875	.799	.076
Meibrys Viloria	L	**.586**	.661	.076
Mike Yastrzemski	L	.671	.746	.075
Khris Davis	R	.870	.796	.075
Aaron Altherr	R	.733	.658	.075
J.T. Riddle	L	**.592**	.666	.074
Mike Freeman	L	**.592**	.666	.074

Note: Splits of .635 or below (Sucking Risk) are shown in bold.

NAME	Bats	OPS vs LHP	OPS vs RHP	Diff
Daniel Descalso	L	**.609**	.683	.074
Tommy La Stella	L	.694	.768	.074
Corban Joseph	L	.661	.735	.073
Joe Panik	L	**.642**	.716	.073
Carlos Correa	R	.925	.851	.073
Yoan Moncada	B	.756	.829	.073
Shed Long	L	.653	.726	.073
Enrique Hernandez	R	.804	.732	.073
Ryan Zimmerman	R	.850	.777	.073
Manny Machado	R	.905	.833	.072
Jedd Gyorko	R	.793	.721	.072
Chris Herrmann	L	**.603**	.674	.072
Scott Schebler	L	**.636**	.707	.071
Adam Duvall	R	.800	.729	.071
Garrett Stubbs	L	**.594**	.665	.071
Eric Sogard	L	**.637**	.708	.071
Trevor Story	R	.932	.862	.070
Derek Fisher	L	.671	.741	.070
Charlie Tilson	L	**.579**	**.649**	.070
Jarrod Dyson	L	**.608**	.677	.069
Maikel Franco	R	.858	.789	.069
Anthony Bemboom	L	**.539**	**.608**	.069
Tony Wolters	L	**.636**	.705	.069
Domingo Santana	R	.802	.733	.069
Tony Kemp	L	.660	.729	.069
Kole Calhoun	L	.692	.761	.069
Tucker Barnhart	L	**.638**	.707	.069
Mookie Betts	R	.979	.910	.069
Taylor Ward	R	.777	.709	.068
Mike Ford	L	.762	.831	.068
Josh Donaldson	R	.913	.845	.068
Ronald Acuna Jr.	R	.933	.866	.068
Luis Guillorme	L	**.614**	.682	.068
Franmil Reyes	R	.885	.819	.067
Jose Pirela	R	.768	.701	.067
JB Shuck	L	**.613**	.680	.067
Mikie Mahtook	R	.756	.690	.066
Jordan Luplow	R	.816	.750	.066
Nick Senzel	R	.794	.728	.066
Mallex Smith	L	**.624**	.690	.066
Eugenio Suarez	R	.882	.816	.066
Christian Walker	R	.811	.746	.065
Brandon Crawford	L	.662	.726	.064
Mitch Garver	R	.833	.769	.064
Matt Kemp	R	.781	.717	.064
Peter O'Brien	R	.660	**.597**	.064
Steve Wilkerson	B	**.597**	.660	.063
Mark Zagunis	R	.698	**.635**	.063
Magneuris Sierra	L	**.588**	.651	.063
Kyle Seager	L	.709	.772	.063
Alex Bregman	R	.977	.914	.062
Harrison Bader	R	.766	.704	.062
Austin Slater	R	.756	.693	.062
Kevin Cron	R	.837	.775	.062
Mike Trout	R	1.087	1.025	.062
Patrick Wisdom	R	.723	.661	.062
Kris Bryant	R	.925	.864	.061
Ian Happ	B	.725	.787	.061
Andrew McCutchen	R	.867	.806	.060

Note: Splits of .635 or below (Sucking Risk) are shown in bold.

NAME	Bats	OPS vs LHP	OPS vs RHP	Diff
Luis Arraez	L	.728	.789	.060
Josh Bell	B	.821	.881	.060
Tim Federowicz	R	.700	**.640**	.060
Tommy Pham	R	.863	.804	.059
Luke Voit	R	.823	.764	.059
Randal Grichuk	R	.832	.773	.059
Nick Ahmed	R	.751	.693	.058
Chris Taylor	R	.760	.702	.058
Anthony Rendon	R	.949	.892	.058
Jordy Mercer	R	.747	.689	.058
George Springer	R	.911	.853	.058
Adam Engel	R	.675	**.617**	.058
Edwin Encarnacion	R	.882	.824	.058
Austin Riley	R	.810	.752	.058
Fernando Tatis Jr.	R	.838	.780	.058
Carson Kelly	R	.800	.743	.058
Charlie Culberson	R	.700	**.643**	.058
Kyle Garlick	R	.705	**.647**	.057
Travis Demeritte	R	.782	.725	.057
Marco Hernandez	L	**.642**	.699	.057
Aristides Aquino	R	.810	.753	.057
Renato Nunez	R	.790	.733	.057
J.D. Davis	R	.822	.765	.057
Sam Travis	R	.752	.695	.057
Willson Contreras	R	.834	.777	.056
Robinson Chirinos	R	.747	.691	.056
Hunter Pence	R	.800	.744	.056
Nick Solak	R	.819	.763	.056
Stephen Piscotty	R	.827	.771	.056
Lorenzo Cain	R	.799	.744	.055
Mark Canha	R	.833	.777	.055
C.J. Cron	R	.860	.804	.055
David Freese	R	.804	.749	.055
Wilson Ramos	R	.813	.759	.055
Yan Gomes	R	.751	.696	.054
Mark Trumbo	R	.785	.730	.054
Tyler O'Neill	R	.774	.720	.054
John Ryan Murphy	R	**.647**	**.593**	.054
Nicky Lopez	L	.658	.712	.054
Jesus Aguilar	R	.779	.725	.054
Curt Casali	R	.739	.685	.054
Martin Prado	R	.706	.652	.054
Kyle Higashioka	R	.725	.672	.054
Tom Murphy	R	.703	**.650**	.054
Jorge Polanco	B	.753	.807	.053
Tim Anderson	R	.783	.730	.053
Evan Longoria	R	.783	.730	.053
DJ LeMahieu	R	.812	.759	.053
James McCann	R	.722	.669	.053
Jon Jay	L	**.600**	.653	.053
Pat Valaika	R	.749	.696	.053
Danny Santana	B	.679	.732	.053
Marcus Semien	R	.845	.792	.053
Teoscar Hernandez	R	.774	.721	.053
Jose Martinez	R	.817	.765	.053
A.J. Pollock	R	.795	.743	.052
Jose Abreu	R	.864	.812	.052
Michael Chavis	R	.789	.737	.052
Jaylin Davis	R	.748	.696	.052

Note: Splits of .635 or below (Sucking Risk) are shown in bold.

NAME	Bats	OPS vs LHP	OPS vs RHP	Diff
Christian Vazquez	R	.761	.709	.052
Jose Ramirez	B	.842	.894	.052
Gleyber Torres	R	.879	.827	.052
Hernan Perez	R	.721	.669	.051
Orlando Arcia	R	.735	.684	.051
Carter Kieboom	R	.774	.723	.051
Tyler Flowers	R	.741	.690	.051
Dansby Swanson	R	.775	.724	.051
Brian Dozier	R	.806	.756	.051
Peter Alonso	R	.903	.853	.050
Lewis Brinson	R	.672	**.622**	.050
Xander Bogaerts	R	.900	.849	.050
Ryan McBroom	R	.755	.705	.050
Jorge Soler	R	.882	.831	.050
Ryan Court	R	**.644**	**.595**	.050
Avisail Garcia	R	.791	.741	.050
Matt Wieters	B	.655	.704	.049
Alex Blandino	R	.705	.656	.049
Trea Turner	R	.857	.808	.049
Marcell Ozuna	R	.871	.822	.049
Gary Sanchez	R	.870	.821	.049
Ramon Laureano	R	.812	.764	.049
Clint Frazier	R	.777	.728	.049
Phillip Ervin	R	.755	.706	.048
Brandon Dixon	R	.719	.671	.048
Dee Gordon	L	**.627**	.675	.048
Tyler Saladino	R	.682	**.635**	.048
Dustin Garneau	R	.691	**.643**	.048
Lane Thomas	R	.760	.712	.048
Roberto Perez	R	.730	.683	.047
Aramis Garcia	R	**.647**	**.599**	.047
Austin Nola	R	.704	.657	.047
Austin Barnes	R	.708	.661	.047
Yasmani Grandal	B	.791	.838	.047
Jose Altuve	R	.876	.830	.047
Kristopher Negron	R	**.633**	**.587**	.047
Matt Chapman	R	.880	.833	.047
Garrett Hampson	R	.758	.712	.046
Kevin Pillar	R	.743	.697	.046
Keon Broxton	R	**.616**	**.570**	.046
Hunter Dozier	R	.790	.744	.046
Jorge Bonifacio	R	.721	.675	.046
Albert Almora Jr.	R	.743	.697	.046
Chad Pinder	R	.761	.715	.046
Vladimir Guerrero Jr.	R	.886	.841	.046
Jake Rogers	R	.687	**.642**	.045
Addison Russell	R	.768	.723	.045
Jorge Alfaro	R	.720	.675	.045
Cedric Mullins II	B	**.637**	.682	.045
Austin Romine	R	.723	.678	.045
Welington Castillo	R	.732	.687	.045
Russell Martin	R	.725	.680	.044
Nick Hundley	R	.669	**.625**	.044
Lourdes Gurriel Jr.	R	.802	.758	.044
Sean Murphy	R	.769	.725	.044
Buster Posey	R	.782	.739	.044
Gorkys Hernandez	R	.683	**.640**	.044
Jose Rondon	R	.695	.652	.044
Bo Bichette	R	.813	.769	.044

Note: Splits of .635 or below (Sucking Risk) are shown in bold.

NAME	Bats	OPS vs LHP	OPS vs RHP	Diff
Mike Zunino	R	.695	.651	.043
Ryon Healy	R	.770	.726	.043
Ryan LaMarre	R	.712	.669	.043
Miguel Cabrera	R	.816	.772	.043
Garrett Cooper	R	.772	.729	.043
Michael Brosseau	R	.743	.700	.043
Yasiel Puig	R	.833	.790	.043
Yandy Diaz	R	.794	.751	.043
Erik Kratz	R	.702	.659	.042
Wil Myers	R	.752	.710	.042
Byron Buxton	R	.799	.757	.042
Jacob Stallings	R	.729	.686	.042
Austin Hays	R	.775	.733	.042
Jake Marisnick	R	.696	.654	.042
Josh Phegley	R	.712	.670	.042
Whit Merrifield	R	.790	.748	.042
Bubba Starling	R	.671	**.629**	.042
Kyle Farmer	R	.683	**.641**	.042
Miguel Andujar	R	.800	.759	.042
Nick Dini	R	.739	.698	.042
Jake Elmore	R	.699	.657	.042
Adeiny Hechavarria	R	.698	.656	.042
David Bote	R	.750	.708	.042
Grayson Greiner	R	.675	**.634**	.041
Randy Arozarena	R	.786	.744	.041
Jose Osuna	R	.778	.736	.041
Chad Wallach	R	**.641**	**.600**	.041
Jack Mayfield	R	.681	**.640**	.041
Phil Gosselin	R	.698	.656	.041
Terrance Gore	R	**.579**	**.538**	.041
Aaron Hicks	B	.751	.792	.041
Rangel Ravelo	R	.763	.722	.041
Mark Reynolds	R	.708	.668	.041
Danny Jansen	R	.776	.735	.041
Dustin Peterson	R	.718	.677	.041
Zack Cozart	R	.728	.688	.041
Jurickson Profar	B	.725	.766	.041
Justin Turner	R	.874	.834	.041
Steve Pearce	R	.757	.717	.041
Franklin Barreto	R	.732	.692	.040
Yuli Gurriel	R	.847	.807	.040
Mac Williamson	R	.688	**.648**	.040
Keston Hiura	R	.848	.808	.040
Cheslor Cuthbert	R	.749	.710	.040
Sheldon Neuse	R	.720	.680	.040
Victor Robles	R	.771	.731	.040
Dylan Moore	R	.676	**.637**	.040
Austin Dean	R	.776	.737	.040
Yu-Cheng Chang	R	.699	.660	.040
Ronny Rodriguez	R	.747	.708	.039
Mitch Haniger	R	.800	.761	.039
Brendan Rodgers	R	.794	.755	.039
Wilmer Flores	R	.842	.803	.039
Eric Stamets	R	**.599**	**.560**	.039
Elvis Andrus	R	.746	.707	.039
Manuel Margot	R	.741	.702	.039
Kelvin Gutierrez	R	.718	.680	.039
Cameron Maybin	R	.731	.692	.039
Sean Rodriguez	R	.697	.658	.039

Note: Splits of .635 or below (Sucking Risk) are shown in bold.

NAME	Bats	OPS vs LHP	OPS vs RHP	Diff
Todd Frazier	R	.770	.732	.039
Starlin Castro	R	.761	.722	.039
Trey Mancini	R	.844	.806	.039
Kyle Lewis	R	.698	.660	.039
Isaac Galloway	R	**.641**	**.603**	.039
Eloy Jimenez	R	.869	.831	.038
Albert Pujols	R	.763	.724	.038
Tomas Nido	R	**.644**	**.605**	.038
Jeff Mathis	R	**.585**	**.547**	.038
Travis d'Arnaud	R	.758	.720	.038
Tim Lopes	R	.684	**.646**	.038
Elias Diaz	R	.728	.690	.038
Luis Urias	R	.741	.703	.038
Guillermo Heredia	R	.686	**.648**	.038
Pedro Severino	R	.724	.687	.038
JaCoby Jones	R	.714	.677	.037
Scott Heineman	R	.740	.703	.037
Bobby Wilson	R	**.615**	**.578**	.037
Richie Martin Jr.	R	.661	**.624**	.037
Alen Hanson	B	**.612**	**.649**	.037
Danny Mendick	R	.718	.681	.037
Logan Forsythe	R	.724	.688	.037
Max Stassi	R	.658	**.621**	.037
Yadier Molina	R	.744	.708	.037
Justin Upton	R	.797	.760	.037
Hanley Ramirez	R	.753	.717	.037
Christian Arroyo	R	.715	.679	.036
Anthony Santander	B	.727	.763	.036
Daniel Robertson	R	.707	.671	.036
Braden Bishop	R	.653	**.617**	.036
Kevan Smith	R	.741	.704	.036
Bryan Holaday	R	.719	.683	.036
Andrew Knizner	R	.745	.709	.036
Austin Hedges	R	.683	**.648**	.036
Amed Rosario	R	.762	.726	.036
Tim Beckham	R	.712	.676	.036
Josh Fuentes	R	.735	.699	.036
Jose Iglesias	R	.716	.680	.036
J.T. Realmuto	R	.828	.793	.035
Adrian Sanchez	R	.683	**.648**	.035
Jose Peraza	R	.730	.695	.035
Isiah Kiner-Falefa	R	.700	.665	.035
Jean Segura	R	.789	.754	.035
Austin Wynns	R	.678	**.642**	.035
Joey Rickard	R	.701	.666	.035
Ian Kinsler	R	.700	.665	.035
Drew Butera	R	.720	.685	.035
Justin Smoak	B	.785	.820	.035
Aledmys Diaz	R	.779	.744	.035
Seth Mejias-Brean	R	**.649**	**.615**	.034
Jonathan Davis	R	.683	**.649**	.034
Will Smith	R	.761	.727	.034
Pablo Reyes	R	.727	.693	.034
Myles Straw	R	.691	.657	.034
Kevin Newman	R	.749	.714	.034
Tyler White	R	.732	.698	.034
Jesus Sucre	R	.674	**.640**	.034
Dustin Pedroia	R	.736	.702	.034
Kendrys Morales	B	.734	.767	.034

Appendix D - Steamer Hitter OPS Splits

Note: Splits of .635 or below (Sucking Risk) are shown in bold.

NAME	Bats	OPS vs LHP	OPS vs RHP	Diff
Miguel Rojas	R	.731	.697	.034
Andrelton Simmons	R	.751	.717	.033
Cole Tucker	B	.652	.686	.033
Michael Hermosillo	R	.671	**.638**	.033
Robel Garcia	B	.693	.726	.033
Kurt Suzuki	R	.802	.769	.033
Yairo Munoz	R	.710	.677	.033
Mauricio Dubon	R	.725	.692	.033
Anthony Alford	R	.656	**.623**	.033
Gordon Beckham	R	.696	.664	.032
Victor Caratini	B	.723	.755	.032
Yonathan Daza	R	.778	.746	.032
Giovanny Urshela	R	.758	.725	.032
Ozzie Albies	B	.853	.821	.032
Howie Kendrick	R	.857	.825	.032
Chris Owings	R	.662	**.631**	.031
Cesar Puello	R	.704	.673	.031
David Fletcher	R	.734	.703	.031
Manny Pina	R	.720	.689	.031
Matt Duffy	R	.732	.701	.031
Oscar Mercado	R	.729	.699	.030
Brandon Drury	R	.724	.693	.030
Delino DeShields	R	.691	.661	.030
Neil Walker	B	.705	.735	.030
Ty France	R	.784	.754	.030
Yadiel Rivera	R	**.582**	**.552**	.030
Adam Jones	R	.751	.721	.030
Ryan Cordell	R	.658	**.628**	.030
Jon Berti	R	.690	.660	.030
Francisco Cervelli	R	.729	.699	.030
Ben Zobrist	B	.709	.738	.030
Kevin Plawecki	R	.708	.678	.030
Jeimer Candelario	B	.728	.758	.029
Jose Trevino	R	.666	**.637**	.029
John Hicks	R	.684	.655	.029
Brian Anderson	R	.779	.750	.029
Pablo Sandoval	B	.706	.734	.029
Yolmer Sanchez	B	**.649**	.678	.029
Erik Gonzalez	R	.658	**.629**	.029
Wilfredo Tovar	R	**.647**	**.619**	.028
Greg Allen	B	**.648**	.675	.028
Thairo Estrada	R	.699	.672	.028
Carlos Gomez	R	.718	.691	.028
Paul DeJong	R	.802	.774	.028
Abraham Toro	B	.721	.748	.027
Michael A. Taylor	R	.698	.671	.027
Cam Gallagher	R	.694	.667	.027
Willy Adames	R	.754	.727	.027
Donovan Solano	R	.708	.681	.027
Scott Kingery	R	.718	.691	.027
Billy Hamilton	B	**.582**	**.609**	.027
Nico Hoerner	R	.745	.719	.026
Juan Lagares	R	.666	**.640**	.026
Caleb Joseph	R	**.623**	**.597**	.026
Jonathan Villar	B	.731	.757	.026
Hanser Alberto	R	.737	.711	.026
Humberto Arteaga	R	**.646**	**.620**	.026
Blake Swihart	B	**.591**	**.616**	.025
Breyvic Valera	B	.687	.712	.025

304

Note: Splits of .635 or below (Sucking Risk) are shown in bold.

NAME	Bats	OPS vs LHP	OPS vs RHP	Diff
Victor Reyes	B	.682	.708	.025
Peter Bourjos	R	.651	**.626**	.025
Luke Maile	R	**.612**	**.587**	.025
Josh Harrison	R	.691	.666	.025
Eduardo Nunez	R	.721	.696	.025
Francisco Lindor	B	.862	.887	.025
Dawel Lugo	R	.714	.689	.025
Rajai Davis	R	**.627**	**.603**	.024
Jonathan Schoop	R	.801	.777	.024
Harold Ramirez	R	.746	.722	.024
Wilmer Difo	B	**.637**	.660	.024
Asdrubal Cabrera	B	.753	.776	.023
Bryan Reynolds	B	.782	.803	.021
Willians Astudillo	R	.787	.767	.021
Leury Garcia	B	.683	.663	.021
Ehire Adrianza	B	.685	.705	.020
Niko Goodrum	B	.720	.700	.019
Luis Rengifo	B	.682	.702	.019
Cesar Hernandez	B	.718	.738	.019
Melky Cabrera	B	.726	.745	.019
Jonathan Lucroy	R	.720	.701	.018
Rosell Herrera	B	**.647**	.666	.018
Sandy Leon	B	**.637**	**.619**	.018
Carlos Santana	B	.840	.858	.018
Abraham Almonte	B	.710	.726	.017
Andrew Knapp	B	**.631**	**.647**	.016
Yangervis Solarte	B	.709	.725	.016
Eduardo Escobar	B	.765	.780	.015
Cristhian Adames	B	**.621**	**.636**	.015
Domingo Leyba	B	.697	.712	.015
Jung Ho Kang	R	.760	.746	.014
Max Moroff	B	.676	.688	.012
Kaleb Cowart	B	**.625**	**.636**	.012
Dexter Fowler	B	.739	.728	.011
Martin Maldonado	R	.661	.651	.010
Johan Camargo	B	.748	.757	.009
Starling Marte	R	.805	.797	.008
Tim Locastro	R	.695	.688	.008
Richard Urena	B	**.636**	**.629**	.007
Adalberto Mondesi	B	.712	.706	.006
Ketel Marte	B	.850	.844	.006
Roman Quinn	B	.674	.680	.005
Willi Castro	B	.688	.693	.005
Francisco Mejia	B	.725	.729	.004
Freddy Galvis	B	.668	.672	.004
Ildemaro Vargas	B	.723	.719	.004
Erick Mejia	B	**.633**	**.635**	.002
Tommy Edman	B	.737	.739	.002
Andrew Velazquez	B	.660	.662	.002
Marwin Gonzalez	B	.772	.773	.001
Robbie Grossman	B	.736	.735	.000

Pitcher	pERA	pERA (Just Pitchers)	ERA	BB%	pERA FF	FF Count	pERA FT	FT Count	pERA SI	SI Count	pERA FC	FC Count	pERA CH	CH Count	pERA FS	FS Count	pERA SL	SL Count	pERA CU	CU Count	Count
A.J. Cole	3.60	3.22	3.81	6.8%	5.44	200	0.00	3	0.00	0	0.00	0	0.00	10	0.00	0	1.22	196	3.00	51	481
A.J. Minter	5.70	3.17	7.06	15.7%	5.20	227	0.00	0	0.00	0	1.96	253	1.56	91	0.00	0	-1.15	2	0.00	0	573
A.J. Puk	4.17	3.18	3.18	10.6%	4.40	130	0.00	0	0.00	0	0.00	0	0.04	19	0.00	0	0.84	49	7.14	4	202
Aaron Brooks	4.88	4.49	5.65	7.1%	6.23	508	4.95	507	0.00	0	8.23	3	3.06	375	0.00	0	2.92	417	5.49	62	1,899
Aaron Bummer	3.05	2.45	2.13	9.2%	3.10	95	0.00	0	2.79	701	0.69	183	1.30	4	0.00	0	2.95	55	0.00	0	1,039
Aaron Civale	4.58	4.34	2.34	7.1%	7.37	28	0.00	0	5.51	302	3.96	257	2.02	57	0.00	0	3.66	122	2.99	96	863
Aaron Nola	4.35	3.57	3.87	9.4%	5.07	1,197	4.85	334	0.00	1	0.00	0	2.28	596	0.00	0	0.00	0	2.25	1,101	3,332
Aaron Sanchez	5.37	4.04	5.89	11.2%	4.97	657	4.83	620	6.96	3	0.00	0	3.13	423	0.00	0	0.00	0	2.65	515	2,220
Aaron Wilkerson	6.40	4.87	7.31	11.3%	5.26	170	0.00	0	0.00	0	0.00	0	2.27	47	0.00	0	5.32	59	5.40	57	333
Adalberto Mejia	6.65	4.64	6.61	14.5%	5.05	269	5.46	70	0.00	0	0.00	0	3.51	99	0.00	0	4.45	186	0.00	5	629
Adam Cimber	3.86	3.36	4.45	7.8%	2.68	122	0.00	0	3.56	397	0.00	0	0.00	0	1.30	8	3.54	243	0.38	9	779
Adam Conley	5.26	4.11	6.53	10.3%	4.46	644	8.23	1	0.00	0	8.23	3	2.95	180	0.00	0	3.94	191	4.00	38	1,061
Adam Kolarek	2.97	2.66	3.27	7.0%	4.15	81	8.23	1	2.28	540	2.20	6	2.58	66	0.00	0	3.92	67	0.00	0	761
Adam Morgan	3.06	2.55	3.94	8.3%	3.26	38	5.28	89	0.00	0	1.30	1	2.33	90	0.00	0	0.78	191	4.33	49	463
Adam Ottavino	5.39	3.68	1.90	14.1%	0.00	10	4.14	471	0.00	0	4.00	155	8.23	2	0.00	1	3.22	515	7.35	1	1,158
Adam Plutko	4.85	4.78	4.86	5.6%	5.41	919	0.00	0	0.00	0	8.23	1	4.77	197	0.00	0	3.78	413	3.83	174	1,705
Adam Wainwright	4.95	4.28	4.19	8.6%	5.46	381	0.00	0	5.30	662	3.98	615	2.38	49	0.00	0	1.46	5	3.43	992	2,876
Adam Warren	4.97	4.09	5.34	9.7%	5.94	169	0.00	0	0.00	0	8.23	1	2.22	99	0.00	0	3.56	254	4.20	24	555
Adbert Alzolay	6.53	4.25	7.30	15.0%	5.47	129	0.00	0	0.00	0	0.00	0	1.85	47	0.00	0	0.00	0	3.32	49	225
Adrian Houser	4.19	3.70	3.72	8.0%	3.70	567	3.46	647	0.00	0	0.00	0	2.54	120	0.00	0	3.68	195	4.89	248	1,777
Adrian Morejon	5.39	4.70	10.13	7.1%	4.72	80	5.93	3	0.00	0	0.00	0	6.01	28	0.00	0	0.00	0	3.74	43	154
Adrian Sampson	4.46	4.17	5.89	6.4%	7.99	11	8.23	1	5.55	1,100	1.30	2	3.06	256	0.00	0	2.24	547	2.57	136	2,056
Alec Mills	3.51	3.13	2.75	7.2%	5.10	170	4.04	130	0.00	0	0.00	0	0.23	106	0.00	0	1.19	61	2.84	86	553
Alex Claudio	3.89	3.15	4.06	9.0%	1.30	8	0.00	0	3.31	437	0.00	0	2.67	348	0.00	0	3.82	182	-2.04	2	978
Alex Cobb	3.45	3.72	10.95	3.3%	5.02	109	0.00	0	0.00	0	0.00	0	0.00	0	1.37	80	0.00	0	4.89	39	229
Alex Colome	4.07	3.37	2.80	9.2%	5.21	269	0.00	0	0.00	0	2.68	679	2.06	25	0.00	0	8.23	1	0.00	0	975
Alex McRae	6.00	4.30	8.78	12.1%	5.10	89	5.39	199	0.00	0	0.00	0	3.90	44	0.00	0	3.19	98	1.90	67	547
Alex Wilson	6.77	4.20	9.53	15.8%	5.59	43	6.68	48	0.00	0	1.30	1	0.00	2	0.00	0	2.65	108	0.00	0	202
Alex Wood	4.22	4.09	5.80	5.9%	0.00	0	4.62	295	0.00	0	0.00	0	3.34	147	0.00	0	0.00	0	3.75	144	586
Alex Young	3.69	3.23	3.56	7.7%	6.31	186	0.00	0	3.80	300	3.36	304	1.84	270	0.00	0	0.94	22	1.75	242	1,325
Allen Webster	3.14	2.09	4.91	9.6%	5.36	61	0.48	12	0.00	0	0.00	0	-0.02	26	0.00	0	0.35	72	0.00	0	171
Amir Garrett	3.72	1.91	3.21	14.2%	3.83	169	4.49	224	0.00	0	8.23	1	8.23	1	0.00	0	0.21	540	0.00	0	978
Andres Munoz	3.88	2.73	3.91	11.3%	4.22	277	0.00	2	0.00	0	0.00	1	0.00	0	0.00	0	-0.26	135	0.00	0	416
Andrew Cashner	4.68	3.94	4.68	8.1%	4.95	1,137	5.19	81	0.00	0	5.93	2	2.38	687	0.00	0	3.04	325	4.35	277	2,511
Andrew Chafin	3.11	2.57	3.76	8.0%	4.32	266	0.00	0	4.48	268	0.00	0	0.00	0	0.00	0	-0.26	338	-6.47	2	876
Andrew Heaney	3.58	3.17	4.91	7.3%	0.00	0	8.23	1	3.82	924	-2.12	3	2.90	251	0.00	0	0.00	1	1.95	428	1,609
Andrew Kittredge	2.41	2.32	4.17	5.7%	4.11	175	3.62	299	8.23	1	8.23	1	-0.12	38	0.00	0	0.28	304	0.00	0	818
Andrew Miller	4.62	3.40	4.45	11.4%	5.06	364	0.00	4	0.00	0	0.00	0	0.00	1	0.00	0	2.40	587	0.00	0	969
Andrew Suarez	5.25	4.33	5.79	9.5%	6.05	163	4.48	146	0.00	0	0.00	0	3.13	76	0.00	0	3.09	117	2.49	37	540
Anibal Sanchez	4.86	4.29	3.85	8.2%	5.62	797	0.00	0	5.71	265	4.80	612	2.34	120	1.76	627	4.09	81	4.88	153	2,690
Anthony Bass	3.73	3.13	3.56	9.0%	5.21	31	4.24	333	0.00	0	8.23	1	0.00	0	1.78	98	1.81	231	0.00	0	718
Anthony DeSclafani	4.35	4.03	3.89	7.0%	4.95	955	4.54	481	0.00	0	0.00	0	4.20	133	0.00	0	2.94	634	2.85	384	2,668
Anthony Kay	4.27	3.66	5.79	7.9%	4.71	159	0.00	0	0.00	0	0.00	0	0.49	50	0.00	0	0.00	0	3.48	49	258
Anthony Swarzak	4.52	3.24	4.56	11.5%	4.97	338	1.30	40	0.00	0	8.23	1	0.00	0	0.00	0	2.31	546	0.00	0	926
Antonio Senzatela	5.13	4.07	6.71	9.8%	4.40	1,400	0.00	1	0.00	0	0.00	1	4.97	164	0.00	0	3.33	434	2.91	237	2,237
Archie Bradley	5.34	4.08	3.52	11.4%	4.95	760	2.57	134	-1.15	2	0.00	0	1.10	70	0.00	0	0.00	1	3.34	316	1,284
Ariel Jurado	4.76	4.44	5.81	6.7%	5.04	472	4.47	839	-2.12	3	0.00	0	4.44	240	0.00	0	3.93	319	3.68	169	2,047
Aroldis Chapman	4.09	3.11	2.21	18.0%	3.93	587	0.00	0	3.05	94	0.00	0	-7.30	2	0.00	0	1.63	305	0.00	0	989
Asher Wojciechowski	4.65	4.12	4.92	7.8%	4.95	795	0.00	0	0.00	0	8.23	2	5.55	42	0.00	0	2.45	323	3.49	305	1,467
Austin Adams	3.55	2.30	3.94	12.3%	4.13	186	6.96	19	0.00	0	0.00	0	0.00	0	0.00	0	0.98	323	0.00	0	541
Austin Adams	6.52	4.01	7.02	16.3%	5.60	171	0.00	10	0.00	0	0.00	0	0.00	0	0.00	7	2.27	117	0.00	0	318
Austin Brice	4.57	3.75	3.43	9.1%	2.96	222	-7.30	2	4.05	165	8.23	1	4.60	33	0.00	0	7.37	4	4.06	333	761
Austin Davis	6.01	3.96	6.53	14.3%	4.64	236	0.00	0	0.00	0	0.00	0	1.51	74	0.00	0	4.90	45	3.54	52	407
Austin Pruitt	3.49	3.34	4.40	6.2%	4.40	311	0.00	0	0.00	0	-1.15	2	2.62	142	0.00	0	1.97	167	3.43	97	720
Austin Voth	3.83	3.49	3.30	7.5%	4.46	419	0.00	0	0.00	0	0.00	0	2.49	65	0.00	0	2.63	61	1.40	138	684
Ben Heller	4.40	3.56	1.23	10.7%	0.00	0	6.58	50	0.00	0	0.00	0	0.34	8	0.00	0	0.73	43	0.00	1	102
Blaine Hardy	4.17	3.85	4.47	7.1%	5.93	147	0.00	6	0.00	0	5.57	70	1.82	287	0.00	0	8.23	2	5.16	130	672
Blake Parker	4.56	3.95	4.55	8.6%	4.16	489	0.00	0	0.00	0	7.48	41	0.00	0	2.65	329	8.23	1	5.04	159	1,020
Blake Snell	2.91	2.23	4.29	9.1%	3.69	893	0.00	0	8.23	1	-5.26	4	1.09	369	1.30	1	1.30	133	0.58	448	1,852
Blake Treinen	5.32	3.48	4.91	13.9%	4.70	211	8.23	4	3.11	442	3.38	185	0.00	0	0.00	0	2.82	136	0.00	0	1,023
Bobby Poyner	5.33	4.41	6.94	10.2%	4.97	148	0.00	0	0.00	0	0.00	0	3.50	41	0.00	0	3.30	34	0.00	2	225
Brad Boxberger	5.56	3.70	5.40	13.9%	4.04	227	0.00	0	0.00	0	0.00	0	2.83	137	1.30	1	4.18	81	7.31	1	487
Brad Brach	5.25	3.68	5.47	12.8%	3.94	464	5.37	54	0.00	0	3.20	66	2.15	179	0.00	0	4.19	186	0.00	0	982
Brad Hand	3.96	3.55	3.30	7.4%	4.92	396	6.23	31	0.00	0	0.00	0	1.30	1	0.00	0	2.30	502	0.00	0	946
Brad Keller	5.00	4.09	4.19	9.9%	4.45	1,100	4.60	644	8.23	3	0.00	0	7.20	41	0.00	0	3.05	826	0.00	0	2,616
Brad Peacock	4.79	4.26	4.12	8.1%	4.87	408	5.09	470	8.23	1	8.23	1	4.20	91	0.00	0	2.94	430	3.61	104	1,510
Brad Wieck	4.61	3.93	5.71	8.8%	3.82	476	0.00	0	8.23	1	0.00	0	0.00	0	0.00	0	4.13	70	4.37	73	621
Brady Rodgers	5.98	4.28	16.20	12.0%	4.94	59	0.00	1	0.00	0	8.23	1	1.95	13	0.00	0	2.95	30	7.43	10	114
Branden Kline	5.09	4.00	5.93	10.4%	4.95	414	0.00	0	0.00	0	0.00	0	1.25	55	0.00	0	2.99	239	0.00	0	708
Brandon Brennan	3.68	2.40	4.56	12.2%	6.82	22	0.69	8	4.73	339	0.00	0	-0.32	297	0.00	0	0.84	45	7.08	1	725
Brandon Kintzler	4.05	4.02	2.68	5.7%	5.74	17	8.23	1	4.57	602	0.00	0	2.22	148	0.00	0	2.89	84	0.00	0	855
Brandon Woodruff	3.56	3.45	3.62	6.1%	3.67	772	3.33	499	0.00	0	8.23	1	2.83	276	0.00	0	3.37	396	6.05	34	1,979
Brandon Workman	5.00	3.17	1.88	15.7%	3.52	420	0.00	0	0.00	0	2.28	263	0.00	0	0.00	0	0.00	4	3.35	557	1,244
Brendan McKay	4.68	4.22	5.14	7.4%	4.61	501	0.00	0	0.00	0	4.15	114	4.09	30	0.00	0	0.00	2	3.44	230	878
Brent Suter	2.15	2.90	0.49	1.8%	5.21	173	5.93	9	0.00	0	0.00	0	2.81	43	0.00	0	0.00	0	7.10	8	233
Brett Anderson	4.33	4.07	3.89	6.6%	5.33	493	0.00	0	4.15	1,158	8.23	4	3.21	356	0.00	0	3.22	506	4.18	141	2,659
Brett Martin	3.18	2.88	4.76	6.4%	3.63	287	3.06	206	0.00	0	0.00	0	8.23	1	0.00	0	2.15	330	2.79	144	1,022

Pitcher	pERA	pERA (Just Pitchers)	ERA	BB%	pERA FF	FF Count	pERA FT	FT Count	pERA SI	SI Count	pERA FC	FC Count	pERA CH	CH Count	pERA FS	FS Count	pERA SL	SL Count	pERA CU	CU Count	Count
Brian Flynn	5.91	4.30	5.22	12.2%	5.89	83	3.79	170	0.00	0	8.23	2	0.00	1	0.00	0	4.05	197	0.00	0	453
Brian Johnson	6.15	4.58	6.02	11.9%	5.83	270	6.96	23	0.00	0	0.00	0	8.23	6	0.00	0	3.32	210	4.02	263	772
Brian Moran	3.13	2.71	4.26	6.9%	2.80	50	-2.12	3	0.00	0	0.00	0	0.00	3	0.00	0	3.13	8	3.02	48	112
Brian Schlitter	4.39	3.52	3.72	9.8%	4.83	54	4.44	15	2.88	61	0.89	12	0.00	0	0.00	0	1.30	6	0.00	0	150
Brock Burke	5.62	4.77	7.43	9.2%	4.81	206	5.52	88	0.00	0	0.00	0	3.50	73	0.00	0	0.00	3	5.06	106	476
Brock Stewart	4.87	4.46	9.82	6.5%	2.02	25	5.30	238	0.00	0	0.00	0	3.83	64	0.00	0	3.85	159	0.00	0	486
Brooks Pounders	4.41	4.19	6.14	5.9%	6.56	47	0.00	0	0.00	0	0.00	0	8.23	6	0.00	0	2.53	82	0.00	0	135
Brusdar Graterol	3.26	3.33	4.66	5.0%	5.41	25	0.00	0	2.59	74	0.00	0	8.23	1	0.00	0	3.29	44	0.00	0	144
Bryan Abreu	2.52	1.96	1.04	9.4%	6.46	46	0.00	3	0.00	0	0.00	0	0.00	1	0.00	0	-0.14	88	0.14	8	146
Bryan Garcia	4.14	1.77	12.15	15.2%	0.00	7	1.30	8	3.53	52	0.00	0	0.19	22	0.00	0	0.75	40	0.00	0	129
Bryan Shaw	4.40	3.58	5.38	9.3%	8.23	2	1.30	1	0.00	0	4.15	886	0.45	85	0.00	1	2.40	187	2.64	18	1,180
Bryse Wilson	6.00	4.75	7.20	10.8%	4.87	237	4.75	19	0.00	0	0.00	0	2.86	48	0.00	0	5.68	44	7.48	8	356
Buck Farmer	3.86	3.26	3.72	8.3%	4.73	555	8.23	1	0.00	0	1.30	1	2.52	288	0.00	0	1.16	287	0.00	0	1,157
Buddy Boshers	5.38	4.13	4.05	11.0%	5.64	12	5.93	5	5.65	135	0.00	0	0.77	26	0.00	0	0.00	10	3.61	196	384
Burch Smith	6.10	4.15	5.48	13.2%	3.90	268	1.30	1	0.00	0	0.00	0	2.64	69	0.00	0	0.00	1	6.24	85	425
Cal Quantrill	4.16	3.94	5.16	6.3%	4.37	392	4.76	632	0.00	0	0.00	0	2.77	317	0.00	0	2.72	370	5.97	68	1,781
Caleb Ferguson	6.02	4.30	4.84	13.2%	4.37	607	-1.15	2	0.00	0	0.00	1	0.00	2	0.00	0	5.93	6	4.12	169	804
Caleb Smith	4.66	3.90	4.52	9.3%	4.71	1,366	0.00	0	0.00	1	0.00	2	3.06	363	0.00	0	2.97	816	-1.96	6	2,661
Cam Bedrosian	3.90	3.28	3.23	8.5%	4.53	481	0.00	0	0.00	0	0.00	0	8.23	1	-1.09	10	2.15	501	7.21	2	1,003
Carl Edwards Jr.	6.99	4.55	8.47	16.7%	5.13	258	5.93	8	0.00	0	0.00	0	0.00	2	0.00	0	0.00	0	2.59	77	346
Carlos Carrasco	2.82	2.92	5.29	4.7%	4.88	421	5.34	164	0.00	1	0.00	0	1.27	233	0.00	0	0.84	432	5.61	22	1,274
Carlos Estevez	3.64	3.20	3.75	7.5%	3.29	841	2.09	35	0.00	0	0.00	0	2.69	44	0.00	0	3.17	320	0.00	0	1,240
Carlos Martinez	3.41	2.74	3.17	9.0%	3.82	223	2.84	155	0.00	0	6.96	16	1.64	137	0.00	0	1.93	217	0.00	0	749
Carlos Rodon	4.94	3.74	5.19	10.8%	5.88	348	4.65	9	0.00	0	8.23	1	1.16	79	1.30	1	1.57	257	7.35	1	696
Carlos Torres	3.60	3.85	7.50	3.5%	1.46	20	8.23	10	0.00	0	4.77	36	0.00	0	0.00	0	0.00	5	3.16	14	115
Carson Fulmer	6.15	3.86	6.26	15.0%	5.92	239	0.00	0	8.23	1	2.17	179	2.83	86	8.23	1	0.00	0	1.28	43	556
Casey Sadler	4.22	3.95	2.14	6.7%	0.00	0	0.00	0	4.54	266	5.07	138	4.14	22	0.00	0	3.93	80	2.31	190	696
CC Sabathia	4.46	3.82	4.95	8.3%	4.89	32	0.00	0	4.88	228	4.05	678	1.86	197	8.23	2	3.71	494	7.36	2	1,635
Chad Bettis	3.94	3.46	6.08	7.3%	4.56	373	5.19	32	0.00	0	3.26	174	2.21	324	0.00	0	4.65	3	3.21	124	1,030
Chad Green	3.55	3.31	4.17	6.4%	3.57	1,022	0.00	0	0.00	0	0.00	0	0.00	0	4.50	25	2.20	271	0.00	0	1,320
Chad Sobotka	4.57	2.62	6.21	14.2%	3.44	318	0.00	0	0.00	0	8.23	1	8.23	1	0.00	0	1.48	242	7.24	1	564
Chance Adams	5.95	5.00	8.53	8.9%	4.81	305	1.30	2	0.00	0	0.00	0	7.37	33	0.00	2	5.46	91	4.45	86	519
Chandler Shepherd	5.12	4.70	6.63	7.1%	4.99	151	0.00	0	0.00	0	0.00	0	2.81	34	0.00	0	5.69	87	3.24	46	318
Charlie Morton	3.44	3.12	3.05	7.2%	3.75	938	3.86	598	8.23	1	3.10	319	8.23	1	3.70	106	5.19	7	2.17	1,168	3,139
Chase Anderson	4.68	4.06	4.21	8.5%	4.09	999	4.89	185	0.00	0	4.40	415	2.90	551	-7.30	2	8.23	1	5.49	235	2,392
Chasen Bradford	3.68	3.60	4.86	5.8%	5.14	72	0.00	0	3.29	44	0.76	9	2.19	28	0.00	0	3.20	82	0.00	0	248
Chaz Roe	5.64	3.90	4.06	13.5%	4.39	56	4.44	216	0.00	0	2.06	40	-1.97	3	0.00	0	3.91	599	-2.89	8	922
Chi Chi Gonzalez	5.74	4.39	5.29	11.9%	4.43	476	5.48	132	0.00	0	4.48	257	1.46	126	0.00	0	5.39	140	7.29	14	1,145
Chris Archer	4.55	3.48	5.19	10.5%	5.24	828	5.81	227	0.00	0	8.23	5	3.23	253	0.00	0	0.84	742	4.01	41	2,098
Chris Bassitt	4.91	4.44	3.81	7.7%	4.86	504	0.00	0	4.74	926	4.20	296	4.26	193	0.00	0	0.00	0	3.09	284	2,331
Chris Devenski	4.03	3.66	4.83	7.1%	5.34	498	8.23	5	0.00	0	8.23	1	1.64	396	0.00	0	3.48	238	0.00	6	1,144
Chris Flexen	8.66	5.38	6.59	18.6%	6.56	129	6.29	16	0.00	0	5.93	3	4.09	30	0.00	0	2.58	45	4.98	11	234
Chris Martin	2.60	3.20	3.40	2.3%	3.48	381	0.00	0	3.93	157	2.66	129	0.67	103	0.00	0	4.17	72	6.57	11	865
Chris Mazza	4.88	4.50	5.51	6.8%	1.33	9	0.00	0	5.19	135	4.00	71	5.64	12	0.00	0	3.74	55	0.00	0	285
Chris Paddack	3.92	3.92	3.33	5.5%	4.52	1,391	0.00	0	0.00	0	0.00	0	2.16	650	0.00	0	0.00	0	5.26	238	2,280
Chris Sale	3.19	3.06	4.40	6.1%	4.14	897	3.58	233	0.00	0	0.00	0	2.27	385	0.00	0	2.26	945	-2.33	4	2,466
Chris Stratton	4.80	3.85	5.57	9.6%	4.73	658	3.83	43	0.00	0	2.02	10	3.18	76	0.00	0	2.57	300	3.03	158	1,363
Cionel Perez	3.94	3.94	10.00	6.0%	4.62	99	0.00	0	0.00	0	0.00	0	2.74	16	0.00	0	2.95	45	0.00	1	163
Clay Buchholz	4.25	4.03	6.56	6.3%	4.97	146	4.10	184	0.00	0	3.58	273	2.95	188	0.00	0	6.96	3	5.03	169	963
Clay Holmes	5.83	3.59	5.58	15.0%	4.62	86	0.00	0	4.01	464	0.00	5	6.96	8	0.00	0	2.54	90	2.68	219	915
Clayton Kershaw	3.27	3.24	3.03	5.8%	5.14	1,118	0.00	0	0.00	2	-10.41	5	3.13	16	0.00	0	1.45	1,010	2.67	421	2,672
Clayton Richard	5.21	4.42	5.96	9.0%	7.34	99	4.27	419	8.23	1	8.23	1	0.97	15	0.00	0	3.47	188	0.00	1	728
Cody Allen	7.78	4.87	6.26	17.2%	5.98	262	8.23	1	0.00	0	0.00	0	0.00	0	0.00	0	8.23	1	3.55	226	491
Cody Anderson	7.10	3.95	9.35	17.4%	6.05	84	0.00	0	0.00	0	0.00	1	2.07	62	8.23	1	0.27	19	4.30	26	193
Cody Stashak	1.45	2.27	3.24	1.0%	4.43	198	0.00	0	0.00	0	0.00	0	1.30	26	0.00	0	-0.50	145	0.00	0	369
Cole Hamels	4.32	3.54	3.81	9.1%	4.58	825	4.49	286	8.23	2	4.60	464	0.33	506	0.00	0	4.57	9	3.50	296	2,394
Cole Irvin	4.89	4.48	5.83	7.2%	5.31	316	0.00	0	0.00	0	0.00	1	2.35	164	0.00	0	4.83	123	7.51	17	624
Cole Sulser	4.64	3.80	0.00	10.3%	4.30	83	0.00	0	0.00	0	0.00	0	3.06	12	0.00	0	2.86	35	0.00	0	130
Colin Poche	3.27	2.61	4.70	9.2%	2.47	740	0.00	0	0.00	1	0.00	0	8.23	4	8.23	5	8.23	1	3.24	85	836
Collin McHugh	4.54	3.73	4.70	9.5%	4.81	418	0.00	4	0.00	0	5.13	158	2.62	48	0.00	0	2.33	555	5.29	110	1,294
Colten Brewer	5.18	3.38	4.12	13.4%	2.96	40	0.00	0	0.00	0	4.74	403	0.00	3	0.00	0	2.68	121	2.37	435	1,016
Conner Menez	6.55	4.38	5.29	16.4%	5.30	194	0.00	0	0.00	0	0.00	0	1.53	45	0.00	0	2.99	53	5.24	26	319
Connor Sadzeck	5.76	3.90	2.66	14.0%	3.88	131	1.95	73	0.00	0	1.30	1	0.00	3	0.00	0	4.67	214	0.00	1	424
Corbin Burnes	3.11	2.27	8.82	8.5%	4.36	476	5.57	29	0.00	1	0.00	4	0.82	35	0.00	0	-2.08	272	4.50	70	903
Corbin Martin	6.04	4.25	5.59	13.0%	4.65	232	0.00	0	8.23	1	0.00	0	2.39	41	0.00	0	3.79	28	4.75	70	372
Corey Kluber	4.48	3.58	5.80	8.9%	6.02	82	0.00	0	4.99	164	2.45	174	4.13	52	0.00	0	-2.12	3	1.79	136	611
Corey Oswalt	8.06	5.01	12.15	17.7%	7.45	54	0.00	1	4.75	38	0.00	0	3.25	25	0.00	0	0.00	4	1.49	15	139
Cory Gearrin	5.22	4.18	4.07	10.4%	5.68	41	0.00	1	4.23	354	0.00	0	3.38	136	0.00	0	4.27	362	7.21	1	916
Craig Kimbrel	4.86	3.25	6.53	12.5%	4.23	251	0.00	0	0.00	0	0.00	0	0.00	0	0.00	0	0.00	0	1.29	126	392
Craig Stammen	3.82	3.99	3.29	4.4%	0.00	0	6.96	3	4.43	857	0.00	0	8.23	1	0.00	0	3.79	193	1.65	148	1,224
Cy Sneed	3.80	3.75	5.48	5.4%	4.02	223	1.30	3	0.00	0	4.35	16	2.95	40	0.00	0	4.72	47	-1.33	15	344
D.J. Johnson	6.48	4.06	5.04	16.4%	5.17	309	0.00	0	0.00	0	0.00	2	0.00	1	0.00	0	0.00	0	2.18	177	489
Dakota Hudson	4.59	3.37	3.35	11.4%	3.91	368	0.00	0	4.09	1,390	0.00	0	2.25	70	0.00	0	1.47	713	4.15	304	2,848
Dallas Keuchel	4.09	3.53	3.75	8.0%	4.44	90	3.51	914	0.00	0	4.84	373	1.90	272	0.00	0	3.01	214	6.93	1	1,864
Dan Altavilla	6.30	3.61	5.52	18.8%	5.12	166	0.00	0	0.00	0	0.00	0	0.00	0	0.00	0	1.42	114	0.00	0	294
Dan Jennings	9.15	3.40	13.50	21.9%	0.00	5	4.52	64	0.00	0	0.00	0	0.00	0	0.00	0	2.31	50	0.00	0	134
Dan Otero	3.88	4.43	4.85	2.3%	5.41	49	0.00	0	4.94	225	0.00	0	3.63	75	8.23	1	2.59	58	0.00	0	416

Appendix E: Pitcher pERA Values, 2017 and 2019 Ball

Pitcher	pERA	pERA (Just Pitchers)	ERA	BB%	pERA FF	FF Count	pERA FT	FT Count	pERA SI	SI Count	pERA FC	FC Count	pERA CH	CH Count	pERA FS	FS Count	pERA SL	SL Count	pERA CU	CU Count	Count
Dan Straily	6.24	5.17	9.82	9.3%	5.59	442	3.58	19	0.00	0	0.00	0	3.52	219	0.00	0	6.11	179	6.26	32	966
Dan Winkler	4.62	3.34	4.98	11.8%	4.83	113	0.15	17	0.00	0	2.75	145	0.00	0	0.00	0	0.00	0	2.96	76	351
Daniel Hudson	4.89	4.23	2.47	8.9%	4.70	752	3.81	111	0.00	1	8.23	1	4.05	72	0.00	0	3.18	280	0.00	0	1,217
Daniel Mengden	6.19	5.15	4.83	10.4%	6.07	359	5.58	192	0.00	0	4.42	148	4.83	116	0.00	0	4.29	130	3.63	103	1,048
Daniel Norris	4.27	4.08	4.49	6.2%	5.61	1,047	4.68	161	0.00	0	7.59	5	1.06	450	0.00	0	3.07	538	5.29	155	2,361
Daniel Ponce de Leon	4.97	3.57	3.70	12.8%	3.35	548	0.00	0	0.00	0	3.92	102	3.86	57	0.00	0	0.00	0	4.60	63	771
Daniel Stumpf	5.55	4.22	4.34	11.1%	4.96	271	0.00	0	0.00	0	0.00	0	4.40	47	0.00	0	3.15	193	0.00	0	522
Daniel Zamora	5.70	4.11	5.19	12.2%	4.75	38	0.00	0	0.00	0	0.00	0	0.00	2	8.23	1	3.89	94	0.00	0	165
Danny Duffy	4.82	4.23	4.34	8.3%	5.13	946	5.53	205	0.00	0	-7.30	2	2.58	249	0.00	0	3.21	563	3.70	196	2,161
Dario Agrazal	5.05	4.94	4.91	5.6%	5.71	141	8.23	1	5.65	628	0.00	0	4.05	161	0.00	0	3.06	218	0.00	0	1,149
Darwinzon Hernandez	5.77	2.91	4.45	17.7%	2.67	506	0.00	0	0.00	0	0.00	0	0.00	1	0.00	0	3.89	161	0.00	11	681
David Bednar	4.35	3.30	6.55	10.4%	4.88	83	0.00	0	0.00	0	0.00	2	0.00	0	1.61	67	0.00	0	3.06	44	196
David Hale	4.04	4.20	3.11	4.5%	5.47	202	4.42	158	0.00	0	0.00	0	3.23	129	0.00	0	0.00	0	2.69	110	602
David Hernandez	4.12	3.01	8.02	10.1%	3.36	194	5.16	203	0.00	0	3.06	24	-2.12	6	8.23	1	1.58	232	1.62	104	787
David Hess	5.44	4.75	7.09	8.2%	5.41	760	5.15	86	0.00	0	8.23	1	4.99	165	0.00	0	3.20	353	4.25	63	1,430
David McKay	7.01	5.10	5.47	14.8%	0.00	7	8.23	1	5.24	285	0.00	0	6.96	8	0.00	0	0.00	2	5.03	170	473
David Phelps	5.88	4.65	3.41	11.6%	5.47	139	5.14	115	0.00	0	4.63	202	0.00	3	0.00	0	0.47	4	3.90	177	640
David Price	4.11	3.77	4.28	7.0%	3.93	501	5.45	501	0.00	0	3.73	321	2.05	485	0.00	0	4.18	9	1.93	44	1,862
David Robertson	6.96	3.91	5.40	18.2%	1.30	6	0.00	1	0.00	0	5.72	71	0.00	0	0.00	0	2.41	28	1.66	30	136
Dennis Santana	5.56	2.96	7.20	14.8%	0.00	0	3.66	59	0.00	0	0.00	0	1.71	15	0.00	0	2.20	30	0.00	0	104
Dereck Rodriguez	4.97	4.34	5.64	8.2%	5.23	649	4.03	139	0.00	0	3.62	225	3.67	333	0.00	0	8.23	2	3.75	274	1,625
Derek Holland	5.14	3.73	6.08	12.0%	5.93	2	1.30	1	4.64	910	8.23	1	5.24	62	8.23	1	1.80	423	2.23	73	1,487
Derek Law	5.38	3.41	4.90	14.0%	5.22	431	0.00	0	0.00	0	0.00	0	1.62	153	0.00	0	1.61	366	4.12	221	1,174
Devin Smeltzer	4.51	4.40	3.86	5.9%	5.58	338	0.00	0	0.00	0	8.23	1	2.86	186	0.00	0	6.58	28	3.43	179	732
Devin Williams	5.12	4.15	3.95	9.0%	4.54	83	6.50	77	0.00	0	0.00	0	2.06	91	0.00	0	3.06	18	0.00	0	270
Diego Castillo	3.32	2.62	3.41	9.0%	4.47	46	0.00	0	3.60	487	1.51	233	8.23	1	0.00	0	1.69	335	0.00	0	1,106
Dillon Maples	4.68	1.82	5.40	18.5%	3.29	79	0.00	0	0.00	0	0.00	0	0.00	0	0.00	0	1.03	141	1.60	17	237
Dillon Peters	5.07	4.44	5.38	8.0%	5.73	585	3.95	58	0.00	0	0.00	0	1.96	286	0.00	0	1.27	30	4.70	315	1,274
Dillon Tate	4.12	3.19	6.43	9.7%	0.00	7	0.00	0	3.59	190	0.00	0	1.98	68	0.00	0	4.57	33	2.86	52	350
Dinelson Lamet	3.98	3.13	4.07	9.6%	4.91	454	5.04	225	0.00	0	0.00	0	0.89	12	0.00	0	0.69	208	1.01	332	1,233
Domingo German	3.69	3.47	4.03	6.6%	5.07	766	4.85	240	8.23	2	0.00	0	3.27	427	0.00	1	0.00	5	1.64	804	2,247
Dominic Leone	4.47	3.03	5.53	12.2%	3.97	235	5.35	77	0.00	0	2.09	239	8.23	2	0.00	0	1.00	90	0.00	0	682
Donnie Hart	2.80	1.45	0.00	13.8%	0.00	0	0.00	0	1.48	63	0.00	0	-0.03	15	0.00	0	2.06	25	6.50	1	104
Dovydas Neverauskas	5.81	3.43	10.61	13.2%	3.80	119	0.00	0	0.00	0	3.30	40	0.00	2	0.00	0	1.30	5	2.97	46	212
Drew Anderson	6.30	2.80	7.50	20.0%	3.30	53	7.73	13	0.00	0	0.00	0	-0.34	3	1.30	1	-5.08	7	1.88	27	104
Drew Gagnon	4.15	3.82	8.37	6.0%	5.13	218	0.00	0	0.00	0	0.00	0	0.90	127	0.00	0	3.69	20	6.27	36	414
Drew Pomeranz	4.69	3.78	4.85	9.7%	3.67	1,018	4.65	147	0.00	0	6.85	81	4.21	22	0.00	0	8.23	3	3.30	581	1,857
Drew Smyly	5.35	4.18	6.24	10.7%	5.11	1,020	0.00	0	0.00	0	4.06	431	3.65	49	0.00	0	6.88	23	2.62	604	2,130
Drew Steckenrider	5.07	4.50	6.28	8.6%	5.21	143	0.00	0	0.00	0	0.00	0	0.00	0	0.00	0	8.23	1	3.27	85	237
Drew VerHagen	4.53	3.74	5.90	8.9%	4.82	110	4.62	389	0.00	0	0.00	0	0.47	4	0.00	0	2.12	288	3.87	154	945
Duane Underwood Jr.	3.57	3.41	5.40	5.9%	4.88	118	0.34	8	0.00	0	0.00	0	1.63	52	0.00	0	0.00	0	1.73	33	211
Dustin May	3.80	4.16	3.63	3.6%	4.50	37	0.00	0	4.56	287	2.83	175	8.23	7	0.00	0	0.00	0	5.40	60	566
Dylan Bundy	4.10	3.48	4.79	8.3%	5.20	1,173	4.60	211	0.00	0	1.30	1	1.78	483	0.00	0	0.96	632	4.11	277	2,778
Dylan Cease	4.80	3.64	5.79	10.7%	3.96	662	3.03	41	0.00	0	3.12	122	0.00	0	0.00	0	3.04	287	3.84	252	1,364
Dylan Covey	5.81	4.66	7.98	10.0%	4.51	126	5.41	362	8.23	1	4.84	133	1.97	185	0.00	0	6.02	111	5.30	101	1,019
Dylan Floro	3.49	3.14	4.24	7.0%	3.81	137	8.23	1	3.02	330	0.21	9	5.66	27	0.00	0	2.65	203	0.00	0	721
Edgar Garcia	5.78	3.78	5.77	15.1%	6.71	312	1.92	45	0.00	0	8.23	1	0.00	9	0.00	0	1.47	346	0.00	0	713
Edinson Volquez	6.93	4.55	6.75	16.0%	0.00	1	8.23	1	5.60	140	0.00	0	3.74	109	0.00	0	0.00	0	3.30	46	297
Eduardo Jimenez	5.82	4.71	5.91	10.2%	4.78	78	6.09	29	0.00	0	0.00	0	5.93	11	0.00	0	3.87	71	0.00	0	189
Eduardo Rodriguez	4.11	3.45	3.81	8.7%	3.94	1,275	3.88	555	5.93	2	4.40	590	1.40	787	0.00	0	5.27	65	4.27	91	3,384
Edubray Ramos	5.82	4.72	5.40	10.1%	4.44	100	0.00	2	0.00	0	0.00	0	3.74	23	0.00	0	5.13	149	0.00	0	276
Edwin Diaz	2.77	2.07	5.59	8.7%	2.71	702	1.30	5	0.00	0	1.30	1	0.00	0	0.00	0	0.83	361	0.00	0	1,073
Edwin Jackson	5.12	3.99	9.58	9.5%	5.81	316	3.48	169	0.00	0	3.80	358	6.73	98	0.00	0	1.70	338	6.52	36	1,315
Elieser Hernandez	4.34	3.92	5.03	7.4%	4.69	785	5.08	14	0.00	0	0.00	0	4.84	162	0.00	0	2.32	480	0.00	1	1,442
Elvis Luciano	6.27	4.07	5.35	15.1%	5.28	340	0.00	0	8.23	1	8.23	1	2.40	108	0.00	0	2.59	163	0.00	0	635
Emilio Pagan	2.12	2.28	2.31	4.9%	2.24	654	0.00	1	0.00	0	2.72	47	0.00	0	0.00	0	2.19	344	5.45	14	1,061
Emmanuel Clase	3.47	3.31	2.41	6.4%	4.33	14	0.00	0	3.26	258	0.00	0	0.00	0	0.00	0	3.31	73	0.00	0	345
Enyel De Los Santos	4.22	3.17	7.36	10.9%	3.58	100	1.30	1	0.00	0	8.23	1	4.57	36	0.00	0	1.92	16	-0.20	22	176
Eric Lauer	5.02	4.49	4.45	7.8%	4.61	1,260	8.23	1	0.00	0	4.01	371	5.30	88	0.00	0	4.28	323	4.52	352	2,510
Eric Skoglund	6.53	5.61	9.00	8.9%	5.99	153	5.35	81	0.00	0	0.00	0	5.50	69	0.00	0	0.00	0	5.27	92	395
Eric Yardley	2.84	2.68	2.31	5.8%	0.00	1	0.00	0	2.87	121	0.00	0	0.00	0	0.00	0	2.34	59	0.00	0	181
Erick Fedde	5.23	4.32	4.50	9.9%	5.02	185	8.23	1	5.28	501	3.59	224	0.00	0	3.70	91	3.13	24	2.66	217	1,287
Erik Swanson	4.29	4.36	5.74	4.9%	4.36	661	0.00	1	0.00	0	8.23	1	4.91	149	0.00	0	3.85	158	0.00	0	971
Ervin Santana	6.51	5.48	9.45	9.4%	6.26	110	4.69	18	0.00	0	0.00	0	5.93	12	0.00	0	4.79	110	0.00	0	250
Evan Marshall	4.55	3.41	2.49	11.5%	6.17	174	5.08	168	2.44	26	8.23	1	1.34	324	0.00	0	3.58	95	1.63	46	834
Evan Phillips	5.88	3.67	6.43	14.3%	3.69	344	0.89	24	0.00	0	0.00	0	4.14	43	0.00	0	4.03	146	0.00	0	567
Felipe Vazquez	2.97	2.99	1.65	5.5%	3.61	563	0.76	9	0.00	0	8.23	2	0.72	73	0.00	0	1.80	164	3.18	127	946
Felix Hernandez	4.68	4.11	6.40	7.7%	6.41	87	8.23	1	5.19	386	6.51	18	3.41	202	0.00	0	2.21	90	3.30	427	1,216
Felix Pena	3.91	3.32	4.58	8.4%	4.18	72	5.33	699	8.23	1	0.00	0	3.16	173	0.00	0	0.97	619	7.29	2	1,570
Fernando Abad	3.08	3.05	4.15	6.4%	0.00	3	3.48	96	0.00	0	0.00	0	3.56	24	0.00	0	0.00	0	2.11	48	171
Fernando Rodney	5.09	3.45	5.66	13.3%	4.54	177	4.39	399	8.23	1	0.00	0	0.99	243	0.00	0	4.29	26	0.00	0	881
Fernando Romero	5.82	3.29	7.07	15.3%	4.75	66	4.70	127	0.00	0	0.00	0	0.00	5	0.00	0	0.05	80	0.00	0	278
Framber Valdez	4.91	3.11	5.86	13.4%	5.03	214	3.63	510	0.00	0	0.00	0	1.19	49	0.00	0	8.23	2	1.62	400	1,175
Francisco Liriano	4.07	2.82	3.47	11.6%	4.67	84	5.04	408	0.00	0	0.00	0	0.91	263	8.23	1	1.10	326	0.00	0	1,110
Frankie Montas	3.59	3.51	2.63	5.8%	4.98	279	4.80	563	5.93	2	5.93	2	0.00	0	0.96	268	2.25	370	0.00	0	1,485
Freddy Peralta	4.56	3.60	5.29	9.7%	3.41	1,255	8.23	1	0.00	0	8.23	1	3.81	24	0.00	0	8.23	1	4.29	317	1,599
Gabe Speier	6.93	4.25	7.36	18.2%	5.11	80	4.09	15	0.00	0	0.00	0	0.00	2	0.00	0	3.21	56	0.00	0	153

Pitcher	pERA	pERA (Just Pitchers)	ERA	BB%	pERA FF	FF Count	pERA FT	FT Count	pERA SI	SI Count	pERA FC	FC Count	pERA CH	CH Count	pERA FS	FS Count	pERA SL	SL Count	pERA CU	CU Count	Count
Gabriel Ynoa	4.19	4.13	5.61	5.4%	5.18	562	3.45	18	4.47	400	0.00	0	4.52	241	0.00	0	2.66	532	0.00	5	1,815
Garrett Richards	6.18	4.06	8.31	14.6%	4.53	64	6.73	28	0.00	0	0.00	0	0.00	0	0.00	0	1.93	46	3.70	19	157
Genesis Cabrera	6.29	4.86	4.87	11.1%	5.75	221	1.30	10	0.00	0	0.00	0	3.08	61	0.00	0	4.67	71	0.46	9	372
Geoff Hartlieb	4.89	3.58	9.00	10.5%	4.16	260	0.81	10	3.65	184	0.00	0	3.54	59	0.00	0	2.60	136	0.00	1	651
Gerardo Reyes	3.65	2.74	7.62	9.4%	3.35	257	0.00	0	2.98	77	8.23	1	0.00	0	0.00	0	1.16	107	1.44	8	451
German Marquez	3.01	3.11	4.76	4.9%	4.69	941	4.62	434	0.00	0	2.44	6	6.08	78	0.00	0	1.72	598	0.33	558	2,616
Gerrit Cole	2.45	2.43	2.50	5.9%	2.72	1,623	4.09	82	5.93	2	8.23	2	2.13	234	8.23	1	1.14	739	3.27	480	3,268
Gerson Bautista	7.83	4.33	11.00	18.4%	5.18	125	0.00	0	0.00	0	0.00	0	0.00	0	0.00	3	2.98	69	0.00	0	197
Gio Gonzalez	4.84	3.94	3.50	10.1%	4.63	375	5.76	345	5.93	2	0.00	0	2.15	442	0.00	0	8.23	1	3.47	232	1,501
Giovanny Gallegos	2.64	2.67	2.31	5.7%	4.42	625	8.23	1	0.00	0	0.00	0	1.14	15	0.00	0	0.49	492	0.00	1	1,141
Glenn Sparkman	5.25	4.90	6.02	6.8%	5.31	1,376	0.00	0	1.30	1	8.23	2	5.20	293	0.00	0	2.61	192	4.36	408	2,275
Grant Dayton	4.09	3.59	3.00	7.8%	3.20	136	0.00	0	0.00	0	8.23	1	0.00	0	0.00	0	2.02	20	5.30	47	204
Greg Holland	5.40	3.37	4.54	15.8%	5.21	283	0.00	0	0.00	0	0.00	0	0.00	0	0.00	0	1.11	260	4.59	55	599
Gregory Soto	5.76	4.19	5.77	12.0%	4.60	84	5.73	37	4.80	653	0.00	0	5.16	58	0.00	0	2.19	265	0.00	5	1,110
Griffin Canning	3.83	3.33	4.58	7.8%	5.06	662	8.23	1	0.00	0	5.93	2	2.89	190	0.00	0	1.12	450	3.03	247	1,552
Hansel Robles	3.58	3.59	2.48	5.7%	4.28	559	4.06	89	0.00	0	0.47	4	1.22	241	0.00	0	4.23	246	0.00	0	1,159
Harrison Musgrave	6.88	4.73	3.60	14.9%	4.94	52	0.00	0	4.97	56	0.00	0	2.80	19	0.00	0	4.88	78	0.00	0	205
Heath Fillmyer	5.90	4.48	8.06	11.0%	4.93	216	3.13	24	0.00	0	0.00	0	3.07	81	0.00	0	3.87	87	6.83	44	453
Heath Hembree	5.35	4.30	3.86	10.4%	5.04	490	0.00	0	0.00	0	0.00	0	0.00	0	0.00	0	1.64	116	3.74	91	718
Hector Neris	2.76	2.16	2.93	8.7%	4.09	285	4.29	92	0.00	0	0.00	0	0.00	1	1.10	713	8.23	2	0.00	0	1,126
Hector Noesi	5.02	3.74	8.46	11.3%	1.58	14	4.43	199	0.00	0	0.00	0	2.91	49	0.00	0	4.91	152	0.00	83	497
Hector Rondon	4.29	3.81	3.71	7.8%	4.03	445	3.63	141	0.00	0	0.00	0	4.29	41	0.00	0	3.53	343	7.15	1	994
Hector Santiago	6.11	4.17	6.68	13.5%	3.58	348	0.00	0	4.50	76	0.00	1	5.11	138	0.00	0	4.21	117	5.66	32	715
Hector Velazquez	5.53	4.29	5.43	11.4%	4.29	245	0.00	1	5.28	272	1.30	1	3.82	266	0.00	0	3.50	174	4.47	19	981
Homer Bailey	4.40	3.94	4.57	7.6%	5.23	1,289	5.63	55	0.00	0	-0.34	3	0.00	4	1.34	674	3.39	406	5.00	231	2,836
Hunter Harvey	4.40	2.56	1.42	15.4%	3.52	94	0.00	0	0.00	0	0.00	0	0.87	23	0.00	0	0.00	0	0.00	20	137
Hunter Strickland	4.57	4.09	5.55	7.6%	4.40	220	3.86	23	0.00	0	0.00	0	4.09	15	0.00	0	3.51	111	0.00	0	391
Hunter Wood	3.91	3.72	2.98	6.2%	4.87	418	0.00	1	5.93	2	5.93	2	3.20	85	0.00	0	1.82	204	2.30	38	752
Hyun-Jin Ryu	2.98	3.39	2.32	3.3%	4.50	746	4.51	354	0.00	0	3.55	527	1.73	743	0.00	0	0.96	9	3.20	326	2,706
Ian Gibaut	5.78	3.64	5.65	15.6%	4.72	152	0.00	0	0.00	0	0.00	0	3.69	60	0.00	0	0.71	57	0.00	0	269
Ian Kennedy	4.16	3.96	3.41	6.4%	4.27	730	8.23	2	0.00	1	3.47	152	3.58	19	0.00	0	1.30	11	3.19	162	1,096
Ivan Nova	4.40	4.27	4.72	5.8%	5.74	518	4.63	1,107	1.30	1	2.52	389	3.25	478	1.30	1	8.23	1	4.30	503	3,005
J. D. Hammer	6.10	4.25	3.79	14.8%	4.72	172	0.00	2	0.00	0	0.00	0	0.00	0	0.00	0	3.77	148	0.00	0	322
J.A. Happ	4.36	4.00	4.91	7.2%	4.37	1,297	3.39	480	0.00	0	1.65	10	3.09	401	0.00	0	4.37	476	4.80	22	2,696
J.B. Wendelken	3.96	3.72	3.58	6.9%	3.56	270	5.19	15	0.00	0	0.00	0	1.83	82	0.00	0	4.33	14	5.57	91	501
Jace Fry	5.22	2.70	4.75	17.1%	4.22	122	3.24	127	1.30	1	1.23	521	3.45	81	0.00	0	1.30	4	5.06	195	1,054
Jack Flaherty	3.40	3.14	2.75	7.1%	4.37	1,474	3.36	390	0.00	0	8.23	1	4.95	55	0.00	0	0.72	875	3.44	384	3,179
Jacob Barnes	6.05	4.02	7.44	13.8%	5.12	283	0.00	0	0.00	0	3.16	374	8.23	1	0.00	0	5.93	3	0.00	0	661
Jacob deGrom	2.68	2.71	2.43	5.5%	3.73	1,529	5.84	47	0.00	0	-10.06	7	1.15	498	0.00	0	1.84	1,005	3.05	90	3,297
Jacob Rhame	9.17	3.77	4.26	30.0%	5.39	75	0.76	9			8.23	1	1.30	23	0.55	13	0.00	0			121
Jacob Waguespack	4.82	4.14	4.38	8.7%	3.26	435	5.82	215	0.00	0	4.03	315	2.59	96	0.00	0	5.05	101	4.83	171	1,333
Jacob Webb	4.15	3.48	1.39	9.2%	5.20	283	0.00	1	0.00	0	0.00	0	0.22	63	0.00	0	2.85	70	1.28	107	536
Jaime Barria	4.98	4.51	6.42	7.4%	5.89	442	6.06	104	0.00	0	5.93	5	3.27	244	0.00	0	3.83	701	7.43	2	1,498
Jairo Diaz	3.38	2.90	4.53	7.8%	5.37	206	4.40	294	0.00	0	0.00	0	0.00	0	0.00	0	0.45	388	0.00	0	888
Jake Arrieta	4.97	4.28	4.64	8.6%	4.52	19	0.26	4	4.83	1,162	0.00	1	2.63	384	0.00	0	4.00	248	4.56	289	2,107
Jake Diekman	4.39	2.56	4.65	13.8%	3.55	312	0.00	1	3.16	304	8.23	1	0.00	3	0.00	0	1.67	541	0.00	1	1,166
Jake Faria	5.46	3.57	6.75	12.6%	5.05	248	0.00	0	0.00	0	0.00	0	0.00	0	0.72	111	2.55	47	0.00	1	408
Jake Jewell	2.95	2.58	6.84	7.0%	4.14	156	2.73	50	0.00	0	1.30	1	0.49	61	0.00	0	1.79	139	0.00	4	412
Jake McGee	4.85	4.65	4.35	6.1%	5.12	517	0.00	0	8.23	1	8.23	1	0.00	0	0.00	0	2.69	128	0.00	0	647
Jake Newberry	4.98	3.66	3.77	11.7%	5.32	282	0.00	1	0.00	0	8.23	1	2.41	16	0.00	0	1.77	238	0.00	0	539
Jake Odorizzi	4.01	3.51	3.51	8.1%	3.24	1,608	8.23	1	0.00	0	4.31	486	8.23	2	2.92	472	2.26	26	5.33	182	2,787
Jake Petricka	6.41	4.03	3.38	16.7%	1.30	1	4.19	76	8.23	1	0.00	0	6.09	29	0.00	0	-2.59	11	0.00	0	118
Jakob Junis	4.53	4.04	5.24	7.5%	5.21	997	8.23	1	4.48	483	7.20	7	3.86	156	0.00	0	2.30	870	4.41	408	2,926
Jalen Beeks	4.69	3.97	4.31	8.6%	4.74	792	0.00	0	0.00	1	2.47	109	3.05	569	0.00	0	8.23	3	4.16	345	1,821
James Hoyt	1.53	1.45	2.16	6.3%	1.30	8	4.29	41	0.00	0	0.00	0	3.13	19	0.00	0	-1.23	55	0.00	0	123
James Marvel	4.20	3.64	8.31	7.1%	4.11	69	0.00	0	4.86	109	0.00	0	1.87	66	0.00	0	0.00	0	3.08	87	331
James Norwood	6.19	3.33	2.89	18.2%	5.25	118	0.00	0	0.00	14	0.00	0	0.00	0	2.04	32	0.05	42	0.00	0	206
James Paxton	3.82	3.18	3.82	8.7%	3.99	1,586	0.00	0	0.00	0	1.46	532	2.03	31	0.00	0	-1.20	6	2.56	493	2,665
James Pazos	3.45	2.71	1.74	10.3%	0.00	0	0.00	0	3.10	102	0.00	0	0.00	0	0.00	0	1.86	47	0.00	0	149
Jameson Taillon	3.43	3.47	4.10	5.1%	3.89	152	3.89	108	0.00	0	0.00	1	4.14	30	0.00	0	2.73	175	3.49	87	555
Jandel Gustave	5.01	4.34	2.96	9.1%	4.24	180	3.87	70	0.00	0	0.00	0	0.00	0	0.00	0	4.86	99	0.00	0	349
Jared Hughes	4.17	3.46	4.04	9.3%	5.62	71	0.00	0	3.33	800	0.00	0	2.30	100	1.30	4	4.71	73	3.22	55	1,143
Jarlin Garcia	4.35	3.93	3.02	7.8%	5.24	294	8.23	1	0.00	0	0.00	0	2.73	129	0.00	0	3.20	321	0.00	0	747
Jason Adam	5.28	4.20	2.91	11.0%	3.26	243	0.00	0	0.00	0	0.00	0	3.99	46	0.00	0	0.00	0	6.44	107	397
Jason Vargas	5.24	4.34	4.51	9.7%	5.71	630	6.31	584	0.00	0	1.30	1	2.23	898	0.00	0	7.20	8	3.98	379	2,505
Javier Guerra	4.80	4.24	5.19	8.3%	5.17	44	3.46	59	0.00	0	0.00	0	0.00	0	0.00	0	4.42	31	0.00	0	134
Javy Guerra	4.75	4.62	4.66	5.9%	5.20	618	0.00	0	0.00	0	8.23	4	1.83	96	0.00	0	3.83	270	6.12	72	1,060
Jay Jackson	3.99	2.32	4.45	13.6%	4.26	222	0.00	0	0.00	0	0.00	0	0.00	3	0.00	0	1.06	335	0.00	0	560
JC Ramirez	3.16	3.60	4.50	2.9%	2.74	57	0.00	0	0.00	0	0.00	0	0.00	0	0.00	0	6.41	17	3.63	33	107
Jeanmar Gomez	5.18	4.42	8.22	8.2%	8.23	2	0.00	0	4.51	110	0.00	0	3.27	47	0.00	0	4.94	48	5.86	8	270
Jeff Brigham	4.54	3.89	4.46	8.7%	3.39	354	0.00	0	8.23	1	0.00	0					-4.19	15	4.82	319	690
Jeff Hoffman	5.59	4.41	6.56	10.8%	5.13	737	0.00	0	8.23	1	0.00	0	3.01	141	0.00	0	0.99	16	3.62	361	1,256
Jeff Samardzija	4.76	4.54	3.52	6.6%	5.20	847	4.48	580	0.00	0	4.84	731	0.00	0	2.05	179	3.78	593	6.65	73	3,006
Jeffrey Springs	6.07	3.87	6.40	14.8%	0.00	0	0.00	0	5.11	357	8.23	1	0.81	191	0.00	0	5.83	69	0.00	0	665
Jefry Rodriguez	5.09	4.06	4.63	10.3%	5.02	226	4.24	304	0.00	0	0.00	0	4.48	71	0.00	0	0.00	0	2.42	182	784
Jerad Eickhoff	4.53	4.14	5.71	7.4%	5.97	379	8.23	1	0.00	0	0.00	0	0.00	1	0.00	0	2.58	286	3.34	307	975
Jeremy Hellickson	6.56	5.25	6.23	10.9%	6.06	214	4.54	47	7.37	24	6.12	120	3.82	179	0.00	0	8.23	1	4.80	90	675

Appendix E: Pitcher pERA Values, 2017 and 2019 Ball

Pitcher	pERA	pERA (Just Pitchers)	ERA	BB%	pERA FF	FF Count	pERA FT	FT Count	pERA SI	SI Count	pERA FC	FC Count	pERA CH	CH Count	pERA FS	FS Count	pERA SL	SL Count	pERA CU	CU Count	Count
Jeremy Jeffress	4.11	3.64	5.02	7.6%	4.15	243	4.12	266	0.00	0	0.00	0	0.00	0	3.39	91	8.23	3	2.60	234	855
Jeremy Walker	4.27	3.34	1.93	10.5%	-0.34	6	0.00	0	3.98	98	0.00	0	0.00	1	0.00	0	0.00	0	2.70	59	164
Jerry Blevins	5.51	4.28	3.90	11.4%	6.70	236	0.00	0	0.00	0	0.00	0	3.70	47	0.00	0	8.23	1	2.28	274	558
Jesse Biddle	6.92	4.39	8.36	14.5%	4.92	328	0.00	0	0.00	2	0.00	0	0.00	0	0.00	1	3.23	121	4.24	149	617
Jesse Chavez	5.15	4.89	4.85	6.5%	4.82	90	5.69	469	0.00	0	4.79	392	3.34	122	0.00	0	4.06	170	0.00	1	1,248
Jesse Hahn	7.48	2.69	13.50	22.2%	0.00	4	3.76	63	0.00	0	0.00	0	0.00	5	0.00	0	1.46	35	0.00	0	107
Jesus Luzardo	2.93	2.81	1.50	6.5%	4.09	30	5.51	53	0.00	0	0.00	0	1.57	35	0.00	0	0.11	37	0.41	16	171
Jesus Tinoco	5.97	4.22	4.75	13.7%	4.94	89	3.92	30	4.76	272	0.00	0	-0.64	7	0.00	0	3.34	187	4.10	31	616
Jeurys Familia	5.74	3.59	5.70	15.3%	5.82	169	0.00	1	4.21	521	0.00	0	0.00	1	1.02	71	1.74	276	0.00	0	1,041
Jhoulys Chacin	5.68	4.68	6.01	9.8%	5.85	250	5.02	617	8.23	1	-7.30	2	5.27	57	3.45	44	4.17	962	7.13	11	1,945
Jimmie Sherfy	4.55	4.32	5.89	6.0%	6.65	114	0.00	0	0.00	0	0.00	0	4.46	21	0.00	0	2.34	159	6.42	22	316
Jimmy Cordero	2.56	2.24	2.89	7.5%	4.84	102	0.00	0	2.13	270	2.54	37	-0.83	94	0.00	0	3.30	39	0.00	0	542
Jimmy Nelson	6.73	4.26	6.95	16.2%	4.73	112	0.00	0	6.35	95	0.00	0	0.00	0	0.00	0	1.61	77	4.03	117	408
Jimmy Yacabonis	6.18	4.55	6.80	12.4%	5.76	43	4.97	422	0.00	0	8.23	3	2.88	50	8.23	1	3.79	215	7.45	1	739
Joakim Soria	3.67	3.37	4.30	7.2%	3.52	718	4.18	23	0.00	0	0.00	0	2.12	73	0.00	0	3.83	138	2.58	130	1,100
Joe Biagini	4.32	3.51	4.59	9.3%	5.15	169	4.36	410	0.00	0	1.50	342	2.29	118	0.00	0	0.34	4	5.73	99	1,142
Joe Harvey	5.93	3.68	5.00	15.5%	4.41	259	0.00	0	0.99	16	0.00	0	1.30	6	0.00	0	2.02	80	0.00	0	361
Joe Jimenez	3.93	3.19	4.37	9.0%	3.62	712	0.00	0	0.00	0	0.00	0	2.86	60	0.00	0	2.13	269	0.00	0	1,056
Joe Kelly	4.22	3.29	4.56	9.7%	4.98	234	3.57	195	1.30	1	0.00	0	2.50	106	0.00	0	0.42	45	2.40	260	872
Joe Musgrove	3.57	3.54	4.44	5.4%	5.26	978	0.00	0	3.88	341	4.28	228	1.80	276	0.00	0	1.63	587	2.04	247	2,657
Joe Ross	5.10	3.78	5.48	11.2%	4.26	282	1.30	1	4.39	436	8.23	1	4.14	83	0.00	0	2.44	252	2.69	83	1,138
Joe Smith	3.90	4.00	1.80	5.2%	4.28	54	0.00	0	3.31	147	0.00	0	0.00	2	0.00	0	4.68	141	0.00	0	344
Joel Kuhnel	3.57	2.25	4.66	11.9%	2.19	60	3.53	47	0.00	0	0.00	0	0.00	5	0.00	0	1.40	54	0.00	0	166
Joey Lucchesi	4.26	3.72	4.18	8.2%	7.21	40	0.00	1	4.35	1,350	4.32	320	2.82	657	0.00	0	2.02	5	1.57	269	2,643
John Brebbia	4.22	3.55	3.59	8.9%	3.57	684	0.00	0	0.00	2	-1.15	2	8.23	8	0.00	0	3.48	516	0.00	0	1,217
John Gant	4.57	3.26	3.66	12.6%	4.22	266	4.19	347	0.00	0	2.63	99	0.47	244	0.00	0	3.13	16	4.81	113	1,105
John Means	4.63	4.53	3.60	6.0%	5.38	1,364	0.00	0	0.00	0	0.00	1	3.43	769	0.00	0	3.46	385	5.15	162	2,681
John Schreiber	3.88	3.50	6.23	6.8%	3.32	134	3.81	21	0.00	0	0.00	0	8.23	16	0.00	0	0.00	0	2.77	80	251
Johnny Cueto	5.73	4.20	5.06	13.4%	5.33	85	2.64	51	0.00	0	0.00	0	2.77	51	0.00	0	5.14	72	2.44	6	265
Jon Duplantier	5.64	4.43	4.42	11.0%	4.67	194	5.19	204	0.00	0	0.00	0	4.57	60	0.00	0	4.08	132	2.48	85	677
Jon Edwards	5.62	3.25	2.25	16.7%	3.92	72	0.00	0	0.00	0	0.00	0	0.00	0	0.00	0	2.07	58	4.90	12	143
Jon Gray	3.90	3.22	3.84	8.8%	4.42	1,185	2.49	13	8.23	1	8.23	2	4.43	65	0.00	0	1.14	757	3.46	255	2,290
Jon Lester	4.71	4.34	4.46	6.8%	5.64	800	0.00	0	3.78	291	4.36	990	3.20	332	0.00	0	1.46	5	3.19	430	2,929
Jonathan Hernandez	5.93	3.42	4.32	16.7%	8.23	8	0.00	0	4.64	153	0.00	0	3.27	53	0.00	0	1.57	118	0.00	0	332
Jonathan Holder	3.77	3.57	6.31	6.1%	3.79	362	0.00	0	0.00	0	2.97	47	3.11	109	0.00	0	3.56	151	0.00	0	673
Jonathan Loaisiga	4.41	3.13	4.55	11.5%	4.24	283	4.81	50	0.00	0	0.00	0	1.86	75	0.00	0	1.80	37	1.40	146	592
Jonny Venters	8.14	3.52	12.38	20.4%	0.00	5	0.00	0	4.02	151	0.00	0	-0.66	5	0.00	0	2.46	35	0.00	0	197
Jordan Hicks	3.33	2.60	3.14	10.0%	0.00	1	0.00	0	3.96	250	0.00	0	-0.47	24	0.00	0	0.74	141	0.00	0	433
Jordan Lyles	4.82	4.06	4.15	9.2%	4.57	1,189	5.18	45	0.00	0	8.23	2	3.49	244	0.00	0	3.76	234	3.45	742	2,456
Jordan Romano	4.58	2.94	7.63	12.0%	3.30	182	0.00	0	0.00	2	0.00	0	0.00	0	0.00	0	2.45	99	0.00	4	287
Jordan Yamamoto	5.50	4.44	4.46	11.1%	5.29	666	5.93	13	0.00	0	3.43	244	5.84	52	0.00	0	2.39	206	4.48	191	1,377
Jordan Zimmermann	4.40	4.40	6.91	5.0%	5.70	589	4.34	196	0.00	0	0.00	0	2.95	46	0.00	0	3.95	560	3.05	323	1,791
Jorge Lopez	4.61	4.08	6.33	7.7%	5.86	644	4.07	471	1.30	1	8.23	1	2.73	145	0.00	0	2.27	134	3.01	654	2,060
Jose Alvarado	6.43	3.38	4.80	18.5%	0.34	8	0.00	0	4.07	455	0.42	108	0.00	0	0.00	0	8.23	1	5.10	14	586
Jose Alvarez	3.96	3.59	3.36	7.1%	4.60	141	4.07	373	0.00	0	4.49	69	1.64	214	0.00	0	3.93	106	3.58	81	984
Jose Berrios	4.03	3.89	3.68	6.1%	4.37	993	4.57	736	0.00	0	0.00	0	2.61	495	0.00	0	8.23	4	3.48	904	3,132
Jose Cisnero	5.04	3.62	4.33	11.7%	3.92	337	5.80	64	0.00	0	0.00	0	3.99	61	0.00	0	2.19	182	0.00	0	646
Jose Leclerc	4.79	3.24	4.33	13.0%	4.09	516	4.00	112	0.00	0	0.47	4	1.42	143	0.00	0	2.61	462	5.54	15	1,294
Jose Quijada	6.19	3.25	5.76	18.1%	2.78	455	0.00	0	0.00	0	0.00	0	3.62	104	0.00	0	-1.09	10	6.17	75	647
Jose Quintana	4.54	4.33	4.68	6.2%	4.92	970	0.00	0	4.41	661	8.23	4	3.61	297	0.00	0	0.47	4	3.76	716	2,826
Jose Rodriguez	5.65	4.14	2.75	13.1%	5.11	133	8.23	19	0.00	0	0.00	0	1.98	55	0.00	0	3.70	69	3.03	53	329
Jose Ruiz	5.95	4.25	5.63	12.1%	4.85	454	0.00	0	8.23	1	8.23	2	2.37	99	0.00	0	3.70	175	3.45	7	739
Jose Suarez	4.96	4.13	7.11	8.8%	5.50	700	0.00	0	0.00	0	0.00	0	1.98	435	0.00	0	3.61	47	4.29	279	1,486
Jose Urena	4.19	3.81	5.21	7.1%	2.69	13	4.61	857	0.00	1	0.00	0	3.09	135	0.00	0	2.31	274	1.91	87	1,372
Jose Urquidy	3.56	3.79	3.95	4.2%	5.29	326	8.23	1	8.23	1	0.00	0	3.15	182	0.00	0	0.75	80	2.43	103	693
Joseph Palumbo	5.38	4.22	9.18	9.9%	4.47	163	0.00	0	0.00	0	0.00	0	4.57	44	0.00	0	0.00	0	3.42	70	277
Josh A. Smith	3.80	3.64	5.81	5.8%	4.30	179	4.72	43	0.00	0	4.17	51	4.92	47	0.00	0	2.33	135	3.10	138	593
Josh D. Smith	7.55	4.64	6.39	17.2%	5.57	154	0.00	0	4.65	24	0.00	0	0.00	1	0.00	0	3.33	106	0.00	0	285
Josh Hader	1.25	1.06	2.62	6.9%	1.15	940	5.08	14	0.00	0	-2.12	3	0.00	3	0.00	0	0.40	193	0.00	0	1,181
Josh Lucas	4.91	3.90	5.74	10.1%	6.90	75	0.00	0	2.68	69	0.00	0	1.30	3	0.00	0	2.85	126	0.00	0	273
Josh Osich	3.55	3.55	4.66	5.5%	5.13	146	5.85	34	0.00	0	3.20	692	3.62	49	0.00	0	2.97	123	0.00	0	1,044
Josh Rogers	6.43	5.55	8.79	8.7%	5.86	110	0.00	0	0.00	0	0.00	0	3.94	45	0.00	0	6.60	52	0.00	3	210
Josh Sborz	5.09	4.09	8.00	10.0%	3.71	119	0.00	0	0.00	0	0.00	0	0.00	0	0.00	0	4.67	53	5.21	13	185
Josh Staumont	6.09	4.76	3.72	11.4%	5.78	207	0.60	7	0.00	0	5.64	12	0.00	0	0.00	0	1.30	1	2.85	99	326
Josh Taylor	3.21	2.69	3.04	8.3%	4.44	396	2.29	115	0.00	0	0.76	199	0.00	0	0.00	0	0.45	102	0.00	13	826
Josh Tomlin	3.95	4.55	3.74	2.2%	5.88	299	0.00	0	6.96	50	4.14	488	4.02	98	8.23	1	8.23	2	3.16	197	1,136
Joshua James	4.16	2.60	4.70	13.2%	3.29	716	0.00	0	0.00	0	0.00	0	0.86	165	0.00	0	1.92	230	0.00	21	1,142
JT Chargois	2.58	2.53	6.33	5.7%	4.78	32	8.23	1	5.68	87	0.00	0	0.00	2	0.00	0	0.49	170	0.00	0	292
Juan Minaya	5.33	4.38	3.90	9.5%	4.60	285	0.00	0	8.23	1	0.00	0	3.17	89	0.00	0	4.57	44	5.22	39	460
Juan Nicasio	5.05	4.06	4.75	9.7%	3.82	319	5.79	120	0.00	0	0.00	1	0.00	5	0.00	0	3.76	361	0.00	0	806
Julio Teheran	5.48	4.34	3.55	11.0%	5.16	1,224	4.64	654	0.00	0	8.23	1	4.08	246	0.00	0	2.84	623	3.15	288	3,036
Julio Urias	3.81	3.29	2.49	8.3%	3.68	783	4.63	29	0.00	0	0.00	2	1.42	216	0.00	0	2.95	233	5.04	81	1,344
Junior Fernandez	2.71	1.40	5.40	11.1%	0.00	0	0.00	0	4.70	91	0.00	0	0.97	69	0.00	0	-3.28	58	0.00	0	218
Junior Guerra	4.63	3.69	3.55	10.5%	4.30	406	4.31	400	1.30	1	0.00	1	0.00	0	2.32	299	3.51	51	3.35	200	1,378
Justin Anderson	5.74	3.68	5.55	14.8%	5.19	395	5.93	24	8.23	3	8.23	1	0.60	7	0.00	0	2.28	465	0.00	0	914
Justin Dunn	9.92	4.84	2.70	30.0%	6.65	77	0.00	0	0.00	1	0.00	0	1.30	11	0.00	0	2.81	47	0.00	0	136
Justin Miller	5.15	5.00	4.02	6.2%	4.90	183	4.07	24	0.00	0	0.00	0	8.23	7	0.00	0	5.29	53	7.78	1	275

Pitcher	pERA	pERA (Just Pitchers)	ERA	BB%	pERA FF	FF Count	pERA FT	FT Count	pERA SI	SI Count	pERA FC	FC Count	pERA CH	CH Count	pERA FS	FS Count	pERA SL	SL Count	pERA CU	CU Count	Count
Justin Shafer	5.64	3.81	3.86	13.7%	4.31	325	0.00	1	4.29	52	3.31	127	0.00	1	0.00	0	3.19	191	0.00	0	697
Justin Verlander	2.57	2.72	2.58	5.0%	3.49	1,613	0.00	0	0.00	0	4.65	3	2.83	137	0.00	0	0.62	930	3.86	606	3,448
Justin Wilson	4.42	3.23	2.54	11.5%	3.67	364	0.00	0	0.00	0	2.98	261	0.00	0	0.00	0	1.76	66	0.00	0	692
Justus Sheffield	4.07	2.82	5.50	10.7%	4.67	323	0.00	0	0.00	0	0.00	0	1.79	108	0.00	0	0.80	238	0.00	3	673
Kelvin Herrera	4.79	3.78	6.14	9.8%	3.99	361	4.81	128	0.00	0	2.86	116	3.12	174	0.00	0	3.87	114	0.00	0	895
Ken Giles	2.51	2.07	1.87	8.2%	4.36	393	2.89	17	0.00	0	8.23	1	0.00	0	0.00	0	-0.27	397	0.00	0	810
Kenley Jansen	2.91	2.77	3.71	6.1%	2.07	145	0.00	0	0.00	0	2.93	762	0.00	0	0.00	0	2.59	132	7.49	1	1,068
Kenta Maeda	3.39	2.90	4.04	8.2%	4.85	821	3.85	86	8.23	2	2.02	5	1.54	577	0.00	0	1.32	761	4.60	175	2,433
Keone Kela	4.47	3.80	2.12	9.2%	4.94	268	0.00	0	0.00	0	0.00	0	0.97	15	0.00	0	8.23	1	2.58	219	504
Kevin Gausman	3.38	2.98	5.72	7.1%	4.31	933	8.23	1	8.23	1	0.00	0	0.26	4	1.04	670	3.90	60	0.00	0	1,671
Kevin Ginkel	3.84	3.18	1.48	9.4%	4.72	214	0.00	0	0.00	0	0.00	0	0.00	4	0.00	0	1.39	178	0.00	0	396
Kevin McCarthy	3.93	3.37	4.48	7.8%	3.48	137	8.23	1	3.41	495	8.23	1	2.64	195	0.00	0	3.68	32	6.64	26	901
Keynan Middleton	7.96	4.85	1.17	21.2%	5.68	82	0.00	0	0.00	0	0.00	0	2.32	31	0.00	0	5.19	30	0.00	0	143
Kirby Yates	2.71	2.75	1.19	5.4%	3.36	572	0.00	0	0.00	0	0.00	0	0.00	1	1.81	423	8.23	9	0.00	0	1,021
Kohl Stewart	4.53	4.11	6.39	7.3%	5.03	25	0.00	0	4.82	189	0.00	0	0.00	10	0.00	0	3.00	124	4.72	35	384
Kolby Allard	5.17	4.29	4.96	9.1%	4.82	390	0.00	0	0.00	0	3.74	276	4.77	126	0.00	0	0.00	1	1.70	45	837
Kyle Barraclough	5.30	3.49	5.61	12.8%	4.48	454	0.00	0	0.00	0	0.00	0	2.06	89	0.00	0	1.88	109	-0.09	41	708
Kyle Bird	8.35	4.02	7.82	23.1%	5.91	42	0.00	0	4.68	72	0.00	0	0.00	0	0.00	0	3.22	118	0.00	8	277
Kyle Crick	5.59	3.38	4.96	15.5%	3.88	469	5.01	115	0.00	0	0.00	0	0.00	0	0.00	0	2.17	350	0.00	0	934
Kyle Dowdy	6.82	4.19	7.25	16.4%	4.93	295	0.00	0	0.00	0	0.00	0	2.57	20	0.00	0	2.65	61	2.70	61	438
Kyle Freeland	4.62	3.93	6.73	8.3%	5.07	737	4.34	184	0.00	0	8.23	3	2.54	194	0.00	0	2.98	550	2.76	112	1,780
Kyle Gibson	3.56	2.99	4.84	7.9%	5.80	482	4.28	856	1.30	2	0.00	0	1.25	434	8.23	1	-0.22	563	3.28	328	2,670
Kyle Hendricks	3.75	3.94	3.46	4.4%	4.04	529	8.23	2	4.32	1,133	8.23	1	3.05	755	0.00	0	4.65	4	4.55	269	2,698
Kyle Keller	6.70	4.33	3.38	17.4%	4.80	132	0.00	0	0.00	0	0.00	0	0.00	0	0.00	0	-1.09	10	4.16	51	193
Kyle McGowin	3.51	3.39	10.13	5.3%	6.96	18	0.00	0	5.80	139	0.00	0	-0.90	17	0.00	0	0.60	120	7.36	2	298
Kyle Ryan	4.78	3.64	3.54	11.2%	3.50	188	0.00	0	3.36	307	4.04	386	8.23	4	0.00	0	1.30	2	3.17	119	1,034
Kyle Wright	6.23	4.26	8.69	14.0%	5.57	189	0.60	21	0.00	0	0.00	0	1.95	26	8.23	1	2.62	83	4.90	31	351
Kyle Zimmer	7.48	3.82	10.80	18.6%	4.68	264	0.00	0	0.00	0	0.00	0	4.50	25	0.00	0	1.58	108	3.73	38	435
Lance Lynn	3.75	3.47	3.67	6.7%	3.21	1,826	3.86	571	0.00	0	3.91	535	5.69	93	0.00	0	8.23	3	2.84	315	3,553
Lewis Thorpe	4.52	3.89	6.18	8.1%	4.94	244	0.00	0	0.00	0	0.00	0	3.40	58	0.00	0	1.05	104	4.68	86	492
Liam Hendriks	2.70	2.59	1.80	6.3%	3.73	889	4.65	17	0.00	0	0.00	0	8.23	1	0.00	0	-0.52	288	0.77	89	1,321
Locke St. John	6.78	5.08	5.40	12.1%	5.93	27	0.00	0	4.38	61	0.00	0	4.69	18	0.00	0	5.69	43	0.00	0	149
Logan Allen	4.93	3.81	6.18	10.2%	5.23	216	0.00	0	0.00	0	0.00	0	2.05	96	0.00	0	2.93	104	2.46	33	450
Logan Webb	4.68	4.09	5.22	8.1%	4.87	296	5.13	85	0.00	0	0.00	0	2.58	136	0.00	0	3.36	159	0.00	0	676
Lou Trivino	4.66	3.33	5.25	11.5%	4.64	317	4.35	163	0.00	0	1.54	327	1.71	45	0.00	0	8.23	2	4.05	99	987
Lucas Giolito	3.51	3.06	3.41	8.1%	4.14	1,493	3.06	6	0.00	0	0.39	8	1.13	698	0.00	0	1.78	411	5.69	107	2,726
Lucas Sims	4.32	3.33	4.60	10.7%	4.47	357	0.00	0	5.53	23	0.00	0	0.84	42	0.00	0	-0.32	90	3.22	239	751
Luis Avilan	4.66	3.69	5.06	9.9%	0.00	0	5.36	176	0.00	0	8.23	1	2.30	347	8.23	1	5.93	2	6.07	73	600
Luis Castillo	3.16	2.30	3.40	10.1%	4.37	884	3.55	621	0.00	0	8.23	1	0.03	971	0.00	0	1.61	594	0.00	0	3,158
Luis Cessa	3.96	3.24	4.11	9.0%	4.81	466	5.19	96	0.00	0	0.00	0	2.81	112	0.00	0	1.95	656	0.00	8	1,339
Luis Escobar	6.08	3.91	7.94	13.8%	6.17	41	2.20	30	0.00	0	0.00	0	1.06	20	0.00	0	0.00	0	5.08	13	104
Luis Garcia	4.60	3.21	4.35	11.9%	4.87	247	3.56	244	0.00	0	8.23	2	0.00	0	1.07	193	2.95	361	0.00	0	1,053
Luis Perdomo	3.94	3.81	4.00	6.1%	5.42	75	4.49	489	8.23	1	0.00	0	8.23	1	3.09	133	2.72	335	0.00	0	1,040
Luis Severino	5.32	4.07	1.50	12.5%	4.58	122	0.00	0	0.00	0	0.00	0	4.31	37	0.00	0	2.87	59	0.00	0	219
Luke Bard	3.74	3.55	4.78	6.5%	5.57	250	4.55	100	8.23	1	0.00	0	3.90	43	0.00	0	1.98	399	0.00	0	818
Luke Farrell	4.98	4.97	2.70	6.3%	5.97	111	0.00	0	0.00	0	0.00	0	0.00	0	0.00	0	2.98	74	6.29	27	212
Luke Gregerson	4.65	4.85	7.94	3.7%	8.23	9	5.28	51	0.00	0	0.00	0	0.00	2	0.00	0	3.01	23	0.00	0	104
Luke Jackson	2.79	2.18	3.84	8.3%	4.00	469	0.00	0	0.00	0	0.00	0	0.00	1	0.00	0	0.97	659	1.71	111	1,241
Luke Weaver	3.88	3.91	2.94	5.4%	4.66	546	0.00	1	0.00	0	4.54	148	1.92	260	0.00	0	-7.30	2	4.29	96	1,053
Madison Bumgarner	3.82	3.89	3.90	5.1%	4.82	766	4.94	634	0.00	0	3.23	1,064	5.23	172	0.00	0	1.93	6	2.39	594	3,244
Manny Banuelos	6.41	4.48	6.93	14.0%	6.63	211	8.23	2	5.07	238	0.00	0	2.49	78	8.23	1	3.29	314	3.72	96	948
Marco Estrada	5.59	5.07	6.85	7.6%	6.51	174	0.00	0	0.00	0	4.19	39	2.70	104	8.23	1	8.23	1	6.67	14	408
Marco Gonzales	4.95	4.71	3.99	6.5%	4.68	23	0.00	0	5.47	1,144	4.78	613	3.74	712	0.00	0	0.39	4	4.29	467	3,136
Marcus Stroman	3.92	3.51	3.22	7.5%	5.08	84	4.09	1,127	0.00	0	3.82	686	4.35	151	0.00	0	2.39	972	1.67	25	3,047
Marcus Walden	3.55	2.70	3.81	9.8%	4.85	246	8.23	1	3.33	217	3.58	328	0.00	1	0.00	0	0.67	470	0.00	0	1,263
Mark Melancon	3.44	3.24	3.61	6.3%	4.33	98	0.00	0	0.00	0	3.87	610	0.00	0	1.72	27	8.23	3	1.82	329	1,068
Martin Perez	4.59	3.76	5.12	9.1%	4.85	510	4.11	692	0.00	0	3.80	816	2.24	611	8.23	1	-0.97	10	4.91	131	2,772
Masahiro Tanaka	3.72	3.73	4.45	5.3%	5.08	735	0.00	0	5.46	151	2.73	42	6.96	3	2.90	744	2.94	1,008	5.81	90	2,787
Matt Albers	5.01	3.82	5.13	11.2%	4.99	114	-2.12	3	3.47	452	0.00	0	3.24	101	1.30	1	4.14	331	0.00	0	1,005
Matt Andriese	4.46	3.74	4.71	8.7%	4.41	596	3.79	7	0.00	0	0.00	0	2.56	441	0.00	0	2.32	17	4.76	137	1,204
Matt Barnes	4.49	2.84	3.73	13.3%	4.19	608	0.00	0	1.30	1	0.00	0	0.00	0	0.73	26	8.23	3	1.63	650	1,288
Matt Bowman	4.32	3.49	3.66	9.5%	3.03	106	2.76	106	1.30	5	3.17	67	1.30	1	2.48	80	5.24	97	4.81	55	529
Matt Carasiti	4.67	3.34	4.66	11.6%	0.00	1	0.00	0	3.23	106	4.19	38	-7.30	2	0.00	0	0.00	0	7.06	1	185
Matt Grace	3.94	3.98	6.36	4.9%	8.23	2	0.00	0	4.74	441	5.39	15	1.87	29	0.00	0	2.56	214	0.00	0	704
Matt Hall	6.18	4.28	7.71	13.3%	5.09	334	0.00	0	0.00	0	0.00	4	4.62	17	0.00	0	2.26	26	2.57	120	501
Matt Harvey	5.29	4.10	7.09	10.9%	5.51	435	5.93	11	0.00	0	8.23	1	3.02	100	0.00	0	2.41	263	3.47	132	999
Matt Koch	4.91	5.04	9.15	4.2%	5.59	174	8.23	1	0.00	0	3.60	101	5.39	60	0.00	0	0.00	0	5.94	28	364
Matt Magill	3.90	3.12	4.09	8.7%	3.90	453	0.00	0	0.00	0	0.00	0	0.00	0	0.00	0	2.08	195	2.49	237	885
Matt Moore	2.02	2.57	0.00	3.0%	3.54	63	0.00	0	0.00	0	0.00	0	1.08	22	-0.80	14	0.00	0	3.60	18	117
Matt Shoemaker	3.41	3.00	1.57	8.3%	3.40	73	6.12	122	0.00	0	0.00	0	0.00	0	-0.14	136	3.68	75	0.00	11	418
Matt Strahm	3.89	4.02	4.71	4.5%	5.14	641	0.00	10	0.00	0	-1.97	3	3.44	231	0.00	0	3.29	537	3.56	281	1,707
Matt Wisler	3.35	2.95	5.61	7.1%	5.68	159	5.83	111	0.00	0	0.00	0	0.00	0	0.00	0	1.76	623	0.00	4	905
Matt Wotherspoon	5.18	4.26	15.43	7.7%	4.70	64	0.00	0	0.00	0	0.00	0	6.58	17	0.00	0	1.17	22	0.00	0	103
Matthew Boyd	3.49	3.27	4.56	6.4%	4.31	1,533	4.17	109	0.00	0	8.23	2	3.31	183	0.00	0	1.60	1,102	4.44	124	3,118
Matthew Festa	5.54	4.13	5.64	11.9%	4.99	179	4.87	21	0.00	0	0.00	0	0.00	0	0.00	0	3.45	155	1.83	23	407
Max Fried	3.51	3.23	4.02	6.7%	3.92	1,392	2.86	62	0.00	0	0.19	12	3.82	63	0.00	0	2.55	400	2.18	637	2,569
Max Scherzer	2.48	2.61	2.92	4.8%	3.84	1,267	0.43	8	0.00	0	2.71	202	1.05	386	0.00	0	-0.02	553	4.78	233	2,653

Pitcher	pERA	pERA (Just Pitchers)	ERA	BB%	pERA FF	FF Count	pERA FT	FT Count	pERA SI	SI Count	pERA FC	FC Count	pERA CH	CH Count	pERA FS	FS Count	pERA SL	SL Count	pERA CU	CU Count	Count
Merrill Kelly	4.53	4.13	4.42	7.3%	5.21	1,153	0.00	0	3.91	300	3.94	493	3.60	379	0.00	0	1.81	5	2.73	632	2,962
Michael Feliz	4.80	3.65	3.99	11.3%	4.60	735	0.00	2	0.00	0	0.00	0	4.52	64	0.00	0	-0.06	202	0.00	0	1,016
Michael Lorenzen	3.51	3.00	2.92	8.2%	3.75	281	4.71	200	1.30	1	4.77	110	0.13	247	0.00	0	3.07	357	2.40	102	1,335
Michael Pineda	3.49	3.63	4.01	4.7%	4.69	1,204	1.30	12	8.23	2	8.23	1	3.71	321	0.00	0	1.64	642	0.00	2	2,278
Michael Shawaryn	4.75	2.87	9.74	12.6%	3.94	197	0.00	5	0.00	0	0.00	0	0.00	4	0.00	0	1.67	160	2.95	95	461
Michael Wacha	4.96	4.00	4.76	9.8%	5.25	1,099	3.91	15	0.00	1	3.98	331	0.95	517	0.00	0	1.30	2	5.00	224	2,199
Michel Baez	5.00	3.88	3.03	10.7%	4.49	306	0.00	0	0.00	0	0.00	0	2.47	173	0.00	0	1.30	4	5.63	38	521
Miguel Castro	5.01	3.50	4.66	12.9%	8.23	1	8.23	3	4.60	598	-1.15	2	1.59	213	0.00	0	2.78	368	0.00	0	1,204
Miguel Del Pozo	7.20	4.34	10.61	17.8%	5.51	104	0.00	0	0.00	0	0.00	0	0.00	6	0.00	0	0.00	0	3.03	73	183
Miguel Diaz	4.31	4.60	7.11	3.5%	4.96	55	0.00	0	0.00	0	0.00	1	3.45	13	0.00	0	4.90	31	0.00	2	102
Mike Clevinger	3.13	2.81	2.71	7.4%	3.60	1,069	0.00	0	0.00	0	0.00	0	2.56	237	0.00	0	1.35	532	2.79	252	2,090
Mike Dunn	4.32	3.80	7.13	8.0%	4.95	134	0.00	7	0.00	0	0.00	0	0.00	0	0.00	0	3.28	131	1.52	25	302
Mike Fiers	5.02	4.73	3.90	7.0%	5.43	935	5.52	554	0.00	0	1.81	5	4.45	358	8.23	1	4.47	483	3.00	493	2,899
Mike Foltynewicz	4.42	4.00	4.54	7.5%	5.66	442	4.84	543	0.00	0	0.00	0	1.68	179	0.00	0	2.31	517	4.46	207	1,888
Mike Leake	3.90	4.29	4.29	3.2%	5.88	404	8.23	2	5.29	556	4.53	784	3.45	603	0.00	0	2.07	339	3.74	271	2,975
Mike Mayers	5.76	4.15	6.63	12.5%	5.68	178	0.00	0	0.00	0	0.00	0	8.23	3	0.00	0	1.36	127	6.48	30	357
Mike Minor	4.19	3.72	3.59	7.9%	4.45	1,489	8.23	1	8.23	4	0.47	4	2.69	822	0.00	0	3.62	646	3.21	380	3,358
Mike Montgomery	4.70	4.02	4.95	8.5%	5.76	241	6.96	3	4.59	392	4.00	268	2.71	329	0.00	0	0.00	0	3.38	335	1,573
Mike Morin	3.62	3.74	4.62	4.8%	4.97	75	4.10	263	0.00	0	0.00	0	2.64	258	0.00	0	4.59	111	0.00	0	724
Mike Soroka	3.57	3.51	2.68	5.9%	5.32	472	3.97	1,129	0.00	0	0.00	0	1.05	317	8.23	1	2.53	615	7.07	1	2,557
Mike Wright Jr.	4.93	4.09	7.98	8.2%	4.24	197	8.23	2	4.73	136	8.23	1	4.98	31	0.00	0	3.34	207	2.77	3	577
Miles Mikolas	3.63	3.84	4.16	4.2%	4.22	778	4.16	658	0.00	0	1.30	1	4.56	106	0.00	0	3.48	658	3.28	600	2,867
Mitch Keller	4.10	3.60	7.13	7.1%	5.05	448	0.00	0	0.00	0	0.00	0	5.69	28	0.00	0	-0.02	158	2.49	120	932
Montana DuRapau	4.95	3.61	9.35	10.0%	4.29	153	0.00	0	0.00	0	4.44	82	1.30	8	0.00	0	-1.76	39	4.84	45	342
Mychal Givens	3.68	2.82	4.57	10.0%	3.07	761	5.93	4	0.00	0	0.00	0	0.61	154	0.00	0	3.64	166	0.00	0	1,092
Nate Jones	5.53	3.48	3.48	14.9%	8.23	3	4.68	117	0.00	0	0.00	0	0.00	6	0.00	0	1.80	80	0.00	0	206
Nathan Eovaldi	5.07	3.74	5.99	11.6%	3.93	557	0.00	0	8.23	1	4.99	274	0.00	0	3.11	167	1.93	47	2.56	218	1,264
Neil Ramirez	5.23	3.53	5.40	13.4%	3.42	219	3.33	38	0.00	0	0.00	0	0.00	0	0.00	0	2.74	146	6.09	58	461
Nestor Cortes	5.10	4.21	5.67	9.4%	4.22	599	3.09	82	0.00	0	0.00	1	4.12	159	0.00	0	4.47	412	4.28	47	1,301
Nick Anderson	2.23	1.98	3.32	4.8%	3.05	656	8.23	1	0.00	0	0.00	0	8.23	1	0.00	0	0.98	39	0.29	399	1,096
Nick Burdi	3.13	2.57	9.35	7.5%	6.29	73	0.00	0	0.00	0	0.00	0	0.00	0	0.00	0	-0.52	88	0.00	0	161
Nick Goody	4.60	3.17	3.54	12.7%	5.13	351	0.00	0	0.00	0	0.00	0	0.00	0	0.00	0	1.07	328	0.00	0	679
Nick Kingham	5.52	4.50	7.28	9.7%	5.94	375	4.34	100	0.00	0	4.18	165	2.76	174	0.00	0	7.59	13	3.47	200	1,027
Nick Margevicius	4.62	4.12	6.79	7.2%	5.17	515	0.00	0	0.00	0	0.00	0	2.97	73	0.00	0	2.76	241	3.15	129	958
Nick Pivetta	5.08	4.21	5.38	9.3%	4.93	788	7.13	46	8.23	1	0.00	1	5.93	14	0.00	0	2.69	220	3.48	545	1,619
Nick Ramirez	4.00	3.02	4.07	10.1%	4.62	192	3.91	20	4.82	194	3.82	378	0.34	406	0.00	0	-0.86	17	5.49	73	1,282
Nick Tropeano	5.20	4.22	9.88	9.1%	6.23	108	5.93	17	0.00	0	8.23	2	1.46	54	3.63	27	2.86	65	0.00	0	273
Nick Vincent	4.04	3.83	4.43	6.2%	3.81	424	2.70	33	0.00	0	3.84	252	6.34	27	0.00	0	1.19	9	0.00	0	751
Nick Wittgren	4.48	4.31	2.81	6.5%	4.48	629	0.00	0	0.00	0	8.23	2	3.40	142	0.00	0	4.38	178	7.35	1	975
Noah Syndergaard	3.36	3.22	4.28	6.1%	4.24	904	8.23	3	3.86	919	5.19	5	2.26	495	0.00	0	1.79	461	1.94	301	3,095
Noe Ramirez	3.63	3.30	3.99	7.1%	3.75	117	0.00	0	3.49	186	8.23	2	1.96	372	0.00	0	-1.15	2	4.33	402	1,099
Odrisamer Despaigne	7.35	5.99	9.45	10.3%	6.99	95	0.00	0	6.73	42	4.28	54	8.23	16	0.00	0	6.58	28	1.69	20	255
Oliver Drake	2.71	2.18	3.21	8.7%	3.17	370	0.00	0	0.00	1	0.00	1	0.00	0	1.50	539	8.23	1	0.00	0	913
Oliver Perez	3.63	3.30	5.06	4.9%	4.30	95	0.00	0	4.17	226	0.00	1	8.23	1	0.00	0	2.31	300	7.27	1	641
Pablo Lopez	3.83	3.74	5.09	5.8%	4.69	729	3.50	320	0.00	0	8.23	3	2.22	389	0.00	0	-10.41	5	3.84	343	1,796
Parker Markel	6.51	4.03	7.77	15.5%	5.05	182	0.00	0	6.64	38	0.00	0	8.23	6	0.00	0	2.71	234	0.00	0	460
Pat Neshek	3.88	4.38	5.00	2.5%	0.00	0	0.00	0	5.40	96	8.23	1	8.23	3	0.00	0	3.71	169	0.00	0	270
Patrick Corbin	3.30	2.74	3.25	8.4%	4.88	641	4.49	1,073	0.00	1	8.23	5	2.19	219	0.00	0	-0.16	1,139	3.97	117	3,198
Patrick Sandoval	4.31	3.14	5.03	11.2%	5.26	331	0.00	0	0.00	0	0.00	0	0.37	221	0.00	0	1.57	66	3.26	96	714
Paul Blackburn	4.47	3.83	10.64	7.0%	6.01	28	4.68	89	0.00	0	0.00	0	3.90	11	0.00	0	2.67	48	2.13	48	224
Paul Fry	4.65	3.38	5.34	11.4%	3.86	555	0.00	3	0.00	0	1.30	1	5.93	9	0.00	0	2.80	481	0.00	0	1,076
Paul Sewald	4.79	5.10	4.58	3.8%	5.32	222	0.00	1	0.00	0	0.00	0	5.71	21	0.00	0	4.56	83	0.00	2	330
Pedro Baez	3.47	2.99	3.10	8.3%	2.52	535	4.65	12	0.00	0	0.00	0	3.61	332	0.00	0	3.12	178	0.00	0	1,103
Pedro Payano	5.74	3.68	5.73	14.6%	8.23	8	0.00	0	5.36	186	0.00	0	3.94	85	0.00	0	0.57	84	1.62	54	417
Pedro Strop	3.99	2.83	4.97	11.2%	5.33	149	6.02	114	0.00	0	2.53	137	0.00	0	1.81	35	0.53	287	0.00	0	737
Peter Fairbanks	4.64	3.50	6.86	10.1%	5.74	168	0.00	1	0.00	0	0.00	0	0.00	0	0.00	0	1.79	218	0.00	0	387
Peter Lambert	5.49	4.68	7.25	8.6%	5.88	838	8.23	2	0.00	0	8.23	2	2.38	353	0.00	0	3.71	182	5.32	204	1,582
Phil Maton	4.07	3.60	6.14	7.4%	4.63	345	0.00	0	1.30	1	2.24	125	0.00	0	0.00	0	5.13	20	1.78	117	608
Phillip Diehl	2.92	2.70	7.36	5.7%	4.57	62	0.00	0	0.00	0	0.00	0	0.00	0	0.00	0	1.17	76	0.00	0	138
Phillips Valdez	5.17	3.64	3.94	12.0%	0.00	1	-1.53	3	4.59	131	0.00	0	2.90	83	0.00	0	3.11	74	0.00	1	293
Rafael Montero	3.35	3.58	2.48	4.4%	5.17	169	3.50	74	0.00	0	0.00	0	1.93	154	0.00	0	3.43	62	0.00	0	459
Raisel Iglesias	3.49	3.08	4.16	7.5%	4.26	421	0.00	0	4.76	113	0.00	0	0.73	232	8.23	1	2.65	335	0.00	0	1,133
Randy Dobnak	2.73	2.93	1.59	4.2%	4.58	99	0.00	0	3.74	154	0.00	0	3.78	55	0.00	0	0.00	0	0.12	119	427
Randy Rosario	4.08	3.51	4.40	7.9%	2.52	33	4.94	120	0.00	0	0.70	40	0.00	0	0.00	0	2.49	26	0.00	0	224
Ranger Suarez	3.74	3.63	3.14	5.9%	5.27	179	3.68	222	0.00	0	0.00	0	2.13	206	0.00	0	3.65	155	0.00	0	763
Ray Black	4.84	4.31	5.06	12.9%	3.93	198	0.00	0	0.00	0	0.00	0	0.00	0	0.00	0	1.85	84	0.00	0	282
Reed Garrett	6.97	4.16	8.22	16.9%	5.01	176	5.93	9	0.00	0	8.23	1	0.00	2	0.00	4	2.70	85	0.00	5	319
Reggie McClain	5.44	3.65	6.00	13.7%	0.00	1	0.00	0	4.01	274	0.00	0	5.93	15	0.00	0	1.63	64	0.00	0	354
Reyes Moronta	5.29	3.67	2.86	13.4%	4.54	590	0.00	0	0.00	0	8.23	1	0.75	71	0.00	0	2.80	352	0.00	0	1,015
Reymin Guduan	6.03	3.65	11.81	14.8%	6.14	54	0.00	0	0.00	0	8.23	1	0.00	0	0.00	0	1.22	57	0.00	0	112
Reynaldo Lopez	4.59	4.00	5.38	8.0%	4.70	1,850	0.00	0	0.00	0	8.23	3	2.98	459	0.00	0	2.49	637	4.64	211	3,163
Rich Hill	4.23	3.85	2.45	7.4%	4.27	494	8.23	9	0.00	0	0.00	3	1.30	3	0.00	0	0.18	27	3.54	404	951
Richard Bleier	3.06	3.41	5.37	3.4%	1.30	11	0.00	0	3.52	464	3.64	167	5.46	29	0.00	0	0.55	45	0.00	0	753
Richard Lovelady	5.00	4.20	7.65	8.3%	4.03	174	0.00	2	4.62	41	0.00	0	2.02	5	0.00	0	4.43	144	0.00	0	366
Richard Rodriguez	4.33	3.75	3.72	8.1%	4.13	937	-2.12	6	0.00	0	0.00	0	0.00	0	0.00	0	1.81	158	0.00	0	1,142
Rick Porcello	4.76	4.60	5.52	5.9%	4.87	892	4.71	721	0.00	0	8.23	4	4.99	356	0.00	0	3.91	527	4.26	364	2,960
Robbie Erlin	4.23	4.01	5.37	6.0%	5.12	286	5.48	203	0.00	0	8.23	1	1.27	152	0.00	0	2.94	90	3.51	209	959

Pitcher	pERA	pERA (Just Pitchers)	ERA	BB%	pERA FF	FF Count	pERA FT	FT Count	pERA SI	SI Count	pERA FC	FC Count	pERA CH	CH Count	pERA FS	FS Count	pERA SL	SL Count	pERA CU	CU Count	Count
Robbie Ray	4.51	3.34	4.34	11.2%	4.98	1,332	4.65	271	0.00	0	7.73	7	5.93	2	0.00	0	1.07	952	2.51	491	3,064
Robby Scott	7.73	4.43	4.91	18.9%	8.23	25	0.00	0	4.50	57	0.00	0	8.23	13	0.00	0	2.50	53	1.59	16	164
Robert Dugger	5.46	4.23	5.77	10.9%	5.04	193	5.51	144	0.00	0	0.00	0	0.92	13	0.00	0	2.28	139	3.87	74	568
Robert Gsellman	4.20	3.58	4.66	8.3%	3.79	28	4.14	157	4.74	366	0.00	0	2.22	98	0.00	0	2.04	277	3.88	125	1,072
Robert Stephenson	2.60	1.93	3.76	9.2%	5.63	362	0.00	0	0.00	0	0.00	0	0.45	61	0.00	0	-0.21	583	1.21	9	1,028
Robert Stock	6.01	3.64	10.13	14.3%	3.88	121	0.00	2	0.00	0	0.00	0	0.06	19	0.00	0	4.19	83	0.00	0	229
Roberto Osuna	2.30	2.47	2.63	4.7%	3.62	413	6.34	34	8.23	1	2.56	137	1.25	172	8.23	1	-0.19	156	0.00	0	950
Roenis Elias	4.68	4.06	3.96	8.3%	4.72	357	4.73	67	0.00	0	8.23	1	2.74	215	0.00	0	8.23	3	3.90	99	826
Rogelio Armenteros	4.13	3.88	4.00	6.7%	4.20	161	0.00	0	0.00	0	0.00	0	2.73	95	0.00	0	6.96	11	4.24	66	333
Ronald Bolanos	5.61	3.86	5.95	13.6%	5.27	189	2.77	28	0.00	0	0.00	0	0.00	18	0.00	0	3.79	35	1.64	74	346
Rookie Davis	6.01	3.63	6.75	15.7%	3.83	77	3.41	62	0.00	0	0.00	0	4.33	28	0.00	0	3.13	16	2.82	7	192
Ross Detwiler	5.29	4.54	6.59	8.6%	5.09	400	0.00	0	4.66	230	4.92	150	3.88	192	0.00	0	2.32	31	3.86	154	1,157
Ross Stripling	3.73	3.74	3.47	5.4%	5.23	496	0.00	0	5.00	24	5.82	46	1.67	205	0.00	0	3.61	215	2.67	383	1,445
Rowan Wick	4.37	3.21	2.43	11.4%	2.86	390	0.00	0	0.00	0	1.30	12	0.00	1	0.00	0	3.21	21	4.20	163	587
Ruben Alaniz	5.26	4.25	9.19	9.9%	4.89	56	4.71	76	0.00	0	0.00	0	3.32	35	0.00	0	3.89	94	0.00	1	263
Ryan Borucki	7.21	4.16	10.80	15.0%	0.00	0	0.00	0	5.38	81	0.00	0	0.47	32	0.00	0	4.61	42	0.00	0	155
Ryan Brasier	3.63	2.93	4.85	8.7%	3.49	536	4.50	38	0.00	0	0.00	0	3.69	86	0.00	0	1.54	305	0.00	0	978
Ryan Buchter	5.37	4.09	2.98	11.6%	4.36	489	0.00	0	0.00	0	3.44	114	0.00	0	1.30	1	0.00	0	3.78	175	795
Ryan Burr	5.17	4.34	4.58	9.3%	4.84	207	0.00	0	0.00	0	3.44	82	0.00	0	0.00	0	3.88	67	0.00	0	356
Ryan Carpenter	5.37	4.93	9.30	6.6%	6.16	155	5.08	152	0.00	0	0.00	0	4.71	103	0.00	0	3.94	192	4.96	81	686
Ryan Dull	6.07	4.58	12.79	9.9%	6.35	134	0.00	0	0.00	0	0.00	0	6.96	15	0.00	0	1.93	103	0.00	0	270
Ryan Eades	5.95	4.57	2.38	12.0%	5.62	98	0.00	0	0.00	0	0.00	0	2.73	28	0.00	0	3.90	77	0.00	0	203
Ryan Feierabend	4.17	4.38	11.12	3.5%	6.51	24	0.00	0	0.00	0	0.00	0	1.33	9	0.00	0	0.00	0	0.00	0	104
Ryan Helsley	4.68	4.21	2.95	7.8%	5.19	330	0.00	0	0.00	0	2.94	184	0.00	12	0.00	0	1.30	1	3.51	50	577
Ryan Pressly	2.12	2.13	2.32	5.7%	4.28	281	0.00	0	0.00	0	0.00	0	1.30	1	0.00	0	0.69	228	1.14	279	827
Ryan Tepera	4.03	3.37	4.98	8.8%	6.20	64	0.00	0	3.54	128	1.99	112	3.21	21	0.00	0	0.32	15	0.00	0	340
Ryan Weber	4.68	4.79	5.09	4.4%	5.84	13	0.00	0	5.40	341	0.00	0	4.93	114	0.00	0	0.34	8	3.78	198	674
Ryan Yarbrough	3.46	3.83	4.13	3.6%	8.23	1	0.00	0	4.54	492	4.95	751	1.87	528	0.00	0	7.59	6	3.16	279	2,057
Ryne Harper	3.31	3.48	3.81	4.4%	4.25	327	0.00	0	0.00	0	0.00	0	5.93	2	1.30	4	8.23	3	2.96	504	856
Ryne Stanek	4.36	3.08	3.97	11.9%	4.58	712	0.00	0	0.00	1	0.00	0	1.71	5	0.00	4	0.54	259	1.77	300	1,284
Sal Romano	6.03	4.82	7.71	10.4%	3.79	21	5.96	151	0.00	0	0.00	0	0.00	0	0.00	0	3.16	88	4.75	46	306
Sam Coonrod	5.47	4.03	3.58	13.2%	4.67	123	0.00	0	4.72	170	0.00	0	1.26	80	0.00	0	0.00	0	4.38	79	454
Sam Dyson	3.81	3.87	3.32	5.2%	5.02	95	8.23	1	4.07	382	2.99	217	2.78	89	0.00	0	5.50	62	0.00	0	848
Sam Gaviglio	3.36	3.33	4.61	5.6%	0.00	0	0.00	0	4.89	604	-1.20	6	2.07	134	1.30	1	1.88	629	6.55	50	1,427
Sam Howard	4.74	3.37	6.63	11.0%	5.47	169	0.00	0	0.00	0	0.00	0	0.00	0	0.00	0	1.72	214	0.00	0	383
Sam Selman	5.62	4.01	4.35	13.6%	5.43	79	0.00	0	0.00	0	0.00	0	0.00	0	0.00	0	2.97	108	0.00	0	187
Sam Tuivailala	5.38	4.23	2.35	11.7%	4.52	129	4.15	112	0.00	0	0.00	0	0.00	0	0.00	0	4.06	83	4.02	66	390
Sandy Alcantara	4.64	3.80	3.88	9.7%	4.65	925	4.65	3	0.00	0	3.14	852	-7.30	2	2.00	381	3.53	655	4.08	270	3,091
Scott Alexander	4.21	3.40	3.63	9.2%	1.30	1	0.00	0	3.68	244	0.00	0	-2.12	9	0.00	0	2.68	24	0.00	0	278
Scott Barlow	4.29	2.92	4.22	11.9%	3.78	471	3.99	95	0.00	0	8.23	1	8.23	3	0.00	0	2.35	566	1.65	164	1,300
Scott Oberg	4.17	3.32	2.25	10.3%	3.76	460	0.00	1	0.00	0	0.00	0	4.21	39	0.00	0	2.71	381	0.00	1	884
Sean Doolittle	4.08	3.95	4.05	5.8%	4.11	908	0.00	0	0.00	0	0.00	0	8.23	1	3.55	64	1.82	58	0.00	0	1,063
Sean Manaea	3.64	3.58	1.21	6.4%	4.27	278	0.00	0	0.00	0	0.00	0	2.94	67	0.00	0	2.05	98	0.00	0	444
Sean Newcomb	4.75	3.84	3.16	9.9%	4.23	759	1.30	1	0.00	0	8.23	1	3.13	80	0.00	0	4.19	105	2.61	222	1,181
Sean Reid-Foley	6.21	4.22	4.26	14.0%	4.53	295	8.23	8	0.00	0	8.23	1	5.68	55	0.00	0	3.07	211	5.11	41	612
Seranthony Dominguez	4.01	2.82	4.01	10.9%	3.19	270	5.41	11	0.00	0	0.00	0	2.40	19	0.00	0	1.97	141	0.00	0	464
Sergio Romo	3.54	3.27	3.43	6.8%	6.22	104	0.00	0	3.66	133	0.00	0	2.36	159	8.23	1	2.90	580	0.00	0	989
Seth Lugo	3.53	3.63	2.70	5.1%	3.55	440	4.01	283	5.93	2	0.00	1	4.10	78	0.00	0	3.05	169	3.58	298	1,275
Seunghwan Oh	3.53	3.06	9.33	6.8%	4.01	157	0.00	0	0.00	0	1.17	133	4.04	17	8.23	1	0.47	12	5.23	51	373
Shane Bieber	2.94	3.10	3.28	4.7%	5.48	1,476	0.00	0	0.00	0	0.00	0	3.68	237	0.00	0	0.90	901	0.55	651	3,332
Shane Carle	7.41	4.07	9.64	18.4%	4.71	85	0.00	0	0.00	0	0.00	0	3.98	41	0.00	0	3.91	27	2.70	34	187
Shane Greene	3.40	3.18	2.30	6.8%	4.33	14	3.77	433	0.00	0	3.00	294	0.00	3	0.00	0	2.16	204	0.00	0	949
Shaun Anderson	4.98	4.20	5.44	8.9%	4.67	719	4.98	214	0.00	0	8.23	1	4.56	135	0.00	0	2.93	467	5.11	45	1,587
Shawn Armstrong	5.19	3.94	5.74	10.7%	3.67	663	0.00	0	0.00	0	3.87	298	0.00	0	0.00	0	5.38	141	2.91	1	1,103
Shawn Kelley	4.10	4.06	4.94	5.4%	6.22	306	0.00	0	0.00	0	0.00	0	0.00	0	0.00	0	2.61	459	7.59	1	768
Shelby Miller	6.76	4.79	8.59	13.2%	4.94	567	4.65	10	0.00	0	2.12	33	4.33	14	0.00	0	8.23	3	4.79	195	823
Sonny Gray	4.22	3.47	2.87	9.6%	5.10	805	3.51	607	0.00	0	0.00	0	3.49	77	0.00	0	1.81	603	3.01	711	2,909
Spencer Turnbull	4.38	3.59	4.61	9.0%	4.17	1,132	8.23	2	3.62	509	1.46	170	4.09	78	0.00	0	3.01	366	3.15	316	2,661
Stefan Crichton	3.66	3.47	3.56	6.5%	2.87	23	8.23	2	3.91	271	0.00	0	5.64	12	0.00	0	0.00	15	2.86	144	467
Stephen Nogosek	5.75	5.40	10.80	15.7%	5.27	88	0.00	0	0.00	1	0.00	0	2.73	7	0.00	0	6.40	35	0.00	0	131
Stephen Strasburg	3.17	2.96	3.32	6.7%	4.20	977	4.21	668	8.23	1	8.23	3	0.78	684	0.00	0	4.21	13	2.39	1,036	3,384
Stephen Tarpley	5.04	3.31	6.93	12.5%	6.54	92	0.00	0	4.11	170	0.00	0	0.00	2	0.00	0	1.44	251	7.40	10	525
Steve Cishek	4.99	3.95	2.95	10.9%	3.05	163	0.00	0	4.17	479	0.00	0	4.10	10	0.00	0	4.03	435	7.14	1	1,090
Steven Brault	5.03	3.93	5.16	10.5%	4.87	1,005	4.93	273	0.00	0	0.54	288	3.95	281	0.00	0	2.21	125	2.60	27	2,001
Steven Matz	4.36	3.90	4.21	7.5%	1.30	9	3.03	7	4.64	1,315	0.00	0	2.77	521	0.00	0	3.53	355	3.30	387	2,603
Steven Wright	6.51	4.67	8.53	12.1%	0.00	0	8.23	6	0.00	0	0.00	0	0.00	0	0.00	0	0.00	0	0.00	8	132
T.J. McFarland	3.71	3.10	4.82	8.0%	0.00	3	0.00	0	3.47	608	0.00	0	1.71	142	0.00	0	2.94	140	6.88	1	897
T.J. Zeuch	4.82	3.63	4.76	11.1%	0.00	12	0.00	0	3.97	200	0.00	0	4.41	79	0.00	0	2.69	79	3.32	34	404
Tanner Anderson	4.60	4.19	6.04	6.7%	5.09	55	0.00	0	4.18	245	2.02	5	3.88	38	0.00	0	3.92	78	0.00	0	422
Tanner Rainey	4.73	2.20	3.91	17.8%	3.51	616	0.00	0	0.00	0	8.23	1	0.32	5	0.00	0	-0.99	253	0.00	0	875
Tanner Roark	4.97	4.58	4.35	7.1%	5.03	752	5.16	844	0.00	0	8.23	3	3.27	280	0.00	0	4.27	621	3.86	370	2,992
Tanner Scott	5.19	2.94	4.78	15.6%	5.07	269	-1.15	2	0.00	0	8.23	1	0.00	0	0.00	0	-0.04	191	0.00	0	463
Tayler Scott	5.54	3.51	14.33	11.8%	5.38	55	0.00	0	4.56	148	0.00	0	0.00	0	0.00	0	1.81	151	0.00	0	354
Taylor Clarke	4.81	4.22	5.31	8.1%	4.72	729	4.28	74	0.00	0	1.30	1	4.22	178	0.00	0	1.42	387	5.53	143	1,512
Taylor Cole	4.60	3.51	5.92	10.4%	4.71	340	8.23	1	0.00	0	4.77	32	1.31	281	0.00	0	4.26	195	3.96	36	885
Taylor Guerrieri	6.93	4.17	5.81	17.9%	0.00	6	0.00	0	4.86	216		1	4.75	49	0.00	0	0.00	0	3.50	219	491
Taylor Guilbeau	3.44	3.35	3.65	5.9%	0.00	0	0.00	0	3.96	115	0.00	0	2.68	54	0.00	0	0.48	12	0.00	0	181

Pitcher	pERA	pERA (Just Pitchers)	ERA	BB%	pERA FF	FF Count	pERA FT	FT Count	pERA SI	SI Count	pERA FC	FC Count	pERA CH	CH Count	pERA FS	FS Count	pERA SL	SL Count	pERA CU	CU Count	Count
Taylor Rogers	3.08	3.36	2.61	4.0%	0.00	0	4.15	518	8.23	1	0.00	0	8.23	1	0.00	0	2.34	439	3.72	78	1,065
Taylor Williams	3.98	2.83	9.82	9.6%	3.82	168	8.23	2	0.00	0	0.00	0	0.95	14	0.00	0	1.01	83	0.00	0	267
Tayron Guerrero	5.70	3.17	6.26	16.7%	3.29	636	2.98	63	0.00	0	0.00	0	0.00	0	0.00	0	2.82	175	0.00	0	884
Thomas Pannone	4.96	4.05	6.16	9.5%	4.14	712	8.23	1	0.00	0	0.47	4	4.06	249	0.00	0	-2.12	3	3.91	286	1,255
Thyago Vieira	6.31	4.10	9.00	13.5%	5.23	112	0.00	3	0.00	0	0.00	0	-0.34	3	0.00	0	2.12	51	0.00	0	169
Tim Collins	5.37	4.81	3.12	7.9%	5.49	74	0.00	0	0.00	0	0.00	0	0.00	0	0.00	0	4.13	53	4.40	33	160
Tim Hill	4.04	3.57	3.63	8.1%	3.05	207	0.00	0	4.26	271	0.00	0	0.00	0	0.00	0	3.02	155	6.97	1	634
Tim Mayza	4.08	2.72	4.91	11.9%	5.82	174	2.44	419	0.00	0	8.23	1	0.00	0	0.00	0	1.39	324	0.00	0	921
Tim Melville	4.62	3.73	4.86	9.8%	5.70	188	0.00	0	0.00	0	0.00	0	5.41	34	0.00	0	2.14	309	5.66	33	564
Tim Peterson	8.34	5.05	4.91	20.0%	5.62	77	8.23	1	0.00	0	0.00	0	3.72	46	0.00	0	5.83	18	0.00	0	142
Tom Eshelman	5.63	5.26	6.50	6.7%	5.83	167	6.19	110	0.00	0	0.00	0	5.75	111	0.00	0	4.31	129	3.84	92	609
Tommy Kahnle	2.55	2.08	3.67	8.1%	4.43	454	0.00	0	0.00	0	1.30	1	-0.08	528	0.00	0	3.98	41	0.00	0	1,026
Tommy Milone	4.32	4.39	4.76	5.1%	6.33	728	8.23	1	0.00	0	0.00	0	2.11	636	0.00	0	3.62	182	5.80	123	1,750
Tony Gonsolin	4.33	3.64	2.93	9.2%	5.32	332	0.00	0	0.00	0	0.00	0	0.00	0	1.72	175	0.83	116	5.17	70	693
Tony Sipp	4.66	3.73	4.71	9.8%	5.58	173	0.00	0	0.00	0	0.00	0	1.30	1	-0.24	73	3.51	115	2.81	1	363
Tony Watson	3.19	3.19	4.17	5.2%	8.23	1	6.96	4	4.13	410	0.00	0	1.79	309	0.00	0	3.51	89	0.00	0	813
Touki Toussaint	5.48	3.68	5.62	13.1%	6.71	201	3.91	5	4.59	183	0.00	0	8.23	2	0.18	161	0.00	1	2.59	203	777
Travis Bergen	6.28	5.22	5.49	10.6%	5.44	251	0.00	0	0.00	0	0.00	0	8.23	1	0.00	0	3.45	18	4.97	105	375
Travis Lakins	4.56	3.63	3.86	9.8%	3.71	156	0.00	0	0.00	0	3.46	143	6.58	14	0.00	0	0.00	0	3.25	77	395
Trent Thornton	5.13	4.35	4.84	9.0%	5.45	1,215	4.47	69	0.00	0	2.80	302	3.36	90	4.03	157	3.61	595	3.42	330	2,759
Trevor Bauer	4.34	3.60	4.48	9.0%	4.73	1,325	3.89	143	0.00	0	3.11	580	3.15	253	8.23	1	2.26	491	2.90	674	3,687
Trevor Cahill	4.39	3.67	5.98	8.6%	3.71	135	8.23	4	4.53	477	2.25	327	3.20	400	0.00	0	8.23	4	4.23	370	1,788
Trevor Gott	4.20	3.75	4.44	7.9%	3.76	606	0.00	0	2.80	91	0.00	0	3.55	32	0.00	0	4.35	8	4.24	159	914
Trevor Hildenberger	4.79	3.86	10.47	8.0%	3.87	17	0.00	0	5.21	104	0.00	0	1.11	120	0.00	0	6.12	84	0.00	0	326
Trevor Kelley	7.57	5.87	8.64	12.5%	0.00	0	0.00	0	5.75	100	0.00	0	0.00	0	0.00	0	6.09	29	6.04	34	163
Trevor May	4.28	3.46	2.94	9.8%	2.79	725	1.33	9	0.00	0	0.00	0	3.99	115	0.00	0	4.61	168	5.18	148	1,166
Trevor Richards	4.68	3.82	4.06	9.7%	4.48	958	0.00	0	0.00	0	5.27	183	2.29	834	-7.30	2	6.29	44	5.67	159	2,182
Trevor Rosenthal	10.77	4.14	13.50	30.6%	4.79	287	5.41	11	0.00	0	0.00	0	0.47	8	0.00	0	2.42	99	0.00	0	405
Trevor Williams	4.48	4.12	5.38	6.9%	4.28	1,106	0.00	0	4.77	332	8.23	4	4.70	266	0.00	0	2.93	447	2.20	19	2,259
Trey Wingenter	4.37	2.90	5.65	12.8%	4.64	498	0.00	0	0.00	0	0.00	0	0.00	0	0.00	0	0.76	407	0.00	0	906
Ty Blach	7.01	5.18	12.00	12.2%	0.00	0	0.00	0	6.09	295	4.65	26	3.66	134	0.00	0	5.93	20	3.66	45	521
Ty Buttrey	3.81	3.38	3.98	7.4%	3.38	689	8.23	2	0.00	0	8.23	2	3.40	163	0.00	0	3.31	354	0.00	0	1,225
Tyler Alexander	4.12	4.54	4.86	3.0%	5.67	301	4.19	200	0.00	0	0.00	0	2.50	106	0.00	0	4.17	144	4.51	167	918
Tyler Anderson	5.12	3.72	11.76	10.4%	4.69	193	1.30	8	0.00	0	3.36	86	2.92	111	0.00	0	0.00	0	1.95	27	428
Tyler Bashlor	6.65	4.18	6.95	16.5%	4.92	225	0.00	0	0.00	0	0.00	0	2.91	42	0.00	0	2.93	94	7.51	1	396
Tyler Beede	4.42	3.65	5.08	8.8%	4.99	1,129	3.06	6	8.23	2	0.00	0	1.76	376	0.00	0	2.22	236	1.96	276	2,028
Tyler Chatwood	4.80	3.63	3.76	11.4%	4.72	387	4.21	497	0.00	0	1.87	119	1.36	87	0.00	0	-3.54	5	1.81	146	1,285
Tyler Clippard	3.43	3.34	2.90	6.2%	2.74	188	4.17	192	0.00	0	0.00	0	4.16	282	1.70	226	1.30	5	6.28	36	937
Tyler Duffey	2.88	2.79	2.50	5.8%	3.26	505	0.92	13	0.90	13	0.00	0	0.00	4	0.00	0	1.78	294	3.58	149	980
Tyler Glasnow	3.38	3.34	1.78	6.1%	4.15	606	8.23	1	0.00	0	0.00	0	3.17	30	0.00	0	-2.57	23	1.86	237	903
Tyler Kinley	5.77	3.49	3.65	16.3%	5.51	365	0.00	0	0.00	0	0.00	0	0.00	0	0.00	0	1.98	488	0.00	0	866
Tyler Lyons	3.72	2.94	6.39	9.3%	4.81	28	0.00	0	5.17	49	0.00	0	1.33	20	0.00	0	1.57	94	0.00	0	191
Tyler Mahle	4.28	4.10	5.14	6.1%	4.59	1,191	8.23	1	8.23	2	4.77	135	1.49	35	2.60	208	3.75	67	3.55	474	2,116
Tyler Olson	4.86	3.52	4.40	11.4%	3.71	215	0.00	0	7.37	16	5.93	2	3.98	71	0.00	0	-1.15	2	2.93	224	533
Tyler Rogers	2.72	2.96	1.02	4.3%	1.07	21	0.00	0	3.92	141	0.00	0	0.00	0	0.00	0	0.00	0	1.94	94	256
Tyler Skaggs	5.06	4.48	4.29	8.4%	5.43	689	0.00	1	0.00	0	0.00	2	4.07	220	0.00	0	-2.12	3	3.33	465	1,386
Tyler Thornburg	6.37	4.96	7.71	11.6%	5.98	209	0.00	0	8.23	1	0.00	0	1.65	72	0.00	0	0.00	1	5.24	99	382
Tyler Webb	4.81	3.93	3.76	10.4%	4.07	341	4.21	207	0.00	0	0.00	0	2.92	169	0.00	0	4.36	94	4.46	39	889
Tyson Ross	5.69	4.40	6.11	11.1%	5.34	201	0.47	4	0.00	0	4.39	212	0.00	0	0.00	0	3.44	177	0.00	0	595
Victor Alcantara	3.89	3.31	4.85	8.2%	0.00	0	6.96	3	3.45	466	0.00	0	2.44	113	0.00	0	3.69	53	0.00	0	677
Vince Velasquez	4.55	3.90	4.91	8.3%	4.06	1,325	4.24	110	0.00	0	0.00	0	1.30	2	0.00	0	3.34	432	3.90	250	2,120
Wade Davis	6.08	4.02	8.65	14.1%	5.04	362	0.00	5	0.00	0	3.09	290	4.81	14	0.00	0	0.00	1	3.47	150	822
Wade LeBlanc	4.39	4.24	5.71	5.8%	6.63	102	5.51	442	0.00	0	4.90	586	2.36	605	0.00	0	-0.54	7	4.14	213	1,955
Wade Miley	4.48	3.84	3.98	8.5%	4.64	472	6.07	174	0.00	0	4.00	1,326	2.23	589	0.00	0	4.39	32	3.66	268	2,968
Walker Buehler	3.46	3.55	3.26	5.0%	4.12	1,501	5.35	218	0.00	0	3.17	362	1.30	5	0.00	0	1.92	406	2.25	337	2,838
Walker Lockett	4.75	4.56	8.34	5.8%	5.71	178	0.00	0	7.50	29	0.00	0	2.16	73	0.00	0	0.00	0	3.28	89	369
Wander Suero	3.78	3.14	4.54	8.8%	3.90	8	0.00	0	0.00	0	3.41	839	2.11	245	0.00	0	-7.30	2	3.60	84	1,197
Wandy Peralta	3.38	2.57	5.67	9.3%	3.59	67	3.97	165	0.00	0	8.23	1	1.90	153	0.00	0	1.74	247	0.00	0	657
Wei-Chieh Huang	8.85	5.88	3.18	15.6%	8.23	60	0.00	0	0.00	0	0.00	0	2.97	27	0.00	0	1.30	3	3.85	24	114
Wei-Chung Wang	5.87	4.83	3.77	10.9%	6.09	224	0.00	1	1.30	1	8.23	1	3.20	82	0.00	0	4.22	187	3.61	23	519
Wei-Yin Chen	4.49	4.31	6.59	5.9%	5.25	559	2.88	29	0.00	0	-12.48	3	5.09	41	0.00	0	3.20	261	3.61	258	1,151
Wes Parsons	6.94	4.17	5.45	18.5%	4.60	129	0.00	0	4.95	236	0.00	0	5.29	35	0.00	0	3.00	236	0.00	0	637
Will Harris	3.16	3.11	1.50	6.1%	0.25	14	0.00	0	3.46	501	0.00	0	0.00	0	0.00	0	8.23	2	2.71	372	926
Will Smith	2.94	2.49	2.76	8.2%	4.64	487	2.02	5	0.00	0	0.00	0	1.30	13	0.00	0	-0.46	427	4.70	105	1,043
Williams Jerez	7.30	4.38	4.35	18.8%	5.38	106	0.00	0	0.00	0	0.00	0	1.60	23	0.00	0	3.72	63	0.00	0	192
Wilmer Font	4.28	3.73	4.48	8.2%	4.10	723	0.00	1	4.11	175	8.23	1	1.30	3	3.02	131	3.09	202	3.37	287	1,541
Wily Peralta	5.40	4.28	5.80	10.8%	4.75	356	8.23	1	0.00	0	0.00	0	4.09	85	0.00	0	3.38	202	7.22	9	673
Yacksel Rios	4.89	3.12	6.92	12.3%	2.53	72	0.94	74	0.00	0	0.00	0	4.27	27	0.00	0	7.03	42	3.55	22	237
Yefry Ramirez	5.56	3.60	7.40	13.5%	4.59	234	1.30	2	0.00	0	0.00	0	1.83	143	0.00	0	3.90	85	0.00	0	464
Yency Almonte	5.14	4.28	5.56	8.9%	5.96	345	8.23	2	0.00	0	0.00	0	1.30	1	5.50	18	1.78	242	0.00	0	608
Yimi Garcia	4.04	4.03	3.61	5.7%	3.46	436	8.23	11	0.00	0	0.00	0	4.17	62	0.00	0	3.24	187	5.25	278	975
Yoan Lopez	4.33	4.07	3.41	6.9%	5.10	499	0.00	0	0.00	0	0.00	0	3.79	21	0.00	0	2.56	335	0.00	0	857
Yohander Mendez	7.77	3.95	5.79	23.8%	4.28	45	0.00	0	0.00	0	0.00	0	2.30	37	0.00	0	6.51	18	0.00	0	100
Yonny Chirinos	3.69	3.75	3.85	5.3%	4.01	32	4.14	11	4.85	1,086	1.33	9	-6.17	6	1.65	415	3.15	425	0.00	0	1,985
Yoshihisa Hirano	3.95	3.08	4.75	9.4%	5.08	447	0.00	0	0.00	0	8.23	1	0.00	0	1.22	481	2.02	5	0.00	0	934
Yu Darvish	3.56	3.15	3.98	7.7%	4.08	813	3.95	337	0.00	1	2.45	985	0.78	44	2.25	59	3.04	410	2.43	198	2,848
Yusei Kikuchi	4.64	4.24	5.46	6.9%	4.90	1,290	0.00	0	0.00	0	0.00	0	3.14	199	0.00	0	2.83	733	5.25	406	2,721

Pitcher	pERA	pERA (Just Pitchers)	ERA	BB%	pERA FF	FF Count	pERA FT	FT Count	pERA SI	SI Count	pERA FC	FC Count	pERA CH	CH Count	pERA FS	FS Count	pERA SL	SL Count	pERA CU	CU Count	Count
Yusmeiro Petit	3.72	4.18	2.71	3.3%	6.19	507	0.00	0	5.93	2	2.63	234	2.13	213	8.23	1	7.37	4	2.68	160	1,139
Zac Gallen	4.53	3.51	2.81	10.8%	5.01	660	0.95	28	0.00	0	2.88	214	0.89	222	0.00	0	0.00	0	2.73	262	1,387
Zac Grotz	4.06	2.99	4.15	11.0%	4.69	95	2.14	14	4.28	36	0.00	0	0.00	3	1.86	112	1.30	22	1.57	17	299
Zac Reininger	6.45	4.88	8.68	11.4%	5.21	214	5.73	107	0.00	0	0.00	0	0.56	20	0.00	0	5.16	128	3.14	64	533
Zac Rosscup	5.88	2.13	5.00	20.2%	2.95	70	4.75	79	0.00	0	8.23	1	0.00	0	0.00	0	0.91	222	0.00	0	402
Zach Davies	5.33	4.90	3.55	7.6%	-2.12	3	5.87	1,362	0.00	0	5.90	315	2.63	813	0.00	0	6.75	21	6.91	90	2,608
Zach Duke	6.84	4.37	5.01	17.0%	5.10	27	0.00	0	5.31	189	8.23	1	0.00	0	0.00	0	3.40	125	2.64	47	408
Zach Eflin	4.53	4.20	4.13	6.8%	4.55	829	4.02	551	0.00	0	8.23	6	4.17	195	8.23	1	3.98	759	3.93	137	2,481
Zach Plesac	4.84	4.28	3.81	8.4%	5.41	955	0.00	0	-7.30	2	0.00	0	3.05	370	0.00	0	2.28	360	4.94	185	1,892
Zack Britton	3.73	2.39	1.91	13.1%	-1.15	2	0.00	0	2.55	800	0.00	0	0.00	0	0.00	0	1.42	129	0.00	0	933
Zack Godley	5.07	4.01	5.97	10.3%	8.23	2	0.00	1	5.37	545	4.29	256	3.61	89	0.00	0	5.93	5	2.79	647	1,548
Zack Greinke	3.49	3.84	2.93	3.7%	5.32	1,246	5.00	160	0.00	0	8.23	1	2.34	649	8.23	2	3.07	488	2.28	445	3,026
Zack Littell	3.52	3.43	2.68	6.2%	4.24	276	8.23	1	0.00	0	3.94	47	0.00	3	8.23	1	2.18	215	6.87	6	551
Zack Wheeler	4.09	3.94	3.96	6.0%	4.27	854	4.22	961	8.23	2	0.00	0	2.72	104	3.51	229	3.65	606	3.40	304	3,159

Pitcher	pERA	pERA (Just Pitchers)	ERA	BB%	pERA FF	FF Count	pERA FT	FT Count	pERA SI	SI Count	pERA FC	FC Count	pERA CH	CH Count	pERA FS	FS Count	pERA SL	SL Count	pERA CU	CU Count	Count
A.J. Cole	3.25	2.86	3.81	6.8%	4.73	200	0.00	3	0.00	0	0.00	0	0.00	10	0.00	0	1.18	196	2.74	51	481
A.J. Minter	5.59	3.06	7.06	15.7%	4.96	227	0.00	0	0.00	0	1.93	253	1.54	91	0.00	0	0.55	2	0.00	0	573
A.J. Puk	4.10	3.11	3.18	10.6%	4.27	130	0.00	0	0.00	0	0.04	19	0.00	0	0.73	49	9.30	4	202
Aaron Brooks	4.83	4.44	5.65	7.1%	5.78	508	5.08	507	0.00	0	6.08	3	3.14	375	0.00	0	2.92	417	6.16	62	1,899
Aaron Bummer	2.83	2.23	2.13	9.2%	3.18	95	0.00	0	2.49	701	0.70	183	-0.62	4	0.00	0	2.61	55	0.00	0	1,039
Aaron Civale	4.56	4.31	2.34	7.1%	6.92	28	0.00	0	5.64	302	3.84	257	2.03	57	0.00	0	3.49	122	3.04	96	863
Aaron Nola	4.28	3.50	3.87	8.4%	4.97	1,197	4.95	334	0.00	1	0.00	0	2.28	596	0.00	0	0.00	0	2.14	1,101	3,332
Aaron Sanchez	5.38	4.05	5.89	11.2%	4.79	657	4.96	620	6.82	3	0.00	0	3.19	423	0.00	0	0.00	0	2.68	515	2,220
Aaron Wilkerson	6.33	4.80	7.31	11.3%	5.06	170	0.00	0	0.00	0	0.00	0	2.31	47	0.00	0	5.35	59	5.53	57	333
Adalberto Mejia	6.43	4.41	6.61	14.5%	4.68	269	5.35	70	0.00	0	0.00	0	3.55	99	0.00	0	4.24	186	0.00	5	629
Adam Cimber	3.79	3.28	4.45	7.8%	2.70	122	0.00	0	3.49	397	0.00	0	0.00	0	-0.62	8	3.50	243	-0.60	9	779
Adam Conley	5.22	4.07	6.53	10.3%	4.40	644	6.08	1	0.00	0	6.08	3	2.98	180	0.00	0	4.00	191	3.88	38	1,061
Adam Kolarek	2.72	2.41	3.27	7.0%	3.63	81	6.08	1	2.02	540	2.26	6	2.63	66	0.00	0	3.78	67	0.00	0	761
Adam Morgan	3.11	2.60	3.94	8.3%	3.22	38	5.41	89	0.00	0	-0.62	1	2.26	90	0.00	0	0.76	191	4.86	49	463
Adam Ottavino	5.37	3.66	1.90	14.1%	0.00	10	4.24	471	0.00	0	3.96	155	6.08	2	0.00	1	3.10	515	8.69	1	1,158
Adam Plutko	4.60	4.53	4.86	5.6%	5.10	919	0.00	0	0.00	0	6.08	1	4.77	197	0.00	0	3.77	413	3.05	174	1,705
Adam Wainwright	4.86	4.18	4.19	8.6%	5.34	381	0.00	0	5.43	662	4.05	615	1.98	49	0.00	0	1.49	5	3.11	992	2,876
Adam Warren	4.85	3.97	5.34	9.7%	5.52	169	0.00	0	0.00	0	6.08	1	2.26	99	0.00	0	3.61	254	3.78	24	555
Adbert Alzolay	6.35	4.07	7.30	15.0%	5.09	129	0.00	0	0.00	0	0.00	0	1.76	47	0.00	0	0.00	0	3.60	49	225
Adrian Houser	4.35	3.85	3.72	8.0%	3.70	567	3.43	647	0.00	0	0.00	0	2.60	120	0.00	0	3.64	195	6.06	248	1,777
Adrian Morejon	5.07	4.38	10.13	7.1%	4.74	80	6.08	3	0.00	0	0.00	0	4.44	28	0.00	0	0.00	0	3.56	43	154
Adrian Sampson	4.43	4.14	5.89	6.4%	6.58	11	6.08	1	5.52	1,100	-0.62	2	3.13	256	0.00	0	2.27	547	2.27	136	2,056
Alec Mills	3.56	3.18	2.75	7.2%	5.01	170	4.09	130	0.00	0	0.00	0	0.24	106	0.00	0	0.75	61	3.56	86	553
Alex Claudio	3.86	3.12	4.06	9.0%	-0.62	8	0.00	0	3.24	437	0.00	0	2.74	348	0.00	0	3.72	182	3.16	2	978
Alex Cobb	3.76	4.03	10.95	3.3%	5.13	109	0.00	0	0.00	0	0.00	0	0.00	0	1.40	80	0.00	0	6.36	39	229
Alex Colome	3.95	3.25	2.80	9.2%	4.64	269	0.00	0	0.00	0	2.74	679	2.09	25	0.00	0	6.08	1	0.00	0	975
Alex McRae	5.99	4.29	8.78	12.1%	5.16	89	5.40	199	0.00	0	0.00	0	3.99	44	0.00	0	3.27	98	1.52	67	547
Alex Wilson	6.44	3.86	9.53	15.8%	5.07	43	5.61	48	0.00	0	-0.62	1	0.00	2	0.00	0	2.72	108	0.00	0	202
Alex Wood	4.09	3.95	5.80	5.9%	0.00	0	4.35	295	0.00	0	0.00	0	3.43	147	0.00	0	0.00	0	3.66	144	586
Alex Young	3.58	3.12	3.56	7.7%	6.05	186	0.00	0	3.86	300	3.22	304	1.86	270	0.00	0	0.94	22	1.44	242	1,325
Allen Webster	3.11	2.06	4.91	9.6%	5.39	61	-0.23	12	0.00	0	0.00	0	0.01	26	0.00	0	0.36	72	0.00	0	171
Amir Garrett	3.73	1.92	3.21	14.2%	3.84	169	4.56	224	0.00	0	6.08	1	6.08	1	0.00	0	0.21	540	0.00	0	978
Andres Munoz	3.86	2.71	3.91	11.3%	4.18	277	0.00	2	0.00	0	0.00	0	0.00	0	0.00	0	-0.24	135	0.00	0	416
Andrew Cashner	4.62	3.88	4.68	9.1%	4.97	1,137	5.32	81	0.00	0	6.08	2	2.44	687	0.00	0	3.11	325	3.45	277	2,511
Andrew Chafin	3.14	2.60	3.76	8.0%	4.31	266	0.00	0	4.59	268	0.00	0	0.00	0	0.00	0	-0.26	338	-7.84	2	876
Andrew Heaney	3.51	3.09	4.91	7.3%	0.00	0	6.08	1	3.74	924	-1.57	3	2.89	251	0.00	0	0.00	1	1.85	428	1,609
Andrew Kittredge	2.42	2.33	4.17	5.7%	4.03	175	3.69	299	6.08	1	6.08	1	0.06	38	0.00	0	0.28	304	0.00	0	818
Andrew Miller	4.60	3.38	4.45	11.4%	5.01	364	0.00	4	0.00	0	0.00	0	0.00	1	0.00	0	2.39	587	0.00	0	969
Andrew Suarez	5.24	4.31	5.79	9.5%	5.78	163	4.59	146	0.00	0	0.00	0	3.21	76	0.00	0	3.12	117	2.76	37	540
Anibal Sanchez	4.74	4.17	3.85	8.2%	5.37	797	0.00	0	5.63	265	4.60	612	2.31	120	1.80	627	4.18	81	4.75	153	2,690
Anthony Bass	3.78	3.19	3.56	9.0%	5.34	31	4.34	333	0.00	0	6.08	1	0.00	0	1.76	98	1.83	231	0.00	0	718
Anthony DeSclafani	4.29	3.97	3.89	7.0%	4.77	955	4.65	481	0.00	0	0.00	0	4.30	133	0.00	0	2.95	634	2.68	384	2,668
Anthony Kay	4.12	3.52	5.79	7.9%	4.81	159	0.00	0	0.00	0	0.00	0	0.50	50	0.00	0	0.00	0	2.40	49	258
Anthony Swarzak	4.49	3.21	4.56	11.5%	5.02	338	-0.62	40	0.00	0	6.08	1	0.00	0	0.00	0	2.37	546	0.00	0	926
Antonio Senzatela	5.26	4.20	6.71	9.8%	4.50	1,400	0.00	1	0.00	0	0.00	1	5.02	164	0.00	0	3.39	434	3.36	237	2,237
Archie Bradley	5.25	3.99	3.52	11.4%	4.84	760	2.28	134	0.55	2	0.00	0	0.83	70	0.00	0	0.00	1	3.39	316	1,284
Ariel Jurado	4.79	4.47	5.81	6.7%	4.89	472	4.57	839	-1.57	3	0.00	0	4.36	240	0.00	0	4.02	319	3.91	169	2,047
Aroldis Chapman	4.11	3.13	2.21	10.6%	3.99	587	0.00	0	2.73	94	0.00	0	-5.39	2	0.00	0	1.66	305	0.00	0	989
Asher Wojciechowski	4.43	3.89	4.92	7.8%	4.68	795	0.00	0	0.00	0	6.08	2	5.03	42	0.00	0	2.42	323	3.24	305	1,467
Austin Adams	3.59	2.34	3.94	12.3%	4.20	186	6.82	19	0.00	0	0.00	0	0.00	0	0.00	0	1.00	323	0.00	0	541
Austin Adams	6.51	4.00	7.02	16.3%	5.56	171	0.00	10	0.00	0	0.00	0	0.00	0	0.00	7	2.30	117	0.00	0	318
Austin Brice	4.75	3.94	3.43	9.1%	2.80	222	-5.39	2	4.15	165	6.08	1	4.67	33	0.00	0	6.92	4	4.54	333	761
Austin Davis	5.49	3.44	6.53	14.3%	4.25	236	0.00	0	0.00	0	0.00	0	1.26	74	0.00	0	4.60	45	1.90	52	407
Austin Pruitt	3.60	3.45	4.40	6.2%	4.50	311	0.00	0	0.00	0	0.55	2	2.65	142	0.00	0	2.02	167	3.80	97	720
Austin Voth	3.75	3.41	3.30	7.5%	4.43	419	0.00	0	0.00	0	0.00	0	2.55	65	0.00	0	1.94	61	1.39	138	684
Ben Heller	4.42	3.58	1.23	10.7%	0.00	0	6.61	50	0.00	0	0.00	0	0.34	8	0.00	0	0.74	43	0.00	1	102
Blaine Hardy	4.05	3.73	4.47	7.1%	5.49	147	0.00	6	0.00	0	5.67	70	1.86	287	0.00	0	6.08	2	4.94	130	672
Blake Parker	4.16	3.55	4.55	8.6%	4.05	489	0.00	0	0.00	0	5.52	41	0.00	0	2.64	329	6.08	1	3.36	159	1,020
Blake Snell	2.82	2.13	4.29	9.1%	3.52	893	0.00	0	0.00	0	6.08	1	-5.39	4	1.11	369	-0.62	1	1.32	133	0.52	448	1,852
Blake Treinen	5.26	3.42	4.91	13.9%	4.31	211	6.08	4	3.19	442	3.45	185	0.00	0	0.00	0	2.69	136	0.00	0	1,023
Bobby Poyner	5.03	4.10	6.94	10.2%	4.62	148	0.00	0	0.00	0	0.00	0	3.03	41	0.00	0	3.38	34	0.00	2	225
Brad Boxberger	5.55	3.68	5.40	13.9%	3.97	227	0.00	0	0.00	0	0.00	0	2.90	137	-0.62	1	4.19	81	8.80	1	487
Brad Brach	5.18	3.61	5.47	12.8%	3.97	464	5.33	54	0.00	0	2.96	66	2.20	179	0.00	0	3.82	186	0.00	0	982
Brad Hand	3.72	3.31	3.30	7.4%	4.54	396	4.60	31	0.00	0	0.00	0	-0.62	1	0.00	0	2.26	502	0.00	0	946
Brad Keller	5.06	4.15	4.19	9.9%	4.50	1,100	4.70	644	6.08	3	0.00	0	6.90	41	0.00	0	3.12	826	0.00	0	2,616
Brad Peacock	4.69	4.17	4.12	8.1%	4.66	408	5.21	470	6.08	1	6.08	1	3.71	91	0.00	0	2.88	430	3.24	104	1,510
Brad Wieck	4.53	3.84	5.71	8.8%	3.71	476	0.00	0	6.08	1	0.00	0	0.00	0	0.00	0	3.93	70	4.59	73	621
Brady Rodgers	5.94	4.24	16.20	12.0%	4.70	59	0.00	1	0.00	0	6.08	1	1.93	13	0.00	0	3.02	30	8.44	10	114
Branden Kline	5.03	3.95	5.93	10.4%	4.96	414	0.00	0	0.00	0	0.00	0	0.99	55	0.00	0	2.87	239	0.00	0	708
Brandon Brennan	3.66	2.38	4.56	12.2%	5.04	22	-0.33	8	4.85	339	0.00	0	-0.33	297	0.00	0	0.70	45	9.48	1	725
Brandon Kintzler	4.12	4.10	2.68	5.7%	5.38	17	6.08	1	4.68	602	0.00	0	2.28	148	0.00	0	2.84	84	0.00	0	855
Brandon Woodruff	3.56	3.45	3.62	6.1%	3.64	772	3.37	499	0.00	0	6.08	1	2.86	276	0.00	0	3.39	396	5.75	34	1,979
Brandon Workman	4.78	2.95	1.88	15.7%	3.51	420	0.00	0	0.00	0	2.33	263	0.00	0	0.00	0	0.00	4	2.85	557	1,244
Brendan McKay	4.22	3.75	5.14	7.4%	4.31	501	0.00	0	0.00	0	4.09	114	3.02	30	0.00	0	0.00	2	2.50	230	878
Brent Suter	2.29	3.04	0.49	1.5%	2.63	173	6.08	9	0.00	0	0.00	0	2.88	43	0.00	0	0.00	0	9.43	8	233
Brett Anderson	4.33	4.08	3.89	6.6%	5.39	493	0.00	0	4.23	1,158	6.08	4	3.28	356	0.00	0	3.30	506	3.03	141	2,659
Brett Martin	3.23	2.93	4.76	6.4%	3.58	287	2.97	206	0.00	0	0.00	0	6.08	1	0.00	0	2.21	330	3.18	144	1,022

Pitcher	pERA	pERA (Just Pitchers)	ERA	BB%	pERA FF	FF Count	pERA FT	FT Count	pERA SI	SI Count	pERA FC	FC Count	pERA CH	CH Count	pERA FS	FS Count	pERA SL	SL Count	pERA CU	CU Count	Count
Brian Flynn	5.84	4.23	5.22	12.2%	5.95	83	3.83	170	0.00	0	6.08	2	0.00	1	0.00	0	3.86	197	0.00	0	453
Brian Johnson	5.71	4.15	6.02	11.9%	5.47	270	6.82	23	0.00	0	0.00	0	6.08	6	0.00	0	3.39	210	3.11	263	772
Brian Moran	3.35	2.93	4.26	6.9%	2.87	50	-1.57	3	0.00	0	0.00	0	0.00	3	0.00	0	3.21	8	3.40	48	112
Brian Schlitter	4.25	3.39	3.72	9.8%	4.91	54	4.55	15	2.91	61	-0.42	12	0.00	0	0.00	0	-0.62	6	0.00	0	150
Brock Burke	5.93	5.07	7.43	9.2%	4.92	206	5.66	88	0.00	0	0.00	0	3.58	73	0.00	0	0.00	3	6.05	106	476
Brock Stewart	4.80	4.40	9.82	6.5%	1.49	25	5.20	238	0.00	0	0.00	0	3.93	64	0.00	0	3.84	159	0.00	0	486
Brooks Pounders	4.04	3.81	6.14	5.9%	5.68	47	0.00	0	0.00	0	0.00	0	6.08	6	0.00	0	2.57	82	0.00	0	135
Brusdar Graterol	2.85	2.92	4.66	5.0%	5.53	25	0.00	0	2.29	74	0.00	0	6.08	1	0.00	0	2.43	44	0.00	0	144
Bryan Abreu	2.26	1.70	1.04	9.4%	5.70	46	0.00	3	0.00	0	0.00	0	0.00	1	0.00	0	-0.13	88	-0.24	8	146
Bryan Garcia	4.01	1.64	12.15	15.2%	0.00	7	-0.62	8	3.61	52	0.00	0	-0.09	22	0.00	0	0.76	40	0.00	0	129
Bryan Shaw	4.49	3.68	5.38	9.3%	6.08	2	-0.62	1	0.00	0	4.26	886	0.45	85	0.00	1	2.43	187	3.49	18	1,180
Bryse Wilson	5.85	4.60	7.20	10.8%	4.60	237	4.87	19	0.00	0	0.00	0	2.92	48	0.00	0	5.61	44	8.31	8	356
Buck Farmer	3.86	3.27	3.72	8.3%	4.71	555	6.08	1	0.00	0	-0.62	1	2.57	288	0.00	0	1.18	287	0.00	0	1,157
Buddy Boshers	5.34	4.09	4.05	11.0%	4.17	12	6.08	5	5.74	135	0.00	0	0.79	26	0.00	0	0.00	10	3.55	196	384
Burch Smith	5.67	3.72	5.48	13.2%	3.70	268	-0.62	1	0.00	0	0.00	0	2.35	69	0.00	0	0.00	1	4.97	85	425
Cal Quantrill	4.24	4.02	5.16	6.3%	4.37	392	4.86	632	0.00	0	0.00	0	2.84	317	0.00	0	2.73	370	6.70	68	1,781
Caleb Ferguson	5.93	4.21	4.84	13.2%	4.35	607	0.55	2	0.00	0	0.00	1	0.00	2	0.00	0	6.08	6	3.75	169	804
Caleb Smith	4.39	3.62	4.52	9.3%	4.23	1,366	0.00	0	0.00	1	0.00	2	3.03	363	0.00	0	2.93	816	-2.05	6	2,661
Cam Bedrosian	3.97	3.36	3.23	8.5%	4.64	481	0.00	0	0.00	0	0.00	0	6.08	1	-0.80	10	2.18	501	9.10	2	1,003
Carl Edwards Jr.	6.24	3.80	8.47	16.7%	4.53	258	6.08	8	0.00	0	0.00	0	0.00	2	0.00	0	0.00	0	1.21	77	346
Carlos Carrasco	2.83	2.93	5.29	4.7%	4.83	421	5.38	164	0.00	0	0.00	1	1.30	233	0.00	0	0.86	432	6.11	22	1,274
Carlos Estevez	3.59	3.15	3.75	7.5%	3.18	841	2.15	35	0.00	0	0.00	0	2.68	44	0.00	0	3.24	320	0.00	0	1,240
Carlos Martinez	3.37	2.70	3.17	9.0%	3.92	223	2.69	155	0.00	0	6.82	16	1.55	137	0.00	0	1.86	217	0.00	0	749
Carlos Rodon	4.84	3.63	5.19	10.8%	5.68	348	4.59	9	0.00	0	6.08	1	1.16	79	-0.62	1	1.58	257	8.67	1	696
Carlos Torres	3.34	3.59	7.50	3.5%	1.49	20	6.08	10	0.00	0	4.68	36	0.00	0	0.00	0	0.00	5	3.27	14	115
Carson Fulmer	6.11	3.82	6.26	15.0%	5.83	239	0.00	0	6.08	1	2.22	179	2.84	86	6.08	1	0.00	0	1.18	43	556
Casey Sadler	4.19	3.92	2.14	6.7%	0.00	0	0.00	0	4.65	266	5.12	138	4.17	22	0.00	0	3.89	80	2.02	190	696
CC Sabathia	4.44	3.81	4.95	8.3%	4.96	32	0.00	0	4.99	228	3.97	678	1.91	197	6.08	2	3.69	494	8.66	2	1,635
Chad Bettis	4.11	3.63	6.08	7.3%	4.67	373	5.27	32	0.00	0	3.32	174	2.18	324	0.00	0	4.59	3	4.27	124	1,030
Chad Green	3.44	3.20	4.17	6.4%	3.45	1,022	0.00	0	0.00	0	0.00	0	0.00	0	3.33	25	2.26	271	0.00	0	1,320
Chad Sobotka	4.61	2.66	6.21	14.2%	3.52	318	0.00	0	0.00	0	6.08	1	6.08	1	0.00	0	1.48	242	9.01	1	564
Chance Adams	5.86	4.91	8.53	8.9%	4.71	305	-0.62	2	0.00	0	0.00	0	6.92	33	0.00	2	5.19	91	4.79	86	519
Chandler Shepherd	4.80	4.38	6.63	7.1%	4.92	151	0.00	0	0.00	0	0.00	0	2.85	34	0.00	0	5.06	87	2.43	46	318
Charlie Morton	3.35	3.03	3.05	7.2%	3.55	938	3.87	598	6.08	1	3.15	319	6.08	1	3.74	106	5.27	7	2.07	1,168	3,139
Chase Anderson	4.49	3.87	4.21	8.5%	3.91	999	4.97	185	0.00	0	4.41	415	2.82	551	-5.39	2	6.08	1	4.38	235	2,392
Chasen Bradford	3.61	3.53	4.86	5.8%	5.03	72	0.00	0	3.19	44	-0.36	9	2.19	28	0.00	0	3.28	82	0.00	0	248
Chaz Roe	5.61	3.88	4.06	13.5%	4.12	56	4.46	216	0.00	0	1.88	40	0.94	3	0.00	0	3.89	599	-3.39	8	922
Chi Chi Gonzalez	5.78	4.42	5.29	11.9%	4.51	476	5.62	132	0.00	0	4.35	257	1.48	126	0.00	0	5.32	140	8.87	14	1,145
Chris Archer	4.49	3.42	5.19	10.5%	5.06	828	5.84	227	0.00	0	6.08	5	3.31	253	0.00	0	0.82	742	4.56	41	2,098
Chris Bassitt	4.85	4.38	3.81	7.7%	4.53	504	0.00	0	4.84	926	4.07	296	4.23	193	0.00	0	0.00	0	3.02	284	2,331
Chris Devenski	3.91	3.54	4.83	7.1%	5.12	498	6.08	5	0.00	0	6.08	1	1.66	396	0.00	0	3.38	238	0.00	6	1,144
Chris Flexen	8.18	4.90	6.59	18.6%	6.11	129	4.65	16	0.00	0	6.08	3	3.02	30	0.00	0	2.62	45	5.25	11	234
Chris Martin	2.65	3.25	3.40	2.3%	3.53	381	0.00	0	0.00	0	4.01	157	2.69	129	0.56	103	4.19	72	7.96	11	865
Chris Mazza	4.82	4.44	5.51	6.8%	0.98	9	0.00	0	5.31	135	3.92	71	4.17	12	0.00	0	3.59	55	0.00	0	285
Chris Paddack	3.80	3.81	3.33	5.5%	4.27	1,391	0.00	0	0.00	0	0.00	0	2.21	650	0.00	0	0.00	0	5.45	238	2,280
Chris Sale	3.14	3.01	4.40	6.1%	3.89	897	3.67	233	0.00	0	0.00	0	2.31	385	0.00	0	2.28	945	4.02	4	2,466
Chris Stratton	4.84	3.88	5.57	9.6%	4.70	658	3.89	43	0.00	0	1.49	10	3.26	76	0.00	0	2.64	300	3.28	158	1,363
Cionel Perez	4.01	4.01	10.00	12.5%	4.70	99	0.00	0	0.00	0	0.00	0	2.79	16	0.00	0	3.02	45	0.00	1	163
Clay Buchholz	4.28	4.06	6.56	6.3%	4.76	146	4.16	184	0.00	0	3.60	273	3.01	188	0.00	0	6.82	3	5.20	169	963
Clay Holmes	6.02	3.78	5.58	15.0%	4.71	86	0.00	0	4.06	464	0.00	5	6.82	8	0.00	0	2.60	90	3.28	219	915
Clayton Kershaw	3.20	3.16	3.03	5.8%	5.05	1,118	0.00	0	0.00	0	0.00	2	-7.69	5	3.21	16	1.49	1,010	2.30	421	2,672
Clayton Richard	5.04	4.26	5.96	9.0%	6.13	99	4.32	419	6.08	1	6.08	1	-0.46	15	0.00	0	3.51	188	0.00	1	728
Cody Allen	7.09	4.17	6.26	17.2%	5.23	262	6.08	1	0.00	0	0.00	0	0.00	0	0.00	0	6.08	1	2.93	226	491
Cody Anderson	6.83	3.68	9.35	17.4%	5.67	84	0.00	0	0.00	0	0.00	1	1.85	62	6.08	1	-0.13	19	4.45	26	193
Cody Stashak	1.10	1.92	3.24	1.0%	3.99	198	0.00	0	0.00	0	0.00	0	-0.62	26	0.00	0	-0.46	145	0.00	0	369
Cole Hamels	4.27	3.49	3.81	9.1%	4.51	825	4.60	286	6.08	2	4.65	464	0.34	506	0.00	0	3.90	9	3.15	296	2,394
Cole Irvin	4.78	4.38	5.83	7.2%	5.15	316	0.00	0	0.00	0	0.00	1	2.36	164	0.00	0	4.58	123	8.21	17	624
Cole Sulser	4.12	3.28	0.00	10.3%	3.66	83	0.00	0	0.00	0	0.00	0	2.26	12	0.00	0	2.73	35	0.00	0	130
Colin Poche	3.02	2.37	4.70	9.2%	2.25	740	0.00	0	0.00	0	0.00	1	0.00	0	6.08	4	6.08	5	2.97	85	836
Collin McHugh	4.56	3.76	4.70	9.5%	4.72	418	0.00	4	0.00	0	5.17	158	2.19	48	0.00	0	2.36	555	5.92	110	1,294
Colten Brewer	4.95	3.15	4.12	13.4%	2.58	40	0.00	0	0.00	0	4.80	403	0.00	3	0.00	0	2.74	121	1.82	435	1,016
Conner Menez	6.30	4.12	5.29	16.4%	4.89	194	0.00	0	0.00	0	0.00	0	1.51	45	0.00	0	2.94	53	5.33	26	319
Connor Sadzeck	5.70	3.84	2.66	14.0%	3.84	131	1.70	73	0.00	0	-0.62	1	0.00	3	0.00	0	4.67	214	0.00	1	424
Corbin Burnes	3.24	2.40	8.82	8.5%	4.44	476	5.64	29	0.00	1	0.00	4	0.84	35	0.00	0	-2.10	272	5.62	70	903
Corbin Martin	5.98	4.18	5.59	13.0%	4.68	232	0.00	0	0.00	0	6.08	1	2.39	41	0.00	0	3.85	28	3.70	70	372
Corey Kluber	4.42	3.53	5.80	8.9%	5.64	82	0.00	0	5.04	164	2.46	174	4.17	52	0.00	0	-1.57	3	1.67	136	611
Corey Oswalt	7.10	4.05	12.15	17.7%	6.09	54	0.00	1	4.87	38	0.00	0	3.33	25	0.00	0	0.00	4	-2.80	15	139
Cory Gearrin	5.13	4.09	4.07	10.4%	5.57	41	0.00	1	4.30	354	0.00	0	3.46	136	0.00	0	3.96	362	9.10	1	916
Craig Kimbrel	4.50	2.88	6.53	12.5%	3.89	251	0.00	0	0.00	0	0.00	0	0.00	0	0.00	0	0.00	0	0.88	126	392
Craig Stammen	3.85	4.03	3.29	4.4%	0.00	0	6.82	3	4.54	857	0.00	0	6.08	1	0.00	0	3.84	193	1.22	148	1,224
Cy Sneed	3.74	3.68	5.48	5.4%	4.04	223	-0.62	3	0.00	0	3.21	16	2.77	40	0.00	0	4.63	47	-0.79	15	344
D.J. Johnson	5.49	3.07	5.04	16.4%	4.70	309	0.00	0	0.00	0	0.00	0	0.00	2	0.00	1	0.00	0	0.29	177	489
Dakota Hudson	4.71	3.49	3.35	11.4%	4.01	368	0.00	0	4.14	1,390	0.00	0	1.55	70	0.00	0	1.48	713	5.07	304	2,848
Dallas Keuchel	4.01	3.45	3.75	8.0%	4.29	90	3.38	914	0.00	0	4.82	373	1.94	272	0.00	0	2.88	214	9.94	1	1,864
Dan Altavilla	6.22	3.54	5.58	18.8%	4.98	166	0.00	0	0.00	0	0.00	0	0.00	0	0.00	0	1.45	114	0.00	0	294
Dan Jennings	9.14	3.39	13.50	21.9%	0.00	5	4.58	64	0.00	0	0.00	0	0.00	0	0.00	0	2.21	50	0.00	0	134
Dan Otero	3.87	4.42	4.85	2.3%	4.68	49	0.00	0	5.06	225	0.00	0	3.68	75	6.08	1	2.63	58	0.00	0	416

Pitcher	pERA	pERA (Just Pitchers)	ERA	BB%	pERA FF	FF Count	pERA FT	FT Count	pERA SI	SI Count	pERA FC	FC Count	pERA CH	CH Count	pERA FS	FS Count	pERA SL	SL Count	pERA CU	CU Count	Count
Dan Straily	5.82	4.74	9.82	9.3%	5.14	442	3.66	19	0.00	0	0.00	0	3.61	219	0.00	0	5.08	179	5.65	32	966
Dan Winkler	4.38	3.09	4.98	11.8%	4.35	113	-0.07	17	0.00	0	2.60	145	0.00	0	0.00	0	0.00	0	2.87	76	351
Daniel Hudson	4.81	4.15	2.47	8.9%	4.53	752	3.91	111	0.00	1	6.08	1	4.11	72	0.00	0	3.23	280	0.00	0	1,217
Daniel Mengden	6.17	5.14	4.83	10.4%	5.87	359	5.59	192	0.00	0	4.49	148	4.95	116	0.00	0	4.36	130	3.86	103	1,048
Daniel Norris	4.24	4.06	4.49	6.2%	5.48	1,047	4.80	161	0.00	0	6.88	5	1.02	450	0.00	0	3.00	538	6.09	155	2,361
Daniel Ponce de Leon	4.79	3.38	3.70	12.8%	3.31	548	0.00	0	0.00	0	4.01	102	3.91	57	0.00	0	0.00	0	2.55	63	771
Daniel Stumpf	5.50	4.17	4.34	11.1%	4.89	271	0.00	0	0.00	0	0.00	0	4.44	47	0.00	0	3.09	193	0.00	0	522
Daniel Zamora	5.66	4.07	5.19	12.2%	4.87	38	0.00	0	0.00	0	0.00	0	0.00	2	6.08	1	3.81	94	0.00	0	165
Danny Duffy	4.54	3.95	4.34	8.3%	4.82	946	5.49	205	0.00	0	-5.39	2	2.63	249	0.00	0	3.18	563	2.16	196	2,161
Dario Agrazal	5.05	4.94	4.91	5.6%	5.43	141	6.08	1	5.74	628	0.00	0	3.95	161	0.00	0	3.07	218	0.00	0	1,149
Darwinzon Hernandez	5.80	2.95	4.45	17.7%	2.72	506	0.00	0	0.00	0	0.00	0	0.00	1	0.00	0	3.88	161	0.00	11	681
David Bednar	4.24	3.19	6.55	4.8%	4.70	83	0.00	0	0.00	0	0.00	2	0.00	0	1.46	67	0.00	0	3.12	44	196
David Hale	4.07	4.23	3.11	4.5%	5.45	202	4.48	158	0.00	0	0.00	0	3.31	129	0.00	0	0.00	0	2.71	110	602
David Hernandez	4.00	2.89	8.02	10.1%	3.15	194	5.17	203	0.00	0	2.26	24	-1.57	6	6.08	1	1.51	232	1.41	104	787
David Hess	5.28	4.59	7.09	8.2%	5.24	760	5.28	86	0.00	0	6.08	1	4.92	165	0.00	0	2.91	353	4.33	63	1,430
David McKay	6.29	4.38	5.47	14.8%	0.00	7	6.08	1	4.67	285	0.00	0	6.82	8	0.00	0	0.00	2	4.01	170	473
David Phelps	5.80	4.57	3.41	11.6%	5.22	139	5.21	115	0.00	0	4.69	202	0.00	3	0.00	0	0.34	4	3.68	177	640
David Price	4.11	3.77	4.28	7.0%	3.97	501	5.39	501	0.00	0	3.77	321	2.08	485	0.00	0	4.01	9	1.70	44	1,862
David Robertson	6.65	3.60	5.40	18.2%	-0.62	6	0.00	1	0.00	0	5.44	71	0.00	0	0.00	0	2.26	28	1.48	30	136
Dennis Santana	5.62	3.02	7.20	14.8%	0.00	0	3.75	59	0.00	0	0.00	0	1.67	15	0.00	0	2.26	30	0.00	0	104
Dereck Rodriguez	4.93	4.30	5.64	8.2%	5.24	649	4.09	139	0.00	0	3.63	225	3.71	333	0.00	0	6.08	2	3.42	274	1,625
Derek Holland	5.16	3.76	6.08	12.0%	6.08	2	-0.62	1	4.72	910	6.08	1	4.80	62	6.08	1	1.77	423	2.40	73	1,487
Derek Law	5.37	3.41	4.90	14.0%	5.34	431	0.00	0	0.00	0	0.00	0	1.60	153	0.00	0	1.65	366	3.80	221	1,174
Devin Smeltzer	4.20	4.10	3.86	5.9%	5.13	338	0.00	0	0.00	0	6.08	1	2.92	186	0.00	0	6.61	28	2.98	179	732
Devin Williams	4.95	3.98	3.95	9.0%	4.38	83	6.22	77	0.00	0	0.00	1	2.10	91	0.00	0	2.26	18	0.00	1	270
Diego Castillo	3.36	2.65	3.41	9.0%	4.58	46	0.00	0	3.64	487	1.55	233	6.08	1	0.00	0	1.72	335	0.00	1	1,106
Dillon Maples	4.28	1.42	5.40	18.5%	3.35	79	0.00	0	0.00	0	0.00	0	0.00	0	0.00	0	0.78	141	-2.22	17	237
Dillon Peters	4.82	4.20	5.38	8.0%	5.31	585	3.99	58	0.00	0	0.00	0	1.98	286	0.00	0	1.06	30	4.49	315	1,274
Dillon Tate	4.09	3.16	6.43	9.7%	0.00	7	0.00	0	3.31	190	0.00	0	2.03	68	0.00	0	4.48	33	3.66	52	350
Dinelson Lamet	3.96	3.11	4.07	9.6%	4.89	454	5.10	225	0.00	0	0.00	0	-0.42	12	0.00	0	0.64	208	1.02	332	1,233
Domingo German	3.60	3.38	4.03	6.6%	4.77	766	4.96	240	6.08	2	0.00	0	3.31	427	0.00	1	0.00	5	1.63	804	2,247
Dominic Leone	4.43	2.99	5.53	12.2%	3.80	235	5.48	77	0.00	0	2.11	239	6.08	2	0.00	0	1.02	90	0.00	0	682
Donnie Hart	2.38	1.03	0.00	13.8%	0.00	0	0.00	0	0.70	63	0.00	0	-0.03	15	0.00	0	2.09	25	11.18	1	104
Dovydas Neverauskas	5.85	3.48	10.61	13.2%	3.76	119	0.00	0	0.00	0	3.36	40	0.00	2	0.00	0	-0.62	5	3.44	46	212
Drew Anderson	6.19	2.69	7.50	20.0%	3.32	53	6.82	13	0.00	0	0.00	0	0.16	3	-0.62	1	-3.75	7	1.54	27	104
Drew Gagnon	3.96	3.63	8.37	6.0%	4.97	218	0.00	0	0.00	0	0.00	0	0.91	127	0.00	0	3.78	20	5.07	36	414
Drew Pomeranz	3.83	2.93	4.85	9.7%	3.50	1,018	4.70	147	0.00	0	5.69	81	4.26	22	0.00	0	6.08	3	1.03	581	1,857
Drew Smyly	5.15	3.98	6.24	10.7%	4.86	1,020	0.00	0	0.00	0	4.09	431	3.74	49	0.00	0	5.08	23	2.39	604	2,130
Drew Steckenrider	4.66	4.09	6.28	8.6%	5.06	143	0.00	0	0.00	0	0.00	0	0.00	0	0.00	0	6.08	1	2.43	85	237
Drew VerHagen	4.73	3.95	5.90	8.9%	4.90	110	4.70	389	0.00	0	0.00	0	0.34	4	0.00	0	2.12	288	4.87	154	945
Duane Underwood Jr.	2.81	2.65	5.40	5.9%	4.82	118	0.34	8	0.00	0	0.00	0	1.67	52	0.00	0	0.00	0	-2.98	33	211
Dustin May	3.87	4.22	3.63	3.6%	4.07	37	0.00	0	4.67	287	2.73	175	6.08	7	0.00	0	0.00	0	6.26	60	566
Dylan Bundy	3.93	3.31	4.79	8.3%	4.85	1,173	4.71	211	0.00	0	-0.62	1	1.82	483	0.00	0	0.99	632	3.67	277	2,778
Dylan Cease	4.66	3.51	5.79	10.7%	4.03	662	3.10	41	0.00	0	0.00	0	3.14	122	0.00	0	2.97	287	2.99	252	1,364
Dylan Covey	5.93	4.79	7.98	10.0%	4.56	126	5.48	362	6.08	1	4.96	133	2.01	185	0.00	0	5.73	111	6.38	101	1,019
Dylan Floro	3.50	3.15	4.24	7.0%	3.66	137	6.08	1	3.08	330	-0.10	9	5.69	27	0.00	0	2.70	203	0.00	0	721
Edgar Garcia	5.52	3.52	5.77	15.1%	6.15	312	1.90	45	0.00	0	6.08	1	0.00	9	0.00	0	1.45	346	0.00	0	713
Edinson Volquez	6.66	4.29	6.75	16.0%	0.00	1	6.08	1	5.66	140	0.00	0	3.79	109	0.00	0	0.00	0	1.35	46	297
Eduardo Jimenez	5.62	4.51	5.91	10.2%	4.90	78	4.50	29	0.00	0	0.00	0	6.08	11	0.00	0	3.85	71	0.00	0	189
Eduardo Rodriguez	4.11	3.45	3.81	8.7%	3.86	1,275	3.96	555	6.08	2	4.46	590	1.40	787	0.00	0	4.91	65	4.78	91	3,384
Edubray Ramos	5.48	4.38	5.40	10.1%	4.03	100	0.00	2	0.00	0	0.00	0	3.51	23	0.00	0	4.81	149	0.00	0	276
Edwin Diaz	2.74	2.03	5.59	8.7%	2.67	702	-0.62	5	0.00	0	-0.62	1	1.00	0	0.00	0	0.83	361	0.00	0	1,073
Edwin Jackson	5.13	4.00	9.58	9.5%	5.81	316	3.49	169	0.00	0	3.86	358	6.38	98	0.00	0	1.72	338	6.79	36	1,315
Elieser Hernandez	4.25	3.83	5.03	7.4%	4.53	785	4.98	14	0.00	0	0.00	0	4.92	162	0.00	0	2.30	480	0.00	1	1,442
Elvis Luciano	6.22	4.01	5.35	15.1%	5.21	340	0.00	0	6.08	1	6.08	1	2.42	108	0.00	0	2.55	163	0.00	0	635
Emilio Pagan	2.06	2.23	2.31	4.9%	2.13	654	0.00	1	0.00	1	2.46	47	0.00	0	0.00	0	2.23	344	6.11	14	1,061
Emmanuel Clase	3.54	3.38	2.31	6.4%	4.14	14	0.00	0	4.44	14	0.00	0	3.33	258	0.00	0	3.37	73	0.00	0	345
Enyel De Los Santos	4.10	3.05	7.36	10.9%	3.65	100	-0.62	1	0.00	0	6.08	1	3.90	36	0.00	0	1.93	16	-0.21	22	176
Eric Lauer	4.98	4.45	4.45	7.8%	4.59	1,260	6.08	1	0.00	0	4.09	371	4.23	88	0.00	0	4.37	323	4.45	352	2,510
Eric Skoglund	6.22	5.29	9.00	8.9%	5.32	153	5.45	81	0.00	0	0.00	0	5.35	69	0.00	0	0.00	0	5.07	92	395
Eric Yardley	3.19	3.03	2.31	5.8%	0.00	1	0.00	0	2.59	121	0.00	0	0.00	0	0.00	0	0.00	0	3.99	59	181
Erick Fedde	5.36	4.46	4.50	9.9%	5.15	185	6.08	1	5.42	501	3.61	224	0.00	0	3.79	91	3.21	24	2.94	217	1,287
Erik Swanson	4.12	4.19	5.74	4.9%	4.07	661	0.00	1	0.00	0	6.08	1	5.01	149	0.00	0	3.95	158	0.00	0	971
Ervin Santana	6.29	5.26	9.45	9.4%	6.25	110	4.80	18	0.00	0	0.00	0	6.08	12	0.00	0	4.26	110	0.00	0	250
Evan Marshall	4.19	3.06	2.49	11.5%	5.71	174	5.06	168	2.03	26	6.08	1	1.31	324	0.00	0	3.66	95	-2.63	46	834
Evan Phillips	5.79	3.57	6.43	14.3%	3.65	344	-0.42	24	0.00	0	0.00	0	3.88	43	0.00	0	4.05	146	0.00	0	567
Felipe Vazquez	2.85	2.88	1.65	5.5%	3.62	563	-0.36	9	0.00	0	6.08	2	0.74	73	0.00	0	1.66	164	2.55	127	946
Felix Hernandez	4.45	3.88	6.40	7.7%	6.02	87	6.08	1	5.30	386	4.81	18	3.49	202	0.00	0	2.21	90	2.66	427	1,216
Felix Pena	3.94	3.35	4.58	8.4%	4.28	72	5.38	699	6.08	1	0.00	0	3.21	173	0.00	0	0.97	619	8.87	2	1,570
Fernando Abad	3.24	3.20	4.15	6.1%	0.00	3	3.52	96	0.00	0	0.00	0	3.62	24	0.00	0	0.00	0	2.54	48	171
Fernando Rodney	5.15	3.51	5.66	13.3%	4.62	177	4.50	399	6.08	1	0.00	0	1.01	243	0.00	0	3.89	26	0.00	0	881
Fernando Romero	5.90	3.36	7.07	15.3%	4.85	66	4.81	127	0.00	0	0.00	0	0.00	5	0.00	0	0.05	80	0.00	0	278
Framber Valdez	4.90	3.10	5.86	13.4%	5.15	214	3.64	510	0.00	0	0.00	0	1.21	49	0.00	0	6.08	2	1.53	400	1,175
Francisco Liriano	4.12	2.87	3.47	11.6%	4.79	84	5.17	408	0.00	0	0.00	0	0.91	263	6.08	1	1.07	326	0.00	0	1,110
Frankie Montas	3.57	3.50	2.63	5.8%	4.67	279	4.89	563	6.08	2	6.08	2	0.00	0	0.97	268	2.29	370	0.00	0	1,485
Freddy Peralta	4.24	3.28	5.29	9.7%	4.26	1,255	6.08	1	0.00	0	6.08	1	3.64	24	0.00	0	6.08	1	3.36	317	1,599
Gabe Speier	6.70	4.02	7.36	18.2%	4.93	80	3.02	15	0.00	0	0.00	0	0.00	2	0.00	0	3.14	56	0.00	0	153

Pitcher	pERA	pERA (Just Pitchers)	ERA	BB%	pERA FF	FF Count	pERA FT	FT Count	pERA SI	SI Count	pERA FC	FC Count	pERA CH	CH Count	pERA FS	FS Count	pERA SL	SL Count	pERA CU	CU Count	Count
Gabriel Ynoa	4.22	4.17	5.61	5.4%	5.11	562	3.53	18	4.59	400	0.00	0	4.57	241	0.00	0	2.73	532	0.00	5	1,815
Garrett Richards	6.13	4.02	8.31	14.6%	4.64	64	6.71	28	0.00	0	0.00	0	0.00	0	0.00	0	1.81	46	3.30	19	157
Genesis Cabrera	5.84	4.40	4.87	11.1%	5.08	221	-0.62	10	0.00	0	0.00	0	3.09	61	0.00	0	4.79	71	-0.84	9	372
Geoff Hartlieb	4.90	3.59	9.00	10.5%	4.22	260	-0.38	10	3.74	184	0.00	0	3.58	59	0.00	0	2.49	136	0.00	1	651
Gerardo Reyes	3.48	2.57	7.62	9.4%	3.16	257	0.00	0	3.03	77	6.08	1	0.00	0	0.00	0	1.18	107	-2.55	8	451
German Marquez	3.08	3.17	4.76	4.9%	4.79	941	4.71	434	0.00	0	2.45	6	6.06	78	0.00	0	1.76	598	0.37	558	2,616
Gerrit Cole	2.15	2.14	2.50	5.9%	2.56	1,623	4.13	82	6.08	2	6.08	2	2.09	234	6.08	1	1.16	739	1.85	480	3,268
Gerson Bautista	7.73	4.23	11.00	18.4%	5.01	125	0.00	0	0.00	0	0.00	0	0.00	3	0.00	0	3.00	69	0.00	0	197
Gio Gonzalez	4.68	3.78	3.50	10.1%	4.46	375	5.75	345	6.08	2	0.00	0	2.21	442	0.00	0	6.08	1	2.70	232	1,501
Giovanny Gallegos	2.55	2.58	2.31	5.7%	4.27	625	6.08	1	0.00	0	0.00	0	1.13	15	0.00	0	0.48	492	0.00	1	1,141
Glenn Sparkman	5.10	4.74	6.02	6.8%	5.19	1,376	0.00	0	-0.62	1	6.08	2	5.26	293	0.00	0	2.61	192	3.86	408	2,275
Grant Dayton	3.76	3.26	3.00	7.8%	3.18	136	0.00	0	0.00	0	6.08	1	0.00	0	0.00	0	1.49	20	4.17	47	204
Greg Holland	5.49	3.46	4.54	15.8%	5.33	283	0.00	0	0.00	0	0.00	0	0.00	0	0.00	0	1.12	260	4.87	55	599
Gregory Soto	5.85	4.27	5.77	12.0%	4.71	84	5.49	37	4.91	653	0.00	0	5.29	58	0.00	0	2.24	265	0.00	5	1,110
Griffin Canning	3.51	3.02	4.58	7.8%	4.56	662	6.08	1	0.00	0	6.08	2	2.96	190	0.00	0	1.14	450	2.31	247	1,552
Hansel Robles	3.45	3.45	2.48	5.7%	4.06	559	3.95	89	0.00	0	0.34	4	1.18	241	0.00	0	4.18	246	0.00	0	1,159
Harrison Musgrave	6.43	4.28	3.60	14.9%	4.84	52	0.00	0	4.58	56	0.00	0	2.77	19	0.00	0	4.05	78	0.00	0	205
Heath Fillmyer	6.05	4.63	8.06	11.0%	5.02	216	3.21	24	0.00	0	0.00	0	3.01	81	0.00	0	3.97	87	7.78	44	453
Heath Hembree	4.90	3.86	3.86	10.4%	4.47	490	0.00	0	0.00	0	0.00	0	0.00	0	0.00	0	1.65	116	3.36	91	718
Hector Neris	2.72	2.13	2.93	8.7%	3.89	285	4.40	92	0.00	0	0.00	0	0.00	1	1.12	713	6.08	2	0.00	0	1,126
Hector Noesi	4.76	3.48	8.46	11.3%	1.16	14	4.27	199	0.00	0	0.00	0	2.98	49	0.00	0	4.50	152	0.43	83	497
Hector Rondon	4.26	3.78	3.71	7.8%	4.10	445	3.48	141	0.00	0	0.00	0	4.40	41	0.00	0	3.40	343	9.28	1	994
Hector Santiago	5.88	3.94	6.68	13.5%	3.39	348	0.00	0	4.17	76	0.00	1	4.98	138	0.00	0	4.16	117	4.10	32	715
Hector Velazquez	5.41	4.17	5.43	11.4%	3.77	245	0.00	1	5.39	272	-0.62	1	3.82	266	0.00	0	3.31	174	5.12	19	981
Homer Bailey	4.48	4.02	4.57	7.6%	5.19	1,289	5.46	55	0.00	0	0.16	3	0.00	4	1.36	674	3.48	406	5.96	231	2,836
Hunter Harvey	4.23	2.39	1.42	15.4%	3.58	94	0.00	0	0.00	0	0.00	0	-0.41	23	0.00	0	0.00	0	0.00	20	137
Hunter Strickland	4.42	3.95	5.55	7.6%	4.34	220	3.50	23	0.00	0	0.00	0	3.02	15	0.00	0	3.38	111	0.00	0	391
Hunter Wood	3.62	3.43	2.98	6.2%	4.60	418	0.00	1	6.08	2	6.08	2	3.17	85	0.00	0	1.78	204	-0.24	38	752
Hyun-Jin Ryu	2.98	3.39	2.32	3.3%	4.57	746	4.62	354	0.00	0	3.62	527	1.77	743	0.00	0	0.98	9	2.70	326	2,706
Ian Gibaut	5.77	3.63	5.65	15.6%	4.71	152	0.00	0	0.00	0	0.00	0	3.78	60	0.00	0	0.59	57	0.00	0	269
Ian Kennedy	3.99	3.78	3.41	6.4%	4.22	730	6.08	2	0.00	1	3.52	152	3.66	19	0.00	0	-0.62	11	2.37	162	1,096
Ivan Nova	4.62	4.49	4.72	5.8%	5.60	518	4.74	1,107	-0.62	1	2.56	389	3.33	478	-0.62	1	6.08	1	5.43	503	3,005
J. D. Hammer	6.10	4.26	3.79	14.8%	4.68	172	0.00	2	0.00	0	0.00	0	0.00	0	0.00	0	3.83	148	0.00	0	322
J.A. Happ	4.23	3.86	4.91	7.2%	4.03	1,297	3.38	480	0.00	0	1.64	10	3.16	401	0.00	0	4.43	476	5.80	22	2,696
J.B. Wendelken	3.89	3.65	3.58	6.9%	3.54	270	5.27	15	0.00	0	0.00	0	1.80	82	0.00	0	4.44	14	5.28	91	501
Jace Fry	5.47	2.95	4.75	17.1%	3.92	122	3.15	127	-0.62	1	1.25	521	3.53	81	0.00	0	-0.62	4	6.59	195	1,054
Jack Flaherty	3.28	3.02	2.75	7.1%	4.28	1,474	3.45	390	0.00	0	6.08	1	4.91	55	0.00	0	0.73	875	2.66	384	3,179
Jacob Barnes	6.12	4.09	7.44	13.8%	5.22	283	0.00	0	0.00	0	3.22	374	6.08	1	0.00	0	6.08	3	0.00	0	661
Jacob deGrom	2.64	2.67	2.43	5.5%	3.59	1,529	5.73	47	0.00	0	-10.31	7	1.17	498	0.00	0	1.89	1,005	3.43	90	3,297
Jacob Rhame	8.22	2.83	4.26	30.0%	4.76	75	-0.36	9	0.00	0	6.08	1	-0.62	23	-0.26	13	0.00	0			121
Jacob Waguespack	4.79	4.11	4.38	8.7%	3.21	435	5.32	215	0.00	0	4.13	315	2.60	96	0.00	0	5.17	101	5.10	171	1,333
Jacob Webb	3.88	3.21	1.39	9.2%	4.89	283	0.00	1	0.00	0	0.00	0	0.22	63	0.00	0	2.92	70	0.73	107	536
Jaime Barria	4.83	4.36	6.42	7.4%	5.43	442	5.87	104	0.00	0	6.08	5	3.36	244	0.00	0	3.78	701	8.46	2	1,498
Jairo Diaz	3.42	2.94	4.53	7.8%	5.40	206	4.48	294	0.00	0	0.00	0	0.00	0	0.00	0	0.46	388	0.00	0	888
Jake Arrieta	5.07	4.38	4.64	8.6%	4.16	19	0.26	4	4.95	1,162	0.00	1	2.69	384	0.00	0	3.97	248	4.79	289	2,107
Jake Diekman	4.44	2.61	4.65	13.8%	3.61	312	0.00	1	3.24	304	6.08	1	0.00	3	0.00	0	1.70	541	0.00	1	1,166
Jake Faria	5.42	3.53	6.75	12.6%	5.00	248	0.00	0	0.00	0	0.00	0	0.00	0	0.72	111	2.46	47	0.00	1	408
Jake Jewell	2.95	2.59	6.84	7.0%	4.24	156	2.49	50	0.00	0	-0.62	1	0.43	61	0.00	0	1.81	139	0.00	4	412
Jake McGee	4.77	4.57	4.35	6.1%	5.02	517	0.00	1	6.08	1	6.08	1	0.00	0	0.00	0	2.75	128	0.00	0	647
Jake Newberry	4.91	3.59	3.77	11.7%	5.25	282	0.00	1	0.00	0	6.08	1	1.78	16	0.00	0	1.74	238	0.00	0	539
Jake Odorizzi	3.92	3.42	3.51	8.1%	3.02	1,608	6.08	1	0.00	0	4.42	486	6.08	2	2.99	472	1.67	26	5.60	182	2,787
Jake Petricka	5.95	3.58	3.38	16.7%	-0.62	1	4.13	76	6.08	1	0.00	0	4.50	29	0.00	0	-2.54	11	0.00	0	118
Jakob Junis	4.58	4.09	5.24	7.5%	5.10	997	6.08	1	4.58	483	6.90	7	3.96	156	0.00	0	2.34	870	4.75	408	2,926
Jalen Beeks	4.60	3.87	4.31	8.6%	4.67	792	0.00	0	0.00	1	2.53	109	3.13	569	0.00	0	6.08	3	3.67	345	1,821
James Hoyt	1.39	1.31	2.16	6.3%	-0.62	8	4.26	41	0.00	0	0.00	0	2.86	19	0.00	0	-1.15	55	0.00	0	123
James Marvel	3.98	3.42	8.31	7.1%	4.21	69	0.00	0	4.98	109	0.00	0	1.77	66	0.00	0	0.00	0	2.09	87	331
James Norwood	6.10	3.24	2.89	18.2%	5.10	118	0.00	14	0.00	0	0.00	0	0.00	0	2.00	32	0.05	42	0.00	0	206
James Paxton	3.74	3.09	3.82	8.7%	3.89	1,586	0.00	0	0.00	0	1.50	532	2.06	31	0.00	0	-1.18	6	2.37	493	2,665
James Pazos	3.52	2.77	1.74	10.3%	0.00	0	0.00	0	3.18	102	0.00	0	0.00	0	0.00	0	1.89	47	0.00	0	149
Jameson Taillon	3.44	3.48	4.10	5.1%	3.79	152	3.99	108	0.00	0	0.00	1	4.24	30	0.00	0	2.78	175	3.46	87	555
Jandel Gustave	4.89	4.23	2.96	9.1%	4.01	180	3.89	70	0.00	0	0.00	0	0.00	0	0.00	0	4.87	99	0.00	0	349
Jared Hughes	4.19	3.49	4.04	9.3%	5.42	71	0.00	0	3.36	800	0.00	0	2.33	100	-0.62	4	4.41	73	4.04	55	1,143
Jarlin Garcia	4.38	3.96	3.02	7.8%	5.35	294	6.08	1	0.00	0	0.00	0	2.64	129	0.00	0	3.21	321	0.00	0	747
Jason Adam	5.19	4.11	2.91	11.0%	3.05	243	0.00	0	0.00	0	0.00	0	4.08	46	0.00	0	0.00	0	6.54	107	397
Jason Vargas	5.07	4.18	4.51	9.7%	5.60	630	6.17	584	0.00	0	-0.62	1	2.21	898	0.00	0	6.90	8	3.37	379	2,505
Javier Guerra	4.73	4.17	5.19	8.3%	5.07	44	3.42	59	0.00	0	0.00	0	0.00	0	0.00	0	4.33	31	0.00	0	134
Javy Guerra	4.55	4.42	4.66	5.9%	5.03	618	0.00	0	0.00	0	6.08	4	1.87	96	0.00	0	3.63	270	5.52	72	1,060
Jay Jackson	3.83	2.16	4.45	13.6%	3.83	222	0.00	0	0.00	0	0.00	0	0.00	3	0.00	0	1.08	335	0.00	0	560
JC Ramirez	2.84	3.28	4.50	2.9%	2.77	57	0.00	0	0.00	0	0.00	0	0.00	0	0.00	0	4.73	17	3.42	33	107
Jeanmar Gomez	5.15	4.39	8.22	8.2%	6.08	2	0.00	0	4.52	110	0.00	0	3.32	47	0.00	0	4.73	48	6.30	8	270
Jeff Brigham	4.58	3.94	4.46	8.7%	3.37	354	0.00	0	4.58	1	0.00	0	0.00	0	0.00	0	-3.10	15	4.89	319	690
Jeff Hoffman	5.41	4.22	6.56	10.8%	5.02	737	0.00	0	6.08	1	0.00	0	2.97	141	0.00	0	-0.47	16	3.28	361	1,256
Jeff Samardzija	4.65	4.43	3.52	6.6%	4.78	847	4.59	580	0.00	0	4.74	731	0.00	0	2.04	179	3.72	593	7.62	73	3,006
Jeffrey Springs	5.82	3.62	6.40	14.8%	0.00	0	0.00	0	4.80	357	6.08	1	0.77	191	0.00	0	5.40	69	0.00	0	665
Jefry Rodriguez	5.23	4.21	4.63	10.3%	4.90	226	4.26	304	0.00	0	0.00	0	4.51	71	0.00	0	0.00	0	3.15	182	784
Jerad Eickhoff	4.25	3.87	5.71	7.4%	5.67	379	6.08	1	0.00	0	0.00	0	0.00	1	0.00	0	2.59	286	2.83	307	975
Jeremy Hellickson	6.35	5.04	6.23	10.9%	5.96	214	4.64	47	6.92	24	5.59	120	3.84	179	0.00	0	6.08	1	4.23	90	675

319

Pitcher	pERA	pERA (Just Pitchers)	ERA	BB%	pERA FF	FF Count	pERA FT	FT Count	pERA SI	SI Count	pERA FC	FC Count	pERA CH	CH Count	pERA FS	FS Count	pERA SL	SL Count	pERA CU	CU Count	Count
Jeremy Jeffress	4.18	3.70	5.02	7.6%	3.91	243	4.10	266	0.00	0	0.00	0	0.00	0	3.37	91	6.08	3	3.14	234	855
Jeremy Walker	4.77	3.84	1.93	10.5%	0.16	6	0.00	0	3.88	98	0.00	0	0.00	1	0.00	0	0.00	0	4.21	59	164
Jerry Blevins	5.01	3.78	3.90	11.4%	6.13	236	0.00	0	0.00	0	0.00	0	3.57	47	0.00	0	6.08	1	1.79	274	558
Jesse Biddle	6.79	4.26	8.36	14.5%	5.00	328	0.00	0	0.00	0	0.00	0	0.00	0	0.00	1	3.19	121	3.57	149	617
Jesse Chavez	5.20	4.93	4.85	6.5%	4.78	90	5.80	469	0.00	0	4.74	392	3.42	122	0.00	0	4.13	170	0.00	1	1,248
Jesse Hahn	7.51	2.72	13.50	22.2%	0.00	4	3.80	63	0.00	0	0.00	0	0.00	5	0.00	0	1.49	35	0.00	0	107
Jesus Luzardo	2.77	2.64	1.50	6.5%	3.02	30	5.65	53	0.00	0	0.00	0	1.59	35	0.00	0	-0.05	37	0.50	16	171
Jesus Tinoco	6.00	4.25	4.75	13.7%	5.03	89	3.99	30	0.00	0	-0.48	7	0.00	0	3.26	187	4.03	31	616		
Jeurys Familia	5.71	3.56	5.70	15.3%	5.36	169	0.00	0	1	4.32	521	0.00	0	0.00	1	0.83	71	1.77	276	0.00	0	1,041
Jhoulys Chacin	5.57	4.56	6.01	9.8%	5.18	250	5.12	617	6.08	1	-5.39	2	5.30	57	3.41	44	4.04	962	7.63	11	1,945
Jimmie Sherfy	4.18	3.95	5.89	6.0%	5.95	114	0.00	0	0.00	0	0.00	0	4.37	21	0.00	0	2.15	159	6.21	22	316
Jimmy Cordero	2.49	2.17	2.89	7.5%	4.78	102	0.00	0	2.01	270	2.59	37	-0.83	94	0.00	0	3.26	39	0.00	0	542
Jimmy Nelson	6.19	3.72	6.95	16.2%	4.56	112	0.00	0	6.08	95	0.00	0	0.00	5	0.00	0	1.49	77	2.61	117	408
Jimmy Yacabonis	6.11	4.47	6.80	12.4%	4.98	43	4.96	422	0.00	0	6.08	3	2.74	50	6.08	1	3.77	215	8.40	1	739
Joakim Soria	3.63	3.32	4.30	7.2%	3.51	718	3.09	23	0.00	0	0.00	0	2.17	73	0.00	0	3.80	138	2.47	130	1,100
Joe Biagini	4.35	3.54	4.59	9.3%	5.10	169	4.46	410	0.00	0	1.53	342	2.24	118	0.00	0	0.34	4	5.69	99	1,142
Joe Harvey	5.72	3.47	5.00	15.5%	4.27	259	0.00	0	-0.47	16	0.00	0	-0.62	6	0.00	0	1.99	80	0.00	0	361
Joe Jimenez	3.73	2.99	4.37	9.0%	3.32	712	0.00	0	0.00	0	0.00	0	2.93	60	0.00	0	2.14	269	0.00	0	1,056
Joe Kelly	3.99	3.06	4.56	9.7%	5.09	234	3.60	195	-0.62	1	0.00	0	2.47	106	0.00	0	0.43	45	1.53	260	872
Joe Musgrove	3.53	3.50	4.44	5.4%	5.16	978	0.00	0	3.96	341	4.26	228	1.83	276	0.00	0	1.67	587	1.77	247	2,657
Joe Ross	5.11	3.79	5.48	11.2%	4.12	282	-0.62	1	4.50	436	6.08	1	3.75	83	0.00	0	2.48	252	2.94	83	1,138
Joe Smith	3.60	3.70	1.80	5.2%	4.02	54	0.00	0	3.29	147	0.00	0	0.00	2	0.00	0	4.05	141	0.00	0	344
Joel Kuhnel	3.53	2.20	4.66	11.9%	2.12	60	3.48	47	0.00	0	0.00	0	0.00	5	0.00	0	1.38	54	0.00	0	166
Joey Lucchesi	4.30	3.76	4.18	8.2%	5.99	40	0.00	1	4.45	1,350	4.43	320	2.81	657	0.00	0	1.49	5	1.56	269	2,643
John Brebbia	4.06	3.39	3.59	8.9%	3.46	684	0.00	0	0.00	2	0.55	2	6.08	8	0.00	0	3.27	516	0.00	0	1,217
John Gant	4.54	3.23	3.66	12.6%	4.06	266	4.29	347	0.00	0	2.68	99	0.47	244	0.00	0	3.21	16	4.54	110	1,105
John Means	4.42	4.32	3.60	6.0%	5.10	1,364	0.00	0	0.00	0	0.00	1	3.35	769	0.00	0	3.36	385	4.65	162	2,681
John Schreiber	3.98	3.59	6.23	6.8%	3.37	134	3.77	21	0.00	0	0.00	0	6.08	16	0.00	0	0.00	0	3.42	80	251
Johnny Cueto	5.45	3.92	5.06	13.4%	5.38	85	2.01	51	0.00	0	0.00	0	2.75	51	0.00	0	5.03	72	-3.96	6	265
Jon Duplantier	5.49	4.28	4.42	11.0%	4.19	194	5.33	204	0.00	0	0.00	0	4.57	60	0.00	0	4.12	132	1.99	85	677
Jon Edwards	5.81	3.43	2.25	16.7%	4.00	72	0.00	0	0.00	0	0.00	0	0.00	0	0.00	0	2.12	58	6.35	12	143
Jon Gray	4.04	3.36	3.84	8.8%	4.53	1,185	2.55	13	6.08	1	6.08	2	4.39	65	0.00	0	1.16	757	4.19	255	2,290
Jon Lester	4.72	4.35	4.46	6.8%	5.38	800	0.00	0	3.86	291	4.40	990	3.28	332	0.00	0	1.49	5	3.54	430	2,929
Jonathan Hernandez	5.85	3.34	4.32	16.7%	6.08	8	0.00	0	4.74	153	0.00	0	2.96	53	0.00	0	1.52	118	0.00	0	332
Jonathan Holder	3.69	3.50	6.31	6.1%	3.60	362	0.00	0	0.00	0	2.95	47	3.17	109	0.00	0	3.65	151	0.00	0	673
Jonathan Loaisiga	4.31	3.03	4.55	11.5%	4.17	283	4.93	50	0.00	0	0.00	0	1.69	75	0.00	0	1.83	37	1.17	146	592
Jonny Venters	8.21	3.59	12.38	20.4%	0.00	5	0.00	0	4.09	151	0.00	0	0.31	5	0.00	0	2.41	35	0.00	0	197
Jordan Hicks	3.30	2.57	3.14	10.0%	0.00	1	0.00	0	3.90	250	0.00	0	-0.46	24	0.00	0	0.75	141	0.00	0	433
Jordan Lyles	4.50	3.75	4.15	9.2%	4.40	1,189	5.31	45	0.00	0	6.08	2	3.56	244	0.00	0	3.80	234	2.64	742	2,456
Jordan Romano	4.63	2.99	7.63	12.0%	3.38	182	0.00	2	0.00	0	0.00	0	0.00	0	0.00	0	2.45	99	0.00	4	287
Jordan Yamamoto	5.45	4.39	4.46	11.1%	5.25	666	6.08	13	0.00	0	3.35	244	5.41	52	0.00	0	2.45	206	4.41	191	1,377
Jordan Zimmermann	4.18	4.17	6.91	5.0%	5.51	589	4.45	196	0.00	0	0.00	0	2.69	46	0.00	0	3.93	560	2.19	323	1,791
Jorge Lopez	4.59	4.06	6.33	7.7%	5.74	644	4.06	471	-0.62	1	6.08	1	2.80	145	0.00	0	2.22	134	3.07	654	2,060
Jose Alvarado	6.50	3.45	4.80	18.5%	0.34	8	0.00	0	4.15	455	0.39	108	0.00	0	0.00	0	6.08	1	5.89	14	586
Jose Alvarez	3.99	3.61	3.36	7.1%	4.64	141	4.17	373	0.00	0	4.26	69	1.68	214	0.00	0	3.71	106	3.70	81	984
Jose Berrios	3.99	3.85	3.68	6.1%	4.15	993	4.67	736	0.00	0	0.00	0	2.67	495	0.00	0	6.08	4	3.48	904	3,132
Jose Cisnero	4.86	3.44	4.33	11.7%	3.66	337	5.26	64	0.00	0	0.00	0	4.00	61	0.00	0	2.21	182	0.00	0	646
Jose Leclerc	4.71	3.15	4.33	13.0%	3.96	516	4.10	112	0.00	0	0.34	4	1.34	143	0.00	0	2.50	462	6.40	15	1,294
Jose Quijada	6.14	3.20	5.76	18.1%	2.66	455	0.00	0	0.00	0	0.00	0	3.66	104	0.00	0	-0.80	10	6.35	75	647
Jose Quintana	4.61	4.40	4.68	6.2%	4.81	970	0.00	0	4.51	661	6.08	4	3.70	297	0.00	0	0.34	4	4.04	716	2,826
Jose Rodriguez	5.41	3.90	2.75	13.1%	5.05	133	6.08	19	0.00	0	0.00	0	2.01	55	0.00	0	3.72	69	2.41	53	329
Jose Ruiz	5.66	3.96	5.63	12.1%	4.43	454	0.00	0	6.08	1	6.08	2	2.28	99	0.00	0	3.68	175	3.81	7	739
Jose Suarez	4.92	4.08	7.11	8.8%	5.26	700	0.00	0	0.00	0	0.00	0	2.03	458	0.00	0	3.54	47	4.60	279	1,486
Jose Urena	4.23	3.85	5.21	7.1%	2.72	13	4.73	857	0.00	1	0.00	0	3.16	135	0.00	0	2.24	274	1.55	87	1,372
Jose Urquidy	3.28	3.52	3.95	4.2%	4.99	326	6.08	1	6.08	1	0.00	0	3.21	182	0.00	0	0.72	80	1.51	103	693
Joseph Palumbo	5.01	3.85	9.18	9.9%	4.19	163	0.00	0	0.00	0	0.00	0	4.48	44	0.00	0	0.00	0	2.66	70	277
Josh A. Smith	3.83	3.67	5.81	5.8%	4.29	179	4.78	43	0.00	0	3.84	51	4.97	47	0.00	0	2.26	135	3.38	138	593
Josh D. Smith	7.38	4.47	6.39	17.2%	5.22	154	0.00	0	4.59	24	0.00	0	0.00	1	0.00	0	3.39	106	0.00	0	285
Josh Hader	1.14	0.95	2.62	6.9%	1.02	940	4.98	14	0.00	0	-1.57	3	0.00	3	0.00	0	0.40	193	0.00	0	1,181
Josh Lucas	4.65	3.64	5.74	10.1%	6.56	75	0.00	0	2.24	69	0.00	0	-0.62	3	0.00	0	2.76	126	0.00	0	273
Josh Osich	3.52	3.52	4.66	5.5%	4.93	146	5.88	34	0.00	0	3.26	692	3.61	49	0.00	0	2.64	123	0.00	0	1,044
Josh Rogers	6.07	5.19	8.7%	5.49	110	0.00	0	0.00	0	0.00	0	4.04	45	0.00	0	5.83	52	0.00	3	210		
Josh Sborz	5.12	4.12	8.00	10.0%	3.60	119	0.00	0	0.00	0	0.00	0	0.00	0	0.00	0	4.78	53	6.18	13	185
Josh Staumont	5.75	4.42	3.72	11.4%	5.40	207	-0.28	7	0.00	0	4.17	12	0.00	0	0.00	0	-0.62	1	2.78	99	326
Josh Taylor	3.13	2.61	3.04	8.3%	4.27	396	2.24	115	0.00	0	0.78	199	0.00	0	0.00	0	0.46	102	0.00	13	826
Josh Tomlin	3.86	4.46	3.74	2.2%	5.60	299	0.00	0	6.38	50	4.12	488	4.11	98	6.08	1	6.08	2	3.23	197	1,136
Joshua James	4.09	2.52	4.70	13.2%	3.21	716	0.00	0	0.00	0	0.00	0	0.86	165	0.00	0	1.81	230	0.00	21	1,142
JT Chargois	2.58	2.52	6.33	5.7%	4.88	32	6.08	1	5.61	87	0.00	0	0.00	2	0.00	0	0.51	170	0.00	0	292
Juan Minaya	4.82	3.86	3.90	9.5%	3.99	285	0.00	0	6.08	1	0.00	0	3.24	89	0.00	0	4.48	44	3.62	39	460
Juan Nicasio	5.12	4.12	4.75	9.7%	3.90	319	5.72	120	0.00	0	0.00	1	0.00	5	0.00	0	3.85	361	0.00	0	806
Julio Teheran	5.42	4.28	3.81	11.0%	4.92	1,224	4.76	654	0.00	0	6.08	1	4.05	246	0.00	0	2.85	623	3.50	177	3,036
Julio Urias	3.82	3.30	2.49	8.3%	3.66	783	4.20	29	0.00	0	0.00	2	1.42	216	0.00	0	2.99	233	5.41	81	1,344
Junior Fernandez	2.85	1.54	5.40	11.1%	0.00	0	0.00	0	4.82	91	0.00	0	0.99	69	0.00	0	-2.97	58	0.00	0	218
Junior Guerra	4.70	3.76	3.55	10.5%	4.14	406	4.42	400	-0.62	1	0.00	1	0.00	0	2.37	299	3.56	51	3.86	200	1,378
Justin Anderson	5.67	3.61	5.55	14.8%	5.07	395	6.08	24	6.08	3	6.08	1	-0.28	7	0.00	0	2.28	465	0.00	0	914
Justin Dunn	9.55	4.47	2.70	30.0%	6.24	77	0.00	0	0.00	1	0.00	0	0.00	0	0.00	0	2.87	47	0.00	1	136
Justin Miller	4.66	4.51	4.02	6.2%	4.26	183	4.17	24	0.00	0	0.00	0	6.08	7	0.00	0	5.27	53	7.42	1	275

320

Pitcher	pERA	pERA (Just Pitchers)	ERA	BB%	pERA FF	FF Count	pERA FT	FT Count	pERA SI	SI Count	pERA FC	FC Count	pERA CH	CH Count	pERA FS	FS Count	pERA SL	SL Count	pERA CU	CU Count	Count
Justin Shafer	5.51	3.68	3.86	13.7%	4.22	325	0.00	1	4.27	52	3.00	127	0.00	1	0.00	0	3.08	191	0.00	0	697
Justin Verlander	2.21	2.36	2.58	5.0%	3.14	1,613	0.00	0	0.00	0	4.59	3	2.90	137	0.00	0	0.62	930	2.81	606	3,448
Justin Wilson	4.44	3.25	2.54	11.5%	3.70	364	0.00	0	0.00	0	3.03	261	0.00	0	0.00	0	1.66	66	0.00	0	692
Justus Sheffield	4.10	2.85	5.50	10.7%	4.79	323	0.00	0	0.00	0	0.00	0	1.73	108	0.00	0	0.77	238	0.00	3	673
Kelvin Herrera	4.71	3.70	6.14	9.8%	3.90	361	4.77	128	0.00	0	2.90	116	3.18	174	0.00	0	3.45	114	0.00	0	895
Ken Giles	2.44	2.00	1.87	8.2%	4.23	393	2.93	17	0.00	0	6.08	1	0.00	0	0.00	0	-0.27	397	0.00	0	810
Kenley Jansen	2.82	2.68	3.71	6.1%	2.03	145	0.00	0	0.00	0	2.80	762	0.00	0	0.00	0	2.66	132	8.27	1	1,068
Kenta Maeda	3.31	2.82	4.04	8.2%	4.82	821	3.94	86	6.08	2	1.49	5	1.58	577	0.00	0	1.26	761	3.70	175	2,433
Keone Kela	4.42	3.75	2.12	9.2%	4.92	268	0.00	0	0.00	0	0.00	0	-0.46	15	0.00	0	6.08	1	2.60	219	504
Kevin Gausman	3.34	2.94	5.72	7.1%	4.24	933	6.08	1	6.08	1	0.00	0	0.26	4	1.05	670	3.82	60	0.00	0	1,671
Kevin Ginkel	3.77	3.11	1.48	9.4%	4.64	214	0.00	0	0.00	0	0.00	0	0.00	4	0.00	0	1.34	178	0.00	0	396
Kevin McCarthy	4.03	3.47	4.48	7.8%	3.55	137	6.08	1	3.43	495	6.08	1	2.70	195	0.00	0	3.60	32	9.07	26	901
Keynan Middleton	7.79	4.68	1.17	21.2%	5.32	82	0.00	0	0.00	0	0.00	0	2.38	31	0.00	0	5.31	30	0.00	0	143
Kirby Yates	2.50	2.54	1.19	5.4%	3.01	572	0.00	0	0.00	0	0.00	0	0.00	1	1.83	423	6.08	9	0.00	0	1,021
Kohl Stewart	4.57	4.15	6.39	7.3%	4.82	25	0.00	0	4.94	189	0.00	0	0.00	10	0.00	0	3.01	124	4.58	35	384
Kolby Allard	4.98	4.10	4.96	9.1%	4.86	390	0.00	0	0.00	0	3.83	276	4.80	126	0.00	0	0.00	0	-2.87	45	837
Kyle Barraclough	5.28	3.47	5.61	12.8%	4.51	454	0.00	0	0.00	0	0.00	0	2.11	89	0.00	0	1.60	109	-0.10	41	708
Kyle Bird	8.37	4.04	7.82	23.1%	5.66	42	0.00	0	4.76	72	0.00	0	0.00	0	0.00	0	3.29	118	0.00	8	277
Kyle Crick	5.64	3.42	4.96	15.5%	3.94	469	5.14	115	0.00	0	0.00	0	0.00	0	0.00	0	2.16	350	0.00	0	934
Kyle Dowdy	6.96	4.33	7.25	16.4%	5.02	295	0.00	0	0.00	0	0.00	0	2.64	20	0.00	0	2.60	61	3.28	61	438
Kyle Freeland	4.72	4.04	6.73	8.3%	5.17	737	4.43	184	0.00	0	6.08	3	2.61	194	0.00	0	3.00	550	3.43	112	1,780
Kyle Gibson	3.59	3.02	4.84	7.9%	5.69	482	4.36	856	-0.62	2	0.00	0	1.28	434	6.08	1	-0.22	563	3.47	328	2,670
Kyle Hendricks	3.74	3.93	3.46	4.4%	3.76	529	6.08	2	4.43	1,133	6.08	1	3.02	755	0.00	0	4.59	4	4.65	269	2,698
Kyle Keller	6.50	4.12	3.38	17.4%	4.54	132	0.00	0	0.00	0	0.00	0	0.00	0	0.00	0	-0.80	10	4.01	51	193
Kyle McGowin	3.55	3.43	10.13	5.3%	6.82	18	0.00	0	5.85	139	0.00	0	-0.67	17	0.00	0	0.60	120	8.65	2	298
Kyle Ryan	4.89	3.75	3.54	11.2%	3.58	188	0.00	0	3.25	307	4.11	386	6.08	4	0.00	0	-0.62	2	4.13	119	1,034
Kyle Wright	6.31	4.33	8.69	14.0%	5.66	189	0.62	21	0.00	0	0.00	0	1.93	26	6.08	1	2.65	83	5.24	31	351
Kyle Zimmer	7.26	3.60	10.80	18.6%	4.71	264	0.00	0	0.00	0	0.00	0	3.33	25	0.00	0	1.57	108	1.83	38	435
Lance Lynn	3.71	3.44	3.67	6.7%	3.18	1,826	3.95	571	0.00	0	3.78	535	5.65	93	0.00	0	6.08	3	2.76	315	3,553
Lewis Thorpe	4.18	3.55	6.18	8.1%	4.67	244	0.00	0	0.00	0	0.00	0	3.29	58	0.00	0	1.07	104	3.56	86	492
Liam Hendriks	2.54	2.43	1.80	6.3%	3.51	889	4.59	17	0.00	0	0.00	0	6.08	1	0.00	0	-0.53	288	0.73	89	1,321
Locke St. John	6.28	4.58	5.40	12.1%	4.38	27	0.00	0	4.29	61	0.00	0	4.80	18	0.00	0	5.03	43	0.00	0	149
Logan Allen	4.97	3.85	6.18	10.2%	5.31	216	0.00	0	0.00	0	0.00	0	2.10	96	0.00	0	2.97	104	2.17	33	450
Logan Webb	4.75	4.16	5.22	8.1%	4.99	296	5.23	85	0.00	0	0.00	0	2.65	136	0.00	0	3.35	159	0.00	0	676
Lou Trivino	4.74	3.42	5.25	11.5%	4.70	317	4.45	163	0.00	0	1.56	327	1.67	45	0.00	0	6.08	2	4.47	99	987
Lucas Giolito	3.46	3.01	3.41	8.1%	4.04	1,493	2.26	6	0.00	0	0.39	8	1.15	698	0.00	0	1.75	411	5.75	107	2,726
Lucas Sims	3.54	2.55	4.60	10.7%	3.80	357	0.00	0	4.09	23	0.00	0	0.62	42	0.00	0	-0.32	90	1.96	239	751
Luis Avilan	4.72	3.76	5.06	9.9%	0.00	0	5.37	176	0.00	0	6.08	1	2.35	347	6.08	1	6.08	2	6.42	73	600
Luis Castillo	3.14	2.28	3.40	10.1%	4.34	884	3.48	621	0.00	2	6.08	1	0.03	971	0.00	0	1.64	594	0.00	0	3,158
Luis Cessa	4.02	2.30	4.11	9.0%	4.89	466	5.32	96	0.00	0	0.00	0	2.88	112	0.00	0	1.99	656	0.00	8	1,339
Luis Escobar	5.96	3.79	7.94	13.8%	6.12	41	2.26	30	0.00	0	0.00	0	-0.50	20	0.00	0	0.00	0	6.56	13	104
Luis Garcia	4.57	3.18	4.35	11.9%	5.00	247	3.62	244	0.00	0	6.08	2	0.00	0	1.10	193	2.72	361	0.00	0	1,053
Luis Perdomo	4.00	3.88	4.00	6.1%	5.39	75	4.58	489	6.08	1	0.00	0	6.08	1	3.15	133	2.79	335	0.00	0	1,040
Luis Severino	5.08	3.83	1.50	12.5%	4.10	122	0.00	0	0.00	0	0.00	0	4.40	37	0.00	0	2.91	59	0.00	0	219
Luke Bard	3.54	3.34	4.78	6.5%	5.13	250	4.30	100	6.08	1	0.00	0	2.88	43	0.00	0	2.03	399	0.00	0	818
Luke Farrell	4.70	4.69	2.70	6.3%	5.50	111	0.00	0	0.00	0	0.00	0	0.00	0	0.00	0	2.96	74	6.10	27	212
Luke Gregerson	4.50	4.71	7.94	3.7%	6.08	9	5.38	51	0.00	0	0.00	0	0.00	2	0.00	0	3.09	23	0.00	0	104
Luke Jackson	2.77	2.16	3.84	8.3%	4.03	469	0.00	0	0.00	0	0.00	0	0.00	0	0.00	1	0.95	659	1.42	111	1,241
Luke Weaver	3.95	3.97	2.94	5.4%	4.67	546	0.00	1	0.00	0	4.61	148	1.97	260	0.00	0	-5.39	2	4.64	96	1,053
Madison Bumgarner	3.52	3.59	3.90	5.1%	4.28	766	4.76	634	0.00	0	3.22	1,064	5.31	172	0.00	0	1.96	6	1.62	594	3,244
Manny Banuelos	6.15	4.22	6.93	14.0%	5.61	211	6.08	2	5.14	238	0.00	0	2.55	78	6.08	1	3.30	314	3.23	96	948
Marco Estrada	4.99	4.47	6.85	7.6%	5.81	174	0.00	0	0.00	0	4.25	39	2.36	104	6.08	1	6.08	1	3.90	14	408
Marco Gonzales	4.79	4.55	3.99	6.4%	4.58	23	0.00	0	5.39	1,144	4.81	613	3.76	712	0.00	0	0.39	4	3.40	467	3,136
Marcus Stroman	3.93	3.51	3.22	7.5%	4.98	84	4.14	1,127	0.00	0	3.89	686	4.27	151	0.00	0	2.44	972	-2.67	25	3,047
Marcus Walden	3.58	2.73	3.81	9.8%	4.93	246	6.08	1	3.30	217	3.64	328	0.00	1	0.00	0	0.68	470	0.00	0	1,263
Mark Melancon	3.26	3.06	3.61	6.3%	4.44	98	0.00	0	0.00	0	3.95	610	0.00	0	1.57	27	6.08	3	1.09	329	1,068
Martin Perez	4.68	3.85	5.12	9.1%	4.87	510	4.18	692	0.00	0	3.85	816	2.29	611	6.08	1	-0.91	10	5.79	131	2,772
Masahiro Tanaka	3.74	3.75	4.45	5.3%	5.01	735	0.00	0	5.48	151	2.80	42	6.82	3	2.93	744	2.95	1,008	6.78	90	2,787
Matt Albers	4.98	3.80	5.13	11.2%	4.83	114	-1.57	3	3.49	452	0.00	0	3.04	101	-0.62	1	4.15	331	0.00	0	1,005
Matt Andriese	4.50	3.78	4.71	8.7%	4.37	596	2.80	7	0.00	0	0.00	0	2.56	441	0.00	0	2.28	17	5.38	137	1,204
Matt Barnes	4.07	2.41	3.78	13.3%	4.03	608	0.00	0	-0.62	1	0.00	0	0.00	0	-0.35	26	6.08	3	0.99	650	1,288
Matt Bowman	4.37	3.54	3.66	9.8%	2.88	106	2.57	106	-0.62	5	3.02	67	-0.62	1	2.55	80	5.37	97	5.98	55	529
Matt Carasiti	4.59	3.27	4.66	11.6%	0.00	1	0.00	0	3.10	106	4.11	38	-5.39	2	0.00	0	0.00	0	9.55	1	185
Matt Grace	3.95	3.99	6.36	4.9%	6.08	2	0.00	0	4.86	441	5.16	15	1.71	29	0.00	0	2.40	214	0.00	0	704
Matt Hall	6.09	4.19	7.71	13.3%	5.12	334	0.00	0	0.00	0	0.00	4	4.73	17	0.00	0	1.67	26	2.22	120	501
Matt Harvey	5.28	4.09	7.09	10.9%	5.43	435	6.08	11	0.00	0	6.08	1	3.10	100	0.00	0	2.45	263	3.53	132	999
Matt Koch	4.89	5.02	9.15	4.2%	5.56	174	6.08	1	0.00	0	3.68	101	5.16	60	0.00	0	0.00	0	6.14	28	364
Matt Magill	3.64	2.86	4.09	8.7%	3.74	453	0.00	0	0.00	0	0.00	0	0.00	0	0.00	0	2.05	195	1.84	237	885
Matt Moore	1.47	2.02	0.00	3.0%	3.63	63	0.00	0	0.00	0	0.98	22	0.38	14	0.00	0	0.00	0	-1.05	18	117
Matt Shoemaker	3.44	3.03	1.57	8.3%	3.46	73	6.17	122	0.00	0	0.00	0	0.00	0	-0.14	136	3.67	75	0.00	11	418
Matt Strahm	3.74	3.87	4.71	4.5%	4.80	641	0.00	0	0.00	10	0.00	0	0.94	3	3.52	231	0.00	0	3.25	537	3.42	281	1,707
Matt Wisler	3.32	2.91	5.61	7.1%	5.54	159	5.89	111	0.00	0	0.00	0	0.00	0	0.00	0	1.73	623	0.00	4	905
Matt Wotherspoon	4.98	4.05	15.43	7.7%	4.46	64	0.00	0	0.00	0	0.00	0	6.61	17	0.00	0	0.87	22	0.00	0	103
Matthew Boyd	3.41	3.19	4.56	6.4%	4.12	1,533	4.27	109	0.00	0	6.08	2	3.06	183	0.00	0	1.63	1,102	4.86	124	3,118
Matthew Festa	5.46	4.04	5.64	11.9%	4.92	179	4.99	21	0.00	0	0.00	0	0.00	3	0.00	0	3.44	155	0.90	23	407
Max Fried	3.49	3.21	4.02	6.7%	4.02	1,392	2.69	62	0.00	0	0.16	12	3.84	63	0.00	0	2.60	400	1.87	637	2,569
Max Scherzer	2.43	2.57	2.92	4.8%	3.75	1,267	0.39	8	0.00	0	2.52	202	1.06	386	0.00	0	-0.02	553	4.91	233	2,653

Pitcher	pERA	pERA (Just Pitchers)	ERA	BB%	pERA FF	FF Count	pERA FT	FT Count	pERA SI	SI Count	pERA FC	FC Count	pERA CH	CH Count	pERA FS	FS Count	pERA SL	SL Count	pERA CU	CU Count	Count
Merrill Kelly	4.26	3.86	4.42	7.3%	5.02	1,153	0.00	0	4.00	300	3.99	493	3.61	379	0.00	0	1.70	5	1.75	632	2,962
Michael Feliz	4.73	3.57	3.99	11.3%	4.49	735	0.00	2	0.00	0	0.00	0	4.58	64	0.00	0	-0.06	202	0.00	0	1,016
Michael Lorenzen	3.29	2.78	2.92	8.2%	3.48	281	4.81	200	-0.62	1	4.80	110	0.13	247	0.00	0	3.07	357	0.14	102	1,335
Michael Pineda	3.37	3.51	4.01	4.7%	4.48	1,204	-0.62	12	6.08	2	6.08	1	3.70	321	0.00	0	1.66	642	0.00	2	2,278
Michael Shawaryn	4.41	2.53	9.74	12.6%	3.38	197	0.00	5	0.00	0	0.00	0	0.00	4	0.00	0	1.70	160	2.41	95	461
Michael Wacha	5.03	4.08	4.76	9.8%	5.30	1,099	3.57	15	0.00	1	4.08	331	0.97	517	0.00	0	-0.62	2	5.32	224	2,199
Michel Baez	4.80	3.67	3.03	10.7%	4.27	306	0.00	0	0.00	0	0.00	0	2.51	173	0.00	0	-0.62	4	4.63	38	521
Miguel Castro	5.06	3.54	4.66	12.9%	6.08	1	6.08	3	4.69	598	0.55	2	1.61	213	0.00	0	2.78	368	0.00	0	1,204
Miguel Del Pozo	6.41	3.55	10.61	17.8%	4.83	104	0.00	0	0.00	0	0.00	0	0.00	6	0.00	0	0.00	0	2.02	73	183
Miguel Diaz	4.08	4.37	7.11	3.5%	5.06	55	0.00	0	0.00	0	0.00	1	2.55	13	0.00	0	4.33	31	0.00	2	102
Mike Clevinger	3.01	2.69	2.71	7.4%	3.54	1,069	0.00	0	0.00	0	0.00	0	2.62	237	0.00	0	1.37	532	1.95	252	2,090
Mike Dunn	3.92	3.40	7.13	8.0%	4.88	134	0.00	7	0.00	0	0.00	0	0.00	0	0.00	1	3.25	131	-2.71	25	302
Mike Fiers	4.83	4.54	3.90	7.0%	5.24	935	5.51	554	0.00	0	1.70	5	4.54	358	6.08	1	4.48	483	2.19	493	2,899
Mike Foltynewicz	4.35	3.93	4.54	7.5%	5.11	442	4.97	543	0.00	0	0.00	0	1.72	179	0.00	0	2.22	517	4.83	207	1,888
Mike Leake	3.91	4.29	4.29	3.2%	5.66	404	6.08	2	5.43	556	4.48	784	3.47	603	0.00	0	2.11	339	3.88	271	2,975
Mike Mayers	5.39	3.78	6.63	12.5%	5.12	178	0.00	0	0.00	0	0.00	0	6.08	3	0.00	0	1.34	127	5.94	30	357
Mike Minor	4.03	3.56	3.59	7.9%	4.39	1,489	6.08	1	6.08	4	0.34	4	2.69	822	0.00	0	3.68	646	2.02	380	3,358
Mike Montgomery	4.85	4.17	4.95	8.5%	5.79	241	6.82	3	4.70	392	4.04	268	2.78	329	0.00	0	0.00	0	3.84	335	1,573
Mike Morin	3.58	3.69	4.62	4.8%	4.44	75	4.20	263	0.00	0	0.00	0	2.61	258	0.00	0	4.50	111	0.00	0	724
Mike Soroka	3.56	3.50	2.68	5.9%	5.12	472	4.01	1,129	0.00	0	0.00	0	1.07	317	6.08	1	2.56	615	9.50	1	2,557
Mike Wright Jr.	4.84	4.00	7.98	8.2%	4.19	197	6.08	2	4.81	136	6.08	1	5.00	31	0.00	0	3.24	207	-4.95	3	577
Miles Mikolas	3.51	3.72	4.16	4.2%	4.16	778	4.27	658	0.00	0	-0.62	1	4.67	106	0.00	0	3.56	658	2.58	600	2,867
Mitch Keller	3.68	3.18	7.13	7.1%	4.81	448	0.00	0	0.00	0	0.00	0	5.72	28	0.00	0	-0.02	158	0.70	120	932
Montana DuRapau	4.36	3.03	9.35	10.0%	4.16	153	0.00	0	0.00	0	3.28	82	-0.62	8	0.00	0	-1.61	39	3.37	45	342
Mychal Givens	3.56	2.71	4.57	10.0%	2.93	761	6.08	4	0.00	0	0.00	0	0.58	154	0.00	0	3.57	166	0.00	0	1,092
Nate Jones	5.55	3.50	3.48	14.9%	6.08	3	4.79	117	0.00	0	0.00	0	0.00	0	0.00	6	1.78	80	0.00	0	206
Nathan Eovaldi	5.18	3.86	5.99	11.6%	3.94	557	0.00	0	6.08	1	5.12	274	0.00	0	3.18	167	1.89	47	2.98	218	1,264
Neil Ramirez	4.97	3.27	5.40	13.4%	3.08	219	2.46	38	0.00	0	0.00	0	0.00	0	0.00	0	2.73	146	5.88	58	461
Nestor Cortes	4.87	3.98	5.67	9.4%	3.85	599	3.17	82	0.00	0	0.00	1	4.18	159	0.00	0	4.44	412	2.37	47	1,301
Nick Anderson	1.97	1.72	3.32	6.8%	2.71	656	6.08	1	0.00	0	0.00	0	6.08	1	0.00	0	0.89	39	0.15	399	1,096
Nick Burdi	2.68	2.12	9.35	7.5%	5.28	73	0.00	0	0.00	0	0.00	0	0.00	0	0.00	0	-0.50	88	0.00	0	161
Nick Goody	4.34	2.91	3.54	12.7%	4.67	351	0.00	0	0.00	0	0.00	0	0.00	0	0.00	0	1.02	328	0.00	0	679
Nick Kingham	5.25	4.23	7.28	9.7%	5.66	375	4.37	100	0.00	0	4.27	165	2.83	174	0.00	0	6.88	13	2.51	200	1,027
Nick Margevicius	4.44	3.94	6.79	7.2%	5.07	515	0.00	0	0.00	0	0.00	0	2.93	73	0.00	0	2.80	241	2.10	129	958
Nick Pivetta	4.46	3.59	5.38	9.3%	4.66	788	6.88	46	6.08	1	0.00	1	6.08	1	0.00	0	2.72	220	2.04	545	1,619
Nick Ramirez	4.09	3.11	4.07	10.1%	4.73	192	3.57	20	4.94	194	3.90	378	0.34	406	0.00	0	-0.74	17	6.05	73	1,282
Nick Tropeano	4.78	3.81	9.88	9.1%	5.69	108	6.08	17	0.00	0	6.08	2	1.48	54	2.68	27	2.41	65	0.00	0	273
Nick Vincent	3.95	3.74	4.43	6.2%	3.65	424	2.54	33	0.00	0	3.91	252	5.95	27	0.00	0	1.12	9	0.00	0	751
Nick Wittgren	4.43	4.26	2.81	6.5%	4.40	629	0.00	0	0.00	0	6.08	2	3.47	142	0.00	0	4.33	178	8.68	1	975
Noah Syndergaard	3.35	3.22	4.28	6.1%	4.09	904	6.08	3	3.95	919	5.27	5	2.31	495	0.00	0	1.84	461	1.89	301	3,095
Noe Ramirez	3.61	3.28	3.99	7.1%	3.57	117	0.00	0	3.09	186	6.08	2	2.01	372	0.00	0	0.55	2	4.45	402	1,099
Odrisamer Despaigne	6.90	5.54	9.45	10.3%	6.34	95	0.00	0	6.71	42	4.02	54	6.08	16	0.00	0	6.61	28	1.41	20	255
Oliver Drake	2.71	2.18	3.21	8.7%	3.16	370	0.00	0	0.00	1	0.00	1	0.00	0	1.51	539	6.08	1	0.00	0	913
Oliver Perez	3.61	3.28	3.98	6.4%	3.87	95	0.00	0	4.27	226	0.00	1	6.08	1	0.00	0	2.34	300	8.91	1	641
Pablo Lopez	3.94	3.85	4.68	5.8%	4.68	729	3.51	320	0.00	0	6.08	3	2.27	389	0.00	0	-7.69	5	4.33	343	1,796
Parker Markel	6.44	3.96	7.77	15.5%	5.04	182	0.00	0	6.23	38	0.00	0	6.08	6	0.00	0	2.70	234	0.00	0	460
Pat Neshek	3.87	4.37	5.00	2.5%	0.00	0	0.00	0	5.39	96	6.08	1	6.08	3	0.00	0	3.75	169	0.00	0	270
Patrick Corbin	3.38	2.82	3.25	8.4%	4.94	641	4.60	1,073	0.00	1	6.08	5	2.22	219	0.00	0	-0.16	1,139	4.81	117	3,198
Patrick Sandoval	4.25	3.07	5.03	11.2%	5.25	331	0.00	0	0.00	0	0.00	0	0.38	221	0.00	0	1.49	66	2.85	96	714
Paul Blackburn	4.30	3.66	10.64	7.0%	4.44	28	4.79	89	0.00	0	0.00	0	3.99	11	0.00	0	2.73	48	1.98	48	224
Paul Fry	4.73	3.46	5.34	11.4%	3.95	555	0.00	3	0.00	0	-0.62	1	6.08	9	0.00	0	2.87	481	0.00	0	1,076
Paul Sewald	4.14	4.45	4.58	3.8%	4.56	222	0.00	1	0.00	0	0.00	0	5.60	21	0.00	0	4.03	83	0.00	2	330
Pedro Baez	3.38	2.90	3.10	8.3%	2.38	535	4.59	12	0.00	0	0.00	0	3.51	332	0.00	0	3.19	178	0.00	0	1,103
Pedro Payano	5.72	3.65	5.73	14.6%	6.08	8	0.00	0	5.28	186	0.00	0	3.93	85	0.00	0	0.58	84	2.00	54	417
Pedro Strop	3.92	2.76	4.97	11.2%	5.14	149	6.09	114	0.00	0	2.47	137	0.00	0	1.14	35	0.54	287	0.00	0	737
Peter Fairbanks	4.42	3.28	6.86	10.1%	5.17	168	0.00	1	0.00	0	0.00	0	0.00	0	0.00	0	1.84	218	0.00	0	387
Peter Lambert	5.49	4.67	7.25	8.6%	5.71	838	6.08	2	0.00	0	6.08	2	2.44	353	0.00	0	3.73	182	5.10	204	1,582
Phil Maton	3.96	3.49	6.14	7.4%	4.57	345	0.00	0	-0.62	1	2.28	125	0.00	0	0.00	0	3.79	20	1.59	117	608
Phillip Diehl	2.53	2.30	7.36	5.7%	3.80	62	0.00	0	0.00	0	0.00	0	0.00	0	0.00	0	1.08	76	0.00	0	138
Phillips Valdez	5.13	3.60	3.94	12.0%	0.00	1	-1.57	3	4.70	131	0.00	0	2.81	83	0.00	0	2.84	74	0.00	1	293
Rafael Montero	3.23	3.46	2.48	4.4%	4.90	169	3.54	74	0.00	0	0.00	0	1.97	154	0.00	0	3.11	62	0.00	0	459
Raisel Iglesias	3.32	2.91	4.16	7.5%	3.94	421	0.00	0	4.72	113	0.00	0	0.75	232	6.08	1	2.48	335	0.00	0	1,133
Randy Dobnak	2.75	2.96	1.59	4.2%	4.69	99	0.00	0	3.79	154	0.00	0	3.59	55	0.00	0	0.00	0	0.15	119	427
Randy Rosario	4.14	3.57	4.40	7.9%	2.49	33	5.05	120	0.00	0	0.69	40	0.00	0	0.00	0	2.55	26	0.00	0	224
Ranger Suarez	3.79	3.68	3.14	5.9%	5.40	179	3.67	222	0.00	0	0.00	0	2.18	206	0.00	0	3.68	155	0.00	0	763
Ray Black	4.62	3.09	5.06	12.9%	3.61	198	0.00	0	0.00	0	0.00	0	0.00	0	0.00	0	1.86	84	0.00	0	282
Reed Garrett	7.02	4.20	8.22	16.9%	5.08	176	6.08	9	0.00	0	6.08	1	0.00	0	0.00	2	0.00	4	2.70	85	319
Reggie McClain	5.45	3.66	6.00	13.7%	0.00	1	0.00	0	4.02	274	0.00	0	6.08	15	0.00	0	1.61	64	0.00	0	354
Reyes Moronta	5.26	3.64	2.86	13.4%	4.57	590	0.00	0	0.00	0	6.08	1	0.65	71	0.00	0	2.68	352	0.00	0	1,015
Reymin Guduan	5.92	3.54	11.81	14.8%	5.92	54	0.00	0	0.00	0	6.08	1	0.00	0	0.00	0	1.25	57	0.00	0	112
Reynaldo Lopez	4.53	3.94	5.38	8.0%	4.59	1,850	0.00	0	0.00	0	6.08	3	2.91	459	0.00	0	2.51	637	4.74	211	3,163
Rich Hill	3.08	2.70	2.45	7.4%	4.06	494	6.08	9	0.00	0	0.00	3	-0.62	3	0.00	0	0.13	27	1.18	404	951
Richard Bleier	2.98	3.33	5.37	3.4%	-0.62	11	0.00	0	3.45	464	3.69	167	5.12	29	0.00	0	0.53	45	0.00	0	753
Richard Lovelady	5.03	4.23	7.65	8.3%	4.09	174	0.00	2	4.73	41	0.00	0	1.49	5	0.00	0	4.42	144	0.00	0	366
Richard Rodriguez	4.35	3.76	3.72	8.1%	4.14	937	-1.57	6	0.00	0	0.00	0	0.00	4	0.00	0	1.81	158	0.00	0	1,142
Rick Porcello	4.66	4.50	5.52	5.9%	4.60	892	4.83	721	0.00	0	6.08	4	4.92	356	0.00	0	3.92	527	4.03	364	2,960
Robbie Erlin	4.15	3.93	5.37	6.0%	5.07	286	5.46	203	0.00	0	6.08	1	1.30	152	0.00	0	3.01	90	3.18	209	959

Pitcher	pERA	pERA (Just Pitchers)	ERA	BB%	pERA FF	FF Count	pERA FT	FT Count	pERA SI	SI Count	pERA FC	FC Count	pERA CH	CH Count	pERA FS	FS Count	pERA SL	SL Count	pERA CU	CU Count	Count
Robbie Ray	4.46	3.29	4.34	11.2%	4.83	1,332	4.70	271	0.00	0	6.82	7	6.08	2	0.00	0	1.09	952	2.53	491	3,064
Robby Scott	6.77	3.47	4.91	18.9%	6.08	25	0.00	0	4.49	57	0.00	0	6.08	13	0.00	0	2.45	53	-2.98	16	164
Robert Dugger	5.37	4.14	5.77	10.9%	4.75	193	5.63	144	0.00	0	0.00	0	-0.44	13	0.00	0	2.33	139	3.85	74	568
Robert Gsellman	4.29	3.67	4.66	8.3%	2.80	28	4.22	157	4.85	366	0.00	0	2.25	98	0.00	0	2.07	277	4.35	125	1,072
Robert Stephenson	2.58	1.91	3.76	9.2%	5.57	362	0.00	0	0.00	0	0.00	0	0.46	61	0.00	0	-0.20	583	1.34	9	1,028
Robert Stock	6.07	3.69	10.13	14.3%	3.97	121	0.00	0	0.00	2	0.00	0	0.04	19	0.00	0	4.21	83	0.00	0	229
Roberto Osuna	2.20	2.37	2.63	4.7%	3.38	413	6.12	34	6.08	1	2.62	137	1.28	172	6.08	1	-0.18	156	0.00	1	950
Roenis Elias	4.31	3.69	3.96	8.3%	4.14	357	4.75	67	0.00	0	6.08	1	2.76	215	0.00	0	6.08	3	3.24	99	826
Rogelio Armenteros	4.32	4.07	4.00	6.7%	4.24	161	0.00	0	0.00	0	0.00	0	2.79	95	0.00	0	6.82	11	5.05	66	333
Ronald Bolanos	5.60	3.86	5.95	13.6%	5.36	189	2.73	28	0.00	0	0.00	0	0.00	18	0.00	0	2.80	35	1.89	74	346
Rookie Davis	6.03	3.65	6.75	15.7%	3.79	77	3.49	62	0.00	0	0.00	2	4.44	28	0.00	0	3.21	16	2.55	7	192
Ross Detwiler	5.44	4.70	6.59	8.6%	5.07	400	0.00	0	4.72	230	5.02	150	3.98	192	0.00	0	2.38	31	4.74	154	1,157
Ross Stripling	3.67	3.67	3.47	5.4%	5.26	496	0.00	0	5.12	24	5.70	46	1.68	205	0.00	0	3.71	215	2.33	383	1,445
Rowan Wick	4.36	3.20	2.43	11.4%	2.92	390	0.00	0	0.00	0	-0.62	12	0.00	1	0.00	0	2.93	21	4.21	163	587
Ruben Alaniz	5.18	4.17	9.19	9.9%	4.59	56	4.82	76	0.00	0	0.00	0	3.16	35	0.00	0	3.81	94	0.00	1	263
Ryan Borucki	7.20	4.15	10.80	15.0%	0.00	0	0.00	0	5.51	81	0.00	0	0.34	32	0.00	0	4.42	42	0.00	0	155
Ryan Brasier	3.55	2.85	4.85	8.7%	3.35	536	4.56	38	0.00	0	0.00	0	3.71	86	0.00	0	1.51	305	0.00	0	978
Ryan Buchter	5.17	3.89	2.98	11.6%	4.03	489	0.00	0	0.00	0	3.48	114	0.00	0	-0.62	1	0.00	0	3.80	175	795
Ryan Burr	5.21	4.38	4.58	9.3%	4.92	207	0.00	0	0.00	0	3.37	82	0.00	0	0.00	0	3.93	67	0.00	0	356
Ryan Carpenter	5.42	4.99	9.30	6.6%	6.01	155	5.16	152	0.00	0	0.00	0	4.59	103	0.00	0	3.93	192	5.71	81	686
Ryan Dull	5.54	4.06	12.79	9.9%	5.36	134	0.00	0	0.00	0	0.00	0	6.82	15	0.00	0	1.96	103	0.00	0	270
Ryan Eades	5.94	4.56	2.38	12.0%	5.51	98	0.00	0	0.00	0	0.00	0	2.80	28	0.00	0	3.99	77	0.00	0	203
Ryan Feierabend	4.03	4.24	11.12	3.5%	5.75	24	0.00	0	0.00	0	0.00	0	0.98	9	0.00	0	0.00	0	0.00	0	104
Ryan Helsley	4.65	4.17	2.95	7.8%	5.05	330	0.00	0	0.00	0	2.95	184	0.00	12	0.00	0	-0.62	1	3.98	50	577
Ryan Pressly	2.11	2.12	2.32	5.7%	4.27	281	0.00	0	0.00	0	0.00	0	-0.62	1	0.00	0	0.70	228	1.12	279	827
Ryan Tepera	3.94	3.28	4.98	8.8%	5.68	64	0.00	0	3.59	128	2.04	112	3.14	21	0.00	0	-0.15	15	0.00	0	340
Ryan Weber	4.52	4.64	5.09	4.4%	4.32	13	0.00	0	5.52	341	0.00	0	4.92	114	0.00	0	0.34	8	3.15	198	674
Ryan Yarbrough	3.54	3.91	4.13	3.6%	6.08	1	0.00	0	4.66	492	4.99	751	1.90	528	0.00	0	6.88	6	3.40	279	2,057
Ryne Harper	3.78	3.96	3.81	4.4%	4.36	327	0.00	0	0.00	0	6.08	2	-0.62	4	0.00	0	6.08	3	3.71	504	856
Ryne Stanek	4.21	2.93	3.97	11.9%	4.31	712	0.00	0	0.00	1	0.00	0	1.67	5	0.00	4	0.56	259	1.78	300	1,284
Sal Romano	5.75	4.54	7.71	10.4%	2.80	21	5.98	151	0.00	0	0.00	0	0.00	0	0.00	0	3.19	88	3.20	46	306
Sam Coonrod	5.35	3.91	3.58	13.2%	4.08	123	0.00	0	4.84	170	0.00	0	1.00	80	0.00	0	0.00	0	4.61	79	454
Sam Dyson	3.84	3.91	3.32	5.2%	4.93	95	6.08	1	4.12	382	3.06	217	2.83	89	0.00	0	5.48	62	0.00	0	848
Sam Gaviglio	3.48	3.44	4.61	5.6%	0.00	0	0.00	0	5.01	604	-1.18	6	2.06	134	-0.62	1	1.89	629	8.43	50	1,427
Sam Howard	4.68	3.31	6.63	11.0%	5.32	169	0.00	0	0.00	0	0.00	0	0.00	0	0.00	0	1.72	214	0.00	0	383
Sam Selman	5.54	3.92	4.35	13.6%	5.24	79	0.00	0	0.00	0	0.00	0	0.00	0	0.00	0	2.96	108	0.00	0	187
Sam Tuivailala	5.16	4.00	2.35	11.7%	4.43	129	4.06	112	0.00	0	0.00	0	0.00	0	0.00	0	3.77	83	3.37	66	390
Sandy Alcantara	4.59	3.74	3.88	9.7%	5.11	925	4.59	3	3.20	852	-5.39	2	2.05	381	0.00	0	3.37	655	4.14	270	3,091
Scott Alexander	4.28	3.47	3.63	9.2%	-0.62	1	0.00	0	3.77	244	0.00	0	-1.57	9	0.00	0	2.45	24	0.00	0	278
Scott Barlow	4.31	2.94	4.22	11.9%	3.76	471	4.09	95	0.00	0	6.08	1	6.08	3	0.00	0	2.38	566	1.81	164	1,300
Scott Oberg	4.23	3.38	2.25	10.3%	3.83	460	0.00	1	0.00	0	0.00	0	4.31	39	0.00	0	2.77	381	0.00	1	884
Sean Doolittle	3.81	3.68	4.05	5.8%	3.81	908	0.00	0	0.00	0	0.00	0	6.08	1	3.54	64	1.84	58	0.00	0	1,063
Sean Manaea	3.66	3.60	1.21	6.4%	4.29	278	0.00	0	0.00	0	0.00	0	2.93	67	0.00	0	2.10	98	0.00	0	444
Sean Newcomb	4.63	3.72	3.16	9.9%	4.32	759	-0.62	1	0.00	0	6.08	1	3.21	80	0.00	0	4.27	105	1.60	222	1,181
Sean Reid-Foley	6.18	4.19	4.26	14.0%	4.40	295	6.08	8	0.00	0	6.08	1	5.71	55	0.00	0	3.14	211	5.68	41	612
Seranthony Dominguez	4.00	2.81	4.01	10.9%	3.25	270	3.99	11	0.00	0	0.00	0	2.46	19	0.00	0	1.92	141	0.00	0	464
Sergio Romo	3.42	3.15	3.43	6.8%	5.63	104	0.00	0	3.74	133	0.00	0	2.41	159	6.08	1	2.77	580	0.00	0	989
Seth Lugo	3.24	3.34	2.70	5.1%	3.41	440	4.11	283	6.08	2	0.00	1	4.18	78	0.00	0	3.00	169	2.48	298	1,275
Seunghwan Oh	3.51	3.04	9.33	6.8%	3.98	157	0.00	0	0.00	0	1.17	133	4.10	17	6.08	1	0.34	12	5.24	51	373
Shane Bieber	2.92	3.08	3.28	4.7%	5.45	1,476	0.00	0	0.00	0	0.00	0	3.77	237	0.00	0	0.91	901	0.48	651	3,332
Shane Carle	7.32	3.98	9.64	18.4%	4.66	85	0.00	0	0.00	0	0.00	0	4.05	41	0.00	0	3.57	27	2.54	34	187
Shane Greene	3.31	3.09	2.30	6.8%	4.44	14	3.76	433	0.00	0	2.90	294	0.00	3	0.00	0	1.90	204	0.00	0	949
Shaun Anderson	5.00	4.22	5.44	8.9%	4.72	719	5.10	214	0.00	0	6.08	1	4.63	135	0.00	0	2.89	467	4.56	45	1,587
Shawn Armstrong	5.00	3.75	5.74	10.7%	3.37	663	0.00	0	0.00	0	3.88	298	0.00	0	0.00	0	5.32	141	-5.36	1	1,103
Shawn Kelley	3.85	3.80	4.94	5.4%	5.60	306	0.00	0	0.00	0	0.00	0	0.00	0	0.00	0	2.59	459	7.98	1	768
Shelby Miller	6.20	4.24	8.59	13.2%	4.57	567	4.59	10	0.00	0	1.94	33	4.44	14	0.00	0	3.06	8	3.02	195	823
Sonny Gray	4.06	3.31	2.87	9.6%	5.03	805	3.58	607	0.00	0	0.00	0	3.58	77	0.00	0	1.86	603	2.34	711	2,909
Spencer Turnbull	4.38	3.59	4.61	9.0%	4.16	1,132	6.08	2	3.57	509	1.49	170	4.14	78	0.00	0	3.08	366	3.17	316	2,661
Stefan Crichton	3.62	3.43	3.56	6.5%	2.39	23	6.08	2	4.01	271	0.00	0	4.17	12	0.00	0	0.00	15	2.76	144	467
Stephen Nogosek	5.66	5.31	10.80	5.9%	5.10	88	0.00	0	0.00	1	0.00	0	2.80	7	0.00	0	6.49	35	0.00	0	131
Stephen Strasburg	3.09	2.89	3.32	6.7%	4.15	977	4.32	668	6.08	1	6.08	3	0.78	684	0.00	0	4.31	13	2.14	1,036	3,384
Stephen Tarpley	4.93	3.19	6.93	12.5%	6.06	92	0.00	0	4.17	170	0.00	0	0.00	2	0.00	0	1.29	251	8.54	10	525
Steve Cishek	5.03	3.99	2.95	10.9%	3.12	163	0.00	0	4.27	479	0.00	0	4.12	10	0.00	0	4.00	435	9.31	1	1,090
Steven Brault	4.91	3.81	5.16	10.5%	4.77	1,005	5.01	273	0.00	0	0.54	288	4.04	281	0.00	0	2.22	125	-4.44	27	2,001
Steven Matz	4.38	3.92	4.21	7.5%	-0.62	9	4.70	1,315	0.00	0	0.00	0	2.82	521	0.00	0	3.60	355	3.14	387	2,603
Steven Wright	6.38	4.54	8.53	12.1%	0.00	4	6.08	6	0.00	0	0.00	0	0.00	0	0.00	0	0.00	0	0.00	0	132
T.J. McFarland	3.67	3.06	4.82	8.0%	0.00	3	0.00	0	3.43	608	0.00	0	1.75	142	0.00	0	2.81	140	10.07	1	897
T.J. Zeuch	4.85	3.66	4.76	11.1%	0.00	12	0.00	0	4.07	200	0.00	0	4.25	79	0.00	0	2.75	79	3.32	34	404
Tanner Anderson	4.58	4.17	6.04	6.7%	5.15	55	0.00	0	4.24	245	1.49	5	3.98	38	0.00	0	3.55	78	0.00	0	422
Tanner Rainey	4.77	2.23	3.91	17.8%	3.58	616	0.00	0	0.00	0	6.08	1	-0.15	5	0.00	0	-1.01	253	0.00	0	875
Tanner Roark	4.85	4.46	4.35	7.1%	4.66	752	5.16	844	0.00	0	6.08	3	3.29	280	0.00	0	4.29	621	3.60	370	2,992
Tanner Scott	5.24	2.99	4.78	15.6%	5.15	269	0.55	2	0.00	0	6.08	1	0.00	0	0.00	0	-0.04	191	0.00	0	463
Tayler Scott	5.62	3.59	14.33	11.8%	5.48	55	0.00	0	4.65	148	0.00	0	0.00	0	0.00	0	1.86	151	0.00	0	354
Taylor Clarke	4.72	4.12	5.31	8.1%	5.22	729	4.39	74	0.00	0	-0.62	1	4.33	178	0.00	0	1.45	387	5.41	143	1,512
Taylor Cole	4.55	3.46	5.92	10.4%	4.67	340	6.08	1	0.00	0	4.47	32	1.31	281	0.00	0	4.29	195	3.40	36	885
Taylor Guerrieri	6.93	4.17	5.81	17.9%	0.00	6	0.00	0	4.97	216	0.00	1	4.20	49	0.00	0	0.00	0	3.51	219	491
Taylor Guilbeau	3.38	3.28	3.65	5.9%	0.00	0	0.00	0	4.01	115	0.00	0	2.51	54	0.00	0	-0.23	12	0.00	0	181

Appendix F – Pitcher pERA Values, 2016 and 2018 Ball

Pitcher	pERA	pERA (Just Pitchers)	ERA	BB%	pERA FF	FF Count	pERA FT	FT Count	pERA SI	SI Count	pERA FC	FC Count	pERA CH	CH Count	pERA FS	FS Count	pERA SL	SL Count	pERA CU	CU Count	Count
Taylor Rogers	3.18	3.46	2.61	4.0%	0.00	0	4.24	518	6.08	1	0.00	0	6.08	1	0.00	0	2.35	439	4.46	78	1,065
Taylor Williams	3.94	2.79	9.82	9.6%	3.89	168	6.08	2	0.00	0	0.00	0	-0.45	14	0.00	0	1.03	83	0.00	0	267
Tayron Guerrero	5.69	3.17	6.26	16.7%	3.35	636	2.94	63	0.00	0	0.00	0	0.00	0	0.00	0	2.59	175	0.00	0	884
Thomas Pannone	4.61	3.70	6.16	9.5%	3.97	712	6.08	1	0.00	0	0.34	4	4.01	249	0.00	0	-1.57	3	2.83	286	1,255
Thyago Vieira	6.20	3.99	9.00	13.5%	5.03	112	0.00	3	0.00	0	0.00	0	0.16	3	0.00	0	2.15	51	0.00	0	169
Tim Collins	5.28	4.72	3.12	7.9%	5.54	74	0.00	0	0.00	0	0.00	0	0.00	0	0.00	0	3.95	53	4.11	33	160
Tim Hill	4.06	3.58	3.63	8.1%	3.13	207	0.00	0	4.25	271	0.00	0	0.00	0	0.00	0	2.98	155	9.81	1	634
Tim Mayza	4.06	2.70	4.91	11.9%	5.56	174	2.48	419	0.00	0	6.08	1	0.00	0	0.00	0	1.43	324	0.00	0	921
Tim Melville	4.67	3.78	4.86	9.8%	5.79	188	0.00	0	0.00	0	0.00	0	5.31	34	0.00	0	2.18	309	5.77	33	564
Tim Peterson	7.79	4.49	4.91	20.0%	4.67	77	6.08	1	0.00	0	0.00	0	3.78	46	0.00	0	5.47	18	0.00	0	142
Tom Eshelman	5.36	4.98	6.50	6.7%	5.63	167	6.20	110	0.00	0	0.00	0	5.49	111	0.00	0	4.08	129	3.02	92	609
Tommy Kahnle	2.57	2.10	3.67	8.1%	4.49	454	0.00	0	0.00	0	-0.62	1	-0.08	528	0.00	0	3.73	41	0.00	0	1,026
Tommy Milone	4.14	4.22	4.76	5.1%	5.95	728	6.08	1	0.00	0	0.00	0	2.14	636	0.00	0	3.62	182	5.55	123	1,750
Tony Gonsolin	4.23	3.54	2.93	9.2%	5.28	332	0.00	0	0.00	0	0.00	0	0.00	0	1.68	175	0.80	116	4.50	70	693
Tony Sipp	4.41	3.49	4.71	9.8%	5.09	173	0.00	0	0.00	0	0.00	0	-0.62	1	-0.23	73	3.54	115	-5.08	1	363
Tony Watson	3.24	3.24	4.17	5.2%	6.08	1	6.82	4	4.23	410	0.00	0	1.79	309	0.00	0	3.53	89	0.00	0	813
Touki Toussaint	5.36	3.55	5.62	13.1%	6.12	201	3.57	5	4.70	183	0.00	0	6.08	2	0.18	161	0.00	1	2.63	203	777
Travis Bergen	5.33	4.27	5.49	10.6%	5.15	251	0.00	0	0.00	0	0.00	0	6.08	1	0.00	0	3.53	18	2.27	105	375
Travis Lakins	4.54	3.61	3.86	9.8%	3.80	156	0.00	0	0.00	0	3.52	143	6.61	14	0.00	0	0.00	0	2.86	77	395
Trent Thornton	4.91	4.13	4.84	9.0%	5.11	1,215	4.26	69	0.00	0	2.85	302	3.42	90	4.13	157	3.54	595	2.93	330	2,759
Trevor Bauer	4.04	3.31	4.48	9.0%	4.45	1,325	3.97	143	0.00	0	3.11	580	3.22	253	6.08	1	2.18	491	1.93	674	3,687
Trevor Cahill	4.36	3.64	5.98	8.6%	3.43	135	6.08	4	4.64	477	2.30	327	3.20	400	0.00	0	6.08	4	4.04	370	1,788
Trevor Gott	4.08	3.63	4.44	7.9%	3.73	606	0.00	0	2.73	91	0.00	0	3.51	32	0.00	0	3.21	8	3.80	159	914
Trevor Hildenberger	4.78	3.86	10.47	8.0%	3.79	17	0.00	0	5.33	104	0.00	0	1.13	120	0.00	0	5.94	84	0.00	0	326
Trevor Kelley	6.21	4.51	8.64	12.5%	0.00	0	0.00	0	4.98	100	0.00	0	0.00	0	0.00	0	4.50	29	3.14	34	163
Trevor May	4.20	3.38	2.94	9.8%	2.69	725	0.98	9	0.00	0	0.00	0	4.08	115	0.00	0	4.52	168	5.10	148	1,166
Trevor Richards	4.60	3.74	4.06	9.7%	4.35	958	0.00	0	0.00	0	5.15	183	2.31	834	-5.39	2	5.70	44	5.50	159	2,182
Trevor Rosenthal	10.70	4.07	13.50	30.6%	4.73	287	3.99	11	0.00	0	0.00	0	0.34	8	0.00	0	2.46	99	0.00	0	405
Trevor Williams	4.36	4.00	5.38	6.9%	4.12	1,106	0.00	0	4.86	332	6.08	4	4.69	266	0.00	0	2.98	447	-3.91	19	2,259
Trey Wingenter	4.31	2.84	5.65	12.8%	4.55	498	0.00	0	0.00	0	0.00	0	0.00	0	0.00	0	0.75	407	0.00	0	906
Ty Blach	6.80	4.97	12.00	12.2%	0.00	0	0.00	0	5.84	295	4.59	26	3.66	134	0.00	0	6.08	20	2.90	45	521
Ty Buttrey	3.84	3.41	3.98	7.4%	3.46	689	6.08	2	0.00	0	6.08	2	3.48	163	0.00	0	3.25	354	0.00	0	1,225
Tyler Alexander	3.86	4.27	4.86	3.0%	5.04	301	4.28	200	0.00	0	0.00	0	2.45	106	0.00	0	4.19	144	4.11	167	918
Tyler Anderson	4.64	3.24	11.76	10.4%	4.48	193	-0.62	8	0.00	0	3.25	86	2.99	111	0.00	0	0.00	0	-3.43	27	428
Tyler Bashlor	6.40	3.92	6.95	16.5%	4.46	225	0.00	0	0.00	0	0.00	0	2.95	42	0.00	0	3.01	94	8.20	1	396
Tyler Beede	4.32	3.55	5.08	8.8%	5.02	1,129	2.26	6	6.08	2	0.00	0	1.80	376	0.00	0	2.25	236	1.04	276	2,028
Tyler Chatwood	4.88	3.70	3.76	11.4%	4.77	387	4.27	497	0.00	0	1.92	119	1.39	87	0.00	0	-3.48	5	2.03	146	1,285
Tyler Clippard	3.22	3.13	2.90	6.2%	2.15	188	4.24	192	0.00	0	0.00	0	3.86	282	1.72	226	-0.62	5	5.96	36	937
Tyler Duffey	2.77	2.68	2.50	5.9%	3.04	505	-0.44	13	0.88	13	0.00	0	0.00	4	0.00	0	1.83	294	3.63	149	980
Tyler Glasnow	3.20	3.16	1.78	6.1%	4.19	606	6.08	1	0.00	0	0.00	0	3.02	30	0.00	0	-1.90	23	1.02	237	903
Tyler Kinley	5.73	3.45	3.65	16.3%	5.36	365	0.00	0	0.00	0	0.00	0	0.00	0	0.00	0	2.02	488	0.00	0	866
Tyler Lyons	3.59	2.81	6.39	9.3%	4.83	28	0.00	0	5.16	49	0.00	0	1.36	20	0.00	0	1.30	94	0.00	0	191
Tyler Mahle	4.26	4.08	5.14	6.1%	4.60	1,191	6.08	1	6.08	2	4.79	135	1.42	35	2.64	208	3.84	67	3.43	474	2,116
Tyler Olson	5.17	3.82	4.40	11.4%	3.80	215	0.00	0	6.92	16	6.08	16	4.06	71	0.00	0	0.55	2	3.55	224	533
Tyler Rogers	2.80	3.04	1.02	4.3%	-0.51	21	0.00	0	3.79	141	0.00	0	0.00	0	0.00	0	0.00	0	2.71	94	256
Tyler Skaggs	4.29	3.71	4.29	8.4%	5.10	689	0.00	1	0.00	0	0.00	2	4.00	220	0.00	0	-1.57	3	1.56	465	1,386
Tyler Thornburg	5.65	4.23	7.71	11.6%	5.18	209	0.00	0	6.08	1	0.00	0	1.68	72	0.00	0	0.00	1	4.12	99	382
Tyler Webb	4.84	3.96	3.76	10.4%	4.17	341	4.32	207	0.00	0	0.00	0	2.86	169	0.00	0	3.78	94	5.46	39	889
Tyson Ross	5.79	4.50	6.11	11.1%	5.46	201	0.34	4	0.00	0	4.50	212	0.00	0	0.00	0	3.50	177	0.00	0	595
Victor Alcantara	3.96	3.38	4.85	8.2%	0.00	0	6.82	3	3.53	466	0.00	0	2.49	113	0.00	0	3.78	53	0.00	0	677
Vince Velasquez	4.25	3.60	4.91	8.3%	3.82	1,325	4.34	110	0.00	0	0.00	0	-0.62	2	0.00	0	3.39	432	2.52	250	2,120
Wade Davis	6.01	3.95	8.65	14.1%	4.87	362	0.00	5	0.00	0	3.14	290	4.83	14	0.00	0		1	3.36	150	822
Wade LeBlanc	4.42	4.27	5.71	5.8%	6.14	102	5.54	442	0.00	0	4.80	586	2.42	605	0.00	0	-0.53	7	4.70	213	1,955
Wade Miley	4.51	3.87	3.98	8.5%	4.69	472	6.17	174	0.00	0	4.10	1,326	2.28	589	0.00	0	4.36	32	3.24	268	2,968
Walker Buehler	3.42	3.50	3.26	5.0%	4.09	1,501	5.46	218	0.00	0	3.20	362	-0.62	5	0.00	0	1.95	406	1.88	337	2,838
Walker Lockett	4.83	4.64	8.34	5.8%	5.83	178	0.00	0	6.91	29	0.00	0	2.17	73	0.00	0	0.00	0	3.54	89	369
Wander Suero	3.64	3.00	4.84	8.8%	3.65	8	0.00	0	0.00	0	3.37	839	2.16	245	0.00	0	-5.39	2	1.91	84	1,197
Wandy Peralta	3.43	2.62	5.67	9.3%	3.68	67	4.06	165	0.00	0	6.08	1	1.93	153	0.00	0	1.78	247	0.00	0	657
Wei-Chieh Huang	7.10	4.13	3.18	15.6%	6.08	60	0.00	0	0.00	0	0.00	0	2.96	27	0.00	0	-0.62	3	1.18	24	114
Wei-Chung Wang	5.62	4.59	3.77	10.9%	5.75	224	0.00	1	-0.62	1	6.08	1	3.28	82	0.00	0	4.17	187	1.63	23	519
Wei-Yin Chen	4.36	4.17	6.59	9.3%	5.18	559	2.12	29	0.00	0	-9.22	3	5.19	41	0.00	0	3.20	261	3.19	258	1,151
Wes Parsons	7.01	4.24	5.45	18.5%	4.68	129	0.00	0	5.05	236	0.00	0	5.42	35	0.00	0	3.02	236	0.00	0	637
Will Harris	3.23	3.18	1.50	6.1%	-0.12	14	0.00	0	0.00	0	3.55	501	0.00	0	0.00	0	6.08	2	2.80	372	926
Will Smith	2.81	2.36	2.76	8.2%	4.68	487	1.49	5	0.00	0	0.00	0	-0.62	13	0.00	0	-0.46	427	3.48	105	1,043
Williams Jerez	7.37	4.45	4.35	18.8%	5.47	106	0.00	0	0.00	0	0.00	0	1.58	23	0.00	0	3.77	63	0.00	0	192
Wilmer Font	3.96	3.41	4.48	8.2%	3.77	723	0.00	1	3.93	175	6.08	1	-0.62	3	3.08	131	3.15	202	2.58	287	1,541
Wily Peralta	5.48	4.36	5.80	10.8%	4.86	356	6.08	1	0.00	0	0.00	0	4.06	85	0.00	0	3.40	202	9.05	9	673
Yacksel Rios	4.56	2.79	6.92	12.3%	2.51	72	0.91	74	0.00	0	0.00	0	4.38	27	0.00	0	6.21	42	1.55	22	237
Yefry Ramirez	5.58	3.62	7.40	13.5%	4.60	234	-0.62	2	0.00	0	0.00	0	1.87	143	0.00	0	3.98	85	0.00	0	464
Yency Almonte	4.93	4.08	5.56	8.8%	5.63	345	6.08	2	0.00	0	0.00	0	-0.62	1	5.39	18	0.00	0	1.78	242	608
Yimi Garcia	3.57	3.56	3.61	5.7%	3.20	436	6.08	11	0.00	0	0.00	0	3.97	62	0.00	0	3.21	187	4.17	278	975
Yoan Lopez	4.36	4.10	3.41	6.9%	5.15	499	0.00	0	0.00	0	0.00	0	2.80	21	0.00	0	2.61	335	0.00	0	857
Yohander Mendez	7.37	3.55	5.79	23.8%	4.02	45	0.00	0	0.00	0	0.00	0	2.36	37	0.00	0	4.81	18	0.00	0	100
Yonny Chirinos	3.75	3.80	3.85	5.3%	3.64	32	4.21	11	4.95	1,086	0.98	9	-6.05	6	1.69	415	3.14	425	0.00	0	1,985
Yoshihisa Hirano	3.89	3.02	4.75	9.4%	4.94	447	0.00	0	0.00	0	6.08	1	0.00	0	1.25	481	1.49	5	0.00	0	934
Yu Darvish	3.50	3.09	3.98	7.7%	3.96	813	4.03	337	0.00	1	2.49	985	0.65	44	2.29	59	3.02	410	1.87	198	2,848
Yusei Kikuchi	4.61	4.22	5.46	6.9%	4.92	1,290	0.00	0	0.00	0	0.00	0	3.17	199	0.00	0	2.87	733	4.95	406	2,721

Pitcher	pERA	pERA (Just Pitchers)	ERA	BB%	pERA FF	FF Count	pERA FT	FT Count	pERA SI	SI Count	pERA FC	FC Count	pERA CH	CH Count	pERA FS	FS Count	pERA SL	SL Count	pERA CU	CU Count	Count
Yusmeiro Petit	3.47	3.93	2.71	3.3%	5.73	507	0.00	0	6.08	2	2.55	234	2.17	213	6.08	1	6.92	4	2.44	160	1,139
Zac Gallen	4.32	3.29	2.81	10.8%	4.74	660	-0.45	28	0.00	0	2.84	214	0.89	222	0.00	0	0.00	0	2.45	262	1,387
Zac Grotz	3.70	2.62	4.15	11.0%	4.78	95	2.12	14	4.37	36	0.00	0	0.00	3	1.72	112	-0.62	22	-2.14	17	299
Zac Reininger	6.39	4.81	8.68	11.4%	5.19	214	5.62	107	0.00	0	0.00	0	-0.27	20	0.00	0	5.14	128	3.15	64	533
Zac Rosscup	5.91	2.16	5.00	20.2%	2.99	70	4.84	79	0.00	0	6.08	1	0.00	0	0.00	0	0.92	222	0.00	0	402
Zach Davies	5.33	4.89	3.55	7.6%	-1.57	3	5.87	1,362	0.00	0	5.85	315	2.63	813	0.00	0	4.99	21	7.34	90	2,608
Zach Duke	6.79	4.32	5.01	17.0%	5.23	27	0.00	0	5.42	189	6.08	1	0.00	0	0.00	0	3.42	125	1.69	47	408
Zach Eflin	4.56	4.24	4.13	6.8%	4.48	829	4.10	551	0.00	0	6.08	6	4.25	195	6.08	1	3.98	759	4.65	137	2,481
Zach Plesac	4.78	4.22	3.81	8.4%	5.29	955	0.00	0	-5.39	2	0.00	0	3.12	370	0.00	0	2.30	360	4.77	185	1,892
Zack Britton	3.54	2.19	1.91	13.1%	0.55	2	0.00	0	2.31	800	0.00	0	0.00	0	0.00	0	1.46	129	0.00	0	933
Zack Godley	5.02	3.97	5.97	10.3%	6.08	2	0.00	1	5.42	545	4.21	256	3.62	89	0.00	0	6.08	5	2.68	647	1,548
Zack Greinke	3.46	3.81	2.93	3.7%	5.15	1,246	5.12	160	0.00	0	6.08	1	2.37	649	6.08	2	3.15	488	2.41	445	3,026
Zack Littell	3.46	3.36	2.68	6.2%	4.07	276	6.08	1	0.00	0	3.96	47	0.00	3	6.08	1	2.24	215	7.09	6	551
Zack Wheeler	4.03	3.88	3.96	6.0%	4.07	854	4.32	961	6.08	2	0.00	0	2.63	104	3.58	229	3.67	606	3.03	304	3,159

Name	Remaining Salary	Name	Remaining Salary
Aaron Judge	$90,000,000	Justin Upton	$72,000,000
Albert Pujols	59,000,000	Kevin Kiermaier	33,500,000
Brandon Belt	32,000,000	Khris Davis	33,600,000
Brandon Crawford	30,000,000	Kyle Seager	37,000,000
Bryce Harper	300,000,000	Lorenzo Cain	51,000,000
Buster Posey	42,800,000	Manny Machado	270,000,000
Carlos Correa	312,000,000	Matt Carpenter	37,000,000
Charlie Blackmon	73,000,000	Miguel Cabrera	124,000,000
Chris Davis	69,000,000	Mike Trout	33,250,000
Christian Yelich	26,500,000	Ozzie Albies	30,000,000
Dexter Fowler	29,000,000	Paul DeJong	21,166,666
Dustin Pedroia	25,000,000	Paul Goldschmidt	110,000,000
Elvis Andrus	43,000,000	Prince Fielder	24,000,000
Elvis Andrus	43,000,000	Randal Grichuk	39,999,999
Eric Hosmer	99,000,000	Robinson Cano	96,000,000
Eugenio Suarez	52,750,000	Ronald Acuna Jr.	89,000,000
Evan Longoria	53,000,000	Rougned Odor	33,000,000
Freddie Freeman	44,000,000	Salvador Perez	26,000,000
Giancarlo Stanton	234,000,000	Scott Kingery	20,500,000
Ian Desmond	23,000,000	Shin-Soo Choo	21,000,000
J.D. Martinez	62,450,000	Stephen Piscotty	21,500,000
Jacoby Ellsbury	21,142,857	Tim Anderson	20,750,000
Jason Heyward	86,000,000	Wil Myers	60,000,000
Jean Segura	42,750,000	Xander Bogaerts	120,000,000
Joey Votto	120,000,000	Yadier Molina	20,000,000
Jose Altuve	130,000,000	Yoenis Cespedes	29,500,000

A Note About These Standings Gain Points

The 2019 and 2018 standings gain points factors are shown below for a variety of league types. Both years are presented due to the notable change in the baseball between the 2018 and 2019 seasons. Having both sets of numbers available will allow owners to choose the set they think will be most applicable for the 2020 season. Better yet, perhaps spring training results in 2020 will point to the set to use next draft season.

By splitting the calculations into separate years, the sample size for is smaller than the authors would otherwise prefer for the OBP-related, NL-only, and AL-only leagues. Normally several years of standings can be averaged together, but that seems unwise given the significant change in the run scoring environment the past several seasons.

One other item to note is it can be misleading to compare SGP factors from separate seasons without first converting them to a relative scale. This is an obscure topic not discussed in the book but becomes more relevant in this appendix after seeing all these calculations side-by-side. Owners wishing to understand more about relative SGP can read this.

15-team Mixed League, Standard

2019

	R	HR	RBI	SB	AVG	W	K	SV	ERA	WHIP
SGP Factor	15.2	6.6	14.8	4.0	0.0012	2.1	22.6	3.8	-0.0522	-0.0101

SGP Average Formula = ((1749 + H) / (6664 + AB) - 0.262) / 0.0012

SGP ERA Formula = (((542 + ER) * 9) / (1188 + IP) − 4.11) / -0.0522

SGP WHIP Formula = ((1488 + HA + BB) / (1188 + IP) - 1.25) / -0.1011

2018

	R	HR	RBI	SB	AVG	W	K	SV	ERA	WHIP
SGP Factor	11.8	5.1	12.6	4.7	0.0012	2.0	22.1	4.2	-0.0524	-0.0100

SGP Average Formula = ((1716 + H) / (6665 + AB) - 0.257) / 0.0012

SGP ERA Formula = (((511 + ER) * 9) / (1201 + IP) - 3.834) / -0.0524

SGP WHIP Formula = ((1478 + HA + BB) / (1201 + IP) - 1.231) / -0.0100

15-team Mixed League, Standard Rosters, OBP Instead of Batting Average

2019

	R	HR	RBI	SB	OBP	W	K	SV	ERA	WHIP
SGP Factor	9.8	6.1	10.0	4.4	0.0014	2.6	15.7	3.0	-0.0670	-0.0114

SGP Average Formula = ((2449 + H + BB) / (7295 + AB + BB) - 0.3357) / 0.0012

SGP ERA Formula = (((535 + ER) * 9) / (1174 + IP) – 4.101) / -0.0637

SGP WHIP Formula = ((1468 + HA + BB) / (1174 + IP) - 1.251) / -0.0108

2018

	R	HR	RBI	SB	AVG	W	K	SV	ERA	WHIP
SGP Factor	8.3	5.1	14.5	3.7	0.0016	2.2	27.9	3.5	-0.0379	-0.0081

SGP OBP Formula = ((2403 + H + BB) / (7242 + AB + BB) - 0.3317) / 0.0016

SGP ERA Formula = (((498 + ER) * 9) / (1152 + IP) – 3.892) / -0.0379

SGP WHIP Formula = ((1413 + HA + BB) / (1152 + IP) - 1.226) / -0.0081

15-team Mixed League, No Transactions (Draft & Hold), Standard Rosters, Standard Categories

2019

	R	HR	RBI	SB	AVG	W	K	SV	ERA	WHIP
SGP Factor	16.9	6.8	16.8	4.5	0.0013	2.4	28.3	4.4	-0.0550	-0.0104

SGP Average Formula = ((1674+ H) / (6384 + AB) - 0.262) / 0.0013

SGP ERA Formula = (((517 + ER) * 9) / (1137 + IP) – 4.10) / -0.0550

SGP WHIP Formula = ((1422 + HA + BB) / (1137 + IP) - 1.25) / -0.0104

2018

	R	HR	RBI	SB	AVG	W	K	SV	ERA	WHIP
SGP Factor	13.7	5.6	15.2	4.5	0.0013	2.4	28.9	4.6	-0.0556	-0.0100

SGP Average Formula = ((1665 + H) / (6454 + AB) - 0.258) / 0.0013

SGP ERA Formula = ((485 + ER) * 9) / (1141 + IP) – 3.828) / -0.0556

SGP WHIP Formula = ((1401 + HA + BB) / (1141 + IP) - 1.229) / -0.0100

12-team Mixed League, Standard

2019

	R	HR	RBI	SB	AVG	W	K	SV	ERA	WHIP
SGP Factor	20.8	8.4	19.0	5.8	0.0016	2.8	31.7	5.0	-0.0707	-0.0135

SGP Average Formula = ((1795 + H) / (6768 + AB) - 0.265) / 0.0016

SGP ERA Formula = (((526 + ER) * 9) / (1187 + IP) - 3.99) / -0.0707

SGP WHIP Formula = ((1459 + HA + BB) / (1187 + IP) - 1.230) / -0.0135

2018

	R	HR	RBI	SB	AVG	W	K	SV	ERA	WHIP
SGP Factor	17.7	7.2	18.0	6.2	0.0016	3.0	31.7	5.3	-0.0725	-0.0132

SGP Average Formula = ((1759 + H) / (6770 + AB) - 0.2597) / 0.0016

SGP ERA Formula = (((493 + ER) * 9) / (1190 + IP) - 3.733) / -0.0725

SGP WHIP Formula = ((1443 + HA + BB) / (1190 + IP) - 1.213) / -0.0132

12-team AL-Only League, Standard Rosters, OBP Instead of Batting Average

2019

	R	HR	RBI	SB	OBP	W	K	SV	ERA	WHIP
SGP Factor	23.0	10.4	20.2	5.2	0.0029	2.3	44.8	4.2	-0.1180	-0.0177

SGP Average Formula = ((2110 + H + BB) / (6472 + AB + BB) - 0.3258) / 0.0029

SGP ERA Formula = (((488 + ER) * 9) / (999 + IP) – 4.399) / -0.1180

SGP WHIP Formula = ((1296 + HA + BB) / (999 + IP) - 1.297) / -0.0177

2018

	R	HR	RBI	SB	OBP	W	K	SV	ERA	WHIP
SGP Factor	8.2	5.6	10.4	5.2	0.0015	2.2	18.2	5.8	-0.1015	-0.0111

SGP OBP Formula = ((2018 + H + BB) / (6295 + AB + BB) - 0.3205) / 0.0015

SGP ERA Formula = (((472 + ER) * 9) / (1055 + IP) – 4.039) / -0.1015

SGP WHIP Formula = ((1,335 + HA + BB) / (1055 + IP) - 1.267) / -0.0111

12-team NL-Only League, Standard Rosters, OBP Instead of Batting Average

2019

	R	HR	RBI	SB	OBP	W	K	SV	ERA	WHIP
SGP Factor	15.7	11.5	21.2	1.3	0.0027	1.7	18.7	6.5	-0.0238	-0.0084

SGP Average Formula = ((2080 + H + BB) / (6221 + AB + BB) - 0.3310) / 0.0238

SGP ERA Formula = (((487 + ER) * 9) / (1058 + IP) - 4.145) / -0.0238

SGP WHIP Formula = ((1337 + HA + BB) / (1058 + IP) - 1.264) / -0.0084

2018

	R	HR	RBI	SB	OBP	W	K	SV	ERA	WHIP
SGP Factor	21.5	8.3	12.2	3.0	0.0018	3.6	31.7	7.5	-0.0483	-0.0158

SGP OBP Formula = ((2077 + H + BB) / (6271 + AB + BB) - 0.3312) / 0.0018

SGP ERA Formula = (((451 + ER) * 9) / (1049 + IP) – 3.875) / -0.0483

SGP WHIP Formula = ((1310 + HA + BB) / (1049 + IP) - 1.250) / -0.0158

12-team AL-Only League, Standard

2019

	R	HR	RBI	SB	AVG	W	K	SV	ERA	WHIP
SGP Factor	27.9	9.3	26.7	4.8	0.0020	3.2	37.6	4.2	-0.1050	-0.0188

SGP Average Formula = ((1492 + H) / (5762 + AB) - 0.256) / 0.0020

SGP ERA Formula = (((478 + ER) * 9) / (984 + IP) – 4.383) / -0.1050

SGP WHIP Formula = ((1272 + HA + BB) / (984 + IP) - 1.295) / -0.0188

2018

	R	HR	RBI	SB	AVG	W	K	SV	ERA	WHIP
SGP Factor	16.9	5.2	16.4	4.9	0.0018	2.8	35.0	4.2	-0.0595	-0.0129

SGP Average Formula = ((1456 + H) / (5778 + AB) - 0.2518) / 0.0018

SGP ERA Formula = (((467 + ER) * 9) / (1033 + IP) – 4.075) / -0.0595

SGP WHIP Formula = ((1306 + HA + BB) / (1033 + IP) - 1.265) / -0.0129

12-team NL-Only League, Standard

2019

	R	HR	RBI	SB	AVG	W	K	SV	ERA	WHIP
SGP Factor	18.6	9.6	27.7	5.8	0.0013	3.1	35.7	6.8	-0.0691	-0.0157

SGP Average Formula = ((1428 + H) / (5498 + AB) - 0.2598) / 0.0013

SGP ERA Formula = (((486 + ER) * 9) / (1042 + IP) – 4.200) / -0.0691

SGP WHIP Formula = ((1331 + HA + BB) / (1042 + IP) – 1.279) / -0.0157

2018

	R	HR	RBI	SB	AVG	W	K	SV	ERA	WHIP
SGP Factor	18.7	5.6	15.1	4.4	0.0014	2.7	27.5	4.9	-0.0578	-0.0104

SGP Average Formula = ((1425 + H) / (5527 + AB) - 0.2577) / 0.0014

SGP ERA Formula = (((426 + ER) * 9) / (1004 + IP) - 3.823) / -0.0578

SGP WHIP Formula = ((1250 + HA + BB) / (1004 + IP) - 1.246) / -0.0104

15-tm, Standard (NFBC Main Event)

								2019					
RK	PTS	AB	IP	R	HR	RBI	SB	AVG	W	K	SV	ERA	WHIP
1	15	7,538	1,381	1,211	387	1,174	148	0.2745	104	1,575	91	3.573	1.153
2	14	7,443	1,371	1,180	375	1,141	135	0.2711	100	1,522	81	3.726	1.180
3	13	7,391	1,381	1,158	363	1,117	129	0.2692	96	1,492	75	3.808	1.195
4	12	7,367	1,383	1,141	355	1,097	125	0.2677	93	1,466	71	3.893	1.209
5	11	7,263	1,342	1,126	347	1,081	120	0.2662	91	1,440	67	3.960	1.221
6	10	7,336	1,350	1,112	341	1,066	115	0.2646	89	1,416	65	4.006	1.234
7	9	7,203	1,336	1,097	335	1,052	112	0.2634	87	1,399	61	4.067	1.246
8	8	7,206	1,370	1,084	329	1,036	107	0.2624	85	1,380	56	4.105	1.254
9	7	7,124	1,347	1,069	322	1,025	103	0.2612	83	1,350	52	4.153	1.264
10	6	7,143	1,317	1,052	316	1,009	100	0.2599	81	1,331	49	4.206	1.271
11	5	6,967	1,311	1,038	309	992	97	0.2587	78	1,313	45	4.265	1.281
12	4	6,980	1,278	1,016	301	977	93	0.2575	76	1,276	40	4.326	1.293
13	3	7,010	1,283	997	294	961	86	0.2554	72	1,233	35	4.398	1.306
14	2	6,830	1,264	973	284	930	80	0.2530	69	1,187	28	4.499	1.319
15	1	6,473	1,184	913	262	882	72	0.2488	63	1,092	17	4.642	1.353

								2018					
RK	PTS	AB	IP	R	HR	RBI	SB	AVG	W	K	SV	ERA	WHIP
1	15	7,453	1,387	1,114	321	1,064	156	0.2703	102	1,544	94	3.333	1.134
2	14	7,372	1,387	1,075	307	1,040	145	0.2664	98	1,489	86	3.435	1.157
3	13	7,463	1,364	1,059	298	1,018	140	0.2641	95	1,458	82	3.538	1.174
4	12	7,374	1,382	1,042	294	1,007	135	0.2624	93	1,431	78	3.603	1.187
5	11	7,363	1,384	1,030	285	988	129	0.2610	90	1,399	74	3.669	1.201
6	10	7,186	1,357	1,017	283	976	123	0.2596	89	1,379	70	3.749	1.214
7	9	7,212	1,347	1,006	278	967	119	0.2584	86	1,359	67	3.805	1.222
8	8	7,152	1,355	994	274	955	115	0.2573	85	1,337	62	3.841	1.231
9	7	7,128	1,375	982	267	941	111	0.2564	83	1,318	59	3.885	1.240
10	6	7,081	1,331	970	262	928	105	0.2553	81	1,297	55	3.933	1.250
11	5	7,114	1,342	959	257	916	100	0.2540	79	1,269	49	3.977	1.259
12	4	6,993	1,286	947	250	902	96	0.2528	76	1,248	42	4.046	1.271
13	3	6,865	1,301	927	243	879	92	0.2512	74	1,219	36	4.126	1.284
14	2	6,838	1,272	905	236	857	87	0.2488	71	1,176	28	4.206	1.299
15	1	6,651	1,241	865	221	831	77	0.2460	64	1,118	15	4.392	1.330

15-tm, OBP (Tout Wars Mixed Drafts)

2019													
RK	PTS	AB	IP	R	HR	RBI	SB	OBP	W	K	SV	ERA	WHIP
1	15	7,211	1,336	1,151	374	1,172	155	0.3494	102	1,545	80	3.520	1.135
2	14	7,360	1,360	1,146	367	1,113	147	0.3460	99	1,491	77	3.726	1.184
3	13	7,271	1,335	1,125	358	1,081	134	0.3436	97	1,437	73	3.803	1.192
4	12	7,499	1,342	1,114	349	1,061	124	0.3422	94	1,420	71	3.892	1.209
5	11	7,189	1,331	1,093	346	1,053	118	0.3386	93	1,406	70	3.927	1.212
6	10	6,938	1,287	1,090	343	1,046	113	0.3374	92	1,395	68	3.981	1.232
7	9	6,860	1,285	1,076	340	1,040	107	0.3367	84	1,378	66	3.993	1.243
8	8	6,770	1,360	1,069	336	1,035	106	0.3353	85	1,359	62	4.048	1.251
9	7	7,198	1,316	1,060	326	1,030	102	0.3342	83	1,342	55	4.092	1.263
10	6	7,105	1,321	1,051	314	1,023	99	0.3332	79	1,336	54	4.294	1.275
11	5	6,717	1,314	1,050	310	1,015	94	0.3323	78	1,329	50	4.297	1.279
12	4	7,102	1,328	1,041	305	995	90	0.3316	76	1,300	49	4.388	1.293
13	3	6,521	1,219	1,013	296	948	86	0.3279	70	1,266	44	4.512	1.314
14	2	7,176	1,398	1,006	287	932	84	0.3275	68	1,178	19	4.556	1.316
15	1	7,066	1,220	942	281	898	44	0.3241	59	1,156	6	4.622	1.352

2018													
RK	PTS	AB	IP	R	HR	RBI	SB	OBP	W	K	SV	ERA	WHIP
1	15	7,239	1,351	1,089	310	1,058	142	0.3458	107	1,483	93	3.120	1.145
2	14	7,399	1,396	1,065	304	1,042	144	0.3445	98	1,462	91	3.397	1.168
3	13	7,178	1,275	1,046	301	1,010	138	0.3400	93	1,433	84	3.663	1.187
4	12	7,288	1,292	1,028	295	1,005	127	0.3389	89	1,421	76	3.766	1.199
5	11	6,861	1,194	1,001	283	988	122	0.3360	87	1,412	72	3.778	1.195
6	10	7,444	1,302	993	279	985	119	0.3346	84	1,369	69	3.793	1.214
7	9	6,936	1,281	992	275	946	116	0.3331	82	1,331	63	3.829	1.218
8	8	6,988	1,336	980	272	936	114	0.3324	84	1,315	57	3.891	1.226
9	7	6,785	1,416	974	264	920	109	0.3297	79	1,299	62	3.935	1.227
10	6	7,002	1,355	970	257	913	104	0.3290	78	1,294	52	3.993	1.244
11	5	6,989	1,285	964	257	902	100	0.3278	72	1,257	52	4.017	1.253
12	4	7,009	1,207	948	252	895	97	0.3241	72	1,163	48	4.029	1.260
13	3	6,773	1,301	941	247	884	96	0.3204	69	1,142	43	4.098	1.285
14	2	6,485	1,291	912	241	850	84	0.3234	65	1,129	35	4.188	1.337
15	1	6,913	1,192	778	203	735	76	0.3107	61	1,056	16	4.499	1.361

15-tm, Draft & Hold (NFBC Draft Champions)

													2019
RK	PTS	AB	IP	R	HR	RBI	SB	AVG	W	K	SV	ERA	WHIP
1	15	7,312	1,367	1,186	382	1,150	147	0.2743	104	1,595	93	3.565	1.144
2	14	7,230	1,350	1,145	364	1,112	133	0.2711	98	1,513	82	3.710	1.176
3	13	7,192	1,329	1,120	352	1,087	127	0.2689	94	1,471	74	3.809	1.195
4	12	7,140	1,315	1,102	344	1,066	120	0.2671	91	1,430	67	3.880	1.209
5	11	7,117	1,318	1,084	336	1,048	115	0.2658	88	1,401	62	3.934	1.221
6	10	7,008	1,305	1,069	329	1,032	110	0.2646	86	1,371	57	3.986	1.232
7	9	6,933	1,301	1,051	323	1,016	105	0.2633	83	1,341	53	4.037	1.242
8	8	6,862	1,287	1,037	317	1,000	101	0.2621	81	1,316	49	4.092	1.252
9	7	6,820	1,262	1,020	311	983	97	0.2609	79	1,287	44	4.143	1.261
10	6	6,753	1,261	1,002	304	967	93	0.2597	76	1,261	40	4.198	1.271
11	5	6,688	1,234	985	296	950	89	0.2584	74	1,235	36	4.259	1.283
12	4	6,552	1,226	965	288	928	83	0.2569	71	1,199	32	4.329	1.295
13	3	6,476	1,194	940	278	906	78	0.2550	67	1,154	26	4.416	1.309
14	2	6,413	1,162	903	266	869	72	0.2530	63	1,093	18	4.513	1.330
15	1	6,167	1,092	848	245	811	61	0.2497	55	995	9	4.683	1.362

													2018
RK	PTS	AB	IP	R	HR	RBI	SB	AVG	W	K	SV	ERA	WHIP
1	15	7,312	1,377	1,092	317	1,055	157	0.2697	104	1,547	102	3.264	1.128
2	14	7,232	1,355	1,055	301	1,022	144	0.2667	98	1,474	88	3.428	1.156
3	13	7,207	1,350	1,034	292	998	136	0.2645	93	1,436	81	3.528	1.174
4	12	7,118	1,330	1,017	285	983	130	0.2631	90	1,398	75	3.601	1.188
5	11	7,134	1,312	1,004	279	967	126	0.2617	87	1,367	70	3.666	1.199
6	10	7,032	1,314	990	272	951	121	0.2605	84	1,334	65	3.727	1.210
7	9	7,007	1,302	978	268	938	117	0.2591	82	1,308	61	3.773	1.219
8	8	6,977	1,276	965	262	924	112	0.2581	80	1,284	56	3.821	1.228
9	7	6,936	1,274	951	257	910	109	0.2569	78	1,255	52	3.877	1.238
10	6	6,884	1,262	938	251	894	104	0.2555	75	1,223	47	3.933	1.248
11	5	6,792	1,233	921	245	876	98	0.2542	73	1,193	42	3.993	1.258
12	4	6,676	1,247	906	239	858	94	0.2525	70	1,164	37	4.060	1.270
13	3	6,581	1,196	884	231	837	89	0.2510	67	1,122	32	4.138	1.285
14	2	6,480	1,175	856	221	813	81	0.2487	63	1,070	25	4.229	1.304
15	1	6,232	1,130	805	204	763	71	0.2451	56	984	14	4.383	1.333

12-tm, Standard (NFBC Online Championships)

								2019					
RK	PTS	AB	IP	R	HR	RBI	SB	AVG	W	K	SV	ERA	WHIP
1	12	7,675	1,492	1,257	405	1,980	156	0.2765	105	1,632	98	3.503	1.130
2	11	7,632	1,447	1,222	386	1,822	143	0.2732	100	1,560	88	3.652	1.164
3	10	7,545	1,419	1,198	376	1,646	135	0.2709	96	1,520	82	3.749	1.182
4	9	7,459	1,394	1,175	367	1,484	128	0.2691	93	1,487	77	3.825	1.197
5	8	7,400	1,373	1,154	360	1,313	122	0.2675	90	1,455	73	3.890	1.210
6	7	7,319	1,351	1,134	352	1,141	116	0.2657	88	1,428	69	3.960	1.223
7	6	7,268	1,330	1,114	344	970	111	0.2643	85	1,399	64	4.028	1.235
8	5	7,200	1,306	1,094	336	790	105	0.2629	82	1,371	59	4.100	1.249
9	4	7,114	1,278	1,075	326	629	100	0.2612	79	1,335	53	4.166	1.263
10	3	7,007	1,235	1,049	316	471	93	0.2593	76	1,289	45	4.254	1.278
11	2	6,859	1,178	1,016	303	295	84	0.2573	72	1,236	38	4.356	1.296
12	1	6,645	1,097	958	282	137	71	0.2537	64	1,138	26	4.541	1.331

								2018					
RK	PTS	AB	IP	R	HR	RBI	SB	AVG	W	K	SV	ERA	WHIP
1	12	7,622	1,403	1,147	339	1,113	166	0.2712	105	1,583	107	3.194	1.116
2	11	7,578	1,392	1,117	323	1,080	153	0.2677	99	1,522	95	3.367	1.147
3	10	7,497	1,395	1,092	313	1,055	144	0.2656	96	1,478	88	3.477	1.166
4	9	7,459	1,369	1,073	304	1,036	139	0.2636	93	1,446	83	3.557	1.181
5	8	7,397	1,370	1,059	298	1,019	132	0.2620	89	1,414	78	3.633	1.195
6	7	7,357	1,357	1,041	292	1,003	125	0.2605	87	1,388	74	3.698	1.207
7	6	7,269	1,325	1,024	284	985	119	0.2589	84	1,360	68	3.762	1.220
8	5	7,214	1,328	1,008	278	969	114	0.2573	81	1,327	64	3.833	1.231
9	4	7,133	1,295	988	271	949	107	0.2557	78	1,293	57	3.907	1.246
10	3	6,999	1,271	965	260	925	101	0.2540	75	1,248	50	4.001	1.261
11	2	6,884	1,220	932	250	890	92	0.2517	70	1,189	42	4.114	1.283
12	1	6,709	1,181	881	231	835	81	0.2478	62	1,076	26	4.275	1.316

12-tm, AL-only, OBP (Tout Wars AL)

							2019						
RK	PTS	AB	IP	R	HR	RBI	SB	OBP	W	K	SV	ERA	WHIP
1	12	6,285	1,212	1,016	330	1,004	114	0.3403	91	69	1,320	3.700	1.173
2	11	6,863	1,231	1,003	323	977	110	0.3368	82	61	1,289	3.800	1.209
3	10	6,479	1,027	992	316	959	110	0.3361	79	54	1,285	3.910	1.232
4	9	6,477	1,146	984	304	953	108	0.3352	74	49	1,260	4.120	1.248
5	8	6,635	1,263	955	286	938	101	0.3288	73	49	1,227	4.300	1.275
6	7	6,410	1,027	945	279	895	90	0.3264	71	48	1,210	4.380	1.286
7	6	6,477	1,159	930	274	885	90	0.3219	71	42	1,121	4.480	1.324
8	5	6,876	1,283	909	260	861	81	0.3219	66	37	1,104	4.530	1.324
9	4	6,076	1,107	873	256	854	79	0.3188	66	35	1,008	4.600	1.327
10	3	5,278	977	817	237	822	77	0.3171	60	20	993	4.870	1.362
11	2	5,177	1,223	723	196	649	45	0.3167	57	12	974	4.890	1.362
12	1	5,970	1,033	657	188	643	37	0.3004	54	9	962	4.920	1.375

							2018						
RK	PTS	AB	IP	R	HR	RBI	SB	OBP	W	K	SV	ERA	WHIP
1	12	6,206	1,183	907	273	902	122	0.3336	86	83	1,307	3.270	1.142
2	11	6,125	1,125	896	260	901	119	0.3310	83	74	1,271	3.570	1.197
3	10	6,225	1,288	886	255	879	111	0.3268	80	65	1,231	3.730	1.229
4	9	6,571	1,383	865	241	844	107	0.3235	77	58	1,189	3.790	1.241
5	8	6,055	1,078	857	240	843	105	0.3235	76	53	1,186	3.820	1.250
6	7	6,580	1,200	853	235	835	98	0.3205	75	48	1,161	4.000	1.256
7	6	6,543	1,203	842	235	835	95	0.3186	73	42	1,136	4.030	1.271
8	5	6,367	1,173	837	235	832	94	0.3182	69	41	1,125	4.230	1.284
9	4	6,228	1,046	827	223	798	80	0.3172	66	30	1,112	4.320	1.295
10	3	5,152	1,127	825	203	792	73	0.3159	65	22	1,097	4.390	1.307
11	2	6,637	1,176	799	188	664	69	0.3134	62	16	1,047	4.510	1.332
12	1	5,974	1,239	664	131	538	65	0.3112	59	15	1,016	4.680	1.337

12-tm, NL-only, OBP (Tout Wars NL)

								2019					
RK	PTS	AB	IP	R	HR	RBI	SB	OBP	W	K	SV	ERA	WHIP
1	12	6,381	1,280	1,025	345	1,051	127	0.3506	91	71	1,438	3.960	1.233
2	11	6,393	1,295	931	314	942	104	0.3473	88	68	1,359	3.980	1.238
3	10	6,069	1,296	921	310	915	94	0.3443	77	68	1,279	4.080	1.244
4	9	6,475	1,087	921	268	900	93	0.3359	73	60	1,233	4.090	1.248
5	8	6,096	1,343	912	259	883	92	0.3349	73	54	1,200	4.090	1.251
6	7	6,040	1,154	909	248	872	92	0.3298	68	52	1,188	4.130	1.252
7	6	5,752	1,114	875	245	842	90	0.3289	67	42	1,177	4.140	1.255
8	5	6,380	1,158	854	234	804	87	0.3254	67	29	1,161	4.190	1.255
9	4	5,753	1,163	838	222	785	86	0.3243	66	27	1,143	4.190	1.301
10	3	6,300	1,209	822	216	781	86	0.3242	64	26	1,137	4.250	1.305
11	2	5,166	1,063	802	207	736	68	0.3193	64	14	1,123	4.400	1.313
12	1	5,734	1,162	734	187	642	34	0.3170	59	11	1,089	4.560	1.344

								2018					
RK	PTS	AB	IP	R	HR	RBI	SB	OBP	W	K	SV	ERA	WHIP
1	12	6,062	1,261	928	251	891	115	0.3487	86	76	1,366	3.300	1.161
2	11	6,500	1,393	899	250	860	110	0.3446	83	73	1,319	3.550	1.204
3	10	6,194	1,241	896	245	839	107	0.3370	82	73	1,242	3.590	1.213
4	9	6,284	1,030	886	240	838	106	0.3358	81	68	1,239	3.840	1.215
5	8	5,699	1,226	860	222	809	106	0.3341	78	57	1,228	3.870	1.218
6	7	6,075	1,202	816	205	789	98	0.3334	76	52	1,227	3.870	1.233
7	6	5,811	1,321	800	199	766	97	0.3286	75	49	1,222	3.890	1.238
8	5	6,139	1,181	777	197	760	96	0.3275	66	42	1,150	3.920	1.255
9	4	6,385	1,207	766	192	730	92	0.3275	62	39	1,063	3.960	1.305
10	3	6,175	1,031	761	191	674	86	0.3253	58	11	1,021	4.060	1.322
11	2	5,815	1,077	700	161	656	74	0.3172	55	5	1,017	4.100	1.327
12	1	5,171	1,353	633	160	627	67	0.3011	55	0	1,006	4.120	1.344

12-tm, AL-only (NFBC AL-only)

								2019					
RK	PTS	AB	IP	R	HR	RBI	SB	AVG	W	K	SV	ERA	WHIP
1	12	6,632	1,224	1,061	342	1,022	137	0.2677	91	1,326	61	3.688	1.156
2	11	6,735	1,167	1,020	314	983	109	0.2652	86	1,271	56	3.840	1.189
3	10	6,337	1,154	977	303	951	100	0.2624	80	1,226	55	4.020	1.216
4	9	6,492	1,188	958	288	927	95	0.2606	74	1,214	51	4.055	1.242
5	8	6,629	1,268	942	280	894	91	0.2591	74	1,163	46	4.221	1.286
6	7	6,423	1,101	922	265	866	86	0.2586	69	1,149	43	4.382	1.292
7	6	6,393	1,157	874	258	849	83	0.2558	66	1,104	37	4.467	1.304
8	5	5,885	1,015	854	253	822	73	0.2533	65	1,070	34	4.594	1.328
9	4	5,923	1,018	815	247	791	72	0.2503	59	1,010	32	4.633	1.340
10	3	5,561	958	790	233	762	67	0.2491	58	966	25	4.695	1.353
11	2	5,514	1,027	743	216	726	60	0.2479	52	889	21	4.896	1.363
12	1	5,118	904	694	206	702	49	0.2445	47	857	14	4.955	1.399

								2018					
RK	PTS	AB	IP	R	HR	RBI	SB	AVG	W	K	SV	ERA	WHIP
1	12	6,444	1,271	928	274	939	130	0.2632	92	1,357	81	3.554	1.189
2	11	6,759	1,147	901	256	887	118	0.2608	86	1,318	70	3.774	1.197
3	10	6,539	1,237	898	241	858	112	0.2594	79	1,252	62	3.900	1.216
4	9	6,554	1,213	881	236	829	104	0.2560	77	1,205	53	3.929	1.234
5	8	6,307	1,151	870	233	824	103	0.2536	74	1,152	49	3.963	1.246
6	7	6,296	1,181	855	225	809	95	0.2522	72	1,129	48	4.018	1.265
7	6	6,271	1,132	840	222	801	95	0.2514	74	1,093	43	4.103	1.270
8	5	6,057	1,129	822	217	793	90	0.2490	67	1,082	37	4.156	1.278
9	4	5,844	1,109	808	212	771	77	0.2479	63	1,015	37	4.220	1.298
10	3	5,909	1,148	769	202	717	79	0.2451	58	1,003	28	4.311	1.311
11	2	5,605	1,100	686	181	643	72	0.2421	51	948	26	4.526	1.330
12	1	4,837	967	655	159	624	59	0.2404	43	876	5	4.791	1.378

12-tm, NL-only (NFBC NL-only)

								2019					
RK	PTS	AB	IP	R	HR	RBI	SB	AVG	W	K	SV	ERA	WHIP
1	12	6,224	1,185	968	328	961	131	0.2682	89	1,396	89	3.594	1.168
2	11	6,483	1,329	917	290	954	117	0.2661	81	1,350	75	3.841	1.205
3	10	6,131	1,248	951	283	928	108	0.2642	78	1,286	70	3.962	1.222
4	9	6,222	1,272	931	278	915	101	0.2629	76	1,268	57	4.063	1.235
5	8	6,373	1,147	845	259	891	97	0.2621	74	1,237	48	4.078	1.262
6	7	6,231	1,227	831	254	849	90	0.2605	73	1,219	41	4.155	1.273
7	6	5,461	1,174	810	245	826	83	0.2595	69	1,184	36	4.206	1.290
8	5	6,022	1,156	929	239	805	78	0.2577	65	1,123	30	4.283	1.302
9	4	5,832	1,085	833	224	768	74	0.2561	60	1,073	25	4.390	1.308
10	3	5,097	1,072	764	216	740	66	0.2553	56	1,051	20	4.462	1.340
11	2	5,528	943	821	211	703	58	0.2531	56	998	13	4.606	1.353
12	1	5,041	980	766	171	630	45	0.2510	49	895	6	4.672	1.343

								2018					
RK	PTS	AB	IP	R	HR	RBI	SB	AVG	W	K	SV	ERA	WHIP
1	12	6,540	1,420	886	239	863	142	0.2647	97	1,320	82	3.267	1.173
2	11	6,012	1,215	865	233	837	116	0.2627	83	1,270	65	3.447	1.193
3	10	6,434	1,227	852	224	816	107	0.2618	78	1,219	62	3.649	1.204
4	9	6,269	1,212	836	218	798	99	0.2600	78	1,195	56	3.663	1.222
5	8	6,149	1,072	844	214	775	97	0.2612	76	1,160	53	3.693	1.230
6	7	5,909	1,162	816	210	772	97	0.2587	75	1,127	51	3.759	1.248
7	6	5,859	1,161	809	206	735	91	0.2580	68	1,097	44	3.918	1.251
8	5	5,872	1,150	766	194	727	87	0.2561	69	1,069	36	3.940	1.261
9	4	5,484	1,041	743	191	723	80	0.2537	63	1,052	36	3.971	1.273
10	3	5,642	1,015	728	185	714	74	0.2520	60	1,035	25	3.994	1.279
11	2	5,392	1,179	714	181	695	71	0.2459	59	994	13	4.071	1.293
12	1	5,308	1,152	699	161	618	59	0.2432	55	959	4	4.298	1.331